AMERICA
in the
WORLD

AMERICA
in the
WORLD

---◆---

A History of
U.S. Diplomacy
and Foreign Policy

ROBERT B. ZOELLICK

TWELVE

NEW YORK BOSTON

Twelve
Hachette Book Group
1290 Avenue of the Americas, New York, NY 10104

twelvebooks.com

twitter.com/twelvebooks

First Edition: August 2020

Twelve is an imprint of Grand Central Publishing. The Twelve name and logo are trademarks of Hachette Book Group, Inc.

The publisher is not responsible for websites (or their content) that are not owned by the publisher.

The Hachette Speakers Bureau provides a wide range of authors for speaking events. To find out more, go to www.hachettespeakersbureau.com or call (866) 376-6591.

Library of Congress Cataloging-in-Publication Data

Names: Zoellick, Robert B., author.

Title: America in the world : a history of U.S. diplomacy and foreign policy / Robert Zoellick. Description: New York : Twelve, 2020. | Includes bibliographical references and index. | Summary: "Ranging from Benjamin Franklin, Alexander Hamilton, and Thomas Jefferson to Henry Kissinger, Ronald Reagan, and James Baker, America in the World tells the vibrant story of American diplomacy, identifying five traditions that have emerged from America's encounters with the world: the importance of North America; the special roles played by trade, transnational, and technological relations in defining ties with others; changing attitudes toward alliances and ways of ordering connections among states; the need for public support, especially through Congress; and the belief that American policy should serve a larger purpose." — Provided by publisher.

Identifiers: LCCN 2019049280 | ISBN 9781538761304 (hardcover) | ISBN 9781538712368 (ebook)

Subjects: LCSH: United States—Foreign relations.

Classification: LCC E183.7 .Z64 2020 | DDC 327.73—dc23

LC record available at https://lccn.loc.gov/2019049280

ISBNs: 978-1-5387-6130-4 (hardcover), 978-1-5387-1236-8 (ebook)

Printed in the United States of America

LSC-C

10 9 8 7 6 5 4 3 2 1

For Sherry

Contents

PART IV
A New Order of American Alliances

PART V
An End and a Beginning

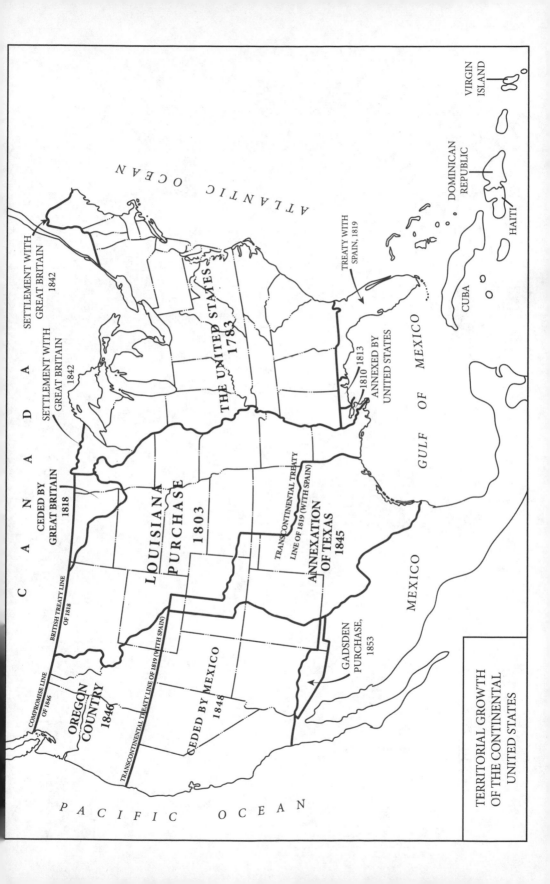

VIRGIN
ISLAND

DOMINICAN
REPUBLIC

HAITI

CUBA

ATLANTIC OCEAN

C A N A D A

SETTLEMENT WITH
GREAT BRITAIN
1842

SETTLEMENT WITH
GREAT BRITAIN
1842

CEDED BY
GREAT BRITAIN
1818

BRITISH TREATY LINE
OF 1818

COMPROMISE LINE
OF 1846

OREGON
COUNTRY
1846

TRANSCONTINENTAL TREATY LINE OF 1819 (WITH SPAIN)

CEDED BY MEXICO
1848

LOUISIANA
PURCHASE
1803

THE UNITED STATES
1783

TREATY WITH
SPAIN, 1819

1813
1810
ANNEXED BY
UNITED STATES

TRANSCONTINENTAL TREATY
LINE OF 1819 (WITH SPAIN)

ANNEXATION
OF TEXAS
1845

GADSDEN
PURCHASE,
1853

MEXICO

GULF OF MEXICO

PACIFIC OCEAN

TERRITORIAL GROWTH
OF THE CONTINENTAL
UNITED STATES

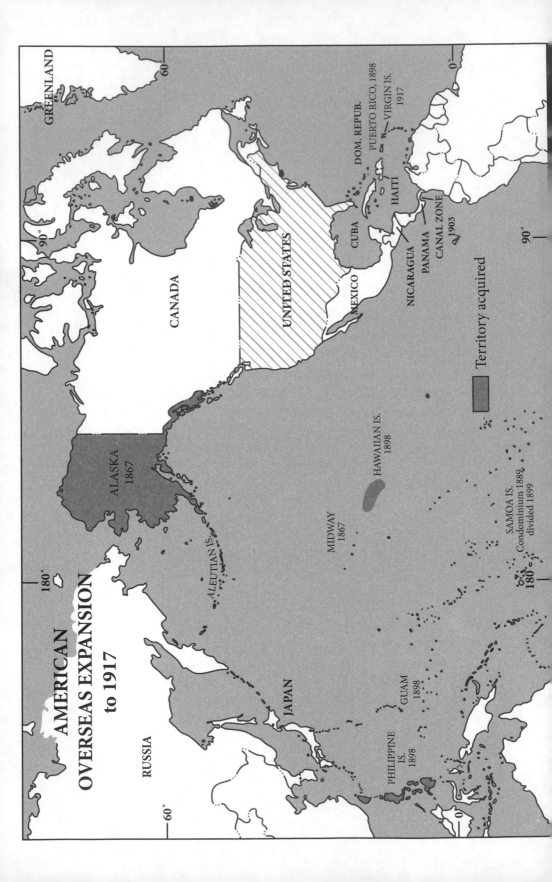

AMERICAN
OVERSEAS EXPANSION
to 1917

RUSSIA

JAPAN

PHILIPPINE
IS.
1898

GUAM
1898

SAMOA IS.
Condominium 1889
divided 1899

ALEUTIAN IS.

ALASKA
1867

MIDWAY
1867

HAWAIIAN IS.
1898

Territory acquired

CANADA

UNITED STATES

MEXICO

CUBA

DOM. REPUB.

HAITI

PUERTO RICO, 1898

VIRGIN IS.
1917

NICARAGUA

PANAMA

CANAL ZONE
1903

GREENLAND

180°

180°

90°

90°

90°

60°

60°

0°

0°

INTRODUCTION

◆

America's First Diplomat

Inventing American Diplomacy

On the evening of February 6, 1778, Ben Franklin arrived at the Parisian offices of the French foreign minister, le Comte de Vergennes, to sign America's first two treaties: a military alliance and a trade accord. Recognition of the new United States, a novel republic, by the venerable and powerful monarchy of France was as momentous as the promise of arms and commerce.

As the delegations gathered, Silas Deane, one of Franklin's fellow commissioners, expressed curiosity about Franklin's suit, a worn blue coat of Manchester velvet. When asked about his attire for this memorable occasion, Franklin replied that his selection was "[to] give it a little revenge."[1]

Four years before, in 1774, Franklin had been humiliated by the British Crown's solicitor general, Alexander Wedderburn, at a hearing of the Privy Council in Westminster. The censure had been in a room known as the Cockpit, describing its function as a place of entertainment during the reign of Henry VIII. For an hour, Franklin had stood motionless before the thirty-six sitting members of the Council while Wedderburn scornfully attacked the sixty-eight-year-old Philadelphian for his release of letters that had embarrassed the governor and lieutenant governor of Massachusetts. The ostensible reason for the assembly was to hear the petition of the Bay Colony to remove the Crown's executives, but Wedderburn instead chastised Franklin.

The Privy Council enjoyed the show. The king's advisers laughed, clapped, and jeered. Franklin remained silent and without expression. The British governing class of 1774 was a select club. The men present knew one another. To lose face was to be stripped of respect and power. The Whig political philosopher and Parliamentarian Edmund Burke, who witnessed Wedderburn's diatribe, described the scolding as "beyond all bounds and measure." Lord Shelburne, who in 1783 would be fated to discharge the unpleasant task of approving the treaty of American independence, wrote former prime minister William Pitt that the solicitor general's performance had been "scurrilous invective." Franklin said it was like "bull baiting." Personal experiences influence diplomats, and this one was a turning point for Franklin. Wedderburn's ridicule had turned a loyal friend of Britain into a determined enemy.[2]

Thus, four years after Wedderburn's verbal execution, on that February night of 1778, Franklin acknowledged to Deane that the suit he had chosen for the treaty ceremony with France was the same one that he had worn in the Cockpit. Diplomacy includes settling scores.

Diplomacy involves deceit as well. Edward Bancroft, Franklin's private secretary, was a British spy. Right after the signing of the treaties in 1778, Bancroft rushed to make copies and deliver them to London within forty-two hours. Bancroft even managed to get word to a London partner in advance of the signing so that they could short stocks and profit handsomely from the news of the French-American alliance. Diplomacy moves markets and attracts scoundrels.[3]

Franklin is "America's First Diplomat." His representation actually began in 1757, when the Pennsylvania Assembly sent the famous printer, publicist, inventor, scientist, community organizer, and politician to represent its interests in London. Over the course of seventeen years, the colonies of Georgia, Massachusetts, and New Jersey also engaged Franklin as an envoy.

Franklin loved England. As tensions increased between the colonists and London, the Philadelphian offered both visionary plans and practical suggestions to preserve and extend the empire of loyal Englishmen. Franklin had urged Britain to retain control of Canada at the end of the Seven Years' War in 1763, one of many Franklin efforts to think of America in continental terms. Later he proposed that the American colonies receive representation in Parliament. Abandoning the idea of Parliamentary supremacy over the colonies, Franklin then proposed a union of separate states, subject to the sovereignty of the Crown, much like the later British Dominions.

Franklin's diplomacy also extended to specific solutions. As late as December 1774, even after Franklin's battering in the Cockpit, he replied to informal emissaries from the king's ministers with seventeen points of "hints" to resolve the crisis between London and the first American Continental Congress.[4] But the two sides turned instead to a contest of arms, will, and international diplomacy.

When Franklin arrived in France in December 1776 to represent the new United States, he faced a challenge even greater than his experience in London. Paris had not recognized Franklin's country—nor had any other capital. The United States was in reality a loose confederation of former colonies; about a decade before, in league with their mother country, the British colonies had warred with France. Franklin's new government, an experimental republic, was untested, starting a war, creating an army and a tiny navy, and trying to raise revenue—all while loudly voicing diverse views. Franklin's mission challenged the most powerful empire in the world. He sought money, weapons, and supplies as well as political recognition. Later he urged the direct commitment of French troops and the assistance of France's fleets. And while wooing the French king, Franklin and his compatriots needed to achieve credibility across Europe in order to seek Dutch loans and perhaps a Spanish alliance as well.

Franklin combined a new type of public diplomacy with the old. While the United States was unknown, Franklin was famous. He personalized his representation of America in ways that appealed to French opinion, even to its sense of style. The 1766 portrait of Franklin in London by David Martin is that of a gentleman scholar, wearing reading glasses and studying a book, and watched over by Isaac Newton. In France, artists painted Franklin as the frontier philosophe in his famous marten fur cap (from Canada), wearing plain brown suits, with no wig, and adored by playful Parisian ladies. Franklin's likeness graced medals, prints, snuffboxes, rings, and even a chamber pot that Louis XVI gave to an enthusiastic Franklin fan. To intrigue the intellectual society of Paris, Franklin highlighted the exceptional nature of America's cause: He arranged for the publication of the Articles of Confederation, state constitutions, and other republican documents. The old publisher also planted anonymous pieces, especially parodies, to feed rumors, amuse, and mock. Franklin's diplomacy appealed to France's sense of self: its respect for the nobility of ideas, culture, and civilization—but also Gallic worldliness, wit, and pride as the historic power of Europe.

At the same time, Franklin was alert to diplomatic verities. For more than four centuries, France and England had been enemies. France yearned to avenge its defeat by Britain in the Seven Years' War of 1756–63, in which Paris lost its American colonies. Now was the moment for George III to lose his. The wealthier plantation islands of the Caribbean might also fall to Paris. A Franco-American victory could restore balance among European empires. France could assert its leadership in Europe by luring Spain and the Netherlands to join the cause against Britain. France might also rely upon future prospects, whether of commerce or power: The vast territory of the new United States was the size of present-day Britain, France, and Germany combined, and the thirteen states, with less than three million people, had room to grow.

Franklin's diplomacy operated through private channels as well as official ones; indeed, he had to proceed indirectly before Louis XVI's recognition of the United States in 1778. Franklin enlisted French officers, materials, and private contributions; he was courting a country while enabling the French government to appear not to take sides. Franklin's friends—the Marquis de Lafayette foremost among them—would assist with the Americans' endless pleas for loans, supplies, and direct military intervention.

Franklin spent seven years beseeching Paris for money. Even after winning independence, Franklin, Thomas Jefferson, and other Americans abroad apprehended that U.S. financial mismanagement cost their new country international respect. In a few years, it was also obvious that France's participation in the American war had proven to be exorbitantly expensive for Louis: By 1787, the French monarchy was devoting half its budget to pay the interest on its war debts, a sum it could not sustain. For the first time in 175 years, the French king had to appeal to the Estates General, sending a signal of weakness that led to a fatal breakdown.[5]

America's First Diplomat, like those to follow, had to work with colleagues of different temperaments, prejudices, and motives. John Jay's skills aptly complemented Franklin's. But Franklin's assessment of the envious and disputatious John Adams in 1783 captured the Massachusetts statesman precisely: He "means well for his Country, is always an honest Man, often a Wise One, but sometimes, and in some things, absolutely out of his senses."[6]

Franklin understood that skillful diplomacy must complement events on the ground. The best envoys have an astute sense of timing—when to act and when to hold back—and how to use the leverage of events to the fullest. Arthur Lee, Franklin's acrimonious colleague, demanded that the Americans twist their defeats in 1777 into an ultimatum to France. Franklin demurred, and then worked the news of the American victory at Saratoga in October 1777 to play Britain and France against one another: Recognizing that spies were ever-present, Franklin let news slip of British emissaries coming to Paris to seek reconciliation with the United States; at the same time, Franklin knew London would learn of the prospects of an American treaty with Paris. Wanting to avoid an apparent Anglo-American rapprochement, France agreed to a military alliance. The key term for Minister Vergennes was a stipulation that the United States would not make peace without France's consent.

After the American-French victory at Yorktown in 1781, Franklin had an opportunity to negotiate with a new British government. Rivalries in London and the vagaries of Parliamentary support created uncertainty, however, about the duration of the opening. Franklin used an informal personal connection to signal good feelings toward Lord Shelburne, soon to be prime minister, without risking French observation. Franklin was taking a long view of American strategic interests while seeking to close the historic deal. With the British, Franklin distinguished peace from reconciliation, arguing that Britain should offer generous terms that began to restore fraternal ties.

Franklin even tried to persuade London to relinquish Canada to the new nation; he suggested that a continued British presence on America's northern border would necessitate stronger U.S. ties with France. In speaking to the French, Franklin reassured that the United States would not seek a separate peace. That posture also countered British maneuvers to play the allies off one another. Furthermore, Franklin knew America's challenges would persist even after peace. He wanted to maintain a friendship with France. Franklin the businessman had an eye for money: Given the insolvency of the U.S. government, America would need even more French aid, if fighting resumed, or to discharge the Continental Army. France deserved respect, Franklin wrote Robert Morris, the U.S. superintendent of finance; Stacy Schiff, the superb historian of Franklin's "Great Improvisation" in France, observed that Franklin recognized that "nations had feelings too."[7]

The French emissaries in America had persuaded (and even paid) the Continental Congress to instruct its negotiators to act only with Paris's consent. Franklin's new colleagues, John Jay and John Adams, were suspicious of France's motives and insisted on negotiating with the British without coordinating with France. Franklin accepted their logic, recognizing France wanted to confine the United States to an Appalachian border and preclude American access to fishing grounds near Canada and Newfoundland. Unlike his colleagues, however, Franklin did not presume bad faith on France's part. Franklin pointed out that the foreign minister had always dealt fairly and never let him down. Franklin's diplomacy included gratitude, too. He wanted peace with Britain while retaining harmony with France.

On November 30, 1782, the Americans signed a provisional treaty with Britain to end the war. Franklin then faced the difficult task of explaining to Vergennes why the U.S. commissioners had ignored their obligation to France as well as the instructions from Congress. Moreover, Franklin even had to ask for yet another French loan.

Franklin's reply to Vergennes's cool protest was a model of artful diplomacy. Franklin apologized gracefully for an "impropriety" without groveling or conceding great error. To help save face, Franklin agreed that the U.S. treaty with Britain would not become binding until France and Britain agreed to terms. Then, in seeking to be excused by the king "whom we all love and honor," Franklin hoped that the "single indiscretion" would not ruin this great achievement of the king's reign. To the contrary, Franklin argued (untruthfully) that nothing in the U.S. agreement was contrary to France's interests. Finally, appealing to France's calculations of power, Franklin claimed that any public dispute would only please the allies' common foe, Britain. Thus, Franklin coated early American duplicity with flavorings of youthful innocence, warm feelings, and cold calculations. Vergennes, a dignified realist, wrote his own assessment: "If we judge the future from what is now passing before our eyes, we shall be poorly repaid for what we have done for the United States of America and for securing them their existence." When Congress inquired if France would file an official complaint against the American commissioners, the secretary to the French legation replied, "great powers never *complained*, but they *felt* and *remembered*."[8]

The U.S. objectives for peace also differed from those of the French and Spanish. At the close of Richard Morris's classic account of great power diplomacy in America's War for Independence, he concludes that Franklin and his colleagues sought a durable peace for a new republican nation and government in a revolutionary age, whereas the French and Spanish looked backward to retrieve influence and properties lost in earlier monarchical contests.[9]

America's First Diplomat "put practice before theory." He "favored modest experience over grandiose hypotheses" and "preferred dialogue to dogma."[10] His statesmanship mixed reason, America's virtues, and, when he enjoyed it, power. Franklin had the critical quality of keeping his eye on the primary objective, avoiding diversions and petty differences. Yet he was attentive to the right details. Franklin wrote Robert Morris that "I find by experience that great affairs and great men are sometimes influenced by small matters."[11]

Franklin recognized that the domestic politics of peacemaking would be frustrating. When Henry Laurens, a fellow peace commissioner, predicted the nation's gratitude, Franklin replied skeptically, "I have never yet known of a peace made, that did not occasion a great deal of popular discontent, clamor, and censure on both sides." "[T]he blessing promised to peacemakers, I fancy, relates to the next world," concluded Franklin.[12]

Even though America's first peace treaty was viewed across Europe as a diplomatic triumph, the Continental Congress found faults anyway. Schiff concluded, "Diplomats make dull heroes." Franklin's experience reminds Americans that they did not attain independence on their own. Franklin's art and artifice have been all too easy to forget.[13]

What This Book Is About

This is a book of stories about the history of American diplomacy.

My idea for this work traces back over twenty-five years, when I read Henry Kissinger's magisterial *Diplomacy*, which draws on history to illuminate the strategy and art of diplomacy. Yet Kissinger's perspective—however wide-ranging and insightful—is rooted in the European experience. Even though Kissinger has been a shrewd practitioner of U.S. statecraft, his sub-text is that America's diplomatic experience reflects, as Otto von Bismarck allegedly observed, that "God always looks after fools—and the United States." In the nineteenth century, according to Kissinger, "the foreign pol-icy of the United States was not to have a foreign policy." He was critical of much of twentieth-century U.S. diplomacy, too.[14] With a different perspec-tive, I believe that the American experience with diplomacy offers valuable insights and ideas.

Kissinger writes that U.S. foreign policy has often overreached—and then overreacted by withdrawing—because Americans have viewed the world as they wished it to be, not as the world really is. Scholars consider Kissinger a "realist" instead of an "idealist" like those who have sought to carry Amer-ica's political beliefs—and, presumably, its virtues—to other lands. I once heard Kissinger wryly observe that "America is the only country where being called 'a realist' is viewed as a criticism."

In fact, Kissinger keeps impressive company. In 1951, George Kennan, the author of "containment" at the start of the Cold War, delivered a series of lectures at the University of Chicago on what he considered the sorry state of American foreign policy. He published these discourses as *American Diplomacy, 1900–1950*, a foundational text for the realist tradition. Kennan decried America's "legalistic-moralistic approach" to world affairs, driven by the "emotionalism" and the "erratic and subjective nature" of Ameri-can public opinion. He viewed the real work of diplomacy as "taking the awkward conflicts of national interest and dealing with them on their mer-its with a view to finding solutions least unsettling to the stability of inter-national life."[15] At the turn of the twenty-first century, Walter McDougall reprised the cautionary wisdom of "realism" in his *Promised Land, Crusader State*. McDougall warned of the dangers of Woodrow Wilson's "idealism" and the recurring pull of America's "global meliorism."[16]

American diplomacy also suffered a withering critique from another direction. In 1959, William Appleman Williams of the University of Wis-consin launched the "revisionist" school with his book *The Tragedy of American Diplomacy*. Whereas Kennan and Kissinger faulted the crusad-ing idealism of U.S. foreign policy, and its incapacity to match means and ends, Williams perceived a single-minded American "imperialism" pursued through economic expansionism.[17] The "New Left" revisionists challenged the "orthodox" views of earlier "nationalist" or "conservative" diplomatic historians, who had celebrated America's achievements. Writing during the frightening nuclear standoffs of the early Cold War and then the Vietnam War, the revisionists challenged Americans to recognize their aggressive past and self-serving motives.

Scholars earn reputations by disputing received wisdom, so the revisionists provoked a reaction among "post-revisionists." The most prominent in Cold War studies was John Lewis Gaddis, who argued against both the platitudes of orthodoxy and the revisionists' excessively narrow focus on economic forces. To understand the Cold War, Gaddis explained, one needed to include "domestic politics, bureaucratic inertia, quirks of personality, [and] perceptions, accurate or inaccurate, of Soviet intentions." In fact, Gaddis maintained, "economic instruments were used to serve political ends, not the other way around as the Leninist model of imperialism would seem to imply."[18]

Since the end of the Cold War, writers have tested other frameworks to categorize the driving impulses of U.S. foreign policy. Walter Russell Mead's *Special Providence: American Foreign Policy and How It Changed the World* identifies the competition among four schools of thought that run through U.S. foreign policy, each emphasizing a different element of the nation's nature, and together producing an adaptive mixture.[19] David Milne's *Worldmaking* tries a new dichotomy, "art versus science," with the "artists" drawn toward cautious assessments based on historical experience and the "scientists" motivated by theories to remake the world.[20] These intellectual histories offer stimulating interpretations and spur creative debates. But intellectual histories risk squeezing messy facts and complex causes to fit theoretical structures. They oversimplify and often fail to explain what in fact happened.

This book takes a different approach. The diplomacy of my experience and study has been about practical efforts to solve problems, often with an eye on domestic politics and sometimes with perspective on the future. The pragmatism of American diplomacy has focused on achieving results in particular matters, not on applying theories.

The idea of pragmatism traces to William James, John Dewey, and a distinctive American philosophy. James and Dewey rejected artificial intellectual conventions, abstractions, and dogmas—as has American diplomacy. In place of a "search for universal, timeless truth," pragmatic philosophers "emphasized instead that a proposition is true if the practical consequences it implies... do in fact follow in experience." Pragmatic philosophers and diplomats alike are "instrumentalists"; they begin with problems, look to experience, and match means with ends to "fix the situation." Pragmatists recognize the powerful roles of chance and contingency, and they appreciate how processes shape practical choices. They account for the dynamism of the world and pluralist perspectives. Pragmatic American philosophers and statesmen share an optimistic belief in progress.[21]

I am not suggesting that pragmatism offers a simple formula for success.

Rather, I will describe the reality of how most U.S. officials approached diplomatic problems. Over two hundred years, U.S. diplomacy has sought out what works, even if practitioners stumbled while discovering what they could accomplish. Franklin, Jay, and Adams struck an opportunistic deal to secure independence and vast territories for a new type of nation. George Washington proceeded carefully with foreign relations, and took the unpopular step of backing Jay's second treaty with Britain in 1795 to give the United States a chance to take root, accrue power under Alexander Hamilton's economic designs, and secure the western frontier. Thomas Jefferson interpreted the Constitution flexibly to complete the Louisiana Purchase when timely. John Quincy Adams focused U.S. energies on transcontinental expansion and pushing Europeans out of the Americas instead of getting involved with European revolutions and alliances. Abraham Lincoln and William Seward employed creative legal reasoning to avoid British and French intervention in the U.S. Civil War, figuring it wise "to fight one war at a time."

At the turn of the twentieth century, when William McKinley could not persuade two-thirds of the Senate to annex Hawaii by treaty, he did so by joint resolution (requiring only majorities) of both houses. Teddy Roosevelt mediated conflicts among great powers in order to maintain balances in East Asia and Europe. Franklin D. Roosevelt cautiously mobilized public support for a global war after the Great Depression. Opposition was intense; in 1941, not long before the Japanese attack on Pearl Harbor, FDR won the extension of the Selective Service Act's draft by only one vote. Dwight Eisenhower calmed the fever pitch of the early Cold War, preparing prudently for the long haul. John F. Kennedy learned to deal pragmatically with crises. Ronald Reagan set ambitious goals, yet was willing to negotiate and accept step-by-step results. George H. W. Bush combined bold moves with careful restraint and constant diplomatic outreach to end the Cold War peacefully and then to organize an unprecedented coalition to reverse Iraq's aggression in the first Gulf War.

The U.S. record also includes tragic failures, especially when leaders lost sight of practical foreign policies. Woodrow Wilson stumbled over his design for collective security, which ignored realities of power politics abroad and the requirements for political support at home. Lyndon Johnson's preoccupation with domestic politics blinded him to making a pragmatic assessment of what the United States could accomplish—and what commitment the American public would support—in Vietnam.

Successful pragmatists consider all available means to achieve results. They pay close attention to realities on the ground—whether of power, economics, military capacity, technology, the attitudes and positions of others, or votes. Pragmatists need to know how institutions work and processes operate; they seek to understand the perspectives and interests of other actors. Knowing when to act—a sense of timing—is vital.

Pragmatic leaders may enjoy intellectual jousts, but they are likely to become impatient with abstractions and long debates about theories when problems demand attention. Pragmatic diplomacy may appreciate the power of rhetoric—especially in effective argument—but will be skeptical of posturing without practical effect.

Pragmatists recognize the need for negotiations and the benefits of imperfect results in a far-from-perfect world. They just keep trying—with a spirit of optimism about fixing things. For them, history offers insights on how to do better, not an acceptance of timeless obstacles.

Pragmatism can include far-reaching visions. The makers of American foreign policy have pursued novel and even exciting ideas, but they have generally been flexible and practical in applying them. Leaders want to accomplish objectives that move the country closer to their vision. Some officials have been attracted to ideologies, but usually not rigidly. American policies have been drawn from the country's traditions of experimentation and contending ideas. Many concepts recur in different forms in succeeding eras.

Pragmatic leaders usually have to juggle multiple issues, domestic as well as foreign. Officials must balance not only time demands, but the allocation of political and personal capital. To do so, most leaders are drawn to practical "solutions" that must be part of a portfolio of positions and a sequence of incremental actions.

Commentators often labeled Secretary of State and Treasury James Baker, my boss for almost eight years, a "pragmatist." Baker understood power and deployed it masterfully—in his own political system as well as around the world. Descriptions of his diplomatic attributes—such as having an iron fist in a velvet glove—signaled respect: Both foreign and American leaders wanted Baker to be their friend, and they certainly did not want to be his enemy. In turn, he demonstrated good humor and amused colleagues with fine storytelling, while maintaining a personal reserve. His focus was on actions—getting things done and solving problems.

"History Is the Memory of States"

Historians reflect the debates of their age. Our experience colors how we view people of earlier times. For example, during the Cold War, proponents of realism viewed Teddy Roosevelt's—and even Alexander Hamilton's—appreciation of power politics through the prism of mid-twentieth-century challenges.[22]

Our own time period is an unstable one, both for the direction of

American diplomacy and because of shifts in world order. President Donald Trump has promised sharp breaks with the past. He proclaims that past policies have failed. Readers who are struggling to understand what lies ahead might reasonably ask why they should turn to a book about the past. Kissinger's wonderful response is that, "History is the memory of states."[23]

Thirty years ago, Ernest May, an esteemed historian of U.S. foreign policy, and Richard Neustadt, a respected scholar of the presidency, wrote a book for policy makers about the uses of history. But May and Neustadt warned about using historical analogies to predict the future: "Human experience," they wrote, "includes discontinuity, sudden, sharp, and hard to foresee, if foreseeable at all."[24] Decisive and divisive moments built American history. An understanding of that process may help readers better understand not only those earlier eras, but the twenty-first century as well.

I hope this book may also serve as an antidote to the apparent decline of diplomatic history as a field of study. The postrevisionist history movement drew out previously unappreciated actors, sources, themes, and perspectives on foreign policy including race, gender, religion, and ideologies. Greater reliance on foreign source materials added to international perspectives. Transnationalism expanded diplomatic horizons to include humanitarians, railroad engineers, missionaries, environmentalists, businesspeople, educators, and diasporas. Yet the new histories led to fragmented analyses and fewer efforts to combine the pieces into coherent accounts of international events and policies. The history of diplomacy is rich with tales of human endeavors, practical problem solving, and political insight. As Fredrik Logevall and Kenneth Osgood put the question not long ago, "Why did we stop teaching political history?"[25]

Insofar as diplomatic history survived, the agenda seemed to focus on understanding the actions at the end of World War II, during the Cold War, and then the confusions of the post–Cold War world. I want to recover ideas, practice, and traditions from the late eighteenth and nineteenth centuries and the first half of the twentieth century. Given the fluidity of foreign relations in this age, we might apply ideas and pragmatic experiences from America's first 150 years in fresh ways.

Stories about pragmatic American diplomacy need to recognize flaws in the experience, too. Pragmatists may fail or be slow to recognize significant shifts in underlying realities. Kissinger has properly pointed out that some problems may not be "solved," only managed, an insight that a practical problem solver may miss.

Pragmatic problem solving can be vulnerable, as Kissinger has also warned, to strategic nihilism. The United States risks conceiving of foreign policy as a series of discrete challenges to be addressed on their merits rather than as part of an overall design.

Five Traditions

America's diplomatic experience has accumulated traditions. This book draws out five diplomatic traditions that have guided America's visions and pragmatism. All five have already made an appearance in Franklin's story. Although these traditions involve topics that are also part of other countries' foreign policies, U.S. diplomacy has given the application of these ideas a distinctly American flavor.

First, the United States has concentrated on North America, its home continent—to determine the country's geography, size, borders, population, nature as a republic, security, economy, and relations with neighbors. Some European and Asian states tried to dominate their regions; only the United States succeeded in winning control of its continent. Today, Americans are again interested in their borders, security, and transborder flows of people, commerce, information, and the environment. In the twenty-first century, North America will be the base of power for U.S. global reach, especially across the Atlantic and Pacific. We want it to be the best possible foundation.

At times, U.S. leaders have expanded their continental perspective to include visions of special bonds among American republics. They hoped that the states of the New World might change the ways of the Old World. The United States is likely to continue to pursue the promise of Western Hemispheric partnerships.

Second, America's trading, transnational, and technological relations have defined the country's political and even security ties—as well as its economic links—with the rest of the world. The United States arose out of protest against the British Empire's infringement of liberties, including taxes on trade. From America's founding, the country drew a connection between economic and political freedoms and embraced the idea that private parties should be the agents of commerce. America's merchants became practitioners of a new type of transnational internationalism. Over time, Americans pressed for "open doors" to trade. In the twentieth century, U.S. officials recognized the connections between trade and finance and healthy economies, politics, and security. The United States created a model of scientific-technological advances, backed by federal funding, that relied on the country's universities and private sector; U.S. entrepreneurialism worked hand in hand with America's transnationalism. In the twenty-first century, America's ties of trade, technology, and finance will provide the foundations of future orders and partnerships.

Third, U.S. diplomacy has reflected changing American attitudes toward alliances and ways of ordering connections among states. For the first 150 years, Americans heeded Washington's and Jefferson's cautions about alliances with European powers. Looking for alternatives, Americans experimented with a range of ways to preserve national independence within safe international systems. The experience of a union of republican states—especially after the preservation of the Union in the Civil War—influenced American thinking about state order for many decades, even to today. Americans looked as well to trade arrangements, international law, arms control, and the mediation of regional balances of power.

After World War II, the United States responded to fears of global breakdown and Soviet hegemony by building an unprecedented alliance network. The American alliances became a new type of political-security system, providing a framework for mutual political and economic benefits. Most of America's alliance partners were free republics, or eventually became democratic states. After the Cold War, for more than twenty-five years, the United States adapted its expanded alliance network to fit new designs.

Today, President Trump and others question the costs and usefulness of U.S. alliances. Although my career involved working with these alliances to advance U.S. interests and values, the United States will probably reassess the scope, commitments, and shared responsibilities of its alliance system. Americans might consider public and private alternatives—or complements—to alliances for cooperation and competition among countries and peoples. If so, they will want to examine why the United States initially agreed to certain alliances and how the United States put alliances to good use.

Fourth, the stewards of American diplomacy have to understand how to lead—and reflect—public attitudes. Fashioning a foreign policy in a democratic republic, and recognizing the powers of Congress, has confounded many exceptional diplomatic thinkers, including George Kennan. The most skilled U.S. statesmen courted key congressional allies. Successful leaders of American diplomacy need to work with the political factors that will establish the foundation for U.S. foreign policy.

Finally, American diplomacy has reflected the belief that the United States is an exceptional, ongoing experiment, both at home and in international relations, that should serve a larger purpose. The founding generations of the United States were attentive students of the world order of their era. They sensed that their republican experiment, if successful, might have the capacity to change the existing imperial order—to "begin the world over again," in the words of Thomas Paine.

When Charles Thomson, secretary to the Congress, presented the design of the Great Seal of the United States for approval in 1782, he described its iconography. (Those unfamiliar with the seal will find it conveniently reprinted on the back of a dollar bill.) Pointing to the uncompleted thirteen-tiered pyramid of states overseen by the eye of Providence and to the Latin phrase below, Novus Ordo Seclorum—New Order of the Ages— Thomson explained that 1776 marked "the beginning of the new American Era." As my first professor of diplomatic history explained, "Much of American history is implicit in [the] question" of "whether the adjective 'American' is to be construed geographically limiting or as broadly descriptive."

The ideas of the Enlightenment, as stated politically through the Declaration of Independence, were internationalist in scope. Over two centuries, American diplomacy would challenge, overcome, and then remake world orders. The ideas of what America's purpose should—or might—be have evolved over the years. Even when U.S. power has been greatest, American diplomacy has not accepted the status quo of the world order. Americans seek change—which they usually believe will lead to improvement.

Americans are now debating again whether and how they should synchronize the national experiment with international purposes. Historically, America's nationalism and internationalism have been two sides of the same coin. The United States again faces the question of whether and how it will shape a "New Order of the Ages."[26]

The stories that follow reflect the research of many historians. This work relies on the scholarship of numerous writers, as explained in the notes. I add my interpretations based on a practitioner's experience. You will also find comments on the conduct of diplomacy and the design of policies. The five traditions emerge from the accounts, and I return to these traditions at the close as I consider recent history. As you think about the future of America in the world, I hope you will enjoy the stories, personalities, and ideas.

I

—

A NEW AMERICAN ERA

Continental Territory, Financial
Power, Neutral Independence, and a
Republican Union

CHAPTER 1

———◆———

Alexander Hamilton

Architect of American Power

Selecting America's First Secretary of the Treasury

In April 1789, George Washington, the newly elected president of the United States, stopped in Philadelphia on the way to his inauguration in New York City. Washington sought out his old friend, Robert Morris, who had served as superintendent of finance of America's revolutionary government. Morris, the country's most powerful merchant-financier, had delivered the monies to keep Washington's Continental Army alive during its darkest hours. He had been an ally of Ben Franklin. Morris had even used his private credit to pay for troops, fund naval privateers, acquire arms, and procure spies.

According to an account written years later by Washington's stepgrandson, the president-elect asked Morris to become the secretary of the treasury of the new U.S. government. Morris turned the offer down, probably because he needed to concentrate on personal financial problems that would eventually lead to his ruin. But Morris offered Washington a suggestion: "I can recommend a far cleverer fellow than I am for your minister of finance," counseled Morris, "your former aide-de-camp, Colonel Hamilton." A surprised Washington replied that he had not known Hamilton "had any knowledge of finance."[1]

Hamilton was only twenty-two when he became an aide to General Washington in early 1777. Some thirty-two aides worked at Washington's headquarters over the eight-year campaign, but Hamilton stood out among this elite cadre. In 1789, Hamilton was only in his early thirties. The New Yorker had been a political ally of Morris in the creation and ratification of the new Constitution, but the two men were not close friends. It appears that Morris had not spoken to Hamilton about his recommendation to Washington.[2]

A Young Strategist

Morris knew the quality of Hamilton's mind and the young man's prodigious appetite for work. In April 1781, shortly after Congress had appointed Morris superintendent of finance, Hamilton had written an unsolicited letter to the older, much more experienced man. The letter consisted of thirty-one printed pages. Hamilton had just resigned his position as an aide to Washington and had retreated to the library of his father-in-law, Philip Schuyler, to reflect on America's cause. He read and reasoned his way to a fresh synthesis of finance, national power, and war. The Hamilton letter to Morris was in fact a refinement and an expansion of two earlier political-financial analyses, one of which he had written to Congressman James Duane in 1780 and the other probably to Schuyler in 1779. Together, the three letters sketch a plan not only to address the problems of war but also to devise systems of financial and economic power for the young United States.[3]

Hamilton had witnessed the trials of an army—and, more important, of a new nation—that suffered for want of money. Troops went without pay, clothes, and even food. They lacked arms and ammunition. Men of courage on the battlefield, such as Benedict Arnold, became traitors in part for money. Hamilton had written Duane that the army had become a mob. In a letter in September 1780 to his close friend John Laurens, also a former aide to Washington, a frustrated Hamilton asserted that the army, the states, and Congress were in control of "a mass of fools and knaves." The want of money, Hamilton recognized in another paper, could lead the army to disband or enfeeble operations so that the public clamored for peace.[4] In other times and places, officers of desperate armies turned their weapons on the politicians who seemed to ignore or disdain them.

Hamilton's missive to Morris, however, looked beyond the field of battle and the encampments of armies. Hamilton made the strategic leap of comparing America's strengths and weaknesses with its enemy's. Hamilton perceived that Britain and the United States were fighting a war of attrition. He analyzed Britain's system of political economy. The colonel concluded that the victory depended not only on mobilizing U.S. resources, but also on eroding London's credit and will.[5]

Ron Chernow, Hamilton's eminent biographer, wrote that the "Revolution [was a] practical workshop in economic and political theory" for Colonel Hamilton.[6] Hamilton's principal insight was that a state needed good credit to wage a long war successfully. The country simply needed to pay its bills. "Power without revenue is a bubble," concluded Hamilton.

Hamilton turned down opportunities in 1781 to work with the new superintendent of finance or to assist Morris by serving in Congress. The colonel preferred a line command in the Continental Army; he would lead a New York battalion that later captured one of two key British redoubts at Yorktown, sealing victory in the last main campaign of the war. Hamilton sought glory, honor, and fame. He differed from other soldiers, however, in recognizing the importance of finance and economic dynamism to national power and resilience.

Hamilton's strategic, political, and fiscal insights fired his drive for a new national Constitution. In his *Federalist* articles, drafted to advocate ratifying the Constitution, Hamilton explained the interconnections among finance, political institutions, and national security. Furthermore, Hamilton's financial and political designs had implications for America's foreign policy and even its conduct of diplomacy. The *Federalist* pointed out bluntly that under the Articles of Confederation the United States had become a pariah country. To succeed in a dangerous world, the new Republic needed foreign commerce, sound money, government revenue, and a peacetime army. As a maritime commercial people, Americans needed a navy, too.[7]

Hamilton's Economic Strategy

The Treaty of Paris, Franklin's legacy, gave the new American Republic vast lands. Virginians, led by Jefferson, were drawn to the ideas of land as the source of wealth, the foundation of liberty through yeoman farmers, and space for security. Hamilton, in turn, understood that the United States needed financial strength, liquid capital, and economic institutions to develop the country's natural bounty.

America's first treasury secretary admired the programs of Britain's William Pitt the Elder and William Pitt the Younger and respected the financial institutions London had developed. Professor Forrest McDonald later perceived that Hamilton took the British example and applied it differently to the United States: Whereas Britain had designed a system to raise money for the government—with *incidental* political, social, and economic by-products—Hamilton's system employed financial means to *attain* political, economic, and social ends. Hamilton was trying to solve a staggering financial problem. At the same time, however, the new treasury secretary was erecting a new architecture of American power.[8] On Independence Day, 1789, Hamilton's eulogy for his former friend and comrade, General Nathanael Greene, alluded to the work ahead: The task, Hamilton explained, was to "[rear] the superstructure of American greatness."[9]

As a younger man, Hamilton had once copied a passage from Demosthenes's Orations that captured his ambition for both military and political leadership: "[Leaders] ought not to wait for the *event*, to know what

measures to take; but the measures which they have taken, ought to produce the *event*."[10] Hamilton would force decisions, not wait for his "inbox"
or meetings to shape his agenda. Moreover, Hamilton's various actions fit
within a design. As an executive, Hamilton turned for guidance to the three-
volume memoirs of Jacques Necker, France's highly respected minister of
finance under Louis XVI. Necker wrote that a great minister must be able
"to perceive, simultaneously, the whole of a system and the relations of all its
parts to one another."[11]

Others have related the history of Hamilton's plans for credit, a national
bank, and manufactures. I want to draw attention to the components of
Hamilton's plan and how the parts fit together. Hamilton's refunding system
established the federal government's debt as a good and reliable credit. The
securities composing the federal debt, in turn, expanded the new nation's
monetary base, creating liquid funds for investment. The new Bank of the
United States facilitated federal finance, expanded the system of private
credit, and supported investment. By refunding the federal debt, financial
and mercantile interests acquired a stake in the success of the new government. Assumption of state debts by the federal government further expanded
support and the credit base. The new revenue system, especially "moderate"
tariffs, linked taxes to interest payments. A "Sinking Fund" offered further
comfort to investors in federal debt. Hamilton's new customs service, Coast
Guard, and information systems demonstrated that the secretary's executive
skills matched his ability to devise plans for a new political economy. Taken
together, the system enabled Hamilton to lower interest rates on refunded
debts—and to raise more foreign loans. Moreover, as Hamilton wrote Morris, "A national debt, if not excessive, will be a national blessing. It will be a
powerful cement of our union."[12]

Professor McDonald points out another aspect of Hamilton's plan that
often has been overlooked: Good credit depends on market psychology—on
confidence—as well as on facts. Hamilton believed that speedy action by the
new government was vital to securing the good faith of public creditors.[13]
And Hamilton recognized that American diplomacy would be a valuable
contributor to the confidence in—and practical success of—his newly created system of political economy.

The Diplomatic Strategy Matches the Economic Plan

The treasury secretary assumed a diplomatic role even before Thomas Jefferson, the first U.S. secretary of state, was on the job. Some later guardians of the prerogatives of the State Department view Hamilton's diplomacy
as stepping beyond his jurisdiction;[14] in fact, Hamilton was demonstrating

that America's foreign policy, from the very start, incorporated economic perspectives and interests, first by necessity and later by opportunity and choice.

The United States, in Hamilton's view, was potentially both a land and a maritime power. Any dream of American isolationism was folly because the United States was part of a wider Atlantic world in which European powers were maneuvering for advantage across both continents. During the Constitutional Convention, Hamilton had argued for a strong national government to counter "the fantasy that the Atlantic Ocean would protect America from future conflicts."[15]

Hamilton recognized the fundamentals of balance of power politics. A European hegemon was not in the U.S. interest. The United States had to guard against continental powers colluding to control the Mississippi Valley and luring settlers in the new western territories and states away from loyalty to the United States.

In the 1790s, the Mississippi Valley, the strategic heart of power for North America, was still a contested buffer region. Hamilton wanted to push Spain out of eastern North America. He wished to secure New Orleans and the Mississippi for the United States. The secretary of the treasury was wary of French designs—whether monarchical, revolutionary, or later imperial—in North America. And Hamilton even postulated that Britain, the leading naval power, might help thwart moves from Paris and Madrid to constrain the United States in North America. Given time, Hamilton believed that the United States would grow into a great power. In the interim, the nation needed to foster its Atlantic trade, preserve internal cohesion, settle western lands, secure the Mississippi Valley, and maintain the confidence of bankers in Holland and London.[16]

Hamilton's economic and foreign policies needed to support domestic peace and tranquility in order to build strength. Hamilton had near-term practical objectives, too: to end hostilities with Native Americans and stop Europeans from encouraging those conflicts; to compel Britain to leave the forts it still occupied on U.S. lands in the west; and to raise revenue from imports to buttress the new credit system. In 1794, trade duties provided about 90 percent of federal revenues; Britain accounted for nearly three-quarters of U.S. imports and half of American exports.[17] The United States needed credit from Britain as well.

A Strategic Dialogue with Britain?

In October 1789, shortly after assuming office, Hamilton began to explain his foreign policy strategy to George Beckwith, a British army major and aide to Lord Dorchester, the governor general of British North America. Beckwith came as an unofficial emissary to warn that the new Congress's tariffs, which discriminated against Britain, would trigger retaliation. But Hamilton engaged Beckwith in a broader exchange about interests.

Today, Hamilton's diplomatic approach would be labeled a "strategic dialogue." The treasury secretary offered his perspective on the domestic and international context. He sketched a vision of what relations might become—indeed, should become. Hamilton pointed to common ground and suggested directions each side might take, factoring in political constraints. Hamilton specified nonnegotiable points—such as exiting British forts and thwarting a Native American buffer region—while dropping other demands, such as the return of slaves who left with British forces after the war. He avoided recriminations, preferring to explain intentions and explore mutual interests.

Hamilton observed that the United States was an agricultural country whose economy fit well with Britain's manufacturing capacities. American purchasing power, already significant, would grow. Britain could expect that U.S. influence would expand; therefore, London should seek political attachments as well as commercial connections. But Hamilton stressed that to forge a community of interest Britain had to respect the United States. The former colonies had been compelled by British policies to ally with France, but Americans preferred bonds with Britain. "We think in English," Hamilton explained to Beckwith, even though Hamilton also spoke excellent French. Hamilton warned that the United States, if spurned, would ally with France and threaten Britain's wealthy West Indian islands.[18]

After eight years of bitter war, Hamilton's overtures to the former enemy were startling. Jefferson and Madison, in contrast, remained hostile to Britain. They wanted to defy the arrogant, corrupt "British lion" and instead commit to a Franco-American connection. When George Hammond arrived as Britain's minister to the United States in late 1791, Jefferson insisted that their communications must be in writing. Before long, that channel of diplomacy degraded into a debate over which country first violated the peace treaty and therefore was to blame for a list of problems. Hamilton viewed Jefferson's outlook as naïve and his diplomatic approach impractical.

In essence, Hamilton was offering to work within the British global trading system, and even to lean toward London in the European struggle for power—if Britain stopped threatening the United States in North America and embraced the country economically through a commercial treaty. Hamilton believed that the United States, the junior partner, would grow into a great power and that close ties to Britain could be mutually beneficial.

In 1782–83, Lord Shelburne, the prime minister who agreed to peace with the independent United States, advanced a similar, farsighted sketch of Anglo-American cooperation. But British enmities against the Americans were too harsh, and Shelburne's government fell. Similarly, Hamilton's vision of a transatlantic "special relationship" with Britain could not gain American public acceptance for another century.[19] By that time, as Hamilton foresaw, the United States was an emerging great power and Britain sought to accommodate American demands.

A Policy of Neutrality

Hamilton's overtures to Britain were unsuccessful, and France's revolutionary turmoil threatened both Europe's security and America's stability. Hamilton's new system required peace. Therefore, the treasury secretary advanced a foreign policy doctrine, neutrality, that would define American diplomacy for more than a century. The greatest challenge for the neutrality policy came in its application. Jefferson and Hamilton jousted over pro-French and pro-British "tilts" when responding to offenses. Neutrality can frustrate countries fighting for great stakes, as the United States would learn during the Civil War and again in 1914. During the Cold War, the United States sometimes objected to countries claiming neutrality.

In the face of British depredations, Hamilton urged President Washington to "[p]reserve peace at all costs consistent with national honor." Hamilton feared war would "cut up credit by the roots," cripple exports, choke off imports and revenue, and lead to debt cancellation. With peace, in contrast, "force of circumstances will enable us to make our way sufficiently fast in trade."[20]

Hamilton's neutrality no doubt had a pro-British bias because the United States needed to operate in a world of commerce ruled by Britain. Paris's revolutionary fervor threatened America's internal cohesion. The French economy could not supply America's needs, and Hamilton wanted to escape the "prison" of past treaties with France. His solution was to "steer as clear as possible of all foreign connections, other than commercial."[21]

Later in the 1790s, when France attacked American ships, Hamilton again urged Washington to maintain peace. He cautioned against responding to rumors, petty sources of frustration, and "pins and needles" with France. Chernow summarized Hamilton's approach as "impassioned pragmatism."[22]

As the years passed and American strength grew, Hamilton's commitment to mutually reinforcing systems of national power influenced his diplomacy. When President John Adams struggled with the Quasi-Naval War with France in 1798–99, Hamilton wanted to build a stronger navy, believing that peace was best preserved by preparing for war. Hamilton maneuvered to lead a large army of regular troops under Washington's over-all command. Hamilton even speculated about working with Britain and the Royal Navy to force the Spanish to concede the Floridas and Louisiana to the United States in order to prevent those territories from falling into French hands.[23]

Washington's Farewell Address and the Admonition Against Alliances

The culminating expression of Hamilton's diplomatic legacy is George Washington's 1796 Farewell Address. Washington and Hamilton worked together closely on this publication. As Chernow observed, the Address states themes that encompassed Washington's approach to the conten-tious issues of the day, including foreign policies and domestic strife. The Farewell Address became the first chapter in the "Holy Writ" of American diplomacy.[24]

Fundamentally, Washington's Address was a plea to preserve the Union. The president identified threats and defended a vigorous national govern-ment. Hamilton made sure to add a passage about the nexus between public credit, backed by tax revenue, and national "strength and security."

The foreign policy that expressed Washington's experience—and vision—was Hamilton's doctrine of neutrality—exhibiting neither "habitual hatreds" nor "habitual fondness" for other countries. In a phrase that reverberated over the years, Washington warned that the United States should avoid "per-manent alliances." Jefferson's subsequent caution against "entangling alli-ances" added to this admonition. The American heritage of hostility toward alliances became so powerful that for more than 150 years, the stewards of U.S. foreign policy sought other organizing concepts for the international order.

Hamilton's Diplomatic Method

Hamilton conducted diplomacy in a reasoned, respectful, and firm but not belligerent fashion. He expected nations to act according to self-interest but knew that individuals conducting affairs of state had feelings and might not act rationally. Emotions could lead officials to miscalculate interests. Hamilton preferred "mildness in the manner, firmness in the thing." A later admirer of Hamilton, Teddy Roosevelt, summarized his similar approach as "speak softly and carry a big stick."[25]

Hamilton did not direct his measured diplomacy solely toward London.

When later dealing with French transgressions, Hamilton cautioned against overreaction, noting "Strut is good for nothing," and calling for "real firmness." "Combine energy with moderation," Hamilton counseled.[26]

Hamilton, like Franklin, observed that "minute circumstances, mere trifles, give a favorable bias or otherwise to the whole." He was attentive that "nations like individuals sometimes get into squabbles from the manner more than the matter of what passes between them." One of Hamilton's biographers properly concluded that Hamilton's diplomacy was marked by "candor, goodwill, and good sense."[27] Secretary of State James Baker offered similar diplomatic counsel: "Pick your shots."

Talleyrand and Hamilton's Realism

A notable character in Dr. Kissinger's studies of European diplomacy, Charles de Talleyrand, offered a calculating assessment of Hamilton and his American diplomacy. In early 1794, Talleyrand, a stateless émigré from revolutionary France's Reign of Terror, fled to America for two years. The Frenchman, a rogue of wit and intellect, greatly admired the American treasury secretary. Indeed, Talleyrand wrote that he considered "Napoleon, [Charles] Fox [of Britain], and Hamilton the three greatest men of our epoch and...I would give without hesitation the first place to Hamilton." Talleyrand concluded that Hamilton had "divined Europe," meaning that the American had assessed the forces shaping the continent's politics and power.[28]

Talleyrand agreed with Hamilton that Britain, not France, could best offer the long-term credit and industrial products America needed to grow. As for the difficulty of the United States aligning with its former enemy, Talleyrand appreciated that "resentments do not subsist when you have won. Satisfied pride reserves no desire for revenge."[29] Neither Hamilton nor Talleyrand fully appreciated that Jefferson, Madison, and other leading Virginians believed that they still had scores to settle with a condescending Britain.

Although Hamilton and Talleyrand respected one another's intellect and shared a commitment to realistic, not sentimental, assessments of foreign policy, their characters were fundamentally different. During the winter of 1795, Talleyrand walked through the cold streets of New York City on his way to a dinner party. The wily genius spied Hamilton working by candlelight in his law office on Wall Street. Hamilton had stepped down as treasury secretary not long before. The Frenchman was bewildered: "I have seen a man who made the fortune of a nation laboring all night to support his family." Shortly thereafter, when Talleyrand returned to France to become foreign minister, he wrote a friend that "I have to make an immense fortune of it." And he did. In contrast, Hamilton's drive for power was combined with a strong sense of republican virtue.[30]

Talleyrand recalled one other feature that dominated Hamilton's perspective: "a persistent faith in America's economic destiny." Hamilton believed ardently in "the day when—and it is perhaps not very remote—great markets, such as formerly existed in the old world, will be established in America."[31] Sadly, Hamilton, the architect of American power, would not live to see that day.

The Hamiltonian Legacy of Economic Statecraft

Alexander Hamilton had a rare ability to understand systems of power. As a strategist, he combined visions with practical steps that moved the United States toward his long-term aims.

The foundation of Hamilton's system was economic and financial strength. He recognized the critical role of national credit—not only for Americans, but also for their enemy in London, which faced the costs of a war of attrition. As treasury secretary, Hamilton built a system of liquid capital, institutions, and even market psychology that launched the U.S. dollar and American financial markets toward preeminent global positions that they enjoy today. Hamilton also comprehended how America's freedom to trade—and its maritime relations—were vital components of the country's economic strategies, foreign and domestic. In part because of the amazing success of Hamilton's vision, later generations of Americans have often taken his accomplishment for granted. When they have done so, the United States has risked the ultimate source of its power.

Hamilton's system also included the federal Constitution, an effective national government, and a standing navy and army. He apprehended how the interconnections of economic capacities, finance, military power, and political institutions created national security and international influence. He even recognized how technology and innovation contributed to economic and military power.

America's first treasury secretary combined his systemic insights with a geopolitical analysis. He knew that the United States needed an economic and a security strategy for the Atlantic world and to dominate the Mississippi Valley. The United States could not realistically pretend to ignore the powers of Europe; it needed ways to maneuver among them, especially during America's early decades, as the country built its power. Hamilton recognized the potential benefits of a partnership with Britain, but politics and honor required mutually respectful relations even though Britain was far more powerful. As it turned out, neither the politics in London nor those in

America would support Hamilton's diplomatic design for at least another century.

Not for the last time, an architect of American statecraft failed to read correctly—or mobilize—public support. Without a British partnership, Hamilton turned instead to a doctrine of neutrality. Neutrality would be the guiding star of American diplomacy for well over a century. Neutrality did not mean, however, disengagement. To the contrary, America's policy of neutrality required agile tactics as U.S. leaders faced the practical problems of their times. As I will relate in chapter 7, when President Woodrow Wilson departed from America's policy of neutrality during World War I, he did so by trying to redefine neutrality as a new type of collective security.

◆

CHAPTER 2

Thomas Jefferson

The Futurist

Expanding the Republic

The Treaty of Paris doubled the territory of the United States. The Confederation Congress then had to decide how these vast western lands would be governed.

During the eighteenth and nineteenth centuries, capitals that secured, settled, and administered new regions viewed matters of territorial governance as questions of both national and international policy. Colonies were part of the old imperial-mercantilist order that dominated European thinking. Czarist Russia, in turn, extended a centralized, autocratic military-administrative state eastward to the Pacific and beyond, as far as North America. Even Parliamentary Britain wanted to retain control over its "white" dominions—such as Australia, Canada, and New Zealand—well into the 1800s and even into the early twentieth century.

Thomas Jefferson had a different idea. The pre–Constitutional Congress, meeting in Annapolis over the winter of 1783–84, had been slow to gather a quorum of states. While waiting, Jefferson, brimming with plans for the new republic, wrote thirty-one reports in four months, including a paper on coinage that led to the adoption of the dollar and decimal system.[1]

On March 1, 1784, Jefferson presented a committee plan for the governance of the trans-Appalachian territories. Jefferson viewed these lands as vital to U.S. security; they offered "defense in depth" against neighboring European colonies. Jefferson had helped organize Virginia's military expedition to seize the Illinois country, and as governor had ceded vast real estate to the Confederation's Western Reserve. But security required settlement.[2]

The key principle of Jefferson's committee report was that new lands should become coequal states with the original thirteen. Indeed, in seeking states of approximately the same size, Jefferson recommended fourteen new states, even outnumbering the thirteen of the Revolution, and

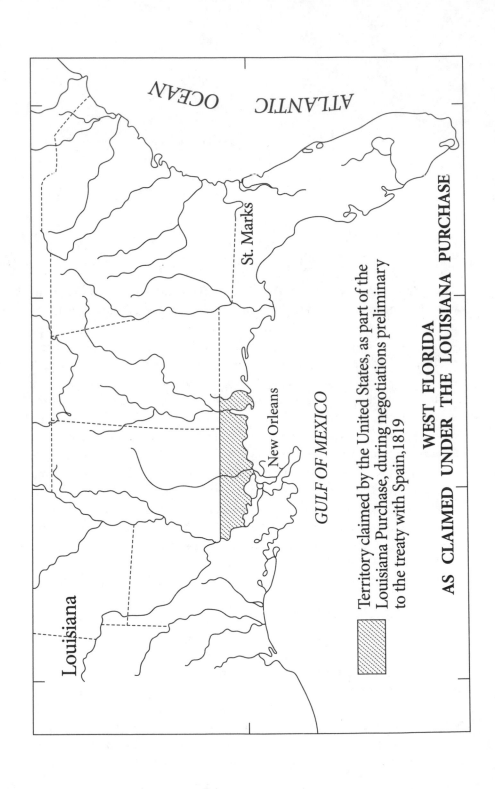

ATLANTIC OCEAN

St. Marks

GULF OF MEXICO

New Orleans

Louisiana

Territory claimed by the United States, as part of the
Louisiana Purchase, during negotiations preliminary
to the treaty with Spain, 1819

WEST FLORIDA
AS CLAIMED UNDER THE LOUISIANA PURCHASE

giving the entrants more votes than their predecessors under the Articles of Confederation.[3]

This powerful republican principle was not Jefferson's alone, although he had first included it in a draft constitution for Virginia in 1776. His plan, however, gave the idea a democratic twist. After the lands were supposed to be purchased from Native Americans, Jefferson envisaged that the territories would step toward statehood in stages, with graduation based on population size. The territories would enjoy self-government at each phase, based on universal white, male suffrage; there would be little interference by the national government. At the time, only Pennsylvania's constitution recognized such a democratic electorate. The territories would share obligations for the Confederation's debt and for the common defense.[4] Jefferson did not want the expansion of the United States to repeat the mistakes of the British Empire by creating second-class colonies.

Jefferson's suggested names for the new territorial-states were a mixture of Native American, classical, and honorific; most, including Cheronesus, Assenispia, and Polypotamia, fortunately fell into history's wastebasket. But Illinois, Michigan, and Washington received their launch from Jefferson's report. Jefferson's interest in geometrical designs led him to ignore geographical features when fixing boundaries, an innovation delayed until the entry of the western states later in the nineteenth century.

Jefferson's report included one other startling idea: After 1800, slavery and indentured servitude would have been illegal in all the new western territories, *south and north*. Jefferson needed seven of the thirteen original states to agree. When the antislavery article came to a vote on April 19, only six states voted yes. The delegate from New Jersey missed the vote because of an illness. Only one other southerner voted with Jefferson.

Two years later, Jefferson wrote to a French historian about the move against slavery: "The voice of a single individual of the state which was divided, or of one of those which were of the negative, would have prevented this abominable crime from spreading itself over the new country. Thus we see the fate of millions unborn hanging on the tongue of one man, and heaven was silent in that awful moment! But it is to be hoped it will not always be silent and that the friends to the rights of human nature will in the end prevail." After that lost vote, Jefferson never again took a bold step against slavery.[5]

Much of the rest of Jefferson's plan was adopted by the Confederation Congress in the Ordinance of 1784, but implementation faltered before the establishment of a new Federal Constitution. In 1787, the Congress superseded the plan with the Northwest Ordinance. That landmark legislation built upon Jefferson's republican principles for new states. The Northwest Ordinance included a ban on slavery, but only north of the Ohio River.

Settlers pushed aside Native American tribes despite George Washington's argument that the First Americans possessed "the right of soil" and that to dispossess them would "stain the character of the nation." The notion of full citizenship—for Native Americans, African-Americans, immigrants, women, and others—in the new American nation would prove a battleground—physically and ideologically—throughout its life.[6]

Taken together, the Treaty of Paris and the Ordinances of 1784 and 1787 laid a foundation for the country's future power. They also planted the seed of an idea about future relations among republican states. The idea of a Union among states became a powerful—even mystical—one for nineteenth-century Americans. Especially after the preservation of the Union in the Civil War of 1861–65, the experience of "Union"—of an expanding "peace pact" among republican states—influenced American speculations about alternatives to the old monarchical and militaristic European international order.[7]

Louisiana and the Mississippi Valley

Thomas Jefferson was a "westerner at heart,"[8] as any visitor to his home at Monticello can see today. When he became the third U.S. president in March 1801, Jefferson faced a conflict between his strategic preferences of westward expansion and friendship with France.

Jefferson's inaugural address embraced American neutrality. He extended Washington's warning against "permanent alliances" to encompass no "entangling alliances." The moment seemed propitious for the dynamic, growing United States to distance itself from Old Europe's strife and wars. Outgoing president John Adams had concluded a treaty on September 30, 1800, to settle the Quasi-Naval War with France. Equally opportune for Jefferson, Adams's diplomacy had badly split the Federalist Party, strengthening the new president's political hand at home.

Unbeknownst to Americans, however, France had signed another treaty—a secret one—with Spain just the day after concluding peace with the United States. Napoleon, who had become first consul of France the prior November, had plans with ominous implications for Jefferson and the United States. In 1761–62, the Bourbon Monarchy of France had ceded Louisiana, its vast western colony in North America, to their fellow Bourbons of Spain; the transfer was part of a compensation settlement at the end of the Seven Years' War. But in 1800, Napoleon wanted Louisiana back; his secret Treaty of Ildefonso reestablished France as an imperial power in North America. The final convention between France and Spain of March 21, 1801, provided a kingdom in Italy for the Spanish queen's nephew (and son-in-law) in exchange for Napoleon's regaining the vast colony on the western border of the United States.[9]

Napoleon thought that his recent peace with Britain and his continental enemies offered an opportunity to extend France's empire far beyond Europe. One option was to return to Egypt and look east. Another was to make the Gulf of Mexico a French lake, uniting the rich islands of the Caribbean with the vast watershed drained by the Mississippi River. Napoleon's foreign minister, Talleyrand, back in Paris after his exile in America, was a proponent of a revived western empire. He had presented a paper before the Institute National, a learned society in Paris, suggesting the commercial benefits of supplying the sugar islands of the West Indies with the produce of Louisiana, in order that France might profit from the "white gold" of Caribbean plantations. After his time in the United States, Talleyrand had concluded that the Americans were an aggressive, expansionist people and that the nominal Spanish overlords of New Orleans and Louisiana would not be able to resist the land-hungry Yankees. But France could do what Spain could not.[10]

Jefferson's ardor for France had cooled in the late 1790s after Europe's republican experiment had turned into Napoleon's virtual dictatorship. Throughout the late 1790s, Americans had heard rumors that France might recover Louisiana. By March 1801, Jefferson's suspicions were stirring, but the government was slow to learn the truth. After failing to uncover the threat to Louisiana, Jefferson's secretary of state, James Madison, finally embraced the dark arts of espionage and set up a small discretionary fund to pay informers in foreign missions.[11]

Jefferson pieced together a troubling picture from scattered reports. The American minister in Madrid, David Humphreys, saw a brief item in a Paris newspaper in August 1800 about a French mission to Madrid to discuss Louisiana. Williams Van Murray, the U.S. minister in Holland, wrote in March 1801 of a rumor that France had taken Louisiana and the Floridas. Minister Rufus King in London reported the same credible hearsay to Jefferson in May. In November 1801, King acquired a copy of the secret treaty. Finally, a paid informant in the Spanish Foreign Ministry sent word that Paris and Madrid had actually signed the treaty of transfer.[12]

In 1801, the Mississippi River was, in effect, the United States' second seacoast, and the Port of New Orleans was the bottleneck for all transit in and out. Napoleon and Talleyrand were well aware that the Americans would object to France's western expedition. Spanish control over New Orleans and the Mississippi had on occasion obstructed U.S. commerce, but Spain's weakness gave the United States the upper hand in any showdown. The powerful French posed an entirely different threat. In 1801, Napoleon wanted to seize his prize before announcing his strike. The first consul needed to ready ships and troops in advance of making his move. In the meantime, he would keep Spanish officials in place to avoid alarming the Americans.[13]

Historians estimate that well over three thousand American sailors and traders passed through New Orleans in 1801. More than half the ships entering the port flew U.S. colors. Many other ships of Spanish registry were owned by Americans. Most of Louisiana's commerce was American. As Jefferson would note, the produce and exports of five U.S. states depended on the channels of the Mississippi. The president wrote Robert Livingston, the U.S. emissary in Paris, "There is on the globe one single spot, the possessor of which is our natural and habitual enemy. It is New Orleans."[14]

American diplomacy in the Louisiana crisis had to weigh the effects of great uncertainties in Europe. The United States had to maneuver among the great powers of Europe while avoiding being drawn into their world war.

Sainte Dominique and the Caribbean Passage

The key that unlocked the door of diplomatic opportunity for Jefferson was France's failure to recapture Sainte Dominique (which became Haiti in 1804) from the freed slaves who had overthrown their plantation owners during the French Revolution. The plantation islands of the West Indies were far richer than Louisiana. Napoleon and Talleyrand's plans considered the islands, the Port of New Orleans, and the unexplored lands of Louisiana as a matched set: The islands produced great sugar wealth and protected Atlantic-Caribbean sea lanes; New Orleans was the port that linked the inland empire with the maritime realm and thus the connection with Europe; and Louisiana represented the promise of agricultural production and mineral wealth that could feed island plantations and enrich the Metropole of France.

Sainte Dominique was led by Toussaint L'Ouverture, a talented and tough former slave. Ruling over half a million former slaves and thousands of mulattoes and whites who had not fled, Toussaint did not surrender power easily. Late in 1801, the first consul sent twenty thousand troops and a large French fleet to subdue Toussaint and the island. The French commander, Charles Leclerc, was an able general as well as Napoleon's brother-in-law. After reasserting control, Napoleon planned to use Sainte Dominique as the base for operations for the occupation of Louisiana and to threaten Jamaica and the British Caribbean islands.[15]

Instead, France's invasion proved disastrous. French duplicity destroyed any hope of winning over the former slaves through an arrangement of local governance within France's empire. Toussaint was tricked and captured; within a year he died in a French prison. His forces retreated to the mountains. But the French were devastated by yellow fever and malaria. Over the course of a year, Leclerc lost twenty-four thousand men. At first, Jefferson sympathized with French efforts to subdue the rebellious former slaves. American slaveholders feared the Africans' success. But when Paris would not answer the president's questions about French plans for Louisiana, the United States permitted merchants to aid the Haitians.[16]

Throughout 1802, Napoleon kept his eye on Louisiana, even amidst his frustrations with Sainte Dominique. In April, Napoleon ordered his minister of the navy, Admiral Denis Decrés, to secretly organize the military and administrative arms of an expedition to Louisiana under the cover of a plan to reinforce Sainte Dominique. The details extended to casting medals with the first consul's likeness—gifts to North American chiefs who were potential allies against the United States.[17]

Jefferson's First Diplomatic Moves

By the spring of 1802, Jefferson's agitation about Napoleon's intentions for Louisiana prompted powerful statements about the stakes involved. Jefferson's letter on April 18 to Livingston in Paris left no doubt about the threat the president wanted to convey to Napoleon. The president wrote that the cession of Louisiana to France "completely reverses all the political relations of the United States...." Although France and the United States had enjoyed a community of interests, the day that France "plac[ed] herself in that door [of New Orleans], [it] assumes to us the attitude of defiance." The United States and France would face "eternal friction." The Americans would be forced to marry the British fleet and nation. And the United States had to turn its "attention to [building] a maritime force." The Anglo-American alliance "would make it impossible for France to reinforce her settlements in the Americas." Britain and the United States would hold sway over all the Americas, with implications for the European power balance. Livingston, probably judging that Napoleon was more likely to be persuaded by logic than threats, softened the message, but there is no doubt that Napoleon heard through multiple channels that France would pay a geopolitical price for its Louisiana adventure.[18]

Robert Livingston, from landed New York gentry, never felt fully accepted or respected by the Virginians. But Livingston might have contributed to solving the Louisiana problem through his uncommon diplomatic style. Livingston tried to build ties with Napoleon, Talleyrand, and Treasury Minister Francois Marbois by offering advice to serve France's interests. Livingston understood, or perhaps just intuited, that in the France of 1800—after the turmoil of the revolution, terror, counterrevolution, and Napoleon's first consulship—the contest for ideas was much more open than during more settled times. If Livingston could pry his way into the small circle that advised Napoleon, perhaps he could shape the leader's thinking.

Livingston prepared a twelve-page paper advising the first consul to reconsider Paris's colonial policy, based on France's own economic interests. The colonies make no sense for France, Livingston wrote, not because of U.S. interests but because colonies are for countries that have an excess population and the inability to produce fine products. France needed its people in Europe. And French wine and craftsmanship offered opportunities for huge profits through exports—including to a friendly United States. Moreover, colonies would prove costly, argued Livingston. Both Talleyrand and Marbois read the paper and recommended it to Napoleon, who was intrigued. The first consul was not prepared to forgo war to make France a peaceful export power, but he could not ignore the costly economics of colonies.[19]

Napoleon even seemed to have an affinity for the New Yorker and the American's willingness to step outside of traditional roles to offer creative, if sometimes incomplete, ideas. Today one would say that Livingston piqued his host's interests by thinking outside the box in ways that might be of help. For whatever reason, the usually impatient Napoleon noticed Livingston was hard of hearing, and he showed the older gentleman special courtesy by articulating his words more clearly when in his presence.[20]

Jefferson sent his own message to Paris through Louis-André Pinchon, the young French chargé in Washington: that the United States "would eventually have Louisiana through the force of things." A French move would drive the United States to ally with Britain, and France would lose both New Orleans and American friendship.[21]

Madison spent considerable time with Pinchon, flattering the twenty-nine-year-old as an intellectual counterpart. The secretary's wide-ranging talks suggested deeper Franco-American ties, but Madison concentrated on the critical risk to the relationship. Madison wanted to delay any French occupation of Louisiana and encourage a deal. The secretary of state warned that France was playing into the hands of the pro-British Federalists.

In the summer of 1802, an angry Madison took a step further. He lectured Pinchon about France's bad faith and dissimulation. Madison had read an article in *La Gazette de France* that argued France must stand up to U.S. expansionism. Countering the notion that French control over the Mississippi would split off the western states, Madison declared that French possession of the territory "would unite Americans, and...France cannot long hold Louisiana against the will of the United States." Madison observed that France had not responded to inquiries about U.S. rights upon the Mississippi and concluded pointedly, "Certainly if people behaved thus toward you, you would regard this silence as a sort of declaration of war."[22]

Jefferson's diplomacy extended to private channels. The members of the du Pont family were thinkers, businesspeople, and investors who operated in both France and the United States.[23] When Jefferson learned that Pierre du Pont planned to travel to Paris, the president suggested that inflated numbers of American militiamen were readying for action on the Mississippi. Meeting with Pierre for two hours, the president warned that his distaste for war should not be interpreted by Napoleon as a lack of resolve. Following the meeting with a letter, Jefferson argued that circumstances permitted no delay. France faced dire consequences: a "war which would annihilate France on the ocean and place it under the despotism of two nations"—the United States and Britain.[24]

Pierre du Pont responded with blunt honesty, which presidents need to hear but often do not. "To say, 'Give up that city or we shall take it from you' is not at all persuasive." "What then are your means of acquiring and persuading France to an amicable cession of her property? Alas, Mr. President... it is payment in money. Consider what the most successful war with France and Spain would cost you. And contract for a part—a half let us say."[25]

The president asked du Pont to destroy his reply, so we do not know his reaction to the proposal to buy what America wanted. But Jefferson did not reject the idea of a purchase. And he kept du Pont informed about U.S. moves.

Du Pont was assessing both France's need for money and Napoleon's temperament. The old gentleman gained an audience with Bonaparte and proposed his simple bargain. Du Pont probably was the man who planted the seed of the idea of a monetary deal with Napoleon. In the spirit of an honest broker, du Pont shared the same view with both parties: Was not this problem really a matter of reaching a fair price for valuable real estate? At this point, du Pont was suggesting several millions of dollars for an agreement on the future of New Orleans and permanent U.S. rights to transit the Mississippi. Yet Napoleon was also hearing messages about Jefferson's impassioned reactions to French moves. Even if the United States might not have had the military means to back up its rash assertions, the president's threats could prove dangerous. When it came time for Napoleon to calculate risks and opportunities, he now had a new option: selling the whole venture and using the proceeds for a land campaign to win the domination of Europe.[26]

The Spanish Spark a Crisis

In the autumn of 1802, an unexpected event forced the Louisiana question higher on everyone's agenda. On October 18, the leading Spanish official in New Orleans ended the Americans' right to deposit goods in the city. This action did not deny Americans the right of free navigation, but it wreaked havoc with transshipment. The news reached Washington in November. Americans were outraged. And they thought they knew whom to blame: Napoleon and the French.

In fact, Paris was surprised by the Spanish official's deed, although at first Napoleon and Talleyrand did not complain. The king of Spain had sent secret instructions to his man in New Orleans. The king was determined to stop American smuggling and welcomed an opportunity to embarrass France. Spain felt bullied by Napoleon over Louisiana and French demands for Florida.[27]

Legislatures across the western states denounced Spain's action. The American Federalists—a party with most of its strength in the Northeast—rapidly embraced the westerners' cause. Calls to arms resounded across the country—against France, Spain, or both. Secretary Madison wrote to U.S. minister Charles Pinckney in Madrid that the Mississippi was "the Hudson, the Delaware, the Potomac, and all other navigable rivers of the Atlantic states formed into one stream." Madison demanded that Spain revoke the suspension immediately.[28]

Madison also wrote Livingston to make sure the French understood that the events in New Orleans had precipitated an explosion that the president could not contain. "There are now or in less than two years will be not less than 200,000 militia on the waters of the Mississippi," wrote Madison, "every man of whom would march at a moment's warning to remove obstructions from that outlet to the sea, every man of whom regards the free use of that river as a natural and indefeasible right and is conscious of the physical force that at any time give effect to it."[29]

Jefferson faced a dilemma when Congress returned to Washington in December 1802. Procrastination would alienate the president's strongest supporters in the west and south; action might trigger a war. Jefferson maintained that the Spanish official in New Orleans had acted on his own and called on Madrid to reverse course. To satisfy his western supporters, the president assembled seven companies of troops at Fort Adams on the Mississippi not far above the Spanish border. Governor William Claiborne of the Mississippi Territory wrote that he had two thousand well-organized militia ready to take New Orleans before the French arrived. Jefferson and Madison thought the French might consider some purchase to resolve the conflict.[30]

Monroe's Mission

On January 10, Jefferson took another step to strengthen his political and negotiating strategies: He asked James Monroe to travel to Paris and Madrid as a special emissary. Monroe was popular in the west, trusted by Jefferson and Madison, spoke French well, and was familiar with France, where he had served as minister (albeit with a questionable record) in the 1790s.[31] Jefferson told his son-in-law that the westerners' "confidence in Monroe will tranquilize them." Assuming that New Orleans must be seized or bought, a committee of Congress also proposed an appropriation of $2 million to buy New Orleans and the Floridas.[32]

Jefferson understood that he was buying time while exploring the option of negotiation. He also searched for more leverage with France and additional options in the event Napoleon would not bargain. The president extended Monroe's mission to include consultations in London, on the recommendation of the British chargé in Washington; Jefferson hoped Paris would recognize the risk of an Anglo-American agreement, perhaps to seize Louisiana. Jefferson convened his cabinet in January to discuss a possible alliance with Britain, an amazing step given the president's long record of hostility. At another meeting, later in April, Jefferson's cabinet actually voted, 3 to 2, to "enter into conferences with the British Government" and "fix principles of alliance" if France would not sell—although the U.S. terms suggest the negotiation might have been meant primarily to signal a threat to Paris.[33]

Jefferson launched one more venture, one that dovetailed with his interests in science and the natural world. The president needed intelligence about the unknown lands west of the Mississippi. On January 18, shortly after Congress concurred with Monroe's mission, the president sent Congress a request for an exploratory corps of discovery to Upper Louisiana. After a discussion behind closed doors, Congress authorized what became known as the Lewis and Clark expedition. With the stated aim of scientific discovery and exploring trade with Native Americans, Jefferson's primary objective was military reconnaissance—a spy mission—in French and Spanish territories to scout possible "purchase...or conquest."[34]

For now, however, the Monroe mission was the critical event. The United States mistakenly thought that France had acquired the Floridas as well as Louisiana. Therefore, Monroe and Livingston were directed to seek "a cession to the United States of New Orleans and of West and East Florida, or as much thereof as the actual proprietor can be prevailed upon to part with." Their fallback was to seek an expanded right of deposit in New Orleans and similar rights at the mouths of other rivers that flowed into the Gulf of

Mexico. To back up his bargaining, Monroe could warn that the people of the United States would seize what they deserved and could not otherwise acquire—an implied but indefinite threat of war.[35]

Jefferson spoke to Monroe in the utmost confidence before his protégé departed. The president said that he would be willing to stretch to a price of 50 million francs—a little more than $9 million—for Mississippi navigation rights and a substantial part of the Floridas. He was more than quadrupling the $2 million figure that a committee of Congress had discussed in a much more limited context. To give some sense of comparison, the total outlays of the federal government in 1801 were $9.4 million.[36]

Developments in Paris, Washington, Madrid, and London

Across the Atlantic, events in early 1803 prodded Napoleon to recalculate his plans. His brother-in-law, General Leclerc, had been felled by yellow fever in November, amidst heavy losses of troops. The French expedition that was supposed to sail from the Netherlands to Louisiana was plagued by postponements and then held back by winter weather. After delaying the formal transfer of Louisiana to France, Spain refused to grant the Floridas. Without Sainte Dominique and control of the Gulf coast in North America, Napoleon's plans looked shakier. "Damn sugar, damn coffee, damn colonies," he reportedly complained in early 1803.[37]

The French had difficulty calculating the latent power of the new United States. Jefferson and Madison pointed to huge population increases in the west, perhaps with timely exaggerations, suggesting a reserve army ready to march on New Orleans. "Population is power," said Jefferson. Pinchon forwarded a summary of the U.S. Census of 1800, which revealed a population increase of 2.5 million—and a growth rate that would rapidly double America's numbers. "These developments boggle the imagination," Pinchon wrote Talleyrand.[38]

Pinchon's reports home fed Napoleon's sense of disquiet. Pinchon believed that Louisiana's security depended on America's goodwill. Unusually for foreign diplomats of this era, he paid attention to Congress, too. The Federalist Party was demanding war. Pinchon warned that if France rejected Jefferson's overtures, Paris should expect conflict.[39]

In February, Senator James Ross of Pennsylvania, a Federalist, offered a series of resolutions authorizing $5 million for the president to call out a fifty-thousand-man militia force to seize New Orleans. The Senate defeated the resolutions, 15 to 11. It passed a substitute, offered by Senator John Breckenridge, a Republican from Kentucky, that authorized the president to call up eighty thousand militia men—but enabled the president to control the timing. Napoleon learned of Ross's belligerent resolutions in early April through a story reported in the *Times* of London. The distinctions of the U.S. Constitution's separation of powers were probably lost on the all-powerful leader of France. But he sensed accurately that relations with the United States had reached a critical point. Monroe would need an answer.[40]

Even as Monroe was departing for Europe, Jefferson's diplomacy was producing results with Spain. Madrid realized that public pressure in the United States could force the president into military action that he wanted to avoid. The Spaniards already saw war clouds gathering over Europe; they had no interest in a conflict with the United States over a colony that Spain was turning over to France in any event. On March 1, 1803, the Crown ordered a restoration of America's right of deposit in New Orleans and dispatched a fast mail ship to Washington with the conciliatory message.[41]

News from London also helped buttress Jefferson's advantage. The British had viewed Napoleon's probe across the Atlantic as a threat to both their Caribbean prizes and, through Louisiana, as a possible move north toward Canada. Britain's Royal Navy sailed along the Dutch coast watchfully, eyeing the Louisiana fleet Napoleon had been assembling. London feared that the French might attempt a landing in Britain instead. On March 2, 1803, King George III informed Parliament that French military preparations necessitated "additional measures of precaution for...security." Napoleon reacted hostilely. Within two weeks of the king's warnings, Napoleon bluntly told the British ambassador in Paris, "So you are determined to go to war."[42]

A French historian has written that a few weeks later, in early April, after reading of the U.S. Congress's moves toward war, Napoleon told a minister, probably Talleyrand, that the game was up. "I will not keep a possession which will not be safe in our hands, that may perhaps embroil me with the Americans, or may place me in a state of coolness with them," determined Napoleon. Then, building on the logic he had heard from Livingston and others, Napoleon added: "I shall make it serve me, on the contrary, to attach [the Americans] to me, to get them into differences with the English, and I shall create for them [the British] enemies who will one day avenge us, if we do not succeed in avenging ourselves." Then, turning to Pierre du Pont's idea, Napoleon explained, "I shall demand of [the United States] a sum of money to pay the expenses of the extraordinary armament I am projecting against Great Britain."[43]

The Negotiation

The pace of diplomacy moved into high gear after the French semaphore system alerted Napoleon of Monroe's arrival in France on April 8. Napoleon called Admiral Decrés and Treasury Minister Marbois to his palace at

St. Cloud to relate his conversation with Talleyrand and to seek their advice. Because Louisiana was a colonial issue, it was formally the responsibility of the navy. Marbois was an alternative to Talleyrand if Napoleon decided to negotiate. Marbois had served in the United States from 1779 to 1785, married a wealthy woman from Philadelphia, and demonstrated loyalty and honesty in cleaning up corrupt army contractors.

Napoleon explained that he expected Britain to seize Louisiana when war resumed. The Americans were asking only for New Orleans, he added, but turning over the whole colony would be more useful to Napoleon's strategy. Yet France did not even hold possession of the place, so Paris could transfer only an empty title. Admiral Decrés protested. Marbois urged prompt action before Louisiana was lost to the British or Americans. Both Napoleon and Marbois echoed points made in Livingston's earlier paper. Napoleon did not reveal his conclusion.[44]

On April 11, Napoleon sent for Marbois at dawn. According to Marbois's later account, Napoleon declared, "Irresolution and deliberation are no longer in season. I renounce Louisiana. It is not only New Orleans that I will cede, it is the whole colony....I direct you to negotiate...with the envoys of the United States. Do not even await the arrival of Mr. Monroe: have an interview with Mr. Livingston; but I require a great deal of money for this war."

Marbois wrote that Napoleon had sketched a draft treaty of sale for 100 million francs (a little less than $20 million), plus a U.S. assumption of the war claims that Americans had made against France for seizures during the Quasi-Naval War. Marbois replied that the Americans could not raise such a sum. Napoleon countered he must at least have 50 million, nothing less, because, "I must have real money for the war with England."[45]

Napoleon probably turned to Marbois because the treasury minister favored the sale, knew the Americans well, and was honest. Speedy action was important—to get the best value before war might lead to a discounted price. Britain or the United States might invade first. Spain could interfere, too, because Madrid had actual possession of Louisiana. And, unfortunately for Paris, in 1802 the French had committed to Spain not to "sell or alienate" the colony.[46]

Talleyrand could not resist positioning himself in the midst of opportunity. On the same day that Napoleon told Marbois to handle the sale, Talleyrand asked Livingston whether the Americans would wish to have the whole of Louisiana. Livingston wrote Madison the next day that he had replied, "No, our wishes extend only to New Orleans and the Floridas." This answer was both accurate and wise bargaining. But Talleyrand pressed for a bid for the whole colony. Livingston supposed about 20 million francs (less than $4 million). Talleyrand said that the figure was far too low and urged Livingston to reflect on the idea. Then Talleyrand sought to protect himself from Napoleon's ire by saying he was not speaking with authority.[47]

Livingston knew that he would have to work with Monroe, who arrived in Paris that same day. But the New Yorker was frustrated at being pushed aside at the moment that fate had offered him a stunning place in history—and perhaps in America's political future as well.

Monroe treated Livingston graciously, but given their relative standing with the president and secretary of state, the responsibility now fell heavily on the Virginian. Marbois launched the negotiation on April 13, offering Louisiana for 100 million francs. The Americans needed to decide whether to wait months to seek guidance from Washington or to move quickly, and if so, with what counteroffer. They also had to figure out what was in fact being sold.

The Americans' principal interest, other than New Orleans, was Florida—East and West—which began on the eastern shore of the Mississippi and defined most of the southern border of the United States.[48] When Livingston later asked Talleyrand about the eastern border of the Louisiana territory in order to learn if it included any of the Floridas, the foreign minister replied enigmatically, "You must take it as we received it." Livingston then logically asked, "But what did you mean to take from Spain?" Talleyrand shrugged and said, "I don't know." "You mean that we should construe it in our own way?" Livingston countered. "I can give you no direction," Talleyrand said. "You have made a noble bargain for yourselves, and I suppose you will make the most of it." When Marbois told Napoleon the boundaries were obscure, Napoleon supposedly replied, "If an obscurity did not already exist, it would perhaps be a good policy to put one there." In effect, France would sell as much as it could, the United States would claim as much as it could, and Spain would protest in frustration.[49]

Monroe's Fateful Decision

Monroe had to decide whether the president and Congress really wanted to double the territory of the United States. The American Republic would become larger than all of Europe. The public and Congress had been focusing on the Mississippi; they could scarcely conceive of the space and lands Monroe might now be able to purchase for future generations. Expansion would pose questions of governance, settlement, migration, economic development, security, and the extension of slavery—issues that would occupy the U.S. political agenda for much of the century that was just beginning. Moreover, the Constitution had not granted the president an explicit right to buy territory. Congress would have to appropriate a huge sum and borrow a good deal of it from foreign bankers.

Monroe struggled to assess what Jefferson would want, reasoning that the authority for the decision would rest with the president. At one point, Monroe thought he should tell Marbois that he needed to seek guidance from Washington. That would have been the safe course. But Monroe recognized the risk in delay and that Napoleon, the sole power in France, might change his mind. The renewal of France's war with Britain could sharply shift priorities and attention. The French might receive news of gains in Sainte Dominique. Napoleon might find another source of quick cash. Talleyrand, Decrés, or Napoleon's brothers, who dreamed of a western empire, might change his mind. Spain might interfere. Monroe eventually recognized that his role—as a minister with "plenipotentiary power"—was not to guess what Jefferson would do, but instead to exercise his own judgment, to the best of his own ability. This was a courageous determination. If Jefferson or Congress disagreed, Monroe's career would end in humiliation.[50]

Monroe knew that the Louisiana Purchase was the right thing to do, and he now resolved to act. He still had to find a price to close the deal. Jefferson had authorized about $9 to $10 million (50 million francs) for New Orleans and as much of the Floridas as possible. The Americans tried that figure, but Marbois reported back that Napoleon's cold response put all their efforts at risk. (Marbois might have handled this offer himself without checking with Napoleon.) The Frenchman urged the Americans to consider that they were not only buying the Mississippi and vast lands, but also the security "of having no neighbors to dispute you, no war to dread." Marbois went back and forth with Monroe and Livingston, finally agreeing on $15 million (80 million francs) for both Louisiana and to pay off French obligations for past seizures of American ships and cargo. Because the U.S. claims against France were for about $3.75 million (20 million francs), the deal actually added $11.25 million (60 million francs) to Napoleon's war chest. Marbois had found a number above the consul's minimum but below his ambition. In line with Marbois's advice, the treaty described "the Colony or Province of Louisiana with the Same extent that it now has in the hand of Spain, & that it had when France possessed it; and Such as it Should be after the Treaties subsequently entered into between Spain and other States." The Americans eventually gained between 827,000 to 875,000 square miles—at four cents an acre, including costs of financing. France and the United States signed the formal treaty on May 2, 1803—quick work for the biggest real estate deal in history.[51]

Jefferson and Madison Sign On

The treaty documents appear to have arrived at the White House on July 3, 1803. At first, Jefferson was overjoyed. Then he began to question his constitutional power to buy the territory. In his battles with Hamilton during the Washington administration, Jefferson had argued that the federal government had only the powers enumerated in the Constitution. He feared that the national government's reliance on "implied powers" threatened liberty. For ten days, Jefferson struggled with the conundrum. He considered asking for a constitutional amendment to give the federal government the right to acquire territory. Madison, the more practical of the two partners, stepped in. Monroe and Livingston were urging prompt action by the Senate on the treaty and the Congress on funding. They warned that Napoleon might change his mind. "Any mention of a constitutional amendment would destroy the whole result," Madison warned. Jefferson opted for a continental United States.

The president called for Congress to reconvene on October 17. Although some Federalists complained, the mood of the American public was patriotic joy. For the first time, Americans began to imagine a continental destiny, and they embraced it.[52] When someone asked Gouverneur Morris, who had drafted the language of the Constitution, whether the Framers favored such a vast expansion of the Republic, he said he could not recollect. But the sharp-tongued Morris added, "I knew as well then as I do now, that all North America must at length be annexed to us—happy, indeed, if the lust for dominion stops there."[53]

The Senate ratified the treaty on October 20 by a telling vote of 24 to 7. The House approved the financial terms by an equally overwhelming vote of 89 to 23.[54]

Geopolitics and Finance

Britain had resumed war with Napoleon's France on May 18. The Louisiana Purchase provided Napoleon valuable funds for lightning campaigns in his principal theater of operations, continental Europe. For over a decade, Napoleon's battles with various coalitions dominated the attention of the transatlantic world. From the vantage point of history, Napoleon's exploration of a new North American empire looks like a sideshow. Perhaps he never could have succeeded. But Jefferson had to deal with the strategic landscape of 1801. Napoleon was a formidable foe, with powerful military capabilities, and a vision that had led to astounding transformations. A French empire on the western border of the United States would have changed history. France might have divided North America along the Mississippi. Britain might have seized it and contained U.S. expansion.

Napoleon forecast presciently for the United States that, "[w]e must expect rivalries in the bosom of the Union. Confederations which are called perpetual last only until one of the contracting parties finds it to its interest to break them." Indeed, the American Union would face a test of survival in 1861. For Britain, Napoleon predicted, "I have just given to England a maritime rival, that will sooner or later humble her pride."[55]

Ironically, Hamilton's financial system—and British banks—made Jefferson's greatest success possible. The United States did not have the cash to pay Napoleon, so the Americans conveyed creditworthy U.S. bonds with an interest rate of 6 percent. Napoleon then turned to Baring Brothers of London and Hope and Company of Amsterdam, the largest handlers of American securities in Europe, to exchange U.S. bonds into coins (after the bankers took a healthy slice). Despite the renewal of war, the British treasury granted Barings permission to ship specie from London to Paris.[56]

Jefferson "the Futurist"

Jefferson's diplomacy, like his approach to governing, was unusual. His interest in ideas, and his ability to foresee historical movements, made him a "Futurist." His gravestone at Monticello reveals what Jefferson believed were his most important contributions: the Virginia Declaration of Rights; the American Declaration of Independence; and the University of Virginia. Each legacy highlights the potential of individuals, secure in liberty, to make a new and more promising state, country, and world. Jefferson's record as an executive—as governor and president—was mixed. But he had a rare capacity to imagine a different future, and he worked to free people and forces that would achieve that posterity.

Jefferson's Ordinance of 1784 imagined an expanding republic of coequal states, populated by free people. In 1803, Jefferson assumed that the expansion of the United States would create an empire of liberty across North America. A growing population, drawn to and strengthened by American freedoms, would prove an unstoppable force.

Jeffersonian Diplomacy

Yet Jefferson the politician had to work within the constraints of his time. He struggled to avoid Europe's conflicts. He had to maneuver among Europe's powers, especially those asserting claims in North America. Jefferson abhorred the armed politics of Europe, and wanted to avoid creating a standing U.S. army, so he experimented with a different approach. The new American diplomacy pressed for peaceful resolution of disputes and preferred ties of commerce over threats of armies. But Jefferson warned Europeans that they needed to take America's power seriously, especially when the country's imperatives were expressed through popular will.

The president had a feel for using the appearance of power, employing threats without the backing of a military establishment. The president's diplomacy simply presumed that France could not withstand America's westward movement or would not want to alienate rising U.S. maritime capabilities. Jefferson may well have believed that—if absolutely necessary—America's latent power could be quickly expressed through mobilized militias. It took the militia's debacle during the War of 1812 to underscore the importance of a regular army and the logistical difficulties of militia campaigns over vast distances. In any event, Pinchon and eventually Napoleon calculated the risks of contravening the will of the United States in the American neighborhood. Throughout the nineteenth and twentieth centuries, others would learn this lesson as well.

Was Jefferson's diplomacy lucky or good? Probably both. Successful negotiators need a clear sense of objective, which Jefferson had. His diplomacy involved considerable agility, varying tactics while keeping a sharp eye on his objective. He kept channels open—with France, Britain, Spain, and his own Congress—while studying the shifting events in Europe and, critically, the Caribbean. He offered France the benefits of American friendship—or the weight of its opposition in league with Britain. The president used multiple channels to gather information and send messages, including unofficially through friends such as the du Ponts. Jefferson was open to bargaining, even buyouts, especially to avoid war. He kept working with all the parties while sending strong messages about the result he wanted. One historian termed Jefferson's policy "threat and procrastination."[57]

The president had a good sense of timing, too. Jefferson's patience permitted calculated delays—in contrast with either a rush to act or inaction through passivity.[58] He felt that time would work against the French plan. He considered how events—in Sainte Dominique, Europe, and within North America—could strengthen his hand with France, pressure Spain, and court Britain. He sent Monroe to France at exactly the right moment.

Jefferson, America's first great party politician, understood and used domestic politics brilliantly in his diplomacy. The public's outcry about foreign intercession in New Orleans and along the Mississippi was a real force with which he and others had to reckon. Jefferson held off Federalist calls for war while using their fervor to threaten France. He shrewdly decided to send Monroe to France both to keep control of the politics in the western states and to force political decisions in Paris. Jefferson might have disliked Hamilton's financial system and the treasury secretary's reasoning about implied constitutional powers, but the Virginian used both when they were necessary to achieve America's ends.

At moments, the tensions between Jefferson's visionary ideas and the practical need to act could confound him. Futurists are still compelled to deal with the here and now. Jefferson was fortunate to have friends and colleagues who complemented him. Madison ended the speculation and delay about seeking a constitutional amendment. Monroe, a sound man who could make decisions, was a better emissary in Paris than Jefferson would have been.

Later in his presidency, Jefferson's search for a "new diplomacy" to avoid Europe's wars was not as successful. His 1807 embargo on the U.S. maritime trade with the warring countries severely hurt the U.S. economy without succeeding diplomatically. U.S. exports did not regain the 1807 level until 1835.[59] Not all visions of the future prove practical. The success of Louisiana, however, dwarfs Jefferson's missteps. The purchase transformed the United States into the dominant power of North America. Henry Adams, the late nineteenth-century historian and descendant of two presidents, called the Louisiana affair "the greatest diplomatic success recorded in American history." He ranked the achievement "next to the Declaration of Independence and the adoption of the Constitution."[60]

After 1803, U.S. foreign policy concentrated on becoming a continental country and pushing possible competitors out, or at least holding them at a safe distance. The greatest challenge would be to preserve the Union of states and to prove that a republic reaching across a continent could survive and prosper. The "abominable crime" of slavery that tormented Jefferson in 1784 would pose a mortal challenge to the Union.

◆

CHAPTER 3

John Quincy Adams and Henry Clay

American Realism and the American System

Canning's Invitation

On August 16, 1823, Richard Rush, the U.S. minister to Great Britain, climbed the stairs of the old brick building that served as the Foreign Office of the world's greatest power. Rush, forty-three, had been attorney general of the United States for three years before assuming the premier American diplomatic post in London in 1817. He was headed toward Foreign Secretary George Canning's office, an imposing room elegantly decorated with three walls of tapestries, overlooking St. James's Park.[1]

Canning had requested to meet Rush at an unusual time. Parliament had just recessed. Canning, who also served as leader of the House of Commons, was exhausted; he might have been expected to have departed for his country home. But instead Canning wanted to meet the representative of the upstart nation that had caused London much trouble during Britain's twenty-year-long war with France. Anglo-American disputes over maritime rights had even led the poorly prepared Americans to declare war against Britain in 1812. The Americans had suffered a succession of military defeats, including the torching of the new U.S. capital of Washington. Nevertheless, the small U.S. Navy distinguished itself on both salt and fresh waters, and American defenses achieved a stalemate. In Ghent, Belgium, on Christmas Day, 1814, the antagonists signed a peace treaty that restored the status quo. Having once again survived the claws of the British lion, and closing with Andrew Jackson's glorious repulse in January 1815 of an invasion of New Orleans, Americans graced the disappointing conflict with the uplifting name of the "Second War of Independence."

There were signs, however, that the two English-speaking countries might learn to suffer one another peacefully. The head of the U.S. delegation at Ghent, John Quincy Adams, had gone on to serve as America's minister to Britain from 1815 to 1817, where he laid the groundwork for President Monroe and Rush (as acting secretary) to complete a treaty with Sir Charles Bagot to limit naval armaments on the Great Lakes and demilitarize the U.S.-Canadian frontier. The Rush-Bagot Treaty was America's first experiment with arms control and the first reciprocal naval disarmament of modern times.[2] It eventually led to the longest peaceful border in the world.

Canning's purpose in meeting Rush, however, pertained to the southern reaches of the globe, not the northern. Spain's American colonies had been declaring their independence and opening their commerce to Britain and the United States when, in 1823, revolutionaries in Spain captured King Ferdinand VII and declared a constitutional monarchy; the Latin Americans appeared close to completing their break with Madrid. But storm clouds were gathering.

The so-called Holy Alliance of Russia, Austria, Prussia, and a restored monarchy in France wanted to reestablish stability in Europe after France's radical revolution and Napoleon's redrawing of the continental map. The countries of the Holy Alliance met with Canning's predecessor, Lord Castlereagh, in a series of congresses to secure the peace of Europe. The Holy Alliance wanted to crush constitutionalists and install "legitimate," reactionary monarchies across the continent. Dr. Kissinger's dissertation and first book, *A World Restored*, recounts the statesmanship that led to the rise of this new world order of Europe.[3]

In 1823, Russia, Austria, and Prussia were encouraging France to send troops to Spain to rescue Ferdinand. Austria had recently routed republican movements in Naples and Piedmont. If France restored Ferdinand's authority in Spain, the Holy Alliance might then turn to help royalist Spain crush the young republics of Latin America.

These were the circumstances that led Canning to make a most extraordinary proposal to Rush: The foreign secretary urged the United States to issue a joint statement with Britain, or at least concurrent declarations, opposing any move by Spain and the Holy Alliance to reconquer Madrid's former colonies in the Americas.[4]

This proposal for an Anglo-American partnership was startling—and flattering. The U.S. Navy had less than 2 percent of the cannon of the Royal Navy, and America's merchant tonnage was but half of Britain's.[5] Yet Canning was behaving as if the United States had earned consideration. Although Americans believed they were exceptional, even potentially powerful, Europeans would have ranked the United States with the Scandinavian states or Switzerland.[6] Moreover, the United States was a distrusted and rowdy constitutional republic, a mere former colony, and distant from the grand chessboard of Europe. Nevertheless, Britain, a power on center stage since the final defeat of Napoleon, with its incomparable Royal Navy, was offering the United States a place within the European, and even the global, arena.

Rush hesitated. He understood the United States' common interests with Britain in Latin America. But given the U.S. dictum of avoiding "entanglement"—as well as a long accumulation of public resentments against London's arrogance—Rush saw a "danger of pledging my government" to any measure "that might implicate it in the federative system of Europe."[7]

Instead, Rush probed for Canning's plans and purposes. Did London intend to recognize the new republics as independent states, as the United States had already done? Canning hedged. In fact, the informal nature of the foreign secretary's proposal reflected his limited room for maneuver. Canning's powerful cabinet colleague, the Duke of Wellington, the victor at Waterloo, remained an influential voice on international topics. The duke was close to King George IV, whose opinions still mattered. Wellington wanted to maintain a working alliance between Britain and the continental monarchies.

In effect, Canning sought to play "an American card" in London by suggesting to his colleagues that Britain needed to recognize the new Latin republics and encourage their friendship in order to ward off U.S. commercial and perhaps territorial aggrandizement. Canning's ears were tuned toward Britain's commercial interests—including in South America—and to parliamentary and literate public opinion, which viewed the Holy Alliance with suspicion. In contrast with Castlereagh's interest in a European system of congresses and order, Canning wanted to reposition Britain as an offshore balancer of continental powers while emphasizing London's global maritime and trade interests.[8] If Canning could present his cabinet colleagues with a British-U.S. declaration, he would likely be able to shift their policy while also constraining the aggressive Americans.

Rush's dispatches reached Washington on October 9. He included a letter from Canning proposing a five-point joint declaration along with Canning's warning of a possible upcoming great power conference about Latin America. Canning was pressing for a U.S. reply. Monroe's cabinet met for a first discussion on October 11, before the president left for a month at his Virginia farm.[9]

U.S. Foreign Policy in 1823: Problems and Principles

The debates that led to Monroe's declaration two months later—which came to be known as the Monroe Doctrine—stemmed from the need to address a problem. Canning had made a proposal about a specific situation; the United States needed to decide on an answer. Neither Monroe nor Secretary of State John Quincy Adams had planned to announce a lasting foreign policy doctrine.

Monroe's response to the problem—under the guidance of Adams—reflected numerous considerations. The president had to assess other foreign policy questions on the agenda, including Russia's assertion of rights along the northwest coast of North America. Prominent Americans also wanted to support Greek revolutionaries fighting for liberty and Christianity against the Ottoman Turks. Monroe had to weigh domestic and political interests, too, including the competition among three of his cabinet, including Adams, for the presidency in the upcoming election of 1824. Finally, the young United States had already developed traditions that would shape the cabinet, congressional, and public debate: This heritage included the neutrality principle of the Farewell Address, past presidential warnings to avoid entanglements with foreign powers, commercial liberties and freedom of the seas, an affinity for fellow republics in a world of monarchies, and a strong spirit of anticolonialism.

The Russia problem also involved foreign intervention in the Americas. Two years earlier, in September 1821, Czar Alexander I had issued an ukase (edict) extending Russia's claim to the Pacific Northwest to the fifty-first parallel (the latitude of present-day Calgary, 160 miles north of the U.S.-Canadian border). Even more important to Washington, the czar's edict prohibited foreign vessels from waters within 110 miles of the coast. The Russian-American Trading Company, whose activities extended to Bodega Bay in California, objected to American competitors operating along the Pacific coast.

In 1812–14, Russia had demonstrated the reach of its power by destroying Napoleon's Grand Armeé and then marching across Europe to Paris. In 1823, Russia, with a population four to five times that of the United States and twice Britain's, was the dominant empire in the Holy Alliance.[10]

Adams knew the czar personally from the secretary's service as minister to Russia during the Napoleonic Wars; he recalled that the absolutist monarch had an odd affinity for the American republic. After the United States and Britain heartily rejected Russia's Pacific claim, Alexander suspended enforcement of his decree, and in late 1822, the czar sent a new minister, Baron de Tuyll van Serooskerken, to Washington to resolve the conflict. The congenial baron and Adams were discussing the question when Rush's report from London arrived. Although President Monroe was open to accepting Russian territorial claims above the fifty-fifth parallel, Adams resisted any Russian hold on the continent. Indeed, Adams pressed his novel idea that there should be no new colonies in the Americas.[11]

Greece posed a different problem for Monroe's administration. Early in 1822, a Greek resistance movement had proclaimed independence from the Ottoman Turks, modeling their declaration on Jefferson's. Greece, the ancient home of democracy, adopted a republican government and pleaded for recognition from European capitals and Washington. Tales of Greek courage and Turkish atrocities moved the American public; republican rhetoric combined with a clash between Christians and infidels to stir a potent political brew. Monroe's annual report to Congress in December 1822—after being toned down by Adams—expressed hope that the Greeks would win independence. But Canning's proposal did not mention Greece.[12]

Monroe's Principles

President Monroe faced these questions as he neared the last year of his second term. His career after the Louisiana Purchase had had ups and downs, making Monroe cautious. At age sixty-five in 1823, Monroe's principal concern was to protect his reputation by "keep[ing] the peace with his cabinet, his party, and his country." His guiding star in 1823 was comity, not bold adventure.[13]

Over the decades, Monroe had forged core principles for his practice of American statecraft. First, like all the leaders of the Revolutionary generation, Monroe recognized the fragility of the new republic; the country was vulnerable to internal strife, whether provoked by slavery, sectional differences, economic interests, or foreign powers. Therefore, Monroe's foreign policies sought to smooth over domestic differences. Second, Monroe believed that the United States had to pursue the game of European politics—to play one power against another—to defend itself. He disagreed with the counsel in Washington's Farewell Address to avoid Europe's political maneuvers. As Monroe explained to Jefferson, "It is important for us to stand well with some power." At first drawn to France as a fellow revolutionary republic, Monroe was willing to consider an English connection when circumstances changed. Americans, who protested the immorality of balance of power politics, were willing to practice such diplomacy even while criticizing it. And third, Madison learned through hard experience that there was a need to build national power. Monroe wanted "to move Europeans to see the United States as a nation of consequence, deserving to be both feared and courted." Having served as a young officer during the Revolution and then bolstering Madison as secretary of war after the embarrassing abandonment and burning of Washington, Monroe believed in military preparedness. Hamilton's ghost must have smiled.[14]

John Quincy Adams: Ambitions and Agenda

Secretary of State John Quincy Adams played the principal role of adviser to Monroe in responding to Canning's proposal. Adams was intellectually combative, drawing on exceptional learning; Adams's flinty personality could spark both admiration for his sincerity as well as frustration with his domineering behavior. As Adams admitted in his diary, "I am a man of reserved, cold, austere, and forbidding manners."[15]

Adams came to office with the most extraordinary international—if not domestic—experience of any secretary of state in American history. After accompanying his father to Paris during the American Revolution, the younger Adams began his diplomatic apprenticeship in 1791 when, at age fourteen, he became the private secretary (and French translator) for the U.S. representative to the court of Catherine the Great of Russia. He then served as his father's private secretary in Paris, the Netherlands, and London. After Adams returned to the United States for nine years to study at Harvard and briefly begin the practice of law, Washington appointed the young prodigy as minister to the Netherlands. This posting was just the first of a series that included assignments in Prussia, Russia, and Great Britain, and as head of the delegation in Ghent that negotiated the peace in 1814. In the spring of 1817, Monroe appointed the worldly diplomat to be secretary of state. The elder John Adams wrote to his son in the blunt Adams style, "You are now approaching fifty years of age. In my opinion, you must return to [your country], or renounce it forever."[16]

Secretary of State Adams was exceedingly well-informed about Europe, including Britain, but also highly critical of Old World societies and presumptions. During his service as U.S. minister in The Hague during the mid-1790s, Adams witnessed firsthand that factions of the Dutch republic were drawn into alignments with foreign powers. Adams believed that the Hollanders, once a maritime power that ranged the Seven Seas, had lost the will to defend their independence. As a result, the Netherlands succumbed to a French invasion. Sweden, Poland, and Geneva suffered similar fates. Adams learned the lesson. In December 1795, Adams wrote his brother Charles that U.S. political dependence on France and commercial dependence on Britain endangered America's freedom. America needed careful diplomacy to win time to build its strength. "[T]en more years will place the United States among the most powerful and opulent nations on earth," he prophesied. If not, the gloomy Adams concluded, the United States would slide into "a parcel of petty tribes at perpetual war with one another, manipulated by European powers."[17]

During Adams's seven years as secretary of state, he pressed incessantly to expand U.S. territory, enhance American prestige, and restrain reckless adventures. He assumed that the United States had a special destiny to dominate North America. In November 1819, Adams told his cabinet colleagues that the world must be "familiarized with the idea of considering our proper dominion to be the continent of North America."[18] In a vigorous exchange with British minister Stratford Canning[19] in January 1821 over control of the Columbia River region, Adams blurted that London could keep its Canadian provinces, "but leave the rest of this continent to us."[20]

Accordingly, Adams's first task was to complete the unfinished business of the Louisiana Purchase: the acquisition of Florida and the drawing of the U.S. border in the west. Adams warned the Spanish that their failure to maintain control over "savage Indians," "runaway negroes," pirates, and traitors in wild Florida threatened American territory—as General Andrew Jackson's recent retaliation across the border colorfully demonstrated. Adams demanded that Spain sell Florida to the United States for $5 million of claims American citizens had against Spain or run the risk that the United States would seize it. When the Spanish balked, Adams hinted that the United States was considering recognition of the United Provinces of La Plata, today's Argentina, which had declared their independence from Spain.[21]

Adams wanted even more. He insisted that Spain accept a western boundary for the United States that would run all across the continent to the Pacific. This line at the forty-second parallel was a geographic placeholder, the borderline between Spanish territory to the south and disputed claims between the United States and Britain to the north in Oregon. The name of the eventual Transcontinental Treaty of 1819 with Spain speaks to the scope of Adams's ambition. He noted in his journal on February 22, the evening of signing (and Washington's birthday), that "the acknowledgement of a definite line of boundary to the South Sea [the Pacific] forms a great Epoch in our History. The first proposal of it in the Negotiation was my own; and I trust it is now secured beyond reach of revocation." Spain, frustrated by the result, took almost two years to ratify the treaty. Adams was willing to use force to press the matter, but Monroe's patience prevailed.[22]

Adams followed in the footsteps of the Founding Fathers by emphasizing the importance of trade. He sought to lower tariffs with Britain and France and urged "a still more expansive liberality" that allowed the foreigner to trade on the exact same footing as the citizen.[23] This was Adam Smith's idea of free trade.

The American commitment to individual liberty envisaged a world very different from the old mercantilism dictated by governments. As Adams explained, "It is the nature of commerce, when unobstructed by the interference of authority, to find its own channels and to make its own way. Let us only not undertake to regulate that which will best regulate itself."[24] Therefore, both economic and political imperatives contributed to Adams's hostility to colonialism. Although Adams's statecraft focused on continental ambitions, he wanted to promote an international order in which U.S. national greatness could prosper.[25]

The master American diplomat had a shortcoming at home, however. From 1803 to 1808, during one of Adams's two intervals back in the United States, the Massachusetts legislature had sent the former president's son to the Senate. But Adams broke with the Federalist Party to support the Louisiana Purchase and Jefferson's embargo. As a Federalist turned Republican, he had few natural political allies on either side.[26] He certainly did not have the personality, charm, and social disposition of most successful politicians. Yet Adams knew that the office of secretary of state had been the stepping-stone to the presidency.

Professor Ernest May's book *The Making of the Monroe Doctrine* develops a powerful case that the administration's answer to Canning's overture of 1823 was driven by domestic politics, and especially Adams's adroit maneuvering to win the presidency in 1824. Adams's most recent biographers respectfully differ. At a minimum, May's study reminds that those crafting diplomacy are not just debating national interests and moral purposes. They calculate and bargain, both bureaucratically and personally, while bringing different perspectives and ambitions to the table. Especially in the United States, public opinion shapes and influences the way policy makers perceive problems and possible solutions. American foreign policy is the outcome of political processes, as exercised through arts of diplomacy and domestic politics.[27]

For Adams, the political irony was that the public perceived him as sympathetic toward America's nemesis, Britain, by reason of his New England background, Federalist history, and haughty manner. In fact, Adams wrote his father in the 1790s that "[b]etween the United States and Great Britain no cordiality can exist." After the Napoleonic Wars, Adams believed Europe and Britain in particular wanted to see the American republican experiment fail.[28]

Adams's "Grand Strategy"

Adams's notes from 1809 state his "grand strategy" for the United States most frankly: "There are two political principles that form the policy best suited to the interests and duties of this country. One in relation to its internal concerns, UNION, the other in respect to its intercourse with foreign nations, INDEPENDENCE. These principles are the keys to my political creed."[29]

On July 4, 1821, Adams used the annual oration at the Capitol in Washington to present his foreign policy principles. Adams was replying to a vision of American foreign policy recently offered by Henry Clay, one of his rivals for the presidency, in a speech in Lexington, Kentucky. Clay, an early advocate of recognizing the Latin American republics, had proposed joining with them in "a sort of counterpoise to the Holy Alliance," in effect, a Republican Alliance to resist the Holy Alliance. As the United States was moving toward greater male and white suffrage and electoral democracy, Clay wrapped himself in the mantle of a new "American System" based on the country's revolutionary creed of liberty.

Adams began his address with a diatribe against Britain, fitting for Americans on July 4 and a convenient antidote to any charge of Anglophilia. He then launched a broadside against colonialism, explaining why peoples' ties to home and community doomed the efforts of distant sovereigns to control them. This was a deft alignment with Clay and the Latin American cause without embracing "romanticism about...kinship" that could lead to unwanted U.S. commitments.

Then Adams summoned the Declaration of Independence to answer recent sniping in the British press about "What has America done for mankind?" Adams rejoined that Jefferson's words had "proclaimed to mankind the inextinguishable rights of human nature, and the only lawful foundation of government." The Declaration was a beacon to the world. It "demolished at a stroke the lawfulness of all governments founded upon conquest." The light of the American example, fired by Jefferson's words and the country's Revolutionary and republican cause, was the proud U.S. contribution to humanity.

Having seized the high ground of American principle, Adams closed by cautioning against foreign interventions. "[America] goes not abroad, in search of monsters to destroy. She is the well-wisher to the freedom and independence of all. She is the vindicator only of her own." Adams warned that intervention in foreign wars would change "the fundamental maxims of her policy" "from liberty to force." "She might become the dictatress of the world; she would no longer be the ruler of her own spirit." James Traub, the author of a recent superb biography of Adams, claimed these were the most famous words Adams ever spoke.[30]

Henry Clay and the "American System"

Henry Clay, Adams's rival for the presidency and a vigorous critic of the Monroe administration's foreign policy, was the foremost U.S. champion of the Latin American republics. Years before, in December 1817, Clay sharply challenged Monroe for his failure to recognize the Latin declarations of independence. Clay drew a direct reference to America's own Revolutionary cause: In 1778–79, when the United States was "skulking" around Europe seeking "one kind look," "legitimacy," and "one great and magnanimous ally," France stepped forward "to recognize us." But neither the United States nor any other nation had offered support to fellow friends of liberty in Latin America.[31]

Clay, age forty-six in 1823, was a Kentuckian who personified the convivial, outspoken, and risk-taking charm of men of the western frontier. Clay was elected to the House of Representatives in 1810 after short stints in the Senate; his new colleagues promptly selected him as Speaker, a perch he used to push for war with Britain in 1812. When President Madison assembled a delegation to negotiate peace in 1814, he asked the "War Hawk" Clay to work with Adams and others.

Clay and Adams were a study in contrasts. Clay's late-night revels and card games in Ghent would be ending in the predawn hours just as Adams was rising to read his Bible and begin his paperwork. Adams's wife, Louisa, described Clay perceptively: "If you watch his character, you almost immediately discover that his heart is generous and good, and that his first impulse is almost always benevolent and liberal. But a neglected education, vicious habits and bad company, united to overweening ambition, have made him blush to act the better part."[32]

When Clay returned to Washington, his colleagues in the House reelected him as the Speaker. Clay used the second-most powerful station in Washington to advance his agenda, conciliate, negotiate legislative compromises, and maneuver for the presidency. Clay was envious when Monroe selected Adams as his secretary of state. Looking to the 1824 election, Clay's political strategy was to fault the administration's foreign policy, stoke public antipathy toward Britain, and stand out as the best friend of the republics of Latin America.[33]

For all his practical political skills, Clay was a man of vision, too, and he represents important ideas in American foreign policy. In a speech to the House on May 10, 1820, Clay had presented the thinking behind his efforts. For the first time, Clay used the expression "American System" to describe the purpose of his policies. In later years, Clay and his supporters in the Whig Party would fill out the meaning of the American System. Their aim was to develop a national market that integrated all sectional interests. The Whigs wanted to bind the nation with internal infrastructure improvements, offer financing through a national bank, and encourage manufacturing with tariffs. From the start, Clay's American System envisaged the United States at the center of a hemispheric network of commerce that would "constitute the rallying point of human freedom against all the despotism of the Old World."[34]

Clay's Lexington speech of 1821, to which Adams replied in his oration of July 4, expanded on his plans for an American System. Clay argued again for recognition of the Latin republics, based on principles of expanding trade and moral duty. Clay was moved by the Greek cause, too. Finally, Clay concluded "that a sort of counterpoise to the Holy Alliance should be formed in the two Americas, in favor of National Independence and Liberty, to operate by the force of example and by moral influence." Clay's republicanism offered an international alternative to the monarchy, mysticism, and oppression of the Holy Alliance.[35]

Clay no doubt had a better feel than Adams did for the aspirations and antagonisms of the American public.[36] Clay had tapped a persistent American impulse to associate with causes of freedom, especially if the efforts could be aligned with U.S. economic and security interests. At the start of the twentieth century, Woodrow Wilson wanted to make the world "safe for democracy." In World War II, FDR pointed to the "Four Freedoms" that should underpin world order. During the Cold War, the United States became "the Leader of the Free World." In the 1990s, Bill Clinton called for the Americas to become the first "Democratic Hemisphere," prospering through a Free Trade Area of the Americas. Most recently, at the dawn of the twenty-first century, the ideal took form as an Alliance of Democracies.

Monroe and Adams shared Clay's hopes for Latin America, but they proceeded cautiously. They were pressing Spain for territorial concessions; the threat of recognition offered leverage—but only if the United States delayed. Monroe gave Spain a face-saving interval of a few months after the final ratification of the Transcontinental Treaty in 1821; the United States became the first country to recognize the Latin American republics in March 1822. Clay claimed credit.

The Making of Monroe's Message

This was the international, ideological, political, geographical, historical, and personal context that formed the backdrop when Monroe first assembled his cabinet on October 11 to consider Foreign Secretary Canning's proposal. The cabinet met again on November 7, two days after Monroe returned to Washington. Within a month, Monroe and Adams had devised an American response and communicated the new policy through three documents: the historic paragraphs in Monroe's annual message to Congress; instructions for Rush's reply to Canning; and a note to Russian minister de Tuyll.

Before Monroe left Washington in October, he had requested advice from Jefferson and Madison. The president's covering note acknowledged that Canning's proposal risked entanglement with Europe's politics and wars, yet explained he was disposed "to meet the proposal of the British government." Although Jefferson was the author of the "nonentanglement" principle and Madison had endured a frustrating war with Britain less than a decade before, both counseled acceptance.[37]

Adams had met with Baron de Tuyll while Monroe was away in October. The Russian minister had delivered a formal note stating that the czar would not receive any representative from revolutionary Latin America, denying the legitimacy of those republican governments. The czar added that Russia did not object to the U.S. view; he hoped Washington would remain neutral. The exchange seemed to plant the seed of an idea with Adams, who told the baron that the United States would remain neutral as long as the Europeans did. Perhaps the secretary began to consider expanding the answers to Russia and Britain into a more general policy statement.[38]

The cabinet meeting of November 7 revealed initial dispositions. Historians rely on Adams's wonderful notes in his journal for the internal debate, while recognizing that policy makers shine brightly in their own accounts. Monroe did not discuss the advice from Jefferson and Madison. He asked Secretary of War John Calhoun to speak first, perhaps knowing of Calhoun's sympathy for accepting the British offer. Indeed, Calhoun, who was genuinely concerned that the Holy Alliance would move against South America, made a case echoing Jefferson and Madison.

Adams counterattacked shrewdly. He pointed out that Canning's proposition included a commitment not to take any territory from the Spanish empire and asked whether Calhoun would be willing to forgo a connection with Texas and Cuba, if in the future those provinces might "solicit a union with us." Adams also played on the anxiety about becoming a pawn in the game of European power politics: Canning had not been willing to recognize the newly independent states, raising the risk Britain might abandon the Latin republics and the United States after London achieved some advantage in Europe. Adams also argued that Britain would claim credit for any joint declaration, enabling London to gain commercial advantage with America's neighbors.

Then Adams used his discussions with the Russians to reshape the question on the table. Adams said the United States had an opportunity "to take our stand against the Holy Alliance, and at the same time to decline the overture of Great Britain. It would be more candid, as well as more dignified, to avow our principles explicitly to Russia and France, than to come in as a cock-boat in the wake of the British man-of-war." In addition to transforming the debate over Canning's proposal into a matter of American principle, Adams thus seized the high ground of American pride.

Adams stayed behind after the meeting to urge Monroe to see the exchange with the Russians and the reply to Canning as "parts of a combined system of policy and adapted to each other." As Professor May pointed out, Adams must also have recognized that a joint statement with Britain would offer Anglophobic opponents of Adams's presidential aspirations a devastating line of attack on him.[39]

During the following week, Monroe learned that the French had captured the last republican redoubt in Cadiz; the monarchists now controlled all of Spain. The president had heard a rumor that a French fleet was preparing to transport Spanish troops to the Americas. Monroe was alarmed. When the cabinet met again on November 15, 18, and 21, Adams was on the defensive. Calhoun, according to Adams, was "perfectly moon-struck" by the report of the Holy Alliance on the move. Adams countered that the Latin Americans were hardly helpless, having won their independence. Moreover, if Europeans could crush the new governments as easily as Calhoun suspected, the United States should not commit its "lives and fortunes in a ship which he declares the very rats have abandoned."

Adams also deployed two new reports to his advantage. Messages from Rush, received on November 16, noted that Canning seemed to have cooled on the idea of a joint declaration, raising the possibility of British mischief as Adams had warned. In addition, on November 17, Baron de Tuyll conveyed a circular by Russian foreign minister Karl Nesselrode congratulating France on its defeat of Spanish revolutionaries; indeed, the Russians heralded a "new political system" of monarchies, favored by God, that would protect legitimate regimes threatened by wrongheaded theories or criminal aims. Adams argued that Russia's triumphant assertion warranted America's reply.[40]

Adams had one other bureaucratic advantage: He controlled "the pen" for drafting dispatches to foreign powers. At the direction of the president, Adams proposed instructions for Rush's response to Canning. The note of guidance concurred with the foreign secretary's five points, but it was conditional and moralizing. Adams's draft instructions concluded with the possibility of independent declarations, if the two governments could reach an understanding on the points Adams had delineated. Rush would have to refer any joint declaration back to Washington.[41] Adams was buying time.

Adams also explained to the president and his cabinet colleagues that he was preparing a paper that would dispute the czar's assertions, summarize U.S. principles, disavow any effort to impose American principles on Europe, and ask Europeans to do the same in the Americas. Adams seemed to be planning to use the reply to Russia to memorialize U.S. policy.[42]

At the cabinet meeting of November 21, Monroe had a draft of his own to share: The annual message that he would deliver to Congress in eleven days. Monroe wanted to explain to the American public—and the world—an international approach that looked beyond the cautious, defensive posture of Washington's Farewell Address.

Monroe included language that Adams had given him recognizing the amicable negotiations with Russia over the northwest coast of America, but also stated the principle that there should be no future European colonization of the Americas. In addition, Monroe proposed to rebuke the French invasion of Spain, affirm Greek independence, and recommend dispatching a minister to Greece.

Adams responded vigorously. He warned that Monroe's language would be "a clap of thunder." "The message would be a summons to arms—to arms against all Europe, and for objects exclusively European—Greece and Spain." He predicted that Spain, France, and Russia would sever relations. The next day, Adams pressed his case with Monroe privately. He invoked the touchstone of all American chief executives, especially ones nearing the end of their terms: presidential legacy. This "golden age of this Republic" must end in peace, not the peril of war, Adams implored. Such a misstep could cloud all of Monroe's achievements. Adams pressed his formula instead: The United States would not interfere with matters that were exclusively European affairs in exchange for Europe leaving South America in peace. It was fine to mention Spain and Greece sympathetically, Adams suggested, but not in a way that the Holy Alliance would read as hostile. The president could let *Congress* speak to the cause of Greece, offering him a way to step back gracefully. Over the years that followed, other astute executives have used the Constitution's separation of powers to their diplomatic advantage as well. Two days later, Monroe read Adams his revised text. The secretary was "highly gratified."[43]

Yet the debate over Monroe's message was not quite over. On November 25, Attorney General William Wirt, who had been absent or silent in earlier discussions, asked whether the president's proposed message should go so far as to link South American independence to the safety of the United States. He doubted that the U.S. public would "support the Government in a war for the independence of South America." How would the United States respond if the Europeans intervened in the Western Hemisphere? No one ever offered Wirt a good answer.[44]

Monroe's Message

On December 2, 1823, at 2:00 p.m., couriers delivered the president's annual message to the clerks of the House and Senate. Since Jefferson's day, presidents had presented their annual "State-of-the-Union" in writing; Woodrow Wilson introduced what has become the modern tradition of a speech before Congress. Given the scope of such annual messages, they often have become a laundry list of activities. Monroe's 1823 paper, for example, ran 6,397 words and included a discussion of the Post Office, the Cumberland Road, and finances, as well as foreign policy.

The three nonsequential paragraphs that came to be known as the Monroe Doctrine took less than one thousand words. To place them in context, however, Monroe's introductory and closing paragraphs are worth recalling. Monroe opened by stating, "There never was a period since the Establishment of our Revolution when...there was a greater necessity for patriotism and union." The country had only recently crafted the "Missouri Compromise" of 1820, maintaining a balance between free and slave states as the nation expanded. Monroe was emphasizing that internal strife posed the greatest threat to national security. Monroe's final paragraph celebrated the twin tenets—Union and expansion—of U.S. foreign policy in the nineteenth and early twentieth centuries: In Monroe's words, the "expansion of population and accession of new States to our Union" will "[augment] our resources and [add] to our strength and responsibility as a power."

In between, Monroe presented three ideas that defined U.S. security—and national purpose—more expansively than in the country's first three decades. First, emerging from the discussions with Russia, Monroe asserted "that the American continents, by the free and independent condition which they have assumed and maintain, are henceforth not to be considered as subjects for future colonization by any European powers." The United States perceived Europeans in the Western Hemisphere as posing a risk to U.S. security, so it wanted to stop—and even reverse—the Old World's expansion. The United States was also criticizing the very idea of colonialism. Adams had objected to the old European system because of its commercial monopoly as well as its political domination. Notably, Washington was now asserting this anticolonial claim on behalf of all the New World.

Second, Monroe recognized U.S. connections, historical and current, with the Old World of Europe. Americans would "cherish sentiments...in favor of the liberty and happiness of their fellow man on that side of the Atlantic," and would be "anxious and interested spectators," but would steer clear of "the wars of European powers." The United States would "not... interfere in the internal concerns of any of [Europe's] powers." The United

States recognized that it was the western star in an Atlantic world, certainly a commercial counterpart and perhaps even a light of hope to people on the eastern shore, but Americans wanted to avoid Europe's old politics, rivalries, and conflicts.

Third, the Western Hemisphere was different. Any effort by the Holy Alliance to extend its political system to the Americas would be "dangerous to our peace and safety." Any effort to oppress or control the independent governments of the Americas would "[manifest] an unfriendly disposition toward the United States." The United States respected the right of South Americans to determine their own governments; so should Europe. The Holy Alliance had asserted that absolutism should be the governing ideology; the United States was standing up—at least with words—to that challenge on behalf of republicanism. Yet the United States was also proposing a new reciprocity to guide international relations: With the brashness of youth, the United States offered not to interfere with Europe if Europeans respected the will of the Americas.

Monroe's message challenged the existing international order in another way as well. Monroe was conducting "open diplomacy." His public message looked to the power of popular opinion, not the statecraft of aristocratic Congresses, drawing rooms, and secret codicils.[45]

Monroe authorized Adams's reply to the Russians and the secretary's instructions for Rush's answer to Canning. The president sought to delete and temper some of Adams's more aggressive language, with mixed results. Still unclear about what action Europeans might take against Latin America, Monroe wanted to keep options open with Britain. In a letter to Jefferson, Monroe described his policies as shaping the form of a possible alliance, if Canning were still interested.[46]

Reactions

Canning was not interested. In September and October, Wellington had argued that France had no intention of marshaling a transatlantic invasion. In October, Canning told the French ambassador, Prince Polignac, that Britain would not permit a European intervention in Spanish America. Without the justification of crisis, Canning would have had difficulty persuading the British cabinet to issue a joint statement with the United States, much less meet the U.S. condition of recognizing the Latin American governments.

Monroe's message caught Canning a step behind, causing some embarrassment. The Whig opposition in Britain accused the government of weakness in standing up to European reactionaries and of ceding leadership to the Americans. Monroe's public diplomacy also revealed an emerging

Anglo-American public opinion. The *Times* of London, rarely a friend of Washington, flattered Monroe's statement as "a policy so directly British." The *Economist* maintained that "the Monroe Doctrine might quite as fairly be called the Canning Doctrine." Canning recovered by releasing the memorandum of his earlier warning to the French ambassador. By early 1825, Britain recognized the Latin American governments and proceeded to develop commercial ties that far exceeded those of the United States. Canning would later boast that he had called the New World into existence to redeem the balance of the Old.[47]

Most continental Europeans knew nothing of the origins of Monroe's declaration and were shocked and offended by its audacious presumptiveness. Count Klemens von Metternich of Austria wrote that the "indecent declarations...have cast blame and scorn on the institutions of Europe," pitting "not only power against power, but...altar against altar." "If this flood of evil doctrines and pernicious examples should extend over the whole of the Americas, what would become of our religious and political institutions, of the moral force of our government, and of that conservative system which has saved Europe from complete dissolution?"[48] Perhaps Metternich was correct to fear republicanism. The liberal revolutions of 1848 in Europe would fail, but they took Metternich down with them.

Czar Alexander judged the American posture as "merit[ing] only the most profound contempt." Like others in Europe, he then decided to ignore it. Some Europeans decided that Monroe's declaration reflected only U.S. politics, in their minds an unfortunate feature of republican foreign policy. Equally terrible, Americans were guilty of "materialism." They had no serious military. They just wanted to make money.[49]

Henry Clay, in contrast, told Adams that the foreign policy paragraphs were the "best part of the [president's] message." Clay welcomed the division with Europe, and even considered "offering a resolution to declare this country an asylum for all fugitives from oppression."[50]

From Declaration to Doctrine

Over the years, Monroe's declaration became the Monroe Doctrine. Later presidents would endow the statement of 1823 with meanings to fit changed circumstances, and those experiences helped define the potential—and pitfalls—of the "Western Hemisphere Idea" in U.S. foreign policy.

At a minimum, Monroe's declaration was the "first public stand by the United States on an [international] controversy that did not immediately touch its own citizens or territory." Dexter Perkins, dean of historians of the Monroe doctrine, wrote that the Doctrine, "in its broad lines, is a prohibition on the part of the United States against the extension of European influence and power to the New World." Writing in 1941, as the United States faced the question of entry into World War II, Perkins added that many connected the Declaration with "the principle of the separation of the New World from the Old...a complement, as a foil, to the principle of no entangling alliances and no binding connection with any European power." Perkins's later editions during the Cold War analogized the Old and New Worlds of the nineteenth century to a globe divided between communist and free states.[51]

More expansively, in the early twenty-first century, James Traub describes Monroe's message as a "distinctive combination of raw assertion of power with a missionary sense of global purpose [that] was to become the animating spirit of American foreign policy."[52] At times, American leaders, and much of the public, treated Monroe's statements as declaring a U.S. "sphere of influence" in the Americas.[53]

I prefer the assessment of Elihu Root and Charles Evans Hughes, two secretaries of state in the early twentieth century, who will make an appearance in chapters 8 and 9. Both were respected international lawyers. Both determined that the Monroe Doctrine was a declaration about acts that would threaten U.S. security, based on the right of self-protection. They eschewed alleged rights to interfere in weaker American states, rights of control, protectorates, or even a claim under international law. The Monroe Doctrine, the two men concluded, should not intrude on Pan-American cooperation or ties with other regions. They stressed that Monroe's words stood for independence, not isolation.[54] Indeed, Henry Ammon, Monroe's biographer, termed the president's statement a "diplomatic declaration of independence."[55] For Adams, the declaration enabled the United States to state anticolonial principles while maintaining the freedom of action to focus on his priority—North America—and avoid European diversions. Monroe had declared what European powers should *not* do, not what the United States *would* do.[56] That was the question Adams and Clay would face, this time working together, two years later.

President Adams and Secretary Clay

John Quincy Adams became the sixth president of the United States after the fiercely contested election of 1824. General Andrew Jackson had a slight edge in electoral votes, as well as the plurality of popular votes, but Jackson had not received the required majority of electoral votes. Under the Constitution, the House of Representatives then elected the president, with each state having one vote. On the first ballot, with the support of Henry Clay, Adams won the votes of thirteen states over Jackson's seven, and four for the ailing William Crawford. After his election, Adams offered Clay the post of secretary of state, and Clay accepted, creating the basis of the Jacksonians' charge of a "corrupt bargain" that thwarted the popular will. Both Adams and Clay would suffer politically, as would their foreign policy.

Adams and Clay shared an interest in expanding U.S. territory in North America and advancing trading ties around the world. Clay also wanted to design a positive U.S. program for the Americas to complement Monroe's defensive message.

From Hemispheric Defense to Initiative: Clay's "Good Neighbor" Policy

As early as 1821, Simon Bolivar, the military liberator of the Andean republics, proposed that the new states of Latin America meet to consider "union, association, and perpetual federation." Bolivar was wary of Washington, but in 1825, Mexico, Colombia, and the United Provinces of Central America, knowing of Clay's advocacy of hemispheric cooperation, urged including the North American republic in a Congress to be held in Panama (which was then a province of Gran Colombia). Clay convinced the more cautious Adams, who, in his first message to Congress in December 1825, announced that the United States had accepted the invitation to attend the Panama Congress.[57]

Clay's instructions for his delegates offer a fascinating vision of a policy for the Americas. Clay believed that this state paper, running about eighteen thousand words, was one of the most important of his life.[58]

Clay's overarching concept was a policy of "good neighborhood," anticipating FDR's Good Neighbor Policy by over a century. Clay believed that Americans had an opportunity to leave behind old prejudices and outmoded practices and to establish new American principles "likely to promote their peace, security, and happiness." Clay was especially interested in establishing principles for commerce, navigation, maritime law, and neutral and belligerent rights. He emphasized free trade without favorable concessions to a foreign power (a point directed against Britain). Property rights on the seas had to have the same protection afforded those on land, a long-standing U.S. interest. Clay favored the liberalization of rights of naturalization and emigration. He even urged "a free toleration of Religion." Clay hoped that U.S. influence and institutional practices could help guide the new Latin republics. If American principles could become hemispheric principles, they might eventually spread even more widely.

Clay believed that America's neutrality policy—in opposition to Europe's old entangling alliances—had persuaded European powers to concede the

independence of the American states. His analysis was suspect, but convenient. Accordingly, the American powers had no need for "an offensive and
defensive alliance" at this time. Clay's hopes for the hemisphere were rooted
in the U.S. experience of independence, economic strength, and neutrality—
bound together to create a new power through union. Not surprisingly, Clay,
the advocate of "internal improvements" in the United States, became the
first American to signal official interest in building a trans-isthmian canal.[59]

Clay's plans for Western Hemispheric cooperation crashed on the rocks
of domestic politics, though the idea seems to have been popular with the
public. The Jacksonians accused Adams and Clay of abandoning the principles of neutrality and independence, entangling the United States in Latin
conflicts, and promoting revolution and race war. The race and religion of
Latin America was too high an obstacle for some. In early 1826, the administration devoted an entire session of Congress to securing Senate confirmation of the U.S. delegates to the Panama Congress and an appropriation to
fund attendance.[60]

Clay's delegation to Panama was ill-starred. One representative died
of a tropical fever along the way. Another got only as far as Mexico City
by the time the Panama Congress had adjourned. The Congress was supposed to reconvene in Tacubaya, Mexico, but never did. The United States
missed the boat, leaving the business to British representatives, who were
delighted to point to the conspicuous absence of the Americans as evidence of U.S. indifference.[61] The diplomatic debacle previewed a frustrating
cycle of U.S. partnership with Latin America—and then detachment and
disappointment—that continues through today.

Legacies

Professor Ernest May wrote that the British offer of 1823 raised a fundamental question for American diplomacy: Would the United States become a
political planet within the European galaxy, or would Washington become a
sun at the center of a separate American system?

John Quincy Adams and James Monroe recognized that the United States
operated within an Atlantic world dominated by European powers. Both
had experience as emissaries in Europe. They knew of the European hostility toward the United States' republican experiment. Monroe was willing to
consider how the United States might manipulate Europe's divisions, as he
had helped to do during the Louisiana Purchase.

Adams preferred to establish a greater distance from Europe's diplomacy. He would maneuver among European powers, too. But he wanted to
avoid entanglement, other than commercial ties, that might offer inroads

for Europeans to hold sway over factions in America. U.S. neutrality and independence would help preserve the new nation's unity as it vindicated republicanism.

Adams's transcontinentalism went hand in hand with national independence. Adams wanted the United States to dominate its home continent. Territorial expansion offered greater security and, with economic and population growth, rising U.S. strength. When Adams became president, he advanced, without success, a national program for infrastructure, education, commerce, and science to build American power.

The challenge of the Holy Alliance to the new Latin American republics offered Adams an opportunity to combine his geopolitical logic with the ideology of liberty and republicanism. He wanted the colonial powers to yield to American republicanism in the Western Hemisphere. In return, he offered brashly to steer clear of European politics.

James Traub explains that later U.S. proponents of realism in foreign policy, such as George Kennan, point to Adams's July 4, 1821, address—with its warning about far-ranging escapades "in search of monsters to destroy"—"as a kind of founding text." Kissinger's *Diplomacy* cites Adams's words as the wise opposite to Woodrow Wilson's idealistic effort to build U.S. foreign policy upon moral principles. These realists respect Adams's differentiation between American interests and its universal aspirations; they share Adams's skepticism about America's capacity, even with the best intentions, to do good abroad.

If Adams is a foreign policy realist, he represents—as Traub points out—a type of American Realism. Adams combined his focus on national interests and the matching of ends and means with a fervent belief in the moral superiority of America and its republican system. Adams could speak as passionately about freedom as John F. Kennedy, Ronald Reagan, or George W. Bush. In the era of the 1820s, however, based on his experience, Adams doubted whether Latin Americans—or Europeans, for that matter—had the political culture, resort to reason, and institutions to sustain the difficult work of building and preserving republican democracies. Over time, Adams was proven both right—and wrong.

The valuable distinction that Adams's American Realism imparted to American diplomacy is that any people's *right* to self-government is not the same as the *capacity* of a society to govern itself democratically. As Adams later explained, freedom must be grounded in a mutual commitment among equals; it cannot be granted or gifted by an outside power. Ben Franklin, with more of a common touch, explained the challenge this way: When asked what type of government the Constitutional Convention in Philadelphia had produced, America's First Diplomat replied, "A republic, if you can keep it."[62]

Later generations of Americans who sought to promote democracy in foreign lands would learn that many of Adams's cautions had merit. Nevertheless, Adams believed republicanism and liberty were the foundations for healthy, prosperous, and free societies. His pursuit of power served his principles. Indeed, in his later, postpresidential years, when Adams recognized that America's slavery had corrupted its republican government, he was willing to risk the Union to extirpate slavery.

Henry Clay took Adams's geopolitical republicanism a step further. Clay envisioned a republican hemisphere. Republics throughout the Americas—North and South—would create new models of governance, domestically *and* internationally. He wanted to give Adams's defensive statements a policy push.

Both Adams and Clay suffered frustrating disappointments. Their ideas, however, reverberated over the years. Their continental nationalism triumphed. America's economic strength, trade, and national power expanded to unimagined proportions. Republicanism succeeded around the world, although not without continual setbacks and threats. The first priority, however, as Adams and Clay both recognized, was the survival of the republican union. By 1861, the Union had reached the breaking point.[63]

CHAPTER 4

Abraham Lincoln and William Seward

Pragmatic Unionists

"One War at a Time"

On April 1, 1861, within a month of President Abraham Lincoln's inauguration, Secretary of State William Seward sent Lincoln a memo of "Thoughts"
proposing what became known as the "foreign war panacea." The secretary
began his paper by stating brashly that after a month the administration
had neither a domestic nor a foreign policy. Six states had seceded, but Fort
Sumter in Charleston Harbor remained in Union hands. Seward knew that
Santo Domingo, the eastern half of the island shared with Haiti (and which
had declared independence in 1821), was struggling economically and facing
public unrest. At the request of the Dominican president, Spain sent forces
to occupy its former colony. Seward wanted to use this expedition to divert
the U.S. public debate from slavery to the cause of the Union. He called for
Spain and France (presumably because of Haiti) to explain themselves—or
face war. Seward threw in unspecified demands to Britain and Russia, too.
To avoid a showdown in South Carolina, he advised Lincoln to abandon Fort
Sumter. The secretary's real aim appears to have been to seize the lead from
Lincoln so as to set a clear policy direction during the secession crisis.

Lincoln, who was ailing, drafted a courteous but curt reply the same
day. The president ignored Seward's suggestion of picking another fight and
plainly rejected Seward's move to take charge of the administration. If a policy needs to be directed, Lincoln concluded, "*I* must do it."

Seward's extraordinary proposal reflects his high state of anxiety during
a crisis of national existence. In April 1861, Lincoln's leadership qualities
were still unknown, and he had not yet demonstrated executive experience. Seward was grasping for a solution to secession—and conveniently
pressing for his own advancement. Lincoln's willingness to put the incident

behind him reveals great self-discipline; Lincoln's policy judgment was also superior.[1]

Before long, Spanish efforts to annex its former colony led to a Dominican rebellion. Seward asked Lincoln whether the United States should support the Dominicans. That move would aggravate tensions with Spain when the administration wanted to prevent Europeans from aiding the Confederacy. Yet a failure to support the Dominicans would appear to accept the reassertion of European empires in the hemisphere, contradicting Monroe's declaration.

Lincoln answered Seward with the story of the preacher who warned his parishioner that he faced two roads: one went "straight to hell," and the other went "right to damnation." The poor man replied that in that case "I shall go through the woods." Lincoln explained that this was not the time "to assume any new troubles or responsibilities." So we will "take to the woods... [and] maintain an honest and strict neutrality."[2]

The shelves of Civil War libraries sink under the weight of books on battles, generals, and, more recently, societal consequences. There are, however, only a few works on a story that decided the fate of the Union: how Abraham Lincoln and William Seward thwarted foreign intervention that might have rescued the rebel Confederacy.[3]

Over four years, Lincoln's pragmatic principle of foreign policy would be "One War at a Time." Its application required a crafty combination of threat and restraint.[4]

The World in 1861

April 1861, when the first cannon of the Civil War blazed, found the international order in flux. The post–Napoleonic Concert of Europe—and certainly the Holy Alliance—were breaking down. The liberal revolutions of 1848 and a revival of national passions had shaken the stability of monarchical regimes. Britain and France had just waged a bloody, indeterminate war with imperial Russia in the Crimea. In 1859, Napoleon III of France battled Austria in the name of Italy's liberation, but all parties were left disappointed. Mutual suspicions plagued the awkward alliance between Britain and France. Prussia's drive toward national unification revived the "German Question" in a new, now powerful form.

Shifts in the European balance of power—and even state borders—were accompanied by destabilizing ideas about sources of strength and progress. Europe witnessed fresh competition over the traditional components of power: territory, resources, and people. New strategists were recognizing capital, banking systems, markets, and technology as ingredients of potential power, in line with Hamilton's observations many years before. Pioneers in science raised expectations for an age of dynamism rather than one of natural equilibria and balance. Charles Darwin's work—applied by Herbert Spencer to societies—transformed perspectives on national competition. Railroads and steamships created a transportation revolution, changing conceptions of time and space. This was a new information age, too, with more literate populations, an explosion of publications, and wide-ranging telegraph and even oceanic cables.

The eruptions were global. Britain had been shocked by the 1857 "Mutiny" in India. During the 1850s, the Taiping Rebellion almost overwhelmed the Qing dynasty of the Manchus in China, at a cost of some 40 million lives. After Commodore Matthew Perry "opened" Japan to trade in the 1850s, the Tokugawa shogunate crumbled, setting the stage for startling reforms by Japanese modernizers and the first rise in this era of an Asian power.[5]

By 1861, the "scramble for America" was not quite over, but the direction of the outcome looked clear. Grumbling Europeans had to defer to the United States. Prime Minister Lord Palmerston of Britain, America's strongest rival in the Western Hemisphere, admitted, "These Yankees...are on the Spot, strong, deeply interested in the matter, totally unscrupulous and dishonest and determined somehow or other to carry their Point." Moreover, the extensive economic ties between the United States and Britain highlighted that economic interdependence had become a force in international relations. The textile industry was one of the principal engines of Britain's economy, with the cotton trade accounting for about $600 million a year (more than half the value of British exports) and about five million jobs. The United States supplied about 75-80 percent of Britain's cotton, rising to 85 percent with the bumper crop of 1860. After Britain opened its market for grain with the repeal of the Corn Laws in 1846, U.S. wheat, flour, and corn supplied about 25 percent of the country's needs, rising to 41 percent in 1861. Britain, in turn, was a huge investor in American canals, railroads, and enterprises, holding about $400 million of U.S. securities.[6] (By way of comparison, the outlays of the U.S. government in 1860 were $63.1 million.)

There were, however, still hot spots in North America that could spark trouble in U.S. and European relations. The Caribbean, in particular, invited rivalries. Mexico's governments had not stabilized after the 1846–48 war with the United States, in which Mexico had lost one-third of its territory. Spain still held Cuba and Puerto Rico, but the islands seemed vulnerable to both local dissension and to being snatched by foreign powers.

Southern Expectations

The secessionist South "expected quick recognition, or judicious interven-tion."[7] Europeans, the Confederates believed, would welcome an oppor-tunity to weaken the North, upset Yankee commercial competition, and create a North American system of competing states that looked more like Europe. The Confederates also relied on Europe's dependence on "King Cot-ton"; Southern leaders tacitly endorsed a cotton embargo in 1861, before the Union blockade took hold, to force European recognition. The rebels also believed that European aristocrats would be attracted to the South's under-dog cavaliers, who were resisting Northern capitalism and radical democ-racy. The ideological defense of slavery, which Southerners had intensified in the antebellum era, blinded them to hostile European attitudes.[8] Britons bought a million copies of Harriet Beecher Stowe's poignant *Uncle Tom's Cabin* in 1852, compared with three hundred thousand sold in the United States. The book spurred a revival of antislavery clubs in Britain. Prime Min-ister Palmerston, who allegedly had not read a novel in thirty years, claimed to have read Mrs. Stowe's story three times.[9]

Secretary of State Seward

Until Doris Kearns Goodwin published *Team of Rivals*, Lincoln overshad-owed his civilian colleagues, including Secretary Seward.[10] The upstate New Yorker was not quite sixty years old when he became secretary of state. After an early visit with Seward, William Russell of the London *Times* wrote that the new secretary was "a slight, middle-sized man, of feeble build, with a stoop...from sedentary habits. A well-formed and large head...projects over the chest in an argumentative kind of way, as if the keen eyes were seeking an adversary...eyes secret but penetrating, and lively with humor." Seward's eyes must have been a dominating feature, peering over a large, beaked nose, topped by gray, grizzly eyebrows, creating the appearance of an alert bird ready to chatter—or strike.[11]

Seward could be "indiscreet, impetuous, and temperamental," not exactly the seminal traits of a diplomat.[12] But he was also "shrewd, diligent, devious, [and tenacious]," as well as warm and charming—all closer to the mark. Certainly, he was never dull. Lincoln no doubt balanced some of Seward's overbearing qualities, and the two formed a strong partnership and even friendship. They both enjoyed humor and stories. They were astute judges of humankind. Having survived and prospered in the rough-and-tumble democratic politics of mid-nineteenth-century America, climbing up the electoral ladder outside the realm of the dominant Democratic Party, they learned how to write, speak, and maneuver skillfully while building new coalitions. Both welcomed immigration and reached out to foreign-born Americans. Both had a feel for the new public diplomacy, at home and abroad, of a more open and democratic era, although their penchant for humor probably confused staid European counterparts. Seward even began a new State Department practice, that continues through today, of publishing a compendium of diplomatic dispatches each year. Most important, Seward grew to respect the president who had defeated him, and they shared insights, tragedies, mutual loyalty, and an unyielding commitment to the Union.

Seward's intelligence ranged far beyond the hustle of political life. He sought to connect history with current developments. He was well traveled, with two extended trips to Europe and the Middle East in 1833 and 1859. Seward framed a geographical outlook, perceiving developments in decades to come based on his assessment of trends in commerce, global politics, and technology. Seward wrote an admiring biography of John Quincy Adams, whom Seward had visited in Adams's postpresidential years. Some scholars have viewed Seward as Adams's "logical successor."[13] Both Adams and Seward believed that if the Union could be preserved, America's energy, dynamism, and spirit of enterprise would create a new system that would overtake Europe's old order. But first the United States had to survive.

Seward's Propositions

Seward feared that the outgoing James Buchanan administration had failed to oppose secession vigorously. Some Lincoln allies warned that U.S. envoys abroad were saying that separation was already an accomplished fact. To counter this drift, Seward's instructions to the new U.S. ministers to Britain and France asserted bold, clear propositions. First, the conflict was emphatically not a contest between two states, but rather an internal insurrection that would be put down by the U.S. government. Second, the government was not waging a moral battle to eliminate slavery. Third, and most important, the United States would view any move toward recognition of the rebels as an unfriendly act.[14]

Throughout the Civil War, London, Paris, and other European capitals were skeptical that the North would manage to reassert control over the South. Europeans believed it was just a matter of time before Washington was compelled to confront reality. The British recalled that Lord Cornwallis had marched across the American South during the Revolution but had failed to control the vast spaces. It seemed inconceivable that the North could now force nine million Southerners to concede. With a smug schadenfreude, the *Times* of London advised the North to "accept the situation as we did 80 years ago." Europeans also had little understanding of the relatively recent rapid growth in the North's material capacity to wage a modern, multi-theater war. As a result, Seward had to argue repeatedly that the North, and its public, was indomitably committed to subduing the rebellion, no matter how long it took and whatever the cost. Any country that challenged the United States in its moment of peril would pay an enormous price. Seward practiced brinksmanship—but he needed to avoid straying over the line into provocation.[15]

Blockade and Belligerency

Lincoln and Seward struck a fine balance in announcing their first international move after the Confederates bombarded Fort Sumter on April 12. Aging general Winfield Scott had recommended an "Anaconda Plan" to strangle the rebellious South into submission. His strategy required the U.S. Navy to choke off supplies to the Confederacy. But the navy had only about forty-two commissioned ships in service, and Secretary of the Navy Gideon Welles reported to Lincoln that only twelve craft were available immediately to operate along the three thousand miles of Atlantic and Gulf coasts.

One option, favored by Welles, was to declare, under domestic law, the closure of Southern ports. The U.S. Navy would then patrol American waters to intercept ships approaching Southern ports—whether rebel or neutral—to collect duties or demand penalties.

Lord Richard Lyons, the British minister in Washington, suggested another route. Lyons warned Seward that seizures of British ships would create tremendous pressure for London to open the ports by force. Alternatively, international law recognized a blockade as a legitimate action between belligerents. The rules for blockades were generally known, especially by Britons who relied on seapower and blockades of their own. Neutrals could continue noncontraband trade, such as cotton. In effect, a blockade could stem war supplies and Confederate shipping, limiting but not stopping trade. International law frowned on weakly enforced "paper blockades," but the British Admiralty had an interest in reinforcing the usefulness of blockades, as Americans had unhappily learned during the Napoleonic Wars.

On April 15, Lincoln explained to his cabinet, "[W]e could not afford to have two wars on our hands at once." On April 16, the president proclaimed the blockade, as Seward had urged. Lincoln then used his executive powers to build what became, by 1865, the largest navy in the world.[16]

By partially closing the gateways to Southern ports, however, Lincoln was unlocking a door to the Confederacy's international status. Although the

North was adamant that the rebels had initiated an insurrection, not created a nation, blockades under the international laws of war were actions between belligerents.

On May 13, London swung the door open. Queen Victoria issued a declaration of neutrality that acknowledged a state of war in America and granted the Confederacy status as a belligerent. The new U.S. minister to Great Britain, Charles Francis Adams, the son of John Quincy Adams, read the news on the train from Liverpool to London right after arriving in Britain to assume his post. Before long, France, Spain, the Netherlands, and Brazil followed Britain's lead.

The British had not recognized the Confederacy's independence. In fact, London was seeking to avoid picking sides in the North-South conflict, at least until the situation on the ground became clearer. Britons were ordered not to join the army or navy of either side, arm or equip their ships, break a lawful blockade, or carry military materials or other contraband. Violators would not receive Britain's protection. On the other hand, Confederate ships could obtain nonmilitary supplies and use British ports. The South could raise money and buy weapons. Just as important, the proclamation raised rebel hopes that recognition of independence beckoned once the Confederacy showed its mettle on the battlefield.

"God damn them, I'll give them hell," exclaimed Seward when he learned of the news. The North's resentment would smolder for many years. Although London could state a reasoned case for its proclamation, the step looked precipitous. No major battle had been fought. To make matters worse, Foreign Minister Lord John Russell had just met unofficially with three rebel envoys. Britain had not even waited to hear from the new U.S. minister. To ease the tension, Russell arranged for Adams to present his credentials promptly and met the American on May 18. The foreign minister explained that Her Majesty's government had no present plans to recognize the Confederacy, but he could not offer assurances about the future.[17]

After learning that Lord Russell planned to meet the Confederate representatives, Seward had begun drafting a biting dispatch for Adams to present to the foreign minister. Further fueling Seward's ire, a member of Parliament had introduced a formal motion to recognize the Confederacy. Seward fumed about the direction of British policy. Accordingly, his missive left no doubt that British recognition of the secessionists' independence would be a cause for war. Lincoln toned down the message. The president wanted a vigorous statement, but a controlled one. He deleted a reference to the British as "enemies," referred to British actions as "hurtful," not "wrongful," and instead of declaring that the United States would not bear the English actions, stated that London's steps would "not pass unquestioned."

Importantly, Lincoln directed that Adams should use the dispatch only as guidance for a face-to-face meeting with Russell—not tender the paper.

Lincoln exercised diplomatic discipline. He wanted to convey severe unhappiness with London's action, while encouraging London to calculate risks of serious consequences. The president viewed the message as part of an ongoing process, which he wanted to direct, leaving room for negotiations. A century later, President Kennedy used similar restraint in a crisis over nuclear missiles in Cuba.

Seward sent the revised dispatch on May 21. (But he kept the original in his files to remind any possible critic of his vehemence.) Adams was taken aback by the language and tone of even the softened version, which he thought signaled that the United States was "almost ready to declare war with all the power of Europe." Adams moderated the communication further when he met with Russell on June 12. Russell still got the message, especially that further contacts with Confederate envoys risked great danger. He did not have another unofficial meeting with a Southern emissary until the following year.

Seward also suggested carrots, as well as sticks, for capitals that worked with Washington. He wrote that he wanted to avoid a foreign war. Nevertheless, Seward's truculence and reputation no doubt created the impression in London and Paris that a misstep could lead to a fall over the precipice, with unpredictable but certainly devastating consequences. Seward thus checked the trend toward Southern recognition.[18]

The United States was playing for the highest stakes. Others, with less definite interests, needed to calculate accordingly. For now, Europeans would remain impartial and careful. (Though to prepare for contingencies, London began to reinforce its troops in Canada.) The Union and rebel armies on the ground would determine what cards Washington had to play.

The *Trent* Affair

Around noon on November 8, 1861, a menacing cannonball shot across the bow of HMS *Trent*, a British mail packet sailing in the Bahamas Channel, 250 miles off the Cuban coast. When the *Trent* stayed on course, a shell from a pivot gun loomed closer. The British ship slowed to a stop.

The *Trent* had been stalked by the USS *San Jacinto*, a screw sloop under the command of Captain Charles Wilkes. Wilkes, sixty-two, was an Antarctic explorer nearing the end of his career. His superiors questioned his judgment and tendency toward insubordination. Indeed, Wilkes was supposed to be sailing the *San Jacinto* from the African coast to Philadelphia. But the captain navigated toward the Caribbean, hoping that he could crown his long career with the capture of Confederate blockade runners. While in Cuba, Wilkes learned that James Mason and John Slidell, Confederate envoys, were sailing from Spanish Havana to Danish St. Thomas on the *Trent*, en route to Europe. Captain Wilkes laid a trap along the only deep-water route between Cuba and the shallow Great Bahamas Bank.

Wilkes's executive officer, Lieutenant D. M. Fairfax, warned that seizing the *Trent* might violate international law. Nevertheless, Captain Wilkes ordered Fairfax to lead a boarding party to seize the envoys as prisoners and the ship as a prize. Fairfax conducted his duty firmly but courteously. He removed Mason and Slidell and their two secretaries, but he persuaded Wilkes not to take the *Trent* as a prize; the British ship was then able to resume its journey to St. Thomas.[19]

Lieutenant Fairfax had not insisted on a forcible search of the *Trent* to seek Confederate dispatches after the British captain had refused permission.[20] Wilkes considered Mason and Slidell themselves to be a type of contraband, "the embodiment of dispatches."

The story of the capture of the Confederate commissioners lit up telegraph wires. After seven months of Northern military setbacks, newspapers across the United States lauded Wilkes as a hero. Turning the tables on Britain—whose searches, seizures, and impressments on the high seas had been a cause of the War of 1812—sweetened the event. Lincoln and his cabinet seemed to share in the exaltation, although there is a report that the president was troubled by the violation of neutral rights. He told a visitor that "the traitors may prove to be white elephants." When Congress reconvened on December 2, the House of Representatives passed a resolution of praise for the aggressive captain. Yet from the start, newspapers and commentators observed that the streets and hotels were filled with would-be experts in international law debating the propriety of the bold captain's exploit.[21]

Lincoln had once remarked that public opinion "is everything in this country." The president certainly could read the wave of public opinion, but he preserved room for maneuver. On December 4, Lincoln told a British official from Canada that he wanted no quarrel with Britain, nor did he want to move against Canada; he expected the problem would pass. The United States would wait quietly to see what London would say.

The crisis was about much more than rights and wrongs under international law. By the time of the *Trent*'s interception, the British lion was primed to roar. In early November, London was rife with rumors that a U.S. warship might seize Mason and Slidell. The Foreign Office sought an urgent legal advisory opinion. Prime Minister Palmerston met with the authors of the opinion, and on November 12 called in Adams to inform him that Britain would be greatly offended by any U.S. removal of envoys from a British ship.

Adams had not yet heard of the boarding of the *Trent*; therefore the minister replied that he knew only of orders to intercept Confederate ships. Palmerston's contemporaneous letter to the queen and his note to the *Times* recognized that a ship carrying enemy dispatches could be taken to a prize court in a belligerent port. But the prime minister's warning to Adams skipped the legal niceties.

News of the seizure of Mason and Slidell reached Britain on November 25. The British press erupted. One American in London reported that people were "frantic with rage, and were the country polled, I fear 999 out of 1,000 would declare for immediate war." Now Seward's aggressive reputation, including statements he had made during his visit to Britain in 1859, came back to haunt him. The mood was further inflamed by accounts—totally false—that Lieutenant Fairfax had conducted the search violently and offensively, bullying Slidell's defenseless daughter.[22] (Policy makers should recall that first accounts of events are rarely correct.)

Palmerston prized cold calculation. One of his best-known statements is, "We have no eternal allies, and we have no perpetual enemies. Our interests are eternal and perpetual, and those interests it is our duty to follow." The old man could pursue moral missions—for example, a campaign against the slave trade—when the cause also suited British interests. His reasoned calculation of interests told him Britain should avoid being drawn into the American conflict.[23]

At age seventy-seven, however, Palmerston's temper prevailed. Even realist statesmen will indulge biases. Palmerston had no love for the United States. He distrusted democracies and resented American rudeness. At the outbreak of the Civil War, Palmerston delighted in seeing the upstart former colonies become the "Disunited States of North America." He was unhappy that the new Republican Congress had boosted tariffs at the start of the Civil War, hurting Britain's exports.[24]

Palmerston believed Seward was spoiling for a fight. On November 12, Palmerston had written that U.S. "policy is to heap indignities upon us, and they are encouraged to do so by what they imagine to be the defenseless state of our North American Provinces." The Yankees had insulted British honor, and Palmerston thought it was no accident. Adams later wrote that the prime minister could not stand to appear to be bullied by Americans. The tension of potential conflict with the United States might also have helped Palmerston hold together support for his government. Palmerston's muscular patriotism prompted him to teach the Americans a lesson. He sent more troops to Canada, beginning with a force of eleven thousand. If need be, the Royal Navy could clear the seas of Americans and open Southern ports. Strong emotions on both sides of the Atlantic narrowed the space for peacemakers.[25]

The British cabinet met on November 29 and 30. The law officers advising the cabinet determined that Wilkes's removal of Mason and Slidell had been illegal. Palmerston wanted the United States to free the two men and apologize. Lord Russell drafted two notes that the cabinet reviewed. One included Palmerston's demands, and the second ordered Lyons to break off diplomatic relations if the United States did not respond satisfactorily within seven days. Reports that Wilkes's action had not been authorized did not calm Palmerston's fervor for a showdown. The prime minister halted exports to the North of gunpowder and saltpeter, which the ever-helpful du Ponts were buying to meet a serious shortage. Palmerston expected that Britain's demands would come as a "Thunder Clap" to Lincoln.[26]

Prince Albert Intervenes

On the evening of November 30, Palmerston sent the two proposed dispatches to the queen with a note reporting that the cabinet had concluded that "a gross outrage and violation of international law had been committed and that your Majesty should be advised to demand reparation and redress." Then a dying man intervened. Prince Albert, the queen's consort, weak with the typhoid that would end his life within two weeks, fought his chills in order to draft a royal note to the prime minister urging the creation of diplomatic space. Albert wrote that the queen would like her government to express hope that Wilkes had not acted with instructions, or that he misapprehended them. Further, Britain should suggest that it did not believe that the United States had intended to insult Britain, which would only add to America's distressing complications. Accordingly, the prince suggested, the Americans would understandably offer the redress Britain sought. Albert did not change the demands; he just smoothed the way for Britain to accomplish its ends with face-saving interpretations instead of haughty orders. Palmerston agreed. The dispatches were sent by ship on the evening of December 1. Poor Albert died before he learned that he had helped stave off a third war between Britain and America. Lord Russell added a third message in a private note, suggesting that Lyons should offer an informal communication to the Americans before triggering the seven-day deadline.

The British government had acted without news of the American reaction to the incident; British despair deepened with recognition that exultant American public sentiment might prevent any administration concessions. Lyons inexcusably forwarded a secondhand, and false, story that Seward had ordered the seizures. Seward's friend and political partner, Thurlow Weed, wrote the secretary from London that the Duke of Newcastle, who was the colonial secretary, was sharing a Seward story from the duke's visit to Canada and the United States (with the Prince of Wales) in 1860. Allegedly, Seward had said that the United States would pick a fight with Britain.[27] The British concluded that Seward had been preparing for war. The military in Canada planned to capture Portland, Maine, in order to block a U.S. invasion from that quarter. The Admiralty prepared to blockade northeastern American cities.[28]

Economic Anxieties

The transatlantic economy also had a vote. U.S. securities tumbled in value, and speculators rushed to buy gold and gunpowder. Britain's stock exchange fell precipitously. Overseas agents warned grain merchants not to ship in American vessels, which might be seized in a conflict. Secretary of the Treasury Salmon Chase, who had been struggling to secure foreign loans, now could not borrow a dime. Uncertainty led Americans to hoard gold and silver, straining the treasury's ability to pay its debts in specie. The New York offices of Barings and Rothschilds closed their doors. In the following year, in part based on the treasury's traumatic experience, Lincoln and Chase sought Congress's authorization for a national paper currency, the new federal "greenbacks," to be sure the Union could pay its bills. As Hamilton had written many years before, fighting wars required money and credit.[29]

On December 13, the *New York Times* carried a story about the sense of outrage in Britain; the next day it reprinted a London newspaper account that underscored the danger. On December 15, Seward appears to have learned about the British demands through letters he had received, and the secretary alerted Lincoln.[30]

Seward's Creative Lawyering

Minister Lyons received the communication from Lord Russell on the evening of December 18, and he called on Seward the next day to deliver the demands for immediate release of the prisoners and a suitable apology. Lyons had to walk a fine line. He had to convey firmness and London's resolve without a bellicosity that might make it harder for Washington to back down. Any miscalculation could trigger a war. Seward asked if there was a deadline for response. Lyons replied confidentially that he had seven days from official delivery. Seward asked for an unofficial copy of the dispatch, which Lyons provided. Seward told Lyons that he appreciated the courteous tone, which reflected the suggestions of the now-deceased Prince Albert. Lyons gave Seward a few days before officially conveying his demarche; he formally presented his note on December 23 and explained that he would have to break off relations if the prisoners were not released.

Lincoln suffered sleepless nights "contriving how to get out of the scrape without loss of national dignity." John Bright, a liberal British MP who was a friend of the United States, had sent a letter to Senator William Sumner, chairman of the Foreign Relations Committee and a rival of Seward's, suggesting international arbitration. But this well-meaning idea created risks. Arbitration was usually a tool to deal with boundary disputes or financial claims, not the resolution of conflicts involving national honor. The British government, impatient with litigious Americans, wanted a clear answer immediately.[31]

Seward, contrary to perceptions in London, recognized that the United States had to release Mason and Slidell. His friend Thurlow Weed, writing from London, reported that a failure to turn over the rebels "means war."[32]

At a cabinet meeting on Christmas Day, Seward read a proposed reply to his colleagues. Senator Sumner, whom Lincoln had invited to attend, read letters from America's British friends, John Bright and Richard Cobden, imploring the United States not to give London a justification for war, and "the breaking up of your country." During the course of the contentious four-hour session, the French legation delivered a message from its foreign minister warning that the rest of Europe backed Britain's position and urging release of the prisoners. Lincoln concluded that they need not decide that day and called for another meeting on the twenty-sixth. A number of accounts say that the president proposed trying his hand on an alternative that would courteously suggest arbitration.[33]

The twenty-six-page draft reply that Seward proposed represented a fine example of creative lawyering. He defended the right to search neutral vessels for contraband, and claimed (mistakenly) that the envoys were a type of contraband. The problem, Seward observed, was that international law required Wilkes to bring the *Trent* to a port for a prize court. International law did not permit a captain to be the judge of his own actions. Then Seward cleverly referenced a letter that Secretary of State James Madison had written to Monroe in 1804, when Monroe had been minister to Britain. Madison had set forth American principles for the rights of neutrals at sea. Seward conveniently reasoned that Britain's position now disavowed its aggravating practice of impressment. Instead, concluded Seward, Britain embraced traditional American views, as articulated by Madison, that a warship could not seize a person from a neutral ship without proper legal process before a tribunal. "We are asked to do to the British nation just what we have always insisted all nations ought to do to us," Seward argued. The United States, according to Seward, should stand by its principles, especially now that Britain accepted the U.S. legal position. Seward transformed a tactical setback into a great success for American principles.[34]

When Lincoln's cabinet met again on December 26, it grudgingly approved Seward's note with a few changes. Lincoln had apparently started a draft, but never finished it. When Seward asked about Lincoln's alternative, Lincoln allegedly replied, "I found I could not make an argument that would satisfy my own mind, and that proved to me that your ground was the right one." Lincoln probably recognized the risk that London would not accept an equivocating reply. Seward's son Frederick later observed that presidents and kings are not apt to see flaws in their own arguments, but fortunately, Lincoln "combined a logical intellect with an unselfish heart." Perhaps. Lincoln also had confirmed Seward as the author of a response that might prove unpopular. Seward recognized that he now had to win his case in the court of public opinion. On December 27, he sent newspapers five diplomatic documents about the incident. Seward's letter to Lyons, for example, which praised Wilkes and referenced Jefferson and Madison, seemed written more for Americans than the British recipients.[35]

On January 1, the United States transferred Mason, Slidell, and their two secretaries to a British warship. After changing to a steamer, the Confederates reached London on January 29. By then, they were old news. London had received Seward's note with a dispatch from Lyons on January 9. Lord Russell concluded that the note and release of the prisoners provided suitable "reparation." The British disputed Seward's legal logic, of course, but those disagreements could be left to lawyers. The British government and public seemed relieved, especially given the gloom after Albert's death on December 14. The American press and public also seemed ready to stand down, encouraged by editors whom Lincoln and Seward had briefed.

Only the Confederates bemoaned the outcome. Many had convinced themselves that the Northern fanatics would not concede. General Robert E. Lee was one of the few who had suspected otherwise. He wrote his wife on Christmas Day that U.S. "rulers are not entirely mad, and if they find England is earnest, and that war or a restitution of their captives must be the consequence, they will adopt the latter. We must make up our minds to fight our battles and win our independence alone. No one will help us."[36]

Lincoln's Recollection

Lincoln deserves the last word. In 1865, the president recalled the *Trent* incident in a talk with General Ulysses Grant. Horace Porter, one of Grant's staff officers, related Lincoln's words in 1897: "It was a pretty bitter pill to swallow, but I contented myself with believing that England's triumph in the matter would be short-lived, and that after ending our war successfully we would be so powerful that we could call her to account for the embarrassment she had inflicted on us."

According to Porter, Lincoln then recounted the story of the dying man who recognized that the time had come to make peace with his enemies. The ailing man asked to see a fellow named Brown, his greatest foe. "In a voice as meek as Moses's," the sick man said "he wanted to die at peace with all his fellow-creatures. And he hoped he and Brown could now shake hands and bury all their enmity." Brown broke down and reconciled, in "a regular love-feast of forgiveness," Lincoln had explained. But as Brown turned to leave the room, the dying man raised himself to call out, "But see here, Brown; if I should happen to get well, mind that old grudge stands." Lincoln then drove the point home: "I thought that if the nation should happen to get well we might want that old grudge against England to stand." The pragmatic Lincoln would fight "one war at a time."[37]

The U.S. diplomacy of December 1861 could have lost the North the Civil War. Instead, Washington and London pulled back from the brink. The British started to perceive Seward differently, distinguishing his adamant defense of the Union from his willingness to avoid a conflict with London. Seward realized, in part through the blunt messages from his friend Thurlow Weed, that his reputation for belligerence could incite disaster. The British government probably concluded that the blustering Yankees needed stern messages, but also that London should pick its fights carefully.

Foreign Public Opinion and Diplomacy

Through the *Trent* affair, Lincoln and Seward became more aware of the importance of foreign public opinion, especially in Britain. France and other Europeans would follow Britain's lead, although Czar Alexander II of Russia, having recently fought a war with the Anglo-French, and disliking revolutionaries and independence movements, leaned toward Lincoln and the Union. British aristocrats were not unified, but they tended to disparage the American republic and its rough-hewn politicians. The Confederacy's valor in battle stirred the nobles' sympathies. Britain's middle class—religious and antislavery in beliefs and republican in spirit—remained reluctant to embrace Southern slaveholders. But in 1861 the North had declared it was fighting for the Union, not to end slavery.

Although the U.S. Constitution had prohibited the importation of slaves after 1807, the antebellum United States had a poor record of enforcing the international ban on the slave trade. When Lord Russell proposed a treaty in March 1862 to permit mutual searches to thwart slavers, Seward worked a deal with Minister Lyons. The number of slaves transported to Cuba, the last major importer, fell from more than 30,000 in 1860 to less than 200 in 1865. The positive response in Europe probably contributed to Lincoln's thinking about establishing the end of slavery as a war aim. The United States also changed its approach toward countries governed by former slaves and finally recognized Haiti and Liberia in June 1862.[38]

The Union defeats in early 1862, followed by Lee's counteroffensive, led to a new diplomatic crisis in the fall of 1862. Both London and Paris contemplated proposals for "humanitarian intervention" to stop the slaughter.

"Humanitarian Intervention"?

The cotton shortage was leading British mills to shut down and textile towns to suffer. The House of Commons received a report of the Poor Law Board in May revealing misery and inadequate assistance. By December 1862, some two million people in Britain were destitute because of the loss of the cotton trade. Other British industries and cities did a booming business because of the war, and alternative supplies of cotton would ease shortages in 1863, but in 1862 politicians worried about the risk of unrest. In July, the Commons debated a motion to offer mediation. The government defeated the move, but both Palmerston and Russell noted the rising sympathy for the South. Fortunately for the North, the French foreign minister hesitated to explore the idea of joint action with Britain that summer. Later in the year, Napoleon, with a new foreign minister, proposed joint intervention to London, but by then Britain had lost interest. The Russians also rebuffed the venture. The following year Seward returned the favor to St. Petersburg by refusing to join a French move to mediate a Polish rebellion against Russian rule, even though Seward sympathized with the "gallant" and "valor[ous]" Poles.[39]

Palmerston and Russell never fully understood Lincoln's and the Union's will to persevere and prevail. The British leaders wanted to avoid being drawn into the conflict, but they speculated on ways to propose separation. One idea was to suggest a temporary armistice. Or the Europeans might offer to mediate. Other possibilities, such as recognition of the South, or a move to lift the blockade, would only seem to incense the North without ending the fighting. In essence, Russell, with Palmerston's acquiescence, searched for a costless peace, perhaps once the North faced the defeatist realities. In 1862, Seward's clear message of resolution loomed large. To have any prospect, a European mediation plan would have to be backed by an implied use of force. Palmerston hesitated while waiting for the outcome of Lee's northern invasion in the late summer of 1862, which the Army of the Potomac turned back at Antietam on September 17.[40]

On September 22, Lincoln declared his intention to issue the Emancipation Proclamation at the beginning of 1863. The president delivered his message primarily to his American audience, but Lincoln hoped he would increase sympathy for the Union in Europe as well.

He was shocked by the initial hostile reaction of Britain's leaders and press. Although the ruling class opposed slavery, they read the proclamation, which applied only to slaves in the secessionist states, as a call for "servile insurrection." With the recent rebellion in India in mind, imperial Britain shivered at the thought of a native uprising. Furthermore, a slave revolt in the South would further squeeze the meager cotton supply reaching Europe. To British leaders, the Emancipation Proclamation looked "cold, vindictive, and entirely political." Palmerston called it "trash."[41]

Lord Russell thought it was time to end the bloodletting. He wanted to impose an arms embargo, and he recommended an offer of "friendly and conciliatory" mediation. In today's context, Lord Russell could be viewed as arguing for a "humanitarian intervention" to protect those suffering from a calamitous civil war.[42]

On October 7, 1862, Chancellor of the Exchequer William Gladstone gave a speech proclaiming that the South would achieve independence. Gladstone was not hostile to American democracy, but he supported the principle of local self-determination. He believed that the Union was too big to survive; the South had made an army and navy, Gladstone asserted, and now was creating a new nation, too.[43]

Fortunately for the Union, members of the prime minister's cabinet pushed back on Gladstone's principles, Russell's inchoate ideas, and Palmerston's inclination. The secretary of war, Sir George Cornewall Lewis, a rival of Gladstone's, asserted that the South had not yet established its independence under principles of international law. He also pointed out that the North would reject mediation, and therefore that ill-considered intervention would likely lead to war with the United States.

Palmerston decided to reach out to Lord Derby, the leader of the Conservative opposition. Derby, Benjamin Disraeli, and the senior Conservatives replied that they opposed mediation or recognition. Such steps would "merely irritate the North without advancing the cause of the South or procuring a single bale of cotton." The Conservatives, who were looking ahead to a "Tory Democracy" with an expanded electoral franchise, also did not want to cross the middle classes who favored the North.

Palmerston's cabinet thrashed out the issue during meetings in October and November. The government decided not to decide, at least for the moment. But a run of Confederate victories could revive the question.[44]

Morality and Realpolitik

By the end of 1862, European public opinion began to shift in response to the Emancipation Proclamation. The Civil War had become a moral cause. The Confederacy carried the banner of slavery, while the Union fought against human bondage. Mass meetings and addresses to President Lincoln spurred a widespread popular movement in Britain. The United States helped draft resolutions and even made secret payments to fund gatherings.

When Parliament reconvened in February 1863, Lincoln wielded the new power of public diplomacy by writing public letters to groups in Britain. The president's letter to the laborers of Manchester thanked their "sublime Christian heroism." While acknowledging that "the duty of self-preservation rests solely with the American people," he urged "forbearance of [foreign] nations." Lincoln drew Britons to his noble cause by recognizing that the workers' meetings provided "an energetic and reinspiring assurance of the inherent power of truth and the ultimate and universal triumph of justice, humanity, and freedom."[45] Diplomacy and democracy mixed to stir a new public opinion that bridged the Atlantic.

Historians debate the ultimate effect of the Emancipation Proclamation on foreign intervention. Lincoln recognized that the military facts on the ground would be determinative. He believed unsentimentally that people acted according to self-interest, so he made clear to London the high price of recognizing the Confederacy. Yet Lincoln also believed that the Union stood for a higher purpose—as an example of government by the people and in opposition to slavery. Lincoln joined those causes to his diplomatic arsenal. Thirty-four years later, Gladstone, a Liberal leader who added moral dimensions to Britain's foreign policy, admitted that his October 1862 speech had been a terrible mistake.[46]

Latter-day experts have wondered why Britain did not pursue a realpolitik strategy of supporting the breakup of its rival for hegemony in the Americas. It is doubtful that Palmerston's government ever seriously considered that idea. A divided America posed dangers. London was concerned that the North might threaten Canada and the Confederacy might expand southward. London thought the war could not last, so it chose not to alienate either side. The Lord Chancellor, Lord Westbury, recommended to "[l]et them tear one another to pieces."[47] Furthermore, uncertainties in Europe counseled against getting dragged into an American war. Giuseppe

Garibaldi, the leader of Italy's unification, had just marched to "liberate" Rome. The wars of German unification were about to begin. At this time, Palmerston and his colleagues, no longer young men, were not disposed to pursue new adventures; instead they just faced problems day by day.

Confederate Raiders... and International Arbitration

One other conflict of Civil War diplomacy is worth mentioning because of later ramifications for the United States and Britain. The Confederacy contracted in Britain to build several "commerce raiders," the most famous of which was the *Alabama*. In the twenty-two months between the *Alabama*'s launch in July 1862 and its sinking by the USS *Kearsarge* off Cherbourg, France, in 1864, the rebel raider took sixty-five merchant prizes. The naval predators virtually eliminated the U.S.-flagged merchant marine, as U.S. owners shifted their ships to foreign flags. The United States merchant fleet took until World War I to recover and never regained its dominance in the maritime carrying trade.[48]

The building of the Confederate vessels in Britain generated enormous—and long-lasting—hostility toward London's "pseudoneutrality." In 1872, London and Washington finally agreed to an arbitration in Geneva for all claims of losses stemming from the *Alabama* and other disputes. In the aftermath of the Franco-Prussian War and with the new tensions in Europe, seafaring Britain became uncomfortable with its own precedent of permitting commerce raiders to be built in neutral ports. The tribunal settled on $15 million of compensation for the damages of the *Alabama* and a sister ship, the *Florida*. Britain objected, but paid promptly. The case came to represent an example of two proud nations willing to resolve differences through negotiation and even arbitration. The diplomacy also reflected Britain's accommodation to the rising power of the victorious United States and London's interest in overcoming ill feelings.[49]

France, Mexico, and the Future of North America

Lincoln and Seward also had to deal with a special French problem during the Civil War. In 1861, the republican regime of Mexican president Benito Juarez had suspended interest payments on debt incurred by a predecessor government. Later in the year, France led an expedition, joined by the British and Spanish, to Vera Cruz to collect unpaid debts. Early in 1862, Napoleon III expanded the mission by marching on Mexico City to "seek our guarantees." Britain and Spain withdrew.

Napoleon had a vision of a Catholic, Latin monarchical empire in Mexico that would contain the warring Anglo-Saxons to the north. Indeed, one of Napoleon's plans for mediation in the U.S. Civil War envisaged an outcome of four states in North America: the North; the South; Mexico; and a new western province incorporating states of northern Mexico and the U.S. Southwest.

The French forces marched into Mexico City in June 1863. The provisional government offered an imperial crown to Ferdinand Maximilian, a Hapsburg prince. Napoleon wanted to secure a suitable monarch for Mexico while persuading the Austrians to yield Venice to Italy, imposing limits on Italy's unification, and safeguarding Austria against Prussia. The bizarre maneuver epitomized exactly the type of monarchical exchanges that the United States had wanted to exclude from North America.

Seward accommodated Napoleon's move without yielding. The United States would continue to support republicanism and self-determination in the hemisphere. Therefore, the administration would not recognize the provisional government and instead withdrew its minister. Yet Seward also accepted the fiction that France was just seeking monies owed under international law and was not conquering territory. The United States used uncertainty to keep France in check, while "compromising nothing, surrendering nothing." As Lincoln explained to Matias Romero, Juarez's representative in Washington, "the settlement of Mexico's present difficulties depended upon a Union defeat of the Confederacy."

Hawks in Congress wanted to confront France, especially as Maximilian and his Empress Charlotte arrived in Mexico in 1864. During that decisive year, Seward held true to the policy of focusing Union armies on the Confederacy. "Why should we gasconade about Mexico when we are in a struggle for our own life?" asked Seward.

By early 1865, French public opinion turned against the Mexican adventure. President Lincoln had been reelected, and the Union Army sensed victory. In February, Napoleon told the American minister in Paris that he wanted to get out of Mexico. After Lincoln's assassination in April, Seward had to restrain resentful generals who aimed to settle a score with France and prevent the rebuilding of a rebel force in Mexico. General Grant ordered General Phil Sheridan to the Rio Grande in order to make a show of force. Grant said he would practice "Neutrality in the French and English sense of the word."

Seward suspected that the French-sponsored monarchy "was rapidly perishing." He believed that American interference in Mexico would only risk prolonging Maximilian's stay and inserting U.S. forces where they were not wanted. Seward was alert to Mexican sensitivities to the U.S. invasion twenty years before. He wondered how the Americans would get out;

in today's language, Seward wanted an "exit plan." When Grant hatched a scheme to place General John Schofield on "leave" and send him to Mexico to recruit a volunteer corps for the Juarista army, Seward convinced President Andrew Johnson to propose Schofield for a diplomatic mission to Paris instead. Napoleon never met Schofield. But Seward's maneuver worked.

In October 1865, Napoleon offered to withdraw all French forces from Mexico in exchange for U.S. recognition of Maximilian's government. Seward declined. He used Grant's threats to push France harder. In April 1866, Napoleon ordered a French withdrawal. Maximilian stayed. Juarez's forces captured the hapless Hapsburg and a firing squad executed Maximilian on June 19, 1867. Juarez had restored the Mexican republic. With the creation of the new Confederation of Canada that same year, a democratic North America appeared possible.[50]

Seward's Strategic Vision

The preservation of the Union did more than sustain the United States as a powerful country that would shape the twentieth-century world. Lincoln's awe-inspiring phrases confirmed the very viability of democratic government. For Seward and later American statesmen, the success of the republican Union suggested a new international system that competed with the old European order of empires and rival states maneuvering for superiority.[51]

Seward—like Hamilton, Jefferson, John Quincy Adams, and Clay—believed that the Union represented an alternative to both centralized empires and rival states jousting in a world of conflict. These early American leaders envisaged a cooperative framework of relations among states based on principles of behavior and law; within this system, freer commerce would maximize wealth. Federations or confederations would encourage the development of overlapping communities. This new type of union among states would protect liberties while respecting varying nationalities.

As early as 1853 and 1854, Seward prophesied an American federal republic extending from the "tropics" to "the polar circle," including "even distant islands in either ocean." Moreover, with widening horizons, Seward could see that "the control of this continent is to be...the controlling interest in the world." Seward wanted to achieve North American union through free choice, not conquest or coercion. He had opposed the war with Mexico in 1846. Seward foresaw that closer ties would be accomplished through "peaceful negotiation" among self-governing states, not annexation through "unlawful aggression." Far ahead of his time, Seward observed, "The intermingling of races always was, and always will be, the chief element of civilization."

Seward believed that expanding trade would boost U.S. influence. Rather than grasp territories hastily, like the European empires, he thought the real prize was "the commerce of the world, which is the empire of the world." The greatest producing and trading nation would be "the great power of the earth." Commerce was the new "god of boundaries." Seward's expectations were global. As early as 1852, he predicted that America's trade with East Asia would someday be as important as trade with Europe.[52]

As Professor David Hendrickson explains, "Seward's visions of national greatness, and of commercial empire...relied on the power of attraction, which 'increases as commerce widens the circle of national influence.'" Ernest Paolino, a Seward biographer, called this concept Seward's "Law of Imperial Gravity."

The tensions over slavery had transformed the experiment of Union into a tense internal balance of power, which imported the conflicts the founding generations had wanted to escape. Ultimately, slavery could not coexist with liberty. For Seward, the success of the Union in the Civil War created a new opportunity to fulfill the potential of the American experiment through enlargement.

The Peaceful Expansionist

Seward's ideas about economic development, trade, and immigration guided his thinking about the territorial scope of the Union. He was a peaceful expansionist who expected that the magnetism of the U.S. economy and the appeal of the federal Union would draw other states closer, whether through annexation, partnerships, or new types of alliances. To bolster these new networks, the secretary wanted America to acquire lands supportive of commerce, ports, and naval bases.[53]

On March 30, 1867, Seward struck a deal with Baron de Stoeckl of Russia to purchase Alaska for $7.2 million. Seward's interest stemmed from Alaska's maritime connections to the whaling industry, which the secretary viewed as supportive of the U.S. Navy, and to Alaska's prospects for resources and trading depots. Seward also recognized Alaska's strategic geography. Seward observed, as did the navy, that ownership of Alaska and the Aleutians would help the United States "extend a friendly hand to Asia." The Senate ratified Seward's treaty within a month, influenced in part by Russia's stalwart friendship during the Civil War, although the House took until the following year to pay up.[54]

The purchase of Alaska positioned the United States on three sides of British Columbia, a geographic advantage noted by supportive newspapers. In 1867, British Columbia was an isolated British colony of only about ten thousand people, many of whom wanted to join the United States. A newspaper in Victoria claimed that "nine out of every ten of our people—sick of the present misrule—look to annexation to the United States as the only hope for our colony." Seward cooked up a plan to exchange the *Alabama* claims for "round[ing] off our North Western territory."

Seward lost this great land deal after Parliament passed the British North America Act of 1867, which created the Canadian Confederation out of the four eastern provinces; London wanted to strengthen the security of the Dominion against the victorious and resentful colossus to the south. The new Confederation thwarted Seward's move with a better bid: Canada offered to assume British Columbia's debts and committed to construct a transcontinental railway to bind the Canadian provinces together. Seward had to console himself with the belief that Canada would grow closer to the United States than to Britain over time.[55]

Seward called the Pacific the "Far West." In 1867, the United States took possession of Brooks Island, later known as Midway Island, under a law that then senator Seward had advanced in the 1850s. As early as 1868, the U.S. Navy told Congress that Midway Island would be valuable, "especially in the event of a foreign war." That report proved prescient in June 1942, when the navy blunted Imperial Japan's maritime onslaught at the epic Battle of Midway.

Seward wanted to annex the Sandwich Islands, as Hawaii was known, but settled for a treaty of trade reciprocity, which the Senate finally ratified in 1875. The United States annexed Hawaii in 1898, and in 1959, Congress added Hawaii as the fiftieth state.

Michael Green, the author of a recent wide-ranging and insightful history of America's "Grand Strategy" in the Asia Pacific, traces the U.S. rise as a Pacific power to Seward's multidimensional vision of "military strength, trade, and republican values." The secretary of state recognized Japan and China as potential independent powers, and sought to thwart European colonial moves on Korea while initiating commercial ties. The Burlingame Treaty of 1868 was China's first "equal" treaty with a Western power.[56]

Given Seward's experiences with Santo Domingo, the *Trent* crisis, and Mexico, it is no surprise that the secretary's strategic eye observed the Caribbean, too. His travel there in January 1866 on a navy steamship was the first official trip by a secretary of state outside the United States. Seward was scouting for a Caribbean port for the navy. In 1867, he arranged for the United States to buy the Danish islands of St. Thomas and St. John for $7.5 million. The Congress, weary of Seward's acquisitions and embroiled in the impeachment of President Johnson, demurred. Late in 1868, the indefatigable Seward tried unsuccessfully to acquire Santo Domingo, now known as the Dominican Republic, over which Seward risked war in 1861. The United States eventually purchased the Danish Virgin Islands for $25 million in 1917, when fears about the German navy's encroachments in the Caribbean revived Seward's plan.[57]

Seward even anticipated President Trump in trying to purchase Greenland and Iceland from Denmark to safeguard the Atlantic approaches. He also needed to link the maritime highways of the Atlantic and Pacific. In 1866, he committed to a treaty with the Colombians to survey a ship canal in Panama, but a change of governments in Colombia stymied the effort. Decades later, Teddy Roosevelt revived Seward's strategy by helping to create an independent Panama after yet another failed deal with Colombia and then building the Panama Canal.[58]

Seward's activist and expansionist U.S. foreign policy after a devastating and costly Civil War was extraordinary. He believed that the Union, unshackled from the internal strife of slavery, was finally freed to achieve its potential at home and abroad. Even amidst the sharp political divisions of Reconstruction, Seward planted fields of diplomatic seeds that later generations would discover and grow.

Lincoln's Strategic Compass

Lincoln's opportunity to shape a post–Civil War world was tragically cut short. The governing classes of Europe never really understood the power of his ideas—or for that matter, the strength of his will—while he was alive. Yet his strategic compass pointed true throughout the war and for 150 years beyond. "The central idea" behind the Civil War, said Lincoln, was to prove to the world "that popular government is not an absurdity."[59]

As early as 1837, Lincoln had contended that the Founding Fathers "aspired to display before an admiring world a practical demonstration of the truth of the proposition which had hitherto been considered at best no better than problematical—namely, the capability of a people to govern themselves." In 1842, he explained that "the capability of man to govern himself—was the germ that has vegetated, and still is to grow and expand into the universal liberty of mankind."[60]

On election night, 1864, Lincoln's impromptu remarks pointed out "how sound and how strong we still are," despite the losses of war, because republican government had risen to the mortal challenge. The nation's true wealth was not gold or guns but patriotic free men. In his brief second inaugural, Lincoln eschewed triumphalism in favor of reconciliation and an acceptance of God's justice in "a just and lasting peace," not between warring regions, but "among ourselves and with all nations."[61]

In the mid-twentieth century, J. William Fulbright, chairman of the Senate Foreign Relations Committee, observed that the American foreign policy tradition is "an expression of two distinct sides of the American character. Both are characterized by a kind of moralism, but one is the morality of decent instincts tempered by the knowledge of human imperfection and the other is the morality of absolute self-assurance fired by the crusading spirit."[62] Abraham Lincoln's pragmatic diplomacy epitomized the first.

II

THE UNITED STATES AND THE GLOBAL ORDER

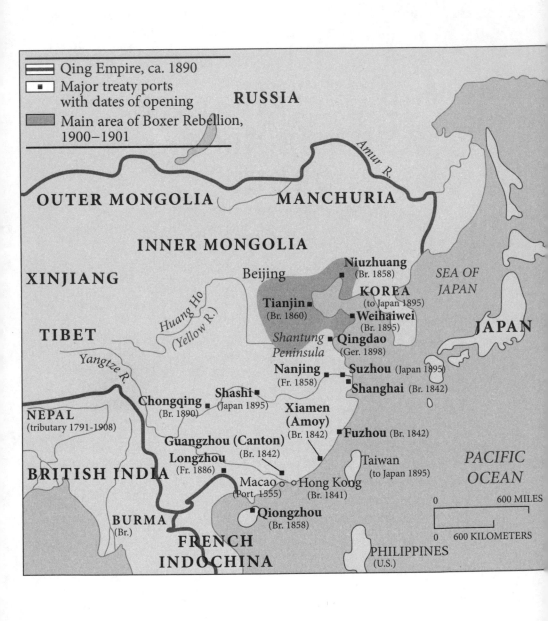

Qing Empire, ca. 1890

Major treaty ports
with dates of opening

Main area of Boxer Rebellion,
1900–1901

RUSSIA

OUTER MONGOLIA   MANCHURIA

Amur R.

INNER MONGOLIA

XINJIANG

Beijing

Niuzhuang
(Br. 1858)

SEA OF
JAPAN

KOREA
(to Japan 1895)

Tianjin
(Br. 1860)

Weihaiwei
(Br. 1895)

Huang Ho
(Yellow R.)

Shantung
Peninsula

Qingdao
(Ger. 1898)

JAPAN

TIBET

Yangtze R.

Nanjing
(Fr. 1858)

Suzhou (Japan 1895)

Shashi
(Japan 1895)

Shanghai (Br. 1842)

Chongqing
(Br. 1890)

NEPAL
(tributary 1791–1908)

Xiamen
(Amoy)
(Br. 1842)

Fuzhou (Br. 1842)

Guangzhou (Canton)
(Br. 1842)

Longzhou
(Fr. 1886)

BRITISH INDIA

Taiwan
(to Japan 1895)

PACIFIC
OCEAN

Macao
(Port. 1555)

Hong Kong
(Br. 1841)

0   600 MILES

BURMA
(Br.)

Qiongzhou
(Br. 1858)

0   600 KILOMETERS

FRENCH
INDOCHINA

PHILIPPINES
(U.S.)

◆

CHAPTER 5

John Hay

The Open Door

The First Open Door Note

On September 6, 1899, Secretary of State John Hay sent a circular note about China to Britain, France, Germany, Italy, Japan, and Russia. China was not on the address list.

The message that became known as Hay's first Open Door note made three points. First, the powers would recognize one another's treaty ports, leased territories, or any vested interest in a "so-called sphere of interest" in China. Second, Chinese tariffs would apply equally to all and be collected by Chinese officials. Third, no power could favor its own nationals with regard to harbor dues and railroad charges. Hay urged each government to endorse the concept and promote it with others. His note never used the term "open door." Hay avoided the nagging issue of territorial integrity. Modest in scope, the note would turn out to have wide-ranging, even unforeseeable, consequences.[1]

Japan and Italy quickly agreed. Britain accepted after clarifying that military ports were not "leased territory." France equivocated over railroad rates but went along. Germany, more focused on European politics, said it would subscribe if all other powers would do so. Russia resisted, perceiving a conspiracy to circumscribe its eastern ambitions. Eventually the State Department told the Russian minister that further delay would be "misinterpreted by the [American] people and would be extremely prejudicial to the friendly relations between the two nations." Russia decided that continued opposition was not worth alienating the United States or isolating Russia from others. In any event, St. Petersburg concluded, the points seemed malleable and unenforceable. By January 4, 1900, Hay had received all the responses; he could usher in the new century by declaring the informal compact "final and definitive" and "proof of…the untrammeled development of commerce and industry in the Chinese Empire." The Chinese drew the practical conclusion that Hay's note meant that if other powers sought to close the door to China, the United States would push back.

Most public reaction was congratulatory. A number of headlines proclaimed a great diplomatic victory, foreseeing a twentieth-century complement to the nineteenth century's Monroe Doctrine. The *New York Post*, an anti-imperialist paper, recognized Hay's and America's diplomatic innovation: "No treaties; just an exchange of official notes. No alliances; no playing off of one Power against another; simply a quiet inclusion of them all in a common policy." The *Times* of London looked ahead, reasoning that the United States was "the last Power in the world to have gone through the trouble of getting paper assurances and then to allow them to remain paper assurances only. [S]he means them to be observed." Hay had launched an idea. That idea would be tested—very soon, and for a century to come.[2]

The World of 1900

By the end of the nineteenth century, the United States was a rising power on the world stage. The country numbered 70 million, reaching from the Atlantic to the Pacific. In 1898, the United States had won a brief war with Spain over Cuba. In doing so, the U.S. Navy had sunk a Spanish fleet in Manila Bay in the Philippines, raising the question of the future of Spain's Pacific colony. In late July, the then American ambassador to Great Britain, John Hay, wrote a congratulatory note to his much younger friend, Colonel Theodore Roosevelt, whose battlefield heroism in Cuba would catapult Roosevelt's political rise even higher and faster. Hay wrote that, "It has been a splendid little war; begun with the highest motives...favored by...Fortune....It is now to be concluded, I hope, with that fine good nature, which is...the distinguishing trait of the American character."[3] Within three months, John Hay would be President William McKinley's secretary of state, with responsibility for helping to guide U.S. policy in the changing global order.

America's international role, along with the domination of "big business" and the trusts, defined the national debate. The American public was proud of its enhanced standing but was uncertain about how to use U.S. power. Finley Peter Dunne, a satirist and sharp-witted writer, captured the public mood through his worldly-wise Irish-American bartender and critic, "Mr. Dooley," who spoke in the dialect of 9009 Archey Road, Chicago, Illinois: "We're a gr-reat people," said Mr. Dooley. "We ar-re that. An' th' best iv it is, we know we ar-re."[4] Mr. Dooley was a tad suspicious of foreigners—especially Englishmen—and of overeducated gentlemen who wanted to misuse American power for selfish, dubious ends.

International power relations were in rapid flux. Brooks Adams, a descendant of the illustrious clan, explained the dislocations in his *American Economic Supremacy*. Britain, supreme for a century, was slipping, and Russia seemed to be gaining from the disequilibrium. London's tribulations in the Boer War looked like a sign of weakness. Germany, finally united after a devastating defeat of France in 1871, posed a more immediate threat, but Adams warned that imperial Russia—extending all across Europe to Asia—represented the principal danger. Adams believed that Russia's push into the northern reaches of the crumbling Chinese empire would require the United States to assume the counterbalancing role that Britain used to play.[5]

Given America's geography, the country's commercial and maritime heritage, and the vastness of the Pacific, it is understandable that a naval officer would offer the first strategic vision of the new era. Alfred Thayer Mahan's 1890 book, *The Influence of Sea Power Upon History*, became a classic. Mahan wanted the United States to become a maritime power with a global perspective. Like Seward, Mahan recognized that the starting point was the U.S. Navy's domination of the Caribbean. America's interest in the security and safety of the nation's west coast pulled it into the Pacific, too. Mahan perceived that the contest for power on the other shore, in Asia, would remain "debated and debatable." The United States would not dominate, as in the Caribbean. But Mahan wanted the United States to sail powerfully in Pacific waters.

Mahan's strategic vision incorporated other diplomatic elements. He wanted to boost trade, including imports as well as exports. Tariffs, Mahan wrote in 1890, were like "a modern ironclad that has heavy armor, but inferior engines and guns; mighty for defence, weak for offence." Trade liberalization would extend American influence. He observed how Seward's trade reciprocity treaty with Hawaii had pulled the islands into the U.S. orbit. Mahan further believed that America's "moral influence"—its values—would gradually encourage political liberalization and indigenous republican institutions that would contribute to a more secure international order.[6]

In 1900, Mahan published a series of essays in *The Problem of Asia*. Mahan wrote that the world rivalries, stoked by fears of Russia's expansion, reflected the conflict between Russia's land power and the sea powers, such as the United States, Britain, Japan, and perhaps Germany.[7] Russia and the United States, the continental nations, were reaching the edges of their natural land boundaries, sparking competition at their borders.

The circle of tension tightened when European and Asian alliances crisscrossed. France, fearful of Germany, yet also dreaming of revenge, bound itself to Russia. Japan, resisting Russia, forged a defensive alliance with Britain in 1902. And Britain and France, anxious about Germany, formed an

Entente Cordiale in 1904—not quite an alliance, but a cooperation intended to rise above centuries of conflicts, if not yet beyond their traditional distrust.[8]

The statecraft of this new era had to recognize the rise of proud, competitive, and aggressive national loyalties, too. Mr. Dooley could meet like-minded patriots, with different flags, around the world. The unification of Germany and Italy transformed once-weak and manipulated German and Italian states into new powers that could challenge their neighbors. Japan demonstrated that Asians could also quickly build modern, powerful countries. Nor was nationalist fervor only for big states; Central and Eastern Europe, including the Balkans, seethed with patriotic societies that recalled glorious, albeit bloody, pasts and foresaw brilliant (and still bloody) futures.[9]

The Scramble for China

John Hay reportedly expressed one of America's great diplomatic challenges from his era to ours. "The storm center of the world has gradually shifted to China," Hay explained. "Whoever understands that mighty empire...has a key to world politics for the next five centuries."[10]

Although Hay knew Europe well, his name will forever be associated with a problem arising from U.S. diplomacy in East Asia: He assumed office as China's last dynasty was crumbling and foreign powers were threatening to carve China into "concessions" and colonies. Hay called it "the great game of spoliation."[11] The European powers were just completing their "scramble for Africa," during which they had divided some ten million square miles and 110 million Africans into thirty new colonies and protectorates.[12] The big powers grasped for pieces of China next.

The starting gun for the scramble for China had been sounded, however, by Japan and Russia, not the Western Europeans. During the Sino-Japanese War of 1894–95, the fast-rising and modernizing Japanese had easily overwhelmed Chinese fleets and troops in a dispute over the Korean peninsula. One recent historian of the conflict explained that this "seismic reversal in the traditional power balance fractured the...harmony within the Confucian world and left an aftershock of enduring territorial and political fault lines."[13] Japan seized the island of Formosa (Taiwan) and the nearby Pescadores Islands, secured access to Chinese ports, and claimed a sphere of influence over Korea. Russia, with a hold in Manchuria and an eye on control of an ice-free Yellow Sea port, pressed Japan to yield some gains, stirring friction that would lead within a decade to the Russo-Japanese War.[14]

The race to seize Chinese ports and privileges became a sprint. Germany secured Tsingtao and mining and railroad rights. To counter Russian control of Port Arthur, the British grabbed a base across the bay and demanded a long-term lease for the Kowloon peninsula, on the landward side of Hong Kong's harbor. France insisted on leasing land north of its new colonies in Indochina.

China's vulnerability had been increasing for fifty years, since the middle of the nineteenth century. Its population had soared from about 150 million in 1700 to some 430 million in 1850, but the Qing dynasty had been unable to expand infrastructure and food production to keep up. Poverty, hunger, and bandits precipitated social breakdowns and uprisings, including the devastating Taiping Rebellion of 1850–64, overlapping with the U.S. Civil War. London had seized Hong Kong as a colony after the first Opium War of 1839–42, and then Britain and France expanded their hold after ending a second conflict with China in 1860. By 1898–99, the Celestial Dynasty was staggering toward its closing chapters. The Chinese people were frustrated and increasingly desperate; foreign powers were playing out their East Asian competition on a map of China.[15]

A headline in the *Washington Post* summarized the emerging crisis: "China Taken by the Throat." A senior European in Beijing told the *New York Times* "that the moment has now arrived for international control of China."[16]

Americans today may not recall or even know of these Chinese tragedies, but the Chinese study and recite them. These decades of the nineteenth century comprise the first half of what Chinese refer to as "the century of humiliation." Today's leaders in Beijing will insist that the twenty-first century's internationalization of China will remain firmly under their control.

The American Experience with China

The American experience with China differed from that of Europeans, Russians, and Japanese. Americans had long indulged dreams of China's commercial potential. In 1784, Robert Morris, the financier who recommended Hamilton to Washington for treasury secretary, commissioned a ship, the *Empress of China*, to carry forty tons of ginseng from Appalachia to Canton (today's Guangzhou). The voyage earned Morris a 400 percent profit. Imitators rushed in. By 1790, Americans had sailed twenty-eight ships to Canton. By the onset of the Napoleonic Wars, the number of U.S. ships in China was second only to Britain's. To gain access, the Yankees had to court Qing dynasty officials or follow in the wake of the Royal Navy and British merchants. In 1844, U.S. envoy Caleb Cushing negotiated a treaty that gave the United States the same commercial rights as those of any "most favored nation." The British East India Company disdained the "Jackal Diplomacy" of the Americans—"eager to feed but never to join the kill."[17]

The shining dream of the great China market always seemed to beckon over the horizon. By 1895, China accounted for less than 1 percent of U.S. trade. Yet over the prior decade, U.S. exports to Asia had almost tripled—from $26 million to $73 million. In the 1890s, China was buying half of America's cotton exports. Businesses saw gains for kerosene, wheat, flour, iron, steel, and textiles. In 1898, U.S. trade doubled with Britain's Hong Kong, the major entry point into southern China.[18]

Americans wanted to save souls as well as earn riches. More than one thousand American missionaries were growing and tending to Christian flocks in China by 1898. These intrepid proselytizers, women as well as men, carried messages of modernity as well as Bibles. The missionaries founded schools and hospitals. They wanted to convert the Chinese to a way of life as well as to an afterlife. Throughout much of the twentieth century, the missionaries and their children became the interpreters of China for other Americans—whether in Sunday schools in small towns or through universities, the diplomatic corps, books, magazines, and even movies.[19]

By 1899, President William McKinley and Secretary of State John Hay had acquired a new interest in China to complement commerce and Christianity: Asia-Pacific security. During and after the Spanish-American War, the United States had acquired stepping-stones of islands leading to China: Hawaii; Pago Pago in Samoa; Wake; and Guam in the Marianas—as well as the Philippines. American diplomacy had to incorporate new geographic dimensions—beyond North America and even *all* the Americas. Whereas the United States still wanted to avoid entanglements with Europe, it was entangling with Asians and encountering Europeans in Pacific waters.[20]

John Hay

John Hay was a man of words. He had served President Abraham Lincoln during the Civil War as one of two private secretaries, assisting with a deluge of correspondence as well as special assignments. Hay wrote poetry, a travelogue, a novel, newspaper editorials, a ten-volume biography of Lincoln (with his former White House colleague John Nicolay), and delightful correspondence, including with literary friends such as Mark Twain, Henry James, and Henry Adams. Hay was a renowned talker and storyteller, too, an art he shared with the martyred president whom he revered. His words made a lasting imprint on U.S.-China policy.

John Hay was an unusual candidate to author an enduring policy toward China. He had never even seen the Pacific, having only journeyed as far west as Yellowstone Park. In 1865, after Lincoln's assassination, Secretary of State Seward assisted Hay's exit from Washington to become secretary to the U.S.

legation in Paris. Hay later served in Madrid and Vienna as well, although his experience was marked more by literary observations than by strategic insights. Hay's marriage in 1874 to Clara Stone, the daughter of a wealthy Cleveland industrialist, relaunched Hay as a man of fortune.

Through his standing in Ohio Republican circles, Hay met a rising talent, Congressman and Governor William McKinley, whom Hay helped financially at key moments. After McKinley was elected president in 1896, he appointed Hay as the U.S. ambassador to Great Britain, where Hay proved to be an inspired choice.[21]

The long era of Anglo-American competition and sometimes conflict was edging toward mutual acceptance and even cooperation. Hay had the ability to flatter British egos as their American cousins insisted on pride of place in North America and the Caribbean. Queen Victoria, who had encountered countless foreign emissaries during her long reign, told the British minister to Washington that Hay was "the most interesting of all the Ambassadors I have known."[22]

One of Hay's modern biographers recognized Hay's "talents as conciliator, problem solver and sounding board."[23] Along with Hay's charm, wit, and skill as a raconteur, he was simply good company; the elder statesman conveyed a sense of history and tragedy.

In the aftermath of the Spanish-American War, McKinley recognized that he needed a secretary of state who could advise and assist with a rapidly widening agenda—in the Caribbean, with European powers, and across the Asia-Pacific. He called Hay home from London, and Hay became secretary of state on September 30, 1898. As one former diplomat and student of this era concluded, "Hay and McKinley were a good fit. They both were friendly, generous to others, and pragmatic in their politics."[24]

Hay's State Department had nearly ninety employees, including clerks, in Washington, and some 1,200 others scattered in embassies, legations, and consulates around the world. Since the days of Lincoln and Seward, presidents had added telephones and electric light bulbs to the White House. Hay's office was in the massive French Empire–style State, War, and Navy building on 17th Street NW, next door to the White House (and still used today as the Eisenhower Executive Office Building).[25]

Hay needed help. He turned to William Woodville Rockhill, a thirty-five-year-old scholar-diplomat-adventurer who would become one of America's storied "China hands."[26] Hay first encountered Rockhill in March 1898, during a visit to Greece, where Rockhill had been posted and was "bored into extinction." To find a place for Rockhill back in Washington, Hay had to appoint him director of the Bureau of American Republics; the deal was that the energetic Rockhill would also find time to serve as Hay's adviser on East Asian affairs.[27]

Rockhill had no particular affinity for the Chinese people. Nor was Rockhill particularly excited about boosting U.S. businesses in the Heavenly Kingdom. He later made the railroad builder E. H. Harriman into a foe by refusing to ask the Qing court to permit Harriman and his companions to tour the Forbidden City. Rockhill's strategic interest was to protect China's territorial integrity, which he viewed as critical to securing America's open relationship with East Asia over the long term.[28]

Seeds of a China Policy

While serving in Britain, Hay's curiosity and enjoyment of the company of thinkers introduced him to two British experts on China. One was Archibald Colquhoun, who published *China in Transformation* in 1899, which Hay read with interest. Colquhoun called for a "room-for-all" doctrine. Hay's other British associate, Charles Beresford—a British admiral, member of Parliament, and author of *The Break-Up of China*—used travels to China and then the United States to promote a plan to save China. While still in China, Beresford wrote Hay, "[I]t is imperative for American interests as well as our own that the policy of 'open door' should be maintained." On a tour of business groups in the United States, Beresford proposed "The Open Door, or Equal Opportunity for All." These British idea merchants believed their own government was too slow to act; moreover, the United States, the power without a colony or concession in China, was best positioned to stop the country's disintegration.

Hay wondered if Britain was maneuvering the United States to counter Russia's advances and protect Britain's commercial interests. (Note the parallel with the skepticism of John Quincy Adams toward another British proposal of partnership in 1823.) He wrote to a friend that the United States opposed China's dismemberment and that American public opinion would not support a grab for "spoliation," "but for the present we think our best policy is one of vigilant protection of our commercial interests without formal alliances." Neither recent immigrants from Ireland and Germany, nor foreign policy traditionalists, would like the idea of an alliance with London on behalf of the British Empire.[29]

During the summer of 1899, Alfred Hippisley, a Briton on leave from his post as inspector of maritime customs in China, visited his old friend Rockhill and Hay. Hippisley followed up with a letter to Rockhill that offered a practical step. The foreign powers controlled the collection of Chinese tariffs within their spheres of influence. Hippisley urged the United States to press an agreement that all foreign powers should apply Chinese tariffs equally. The plan promoted nondiscrimination while accepting the existing authority of foreign powers.[30] In August, Jacob Schurman, Cornell University's respected president and an anti-imperialist, observed that China was on the verge of being devoured. He said China's future was "the one overshadowing question" of U.S. foreign policy: China must maintain its independence and "its doors should be kept open."[31]

Hay and Rockhill decided to move. Rockhill asked Hippisley to prepare a memorandum presenting the points on which the foreign powers might concur. Rockhill urged Hippisley to address China's territorial integrity and independence, but the Englishman demurred in favor of "the irreducible minimum." Hay liked Hippisley's approach of finding the common ground, building upon it ever so slightly, and then holding the whole together with the weak gravity of international cooperation. The secretary asked Rockhill to distill Hippisley's memo and other contributions into a new document. The two Americans recognized that they needed to be the authors of the U.S. policy toward China, whatever its lineage. A week later, Rockhill produced the first Open Door note, which Hay dispatched in early September.[32]

A Rebellion in China

Within a matter of months, the Chinese decided to have a say about the foreigners in their country. The Emperor Dowager Cixi had deposed her reformist emperor-nephew, Kuang Hsu, in 1898. The traditionalist court and military, recently humiliated by the upstart Japanese, were in no position to confront the brazen foreigners. Events had challenged the dignity of the Celestial Empire, a condition that had proven an awful omen for past dynasties. A drought in 1899 led to famine across northern China, adding to public desperation.

Starting in Shantung Province in northern China, the Fists of Righteous Harmony—belittled by foreigners as the "Boxers" because of their martial arts rituals—arose like a quick, violent storm to attack "foreign devils," whom they blamed for all ills. The Boxers slaughtered missionaries, who were located throughout rural China. The rebellion also rampaged against "rice Christians," the nearly one million Chinese converts. The uprising attacked signs of modernity—which the Boxers associated with foreigners—such as railroads, telegraphs, and churches. The fearful Empress Dowager and her court, despite her claims to the contrary, decided to embrace the rebellion and ordered imperial troops to join the Boxers.

The violence surged so quickly that foreign envoys failed to comprehend the danger. On June 5, 1900, the Boxers cut the railroad from the port city of Tianjin to Beijing. The Qing army joined the rebels, swelling the numbers of attackers. On June 15, U.S. minister Edwin Conger reported that "we are besieged in

Peking." Then the telegraph wires went dead. For the next fifty-five days, 435 soldiers and three thousand foreigners and Chinese Christians were trapped in the diplomatic quarter next to the Forbidden City. (The scene of this drama, located just to the east of today's Tiananmen Square, was later razed.)

There was a ray of hope from southern China. The mandarins in Guang-zhou and the provinces below the Yangtze River ignored the Qing court's order to attack foreigners. U.S. officials negotiated secretly with the southern mandarins to keep the peace, saving Chinese and foreign lives. On July 3, the southern officials told Hay that only the United States could head off a full-scale war, a remarkable recognition of America's new standing.

The Second Open Door Note

After chairing a cabinet meeting (in the president's absence) that same day, Hay stated that the United States did not consider itself at war with China. He also issued a declaration that became known as the second Open Door note.

Hay was walking a diplomatic tightrope. He needed to rescue the Americans in Beijing and throughout China while containing the conflict. He wanted to avoid the appearance of joining the vengeful imperial powers that had preyed on China's weakness. While supporting a military relief force, Hay had to maintain communications with Chinese officials in order to signal that the powers wanted only to suppress the Boxers and save their citizens. An escalation would be disastrous for China.

The Boxer Rebellion and siege of Beijing and other cities could open a new, ugly door: to the division of all of China. The United States wanted neither territory nor to overthrow the Chinese government. "What I want," Hay told a friend, "is the friendship of China when the trouble is over." On the home front, Hay needed to save the lives of American missionaries while avoiding a long intervention that would stir the anti-imperialist opposition to President McKinley's reelection that fall.

Hay's second Open Door note of July 3 was another circular to the foreign powers. The message explained U.S. policy toward China in the midst of extraordinary, dangerous, and uncertain circumstances. Although the addressees were the foreign powers, Hay directed his opening sentences toward Chinese readers. He stated that the United States would hold anyone who wronged its citizens to the "uttermost accountability." Then he offered the Qing court a fiction to save face. As long as the Chinese authorities were not in overt collusion with the rebels and "use their power to protect foreign life and prosperity," the United States would "regard them as representing the Chinese people, with whom we seek to remain in peace and friendship."

Then Hay explained the immediate purpose of U.S. policy: "to act concurrently with the other powers, first in opening communication with Peking and rescuing the American officials, missionaries, and other Americans in danger; secondly, in affording all possible protection everywhere in China to American life and property."

Finally, Hay looked to the future. He took the opportunity to assert the fundamental point that Rockhill had wanted to include in the first Open Door note: Whatever the outcome of the rebellion and even the fate of the legations, the United States would "preserve Chinese territorial and administrative entity, protect all rights guaranteed to friendly powers by treaty and international law, and safeguard for the world the principle of equal and impartial trade with all parts of the Chinese Empire."

Hay did not ask for a response to this note. His diplomacy signaled, and suggested, suitable short- and longer-term outcomes for both China and the treaty powers.

The Relief of the Foreign Legations

Now actions mattered more than words. On July 5, the *New York Times* reported, "All Foreigners in Peking Dead." They were not. Hay worked anxiously to reestablish contact with the Americans and other foreigners in Beijing. Throughout the crisis, Hay had maintained respectful relations with the Chinese minister in Washington, Wu Tingfang. Working through a Manchu general who opposed the siege, Wu arranged for the United States to send a coded message to Minister Conger in the barricaded legation quarters. Conger replied with a description of the dire circumstances and a plea for quick relief. To confirm the authenticity of his reply, Conger had been asked to send the name of his sister, "Alta." Hay received the good news from "Alta" on July 20.

The United States had to decide what forces it would contribute to the relief. Fifty U.S. Marines from the USS *Newark* (out of a total of 435 foreign troops) already held the legation walls in Beijing. McKinley's government strained to avoid a formal alliance with the treaty powers, but it had to commit ships and troops. McKinley dispatched 2,500 soldiers and Marines from the Philippines, demonstrating early in the century the benefit of forward-stationed forces in East Asia.

A multinational force of about twenty thousand troops rescued the foreign community in Tianjin, including Herbert Hoover, then a mining engineer, and his wife. After one failed attempt, an expedition of eight nations fought their way to Beijing. To avoid the impression that the United States was at war with China, the Americans termed their operation the "China Relief Mission."

The multinational force broke through Beijing's outer walls on August 14–15, and each contingent fought its way independently through fierce resistance to the legation quarter. The Boxers had launched a fierce attack on the surrounded survivors during the final days, but the rebels melted into the countryside after the relief broke through. The resolute defenders had lost 65 people, with another 150 wounded. Seven U.S. Marines had fallen. Then the looting, destruction, and slaughter of innocent Chinese began. Rockhill had left for China during the crisis so as to be on hand to take part in the negotiations to follow. He wrote in disgust, "The 'disciplined armies of Europe' are everywhere conducting operations such as the Mongols must have done in the 13th century."[33]

Peace Terms

The United States wanted to keep China whole and sovereign. McKinley aimed for an "indemnity for the past and security for the future," according to the *New York Times*. On August 28, after the longest cabinet meeting of his presidency, McKinley issued a statement that reiterated Hay's principles for China. The president wanted to withdraw U.S. forces right away, but Hay persuaded McKinley to maintain a U.S. presence a little longer to send an important signal to the other foreign powers. Hay had to block a move by the navy to seize the Zhoushan Islands, just south of the mouth of the Yangtze River, for a base. In later years, American officials ignored Hay's prudence and extended America's Pacific perimeter into mainland Asia, with costly consequences.

On October 19, Chinese envoys offered terms that recognized China's violations of international law, accepted the idea of an indemnity, and promised the safety of foreigners. The United States promptly accepted the proposals as a basis for negotiation.

Almost a year later, on September 7, 1901, the Qing court and the foreign powers signed the "Boxer Protocol." The Boxers had killed the German minister to China, and Berlin wanted vengeance. Rockhill and Conger thwarted a German demand that all Chinese officials who had supported the rebels should be put to death; only four midlevel mandarins paid that price. The Americans also blocked the construction of an international fortress next to the Forbidden City. The protocol permitted the foreign powers to station troops in north China. The U.S. Army's Fifteenth Infantry Regiment, stationed in Tianjin in the early twentieth century, became a training ground for American generals, including George Marshall, Joseph Stilwell, and Matthew Ridgway, each of whom would return to historic duty in Asia.

Finally, the American diplomats argued the indemnity down to 335 million gold dollars, about $7 billion today.

The United States took the smallest share of the indemnity, 7.5 percent, for about $25 million. In 1908, at the instigation of the U.S.-educated Chinese minister to the United States, Congress decided to return $14 million through scholarships and the building of Tsinghua University, today one of China's top centers of learning. The first fifty Chinese students arrived in the United States in 1909, the vanguard of some 30,000 men and women. The Boxer Indemnity Scholarship Program, the forerunner of the Fulbright Fellowships, may have turned out to be America's greatest contribution to modernizing an independent China.[34]

Rockhill urged economic reforms, too. He wanted China to open up to American investment, establish a stable currency, and protect U.S. trademarks—all issues that the two countries still debate today. In 1903, China and the United States signed a commercial treaty. Sadly, prospects dimmed as America turned against Chinese workers in the United States, expelling, banning, and even murdering the "yellow peril." The Congress passed the Chinese Exclusion law in 1904, violating U.S. treaties with China. Shanghai began a boycott of U.S. products. Boatmen on the Pearl River refused to carry American goods. Rickshaw drivers ignored Yankee passengers. The United States had provoked the mobilization of the first political campaign by Chinese around the world. In 1905, President Roosevelt tried to counter the anti-Chinese wave by explaining, "We cannot expect China to do us justice unless we do China justice." But the damage had been done.[35]

The Significance of Hay's Open Door Diplomacy

Scholars and policy makers have long debated the significance of Hay's Open Door diplomacy. At the time, Hay recognized that he was playing a weak hand: "[W]e do not want to rob China ourselves, and our public opinion will not permit us to interfere, with an army, to prevent others from robbing her.... The talk of the papers about 'our pre-eminent moral position giving us the authority to dictate to the world' is mere flap-doodle."[36]

Yet diplomacy involves shaping the foreign policy landscape—in the eyes of supporters at home and internationally—often without wielding dominant power. Countries face ambiguous situations; expedient solutions can nudge conditions positively, even if not definitively. Over time, statements of intention and direction can become doctrines that influence future assessments and decisions.

American opinion leaders and the public sensed that China was, or would be, important to the world. They turned out to be correct. Secretary of War (and later Hay's successor as Secretary of State) Elihu Root told his wife that China's breakup "would be second to no event in its effect upon mankind since the fall of the Roman empire."[37]

Michael Green observes that the United States focused on both China itself and on dampening great power competition within China that might incite Pacific rivalries. Admiral Mahan noted years later that the Open Door policy depended on "the opposition of interests, in relation to [China], of other states; those of Europe, the United States, and Japan." Mahan knew that the relative power positions of those states would change over time, as they have. Mahan concluded that the factor that would lend consistent weight to the U.S. position was, not surprisingly, America's "naval power."[38]

Teddy Roosevelt wrote his successor, President William Howard Taft, framing Hay's creation in strategic terms: "The Open Door policy in China was an excellent thing, and I hope it will be a good thing in the future, so far as it can be maintained by general diplomatic agreement; but, as has been proven by the whole history of Manchuria, alike under Russia and under Japan, the 'Open Door' policy... completely disappears as soon as a powerful nation determines to disregard it, and is willing to run the risk of war."[39]

As the next chapter recounts, one of TR's diplomatic answers to this conundrum was to manage the balance between the competing powers of Japan and Russia. Britain chose another course by forging a naval alliance with Japan in 1902. After World War I, in the 1920s, the United States tried to maintain balance through a combination of treaties and naval arms control because America was not willing to commit the necessary naval power to protect its interests. The Open Door policies found their way into international treaties negotiated by Charles Evans Hughes some twenty-five years after Hay first pronounced them.[40]

The failure of these later diplomatic efforts led George Kennan in the 1950s to point to the Open Door as a prime example of a faulty lack of realism in U.S. foreign policy. "It was like asking every man who believes in truth to stand up. The liars are obliged to be the first to rise." Nor, Kennan pointed out, was the United States willing to back its words with deeds. "It was not a policy that we Americans cared enough about to support in any determined way or for the results of which, if implemented, we were prepared to accept any particular responsibility."[41]

William Appleman Williams found fault with the Open Door from a different perspective. In his book *The Tragedy of American Diplomacy*, Williams argued that the Open Door policy constituted a "non-colonial imperial expansion... designed to clear the way and establish the conditions under which America's preponderant economic power would extend the

American system throughout the world without the embarrassment and inefficiency of traditional colonialism."[42] Williams's neo-Marxist economic determinism has little foundation. While some U.S. capitalists had long looked to the prospects of the China market, in 1890 U.S. sales to China constituted only 0.3 percent of U.S. exports, all of which contributed modestly to the vastly larger U.S. economy.[43] Moreover, if we are to label all trade and foreign investment as "imperialism," the term loses meaning. Throughout the second half of the twentieth century, many developed and developing economies alike relied on trade and foreign investment to boost growth, living standards, technological diffusion, and cooperation on other issues. The U.S. withdrawal from international trade and investment in the 1930s certainly did not boost the prospects of China, or for that matter Europe. Indeed, liberals of different eras associated the extension of "the American system" to include human, religious, and women's rights along with democratic and good governance.

In contrast with the critics, economic historian Adam Tooze believes that the Open Door policy reflected "one deceptively simple but far-reaching principle": "equality of access for goods and capital." This distinguished America's strategic outlook from the aims of either the old colonial powers or the rising nations of 1900. As Tooze explains, America resisted dividing the world; instead, U.S. soft power of economics and ideology expanded with open doors.[44]

The Open Door policy in fact reflected diverse interests: economic, certainly, but also U.S. security; China's territorial integrity and modernization; constraining the aggression of other powers; and the missionaries' desire to save souls and lives.

In the world of 1900, Hay's words and maneuvers showed that the United States had entered the ranks of the great powers. But that international system teetered on the precipice of the world's most destructive century.

CHAPTER 6

Theodore Roosevelt

Balancer of Power

War in Northeast Asia

On February 8–9, 1904, Japanese torpedo boats launched a surprise attack on Russia's Far East fleet in the roadstead of Port Arthur. Japan formally declared war on February 10. Over the next few weeks, the Japanese severely damaged much of the Russian fleet and contained the rest. A day before the naval attacks on Port Arthur, a division of the Japanese fleet brushed aside a Russian gunboat to land elements of the Japanese First Army on the Korean coast near Seoul. The forty thousand troops moved toward the Yalu River in the north, where they overwhelmed a Russian force in the first major land battle. The way to Manchuria was open to Tokyo's legions.[1]

Over the course of the following century, these Asian names, and the experience of surprise Japanese naval attacks, would become more familiar to Americans. The Russo-Japanese War of 1904–05 was waged in the cockpit of Northeast Asian security—the historic crossroads of China, Russia, Japan, and Korea, as we are relearning today through nuclear diplomacy with North Korea. In 1982, Japan's national TV network, NHK, reminded its viewers of the 1904–05 war with an eight-hour TV docudrama titled *Flags over Portsmouth*. As the title made clear, key scenes of the story took place halfway around the world in the small town of Portsmouth, New Hampshire—because of Teddy Roosevelt.[2]

The conflict between Japan and Russia had been brewing for some time, at least since Russia and the European powers had forced Japan to yield Tokyo's territorial gains over China in the 1894–95 Sino-Japanese War. To add insult to injury, during the Boxer Rebellion, St. Petersburg had moved fifty thousand troops into Manchuria and taken over concessions that Japan had vacated under Russian pressure. Over the next few years, the Russians solidified their hold on China's three eastern provinces and edged toward Korea and Beijing. Russia extended the Trans-Siberian Railway into

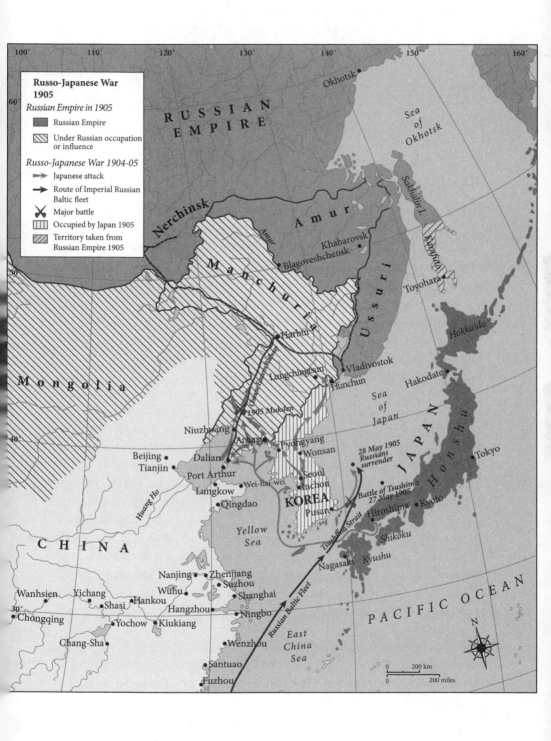

Russo-Japanese War 1905

Russian Empire in 1905

- Russian Empire
- Under Russian occupation or influence

Russo-Japanese War 1904-05

- → Japanese attack
- → Route of Imperial Russian Baltic fleet
- ✕ Major battle
- ▥ Occupied by Japan 1905
- ▨ Territory taken from Russian Empire 1905

100°   110°   120°   130°   140°   150°   160°

60°

RUSSIAN EMPIRE

Okhotsk

Sea of Okhotsk

Nerchinsk

Amur

Manchuria

Amur

Blagoveshchensk

Khabarovsk

Ussuri

Sakhalin I.

Karafuto

50°

Toyohara

Harbin

Lungchingtsun

Vladivostok

Hokkaido

Mongolia

Chinese Eastern Railway

1905 Mukden

Hunchun

Hakodate

Sea of Japan

40°

Niuzhuang

Antung

Pyongyang

Wonsan

Beijing

Dalian

Tianjin

Port Arthur

Wei-hai-wei

Seoul

Inchon

KOREA

28 May 1905 Russians surrender

JAPAN

Honshu

Tokyo

Lungkow

Qingdao

Pusan

Battle of Tsushima 27 May 1905

Hiroshima

Kyoto

CHINA

Huang Ho

Yellow Sea

Tsushima Strait

Nagasaki

Kyushu

Shikoku

Wanhsien

Yichang

Shasi

Hankou

Nanjing

Zhenjiang

Suzhou

Wuhu

Shanghai

Hangzhou

Ningbo

30°

Chongqing

Yochow

Kiukiang

Chang-Sha

Wenzhou

East China Sea

PACIFIC OCEAN

N

Russian Baltic Fleet

Santuao

Fuzhou

0   200 km

0   200 miles

Manchuria; it secured a twenty-five-year lease to build a naval base at Port Arthur, connected by another rail link to its prime trunk line.[3]

Tokyo had tried to resist St. Petersburg's moves peacefully. In 1902, Britain's treaty with Japan pledged assistance if Tokyo became involved with more than one enemy in a conflict over Korea and China. In 1903, Japan pursued comprehensive negotiations with Russia, but Russia would not agree to China's territorial integrity and control of Manchuria. Tokyo suspected Russia would press for a "neutral zone" in northern Korea, which Russia would in fact control. Japan determined Russia must be forced from Manchuria, even if Tokyo had to go to war.[4]

Roosevelt and his secretary of state, John Hay, were surprised by Japan's attack on Port Arthur. But they were well aware of the rising tensions in Northeast Asia. Roosevelt, with his sense of history, respected Russia's past friendship with the United States in the Revolution and the Civil War, and through the sale of Alaska. "Russia, and Russia alone, of European powers, has been uniformly friendly to us in the past," he wrote in 1898. But as president, Roosevelt became angry when Russia failed to keep Manchuria's ports open, as it was supposed to do according to Hay's Open Door notes. The president was forming a personal dislike for the haughty behavior of Russia's absolutist regime. He publicly criticized the wave of violence against Russian Jews in 1903.[5]

That same year, Roosevelt told Hay that Russia's conduct in Manchuria had to be resisted, and that he believed the American public would back him in "going to an extreme in the matter." But TR recognized that Hay's practical assessment was correct: "I take it for granted that Russia knows as well as we do that we will not fight over Manchuria," Hay wrote the president, "for the simple reason that we cannot." Congress would not support a conflict. Nevertheless, Russian behavior rankled. Both Roosevelt and Hay considered Russia guilty of "extraordinary mendacity." They were especially frustrated by the obdurate and cunning behavior of Russia's minister in Washington, Count Arturo Cassini (grandfather of the dress designer, Oleg). Hay teased Roosevelt with the idea of giving Japan a "wink" to "seek a violent solution." St. Petersburg placated Washington with some port concessions and pledged again to withdraw its troops in Manchuria. Russia's true clash of interests was with Japan.[6]

We do not know whether the Roosevelt-Hay antagonism toward Russia encouraged Japan to act. After Japan had struck, Roosevelt wrote his son, "I was thoroughly well pleased with the Japanese victory, for Japan is playing our game." TR recognized that Japan could be an effective counterbalance to Russian power in the Far East. As Japanese victories gained momentum, however, the president perceived the risk of Russia's destruction in the region. After the first month of war, Roosevelt wrote his close British friend (and groomsman at TR's second wedding) Cecil Spring-Rice, then serving in London's embassy in St. Petersburg, that Japan's startling success created a "great new force in eastern Asia." Perhaps the two sides would fight on until both were exhausted, creating the basis of a peace with neither "a yellow peril or a Slav peril."[7]

Roosevelt and the Global Balance of Power

Roosevelt viewed the world of 1904 as composed of "civilized nations" and "backward peoples." He sometimes described the latter in racial or ethnic terms, but he perceived their "barbarism" as a stage of development, not a matter of genetics. For example, he admired and respected Japan's modernization and role as a civilized power. The civilized powers might need to "police" and "lift up" peoples in troubled places who had not yet achieved an ability to govern themselves, but Roosevelt assumed other peoples could eventually become civilized. This view guided TR's interventions in the Caribbean, where outside powers threatened to capitalize on weakness, posing risks to the United States.

The president's principal concern was the competition among the large civilized states. Roosevelt believed power was the most important factor in world affairs. He read the signs of rising nationalisms. He viewed them within the context of two thousand years of movements of peoples and technological and social progress. Indeed, TR imagined nationalism could be a "cure" for the "degenerative materialism" of the industrial economy. At the same time, Roosevelt recognized that the modern instruments of national strength extended far beyond the latent powers of Jefferson's age or even the systemic power that Hamilton longed to establish. The Roosevelt scholar John Blum referred to TR's sweeping speculations as "an eclectic intellectual home, its parts connected, but the whole more comfortable than integrated."[8]

Given this tempestuous global order, the president believed he—and the United States—had a responsibility to promote peace among the great powers. In another letter to Spring-Rice, Roosevelt avoided judgments about whether national interests were right or wrong. He could understand why others pursued ends in their interest, even if the United States disagreed with and would contest them. "Nations may, and often must, have conflicting interests, and in the present age patriotism stands a good deal ahead of cosmopolitanism."[9] Yet Roosevelt believed that a war among the major powers would precipitate a calamity. He was drawn, therefore, toward restraining international rivalries through peaceful balances of power. The United

States need not dominate; instead, America needed to be alert to shifts and threats in order to counter them and reestablish peaceful cooperation.

During 1905–06, Roosevelt mediated two great power conflicts—one in Northeast Asia and another in Europe concerning Morocco. His efforts secured peace and demonstrated America's diplomatic skill at balancing great power politics.

TR Considers Mediation Between Russia and Japan

The Russo-Japanese War posed a threat to China's integrity and the U.S. Open Door policy. Three weeks before the war began, Roosevelt had obtained private assurances from both sides that in the event of war each would respect China's neutrality.[10]

Roosevelt knew that a sweeping Japanese victory could fuel an assertiveness that Tokyo might direct toward China—or even U.S. interests in the Pacific. Japan, TR wrote Spring-Rice early in 1904, would only have one interest—East Asia—while the United States and others would have to tend to multiple interests. The president had taken note of Japan's military audacity and might, especially its naval power.[11]

Throughout 1904, Roosevelt considered possibilities for mediation between Japan and Russia. Shortly before the first shots were fired, he had tested the prospect with the U.S. minister in Tokyo and with the French government through Paris's minister to the United States, Jean Jules Jusserand, another Roosevelt companion. But the president had other priorities: He faced reelection during the first year of the war. Roosevelt yearned to win the presidency in his own right. Then he would have greater freedom to act.

Nevertheless, the restless Roosevelt was thinking ahead throughout 1904. At a long lunch at Sagamore Hill, his home in Oyster Bay, in June, he discussed the international outlook with Takahira Kogoro, Japan's minister to the United States, and Baron Kaneko Kentaro—a contemporary of Roosevelt's at Harvard and now a special envoy to the United States. The president predicted a great future for Japan. TR compared Japan's interest in the Yellow Sea with America's in the Caribbean. But he counseled Japan not to overreach beyond its initial war aims or to divide China. Insolence and aggression would backfire.[12]

Roosevelt recognized that Tokyo would oppose a "congress" like the one that had humiliated Japan in 1895. The president also worried that a congress would invite all the powers to apportion China. Japan wanted direct negotiations with Russia but did not believe Russia could be trusted.[13]

Roosevelt considered how to bring the antagonists together through "good offices," a neutral role recognized by the recent Hague Convention of 1899 and acknowledged in various U.S. treaties.[14] After his reelection in November 1904, TR moved George von Lengerke Meyer from the U.S. post in Rome to St. Petersburg so that the president would have a trusted emissary to the czar.[15]

Throughout 1904, Kaiser Wilhelm of Germany had urged the czar to fight on. Berlin gained from the absorption of France's ally, Russia, in an eastern war. The kaiser also felt a bond with his autocratic cousin in St. Petersburg and wondered if he could lure Russia into a new imperial partnership. TR sought the kaiser's opinions, kept Berlin well-informed about his thinking, and courted Wilhelm's friendship. At the proper time, the kaiser might be of assistance to Roosevelt with Czar Nicholas II.[16]

On New Year's Day, 1905, the fortress at Port Arthur surrendered. Japan captured almost twenty-five thousand Russian prisoners. St. Petersburg had lost a principal Pacific port as well as a powerful symbol. Signs of revolution within Russia flared; a march on the Winter Palace in St. Petersburg to plead with the czar led to a shocking massacre on what became known as "Bloody Sunday." Foreign capitals expected Russia to sue for peace with Japan, but the czar's resolve to reverse ill fortune just increased. The kaiser began to wonder if it were time for an armistice or even a peace settlement.[17]

Roosevelt sounded out Japanese emissaries, London, and other European capitals about peace terms. The president sensed Japan would demand Port Arthur and take Korea under its sphere of influence; indeed, the president wanted Tokyo to do so to constrain Russia. Japan's foreign minister, Komura Jutaro, wanted Manchuria restored to China's control. Japan also hinted at a need for Russia to pay a financial indemnity. Japan even eyed Russia's Trans-Siberian Railway across Manchuria to Vladivostok, the czar's remaining significant port on the Pacific. Japan did not want any foreign mediation, however; Tokyo feared any suggestion of peace would signal weakness. The Russians rejected TR's informal advice, through unofficial channels, that it was time to end the war.[18]

Stalemate

The facts on the ground created their own complex diplomatic logic. On March 10, 1905, after a two-week-long clash between two massive armies, in the largest battle in modern history up to that time, Japan captured Mukden (today's Shenyang) in southern Manchuria. The disorganized Russians fled north; the exhausted Japanese were unable to encircle or pursue their enemy. Now economics had a say: Japan had consumed its war resources and faced financial strains. The two sides had reached a strategic stalemate in the land war in Manchuria.[19]

Right before Japan marched into Mukden, the Japanese minister of war told the U.S. minister in Tokyo that it was time to stop the fighting. The military was actually ahead of Foreign Minister Komura, who believed Russia had to make the first move. Komura expected, correctly, that St. Petersburg needed first to see whether its Baltic fleet, which had sailed all the way to Asia, could salvage victory.[20]

On March 30 and April 2, Roosevelt wrote letters to the ailing Hay, explaining that officials from Japan, Russia, France, and Germany had spoken about peace negotiations, but that no one was ready to move. Roosevelt urged Cassini, the Russian minister in Washington, to recognize that Japan had not yet taken any Russian territory; once Tokyo had done so, Russia would need to yield more to end the fighting. In frustration, TR concluded that "[t]he Czar is a preposterous little creature as the absolute autocrat of 150,000,000 people. He has been unable to make war, and he is now unable to make peace."[21]

First Steps

Roosevelt left for a six-week hunting trip. If he could not guide the Russian bear in St. Petersburg, he would shoot real bears out west. He left instructions for Secretary of War William Howard Taft in his absence. But diplomatic pieces were assembling in a new shape. Russia, having failed to negotiate a new loan in Paris, asked the French to assist with peace, although St. Petersburg hinted at only minimal concessions. The French, however, faced a new crisis with Germany over Morocco, raising the prospect of a widening world conflict. (Before long, TR's foreign counterparts would approach him about assisting quietly with Morocco and the European power balance, too.)

The French exploration of mediation prompted the Japanese cabinet to decide, after meetings on April 8 and 17, to assess whether Roosevelt would use his "good offices" to bring the belligerents directly together. Yet Komura's message of April 18 did not quite make a straightforward request. The president's replies from the West concurred in the need for direct negotiations but sought to draw out Japan's positions on the Open Door, China, and a specific request for his assistance. The president had his own aims—and would need leverage and a sense of obligation to be useful. The Japanese then delivered an unequivocal private request for TR's assistance. But TR judged the time was still not ripe. News from St. Petersburg communicated the czar's resolve to fight on. Japan's demands for a financial indemnity and Russian territory also troubled the president: They were unrealistic and of little benefit to Japan. Further, Roosevelt pointed out to Tokyo that Russia's Baltic fleet, after a long passage, was nearing Japan's home waters. The Russians would read an overture now as a sign of fear.[22]

Franklin suffers humiliation standing in silence in the Cockpit. (His suit should be blue.) *Benjamin Franklin Appearing before the Privy Council*, by Christian Schussele, n.d. (1)

Franklin in London, under Newton's watch, by David Martin, 1767. (2)

Franklin and the ladies of Paris. The rustic emissary of a new republic charms society. This nineteenth-century engraving reflects the image over the reality. *Franklin's Reception at the Court of France, 1778*, by Anton Hohenstein, n.d. (3)

Franklin, the philosopher from the backwoods, in his marten fur cap (from Canada), by John Trumbull, 1778. The hat mattered more than the likeness. (4)

American Commissioners of the Preliminary Peace Negotiations with Great Britain, by Benjamin West, 1783. Pictured are John Jay, John Adams, Benjamin Franklin, Henry Laurens, and William Temple Franklin. West could not finish the painting because the British commissioners declined to sit. (5)

Architect of American power and economic diplomacy. Portrait of Alexander Hamilton, by John Trumbull, 1805. (6)

Purchasing the future. *Hoisting of American Colors over Louisiana*, by Thure de Thulstrup, 1904. (7)

Westerner and futurist. Portrait of Thomas Jefferson, by Rembrandt Peale, 1805. (8)

The Birth of the Monroe Doctrine, by Clyde O. DeLand, 1912. John Quincy Adams, to the left of the globe, sits uncharacteristically silent. (9)

American realist. Daguerreotype of John Quincy Adams, by Philip Haas, 1843. (10)

Henry Clay, 1848. Latin America and the American system. (11)

The *San Jacinto* stopping the *Trent*—and almost starting a second war—in 1861. (12)

"Look out for squalls." John Bull warns Uncle Sam: "You do what's right, my son, or I'll blow you out of the water." *Punch*, December 7, 1861. (13)

LOOK OUT FOR SQUALLS.

Jack Bull. "YOU DO WHAT'S RIGHT, MY SON, OR I'LL BLOW YOU OUT OF THE WATER."

One war at a time. Lincoln and his secretaries, John Nicolay and John Hay, by Alexander Gardner, 1863. (14)

Pragmatic unionist. William H. Seward, by Matthew Brady, ca. 1860–65. A beaked nose and keen eyes, like an alert bird ready to chatter—or strike. (15)

John Hay and the Open Door Notes for China. "Putting his foot down," by J.S. Pughe, 1899. (16)

A man of words. Portrait of John Hay, by John Singer Sargent, 1903. (17)

Mediating balances of power in East Asia and Europe. Theodore Roosevelt with the Russian and Japanese delegations at the signing of the Treaty of Portsmouth, 1905. (18)

HELPING THE PRESIDENT.

Balancing the "double wish" of the American public. Cartoon of Woodrow Wilson between William Jennings Bryan and Theodore Roosevelt, by Rollin Kirby, *New York World*, 1915. (19)

The international law tradition. Elihu Root, ca. 1902. (20)

THE SENATE—"IT DOESN'T MATTER WHICH; I EXPECT TO BOSS THE FOREIGN POLICY MYSELF"

The Senate expects to run foreign policy, as President Harding weighs selecting Hughes or Root as secretary of state. Cartoon in New York *Evening Post*, January 20, 1921. (21)

(A cartoon in the New York *Evening Post*, January 20, 1921)

Naval arms control and regional security in East Asia. American delegation to the Washington Conference, 1921–22, including (*left to right*) Elihu Root, Henry Cabot Lodge, Charles Evans Hughes, and Oscar Underwood. General Pershing stands in the second row between Lodge and Hughes. (22)

Washington Naval Conference in Washington, DC, 1921. The hosts specially designed the U-shaped table to encourage practical exchanges. To fit the French premier on the bottom leg, the delegates shifted to their left, so Charles Evans Hughes is slightly to the right of the middle. (23)

Cordell Hull and reciprocal trade. President Roosevelt speaks with Hull after the latter's return from the London Economic Conference of 1933. (24)

President Truman addresses Congress to request $400 million and American military advisers for Greece and Turkey, March 12, 1947. Congress rose to applaud his courage, but not necessarily his proposal. (25)

R4D/C-47 aircraft unload at Tempelhof Airport during the Berlin Airlift, 1948–49. General William Tunner mastered the logistics of Berlin's survival as freedom's city. (26)

George C. Marshall (*left*) with Arthur Vandenberg, February 26, 1948. Marshall said that Senator Vandenberg "never received full credit" for the Marshall Plan and that Vandenberg's "name should have been associated with it." (27)

William L. Clayton arrives for the Potsdam conference, July 24, 1945. The least recognized architect of the new economic and alliance system of 1947–49. (28)

"Cotton's Clayton." William Clayton, *Time* magazine cover, August 17, 1936. (29)

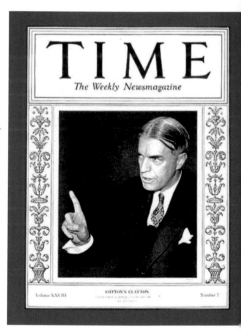

Inventor of the future. Vannevar Bush and the differential analyzer, ca. 1935. (30)

"General of Physics." Vannevar Bush, *Time* magazine cover, April 3, 1944. (31)

The crisis manager perceives Berlin as an asset. JFK in Berlin, June 26, 1963. (32)

Vietnam: learning from defeat. LBJ and McNamara, n.d. (33)

"The week that changed the world." Nixon shakes hands with Mao, February 21, 1972. (34)

Realpolitik and triangular diplomacy. Henry Kissinger shakes hands with Mao in Beijing, 1973. (35)

Setting out a strategy to win the Cold War through a contest of ideas. Reagan addresses the British Parliament in the Royal Gallery at the Palace of Westminster in London, June 8, 1982. (36)

Reagan with Gorbachev in Red Square, May 31, 1988. The revivalist sought to convert, not defeat, his adversary. (37)

George II. W. Bush, James Baker, and advisers in Kennebunkport, Maine, May 1989, shortly before the NATO summit. The author is second from the right. (38)

James Baker (*left*) with the author, 1988. Bush and Baker had a unique bond and partnership: practical American leadership, exercised with restraint, creating an aura of even more strength in reserve. (39)

The two great fleets clashed on May 27–28 in the Korean Strait near the island of Tsushima. Admiral Togo's battle fleet "crossed the T" in front of the Russian line of warships; Japanese gunnery sank four Russian battleships. That night Japanese torpedo boats shattered the rest of the czar's fleet. Tokyo did not lose one major ship. As Roosevelt concluded in a letter to Senator Henry Cabot Lodge, "No one anticipated that it would be a rout and slaughter rather than a fight." The epic battle ascended to the spiritual heights of Japanese warrior myth; in December 1941, the Japanese fleet that attacked Pearl Harbor flew the 1905 command flag from the mast of its leading aircraft carrier.[23]

Roosevelt's Diplomatic Offensive

Roosevelt now made his move, enveloping the czar in a diplomatic offensive. The president's close friend Speck von Sternberg, Germany's minister in Washington, pressed his Russian colleague, Cassini, to face realities. The kaiser jumped to TR's side, too. Wilhelm feared that "they [the Russians] will kill the Tsar," endangering all monarchs. Roosevelt welcomed the kaiser's appeal to Nicholas, even though the president was careful not to encourage the German expectation that the United States could squeeze Japan. TR hoped for assistance from France, too, but Paris, anxious about Morocco, wanted to pay no diplomatic price with Russia.[24]

Roosevelt met with Cassini on June 2 to convey his request to the czar to accept peace talks. TR spoke bluntly about Russia's hopeless position; he then offered to invite both states to meet directly if neither would take the first step. The president said he thought he could persuade Tokyo to agree, without adding that he already had Japan's agreement in his pocket. Not trusting Cassini to have the courage to convey the full direct message, Roosevelt directed Minister Meyer, new to his post, to present the proposal to the czar in person. TR was urging direct talks, "without intermediaries." After the protagonists met, there would be "time enough," if need be, to consider "suggestions" from outsiders. The president proposed a meeting someplace between Harbin and Mukden in Manchuria, explaining to his friend the French minister that he had done so in order "that no one would believe he was hoping for the choice of Washington." TR had to get the parties to commit to meet and to state their positions. He did not want to let Tokyo and St. Petersburg avoid difficult decisions by looking to others to solve their problems. Yet TR's reference to a Washington meeting, where he could serve a role, suggests that the option, while risky, was on the president's mind.[25]

Meyer met with Czar Nicholas II for an hour on June 7, the day after a disputatious conference between the czar and his advisers. A wary Nicholas decided that he should explore the possibility of peace before Japan had seized any Russian land. The czar had just heard from the kaiser, too. Nicholas had to trust Roosevelt to keep the czar's concession "absolutely secret." Near the end of their exchange, Meyer sensed that Nicholas seemed relieved. The czar asked Meyer to convey to the president Nicholas's hope that the two countries could renew their friendship. TR had won the czar's trust. Meyer had delivered.[26]

Yet Roosevelt was not leaving the diplomatic positioning to high-minded feelings and talk. Only the day before Meyer met the czar, Cassini had delivered Russia's earlier official, and negative, reply to Roosevelt's overture. Unimpressed, the president recommended to Baron Kaneko that Japan invade Russia's Sakhalin Island immediately, to gain possession and sharply remind Russia of the price of continuing the war. After Meyer cabled the good news of the czar's agreement to the president, Roosevelt immediately called Minister Takahira to share the report. Roosevelt was building personal capital with the Japanese, as well; he knew he would need to draw on it later.[27]

A Meeting in Portsmouth

On June 8, the president sent an official invitation to Japan and Russia to meet. He offered to assist in arranging the time and place. Both parties began to quibble over secondary details, to maneuver for the appearance of advantage, and even back away from their commitments. Such aftershocks are not unusual after countries undertake difficult decisions. But TR, impatient in the calmest times, was temperamentally unsuited for dithering. In the case of Russia, part of the problem was that TR had had to go straight to the czar for a decision; Russia's emissaries were either ill informed, in ill humor about the war and the czar's decision, or protecting themselves. As the president wrote Lodge, "Russia is so corrupt, so treacherous and shifty, and so incompetent, that I'm utterly unable to say whether or not it [will] make peace, or break off the negotiations at any moment." The ever-direct Roosevelt was particularly put off by "the way [the Russian] will lie when he knows perfectly well that you know he is lying." (One of the challenges of diplomacy is distinguishing intentional moves—good or bad—from inevitable blunders, miscommunications, and delays. Another is recognizing liars.)[28]

After sifting through various meeting locations, Tokyo and St. Petersburg agreed on their second choice, Washington. Recognizing the perils of negotiating in Washington's summer heat and humidity (before air-conditioning), Roosevelt suggested that the parties meet at the Portsmouth Navy Yard, adjacent to Portsmouth, New Hampshire. The facility was actually on an island that was part of Kittery, Maine. The delegations could stay in Portsmouth and meet at the guarded Navy Yard, which had international communications capabilities.[29]

Given the travel distance, the conference could not begin until early August. Russia wanted an armistice, but Japan refused. TR understood Tokyo's reasoning. Japan was in fact now poised for an attack on Sakhalin Island, north of Japan's main islands and just off Russia's coast. In 1875, Japan had agreed that Russia could acquire Sakhalin in exchange for Japan's control of the small Kuril Islands to the south. Japan proceeded to invade in early July to remind St. Petersburg of the price of stalling and to further shrink the Pacific coast that Russia might someday use to revive naval operations near Japan. (After World War II, the USSR seized both Sakhalin and the Kurils; Japan has tried to recover the small islands since the end of the Cold War, to no avail.)

Foreign Minister Komura and minister to the United States Takahira would lead the Japanese delegation. Komura recognized that any peace settlement was unlikely to match public expectations created by Japan's smashing victories on land and at sea. In April, the Japanese cabinet and senior leaders decided that holding Sakhalin Island and forcing Russia to pay a financial indemnity were not indispensable objectives. But Komura badly wanted both. Roosevelt remained troubled by Komura's plans, especially by the demand for money.[30]

Witte Steps onto the Stage

Nicholas faced more difficulty composing Russia's delegation. He wanted to avoid Sergei Witte, the once-powerful former finance minister, modernizer of the Russian economy, and devoted counselor to Alexander III, the czar's father. The gruff, blunt Witte, a huge six foot six, had fallen out of favor with the younger czar. Witte had been the architect of Russia's railways in the east but had worked to avoid conflict with Japan. The czar felt compelled to summon Witte only after others turned down the assignment. Nicholas declared that he wanted peace, but "would not pay one kopeck of indemnity or cede an inch of Russian territory." Witte told his successor as finance minister that "when a sewer had to be cleaned, they send Witte." Witte must have suspected that his duty would likely end up being to play the scapegoat rather than the negotiator.[31]

Even as Witte prepared for his mission, Russia's situation weakened. During the summer of 1905, strikes broke out in many cities, and more than half the provinces reported outbreaks of peasant violence. The crew of the battleship *Potemkin* mutinied in Odessa harbor, turned their guns on the czar's forces, and fled to a Romanian port. The country needed peace, but the czar felt he dared not show weakness—either at home or in the Far East. The dynasty recalled that it had triumphed over foreign invaders, even Napoleon, who had captured Moscow. The Japanese were a long way from Moscow or even from the heart of Siberia. Perhaps Russia could wait out an overextended Japan. Roosevelt sensed the problem: "Japan has a right to ask a good deal and I do not think that her demands are excessive; but Russia is so soddenly stupid and the Government is such an amorphous affair that they really do not know *what* they want."[32]

More than a century later, I asked young, modernizing officials in Russia's Finance Ministry about Witte's reputation. They respected his impressive but ultimately futile efforts to reform Russia before the 1917 Revolution. Indeed, the twenty-first-century Russian financial experts seemed proud to be following in the great man's footsteps. But they cautioned me that Russian history was ambivalent about Witte's role in ending the Russo-Japanese War. Even excellent negotiators are fated to fade into the shadows if they are on the losing side.[33]

Roosevelt's Preparations

Roosevelt prepared for the August meeting by seeking to reason with the parties, especially Japan, about what Tokyo should want. An extended war, he pointed out, would cost too much, just to gain Russian territories that would be of no use to Japan. Tokyo would then need to defend these lands, while Russia would look for an opportunity to regain them. TR also certainly recognized that Japan's dominance of East Asia would threaten U.S. interests in the Asia-Pacific.

Roosevelt did not fully appreciate—although Hamilton might have—that Japan's costs of war, debts, and shrinking credit pushed Tokyo to the brink of bankruptcy. Governments had not yet learned the tricks of self-financing extended wars as they would in the two world wars to come.

The president urged Britain to press its Japanese ally to moderate its demands, but to no avail. Britain's long "Great Game" with Russia in Central and South Asia blinded it to the benefits of reestablishing a security balance in East Asia. London also rated Roosevelt's odds of success as low. When Komura and Takahira visited Roosevelt at Sagamore Hill shortly before the launch of the conference, they listed their demands without ranking priorities. The president recommended that they drop secondary issues such as the disarmament of Vladivostok or the surrender of Russian warships in neutral posts. TR focused primarily on Komura's demand for an indemnity. He again warned of strong Russian resistance. At various times, Roosevelt suggested avoiding using the term "indemnity," instead linking payments to reimbursements (such as for care of Russian POWs) and drastically cutting any amount. He needed flexibility to find a deal.

Roosevelt's session with Witte was frosty. Witte, who had grown to expect the manners of old European deference, was not charmed by the president's informality. Most important, TR sensed little give in the Russian's position—because Witte had no room to be reasonable. The discouraged Roosevelt thought the Russians were both ignorant of the danger they faced and uninterested in peace. He told Taft that the chances for peace were no more than a "tossup."[34]

In fact, Witte wanted peace. At his stopover in Paris, the French made clear that they would not make further loans for war, although perhaps they would help finance an indemnity. Witte sought room to maneuver by finding new alignments that could change the arrangement of pieces on the chessboard. In Paris, he suggested a new combination among Russia, France, and Germany. In London, Witte tested the prospect of new Japanese-Russian ties, which the emissary had also mentioned to the czar before leaving.

While traveling to the United States, Witte drew up a plan: He resolved to court the American press and public upon arrival "with democratic simplicity and without a shadow of snobbishness." He visited the New York Stock Exchange, Tammany Hall, and even immigrant communities where he spoke with Russian Jews. The whole delegation attended a Russian Orthodox Church in New York City. He sought peace, Witte made clear, but not at any price. In fact, Witte's protestation of honor and readiness to fight a prolonged war, which so infuriated Roosevelt, were evidences of the small amount that the czar had authorized Witte to pay to reach a deal.[35]

The Negotiations Begin

The president tactfully introduced the delegations aboard the presidential yacht *Mayflower* in Oyster Bay on August 5, 1905. TR hosted a stand-up luncheon to avoid friction on seating precedence. He proposed a single toast to both sovereigns and peoples so that neither side would be honored first. The youthful president sought to ease the tension with his avuncular spirit.

Now it was up to the delegates, who moved on to Portsmouth. Witte managed to visit Boston and Harvard along the way, traveling on a special train supplied by J. P. Morgan. When Witte left his car, he shook hands with the railway crew. A reporter claimed that the giant Russian kissed the engineer, a story that probably was not true but which boosted Witte's popularity. Nevertheless, most American public opinion remained pro-Japanese throughout the days to follow.[36]

Roosevelt stepped back while the two delegations discussed procedure and made their initial verbal sorties, but the president kept a watchful eye. The Japanese opened with their demands: control of Korea; mutual evacuation of most of Manchuria and the return of Chinese sovereignty; Russia's transfer of the Port Arthur leasehold and associated rail lines to Japan; the cession of Sakhalin Island; the demilitarization of Russia's trans-Manchurian railway; the surrender of Russian warships in neutral ports; limits on Russia's naval strength in the region; fishing rights; and payment for "actual expenses of the war," avoiding the word "indemnity," as Roosevelt had urged.[37]

Witte responded with a strategy of careful concession, indirection, and unusual initiative. He assumed a posture: As the representative of the world's greatest empire, which was coping with a temporary setback, Witte tried to convey a cool, measured, yet commanding tone that recognized neither victory nor defeat. He yielded on the realities of Port Arthur and Manchuria, but initiated a small diplomatic counteroffensive by pressing for recognition of China's and Korea's sovereign rights. He pushed back on secondary issues, raising the cost to Japan of persisting with them. Witte also offered a "long view," even proposing his idea of an alliance between Russia and Japan against other contenders; while the Japanese ignored that idea in 1905, the two countries edged toward such a policy over the following few years. Further, even though Witte agreed to keep the negotiations secret, the Russians actively briefed the press informally. Witte wanted to appear reasonable and positive to wider publics, while isolating Japan in the event of a breakdown.[38]

Witte struggled inwardly to maintain his disciplined composure. Like many negotiators, he simultaneously had to battle with his own capital, including by responding to personal instructions from the czar, who sought to withdraw agreed concessions. Moreover, Witte's number two, Baron Roman Rosen, the czar's new minister to the United States, and other members of his delegation probably favored continuing the war. Witte pushed back successfully. He sought to prepare St. Petersburg for flexibility on Sakhalin Island. Witte knew that a Japanese demand for any payment, an indemnity in any form, was the red line he could not cross. When the Japanese reminded Witte that France had paid an indemnity after the Franco-Prussian War, Witte countered that the Japanese, unlike the Germans, were still thousands of miles away from their foe's capital. Russia had absorbed—and ultimately defeated—proud aggressors many times before.

The Critical Issues

By August 17, the critical issues centered on Sakhalin Island and the indemnity. Witte suggested that Monday, August 21, should be their concluding session, hinting at a breakup. At this point, as is often the case with tense negotiations involving a number of actors, multiple efforts and communications confused the situation. Baron Kaneko rushed to see TR to argue that this was the moment for the president to step in. Roosevelt said he was willing to contact the czar, the kaiser, and the French president, but first needed to meet Witte or Russia's minister Rosen. The president also urged Japan, once again, to scale back its demand for money.

Meanwhile, on August 18, Witte asked to speak privately with his counterpart, Foreign Minister Komura. Recognizing that Japan had already occupied all of Sakhalin, Witte suggested dividing the island. Komura countered that Russia should pay a (large) sum to recover the northern half. Witte conveyed the possible compromise to St. Petersburg but recommended that Russia just cede the whole island. He wanted to maneuver Japan into the position of prolonging war only to win money.

When Roosevelt met Russia's minister Rosen at Sagamore Hill on August 19, the Americans were not aware of the Witte-Komura exchange from the eighteenth. Rosen did not inform the president of the possible compromise, perhaps because he expected the czar would reject the prospect. Roosevelt proposed ceding Sakhalin and then seeking nonbinding arbitration on the question of payment. By the time the arbitration was finished, TR reasoned, Japan would not want to prolong the war and Russia could likely escape any payment. Roosevelt asked that his suggestion be considered as coming from a private person, not from the U.S. president; TR was trying to hold one more bullet of compromise in the chamber of his diplomatic gun.

On Monday, August 21, Witte learned that the czar, encouraged by most of his advisers, had rejected the idea of paying for the return of half of Sakhalin. Russia had not paid an indemnity even to Napoleon! The czar's advisers seemed more ambivalent about the island itself. The foreign minister informed Witte that St. Petersburg would send final instructions the next day on ending the conference.

Roosevelt Buys Time and Pushes Russia

The indefatigable Witte now used the "interfering" Roosevelt to buy time. Witte urged St. Petersburg to take Roosevelt's opinion into account before closing negotiations with Japan. That same day, August 21, the president tried again. He drafted a final appeal to the czar (copied to Witte) "in principle" on a Russian recovery of northern Sakhalin in exchange for payment, with the amount subject to negotiation. The president directed Minister Meyer to deliver the proposal to the czar personally. Roosevelt urged Berlin, Paris, and London to assist, explaining that he would advise Tokyo to agree to peace regardless of how little money it obtained. The kaiser and Prime Minister Maurice Rouvier of France sent supportive messages; London, wary and perhaps jealous of TR's activity, remained quiet.

Meyer could not gain an audience with the czar until August 23. On the twenty-second, Witte received the czar's instructions to break off the conference. The czar also rejected Roosevelt's first suggestion of August 19—the one made as a "private person." Russia's foreign minister told Witte not to make arrangements for a new conference, because such a step might create an obligation for Russia and another chance for Roosevelt to intrude. Witte then took a step that only a confident man, used to exercising power, would try: He seized upon the president's second message to justify not ending the negotiations. Witte acknowledged to St. Petersburg that Roosevelt's action was "hardly corresponding to European etiquette," but he urged the Russian autocrat to consider the president's views. To break off before replying might offend the president and build public sympathy for Japan, Witte argued.

The final plea was now in the hands of America's minister Meyer, who met the czar at 4:00 p.m. on August 23 to present Roosevelt's case. Nicholas had received the president's proposal earlier through Witte and promptly countered the American views. Meyer responded creatively that Sakhalin was different from Russia's mainland—because it was offshore and St. Petersburg had negotiated with Japan for title to the island as recently as 1875. The czar, for the first time, yielded a bit, saying he could accept the cession of the southern half of Sakhalin if Japan retreated from the northern part. He would not bend on any payment, but seemed, according to Meyer, to sincerely appreciate the spirit that motivated the president's efforts. Witte now had an opening to continue. Roosevelt's persistence and Meyer's advocacy had kept the negotiation alive and gained half an occupied island as a concession.

The Final Week

The next, and final, week drifted toward disaster. Even before learning of the czar's concession, Witte had maneuvered Komura into a statement that Japan would insist on money even if Russia ceded all of Sakhalin. Witte was now shaping the public diplomacy of failure. Roosevelt pressed the czar again, to no avail. The president argued to the Japanese that the United States had paid money to Mexico and Spain despite defeating them. Even if

Tokyo occupied Vladivostok, Harbin, and the whole Maritime Province of Russia, it could not compel Russia to pay. The president combined flattery with pressure: Given Japan's success and standing, he argued, the civilized world expected Japan to act for a higher, ethical purpose of peace. By now, both Russians and Japanese were complaining about Roosevelt's badgering.

Witte had communicated the czar's concession of half of Sakhalin to Komura on Saturday, August 26, in a private, informal session from which secretaries (notetakers) were excluded. For some reason, Tokyo never got the word. Komura failed to draw attention to that option, perhaps because he was absorbed by seeking a more ambitious deal. That same day, he sent a telegram to Tokyo announcing his intention to break off negotiations. Witte's frequent exchanges with St. Petersburg must have been painful, but he knew his master's mind. Komura had lost touch with his superior. The foreign minister's news of failure came as a shock to Tokyo.

Over the next couple of days, Prime Minister Katsura Taro, his war cabinet, and Japan's senior statesmen decided to pull Komura back. After all, their original instructions had not insisted on either Sakhalin or an indemnity. But the small window of time was closing. Late on Monday, August 28, Witte received the czar's direct instruction: "Send Witte my order to end discussion tomorrow in any case. I prefer to continue the war than to await gracious concessions on the part of Japan." Witte and Rosen agreed on the meaning of the directive. But they disagreed on what to do. Witte wanted to meet the next day to repeat his offer to achieve peace by giving up half of Sakhalin; he wanted to make absolutely clear that Russia had stretched for peace. Witte informed St. Petersburg what he planned to do. The Russians packed their bags and paid their hotel bill.

The Japanese had also paid their bills on Monday. Late that afternoon, Komura received a shocking message from home instructing him to yield the demands for both Sakhalin and money if necessary to achieve peace. Then he received an intriguing revision: Tokyo had learned of the czar's concession of half of Sakhalin, almost by accident, and directed Komura to hold out for Southern Sakhalin. (The British minister in Tokyo, Sir Claude MacDonald, had learned of the czar's concessions through a report from his colleague in St. Petersburg, who had spoken to U.S. minister Meyer. The Japanese had almost dismissed MacDonald's request to relay his timely information.)

On Tuesday, August 29, Witte and Komura sealed the deal. They signed the six-page Treaty of Portsmouth on September 5. The czar was shocked—and unhappy. The ruling circle in St. Petersburg thought Russia should fight on, but Russians elsewhere were pleased and relieved. The czar eventually honored Witte with the title of Count, but Russians wanted to forget the whole tragic business: Witte's critics called him Count Half-Sakhalin. The Japanese public was stunned, and newspapers exploded in criticism. Not for the last time, the media declared that a military "victorious in the field has been defeated in the conference chambers."[39]

The other capitals around the world greeted the peace treaty enthusiastically. President Roosevelt basked in high praise. In 1906, he became the first American to receive the Nobel Prize for Peace, which today is on display in the Roosevelt Room in the West Wing of the White House—beneath a painting of Colonel Roosevelt on a charging horse, rearing in pride. The president appreciated the praise but was reflective about the work still to be done.

A European Crisis in Morocco

Roosevelt's recognition of other threats to peace proved perceptive. Even as the president was mobilizing efforts to conclude the Russo-Japanese War, another crisis brewed in Europe. This time France and Germany turned to Roosevelt to find a path out of a conflict that risked spinning out of control.

At the Madrid Conference of 1880, the European powers—except Germany—had blessed France's reach into Morocco at the expense of the local Sharifian Empire. In 1904, Britain accepted French designs for "pacific penetration" over Morocco in exchange for London's dominance in Egypt. By 1905, France had begun a new phase of its "civilizing" mission by pressing military and financial reforms in Morocco that would give Paris extensive control of its North African neighbor.

On March 31, 1905, Kaiser Wilhelm made an unexpected call at Tangier during a Mediterranean cruise. Urged on by his advisers, despite Wilhelm's personal reluctance, the kaiser threw down a gauntlet to Paris with an energetic speech. Germany called for an "Open Door" for Morocco and for respect of the country's sovereignty. With one Teutonic swipe, Berlin might accomplish three objectives: diminish France; challenge Paris's recent Entente Cordiale with Britain by testing London's resolve to back France; and undermine the Franco-Russian alliance when St. Petersburg was struggling with Japan and internal insurrections.

At the instigation of Berlin, Sultan Moulay Abd al Aziz proposed a conference. At first, Paris resisted this call, complaining it would not appear before "the tribunal of Europe." Roosevelt's initial reaction was "not...to take sides in the matter," because the United States had "no real interest" in Morocco, and the president had "other fish to fry."[40] Before long, however, TR began to perceive that the dispute was about European security, not North African sovereignty.

TR Maneuvers Quietly

TR began to act quietly, behind the scenes, to bring the protagonists together. He needed to stroke Wilhelm's ego while protecting France's pride, Paris's position in Morocco, and its larger security interests. Historians debate whether the president's initiatives were decisive in convening the parties, but there is no question that TR positioned himself to sway the players in the second act.

The kaiser was drawn to Roosevelt, who at this moment was also urging Berlin to assist with the czar. Wilhelm assumed TR would be a constructive partner in the Moroccan conflict because Germany was standing for an "open door" and fair access. If the United States would not side with Berlin, at least the president could play another mediating role. Roosevelt responded with enthusiastic words of friendship and even flattery. Yet TR recognized the kaiser's "irrational zig zags" and "sudden vagaries."[41] Roosevelt had the diplomatic skill of knowing his counterpart's personality while also recognizing the actions that might flow from another's temperament. By June 1905, the president had concluded that "it really did look as if there might be a war" over the Moroccan dispute. In conjunction with the ongoing Russo-Japanese War, Roosevelt speculated that the combination of events could lead to "a world conflagration."

At the beginning of June, France's premier, Maurice Rouvier, forced the resignation of his foreign minister, who had led a policy hostile to Germany. French diplomats began to warm to the idea of a properly structured international conference as a possible "gate of escape" from Wilhelm's trap. Berlin, in turn, seemed emboldened by the course of events. Ambassador Jean Jules Jusserand, Paris's man in Washington and TR's close friend, suggested to Premier Rouvier that the American president might be the ideal mediator. Roosevelt was well-disposed toward France. He had trusting and effective relations with both Jusserand and Germany's minister in Washington, Speck von Sternberg, who offered an excellent channel to the kaiser. TR recognized that Paris might object to his "meddling," but he told Jusserand frankly that France could only lose in a showdown with Germany.

The pieces of TR's puzzle were falling into place. On June 11, 1905, Sternberg asked Roosevelt to persuade Paris to attend an international conference; Berlin had calculated that London posed the obstacle to such a conference and determined that Roosevelt could sway both Britain and France. On June 23, Premier Rouvier, having agreed to the principle of a conference, asked the president to assist. With Jusserand present, Roosevelt promptly dictated a congratulatory message to the kaiser on his "great triumph," while urging flexibility on "minor details" that stood in the way of actually convening.

Then on July 1, Jusserand sent Paris news of an amazing development: Sternberg had informed Roosevelt that if the proposed conference deadlocked, Berlin "would, in every case, abide by the decision which [the president] would regard as most practical and fair." In fact, Sternberg, perhaps overenthusiastically reflecting the warm words between kaiser and president, had overstated his instructions. Nevertheless, TR promptly pocketed—and later deployed—the German concession, whether or not Berlin had intended to grant it.

The Conference in Algeciras

The conference opened in Algeciras, Spain, on January 16, 1906. Roosevelt, by now basking in the glow of the Portsmouth success, spent his enhanced diplomatic capital carefully and quietly. Henry White, one of Roosevelt's diplomatic cadre, represented the United States, and Secretary of State Elihu Root guided the delegation's work. Roosevelt wanted to keep good relations with all the parties and needed a low profile at home to assuage senators troubled by any U.S. involvement in European affairs. The main U.S. aim, TR instructed White, was "to prevent a rupture between Germany and France." As frequently happens in negotiations, major differences of interest took the form of disputes over complex, even technical arrangements. At Algeciras, the debate bogged down over the composition of foreign police in the eight Moroccan ports open to commerce. On February 19, the United States proposed a detailed compromise. Germany responded graciously, but wanted modifications. The conference stalled. On March 7, Germany threatened to adjourn over the makeup of the police force. Having lost majority support in the National Assembly, Premier Rouvier of France resigned. Europe faced crisis.

Roosevelt stepped up boldly. After courting Wilhelm by saying that he had given serious thought to Germany's proposals, the president reminded the kaiser of the (overstated) promise to accept TR's judgment in the event of deadlock. Within five days, Germany tried an Austrian proposal. Roosevelt told Sternberg that he considered the Austrian plan "absurd" because it favored spheres of influence and partition, which contradicted the whole diplomatic purpose. After two more rounds with the German ambassador, the president remarked that Berlin's obstructionist tactics seemed designed to humble France. If the conference collapsed, the president would be compelled "to publish the entire correspondence" with Berlin to make clear the role the United States had played. On March 19, Berlin stepped back and agreed to the U.S. proposal of February. Roosevelt helped the kaiser save face by praising Berlin's success and the kaiser's unselfish policy.

TR's labors were not yet over. To his frustration, he learned that France had complaints about the U.S. proposal, problems which Paris had failed to clarify earlier. An embarrassed Jusserand exploded at his superiors in Paris. Nevertheless, the United States, working with Italy, smoothed over the differences, and the parties signed the agreement on April 7. France retained—and in time would extend—its preeminent position in Morocco.

The Crisis Defused, Not Solved

Of greater global importance, Berlin had failed to browbeat Paris, the entente with Britain held, and Europe breathed a sigh of relief at avoiding one of the great power confrontations that periodically loomed over the early twentieth century. Both France and Germany expressed gratitude to the president. As for Roosevelt, he came away with a "not very exalted opinion of either French or German diplomacy."[42]

Roosevelt recognized that what became known as the "First Moroccan Crisis" was only a brief rain shower amidst a season of potentially violent tempests. Not since German unification in 1871 had Europe faced the prospect of a general war. The military historian A. J. P. Taylor contended that the affair "shattered the long Bismarckian peace." Some Germans regretted not capitalizing on Berlin's military advantage and even risking war. German diplomacy would take a harder line. The British and French, in turn, decided to deepen military cooperation and even tactical planning in the face of German aggressiveness. Within a decade, the blustery diplomatic weather would build toward a deluge. By then, to his great regret, TR was no longer at the helm of the United States, nor in a position to balance or mediate.[43]

Assessing TR's Diplomacy

The years of 1905–06, right after Roosevelt's election, represent a defining period for his presidential diplomacy. In addition to TR's mediation of the Russo-Japanese War and the Moroccan crisis, Roosevelt stepped in to "police" a troubled Santo Domingo (creating a "corollary" to the Monroe Doctrine) and organized the engineering project to dig the Panama Canal, his great achievement. The president had protected the North American and Caribbean homeland against threats of disorder, ended a dangerous conflict in the Asia-Pacific theater, headed off a confrontation in the Euro-Atlantic region, and changed the global maritime map by linking the Atlantic and the Pacific.[44]

TR found mediation to be exasperating; he had to channel and balance the power of others indirectly instead of using America's power forthrightly. The president demonstrated his diplomatic skill, however, in achieving practical results that served strategic purposes. Roosevelt mastered processes that achieved respectable outcomes. His initiatives brought conflicting parties together. He persuaded antagonists of the need, in terms of their own interests, to reach cooperative solutions. Then Roosevelt helped devise moderate terms—and pressed for them—with an eye on possible compromises. When the inevitable frictions threatened to grind deliberations to a halt, the president kept the parties at the table through contacts with the lead negotiators and their home capitals.

Roosevelt supported his mediation by energetically organizing pressure from other countries.[45] He had the personal touch, magnetism, openness, and power of reason that drew others, including foreign emissaries, to his side; his French, German, and British friends—Jusserand, Sternberg, and Spring-Rice—seemed to be working for Roosevelt as much as for their own governments. They did so not just out of friendship, but because they respected Roosevelt's arguments and realized that he was offering them an opportunity to shape larger events constructively. Once the United States stepped into the role of alliance leader after World War II, its most able diplomats fully appreciated the art of extending American power by drawing other countries—and individuals—to work with Washington as partners.

A critic of Roosevelt's diplomacy might contend that his mediation did not solve the fundamental conflict that sparked the war in Northeast Asia or the crisis in Morocco. Keepers of diplomatic scorecards are free to set their own standards, but if statesmen must achieve perpetual peace, many positive results will go unacknowledged. A pragmatic foreign policy addresses the problems of the day while creating a basis for positive action in the future.

In 1908, Secretary Root and Ambassador Takahira reached an understanding about maintaining the status quo in East Asia through Japan's dominance of Korea and America's position in the Philippines. Eventually, the rise of militarism in Japan, the draw of the unruly yet potentially wealthy Manchuria, the actions of a new republican regime in China, and the economic and political breakdown of the Great Depression led to a decisive contest of power between Tokyo and Washington. Decades later, China would find its footing and reestablish itself as a continental power in East Asia. Northeast Asia would remain a hot spot through today.

As for Europe, Roosevelt believed that war was "imminent" in June 1905. After all, within a decade another small country on Europe's periphery would be the scene of a crisis that pushed great power rivalries over the edge. If war had begun, TR believed it "would probably have extended through a considerable part of the world." The president had gained time for the European powers to avoid the catastrophe that would eventually destroy Europe's preeminent place in the world order.[46]

Roosevelt was keenly aware that his diplomacy and mediation could not alone achieve security and America's national interests. In July 1908, shortly before TR ended his term as president, he reflected on his foreign policy experience in an address at the Naval War College: "Diplomacy," he explained, "rests on the substantial basis of potential force."[47]

In typical Roosevelt style, TR "helped" historians of his presidency by listing his six most important accomplishments. He ordered them as follows: doubling the size of the U.S. Navy and sailing the "Great White Fleet" around the world; gaining access and beginning construction of the Panama Canal; mediating the end of the Russo-Japanese War and helping calm the Moroccan crisis; beginning the conservation of natural resources; conducting a strong, active foreign policy; and pressing the regulation of big business.[48] Note how Roosevelt began with his principal instrument of power: Because of TR's building program, the U.S. fleet expanded from eleven battleships in 1898 to thirty-six in 1913, behind only Britain and Germany.[49]

Roosevelt wielded his "big stick" to serve multiple purposes. TR expected his armada's circumnavigation of the world over the course of more than a year to impress foreign capitals while sharpening the navy's seamanship. But years later the former president explained, "My prime purpose was to impress the American people; and this purpose was fully achieved."[50] Roosevelt understood that an active U.S. foreign policy had to be built upon the foundation of both military might and the pride of the American people in assuming a global role.

CHAPTER 7

Woodrow Wilson

The Political Scientist Abroad

A War to Make the World Safe for Democracy

At 8:20 p.m. on the evening of April 2, 1917, President Woodrow Wilson left the White House for a brief ride to the Capitol. A light spring rain did not dampen the interest of the crowds lining Pennsylvania Avenue. As the president's car approached, floodlights shone upon a massive U.S. flag waving above the Capitol, lit against a darkening sky, creating a scene both somber and grand.

The president walked to a private room to collect his thoughts briefly before giving the most important address of his life. As was his way, Wilson had prepared his remarks alone, except for the company of his second wife, Edith Galt Wilson. Two days before, Wilson had begun with an outline, which he expanded to a shorthand draft, corrected, and then typed on a Hammond typewriter.

Unobserved by Wilson, Ellery Sedgwick, editor of the *Atlantic Monthly*, spied the president as the grim leader walked over to a large fireplace, topped by a big mirror. Wilson stared at himself, chin shaking, face flushed. The president leaned his left elbow on the mantel, looking into the mirror until he had composed his features, if not his emotions. Woodrow Wilson, the twenty-eighth president of the United States, was about to commit his country to the cruelest of endeavors, a modern world war.

At 8:32 p.m. the Speaker of the House announced the president to the 1,500 people who had filled the historic chamber. In addition to the senators, representatives, Supreme Court justices, members of the cabinet, and special guests, Congress had invited the diplomatic corps as a group for the first time. Led by the justices, the audience rose when Wilson entered, giving the president a resounding two-minute welcome. Then all sat and were silent. Mrs. Wilson later said one could hear people breathing.

The president—one of the great orators of an era when eloquence was a respected, and even expected, political art—began with a low, quavering voice. His fingers trembled. Wilson's nervousness complemented his opening message: There were "serious, very serious choices" to be made, "immediately." The president recounted a list of German atrocities to a quiet house. Then he raised the stakes: The "present German submarine warfare against commerce" was "a war against all nations." This conflict was a "challenge to all mankind," not just an assault on U.S. lives and property.

Rather than lead a charge, Wilson explained that each nation must decide how to meet this threat. America's motive "will not be revenge or the victorious assertion of the physical might of the nation, but only the vindication of right, of human right, of which we are only a single champion." The United States, he continued, "will not choose the path of submission." The chamber erupted, led by Chief Justice Edward White, who dropped his big, soft hat so that he could raise his hands above his head to clap.

The president seemed reassured by the response. He wanted Americans to know that the next step was "solemn and even tragical." He asked Congress to declare war on Imperial Germany. Justice White leapt up, leading an even louder ovation.

Wilson now spoke confidently, but expounded an unusual call to arms. The president reasoned that neutrality was no longer possible, or even preferable, when an "autocratic government backed by organized force" threatened peace and freedom. Yet the United States had no quarrel with the German people. America would wage war "without rancor" and "without passion."

The response to the German leaders, Wilson urged, "must be a league of honor" and "a partnership of opinion," including an affiliation of democratic nations. He welcomed recent events in Russia, whose people, having removed its autocracy, were now a "fit partner." Wilson dutifully warned that America must pay the costs of war. If necessary, America must "spend the whole force of the nation" to overcome Germany's "pretensions and its power." America would fight for "the ultimate peace of the world and for the liberation of its people," including the Germans, and "for the rights of nations great and small and the privilege of men everywhere to choose their way of life and obedience."

The president added a simple but powerful justification for war: "The world must be made safe for democracy." At first, the crowd sat still. But then old senator John Sharp Williams of Mississippi, whose Confederate father had died at the Battle of Shiloh, grasped Wilson's meaning—and he began to clap. Applause rose like a wave. Senators, who had been given small silk flags, waved them fervently.

Wilson's eight-word explanation would reverberate across American diplomacy for the next century, and I expect for even longer. Yet echoes can be heard slightly differently. As Wilson's biographer John Milton Cooper observed, the president, "the most punctilious stylist ever to sit in the White House," had chosen to express this ringing phrase in the passive voice. Wilson did not call on the United States to impose democracy on other peoples and certainly not by force. The president wanted to defend democracy where it existed. If America could aid others in turning to democracy, the world would be both safer and more supportive of human rights.

Wilson expanded this point. The United States "desire[s] no conquest, no domination...no indemnities for ourselves, no material compensation." America was "but one of the champions of the rights of mankind." World peace would grow "upon the tested foundations of political liberty."

After thirty minutes, the president reached his peroration. He reminded Americans of the dangerous uncertainties ahead—for the world but also for the effects of war on America—while explaining that the country could not avoid this destiny. "It is a fearful thing to lead this great peaceful people into war, into the most terrible and disastrous of wars, civilization itself seeming to be in the balance. But the right is more precious than the peace." To rally Americans to this new cause, Wilson reached back in history: "God helping her, she can do no other." According to tradition, in 1521 Martin Luther closed his defense against charges of heresy by proclaiming, "Here I stand, I can do no other. God help me, Amen." Luther's conscience had led him to make an inescapable choice, a direct challenge to the established order of the Pope and the Holy Roman Emperor, launching a great Reformation. Wilson was calling for another historic reformation; the president was also reminding the world of Luther's determination: If one must break with the old order, Luther and Wilson insisted, one should "sin boldly."

Wilson's message asserted that the country could justify the appalling costs of war only if America sought great results. Wilson's war would be a costly but elevated enterprise.

Senator Henry Cabot Lodge, who had long demanded that the president join the Allies in war, understood Wilson's message. As the president stepped away to leave, Lodge intercepted his political foe and extended his hand, saying, "Mr. President, you have expressed in the loftiest manner possible, the sentiments of the American people."

Back in the West Wing of the White House, the president sat for a few minutes in the cabinet room alone with Joseph Tumulty, his secretary and political adviser. "Think of what they were applauding," muttered Wilson, "a message of death for our young men. How strange it seems to applaud that." Wilson said he had known the country could not remain neutral, but he had needed to respect "our traditional policy of steering clear of European embroilments." Few had sympathized with the trying and emotional journey, said Wilson. He started to read aloud an empathetic note from a newspaper editor. The president's eyes welled up. Then, Tumulty recalled, Wilson lay his head on the cabinet table and sobbed "as if he had been a child."[1]

The Decision to Go to War

Wilson was the first Southerner elected president since the Civil War. He knew the price of war. Early in 1916, when the United States was on the brink of war with Mexico, the president explained to Tumulty that he would do all he could to prevent conflict: "I came from the South and I know what war is, for I have seen its wreckage and terrible ruin." During the peacemaking at Versailles, the president reminded Prime Minister David Lloyd George of Britain that Wilson had grown up in a "conquered and devastated country."[2]

How then did Woodrow Wilson and the United States reach the most serious of diplomatic decisions—a judgment to go to war? His explanation to Tumulty sounds like the rationalization of a sad leader, emotionally drained by a charged night, who had tried his best but could not escape a fateful verdict.

The guns of August 1914 had first thundered almost three years earlier. By 1917, no one could doubt that World War I was a dehumanizing, mechanical, and even chemical slaughter. European battlefields were scenes of stark and primitive ruin, not glory. From Europe, through the Middle East and on to East Asia, every major power had joined the struggle—except the United States. Only America still had the strength to try to end the twentieth-century Armageddon and lead in rebuilding a new order out of the catastrophe. As Wilson also recognized, going to war would halt, and perhaps reverse, the progressive domestic reforms that he had hoped would be his legacy.

As Wilson told Tumulty on the night of April 2, two of the deepest traditions of American foreign policy were neutrality, dating to Washington and Hamilton—and staying away from Europe's conflicts, recalling Washington, Jefferson, and especially John Quincy Adams. The horror of World War I certainly affirmed the Founding Fathers' rejection of the militarized ways of the Old World. As late as April 1, a majority of Americans probably favored peace. Of the 100 million Americans in 1915, some one-third were immigrants or first-generation citizens, most of whom had escaped Europe's wars, conscriptions, and miseries.[3]

Nor was the U.S. military prepared for war in 1917. The U.S. Army was smaller than Portugal's. America was ready to ship only some twenty-four thousand men to Europe, with ammunition for perhaps a day and a half of combat.[4]

When Wilson finally decided to take the momentous step toward war, he still hesitated to march forward with others. The United States would be an "Associated" power, not a full-fledged ally of Britain and France. Washington would not declare war on Austria-Hungary until December 7; the Americans never crossed the threshold of war with the Ottoman Empire and Bulgaria. The president believed America could restrain the Allies while helping defeat Imperial Germany. Even as the face of battle loomed, Wilson considered how he might lay the groundwork for ending the war and fashioning a peace without victory. At first, Wilson wanted to avoid high-level meetings with the Allies, although he could not maintain that reserve. Wilson's way of war moved Britain's king, George V, to ask, "Do we have a co-belligerent or an umpire?"[5]

The story of Wilson's and America's journey to war between 1914 and 1917 reveals an intellectual president making practical choices about dangerous problems that Europe's combatants forced upon his country. He was reacting.[6] In doing so, Wilson had to consider a public mood shocked by brutal events on land and sea, but also reluctant to face up to the consequences of action. Wilson called this duality the public's "double wish." He also had to establish leadership of his Democratic Party in foreign affairs, which necessitated turning his compatriots away from a long reluctance to act outside North America and the Caribbean. Wilson faced a challenging reelection in 1916, too; the split in the Republican Party in 1912 had created an opening for Democrats to regain the presidency with 42 percent of the vote, but Wilson had to secure and expand his new electoral coalition. In the midst of these public dramas, Wilson faced the death of his wife and the courtship (under the public eye of life in the White House) of a new partner, whom he married in 1915.

Wilson the political scientist needed to explain his practical actions and to articulate how the decisions fit together, yet Wilson the politician recognized the limits of intellectual speculation. He wanted to understand the great drama and tried to anticipate its possible consequences. Not surprisingly, Wilson considered public education to be a primary presidential responsibility. Yet he preferred to face problems when they ripened. In 1915, he wrote Edith Galt that, "I never had had any patience with 'ifs' and conjectural cases. My mind insists always upon waiting until something actually does happen and then discussing what is to be done."[7]

In 1916, the president told the journalist Ida Tarbell, "It bores me to have men waste my time in general terms. What I want to know is how it is to be done. I am never interested until the point is reached. . . . I am not interested until a practical method is proposed—that is, I suppose that in government I am a pragmatist: my first thought is, will it work?"[8]

Contrary to the image of the rigid president who, after the war, could not compromise in order to save his League of Nations, Wilson could be flexible, as his domestic record confirms. Wilson was neither a failed idealist nor a manipulative opportunist. He was a man taking actions that he considered to be practical. He deployed words to explain, justify, and even inspire. As public moods shifted, in a frightening world at war, Wilson adapted; one can recognize themes that evolve. As a democratic leader, Wilson had to recognize public sentiments and speak to them. His greatest weakness seems to have been operational: Neither he nor his key colleagues were artful in translating plans into results.[9]

A Domestic President

Shortly after Wilson won the 1912 election, he commented to a faculty friend, "It would be an irony of fate if my administration had to deal chiefly with foreign problems, for all my preparation has been in domestic matters." His inaugural address in March 1913 did not include one word on foreign affairs.[10]

Wilson produced an astounding domestic record, almost all of which he accomplished in his first term. He benefited from a tailwind of Progressive-era politics, but navigated boldly and speedily. Congress enacted the Federal Reserve Act in 1913 and the Clayton Antitrust Act in 1914; it also created a new Federal Trade Commission to ensure fair competition. Wilson pushed for the first successful lowering of tariffs in four decades. He achieved the first federal aid to farmers; the first permanent, graduated income tax; the first federal inheritance tax; and the first federal eight-hour day (for railway workers). Congress outlawed child labor. In 1916, facing reelection, the president successfully steered the confirmation of Louis Brandeis to the Supreme Court; Brandeis, an activist Progressive and advocate, had many enemies. Wilson never hesitated in making him the first Jewish justice. The president moved more cautiously on women's suffrage, but he endorsed what became the Nineteenth Amendment to the Constitution (in 1920), which provided women the right to vote.[11]

Wilson's leadership with Congress drew from his studies of party leadership in parliamentary democracies. Early in 1913, the president came in person before Congress to argue for lower tariffs, the first time a president had spoken to Congress since John Adams in 1800. Wilson appeared before

Congress more frequently than any other president. He attempted, in effect, to overcome the separation of powers; his later effort to supplant the "balance of power" in international politics was consistent with his views about domestic politics. His method—plus Democratic majorities—made Wilson a masterful legislative forerunner of FDR and LBJ.[12]

Revolution, War, and Neutrality

Wilson faced frustrating choices regarding Mexico early in his term. The Mexican Revolution of 1910 led to a succession of governments, assassinations, upheavals for U.S. businesses, insults, and an American military intervention in Veracruz. A nationalist backlash in Mexico pushed the North American neighbors to the brink of war by the spring of 1914. Prodded by Latin American mediators, Mexico established a provisional government, and the United States escaped a mistaken escapade. Wilson learned a lesson about foreign interventions, and especially about trying to redirect "a profound revolution."[13]

In August 1914, America faced a different type of revolution in Europe, with militaries in the front lines. Germany declared war on Russia on August 1 and on France on August 3, the same day that the kaiser's armies assaulted Belgium. Britain joined in on August 4. Japan, bound by treaty to Britain, entered as well, snatching German outposts in Asia. Everyone seemed stunned by the suddenness of the war.

On August 4, Woodrow Wilson was at the bedside of his wife, Ellen, one hand holding that of his dying spouse, the other writing to European leaders with an offer to "act in the interest of European peace." Ellen expired on August 6. Wilson wrote a friend the next day that "God has stricken me almost beyond what I can bear." As the light faded in the autumn, so did his spirit.[14]

The president issued a proclamation of neutrality on August 4; it was a traditional American statement of detachment from foreign wars. On August 18, the president released a press statement that explained neutrality to his home audience. The United States, a country of immigrants, must not become "divided in camps of hostile opinion...against each other." Wilson recalled that in the past the greatest risk to Union arose from internal strife. Americans "must be neutral in fact as well as in name.... We must be impartial in thought as well as in action, must put a curb upon our sentiments as well as upon every transaction that might be construed as a preference of one party to the struggle before another."[15]

The president's brother-in-law later recalled that even during that first month of war Wilson foresaw that this clash of empires would transform international relations. To achieve peace, Wilson considered, there must be no more conquests, no more private manufacturers of munitions, equal rights for all nations, and an association of all nations to protect the integrity of each and all.[16]

At the end of August, Wilson decamped to an estate in Cornish, New Hampshire, for two days of wide-ranging talks with Colonel Edward House, his close adviser, sounding board, and sometimes friend. House had just returned from a European tour. Wilson hungered for the details of European politics; he did not have good intelligence networks, as had TR, whether from personal ties or his own government. Wilson guessed about broad geopolitical shifts and worried that a German victory would force the United States to become "a military nation."[17]

At first, former president Roosevelt stated that he was "not taking sides one way or the other" in the war. He focused on the need for military preparedness and the weakness of international law, as Belgium's fate amply demonstrated. Reflecting his appreciation of power balances, TR initially did not want either side to win. Although he admired Britain's defense of Belgium, the former president disliked the possibility of gains by two of the Allies, Russia and Japan. Before long, however, the combination of Roosevelt's visceral dislike of the "college president" in the White House and Germany's abominable conduct in Belgium led TR toward a "militant idealism." The old Rough Rider preferred a noble fight to strict neutrality.[18]

The war was also an economic event. The shocks of conflict disrupted trade. Europeans sold U.S. bonds to gain cash, leading to a drop in the dollar exchange rate and a run on gold. The New York Stock Exchange closed for more than four months. By the end of the year, however, fortunes reversed as foreigners raced to buy American agricultural products and goods related to military needs, pulling the United States out of recession and into a long boom.[19]

Neutral Rights on the High Seas

Unfortunately, war in Europe revived century-old ghosts of Neptune's sea dogs. The belligerents' blockades, and soon submarines, threatened the American supply line to Europe. America's merchant marine had never fully recovered from the depredations of the *Alabama* and its fellow commerce raiders during the Civil War, so much of the flow of U.S. goods and people sailed to Europe in foreign bottoms. In an early sign of Congress's disputatious nature about war measures, a Senate filibuster held up Wilson's effort for two years to buy ships. That was Wilson's first major legislative setback, an inauspicious sign.[20]

The British blockade bit into American commerce long before German U-boats sparked tensions. Wilson knew his history; indeed, he had written it. The scholar-president read to Colonel House from his own *History of the American People* about how public anger over naval incidents had forced President Madison into war in 1812. The president added, "Madison and I are the only two Princeton men that have become President. The circumstances of the War of 1812 and now run parallel." Wilson told his brother-in-law, "I am afraid something will happen on the high seas that will make it impossible to keep out of the war."[21]

Suitably warned by his own book, Wilson protested practices that violated American interpretations of neutral rights, but he did so tactfully and without threatening retaliation. The president tilted toward the Allies, but he justified doing so by pointing out that the trade gains during the conflict far exceeded the modest interference. The British shrewdly adjusted their nineteenth-century approach: At first, London removed cotton from the contraband list, and then bought up the bales and other commodities to keep the Germans out of the market and American farmers onside. Critically, the British actions did not involve the loss of American lives.[22]

The Allies needed money in order to buy from the Americans. Early on, the British and French governments retained J. P. Morgan to float $100 million in debt. Morgan approached the State Department. Secretary of State William Jennings Bryan (the populist who in 1896 decried the crucifixion of mankind on a "cross of gold") responded true to form: "Money is the worst of contrabands because it commands everything else," he declared to Wilson. Cutting off money would shorten the war, reasoned Bryan. Wilson accepted Bryan's ban on loans to belligerent governments—for a brief time. Bryan adjusted to permit shorter-term commercial credits to buy U.S. goods. By early 1915, bankers were handling large financings for the warring parties, establishing a web of influence that would entangle policies of peace for years to come. Events vindicated Hamilton's insights about credit, war, and the capacity to borrow, although the transatlantic flows had been reversed from the eighteenth century. Wilson and his successors would struggle to learn how to use financial power successfully.[23]

Wilson tacked to and fro while seeking to keep the war away from America. He sensed the public mood, which the *Literary Digest* described as "that of a detached observer": generally sympathetic to the Allies and negative about Imperial Germany, but wholeheartedly wanting to avoid conflict. In the November midterm elections of 1914 (the first requiring the direct election of senators), Wilson's Democrats won seats in the Senate and held the House, albeit with a smaller majority. Yet the gubernatorial elections and losses in Midwestern and northeastern states raised questions about

Wilson's prospects in 1916. In his December State of the Union address, Wilson resisted Republican calls for large increases in military spending. This was a "war with which we have nothing to do," he explained. Its "causes cannot touch us." He called for "self-possession," wanting to cool public feelings and also invoking a common American diplomatic practice of applying standards of personal conduct to relations among nations. Democrats rallied to his side; Republicans divided. But Wilson stood on sinking ground.[24]

Wilson Considers Mediation

In early December 1914, Secretary Bryan gave Wilson a memorandum urging America to offer to mediate among "these Christian nations." The note was longer on good intentions than practical insights. Neither Bryan nor Wilson had TR's skill as a mediator. Colonel House warned that given the Germans' territorial advantages and implacable militant spirit, the Allies would consider the proposal "an unfriendly act."[25]

Bryan's memo seemed to stir Wilson's thinking. In a confidential interview with a reporter in mid-December, Wilson speculated that the current stalemate could offer an opportunity to end the war quickly. He welcomed a deadlock. Germany was not solely to blame. Victory by either side would lead to a cycle of revenge and more war, although Wilson was less troubled by an Allied success. Wilson would germinate the seeds of these ideas two years later in his "peace without victory" speech of January 1917.[26]

The president needed better information about what European leaders were actually thinking. At the start of 1915, he asked House to return to Europe "to ascertain what our opportunities as neutrals and disinterested friends" might be to assist the warring nations with a first step toward peace. Yet House would travel as the president's "private friend and spokesman without official standing or authority." That type of diplomatic charge was likely to lead to confusion, especially because House's pro-Allied views were closer to Roosevelt's than Wilson's, a difference House did not clarify with the president. On January 31, 1915, House left on the luxurious—soon to be infamous—Cunard liner *Lusitania*.[27]

U-Boat Attacks

That same month, the Germans destroyed the *William P. Frye*, an American ship carrying wheat to Britain. On the other side of the world, Japan confirmed Wilson's fear about geopolitical upheaval when it marched into German-held areas in China and demanded control over much of northern China.

On February 4, 1915, the German admiralty announced that in two weeks its U-boats would attack all merchant ships, whether neutral or belligerent, in a watery war zone around Britain. Civilians traveled in this area at their own risk, warned Berlin. Yet Germany had only thirty slow submarines in early 1915; just about a third could deploy at any one time. The Germans seemed to be acting out of frustration as Britain's blockade tightened and the kaiser's costly surface fleet remained bottled up in the North Sea. Berlin sent secret orders to avoid American ships.[28]

At the end of March, a U-boat sank the small British passenger ship *Falaba*; one American died. In April, a German airplane attacked the *Cushing*, an American steamship, and on May 1 a U-boat sank the American tanker *Gulflight*.

The loss of American life triggered a dispute between the president and Bryan. At the beginning of March, Wilson was still preaching "self-control," "patience," and acting "without excitement." But Wilson figured that he needed to demand that the combatants not endanger U.S. lives. Bryan, in turn, questioned whether any American should put his own "business above his regard for his own country" by assuming "unnecessary risks" and "involv[ing] his country in international complications." Wilson rejoined with the idea of a note that suggested, firmly but diplomatically, that submarines conform to established practices of providing for the safety of neutrals and noncombatants. He argued the case based on "the interests of mankind," rather than on the loss of one man's life. Bryan countered with a proposal for mediation, asking why the nation should risk war over the loss of one man's life. The president decided not to send any note to Berlin.[29]

"America First"

Instead, Wilson gave a series of speeches in April to urge the public to exercise "self-control and self-mastery" in the face of threats from Europe: "I am not speaking in a selfish spirit when I say that our whole duty, for the present, at any rate is summed up in this motto: 'America first.'" In light of later usage of that slogan, it is ironic that Wilson's unselfish message was twofold: First, Americans should unite for their country instead of permitting old national or ethnic ties to divide the Union; and second, America needed to stay neutral so that "we may be Europe's friend when the day of tested friendship comes." The United States had to remain cohesive, and stand for a higher peaceful purpose, in order to help the world overcome its old, militant order.[30]

In March, during the midst of this drama, the fifty-eight-year-old president met Edith Galt, a forty-two-year-old widow. Edith was a confident, capable, and exuberant businesswoman who had mastered her late husband's jewelry enterprise; she was the first woman in Washington to drive her own car. By May 3, Wilson professed his love and proposed to Edith.[31]

The Sinking of the *Lusitania*

A few days later, on Friday, May 7, the president was about ready to leave the White House to play a round of golf when he learned that a U-boat had sunk the *Lusitania*, Cunard's fastest and grandest liner.[32] Its fate brought to mind the sinking of the *Titanic* by an iceberg almost exactly three years before. But the *Lusitania*, hit by a German torpedo, went to the bottom in only eighteen minutes, killing 1,198 people, including 128 Americans. The event transformed the distant war in Europe from just another of the continent's battles into a very real, dangerous—and confusing—tragedy.

TR roared that the sinking was "an act of piracy." He asserted, "We earn as a nation measureless scorn and contempt if we follow the lead of those who exalt peace above righteousness." House, in London, cabled that the United States must demand "that this shall not occur again" and should consider going to war.[33]

Bryan disagreed. Germany had published advertisements below the Cunard schedules in newspapers warning of the risks. The world learned many years later that the *Lusitania* had been carrying munitions in addition to passengers. The secretary of state wanted the administration to warn U.S. citizens not to travel on ships of the warring countries.[34]

Americans were outraged, but uncertain. They had seen photos of the butchery at the Western Front and of the pitiful victims of poison gas. Newspapers in New York asked editors around the country to send their views on how the United States should respond. Only six out of one thousand replies called for war.[35]

The technology of war had twisted traditional beliefs—and principles of warfare—beyond recognition. Submarines could stop to warn or search ships only at risk of their own survival. Battlefields had become trenches in treeless moonscapes that stretched the length of Europe, while powerful machines of destruction massacred a generation of young men. A month after the *Lusitania* attack, Wilson summarized perceptively the public tension to Bryan: "I wish with all my heart that I saw a way to carry out the double wish of our people, to maintain a firm front in respect of what we demand of Germany and yet do nothing that might by any possibility involve us in war."[36]

Events were buffeting Wilson. He might have tried to step back to reflect on America's principal interests and aims. For example, if he had decided not to pay the price of war—perhaps with the aim at some point of using America's power, including its financial leverage, to compel a stop to war or to direct the postwar future—he might have followed Bryan's logic. Alternatively, Wilson might have joined the Allies to pursue a speedier victory and shape the postwar order.

Instead, Wilson temporized. He tried to work with frayed principles of neutrality. He knew that the United States could not divorce itself from the cascading effects of this World War. But he wanted to keep his country out of war. In doing so, he had his finger on the pulse of public opinion.

The Break with Bryan

Wilson drafted a note to Germany demanding an apology, reparations, and immediate steps to prevent any more such attacks on neutrals and noncombatants. Bryan resisted strenuously. He wanted the United States to condemn Allied violations of international law, and to urge arbitration. Wilson sent his note, but apparently supplemented it by meeting with the German ambassador, Johann-Heinrich von Bernstorff, to emphasize his wish for a peaceful resolution. Bernstorff reported Wilson's thinking about terms of peace, including a return to the prewar status quo and a "freedom of the seas" that would amount to a "neutralization of the seas." Wilson also planted news stories suggesting the White House hoped for a peaceful result.[37]

The battle over notes and principles continued over the following eleven months, while sailors waged the conflict at sea. Berlin responded to Wilson at the end of May. The Germans expressed deep regret about the loss of lives of neutrals, but urged the United States to examine the facts of Britain's perfidy in using the *Lusitania* to carry arms. The Germans reaffirmed their pledge to avoid attacking neutral ships. Berlin also sent secret notes to its captains to spare large passenger liners.

Wilson drafted a second note. He challenged German assertions about the *Lusitania* and repeated that the principles of humanity ruled out sinking passenger ships without warning. The president refused Bryan's entreaties to go further: to protest British actions, to ban Americans from traveling on ships carrying ammunition, and to offer mediation. Bryan pointed out that Wilson's second note left no room for Germany "to do anything but refuse to discontinue her submarine warfare." Bryan would not sign the note. Instead, he resigned on June 8, 1915.[38]

The president had not wanted to lose Bryan, the "Old Commoner." His resignation signaled division within the United States and even a breach within Wilson's own party. Shortly before Bryan stepped down, two senior Democratic chairmen from the Senate and House warned Bryan privately that neither body would be willing to declare war. Now the president would have to face external challenges to his leadership.[39]

Wilson sent his second note to Germany on June 9, the day after Bryan departed. The president carefully avoided any steps that Bryan or others could attack as edging toward hostilities. Wilson nominated Robert Lansing as Bryan's successor as secretary of state. Wilson appears to have considered Colonel House, but decided that House's health was uncertain; the president also seemed to prefer House's capacity to assist informally. Lansing had served in the number two State Department post at that time, counselor of the department, and ably supervised a wide range of activity. He was an expert on international law and diplomatic procedures, having helped to found the American Society of International Law. Wilson seems to have been unaware that Lansing's views were closer to those of Roosevelt and House. Lansing believed a German victory would endanger U.S. security. At first, Wilson said he did not think Lansing was "big enough" for the post; Wilson might have been intending to serve as his own secretary of state. He treated Lansing like a clerk, adding to poor chemistry and Lansing's disposition to cause trouble for the president. Wilson was narrowing his council of foreign policy advisers and senior diplomatic agents, with unfortunate consequences in years to come. Edith Galt, who had accepted Wilson's proposal of marriage on June 29, would increasingly serve as his sole sounding board.[40]

Germany responded in mid-July to Wilson's second note. Berlin's efforts to distinguish special circumstances from submarine warfare—such as American ships and Americans on neutral ships, as long as the ships were not carrying contraband—seemed evasive. Wilson began drafting a third note, in which he would demand an end to surprise attacks at sea. But the president would still not issue an ultimatum to Berlin.

"Preparedness" and the "*Arabic* Pledge"

The president decided it was time to back his diplomacy with military muscle. In late July 1915, he directed the secretaries of war and navy to provide recommendations on expanding the army and navy; Wilson approved their plans in October. Wilson's reversal of his earlier stand against preparedness precipitated his largest political fight yet. Wilson's own Democratic Party would prove to be the biggest obstacle. And Wilson's reelection loomed in a year.[41]

On August 19, a U-boat sunk the British liner *Arabic*, killing forty-four people, including two Americans. Based on Wilson's coaching, U.S. newspapers reported "speculation in Government circles" about a break in relations with Germany. Germany stepped back and announced it would follow the traditional rules of "cruiser warfare" under international law. This *Arabic* pledge," even with its ambiguities, prompted a wave of praise for Wilson. The president had forced Germany to back down, the story went, through skillful diplomacy, not military means. But Wilson was wary of the German pledge, and wisely so.[42]

On December 18, 1915, the peacemaking president and Mrs. Galt married in a private ceremony. Shortly thereafter, House departed on another mission to Europe on Wilson's behalf. Ambassador Bernstorff had used the management of the crises to suggest to House and Wilson that Germany was interested in larger principles, such as freedom of the seas. House speculated that the United States might be able to escape nerve-wracking ship incidents by changing the topic: He believed a general disarmament could end both German militarism and British navalism.

Near the end of 1915, the Germans apologized for sinking two ships. Lansing wanted Berlin to concede fault for the *Lusitania* as well. He again threatened a break in relations, even as senior congressional Democrats publicly opposed any such step. In mid-February 1916, Germany partially acknowledged liability for sinking the *Lusitania*, but the parties understood that they would defer claims until after the war. This solution seemed to conclude the battle of *Lusitania* notes, but without facing the fundamental problem.

Meanwhile, Bryan was wooing congressional Democrats with the simple call to keep Americans off belligerents' ships. Tumulty, Wilson's political adviser, warned the president to take his case for military preparedness to the country.

Wilson Prepares the Public

During February 1916, the president found his voice in fifteen speeches on a trip through the Midwest. Wilson explained that with the world in flux, he had to be able to change his mind. He warned that the world was on fire, with tinder everywhere. He said that the United States was not preparing for war, but instead building "an adequate national defense." As president, he would uphold "peace and honor." Nevertheless, Wilson cautioned, he could not control the actions of others. Dangers were "infinite and constant."

Yet Wilson was not content with playing defense. He wanted to share his vision for America's role in the world. He told German-Americans in Milwaukee that "America has no reason for being unless her destiny and her duty be ideal." Wilson's argument for preparedness expanded America's cause from national safety to a higher plane of "national dignity" and even national purpose.

Wilson enjoyed educating the public. With practice, he used punchier lines. The trip recalled his travels as a New Jersey governor pressing for reform and his 1912 campaign. Wilson was also honing his public skills at the start of the presidential election year.[43]

Wilson Takes Command of His Party

Even as the president made his case to the country, he had to beat back a Bryanite rebellion in Congress. With Wilson's consent, Lansing had been exploring a plan for Germany to give up surprise submarine attacks in exchange for Britain not arming merchant ships. Neither side agreed. But Democrats in Congress suspected that the administration had abandoned its own plan. Some Democrats thought Wilson's barnstorming for preparedness "[s]ounded too much like Roosevelt." Prominent Democrats of the old school introduced resolutions to prohibit American citizens from traveling on armed merchantmen or ships of belligerents. The resolutions gained steam. Wilson pushed back hard, explaining that he was doing all he could to resist war, but he needed to hold the line against uncivilized submarine warfare. He connected neutral rights with the very idea of American independence. The president raised the stakes by calling for an early vote. Uncertain Democrats urged delay (Congress's preferred option when facing unpleasant choices). The president would not yield; he insisted that a vote must overcome "the present embarrassment of the Administration." Wilson won in both the Senate and House by overwhelming margins. The president, not Bryan, was now the unrivaled commander of his party.[44]

That spring of 1916 Wilson successfully navigated to passage major navy and army bills. The navy bill moved forward relatively smoothly, but it would take until the early 1920s to build the new fleet of capital ships. The army bill required compromises, and the eventual result, passed in May, focused on continental defense and increased professionalization, not on building an expeditionary force. Wilson had begun reversing decades of Democratic Party resistance to a large military and overseas commitments. On the other hand, World War I was almost two years old before the United States started to prepare to fight.[45]

Colonel House's Diplomacy

While Wilson was solidifying his U.S. base of support, House had been pursuing Wilson's diplomatic track. Americans still wanted to avoid entanglements with the traditional European aims of war, such as territory and indemnities. The White House preferred to explore ideas about "the future peace of the world." Wilson wanted to promote a new approach: military and naval disarmament and "a league of nations to secure each nation against aggression and maintain the absolute freedom of the seas." This initiative was a far cry from Roosevelt's model, a decade earlier, of practical mediation.

House encountered skepticism in both London and Berlin; he concluded that Berlin would pursue victory to achieve bold war aims, including through "an aggressive undersea policy." House sensed danger to the United States and decided, on his own, to lead the United States toward supporting the Allies. He drafted a memorandum with Britain's foreign secretary, Sir Edward Grey, that outlined a plan. At an opportune moment—in effect, if the Allies faced setbacks or worse—the United States would propose a peace conference. If Germany refused, the United States would probably, even inevitably, join the war with the Allies. House explained to the British and French that if Germany agreed to attend the conference, the United States would insist on terms favorable to the Allies. If Germany balked, the United States would leave the conference on the side of the Allies. To win support in London and Paris, House specified territorial terms that Wilson had told him to avoid. The colonel dropped "freedom of the seas," did not raise disarmament, and only briefly discussed the idea of a league of nations with Grey. House had stretched Wilson's instructions beyond recognition in pursuit of a totally different objective. Moreover, House's representations to the Allies and explanations to Wilson diverged.

House delivered the House-Grey Memorandum to Wilson on March 6. Wilson seemed appreciative of House's efforts, but changed the whole thrust of the plan by adding the word "probably" before any U.S. commitment to enter the war. Most likely, Wilson liked the idea of a peace conference but expected to retain his flexibility. House's statements of sympathy with the Allies probably reflected Wilson's disposition, but not his decision.

Furthermore, London had tapped the U.S. cables and broken America's diplomatic codes. The British probably knew that House was not speaking for the president. When Grey presented the memorandum to the cabinet's war committee in March, his colleagues rejected it. They did not want to risk a peace conference that could stall, leaving the Germans with an advantage on the ground. Wilson did not seem to pursue the memorandum, either; in any event, new crises promptly demanded the president's attention.[46]

The *Sussex* and a Brush with War with Germany

On March 24, a U-boat torpedoed but did not sink a French channel steamer, the *Sussex*, with eighty killed or injured, including four wounded

Americans. The *Sussex* had never been armed; its habitual trip avoided the Allied routes to ship troops and supplies. People were shocked by Germany's barbarism—the *Sussex* was the *Lusitania* on a smaller scale.

Wilson no longer had Bryan to hold him in check. To the contrary, Lansing, House, and now Edith Wilson favored a harsh ultimatum either to break relations or to threaten to do so unless Germany's submarines stopped attacking merchant ships. Lansing did not bother to tell the president that Bernstorff had sent a message hinting at conciliation.

Congress remained badly divided. The president needed to hold the legislators with him. He sent his note to Germany late on April 18, met congressional leaders early on the nineteenth to explain his approach, and then spoke to a joint session of Congress at noon. The president told Congress that he had regretfully threatened to break relations with Germany unless it immediately declared an end to attacks on passenger and merchant vessels.

Chancellor Theobold von Bethmann-Hollweg threatened to resign. The admirals had admitted to the kaiser that the German navy was not yet ready for a victorious submarine assault. The Germans backed down.

The president had apparently achieved a momentous result. Yet his diplomacy signaled future dangers. Neither American diplomats overseas nor House's informal efforts revealed the battling opinions in Berlin, the Germans' changing assessments of the possibilities of submarine warfare, or the power relations in the kaiser's council. Unlike Roosevelt in 1905–06, Wilson seemed incapable of drawing from, and working with, the capable German ambassador in Washington.[47]

For Wilson, the timing of Berlin's concession was extremely fortuitous. In April, Irish nationalists had launched their surprise "Easter Rising" in Dublin, the start of a six-year clash that eventually led to Irish independence. The brutal British suppression and summary executions incensed Irish-Americans and inflamed an Anglophobia that had long simmered. The Allies' claim to moral standing suffered.

Wilson's League: A "Disentangling Alliance"

Wilson recognized that neutrality would not offer a safe haven in a world at war. Wilson told a visitor, "This is a year of madness.... [I]t is America's duty to keep her head." His restless intellect searched for a way to promote peace.[48]

The president decided to express his thinking before the League to Enforce Peace's (LEP) annual dinner on May 17. Former president Taft had helped organize the LEP and assumed its leadership in June 1915. In effect, the LEP was the principal group in the United States arguing for "internationalism."

Its members debated a wide range of ideas that coalesced around some type of "international enforcement." In general, the LEP's leaders believed that the Allies would have to win the war before the world could create a new league.

The president used the LEP forum to discuss the transformations in the world and to offer the principles America should apply in mastering the changes. Wilson generally bypassed the causes and objects of the war, although he objected to "secret counsel" that had twisted the world into alliance systems ready to rely on force.

Wilson highlighted three fundamentals for a new and better world order. "[E}very people has a right to choose the sovereignty under which they shall live." All nations, small and large, should have sovereign rights and enjoy territorial integrity. And the world should be free from aggression. Not surprisingly, given America's oceanic ordeals, Wilson also demanded "the inviolate security of the highway of the seas."

With these principles in mind, the United States, along with other "great nations," needed "some feasible method of acting in concert when any nation or group of nations seeks to disturb those fundamental things." Wilson used general language, but took a bold step for a country whose diplomatic tradition eschewed "entanglements." Indeed, three days later, in a Decoration Day (now Memorial Day) address at Arlington National Cemetery, the president connected the past to the present in a new way: "I would never consent to an entangling alliance, but I would gladly assent to a disentangling alliance—an alliance that would disentangle the peoples of the world from those combinations in which they seek their own separate and private interests and unite the peoples of the world to preserve the peace of the world upon a basis of common right and justice."

Wilson had not embraced the LEP's legal designs for arbitration and courts. He seemed to favor a political body, although not just one representing the interests of the great powers. The president's message previewed his famous Fourteen Points of January 1918. He pointed toward what would become Article X of the League of Nations. Just as important for the president in the near term, the Democratic Convention of 1916 adopted his language as the party's new political testament.[49]

Reelection: "Peace, Preparedness, and Progressivism"

To pursue his ideas, Wilson first had to win reelection. His Republican foe was Charles Evans Hughes, a two-term governor of New York and associate justice of the Supreme Court (and the subject of chapter 8). Hughes, like

Wilson, was not a gregarious politician. However, the combination of the New Yorker's swift speech, active expressions, and distinctive beard led to the celebrated sobriquet, "Animated Feather Duster." Hughes was reserved in manner, but he had a dry and sharp wit. As the nominee's stump style improved on the campaign trail, his attacks on Wilson landed stronger blows. One North Dakota farmer reportedly observed, "Gosh! He ain't so inhuman after all."

A frustrated TR, who had not yet recovered the confidence of the Republican faithful after his Progressive apostasy in 1912, called Hughes a "whiskered Wilson." But Hughes's real problems were the Republican Party's internal divisions after the Progressive-Regular split and the party's uncertainty about how to handle the war and U-boats. Republicans could agree that Wilson had mishandled foreign policy, but few other than TR wanted to run on a war plank. Wilson had shifted toward preparedness, and Germany's stand-down after the *Sussex* crisis preserved hope that the president's tactics were working.[50]

Indeed, by the summer of 1916, American frustrations with Britain seemed to supplant complaints about Germany. The United States protested Britain's practice of intercepting and opening the mail of Americans who might have ties with Germans. London ignored the demarche. In July, Britain published a blacklist of American firms suspected of trading with Germany with an eye toward blocking business with double-dealing Yankees. Wilson told House that he was "about at the end of my patience with Great Britain and the Allies." He even speculated about seeking authority to block loans and trade, a recognition of America's increasing economic leverage.[51]

Having restrained German submarines and pushed back against Allied depredations, Wilson stood as the champion of neutrality in late 1916. "Peace, preparedness, and progressivism" was an electric campaign message. The economy thrived, too. And, unlike the Republicans, Wilson had unified his party behind him.[52]

On November 7, Wilson became the first Democrat since Andrew Jackson to win a second consecutive term. He had boosted his popular vote to 49.26 percent and eked out an electoral vote win of 277 to Hughes's 254. (Wilson had won California by only 3,806 votes out of almost one million cast, and the Golden State gave the president his margin of victory in the Electoral College.) Wilson's success no doubt depended on the motto of the party convention: "He kept us out of war." But Wilson knew that he was not in control of that decision.[53]

Wilson's Peace Initiative

On Wilson's first day back at work after reelection, he cleared his schedule, gathered his papers, and summoned Colonel House. A few days before the election, Wilson had written a friend, "The minute the campaign is over… I shall be obliged to prepare some of the most important papers I have yet had to prepare." As soon as House arrived, Wilson told him of a plan to send a note to the warring parties "demanding that the war cease." "[U]nless we do this now, we must inevitably drift into war with Germany upon the submarine issue."[54]

Over the next two months, the president tried to push the parties toward a negotiated peace. Historians have recognized that the end of 1916 marked a critical point in the war. The German plan of attrition at Verdun had exhausted both sides. The British, French, and Italian offenses of 1916 had failed miserably. Some French regiments refused to fight the following year. Germany and Austria had successes in the east, but no clear prospect of victory. Although a subject of debate among historians, German political leaders seemed to be signaling to the United States that Berlin would welcome a settlement. On the other hand, Germany's military chiefs were pressing for unrestricted submarine warfare as part of a final, decisive push.

The events of 1917–18 would smash the pillars of the old European order, destroying any prospects for evolutionary political change in the twentieth century. Russia would collapse into revolution. The Austro-Hungarian and Ottoman empires would dissolve, opening new fault lines across Europe and the Middle East. Germany would crack into dangerous fragments, and its resulting chaos would lead to a new series of questions about German security and hostility for most of the twentieth century. Britain and France would be bled white, with their confidence and finances ruined, ending Europe's global dominance.

Many scholars treat Wilson's peace offensive of November 1916–January 1917 as a forlorn escapade.[55] They have history's determination on their side. Nevertheless, Professor Philip Zelikow recently researched the record again and argues that Wilson might have succeeded at this propitious moment.[56]

Roosevelt had ably demonstrated the U.S. capacity to mediate a decade before. No doubt this World War presented a much thornier problem. Yet Wilson perceived that stalemate offered an opportunity to find a "peace of understanding" in which the warring parties would accept limited aims over victory.[57]

Chancellor Bethmann-Hollweg, aided by the able Ambassador Bernstorff, maneuvered Germany's complex power elite, including the kaiser, to secretly seek Wilson's mediation without preconditions in August 1916. But

Wilson was preoccupied with reelection. The chancellor sent more signals in the Autumn, including through the U.S. embassy in Berlin, which reported Berlin's interest in using Roosevelt's model from 1905. The kaiser sent a personal message urging Wilson to move soon.[58]

Bethmann-Hollweg expected that German public opinion would never permit the government to resume the war once Wilson had convened a peace conference. But the chancellor needed to avoid a public presentation of aims. Maximal objectives would doom the effort; minimal ones would cause an uproar at home. Nevertheless, the chancellor suggested restoring Belgium's sovereignty and neutrality. Bernstorff, acting beyond instructions, spoke of evacuating German troops from France. The U.S. embassy in Berlin reported ideas such as compensating France with parts of Alsace-Lorraine, creating an independent Poland as a buffer with Russia, and yielding German colonies to Britain if Berlin could secure influence in the Balkans. In early December 1916, Bethmann-Hollweg had persuaded the kaiser to issue an order directing U-boats not to take any actions that would interfere with the outreach to Washington. But the chancellor had only a narrow window in which to urge Wilson to move. The German High Command wanted new offensives; the military believed it now had the U-boat capability to use unrestricted warfare to force Britain to sue for peace within five months, before the Americans could come to the Allies' aid.[59]

The complex currents in London might have offered an opening. Key Liberal leaders of the British government in 1916 seemed interested in the idea of a compromise peace, especially after the debacle on the Somme. But the posture of the Liberal David Lloyd George, who became prime minister in December 1916, is harder to read. He saw the huge costs of war to Britain and its future standing in the world. Lloyd George was also a scathing critic of the British generals. Though he relied on Conservative support to become prime minister and positioned himself as the leader who would win the war, almost a year earlier he had told Colonel House that only U.S. mediation could end the war and that America would be able to dictate terms of peace. At that time (early 1916), Lloyd George had cautioned that the time was not ripe for mediation because great new offenses were in motion. The Welshman had speculated that September 1916 might be the right moment.

In September 1916, however, Lloyd George gave an interview rejecting the idea of a compromise peace. The evidence suggests an intriguing political and diplomatic possibility, especially for an energetic, restless, and powerful figure such as Lloyd George: The wily Welshman was positioning himself as Britain's Mister "Fight to the Finish," while remaining open to private exchanges about how to end the war on terms that satisfied Britain.[60]

A Poor Mediator

The principal theme of Zelikow's analysis is how poorly Wilson's aides served the president as the lonely chief executive devised and executed his peace offensive. House and Lansing actively opposed the president. They failed to provide useful intelligence about the possibilities in London and Berlin, and House actually misled the president about Germany. Neither the German nor British government reflected a consensus; Wilson needed guidance about how to empower the peacemakers. "No one analyzed the options for how [Wilson] might design such a [peace] move or choreograph a mediation." As Zelikow notes, "A principal purpose of diplomacy is to clarify or test another government's interest." No one tried to figure out the minimums each party needed. Even worse, when Wilson crafted an initiative on his own, Lansing and House made public and private statements that undercut the president. The best that can be said about House and Lansing is that they wanted the United States to join with the Allies and feared any overture might disadvantage London and Paris.[61]

Wilson's team also failed to consider seriously how the United States could use financial as well as political leverage. By late 1916, Britain's treasury was nearly bare. London would no longer be able to supply collateral for loans. John Maynard Keynes, working at the treasury, observed that "in a few months" Washington could control Britain's policies. Responding to J. P. Morgan's request to make unsecured loans to the Allies, the new Federal Reserve Board suggested to the president in late November 1916 that regulatory authorities should warn against such loans. Wilson urged a stronger warning, not just a caution.[62]

Wilson worked intensively on his peace note in November, while Lansing and House sought to stop or at least divert him. No one reached out to London. By the second week in December, Berlin was losing hope in Wilson's possible mediation. Having defeated Romania, Germany could make a move toward peace without looking weak. Berlin stated publicly that it was prepared to discuss peace. The Allies rejected the approach, demanding to see German proposals.

On December 18, Wilson sent his peace note to the capitals, and he released the text to the press two days later. The president asked the warring countries to state publicly their preferred peace terms, reviving the idea that William Jennings Bryan had first proposed long ago. That step alone sabotaged the necessary private diplomacy. Neither side could suggest publicly results they might reluctantly accept.

The rest of the note failed to convey a practical presidential commitment.

Advised by House and Lansing, Wilson had deleted a suggestion for a conference. With an abundance of caution, the note stated, "The President is not proposing peace; he is not even offering mediation." Wilson's grand move landed with a thud. Then Lansing further buried Wilson's message by issuing a press statement explaining that the diplomatic move showed "we are drawing nearer the verge of war ourselves." An angry Wilson almost fired Lansing, but instead accepted a second Lansing statement repudiating the first.[63]

Wilson would not give up. He finally started to explore the parameters of peace terms privately through House. House misled Bernstorff again by saying Wilson was interested in postwar security guarantees for the future, not the territorial settlement. The German ambassador replied anyway that Berlin's "moderate terms" "did not [include] any part of Belgium." House still did not explore terms with London, but Lloyd George took the initiative with the pro-British U.S. ambassador Walter Hines Page. Lloyd George encouraged a private, confidential dialogue with the president through Page. "I wish[,] if the President will permit me[,] to know his mind through you and I will open my mind to him through you." He would have welcomed an understanding before the president had sent his note. In any event, Lloyd George said that only Wilson could apply pressure on both sides to end the war. He was offering a quiet exchange—away from his colleagues—in which he might divulge his real needs. Wilson and House did not even reply to Lloyd George. They had lost confidence in their own ambassador in London, and perhaps concluded Page was maneuvering for a central role for himself.[64]

"Peace Without Victory"

Having failed to conduct business through diplomatic channels, the president turned to the method with which he was most comfortable: He drafted what would become known as his "Peace Without Victory" speech. Wilson gave the State Department a week to cable and present his remarks in foreign capitals at the time of his delivery (with only an hour's notice) in the Senate on January 22.

The president's powerful speech spoke to "the silent mass of mankind everywhere" rather than to officials or chanceries. He set out the basis for a negotiated peace, a "peace without victory." He argued that "[o]nly a peace between equals can last." The aim must be "not a balance of power, but a community of power; not organized rivalries, but an organized common peace." Wilson explained that lasting peace must be founded on principles, including equality of rights among nations, freely chosen government, freedom of the seas, and limitations on armaments. He pledged that the United States would "guarant[ee] the permanence of [such a] peace."

The president was also speaking to the American people and their elected representatives. His idea, Wilson explained, was to propose the Monroe Doctrine "as the doctrine of the world." He rejected the intrigues and selfish rivalries of entangling alliances not only for America, but for the world. "There is no entangling alliance in a concert of power.... These are American principles, American policies."

Former president Taft and former secretary of state Bryan embraced the inspirational speech. TR bluntly argued the alternative view, relying on his reading of history: "Peace without victory is the natural ideal of the man who is too proud to fight.... The Tories of 1776 demanded peace without victory. The [pro-Confederate] Copperheads of 1864 demanded peace without victory. These men were Mr. Wilson's spiritual forebears."

As a means of practical diplomacy, the speech missed the target. The British government decided that the address "demanded little official attention." The Germans had already decided on their course of action.[65]

Unrestricted Submarine Warfare

On January 9, the kaiser's imperial council met at his Silesian castle. The German navy now had the U-boats and crews, the military argued, to choke off the Atlantic passage. The military leadership wanted to resume the naval offensive because the British blockade would eventually starve Germany. The kaiser signed the order for unrestricted submarine warfare, expecting America to declare war.

Bethmann-Hollweg had resisted until the end, but his peace moves had not borne fruit. He doubted Wilson's intentions. Ambassador Bernstorff had relayed House's uncertainties about Wilson's peace initiative. The U.S. ambassador to Germany admitted to the chancellor that he had no idea whatsoever about the president's plans for peace. Bethmann-Hollweg later testified that "I was wholly powerless to dissipate the deep distrust of the Supreme High Command of the Army for President Wilson." On January 31, Bernstorff presented a demarche to Lansing: As of February 1, "all sea traffic will be stopped with every available weapon and without further notice... around Great Britain, France, Italy and in the Eastern Mediterranean."[66]

The president still resisted the slide to war. On February 2, an anguished Wilson pondered with his cabinet whether entering the slaughter in Europe would enable "the yellow races to take advantage of [the depletion of white men's power] and attempt to subjugate the white races." On February 3, the president told a joint session of Congress that he had "no alternative" but to break diplomatic relations with Germany, although he would wait for "overt acts" before preparing other steps. The Germans stepped up attacks on merchant ships and, for the first time in two years, targeted American vessels.[67]

The Zimmermann Telegram

Within a few weeks, a tangled tale of espionage added insult to injury. On January 16, German foreign secretary Arthur Zimmermann had sent a cable to Germany's mission in Mexico City with a shocking proposal: Berlin offered an alliance with Mexico "to make war together" against the United States. Germany also urged Mexico to draw Japan into the new alignment. In return, "Mexico [would] reconquer the lost territory in Texas, New Mexico and Arizona." (They seemed to have forgotten California, or perhaps had other plans for it!)

Amazingly, the Germans had sent their coded message over the American transatlantic cable network, a courtesy granted by Washington. In an ironic twist, the British had tapped the U.S. cable and broken the German code. But London had to figure out how to relay the intercept without revealing how Britain had acquired it. The ingenious spymasters managed to steal a decoded copy of Zimmermann's note from the German embassy in Mexico. By February 24, Britain's foreign minister shared a copy of his prize with U.S. ambassador Page, who promptly forwarded the text to the president.

After a few days, the administration released the shocking news to the press. Newspapers across the United States exploded at the affront. Some German-American leaders countered that the dispatch must have been a mendacious British trick. But on March 3, Zimmermann acknowledged that he had indeed posted the offer to Mexico.[68]

The House of Representatives promptly and overwhelmingly passed a bill to arm U.S. merchant ships. Yet the resistance to war ran deep. Eleven senators—six Republicans and five Democrats—filibustered the bill until the end of the congressional session on March 4, killing the measure as Wilson waited to take the oath of office for his second term in a private, Sunday ceremony.[69]

War

Wilson's second inaugural address the next day contrasted sharply with his first in 1913, which had called for speedy domestic action without a word on the international context. The president's words just marked time, as Wilson resisted the pull of fate. He struggled. Tragic events had made Americans "citizens of the world." The country would assume a greater role in the dark drama. But the president did not yet know what that part should be.

Over the rest of March, global upheavals continued. The revolution in Russia swept away the Romanov empire. U-boats sent shocking numbers of ships to the bottom of the ocean. The president federalized the National Guard, increased the size of the regular army, authorized the navy to defend against submarines, and opened the way for cooperation with the Royal Navy. The Federal Reserve quietly stepped back from its warnings about unsecured loans to the Allies. Wilson fell ill for more than a week after the inauguration. Still he hesitated to go to war. The president told one editor privately that he feared that "a dictated peace, a victorious peace" would mistakenly "attempt to reconstruct a peacetime civilization with war standards." He shuddered at the thought of what war would do to "the very fibre of our natural life." He strained to find an alternative.[70]

Historians cannot know for sure when Wilson decided to go to war. On March 21, he summoned Congress into session on April 2. Not long thereafter, the president withdrew to his study to write his speech asking Congress to declare war.

Neutrality: Old and New

With the distance of more than a century, including seventy years during which American policy frequently disdained neutrals for not choosing the U.S. side, people today may have a hard time appreciating the U.S. commitment to the "immutable principles" of the "rights of neutrals." We might also find it odd that Wilson, Bryan, and others concentrated their attention on how to apply these principles amidst changing circumstances and technologies instead of arguing about national interests, ends, and means. But the Americans of 1915 deemed the "rights of neutrals" to be a critical national interest. They recognized neutral rights as the defense of a humane international order that regularly had to cope with nations at war.

David Hendrickson has explained that Wilson was holding on to America's tradition of neutrality, while recognizing the need for a "new type of neutrality."[71] Both "old" and "new" neutralities assumed an international society of states. The old neutrality accepted wars as inevitable, but imposed rights and duties to try to confine the consequences of war to the belligerents. Neutrality was a form of regulation to impede the slide into universal conflict.

Wilson could see that the old regulations of neutrality were breaking down. But he wanted to preserve neutrality for the United States and others. He struggled to halt the expansion of war into a global conflict.

Wilson, the political scientist, explored the concept of a new type of security system. Like the national governmental systems he had studied, the international system would be primarily political, although, in Burkean evolutionary fashion, it might develop laws over time. The system required adherence to basic principles. It would operate through "open diplomacy." The collective security of the order would safeguard the neutrality of states, sovereignty of people and states, territory, and freedom of the seas.

Even after America joined the war, Wilson would not give up his belief in the need for a new international system and a new neutrality. He challenged the old order's assumption that belligerents were morally equivalent and that their wars stemmed from structural causes, instead of internal drives. Wilson suggested that the internal order of states—a reliance on democracy—should contribute to an international structure of peace. He did not believe outsiders could impose democracy, but he wanted to create a system conducive to democracies and their spread to other peoples.[72]

As wars, hot or cold, became more ideological and wide-ranging, Americans shifted from notions of neutrality to believing that the humane and even stabilizing decision for states was to choose the "right" (i.e., American) side. The United States would still stand for rights, including human rights, but rights of neutrals would no longer rank so high. The years 1914–17, and Wilson's words and deeds, reflected the start of a transition from the early American diplomatic tradition of neutrality to a new tradition of international leadership.

"Wilsonianism"

Scholars are fascinated with Woodrow Wilson, the professor turned president. So are many others. Even Sigmund Freud coauthored a biography on Wilson.[73]

The foreign policy ideas of the twenty-eighth president have merited a personalized descriptive term, "Wilsonianism." Tony Smith defined that concept as "the conviction that American national interest could be best pursued by promoting democracy worldwide."[74] If so, the story of the president's decision to enter World War I suggests that from 1914 to 1917, Wilson was only starting to work his way toward "Wilsonianism."

Wilson's words and actions have greatly influenced American thinking about foreign policy for a century. In the debate posing realism against idealism, Wilson serves as the standard bearer of the latter. We should assess Wilson, however, in the context of his time. As John Milton Cooper points out, nearly every American political leader of the era of Roosevelt and Wilson was an idealist, "apart from the most hard-bitten standpatters and machine types."[75]

With a touch of irony, many scholars who have defended Wilson's work have co-opted the preferred label of their opponents. Arthur Link concluded that Wilson practiced a "higher realism." Ernest May pointed to Wilson's "sublime realism." Frank Gavin concluded Wilson worked with a "meta-realism." And David Halberstam determined that Wilson represented an "ultra-realism."[76]

These linguistic markers convey slightly different meanings. Their general thrust is that Wilson reached for progressive goals in a practical and hard-headed fashion. These writers point out, as does this story, that Wilson had to work his way through terrible problems while facing the realities of European powers, contingent events, public opinion, Congress, and inherited traditions about America's role in the world—all at a moment that the world faced a crisis and the United States attained a new level of power. In seeking to solve problems, Wilson thought through new types of international systems. He tried to persuade the public, at home and overseas, to support his efforts by aspiring to higher purposes. Wilson was an educator. His reputation as a scholar rested on his appealing syntheses and his ability to explain rather than on original research or thought. As president, Wilson applied his methods and conclusions as a political scientist to a world pushed to extremes.

Trygve Throntveit places Wilson within the Progressive Pragmatist tradition by emphasizing the president's reliance on humane empiricism to challenge outmoded political ideas. Throntveit's Wilson looked to history over theory and believed in contingency over determinism. Throntveit argues that Wilson's pragmatism was incrementalist and based on his assessments of policy experience.[77] The president's course during 1914–17 was without doubt incremental, experimental, and adaptive.

Even the true realists seem compelled to give Wilson his due, as Kissinger did in *Diplomacy*. George Kennan was moved to say late in life, "I now view Wilson...as a man who like so many other people of broad vision and acute sensitivities, was ahead of his time, and did not live long enough to know what great and commanding relevance many of his ideas would acquire.... In this sense, I have to correct or modify...many of the impressions I had about him at an earlier stage."[78] Walter McDougall is more grudging but still recognizes the instrumentality of "Wilsonianism": "As a blueprint for world order, [it] has always been a chimera, but as an ideological weapon against 'arbitrary power anywhere,' it has proved mighty indeed."[79]

Lloyd Ambrosius revived the realist critique of Wilson by distinguishing the president's practicality, and even shrewdness, from his lack of realism about Europe and its conflicts. According to Ambrosius, Wilson's liberal internationalism, in particular his experimentation with collective security, failed to match "the modern world's combination of interdependence and pluralism." Wilson suffered from a disconnect between his idealistic, universalist ends and the means and methods the president could realistically apply. At heart, Ambrosius concludes, "there was a dissonance between his American ideals and European realities."[80]

Martin Walker, a British observer of U.S. foreign policy, probably best captures most American practitioners' view of Wilson's legacy, at least until recently: "They have almost universally seen Wilson as a highly useful embodiment of a higher American purpose in the country's engagement with other countries and as a standing symbol of an America that seeks a just and fairer world."[81]

The Operational Art of Diplomacy

My story reveals a different dimension of Wilson's diplomacy. As a politician and student of power, Wilson could be a master tactician. As professor and leader, Wilson could inspire, explain, and point toward noble goals. As a conductor of diplomacy, however, Wilson did not understand the operational arts. He did not know how to unite observations, assessments, goals, and tactics to increase the likelihood of successful outcomes.[82]

In the early part of the twentieth century, the United States did not have the national security machinery to act like a world power.[83] Roosevelt compensated with talented colleagues, an extensive personal network, and a feel for the practical operations of diplomacy. TR earned trust and respect—and even a little fear—from foreign counterparts. As Secretary Baker frequently remarked, "Success breeds success."

Wilson's foreign policy team was weak; moreover, it consciously and consistently undermined his efforts. The president suffered from poor intelligence about competing opinions in London, Berlin, and Paris. He did not get a fingertip feel for foreign fears and changing views on objectives. He did not know how to test ideas privately. Therefore, Wilson was not prepared to address foreigners' calculations of risks and rewards, help them recognize unpleasant realities, and assist in devising explanations for difficult actions. Nor was Wilson well armed to use leverage, such as America's growing financial power, most effectively.

The president overlooked an executive's responsibility to guide processes that extend one person's reach, draw on other talents, and operate a network of actors—or to appoint others who will do so on the leader's behalf. Time and again, Wilson recognized a problem, but then withdrew to draft a note or write a speech. The notes and speeches were critical tools. Historians revel in sorting through them. But as professor and practitioner Philip Zelikow observes, historians have a harder time identifying and studying things that were not done. Wilson either ignored—or, more likely, did not understand—the practical work of diplomacy.[84]

Wilson's Failure: The Practical Politics of Diplomacy

Consider Wilson's peace offensive in late 1916. We will never know for sure, but it appears possible that Wilson could have convened a peace conference based on a private understanding with Berlin to evacuate Belgium and perhaps France as part of a wider accord. As Keynes observed after the war, Washington's hold on financial credit would have enabled it to squeeze the Allies' stream of munitions and foodstuffs—the very aim of the U-boat campaign—without America ever entering the war.[85]

Quiet American discussions with London could have provided assurances to the Allies that Germany would evacuate territories and that the Allies would not be stuck with the status quo on the ground. Germany would have achieved a buffer in the East, including an independent Poland. The stories of TR's mediations in the Russo-Japanese War and the First Moroccan Crisis demonstrate the difficulty of the work. Yet Wilson could not even start because he was blind to the possibilities, unaware of the channels to use, and oddly detached from the territorial compromises that had to be reached. His speeches tried to mobilize international public opinion, but his diplomacy failed to pull the strings with fellow leaders in capitals.

As a domestic politician, President Wilson knew how to maneuver the principal actors astutely to achieve his ends. He used speaking tours to shape public opinion at home and win critical votes in Congress. Wilson coped with the tactics of submarine crises well enough but did not look beyond the incidents—either to avoid the looming tragedy or enter the war prepared to shape its outcome and aftermath. Wilson continued to stumble operationally in shaping and executing foreign policies after entering the war. The Paris Peace Conference demonstrated the peril of trying to conduct U.S. diplomacy alone. In the end, the president's lonely struggles abroad—and his unwillingness to include Republican opponents or address some of their complaints—weakened his ability to win votes at home to sustain his grand design. Winning crucial votes is the elemental test for practical democratic politicians.[86] Facing defeat, Wilson tried one last time to rally public support—with fatal consequences.

Historians might reasonably contend that the United States could not possibly avoid being drawn into World War I. They might determine that

Wilson overestimated America's ability to remold world politics in the first decades of the twentieth century and yet still admire his aspirations. A pragmatist would conclude that ultimately President Wilson failed at the practical work of the politics of diplomacy. As a result, U.S. diplomacy carried the burden of deep public disillusionment, especially among a generation that had just started to embrace a wider international role for America.

III

—

INTERWAR
INTERNATIONALISTS

———◆———

CHAPTER 8

Charles Evans Hughes

Arms Control and the Washington Conference

The Speech That Sank More Battleships
Than All the Admirals

On the chilly and blustering morning of Saturday, November 12, 1921, delegates from eight countries assembled within the recently completed Daughters of the American Revolution building, right off Washington, D.C.'s Mall. Well over a thousand guests watched from galleries in Constitution Hall. For the first time, Washington was hosting a momentous conference on the world stage.

The day before, on the third anniversary of the armistice that had ended the Great War of 1914–18, President Warren Harding had invited the guests to the dedication of a tomb at Arlington Cemetery for an unknown American soldier. The president's respectful words recounted the cataclysmic recent past with a message for the future: "It must not be again." No one could have imagined that later in the century the nation would enlarge the tomb to honor unknown soldiers from two more wars and that the Mall would become hallowed ground for numerous memorials to many more fallen Americans.[1]

The Washington Conference was convened to discuss the limitation of armaments "in connection with...Pacific and Far Eastern questions." Two prior great power disarmament conferences in The Hague in 1899 and 1907 had produced little. Expectations for this gathering were low. The world had recently been disappointed that Washington had rejected the Treaty of Versailles and Woodrow Wilson's plan for a League of Nations. The inexperienced Americans had said little publicly about the conference's purposes since issuing invitations in July.

The conference arrangements inside the building appeared unusual. Based on a suggestion from Lord Curzon, the British foreign minister, the

American hosts seated the five arms control delegations alphabetically around the outside of a specially constructed walnut table shaped like a block U. The chair of the conference, U.S. Secretary of State Charles Evans Hughes, had requested that each country send only four delegates, creating a group, in the words of the correspondent H. G. Wells, "not too big for intimacy, not too small for a sufficient gathering of people."[2]

As the delegates settled into their places, a stir disturbed the hall. The place assignments had posted Chairman Hughes at the bottom center of the U, with his three U.S. colleagues sitting to his right. The four British delegates, led by former prime minister Arthur Balfour, assembled to Hughes's left. The British staff, ever sensitive to detail, had carefully supplied Balfour with a set of envelopes, his preferred method for taking notes.[3]

Unfortunately, these arrangements left France's premier, Aristide Briand, just around the right corner from the Americans. The indignant Briand demanded a seat at the "table of honor" at the bottom of the U. Hughes answered that there was no such table, but diplomatically suggested that everyone shift one place to the left, enabling Briand to move to the bottom of the U, next to the Americans.[4]

At 10:30 a.m., a Baptist minister opened the conference with a prayer. President Harding then gave his welcoming speech, a blend of the spiritual with the will of the people. The audience cheered, disturbing the Europeans' sense of decorum. Hughes grasped Harding's hand, as did other heads of delegation nearby, and the crowd settled down.[5]

Balfour arose to propose formally that Hughes chair the conference. The secretary stood to offer his welcome. The delegates and audience expected Hughes to follow the traditional course of greeting and offer general guidance. The real work would begin the following week.

Hughes had an idea, however, about how his speech could build momentum for the conference negotiations. He understood how public opinion—not only American, but global—could be a powerful factor in diplomacy. Only nine men, including the president, knew what Hughes planned to say.[6]

Hughes began with appropriate courtesies. He emphasized that the conference's dual purposes—consideration of arms limits and discussion of questions pertaining to the Far East—should be considered simultaneously and without delay. Applause signaled that some in the audience expected the secretary to close with this general exhortation.

But Hughes continued with a brief review of the failed efforts at The Hague to address arms limits. He drew a sharp contrast of those disappointments with the bitter "victory" in the "greatest war in history." Hughes's delivery sharpened as he pointed to the "vital necessity" of the day. "[C]ompetition in armament must stop." His audience now really paid attention.

Hughes signaled a new procedure for the conference. Reports would not suffice. Nor would general resolutions do. "Power and responsibility" needed to forge "a practicable program which shall at once be put into execution."

Hughes recommended a focus on naval arms. Battleships, in particular, were the strategic weapons of the age (similar to the bombers and missiles of later eras). The only way to end competition in the production of ships, declared Hughes, "is to end it now." To be fair, the sacrifices had to be based on existing naval strength. To be definite, Hughes proposed stopping construction of capital ships for a period not less than ten years, establishing "a naval holiday."

Before the audience could reflect on Hughes's headline, he moved on to concrete recommendations for the United States, Britain, and Japan, with applications for France and Italy to be developed. The parties should abandon all programs to build capital ships. They should scrap older ships, too. They should base new limits on existing naval strength. And then the parties should apply the capital-ships methodology to other vessels.

As bold as these principles might sound, Hughes turned shockingly specific. He listed the ships the United States would not build and those it would scrap. He targeted thirty capital ships of 845,740 tons. Clamor filled the hall. Even the skeptical British journalists who had "exuded gloom" about the American show were astonished. The audience expected the ceremonial day would close with Hughes's bold specification of U.S. leadership.

Yet Hughes now directed his rhetorical guns on the Royal Navy and Japan's fleet. Balfour raced to scribble notes on his envelopes. Hughes took aim at 583,375 tons of British and 448,928 tons of Japanese capital ships. In sum, Hughes's plan would destroy sixty-six U.S., British, and Japanese capital ships, built and in process, totaling 1,878,043 tons.

Further, Hughes stipulated no replacements of capital ships for ten years, with a maximum tonnage for Great Britain and the United States of 500,000 tons each and 300,000 tons for Japan. No ship should be larger than 35,000 tons. The conference should also establish limits for other ships, submarines, and aircraft carriers. The secretary closed his naval arms control broadside with a flourish: "Preparation for offensive naval war will stop now."[7]

Contemporaries reported "a tornado of cheering." Former secretary of state William Jennings Bryan, now a correspondent in the balcony, had "tears streaming down his face." A quarter century later, the editor William Allen White wrote that "the Disarmament Conference in Washington furnished the most intensely dramatic moment I had ever witnessed."[8]

Not everyone exalted. One British admiral "turned red, and then white, and sat immovable." Another "leaned forward with the belligerent expression of a waking bulldog that had been 'poked in the stomach.'" The reporter for the *Manchester Guardian* captured the moment: Hughes had sunk more British battleships than "all the admirals of the world had destroyed in a cycle of centuries."[9]

Shock waves reverberated around the world. Japanese correspondents cabled all of Hughes's speech to Tokyo at a cost of $1.50 per word (about $22.00 per word today). The *New York Times* gave the story thirteen pages of coverage. Ring Lardner expressed his review: "I'm going home. This is going to be a bum show. They've let the hero kill the villain in the first act."[10]

Hughes had taken a huge diplomatic risk. Normally, a statesman presented positions carefully behind closed doors, usually after preliminary soundings to gain intelligence and test ideas. The secretary's initial, audacious proposal might have undermined his bargaining position. Hughes had combined an American penchant for open diplomacy with precise, pointed, and yet, just possibly, practical offers and demands.[11]

The secretary of state read shrewdly the constraints—and possibilities—created by changing congressional and public opinion. He also sensed the public and political moods in key European countries and Japan. Hughes's masterful presentation compelled a serious—and prompt—response. He had created his own diplomatic impetus with a whirlwind of substance, presentation, politics, and drama.

Reactions and Results

Delegates toiled over the weekend to assess the American presentation and seek guidance from capitals. The leaders recognized that public acclaim made any direct rejection politically impossible. On Tuesday, November 15, Balfour graciously flattered the U.S. initiative and the opening day as "one of the landmarks in human civilization." Britain accepted Hughes's plan "in spirit and in principle," recognizing the need for a few exceptions. Balfour was balancing interests different from America's. The Royal Navy had to maintain maritime hegemony in Europe while safeguarding the sea-lanes of the Empire. To preserve leadership in ship technology, Britain also needed active construction yards.[12]

On November 18, Prime Minister Lloyd George took another step after recognizing the political opportunity: The British government ordered a production halt of the four new Super-*Hood* battleships that it had just approved in August. The $160 million in savings approximated the annual interest London owed the United States for war debt. With Germany's fleet scuttled in the depths of Scotland's Scapa Flow, Lloyd George concluded that Britain could retain naval dominance in Europe at a much lower cost if Hughes were able to extend his plan to France and Italy, too.[13]

Admiral Baron Kato Tomosaburo, minister of the navy, responded for Japan. Hughes had asked countries to send civilian delegates, reserving military and financial experts as technical advisers. But Japanese prime minister Hara Takashi, a lifelong advocate of cooperation with the United States, had wisely asked Kato to guide Tokyo's approach toward a secure but less costly navy. Kato had accepted, but was subsequently shocked by the prime minister's assassination on November 4.

The new prime minister, Takahashi Korekiyo, remained committed to Hara's strategy but lacked his political strength and skill. Admiral Kato's status loomed even larger, but he had to proceed carefully. Kato followed Balfour's path of endorsing the need for straightforward action, praising Hughes's example and accepting the U.S. principles, subject to "a few modifications." He also prepared a cable to Tokyo outlining alternatives, letting others identify objections to the U.S. proposal.[14]

Within three months, Hughes, Balfour, Kato, and the French and Italians agreed on a landmark treaty to limit their fleets of capital ships for ten years. Their final ceilings included eighteen ships for the United States (525,850 tons), twenty-two ships for the British Empire (580,450 tons), and ten ships for Japan (301,320 tons)—close to Hughes's proposal. The three agreed on a ratio principle of 5-5-3 for their respective tonnage of replacement ships. France and Italy accepted ratios of 1.75 each for their capital ships. The U.S. Senate ratified this five-power naval treaty on March 29, 1922, by a vote of 74 to 1, and twenty of the twenty-one senators who were unable to vote said they would have supported it.[15]

The Washington Conference led to eight other security and arms control treaties, seven of which involved the United States. The agreements and accompanying declarations covered a diverse range of topics, including rules for submarines and a ban on poison gases, Pacific security consultations, China's independence and territorial integrity (including the Open Door principles), Chinese control of its customs charges, undersea cable rights across the Pacific, and a Sino-Japanese accord to restore the Shantung Peninsula to China. The four-power accord among the United States, Britain, Japan, and France to consult on aggressive actions and controversies in the Pacific sparked opposition from senators fearful of commitments to "guarantee" security. In reality, the treaty offered diplomatic cover for ending the Anglo-Japanese alliance, a prime U.S. objective. As Senator Lodge clarified in presenting the treaty, the agreement merely "substituted a four-power agreement to talk for a two-power agreement to fight." Nevertheless, the Senate ratified the treaty by a vote of 62 to 27 (only a four-vote margin under the Constitution's requirement of a two-thirds majority). The Senate ratified all the other U.S. treaties with only one dissenting vote.[16]

The Antidote to Wilson

Charles Evans Hughes had captained a stunning turnaround in U.S. foreign policy from the Senate's defeat of the Versailles Peace Treaty in 1920. The United States remained outside the League of Nations but had offered a positive alternative. The Americans continued to steer clear of military alliances. Instead, the United States had led in combining naval arms control with obligations in China and the Pacific to establish a new regional security system.

Hughes's diplomacy combined an astute assessment of congressional and national inclinations with a sense of European and Asian needs and possibilities. He perceived an opportunity for an American initiative to reorder both naval capacities and foreign policy relationships among the principal powers in East Asia. He designed a proposal that matched his president's inclinations with the support of key senators and at least the acquiescence of the U.S. Navy. Then he used public diplomacy, personal relationships, and his drive and attention to detail to push relentlessly for closure on specific results. In December 1921, the *Literary Digest* noted that the Washington correspondent of the *New York Evening Post* had observed: "Wilson hitched his wagon to a star. Hughes has chosen rather to hitch his star to a wagon."[17] Hughes was the antidote to Wilson.

Within ten years, the Great Depression, political shifts in Japan and China, and shortfalls in U.S. diplomatic and military commitments would shake and then break the politico-security framework of the Washington Conference. Hughes's handiwork had forged a convergence of some national interests, but could only temporarily bridge other conflicts. Effective diplomacy requires ongoing reassessment and reinforcement—and sometimes redirection. Within a few more years, the storm of war would envelop the world again.[18]

The United States and the World in 1921

The story of Hughes and the Washington Conference begins with the American reaction to Wilson's failure to ratify the Versailles Treaty. The incoming Harding administration, assuming office in March 1921, faced both a disaffected public and a long list of practical problems. The Senate, having bested a president over foreign relations, was pressing its advantage versus the executive branch. Congressional Republicans enjoyed large majorities, but were badly split on international topics, especially in the Senate.

In March 1921, the *Times* of London reported, "The murk of the Paris Peace Settlement lay over [America's] international relationships." In April,

Current Opinion observed that, "There is hardly a phase of our foreign policy that is not hanging in mid-air." The British ambassador reported home that the new Harding administration seemed fearful of formal international contact and any "public references to international cooperation" and that "Americans are fed up with all other nations." He added: "They are for America first and no one second," although Britain might squeeze in "if there has to be a second."[19]

The gloom extended deeper. The cruelty and sacrifices of war had stirred expectations of a more promising peace, hopes that were stillborn. As a legal matter, the United States was still at war with Germany and Austria. No one knew what relationships, if any, Washington would have with the League or its various committees. Reparations and debt payments were a tangled mess. The United States had not agreed to League mandates for Pacific islands, including the Pacific cable center of Yap, or for lands in Mesopotamia (including today's Iraq).

To the south, the United States had not figured out a workable relationship with yet another new government in Mexico, and flare-ups in Central America endangered American businesses and property. Across the Pacific, Japan's activities in China, troops in Siberia, and seizure of Germany's Pacific islands threatened to reshape the security and economic landscapes of the Asia-Pacific. Distrust and suspicions were rising. The British and Japanese appeared primed to renew their security alliance. London and Tokyo had extended their 1902 accord in 1905 and 1911 in order to counter Russia and Germany. Neither country now posed threats, so Washington wondered whether Japan and Britain wanted to keep America in check. Furthermore, the United States had not recognized the Bolshevik government in Russia, a vast territory of ongoing revolution and counterrevolution.[20]

Powerful senators were disposed to run U.S. foreign policy themselves. Senator Boies Penrose, a Pennsylvania Republican, welcomed the new administration by reportedly saying, "I do not think it matters much who is Secretary of State, for Congress, especially the Senate, will blaze the way in connection with our foreign policies." With the same spirit, Congress passed a resolution on July 2 declaring an end to the war with Germany, while reserving all rights and advantages as a victorious power—without even bothering to consult the State Department. Congress's unilateral declaration could not secure U.S. rights or establish peaceful relations with Germany; the two countries still needed a treaty.[21]

Hughes came up with a creative solution. He devised a treaty that "looked new to the Senate and old to Germany." His draft incorporated the language of Congress's joint resolution and specified, without any changes, the parts of the Treaty of Versailles that stipulated the rights and privileges available to the United States. As a result, the United States acquired all the benefits of the Versailles Treaty, but none of the responsibilities. Germany assented on August 25, and the Senate ratified the new treaty in October 1921.[22]

America's detachment from international politics in 1921 contrasted with its economic preeminence. The United States enjoyed unmatched resources, mighty industrial capacity, and a skilled labor force. During the war, America had rapidly switched from owing international debts of $3 billion to owning $9 billion of foreign government and private credits. But the Americans of 1921 did not feel so positive. A sharp deflation after the war preceded a recession and an increase in unemployment of 3.5 million between January 1920 and February 1921. Business conditions were weak. Agriculture began its long slide into the farm depression of the 1920s. The challenge for Harding and Hughes was how to assert U.S. leadership, backed by Congress and the public, under trying circumstances.[23]

The world map of 1921 looked much different from the design of 1914. New states—some with old heritages and enmities—colored the globe, while national and ethnic rivalries spilled over borders. The Austro-Hungarian, Russian, and Ottoman Empires were gone. A prostrate Germany, shorn of lands on its frontiers, struggled to create a new republic.[24]

Even the victors appeared uncertain. France was shell-shocked from the past and fearful of the future. The prospect of a revived and vengeful Germany loomed ahead. The old partnership with Russia had vanished. London and Washington had backed away from the security guarantees that Paris desperately wanted. France's priorities were continental security and a settlement of inter-Allied debts, even as it tried to man the thinning outposts of its empire.[25]

Britain's Empire reached its apogee around 1919. London struggled with independence movements in Ireland and India. Fighting in Egypt, Afghanistan, and the Middle East strained a demobilized military. The Dominions of Australia, Canada, and New Zealand had earned a large say on international issues. A postwar slump, the switch from wartime to peace production, unemployment, pent-up frustrations, and huge debt contributed to housing problems, social unrest, coal strikes, and budget pressures. Lloyd George tried to focus on politics at home and the creation of a new center party while avoiding choices abroad.[26]

The World War had destroyed the imperialist balance of power in the Far East. China remained weak and riven by internal conflicts. Japan stood unchecked, but also uncertain. The imperial house faced a transition. Tokyo recognized the power shift from a known and reassuring London to an unknown Washington and New York. In many respects, Japan, with 60 million people, ranked as the third global power. It ranged across both continental and island empires. But Tokyo faced economic pressures, with a military budget totaling about one-half of governmental expenditures. Some Japanese strategists and political leaders argued that long-term national strength depended on economic and financial power, which necessitated cooperation with the United States and Britain.[27]

The horrifying totality of the Great War cast a dark shadow far beyond the politics of states. Four catastrophic years of war had shocked and demoralized societies. Humankind had revealed its most frightening gruesomeness. The release of an estimated fifty varieties of poison gas had killed or disabled more than one million men, with unknown long-term effects. Modern war left vast territories across Europe as ghastly wastelands. As if stirred to match man's savagery, the Spanish influenza of 1918–20 wreaked a follow-on vengeance, with an estimated 50–100 million lives lost, equivalent to 3–5 percent of the world's population.[28]

This twentieth-century apocalypse left its mark on diplomacy, too. The ruin of modern war discredited classical tenets about world order, state and military competition, and political statecraft.[29] Wilson had recognized the need for a changing of the old guard, but he had faltered in attempting to direct it.

Navies in 1921

Navies were powerful symbols of the old order. Mahan had provided the strategic underpinnings for the fleets of capital ships that represented a race for European and global dominance. Wartime innovation had expanded the competition with new technologies, especially submarines and airplanes.

Unimpressive performances in battles at Jutland and the Dardanelles had tarnished Britain's trident. The Royal Navy had been slow to recognize the dangers of the U-boats. The pale inheritors of Nelson's tradition faced inquiries and were lost in squalls of controversies with one another.[30]

While Britain's traditional policy toward Europe sought a balance of power, its global policies preferred regional hegemonies or at least dominating partnerships. The Anglo-Japanese alliance, for example, had been the strategic buttress for Britain's Far Eastern policy for twenty years.[31]

Britain and the United States could now operate safely in the North Atlantic, which had historically been the U.S. Navy's primary interest. In recent years, the U.S. Navy had demanded parity with the Royal Navy. But the American admirals now viewed themselves as the commanders of a two-ocean navy. The War Plans Division of the U.S. Navy looked toward the Pacific and contemplated the need for new ships and fortifications in Hawaii, Guam, and perhaps the Philippines. The huge spending boost for the U.S. Navy in 1916 had it contemplating building sixteen capital ships, but the demands of submarine warfare had prioritized destroyers over battleships. The U.S. admirals had not yet agreed on the lessons of the Great War, so they compromised by fulfilling the old battleship plans. During the transition between the Wilson and Harding administrations, however, Congress signaled that it had different designs.[32]

For the Royal Navy, grudging acceptance of parity with the Americans did not mean equality. Britain's empire required a different force structure. Supremacy of the seas remained totemic for London. The United States looked like an unreliable partner. While pulling back from European security, the Americans had made it clear that Britain's regional partnership with Japan in the Pacific conflicted with any Anglo-American global association. Lloyd George preferred to defer hard choices on postwar naval policies. The Imperial Conference assembling in London in June 1921 offered a handy justification for delaying commitments.[33]

Japan's experience in and lessons from the Great War appeared more promising to the Imperial Navy. Over the course of twenty years, Nippon's fleets had operated successfully against China, Russia, and then Germany. The navy and its battleships matched Japan's rising nationalism and sense of place in the international political and security system. The government expanded the fleet significantly in 1915 and in 1920 authorized 103 new ships, including eight new battleships and eight new battle cruisers.

Japan recognized the rise in U.S. naval power, but also assessed that technological developments, such as submarines and airplanes, would offer Japan an advantage in the Western Pacific against a large expeditionary force. In 1918, Japan's Imperial Navy classified the United States "as probable enemy number one." Japan's fortification of positions in the region would provide a wider base for secure operations.

Nevertheless, Japan's political leaders, prodded by Prime Minister Hara, perceived a different, attractive possibility. With a policy of international cooperation, Tokyo might become part of a "Big Three" with the United States and Britain—without bearing the full weight of all-out military competition. Japan faced economic strains and social unrest. As Japan would demonstrate later in the twentieth century, economic and industrial strength was the prerequisite for both national well-being and sustainable international influence. Naval strength alone would not suffice.[34]

Some leaders in Tokyo recognized dangers in being drawn into China's internal struggles for power. A policy of noninterference in China could still enable Japan's industry to compete prosperously because of advantages of geography. But Japan's policy of restraint would only apply south of the Great Wall. Japan viewed Manchuria—the northern provinces of China—with more avaricious eyes. These territories were a resource and industrial base and perhaps an outlet for Japan's burgeoning population.[35]

The Movement to Reduce Naval Arms

The second of Wilson's Fourteen Points stressed freedom of the seas and the fourth called for arms limits. The compromise in Paris had settled upon Wilson's principle of freedom of the seas, along with Lloyd George's paean to Britain's naval supremacy and Hara's practical acquisition of Germany's Pacific islands for Japan.[36] But late in 1920, after Harding's election, the new League in Geneva proposed a discussion of arms limitations. President Wilson rejected an invitation to participate.[37]

Senator William Borah of Idaho, an "irreconcilable" opponent of the League, perceived an opportunity to awaken a powerful but latent public sentiment. On December 14, 1920, Borah offered a resolution calling upon the president to negotiate a 50 percent reduction in naval construction by Britain, Japan, and the United States over the next five years. The senator said he wanted to test the sincerity of the three great powers. His resolution unleashed an outpouring of support—in Congress, across the United States, and even internationally. Borah ascended to become "the angel of peace."

Senate Majority Leader Lodge, long an ardent supporter of a big U.S. Navy, managed to delay, amend, and then finally permit passage of a weakened Borah resolution. Then Borah proposed a second resolution to study the worth of battleships and consider a halt in their construction for six months. Borah had managed, for the first time in five years, to force the issue of naval armaments on the public agenda. He had tapped a wellspring of public feeling that flowed from disaffection. Borah's new cause preempted the incoming president. Despite President-elect Harding's urging, the Naval Appropriations bill died after a debate that ran past midnight on Harding's inauguration day. The Senate thus managed to reject the leadership of the first of its sitting members to be elected president.[38]

Charles Evans Hughes

Given the fractious domestic politics and complicated international context, the *Literary Digest* of March 5, 1921, reported that Harding's selection of a secretary of state would be the president's most important appointment. The media treated the president's nomination of Charles Evans Hughes with respect. But the *New York Times* reported that "if a ballot of Senate Republicans had been taken, Hughes in all probability would not have received one vote." The former governor of New York, Supreme Court justice, and presidential candidate was neither a man of hearty political manners, nor someone who would defer easily to senators. The editors of Hughes's autobiographical notes determined that the new secretary found practical politics "repugnant" but "fascinating."[39]

Hughes's legal mind had the capacity to assimilate vast amounts of information, sort and organize, analyze logically, and devise sharp arguments and policies. One of his colleagues on the Supreme Court later observed that Hughes was an "intense man," and that "nothing interfered when focused on serious business." At the same time, Hughes had a range of cordial personal relations and a keen sense of humor.[40]

Robert Jackson provided the sharpest portrait of Hughes. Years later, FDR was meeting with a few close advisers on January 1, 1939, to consider whom the president should nominate to the Supreme Court. Hughes was chief justice. Jackson argued for a strong figure, Felix Frankfurter, rather than someone who would represent an appealing constituency or region of the country. "[Hughes] looks like God and talks like God," said Jackson. Any choice other than Frankfurter "would be completely unable to face Chief Justice Hughes in conference and hold his own in discussion." Whereupon FDR replied, "I think Felix is the only man who could do that job, Bob." Frankfurter joined the bench. Two years later, in a private assessment, Frankfurter wrote that Hughes "is among the very few really sizeable figures of my lifetime. He is three-dimensional and has impact. And his exterior rather hides a good deal of shrewd insight and humor.... That the settled verdict will appraise him as a great Chief Justice I have not the slightest doubt."[41]

Hughes defined his role of secretary of state in legal terms: "I am counsel for the people of the country." He was "[d]etermined to act as advocate for the United States within the limits set by public opinion." Either Secretary Hughes or his under secretary (then the number two post) briefed the press twice each day. Hughes also had a "sophisticated sense of American power and limits imposed...in its use."[42]

Like other successful secretaries of state, Hughes recognized that he was the president's advocate and counselor. Hughes wrote that he met the president almost daily to keep him advised "of everything of importance that was done, ascertained, or proposed in department affairs." Even during the three-month-long Washington Conference, Hughes briefed Harding every morning on the prior day's events.[43]

Secretary Baker followed a similar pattern with President George H. W. Bush, even though they enjoyed a long-standing friendship and trust. The State Department grumbled when Baker said early on that he was the president's man at the Department, not the Department's representative to the White

House, but Baker knew what he was doing. As a result, the State Department had much greater influence. Especially after the growth of White House and National Security Council staffs, effective secretaries of state need frequent, personal, private conversations with their boss.

Hughes's own account explains how he treated the president respectfully while taking initiative. Hughes looked for ways to advance the president's cause: "I did not go to him with a statement of difficulties and ask him what should be done, but supplemented my statement of the facts in particular cases by concrete proposals upon which he could act at once."[44] In return, Harding gave Hughes the authority he needed to succeed.

The Washington Conference stands as a striking example of Hughes in action. He connected the Borah resolutions, budgetary realities, a convergence of international opportunities, and a public yearning for intrepid change after the disappointments of Versailles. His leadership reshaped the security system of the Far East, reordered competition among navies, built ties with Britain while ending the Anglo-Japanese alliance, and reestablished the executive branch's preeminence in foreign affairs.

Hughes's Initiative

It appears that Hughes suggested to Harding during their first weeks that the administration should pursue a disarmament conference. The president looked to the secretary to determine the timing. Harding's address to the new Sixty-Seventh Congress on April 12 opened the door to cooperation on disarmament but stated the United States should not act alone. He pressed Congress to approve the naval spending bill. Borah responded the next day with a new resolution on naval disarmament and an attack on the "merchants of death." Church organizations, women's groups, and other supporters flooded Congress with petitions; Borah's congressional support surged.[45]

Between May and July, the administration worked out a deal: It achieved $410 million for the navy, keeping alive most of the 1916 building program, and Borah got his resolution by a vote of 74 to 0.[46]

As the administration worked through the final weeks of its negotiation with Congress, Hughes was laying the groundwork for his diplomatic offensive. On June 23, Britain's ambassador Auckland Geddes explained to the secretary that London was reluctant to end its treaty with Japan. Hughes exploded, perhaps for dramatic effect. How could Britain speak of obligations to Japan when the United States' entry in the war saved England and won the victory? If not for the United States, the kaiser would be the one speaking to Washington. If Britain maintained an alliance with Japan to support Tokyo's special interests, Hughes claimed, a militaristic party in Japan might seek to isolate the United States. Adding even more power to his punch, the secretary pointed out that Congress would face a resolution to recognize the Irish Republic. He did not expect the resolution to pass, but Britain's enemies would pounce on London's alliance with Japan. Cooperation with the United States in the Far East would, in contrast, aid the opponents of a resolution on Ireland.[47]

The secretary knew the Anglo-Japanese treaty was extremely unpopular in the United States, and its continuation would pose a huge obstacle to the administration's efforts to reengage internationally. He might also have suspected that a strong message would be heard by Britain's Dominions meeting at the Imperial Conference in London. Ambassador Geddes reported to London that the secretary of state had gone mad.

In fact, Hughes was maneuvering to launch his plan for the Washington Conference. The account of how he did so is instructive because it highlights the miscues and mistakes that often confuse diplomacy.

At the Imperial Conference in London, Australia's prime minister joined Britain in pressing for a renewal of the Anglo-Japanese Treaty. Canada's man disagreed adamantly, in part reflecting his reading of American hostility. Lloyd George convinced the Dominion prime ministers to suggest to the Americans a conference on both the Far East and naval problems. On Tuesday, July 5, Lord Curzon, the foreign minister, proposed to the inept U.S. ambassador, George Harvey, a Harding friend whom Hughes had tried to block, that the president should convene such a conference. But Harvey did not bother to send a cable to Washington. Lloyd George then told the House of Commons that he hoped to make a statement about a conference the following Monday if the United States, Japan, and China responded favorably. The Foreign Office rushed to explain that it had not really asked those countries to reply.

On Thursday, July 7, reporters peppered Hughes with questions about the reports of Britain's conference on Far Eastern problems. Hughes thought London was preempting his plan for a disarmament event. After asking if the countries would accept an invitation to a conference on arms limitations in Washington, Hughes rushed to get Harding's approval to send cables to London, Paris, Tokyo, and Rome late on Friday the eighth. Hughes's proposal crisscrossed with the dilatory report from Ambassador Harvey about Britain's suggestion of a conference. Meanwhile, Britain's ambassador Geddes in Washington, who had faced the full blast from Hughes on the Anglo-Japanese treaty, was horrified to learn that his U.S. counterpart in London had been misleading Lloyd George and Curzon. Geddes rushed to see Hughes to explain.

Hughes sent a second message to London proposing an enlargement of the arms limitation conference to include Far Eastern problems, with China as an additional participant. On Saturday, Hughes got Harding's approval to issue a formal presidential invitation. On Sunday, Lloyd George praised the idea of a combined conference as "admirable." Getting that news the same day, Hughes directed the State Department to send the president's invitations and notify the press. By Monday, the world had learned of Harding's initiative for a great conference.[48] By the end of July, all the invited states had agreed to come, including China. Belgium, the Netherlands, and Portugal pressed for invitations to take part in discussions of East Asian security, and the United States added them on August 11.

British Expectations

Now the world had to decide what the conference would be about. London's priority was Far Eastern issues, not disarmament. Both Senators Borah and Lodge, from different perspectives, opposed adding the Pandora's Box of East Asian politics to the arms reduction agenda. Britain pressed Hughes hard to permit London to host a "preliminary conference." Lloyd George treated Harding's invitation as a secondary matter; Eamon DeValera, the leader of the Irish independence movement, had just agreed to come to London to begin negotiations. By the autumn, when the Washington Conference convened, the prime minister's negotiations with the Irish neared collapse, threatening his government's existence.[49]

British expectations for Washington's first global conference were low, especially after Hughes rejected London's offers to guide the Americans; the American invitation to the French and Italians was a further aggravation. These were not yet the years of the "special relationship" between Washington and London, although the Washington Conference contributed to building such ties. In 1920, Austen Chamberlain had summed up elite British opinion about their American cousins in a comment to the cabinet: "It is useless and worse than useless to criticize their insularity, blindness, and selfishness, and it is not compatible with our dignity to appear as suitors, pressing for a consideration which is not willingly given." More charitably, as the conference opened, the *Spectator* observed that, "The American nation has a dual personality. Americans are at once the most idealist and the most practical people in the world. They vibrate between Emerson and Edison."[50]

London recognized that it had to send a high-ranking official to lead its delegation, but no one wanted the assignment. It appears that the cabinet chose Lord Balfour because he was abroad in late September when the government finally got around to deciding. But Balfour turned out to be an excellent selection. He was a former prime minister, First Lord of the Admiralty, and foreign minister, who in 1921 served in the cabinet as Lord President of the Council. He was a defender of the Empire and friend of the United States who also had experience with the Anglo-Japanese alliance. When the Committee on Imperial Defense failed to agree on negotiating proposals—because of disparate views and a lack of respect for the Americans' plans—Balfour skillfully suggested his own general negotiating instructions. His aim would be to preserve the status quo in the Far East and conclude a naval limitation agreement that kept Britain equal with any other power.[51]

Japanese Preparations

Japan was the other key player. Tokyo was open to talks on naval limitations, but discussions of Far Eastern problems were less welcome. Japan wanted to avoid condemnations of its past actions or challenges to its positions in Russia or China. The Anglo-Saxons, plus the Chinese, might seek to isolate Japan. The business community, however, welcomed the opportunity to lower defense costs and improve ties with the United States and Europe. Liberal, internationalist voices argued that Japan should recognize an opportunity to state frankly its aims and aspirations instead of acting defensively.

The Japanese ambassador in Washington, Shidehara Kijuro, who would become an influential figure in Tokyo's international outlook over the next decade, explained Japan's reservations. Secretary Hughes assured Shidehara that his purpose was not to provoke public criticism, but "to reach a common understanding in regard to general principles and policies in the Pacific and Far East" that would promote peace. Hughes agreed not to take up certain matters, such as immigration and the opium trade. Having received a report from the U.S. embassy that Tokyo would accept the invitation in any event, Hughes resisted other limits. On July 23, Japan agreed to attend, with the understanding that specific problems between the parties would be "scrupulously avoided." In particular, Japan wanted to shield its bilateral relations with China from foreign interference. Like TR, Hughes wanted to encourage Tokyo to act responsibly as a world power. The pursuit of economic opportunity would be more promising than military adventures.

Prime Minister Hara had a constructive grasp of changing international conditions—and a sensitive reading of Japan's shifting public opinion favoring arms control. But he needed a military ally. Admiral Kato, the navy minister, directed his colleagues to review the major powers' respective building plans. Japan would not gain relative strength if the United States kept up its pace of building. Hara and Kato recognized an opportunity to secure the navy's national support and its security interests, improve civil-military relations, cut costs, and devote more resources to Japan's long-term sources of national economic power. At the same time, agile diplomacy could strengthen Japan's international position by winning foreign respect as the newest great power. Admiral Kato might have been the only person with the standing and vision to navigate among the shoals of power and interests in Japan.[52]

French Preoccupations and Chinese Problems

France was preoccupied with continental European security. Germany's industrial base and population raised the specter of a future threat. Neither Germany nor Russia would be bound by any armament limits. Paris preferred to strengthen the League of Nations and did not want a new effort by the United States to usurp the League's role. Equally important, the impertinent Americans had designated English as the official language of the conference, ignoring the status of French as the language of diplomacy. Washington readily clarified that French would be a coequal official language. The French agreed sullenly to attend; Paris was doubtful about the conference's prospects, but expected to contribute on the Far Eastern topics. Italy, concerned with Mediterranean stability, looked to the conference as an opportunity to boost its standing as a European power.[53]

China posed a different problem. Its central authority over 400 million people had been fracturing for a decade. A patriotic movement, encouraged by nationalists in the south, had pushed the government out of Beijing in January 1921. In April, warlord factions resumed fighting. There was no central authority to direct negotiations. Nevertheless, Wellington Koo, China's ambassador in Washington (and a graduate of Columbia Law School), would try to press for recognition of China's sovereignty and an end to foreign interference. Turmoil at home, which fed internal divisions within the Chinese delegation, would make it hard for Koo and others to accept any compromise.[54]

Hughes's Plan

Hughes had demonstrated that the United States would run this conference. Hughes's political imperative was to keep arms limitation in the forefront. Hughes dismissed Britain's preference for a preliminary conference because he expected London would prioritize Far Eastern questions; furthermore, a preparatory meeting would encourage early statements of position that might become locked in.

The old ways of European diplomacy did not impress Hughes. He would consult about the agenda, but not concede items that diverted from American objectives. When Ambassador Geddes wanted to raise the matter of tolls for the Panama Canal at the conference, Hughes cut him off: "[T]he time had come when the constant sentiments and cordial expressions which were made at dinners and on various occasions with respect to friendly cooperation between the two Governments should be translated into something definite."[55]

Hughes recognized that the resolution of Far Eastern issues was important to his domestic political support. He needed to end the Anglo-Japanese treaty. The Senate also did not like Japan's occupation of Shantung and Siberia. The United States looked for international recognition of its Open Door principles for China. And Hughes had to secure U.S. interests with the Pacific islands that were under League of Nations mandates. All these items were part of Hughes's agenda, but the secretary knew he had to set the stage with naval arms limitations.

Hughes urged the countries to send small delegations so that the participants could focus on the business at hand. They could be backed by military experts and technical advisers who could assist with subcommittees. The secretary wanted the Washington Conference to achieve results, not just exchange views.[56]

Hughes left no doubt that he would run the show. He wanted the responsibility. But the United States would now have to take the initiative to produce action.

The secretary selected his own U.S. delegation with a sharp eye on power and performance. With Harding's agreement, Hughes asked Senator Lodge, Republican majority leader and chair of the Foreign Relations Committee, and Senator Oscar Underwood, minority leader and ranking Democrat on the committee. In choosing these two, the contrast with Wilson's inattention to the Senate and the opposition party could not have been sharper. For the fourth delegate, Hughes requested seventy-six-year-old Elihu Root to help. Root had served as secretary of war, secretary of state, and senator from New York. He was regarded as America's preeminent statesman and had even attended the most recent disarmament conference, in 1907 (as will be discussed in chapter 9). Harding hesitated, because Senate "irreconcilables" disliked Root's internationalism. But Hughes insisted.

He was taking a risk. His three colleagues were strong individuals who would have their own well-founded opinions. Yet if Hughes could weld them together as a small group, then the United States could act decisively. The secretary could get the best advice about what was politically possible. And he would have superb Senate allies to ratify any treaties.

Hughes also needed a partner with the navy. He recruited Assistant Secretary of the Navy Theodore Roosevelt Jr. into the fold to help with the admirals. Hughes worked closely with the uniformed navy and pored over the details of their proposals and responses to his requests for data. Yet the secretary made sure that he—and his three other civilian delegates—kept control over political-military strategy.[57]

The Secretary of State and Arms Control Negotiations

The secretary of state's duty in leading arms control negotiations is excruciatingly difficult. The hardest part might be working with defense officials (and their experts) and the uniformed military to come up with negotiating proposals and objectives—with Congress looking over one's shoulder.

Ambassador Richard Burt relayed a telling story from a session in Moscow with Secretary Baker in the START (Strategic Arms Reduction Talks) negotiations with the Soviet Union. In 1990, Soviet foreign minister Eduard Shevardnadze was in a weakened position. He was struggling to persuade his military to accept U.S. demands for limiting the number of Backfire bombers. Baker had already achieved the agreed U.S. objective. But he kept pushing for a lower number. At a break in the talks, Baker said to Burt, "You think I'm pressing him too hard, don't you?" Burt replied, "Frankly, Mr. Secretary, I do. You've already achieved our objective, and Shevardnadze is clearly in a difficult spot." "You want to know why I'm doing it?" asked Baker. "Because I want to prove to those sons-of-bitches at the Defense Department that I could do even better than they expected." And he did.[58]

Developing a Proposal

Secretary Hughes turned to the navy's General Board, composed of senior admirals, for a disarmament proposal. Hughes asked for a "yardstick" for evaluating current naval strength and assessing reduction plans. The navy board resisted. They wanted to finish building the battleships under the 1916 Plan. When pressed, the navy board suggested a tonnage ratio for capital ships of one hundred for Britain and the United States, and fifty each for Japan, France, and Italy. In October, the board finally proposed a modest but inadequate reduction from prospective levels. So weeks away from the start of the conference, Hughes still did not have a proposal.

At one of the first preparatory meetings of the U.S. delegation, the shrewd and experienced Root asked about the likelihood that Congress would continue to appropriate funds for the navy's building program and for the fortification of the Philippines. "Senators Lodge and Underwood were emphatic in asserting there was no possibility."

Hughes shifted his method of operation with the navy board. Working with Admiral Robert Coontz (chief of naval operations), Roosevelt, and Coontz's assistant, Captain (later Rear Admiral) William Platt, Hughes posed questions to the board and asked for calculations. He asked for comparative strengths if a "stop now" agreement halted future construction. The result was one hundred each for Britain and the United States and sixty for Japan. Then Hughes asked the board to calculate the ratios for 1928, assuming the three countries completed their building programs. Great Britain would account for 106, the United States reached 100, and Japan 87—even if Congress continued full funding, which was a heroic assumption.

The secretary worked with his three colleagues through twelve long preparatory sessions to understand the problems, the navy's data, and possible solutions. They concluded that an agreement that would hold the United States' relative position was superior to both a fully funded arms race and far better than the building competition that Congress would pay for. A number of navy men agreed. The president signed off.

Hughes now had the fundamentals for the plan he announced on November 12. Roosevelt and Captain Pratt mimeographed Hughes's presentation themselves and locked up the stencil in Hughes's safe. They waited to make copies until the morning of Hughes's speech. Hughes had a bold proposal, a plan for surprise, an excellent reading of congressional and public opinion, and a conference organized to capitalize on his diplomatic strike.[59]

Negotiating over Battleships: The Five-Power Treaty

Hughes's blockbuster proposal, and the favorable British and Japanese statements the following week, launched an intensive phase of practical bargaining, as the United States had hoped. The heads of delegation operated as an unofficial steering committee. Two committees guided work on arms control and on Far Eastern and Pacific matters. Each committee had numerous subcommittees and working groups. Hughes held separate meetings with the president and the U.S. delegation every morning. Every afternoon, he hosted a press conference to keep public opinion informed; he needed civic interest to urge specific action. Hughes kept a watchful eye over more committee meetings than seemed possible and met privately with key players as well.[60]

Especially in multiparty negotiations involving numerous issues, the sheer friction of diplomacy can bog down processes. Frustrations build. People need to see a reason to alter established (and professionally safe) positions. Participants also need to sense movement—and the resolution of problems—if they are to remain engaged in devising solutions. Hughes kept up the pressure and set an example.

Japan's experts had established a standard of security through a capital ship ratio of 10:7 with the United States. Hughes had advocated 10:6. Admiral Kato, however, sensed a way around the problem. The navy minister told Balfour, who then spoke to Hughes, of his interest in preventing the fortification of Guam, the Philippines, and Hawaii, for which Japan would forgo coastal defense plans for Formosa (Taiwan), the Pescadores, and Amami Ōshima island. In addition, the Americans had erred in stating that the new battleship *Mutsu* was not complete; in fact, the *Mutsu* was well into sea trials. Having been paid for through a public subscription, including pennies from Japanese schoolchildren, Tokyo could not scrap the *Mutsu*. Kato was expanding the number of variables in play, creating more possibilities for a solution. He hinted that he could scrap an older ship to accommodate the U.S. target ratio.

Hughes had had some inkling of Japanese thinking because the United States had been intercepting and decoding Tokyo's cables. At first, Hughes rejected the nonfortification plan. But Lodge, who had pressed the navy's case for twenty-five years, said, "You're not giving up anything"; Congress would never agree to spend the vast sums to fortify Guam and the Philippines. Underwood and Root agreed. Hughes exempted Hawaii as a "defensive" location. As events turned out, Congress would not fortify the Philippines and Guam in the 1930s even when the treaty limits had expired and dangers had increased.

Admiral Coontz acknowledged that the U.S. experts had mistakenly listed the *Mutsu* as incomplete. Kato said he could not give up the pride of the Japanese navy and still defend the 60 percent ratio. Hughes wanted to avoid new construction but recognized that the United States would need to complete two new battleships, while scrapping two older ones, to hold modernization constant with Japan. But Britain posed a harder problem of adjustment. The new Super-*Hood* vessels it would build to offset the more modern U.S. and Japanese ships would each displace 49,000 tons. The British admirals said they could not reengineer the ships to match Hughes's 35,000-ton limit. Hughes pressed Balfour: How could an arms control conference defend building such new, gigantic battleships to the public? The naval rivalry would turn to larger ships. A shaken Balfour consulted with his admirals. They would not budge. But when Balfour returned, he told Hughes that the American proposal was "manifestly just" and "I am so impressed with the importance of avoiding further delay." He agreed to limit Britain's two new battleships to 35,000 British tons—which, because of methodology, the Americans calculated as amounting to 37,000 American tons.[61] Balfour won "Hughes' unbounded admiration," and the experience contributed to a close working relationship for the rest of the conference. As Alexander Hamilton had said years before, both countries thought in English. The "special relationship" of the twentieth century was built on shared attitudes about fairness to one another and reasoned argument as well as overlapping interests and outlooks.

On December 15, the Big Three announced an agreement on a 10:10:6 ratio, a ten-year naval holiday except for two new U.S. and British battleships to offset the *Mutsu*, and a status quo on fortifying naval bases "in the region of the Pacific." Buoyed by the success of his Irish negotiations, Lloyd George backed Balfour over the Admiralty.[62]

Now Hughes had to bring France and Italy on board. Rome readily agreed to a ratio of 1.75. But Paris objected zealously. France had not been building new capital ships, so in fact the ratio's tonnage exceeded the current French fleet. But France had not invested in the fleet because of the priorities in the Great War. Paris demanded a level higher than Japan's—whether or not it built new capital ships.

Hughes recognized that the problems with France stemmed in part from other causes. Paris despised being excluded from the Big Three. It choked at the idea of an American secretary of state dictating a naval ceiling to France. The linkage to Italy added further insult. France had an overseas colonial empire second only to Britain's; it asserted that Paris had a right to a commensurate fleet. To make matters even worse, the bottles of wine and champagne that the French delegations had carefully brought with them for comfort amidst America's Prohibition against alcohol had disappeared.

Assistant Secretary of the Navy Theodore Roosevelt Jr., who had been decorated for courageous military service in France during the Great War,[63] encountered a furious tirade from the "emotional, wide-eyed" French delegation. In effect, they said Harding and Hughes were traitors.

More fundamental, Premier Briand, who had returned to France, was troubled by signs of instability in Europe. He was an arms control skeptic. On December 16, Hughes contacted Briand directly, going over the heads of the French delegation in Washington. Hughes explained that "the attitude of France will determine the success or failure of these efforts to reduce the heavy burden of naval disarmament." The American public would not understand a French "non." Briand replied on December 18. France would agree to the limits on capital ships, which were "offensive" weapons. But the premier would not approve a reduction in lighter ships because they were "defensive." Briand had probably stretched as far as his Parliament could agree.[64]

Hughes had hoped that the countries would also apply the ratios to smaller cruisers, destroyers, submarines, and aircraft carriers. Yet technology and new military tactics were challenging the old order. The delegates could not agree whether submarines were "offensive" or "defensive" weapons or scouts for reconnaissance. Aircraft carriers were still experimental; the delegates managed to set overall tonnage limits, as well as a maximum displacement for individual flattops and a prohibition against carrier guns with over-eight-inch shells. Roosevelt and Admiral Coontz managed to gain approval for converting two battle cruisers into the aircraft carriers *Saratoga* and *Lexington*, which would serve vital roles in the early months of World War II.[65]

Unable to limit the number or overall tonnage of cruisers and destroyers, the delegates specified that those vessels could not exceed ten thousand tons or carry larger than eight-inch guns. Root proposed rules to protect civilians and noncombatants in submarine warfare, a nod to public cognizance of the bitter events leading to America's entry in the Great War. He also urged the prohibition of lethal gases. The delegates included both provisions in a separate treaty signed by the five naval powers (but never ratified by all, so never in force).[66]

Almost from the start of the conference, Hughes had commissioned a group of experts to draft the naval arms limitation treaty. He personally examined the drafts and sharpened the language with pencil edits. After completing all the detailed articles, the hosts prepared to print the English and French texts in parallel columns. The French ambassador was aghast. The Americans had planned to put the English column on the left, another "place of honor." The French threatened not to sign. Hughes was at the end of his tether when Senator Lodge remarked, "Mr. Secretary, what's the difference?" (Even the most indefatigable negotiators reach a point when they lose perspective.) On February 1, the Conference reconvened in Constitution Hall to bless the new Five-Power Naval Armaments Treaty.[67]

Negotiating Regional Security: The Four-Power Treaty

Hughes understood that the ultimate success of naval arms control in the Pacific depended on overcoming sources of regional security tensions. The debate on Senate ratification would focus on improvements in America's position in the Asia-Pacific. The secretary's principal foreign policy aim was to terminate the Anglo-Japanese treaty.

When Balfour had first met with Hughes before the conference opened, he raised the dispute over the treaty. Balfour explained that he was looking for a solution that would respect Japanese sensitivities, check Japanese behavior, and protect Australia and New Zealand. He offered a memorandum that in effect created a tripartite alliance.

Hughes assured Balfour that the United States wanted friendly relations with Tokyo. America's purpose was to direct Japan toward economic opportunity instead of military expansion. Hughes insisted that the old alliance must end and could not be revived in any way that bound the parties in time of war. He suggested adding France to avoid any suspicion that Britain and Japan would maintain the old partnership under a new guise. A Four-Party arrangement would look better to the Senate, too. Hughes added that any new agreement must avoid the word "alliance."

The secretary had already worked with his legal advisers to prepare a short, simple draft. By the start of December, after London and Tokyo had accepted the U.S. approach, Hughes sat down with British and Japanese proposals, as well as the U.S. draft, and composed a short treaty with four articles. The new ten-year arrangement pledged to respect one another's rights in the Pacific. In the event of controversies, the parties could convene a conference. In the event of aggression, the parties would consult with one another. And the British and Japanese would terminate their alliance. The new treaty did not reference sanctions or use of force.

Hughes tactfully suggested that Senator Lodge have the honor of presenting the new Four-Power treaty to the conference on December 10. The suspicious U.S. Congress scrutinized the text for guarantees and, finding none, imagined secret ones. Some senators alleged British or Japanese draftsmanship until Hughes revealed that he had been the author. Lodge labored to achieve the narrow two-thirds passage by the Senate, even with a reservation that the treaty involved "no commitment to armed force, no alliance, [and] no obligation to join any defense." Lodge persuaded a two-thirds majority of the connection of the Four-Power agreement to the other packet of treaties, and the Senate ratified all of them.[68]

More important for the future, the United States ended Britain's twenty-year-old partnership with Japan in the Far East and began to substitute practical, if not legal, Anglo-American cooperation. The new arrangement also opened the way for a greater calculation of common interests with Australia, Canada, and New Zealand in the Pacific.

Together, the Five-Party and Four-Party treaties established a security balance in the Pacific with much lower levels of naval arms expenditures. Japan also had the opportunity to fashion ties with the United States and the British Empire that reflected an adaptation to changed circumstances.

Negotiations Concerning China

Nevertheless, the key countries had fundamentally different perspectives on China. Japan wanted to dominate China's raw materials, monopolize its markets, and prevent Western intervention. Tokyo was especially sensitive to its prerogatives in Manchuria and the rights it believed it had fairly acquired after the Great War and earlier conflicts, including with Russia in 1904–05.

Britain knew that its influence in China was fading. London hoped to consolidate its overstretched position. It decided to build a powerful base in Singapore that could support Royal Navy ships sent from Europe in a time of crisis. London was comfortable with Open Door access. It hoped to "rehabilitate China"—so that China could preserve its independence and enhance stability. Britain could pursue such a "developmental" policy only with the help of the United States.

The United States wanted to preserve influence in China and constrain Japan. John Hay's Open Door principles continued to define U.S. interests. But America was wary of entanglements. Moreover, U.S. trade with Japan exceeded business with China. As in the days of Teddy Roosevelt, Washington hoped to dampen great power competition in Asia without committing to enforce security.

Political leaders in Japan in the early 1920s recognized that international cooperation might offer Japan a more effective route to achieve its security and economic objectives with minimum force. Japan's trade with the United States was growing more quickly than Tokyo's commerce with China. The Japanese did not want China to interfere with achieving a strategic security balance in the Pacific. Tokyo also recognized the risks of political-military entanglements in China south of the Great Wall and the costs of Chinese boycotts of Japanese goods. Japan's infamous "Twenty-One Demands" on China in 1915 had backfired. But international cooperation did not mean that Tokyo shared a conception of China's future with Washington and London. The Westerners wanted an independent, growing China to contribute to regional stability, balance, and prosperity, along with open access to build fortunes and save souls. Japan could benefit from China's territorial and administrative integrity, too, but Tokyo had claims for special interests.

The representatives from China wanted to regain full sovereignty, dignity for their country, and international respect. But even China's friends were loath to yield authority and full equality to a government struggling to function. The rising waves of China's "assertive nationalism" prompted worries that China would exploit Russia's weakness or act irresponsibly because of "patriotic grandstanding."

The Washington Conference produced two treaties and nine declarations concerning China. Root and Hughes took the lead in forging a Nine-Power Treaty that enshrined the U.S. Open Door principles in an international agreement. But the powerful language lacked provisions for enforcement. The treaty in effect provided guidelines for future policies toward China without referencing vested rights. Japan resisted translating the principles into pledges and obligations.

A separate treaty partially returned authority to China to set customs tariffs in order to strengthen the central government's source of revenues. Other agreements addressed China's control over post offices, railway practices, the stationing of foreign troops, the regulation of radio frequencies, and a commission to study the extraterritorial application of foreign laws in China.[69]

The Versailles Treaty had granted Tokyo control over Shantung Province as part of the spoils of victory over Germany. Wilson's concession on this point contributed to the Senate's defeat of the treaty. In China, frustration with the treaty in 1919 had sparked the May Fourth movement of youthful nationalist patriotism. Hughes knew that the Senate expected a Japanese reversal on Shantung. The Chinese refused to negotiate on the basis of Versailles and wanted to inject the controversy into the Washington Conference. Ambassador Shidehara signaled to Hughes that Japan would reach a satisfactory settlement if it could do so bilaterally with China.

The Chinese representatives insisted on the full restoration of Shantung without any strings. After the Americans and British finally persuaded the Chinese to meet the Japanese on December 1, the Chinese delegation failed to appear. An angry crowd of Chinese students who were opposed to direct negotiations with Japan had besieged the delegates in the bathroom of the Chinese legation on Massachusetts Avenue. Two State Department officials helped free their Chinese counterparts from the students' cordon.

After thirty-six meetings, assisted by the Americans and British, Japan agreed to restore China's full sovereignty over Shantung. Japan withdrew its troops. China received control over the critical Shantung Railroad, with Chinese payments to Japan of financial notes over time. Japan retained economic influence in the province, but China had achieved a significant gain. The two countries signed the treaty in Washington on February 4, 1922, with Hughes and Balfour looking on.

Japan was not willing to accommodate Chinese demands about Manchuria. Tokyo had gained rights in Port Arthur and Kwangtung Province, including over railroads, through the Treaty of Portsmouth after the Russo-Japanese War. The area had become a prosperous industrial base for Japan. Elihu Root observed that "Port Arthur had become a national symbol in Japan, and the Japanese indicated that they could not remain in the Conference if that subject were ever discussed." One might add that Britain showed no willingness to cede rights in Hong Kong and Kowloon. Tokyo viewed the three Manchurian provinces as a resource-rich buffer zone for Japan and Korea against China and Russia. It promised to withdraw Japanese troops from Russia and expand the roles of Chinese workers.[70] But Tokyo held its ground. On two more occasions in the twentieth century, international strife in this Northeast Asian hot spot would spark devastating wars. Even today, American strategists contending with threats from North Korea need to recognize the interlocking security dangers in this borderland of Korea, China, Japan, and Russia.

Historians debate what the Washington Conference achieved for China. In total, the scope of foreign commitments to support China and limit intrusion extended much further than before.[71] They might have provided a basis for a Nationalist China to consolidate authority, unify the country, and develop the economy. That success could have enabled a stronger Chinese government to demand even greater equality. But France blocked the convening of a customs conference that might have given China greater control over its primary source of revenue. The foreign powers could not agree on consolidating China's debt, much less providing it critical new loans. Foreign policy strategists often struggle to create the economic basis for security in troubled lands.

By the time Chiang Kai-shek's Kuomintang government extended its reach across much of China later in the decade, external circumstances had changed. The international diplomacy of Shidehara and his Japanese colleagues had produced neither economic gains nor constructive relations with China. The United States insulted Japan by banning all Japanese immigration on racial grounds. Chiang's Northern Expedition positioned China to test Japan's hold on Manchuria. The Soviets built ties with both the Kuomintang and the Chinese Communist Party, further worrying Tokyo. The collapse of world trade after 1929 and the Great Depression probably sealed the fate of Japan's liberal internationalists. In 1931, Japanese militants boldly seized Manchuria, ending the Japanese diplomacy of conciliation. The foreign, security, and economic policy assumptions upon which the Washington Conference had been based had broken down.[72]

Assessing the Washington Conference System

The Washington Conference adjourned on February 6, 1922. On February 11, Hughes and Shidehara signed a treaty ensuring free access for cable and radiotelegraphic traffic and personnel on Yap, the mid-Pacific island controlled by Japan under a League mandate. Another treaty allocated the former German cables across the Pacific to the United States, Britain, Japan, China, France, and Italy. Hughes had nimbly closed out the foreign policy topics that needed to accompany his venture in naval arms control.

Charles Evans Hughes and the United States had displayed world leadership through a new type of diplomacy, combining arms control with a complementary regional security system. The Washington Conference offered a positive alternative to the ill-fated League of Nations. Hughes had relied on a group of the principal powers, supplemented by a limited number of other interested states. The secretary had steered clear of entangling alliances. In fact, the United States managed to end the disfavored Anglo-Japanese pact.

The negotiations advanced Anglo-American understanding. Later success in working together obscures the historic American suspicions of a haughty and perfidious Britain. At the start of the century, both Germany and Britain had ignored America's maritime interests. As a continental seafaring country, the United States had long treasured the freedom of the seas. Rights of navigation were a geopolitical interest. Their defense had become a storied diplomatic tradition. By 1921, Germany's naval threat had vanished. After the Washington Conference, Britain abandoned its claim of naval dominance. This historic shift provided a foundation for a new U.S.-British partnership in the twentieth century. For its part, Britain made a down payment on an insurance policy that benefited it handsomely by the middle of the century.[73]

The historian Akira Iriye viewed the Washington Conference as the start of a new era of "economic foreign policy" after an age of imperialism in the Far East. The new U.S.-led system offered Japan and others a means to reconcile and promote interests after the breakdown of imperialist diplomacy. Indeed, the United States became Japan's biggest customer. Yet New York's influence over Tokyo never matched London's earlier financial power during the first decades of Japan's modernization. U.S. economic strategy depended on keeping America's markets open to Japan's trade. The highly protectionist Smoot-Hawley Tariff Act of 1930 choked off that possibility.

Iriye points out the risks posed to the Washington system by the exclusion of the Soviet Union and Germany, and the uncertain place of China. The Washington Conference's system offered prospects for China but did not prove flexible enough to cope with Chinese aspirations for full sovereignty. The Nationalist movement to unify China in the 1920s unsettled Japan's sense of security. In combination with the economic calamity in the West and the breakdown of international finance and trade, Japanese suspicions about China favored forces arguing for imperial security and economic self-sufficiency. The Japanese militarists prioritized the dominance of Manchuria and Mongolia over Shidehara's policy of developing mutually beneficial ties with China and the West. Tokyo's alternative to the Washington Conference system became the Great East Asia Co-Prosperity Sphere.[74]

Ernest May pointed out that the system of the Washington Conference was one of a number of piecemeal efforts to cope with regional conflicts after the Great War. Poland and the Soviet Union signed a treaty in 1921 giving space for the new Bolshevik regime to consolidate power. The Lausanne treaty of 1923 sought to circumscribe the breakdown of the Ottoman Empire. The Locarno treaties of 1925 tried to reestablish a regional peace in Europe. The Naval Arms Limitation Treaty connected the balance in Europe to the Pacific. Yet, as May notes, "[t]hese interlocking systems proved fragile." They depended, in various ways, on healthy economies, most of which traced their prosperity to the engine of American production, consumption, and finance. When that motor ground into reverse, the regional systems could not withstand the shocks.[75] Historians of our era may similarly ponder how the global financial crisis of 2008–09 and the pandemic of 2020 shook the precepts of the seventy-year-old system forged after World War II and extended after the Cold War.[76]

The Washington Conference also depended on Hughes's shrewd reading of the limitations Congress imposed on the president's diplomacy. Congress was of no mind to pay for a buildup of the navy. It had rejected the League. But Congress expected the executive to end the Anglo-Japanese alliance, limit Japan's incursions in China, and protect U.S. interests in territories mandated by the League. Secretary of State Hughes assembled a masterful package to promote U.S. interests with the resources available. He drew Senators Lodge and Underwood to his side to assist in negotiations with the navy, participate in the conference, and advocate ratification of the treaties. The secretary also kept public opinion active on his behalf. As a result, Hughes reestablished the president's leading role in U.S. foreign policy.

The Washington Conference constrained the hard power of the U.S. Navy. But the United States never even built enough ships to reach its ceilings under the treaty. Naval competition shifted to less regulated classes of ships. Admirals had to develop technological and tactical alternatives to relying on fixed and fortified forward bases. Chester Nimitz, who would command the Pacific fleet in World War II, wrote his Naval War College thesis in 1923 about the problems of not having fortifications. The U.S. Navy also had to innovate to overcome the limits on capital ships; it planned battle tactics around aircraft carriers. The U.S. Marines experimented with amphibious warfare to compensate for the lack of reliable bases across a vast ocean domain.[77]

In a December 1922 speech, Hughes offered his personal assessment of the diplomacy of the Washington Conference. The secretary traced the lineage of his work to a proposal by Alexander Hamilton to limit armament on the Great Lakes, one facet of the strategic peace that Hamilton tried to advance with Great Britain. Hughes then pointed to the Rush-Bagot agreement of 1817 as a step on the path toward new political-security arrangements in North America.

As for his recent effort, Hughes stressed the importance of working with "a small group of Powers dealing with problems in which they had common interests." The delegates focused on a single conference addressing both arms limits and Far Eastern questions, instead of separating topics with a preliminary meeting. The U.S. proposal led the way in suggesting proportionate sacrifices. And the delegates concentrated on "limited and practical aims." His comments recognized the interdependence among issues. The secretary wanted the United States to build up its navy with the treaty terms. American security required maintaining the country's relative military strength. The pragmatic Hughes knew how to close deals and get results.[78]

Presidents Calvin Coolidge and Herbert Hoover tried to pick up the naval arms control baton in 1927 and 1930, respectively. They wanted to extend the ratios to other types of ships and lengthen the ten-year term that the parties had set in 1922. Their diplomacy mistakenly focused on percentages instead of politics, power, and policies. By 1936, the experiment in naval arms control and security had run aground.[79]

Historians have highlighted various interpretations of the Washington Conference over the years, reflecting, not surprisingly, the experience of their times. Professor May explained that in the 1920s "the conference served as an example of how bold risk-taking could advance disarmament." In the 1930s, naval officers, sensitive to the rising dangers of war, stressed that military forces need to match potential threats. They argued against limits determined by domestic politics, budgetary constraints, and wishful thinking. In 1940, before Pearl Harbor, Harold and Margaret Sprout published *Toward a New Order of Sea Power*, the first serious history of the Washington Conference. The Sprouts respected Hughes's initiatives for peace and his ability to constrain an arms race, but they warned to pay close attention to military details, verify, and enforce agreements. They cautioned against illusory expectations for arms control.

Arms Control Lessons

In the early days of the Cold War, skeptics cited the Washington Conference as a warning against international schemes to control nuclear weapons. A bit later, political scientists examined the unintended technical effects on weaponry, with an eye toward fashioning rules that could contribute to nuclear stability. Other scholars understood how the technical arts of nuclear arms control related to domestic politics, conveying messages to foes, and security stability.[80]

With the end of the Cold War, researchers retrieved lessons about combining arms control with strategies to counter regional dangers.[81] Security strategists sought to rescue arms control from the technical nuclear experts. They argued for analyzing arms control as part of the wider political and security context. As Roger Dingman noted, arms control should be a process, not an event. Arms control, and associated treaties, are instruments in the diplomatic toolbox, but the tools must be used with others, in the cause of a larger blueprint.[82]

Advocates of hard power dislike the limits of arms control. Some Americans prefer the primacy of power and military means, especially when the U.S. military dominates all others. Yet diplomats have had to return to the tasks of controlling or even eliminating arms amidst regional dangers in Northeast Asia and the Middle East. Efforts to control nuclear and missile proliferation require integration with regional security diplomacy and the underlying dynamics of power and purpose. In that sense, the experience of the Washington Conference should inform today's efforts with North Korea and Northeast Asia, Iran and the wider Middle East, and South and East Asia. The United States needs to connect its arms control efforts to plans to address the underlying security disputes. As Ambassador Burt, the U.S. START negotiator, observed, arms control agreements do not change power balances, but they may codify understandings at lower and more stable levels.[83]

Finally, the Washington Naval Conference merits recognition as a checkpoint along the U.S. Navy's long journey to maritime primacy. Many accounts of American diplomacy during the country's first 130 years involve the freedom of the seas. Over America's subsequent hundred years, the navy became a primary instrument of the nation's foreign and security policy. As a maritime power, the command of the seas safeguards America's vital passages to Europe, Asia, and strategic gulfs and seas around the world. Future American diplomacy will depend on preserving the country's ability to project power and protect commerce on the oceans and across skies and space.

CHAPTER 9

Elihu Root

International Law

The United States and the World Court

In early September 1921, shortly before Secretary of State Charles Evans Hughes and former secretary Elihu Root worked together at the Washington Conference, they met to discuss another common interest: the creation of the new Permanent Court of International Justice, a "World Court."

In June, the secretary general of the new League of Nations had written Root to request nominations for judges to the new World Court.[1] Root had been deeply committed to the establishment of a World Court. As secretary of state in 1907, he had led the U.S. delegation to the Second Hague Conference, where he pushed a plan to strengthen the arbitration system created at the First Hague Conference, in 1899. One of his principal criticisms of President Wilson's Versailles Treaty was the president's inattention to the development of international law and lack of interest in creating an institution of international justice. In 1919, because the Senate had not yet acted on the Versailles Treaty, Root had declined an invitation to serve on an international commission to frame the new World Court. But in 1920, after the Senate rejected the treaty, Root joined nine other legal experts in The Hague to attend the postponed session to design the Court. Root hoped the United States would join the World Court at a later point.[2]

Yet when Root sat down with Hughes in September 1921, the two lawyer-diplomats let their pragmatic political judgment dominate their goal of building an international legal system. Root had already agreed to join Hughes's delegation to the upcoming conference on naval arms control and the Far East. Both men recognized that senators might object to any perceived U.S. cooperation with the League, even if that cooperation involved only nominations for judges on the World Court, which was generally popular in the United States. Distrust of the new administration could doom Senate ratification of any treaties that the United States might negotiate at the upcoming Washington Conference.[3] So after meeting with Hughes, Root persuaded his three colleagues to "reluctantly" decline the opportunity to nominate judges.

For the rest of his long life, until 1937, Root sought to resolve problems so that the United States could join the World Court. He never succeeded. Nevertheless, one of Root's three colleagues, John Bassett Moore, became a judge on the World Court in 1921. Charles Evans Hughes succeeded Moore in The Hague in 1928, serving almost two years before becoming chief justice of the U.S. Supreme Court in 1930. Former secretary of state and senator Frank Kellogg followed Hughes on the World Court, sitting until 1935. The United States eventually joined a revised International Court of Justice, part of the new United Nations, after World War II.

The Root-Hughes experience distills the venerable but vexed tradition of international law and American diplomacy. The U.S. lawyer-diplomats of the early twentieth century do not deserve George Kennan's jibe about a failed "legalistic-moralistic approach to international relations," because they were practical men who understood how to exercise national power. The lawyer-diplomats looked for a path between the old European balance of power diplomacy and Woodrow Wilson's dream to transform world politics through a new League of Nations.

The nineteenth- and twentieth-century lawyer-internationalists were pragmatic idealists who believed history evolved through stages of progress. They expected to work within an international order of sovereign states. They were skeptical that transnational ties, such as the international peace movement, would supplant the traditional order. They certainly were not utopians. The lawyer-diplomats were in fact institutionalists, as was Wilson. But the lawyers believed America could redirect the international order gradually through case-by-case experience. That was how they interpreted the history of the American experiment.

The American International Law Tradition

From the beginning, the United States presented its case to the world in legal terms. The opening of the Declaration of Independence appeals to "the Laws of Nature and of Nature's God" and acknowledges "decent respect to the opinions of mankind." The statement of facts in the Declaration stands as an indictment of King George III's despotism.

America's founding generation was in the vanguard of new ideas about foreign and trade relations. In 1758, the Swiss jurist Emer de Vattel had proposed arbitration among states as a reasonable method for resolving disputes that did not involve national "safety."[4] American diplomats would put this suggestion to practical use. In 1786, the Briton Jeremy Bentham (who invented the term "international") called for a Permanent Court of Judicature to resolve conflicts between nations. Bentham also advocated free commerce, arms reductions, and the emancipation of colonies—all ideas that the new Americans embraced.[5] The "Law of Nations" tradition, which had evolved from European practice, included concepts such as neutrality that were vital elements of early American foreign policy. These international legal principles became the first "multilateral norms."[6]

In 1824, Daniel Webster surveyed the vastly expanded connections among states and declared, "We have as clear an interest in international law, as individuals have in the laws of society." Webster, like the lawyer-diplomats who followed him, was searching for a practical yet imaginative path of international relations. On the one hand, Americans were uncomfortable viewing interstate relations as a condition of lawless anarchy, an outlook later associated with concepts of realpolitik. On the other, the violence of the revolutionary causes in Europe in the early nineteenth century left Americans wary of popular movements that might destroy both the system of states and individual liberties.[7]

Even that hard-headed master of balance of power politics, Teddy Roosevelt, understood that an international system based on the rule of law might be an outgrowth of the American experience. In his 1910 speech accepting the Nobel Peace Prize for his mediation of the Russo-Japanese War, the former president declared that the Hague Conference of 1899 had "framed a Magna Carta for the nations." He added, "I cannot help thinking that the Constitution of the United States, notably in the establishment of the Supreme Court and in the methods adopted for securing peace and good relations among and between different states, offers certain valuable analogies [looking to the goal of] a species of world federation."[8]

The practical experience of America's diplomacy contributed to the development of international law. The Jay Treaty of 1795 established the first international arbitration to resolve unsettled claims. The Rush-Bagot Treaty of 1817 limited naval arms on the Great Lakes, leading eventually to complete disarmament of the U.S.-Canada border in the Washington Treaty of 1871. That 1871 agreement also provided for the arbitration of U.S. claims against Britain from the destruction of American shipping by the *Alabama* and other Confederate raiders. The *Alabama* claims, arbitrated in Geneva, set a new precedent by involving foreign judges from neither of the disputing countries.[9]

The momentum behind international law and arbitration gained steam in the late nineteenth century, coincident with the rise of American power. In 1888, perhaps moved by the "Spirit of Geneva"—along with $15.5 million

the United States had won in the *Alabama* claims—Congress funded negotiations for general arbitration treaties with Britain and France.[10] Secretary
of state and former attorney general Richard Olney signed an arbitration
treaty with Britain in January 1897. But the Senate insisted on consenting
to each case of arbitration, in effect rejecting Olney's treaty. This experience
was the first of a long series of Senate refusals to authorize arbitrations without approving each case in advance.[11]

The First Hague Conference (1899)

The interest in international law and arbitration kept gaining adherents. In
1898, Czar Nicholas II invited countries from Europe, the Americas, and
Asia to a peace conference to discuss disarmament and new means to resolve
disputes. It appears that the czar's move was inspired in part by a novel
written by Bertha von Suttner, the president of the Austrian Peace Society.
Suttner's book, *Lay Down Your Arms*, had an effect on world public opinion
like that of *Uncle Tom's Cabin* a half century earlier. Suttner aroused outrage over the waste and injustice of war, and she offered the alternative of
international arbitration. In 1905, Suttner became the first woman to receive
the Nobel Peace Prize.[12]

The twenty-six nations that responded to the czar's invitation to meet at
The Hague in 1899 achieved few practical results, but they planted an allur-
ing idea about how international bodies could contribute to peace and rules
of civilized behavior. The countries were not meeting to settle terms after a
war. Instead, they experimented with ways to improve the inter-state order
to avoid the risks of war. The delegates included non-Europeans. And they
were joined by unofficial groups.[13]

The First Hague Conference managed to create the Permanent Court of
Arbitration, the first global body to resolve national disputes through legal
means. The new body was in reality a roster of approximately one hundred notables; states could voluntarily agree to ask them to serve on panels of arbitrators. Former U.S. president Benjamin Harrison was one of the
members.[14]

The United States Experiments with Arbitration

The Court of Arbitration did not receive a request for three years. But in
1902, President Teddy Roosevelt decided to spark the new mechanism into
life. He submitted an old financial claim against Mexico, which the United
States won. In 1903, Roosevelt aimed at a bigger target. Britain, Germany,
and Italy had shelled Venezuela in an effort to collect debts. TR persuaded

all four countries to rely on arbitration instead of a blockade. The final ruling required Venezuela to set aside 30 percent of customs revenues to pay its foreign debts and gave priority to the three claimants.[15]

TR's commitment to international arbitration had, however, distinct limits. In 1903, Roosevelt agreed reluctantly to arbitrate a dispute over the Alaskan-Canadian boundary along the coastal strip. The president wanted to help London save face. Yet Roosevelt also made clear to all parties that he expected the U.S. position to prevail. The president appointed Root, the U.S. secretary of war, as one of three "impartial" U.S. "jurists." The British lord chief justice broke with his two Canadian colleagues to side with the Americans, although the evidence suggests that he genuinely agreed with the U.S. legal argument.[16]

Building on the Hague Conference's procedures, Secretary of State John Hay negotiated arbitration treaties with eleven countries between 1904 and early 1905. Following an Anglo-French model, the U.S. treaties included exceptions for "vital interests, the independence, or the honor of two contracting states" or which "concern the interests of third parties." In effect, either country could rely on those terms to excuse any matter. But the U.S. Senate, wanting to preserve its judgment of whether an exception applied, insisted on approving each arbitration. TR refused to "[make] the treaties shams" and withdrew them.[17]

Elihu Root

Elihu Root succeeded Hay as secretary of state in July 1905. For the next three decades, Root served as the leader and principal problem solver for Americans seeking to fuse law with diplomacy. In the 1986 classic *The Wise Men*, Walter Isaacson and Evan Thomas extol the six men who became the "architects of the American Century" and the founders of the U.S. foreign policy establishment after World War II. Issacson and Thomas acknowledge that Elihu Root was in fact the "founding father of the line."[18]

Born in 1845, Root was the son of a professor of mathematics and science at Hamilton College in upstate New York, and he graduated from Hamilton in 1864. His forebears included a maternal grandfather who ordered the minutemen to fire on the redcoats at Concord Bridge in 1775. He served briefly in the New York militia during the Civil War after the army rejected the frail boy's enlistment at age seventeen. He earned his law degree in 1867 from New York University, where his mentor was a leader in the development of the new case method of legal education. Root's rise to legal prominence coincided with a legal reform movement. Legal education would professionalize legal practice and new bar associations would raise standards. Root played a role in the creation of both the Bar of the City of New York and the American Bar Association. He became the first president of the American Society of International Law in 1907, a post he held until 1924. In later years, Root became a cofounder of the Council on Foreign Relations and the Carnegie Endowment for International Peace.

Root insisted that he was not a political man, but he applied his reformist spirit to good governance and citizen service. In a commencement speech at Hamilton College in 1879, he told the graduates, "The evil which makes all other evils possible... is the withdrawal of good citizens from the exercise of the governmental duties and the indifference to political affairs." Root followed his own advice. He joined the Union League, the home of staunch and respectable Republicans. He taught Sunday school and participated in the YMCA. In 1883, President Chester Arthur, a friend from New York politics, made Root the U.S. attorney for the Southern District of New York (a part-time post in that era). Root took part in two New York State Constitutional Conventions. He gained the respect of party leaders, even as he worked to shift power from political machines to the rank-and-file party members. Root understood elected politicians. After Root had served in two cabinet posts, Senator Henry Cabot Lodge wrote that Root "has managed Congress better than any Cabinet Minister I have known."[19]

The late nineteenth century was an era of great corporate trial lawyers, and Root stood in the front rank. His biographer, the legal scholar Philip Jessup, wrote, "There was no lawyer practising at the American Bar in the 1890's who was more sought after than Elihu Root." Root's fee income ranged from $50,000 to $110,000 a year, astounding sums for late nineteenth-century America. He defended the conservative order and wanted to counter populist political impulses, but he also respected the need for reforms. He championed the causes of the downtrodden. In 1903, Root called for a revival of the "failed" post–Civil War Thirteenth, Fourteenth, and Fifteenth Amendments to achieve African-American citizenship, suffrage, and equality. He resisted measures against Japanese and Chinese immigrants. He worked to help Jews in Russia and Morocco. Whether the cause was reform or restraint, Root was a man who got things done.[20]

Root identified and inspired younger talent. Future secretary of state and of war Henry Stimson, a mentor to the post–World War II "Wise Men," venerated Root. Root's most promising youthful colleague turned out to be twenty-three-year-old Teddy Roosevelt, whom Root assisted in TR's first race for the New York Assembly in 1881. TR later wrote Andrew Carnegie that Root "is the ablest man I have ever met." When Roosevelt turned over the presidential reins to William Howard Taft in 1908, he urged his successor to rely on that "ever present help in time of trouble, the beloved Root."[21]

Root's contemporaries respected his incisive arguments, ingenious problem solving, irrepressible humor, genius at conciliation, and stern sense of duty. "Above all things," Root once concluded, "let us be just."[22]

A Lawyer as Secretary of War

Root's legal skills led to his first cabinet appointment, as secretary of war, in July 1899. The United States had just routed the Spanish forces in Cuba and the Philippines. According to Root, a McKinley associate called him over a new device, the telephone, to explain that the president wanted Root to become secretary of war. Root asked the caller to convey his deep appreciation to the president, but added that "it is quite absurd, I know nothing about war, I know nothing about the army." After a moment, the caller returned to the line to explain that "President McKinley directs me to say that he is not looking for any one who knows anything about the army; he has got to have a lawyer to direct the government of these Spanish islands, and you are the lawyer he wants." At age fifty-four, Root began his service in Washington.[23]

Root's immediate mission was to figure out what to do with Cuba, Puerto Rico, and the Philippines, where the U.S. Army was still waging a bloody struggle with Filipinos who wanted independence. As Root prepared to assume his new post, he wrote Attorney General John Griggs that his main effort seemed to be "the formation of a new law firm of 'Griggs and Root, legal advisors to the President, colonial business a specialty.' "[24] Within less than six months, Root had devised a colonial policy for the United States. The new secretary studied various precedents, especially British, but he settled on a new model that incorporated American legal traditions. Root was the first of a long line of Americans who experimented with "state building" during and after conflicts in foreign lands.

In his 1899 Annual Report as secretary of war, Root stated the guiding principles for the United States: "I assume...that it is our unquestioned duty to make the interests of the people over whom we assert sovereignty the first and controlling consideration in all legislation and administration which concerns them, and to give them, to the greatest possible extent, individual freedom, self-government in accordance with their capacity, just and equal laws, and opportunity for education, for profitable industry, and for development in civilization."[25]

Legal "State Building" in the Philippines

Root did not believe that the Filipinos were ready to govern themselves. He directed the policy of quelling the insurgency by force in a brutal conflict.

But Root rejected the idea that the U.S. military should rule the islands. He decided that the United States needed to provide a civil government that could operate at municipal, departmental, and central levels while respecting the rights of Filipinos. The experience of civil government, Root expected, would build the principles of citizenship—duties as well as rights—preparing the Philippines for eventual independence. At the same time, Root understood that the American public expected the colonial administration would respect certain individual rights, with the U.S. Bill of Rights serving as a rough guide.

President McKinley had enlisted William Howard Taft, a federal appellate judge, to lead the U.S. civilian commission in the Philippines. Root drafted the president's instructions to Taft and the commission. The instructions emphasized that the purpose of the government should not be for the satisfaction of U.S. views or theories, "but for the happiness, peace, and prosperity" of the Filipinos. Government measures should "conform to their customs, their habits, and even their prejudices, to the fullest extent consistent with the accomplishment of the indispensable requisites of just and effective government." The practical Root recognized that Americans needed to gain local support to govern civilly. The legal Root wanted to instruct the Filipinos on basic rights that were the foundation of effective self-government.

The Philippines commission eventually exported freedom of speech and the press, due process, protection of property, public trials—and all of the U.S. Bill of Rights except the rights to jury trials and to bear arms. Under Taft, Root, and their successors, the United States emphasized a "policy of attraction": good roads, sanitation, free public education, development projects, and responsive governance—but only limited representative government. English became the country's common language. After a 1901 decision by the U.S. Supreme Court determined the legal status of "insular" possessions such as the Philippines, Root offered a pithy summary: "[A]s near as I make out the Constitution follows the flag—but doesn't quite catch up with it."[26]

The American Congress and public turned out, however, to be reluctant colonialists. In 1916, Congress committed to Filipino independence. In 1934, Congress decided to grant the Philippines complete independence over ten years, a goal delayed until 1946 because of World War II. Root and Taft, who did not believe the Philippines was ready for full sovereignty, had nevertheless left a legacy of literacy, health, infrastructure, and legal rights and courts.[27]

Cuba

Root faced a different international legal problem with Cuba. By congressional resolution, the United States had pledged to secure Cuba's independence. Root concluded that the United States was acting "in trust for the people of Cuba," until Cubans could establish a representative government that could "maintain order and discharge international obligations." Root's plan provided for municipal elections of local governments that would establish a convention to draft a constitution and form a government.

Cuba's independence came with a catch, however. The Caribbean was the United States' southern flank and the pathway to the isthmian canal that the United States hoped to build. Latin American republicans had fallen afoul of domestic instabilities and foreign powers, especially when outsiders had claims for unpaid debts.

Having freed Cuba from Spain, the United States wanted to keep the island independent. Root recognized that Cuba would be a foreign country within the United States' external defense perimeter. The United States might need to intervene to prevent foreign intrusions. Root felt that U.S. policy needed a legal footing. The Monroe Doctrine, Root understood, was a statement of U.S. policy, not international law.

The peace treaty with Spain had transferred sovereignty over Cuba to the United States. By 1901, Congress was ready to grant Cuba independence, but subject to the Platt Amendment, largely drafted by Root. To be safe legally, the United States urged Cuba to incorporate the Platt language into its constitution, and then included the Platt Amendment authority in the 1903 U.S.-Cuban treaty recognizing the new, somewhat "independent and sovereign government."

The heart of the Platt Amendment granted the United States "the right to intervene for the preservation of Cuban independence, [and] the maintenance of a government adequate for the protection of life, liberty, and property." Root's pragmatic solution was no doubt offensive to Cubans who wanted full sovereignty. It was also, however, innovative in an era when big powers jostled to control more territories, not grant them independence.

Root explained in the 1930s, "You cannot understand the Platt Amendment unless you know something about the character of Kaiser Wilhelm the Second." The United States had watched Imperial Germany's global adventures warily; Washington did not want Berlin to seize a foothold in the Caribbean. Root had expected that America's grant of authority should be combined with restraint and used only "in a case of urgent necessity" or "anarchy." While Root was on a long trip to South America in 1906, a violent opposition movement deposed the Cuban government. President Roosevelt ordered U.S. forces to restore order, and the Americans stayed until 1909. When Root returned to Washington and learned of the events, he paced his office with folded arms, as if they contained "something" and complained, "They have killed my baby! They have killed my baby!"[28]

Root as Secretary of State

When Root became secretary of state after Hay's death in 1905, Roosevelt was in the midst of his balance of power mediations. Root proved to be an excellent, sometimes restraining, partner. He also recognized Latin America as a geographical interest of the United States and worked to overcome past tensions, especially with Mexico and Brazil. Root took a three-month trip to Latin America, the longest ever by a secretary of state. He conveyed a sincere interest in the region and avoided patronizing attitudes. In 1907, Root coined the phrase "Good Neighbor," a term that FDR would revive. Latin Americans recall Root as a U.S. secretary in the spirit of Henry Clay—and later James Blaine—who worked for hemispheric partnership.[29]

Secretary of State Root's principal interest was to seed world politics with legal norms and institutions. He understood human nature. He recounted that "diplomacy consisted chiefly of bargaining and largely cheating in the process." Root believed that "selfishness and greed," and the world's other evils, created the basis for conflict. "Self-preservation and self assertion… the struggle for existence" was a principal driver of national conduct. Yet Root also believed in "ethical, altruistic, [and] humane impulses" that could press toward ideals, principles, and standards.[30]

In the domestic sphere, Root reasoned, human frailties and strife had been gradually tempered and ordered through rules, institutions, and accepted impartial judicial procedures. The challenge for modern diplomacy, Root argued, was to promote the evolutionary process of building international rules and mediating institutions, beginning with arbitration and expanding to judicial bodies. He had a historical view of law and society that he would pursue patiently, both domestically and then internationally.

The Second Hague Conference (1907)

In 1907, the Second Hague Conference offered Root an opportunity to practice legal statecraft globally. Root wanted the conference to develop a general treaty listing a set of topics subject to compulsory arbitration. The old Court of Arbitration, created eight years earlier, arranged for ad hoc panels when countries agreed to arbitrate disputes; Root wanted to *require* countries to arbitrate specified matters.

Root also wanted to found an institution of international justice, a standing judicial body. Root believed that arbitration often crafted expedient solutions instead of decisions based on an emerging body of international legal principles. Countries with strong legal cases could seek, through a judicial institution, to avoid the "compromises" of arbitration.

Root's instructions expressed the historical experience that motivated his plan: "If there could be a tribunal which would pass upon questions between nations with the same impartial and impersonal judgment that the Supreme Court of the United States gives to questions arising between citizens of different states...nations would be much more ready to submit their controversies to its decision." The new court's charter would define the types of controversies it would consider. The judges, limited in number, would serve full-time and create a culture of judicial responsibility. In sum, Root hoped the 1907 conference would move a step beyond case-by-case dispute settlement in order to create a fledgling international judicial institution with regular sessions of full-time jurists.

The Germans thwarted Root's initiative to launch compulsory arbitration. The delegates also could not agree on how to select a limited number of judges for the new tribunal. This was the problem that Root eventually helped solve in 1920 for the new Permanent Court of International Justice.[31]

Practical Steps Toward International Law and a North American Vision

Root was not discouraged. On matters of international law, he took a long view and looked for practical ways to press forward. If the United States could not persuade a multilateral body to agree on a new arbitration treaty, it would work country by country. In 1908–09, Root negotiated twenty-five arbitration treaties, excepting matters of national honor, independence, or vital interests. Root relied on the model John Hay had tried earlier in the decade. This time, Root persuaded President Roosevelt to accept the Senate's insistence on passing on each case in advance.[32]

Root used international law to strengthen North American and hemispheric ties. He worked with Mexico to persuade Costa Rica, Guatemala, Honduras, Nicaragua, and Salvador to create the Central American Court of Justice, "the first international court in modern history to be endowed with continuing functions."[33]

Root also wanted to ease the way for Canada to draw closer to the United States while remaining loyal to London.[34] He used good faith negotiations and legal principles to address a range of binational disputes with Canada—from tariffs and border transit to boundaries, fisheries, and migratory birds.

The most sensitive topic was the arbitration of a dispute over access of New Englanders to Newfoundland's fisheries; the problem traced back to Franklin's Treaty of Paris in 1783. Root's larger aims with Canada bore fruit. During World War I, Canada began sending its own minister to Washington, starting a special relationship that served both countries' interests for the century to come. Root believed that North America could become a partnership of shared values and respect for the rule of law.[35]

International Law and National Honor

After leaving the State Department, Root served as a U.S. senator from New York from 1909 until 1915. One incident as a senator underscores Root's commitment to international law in diplomacy. The Hay-Pauncefote Treaty of 1901 had given the United States the exclusive right to construct and operate a transisthmian canal, but the treaty bound the United States to ensure equality of access. In 1912, an act of Congress declared that U.S. vessels engaged in the coastal trade would be exempt from tolls. London objected to this preferential treatment of U.S. ships. In 1913, Senator Root demanded that the United States either repeal the toll exemption or submit the dispute to international arbitration. He challenged the "revolting hypocrisy." The heart of Root's argument was that "size alone is not enough to make a country great. A country must be great in its ideals, it must be great-hearted; it must be noble; it must despise and reject all smallness and meanness; it must be faithful to its word; it must keep the faith of treaties; it must be faithful to its mission of civilization in order that it shall be truly great."

A year later, when the Senate debated repeal of the toll exemption, Root quoted Alexis de Tocqueville's observation that democracies were inferior in the conduct of foreign affairs because of the vagaries of public sentiment. Root denied Tocqueville's charge, but put his Senate colleagues to the test. The question they faced was not a petty matter of tolls, he told them. The question was one of national honor. Root believed that American democracy must put its diplomacy on a higher plane. "Our conscience must be our monitor."[36]

Skeptics will sneer at Root's high-minded rhetoric. But his aspirations have been a force in American diplomacy. Congress repealed the toll exemption—although the political compromise reserved the right for the future. I recall that decades later, in a meeting with Senator John McCain, Richard Armitage summarized the U.S. position on a difficult commitment: "Great countries keep their word," Armitage said. "The United States is a great country. It should keep its word."

In Cuba and the Philippines, Root demonstrated his willingness to wield U.S. power on behalf of American interests. He aspired, however, to act fairly.

Root once told James Brown Scott, a close legal colleague, "We must always be careful, and especially so in our relations with the smaller states, that we never propose a settlement which we would not be willing to accept if the situation were reversed." His attitude contrasts sharply with Thucydides's description of the Athenian directive to the Melians: "[Y]ou know as well as we do that right...is only in question between equals in power, while the strong do what they can and the weak suffer what they must." No doubt at times Root fell short of his own principle. Yet it has been a principle that many American diplomats weigh seriously—both to draw more countries to the side of the United States and to uphold national honor.[37]

In 1913, the Nobel Committee awarded the Peace Prize to Root for his contributions to arbitration, the defense of treaties, and peace in the Western Hemisphere. He was the second American, after his friend Roosevelt, to receive the honor. The Norwegians scheduled his speech for December 1914. A Great War intervened.[38]

World War I and the Future of International Law

Root, like everyone else, was surprised by the outbreak of war in 1914. From the start, he blamed Germany. He had watched the rise of the kaiser's militant spirit his whole adult life. By coincidence, Root was in Dresden with his ailing brother in 1870 when Prussia provoked war with France. Root observed the Prussian king, Otto von Bismarck, and Field Marshal Helmuth von Moltke arouse a crowd of one hundred thousand; he left with the forlorn hope that France would win.[39]

As secretary of war and of state, Root had encountered German belligerence all over the world: in Europe and Morocco, in the Caribbean, and across the Asia-Pacific. Germany stood out at The Hague as a loud opponent of Root's vision of international law. In the first week of August 1914, Root concluded that "[t]he real issue...is whether the German Emperor shall be the dominant power in Europe and this in its present stage can only be settled by force." The kaiser was "a big, destructive, intolerable bully...." Berlin's march through neutral Belgium displayed its utter contempt for international law.[40]

Roosevelt, Root, Lodge, and Taft all believed that the United States had a great stake in the European conflict. But they differed on the timing and means of action. Root argued for greater military preparedness, including universal military service. Yet Root did not speak out until February 1916 and did not openly advocate entering the war until February 1917. By temperament, Root was not the man to lead a charge against the president's policies.[41]

From the start of the war, Root's mind turned to the eventual settlement, including the reestablishment of a new political order in Europe. As one of Root's colleagues in the cause of arbitration observed, "the vogue... [was to] ridicule the two Hague conferences and the efforts made to avert the catastrophe... [but] the failure of the militarists has certainly been as decisive and infinitely more appalling."[42]

In his 1915 presidential address to the American Society of International Law, Root offered his assessment. The concerts of Europe, alliances, ententes, and balance of power had ultimately led to war. International legal institutions seemed the only way, consistent with the independence of nations and liberty of individuals, to avoid repeating the calamity. But those institutions needed powerful sanctions, which could only derive from clear, simple rules backed by strong public opinion. "When this war is ended... [t]he civilized world will have to determine whether what we call international law is to be continued as a mere code of etiquette or is to be a real body of laws imposing obligations much more definite and inevitable."[43]

By 1918, Root expanded the idea of international sanctions through an analogy to the distinction between civil and criminal law. The principles of international law, Root explained, had been based on the civil notion of contracts; violations were only matters between the contracting parties. But criminal law was a matter of keeping the peace for the community. Violent conflicts between nations must be regarded as concerns for all states because they involved the maintenance of order in the community of nations. Root offered a historical analogy to support the evolutionary nature of legal systems. "It used to be the fashion, when I was a boy (before the Civil War), to sneer at the Declaration of Independence as being 'a lot of buncombe.'" But the Declaration formulated the principles of freedom and American institutions upon which later generations built the edifice of a new legal and governmental order. Root's legal logic was that if a community could agree on the right theory of law, and then erect the appropriate implementing institutions, it could, over time, transform the society. Whenever you hear of American debates about "rules-based" international orders, think of Root.[44]

As a statesman in a democracy, Root recognized that the U.S. commitment to international law needed public backing. This caution led Root to break with former president Taft's plan for a League to Enforce Peace. Root welcomed the LEP's planks calling for arbitration, a Council of Conciliation, and periodic conferences to codify international law. But he would not sign on to a U.S. commitment to use force against a state that went to war with disregard for the rules. Root thought that the public would not back such a pledge; a promise that the United States would likely repudiate would be worse than no promise at all. The word of the United States had to be reliable, and Root knew that American pledges depended on the national democratic will. Better to proceed pragmatically—building experience and sustainable public support—than to rush to create an appealing but unreliable dream. On that point, Root and Wilson, both internationalists with visions, would differ.[45]

The Versailles Treaty and a Policy of "Reservations"

Root had fundamental disagreements with Wilson's diplomatic handiwork in Paris after the war. He believed Wilson had mistakenly connected the immediate demands of achieving peace terms with the longer-term challenge of building new international institutions. Root would have kept the creation of the League of Nations separate from any peacemaking. By fusing them, Root thought (with considerable wisdom) that the new League became a tool of the victors to perpetuate their power—a decision that would inevitably provoke antagonism from Germany and the other losers. Furthermore, Wilson's League was a quasi-legislative body with far-reaching authorities, and Root was shocked by Wilson's failure to consult the Senate seriously during the negotiations.

Nevertheless, Root's nature was to fix problems and not just complain about them. Root's Republican colleagues, especially in the Senate, looked to him to offer a program around which they could unite. The experience of a fractured party in 1912 was still fresh in their minds, and Republicans needed to hold together to win in 1920.

At first, Root recommended amendments to the Treaty of Versailles. After Wilson rejected them, Root devised a strategy of seeking reservations in a form that the president could reasonably accept. The reservations would offer interpretations of obscure articles and register objections to troublesome provisions. In particular, Root wanted to modify Wilson's overreach of executive authority to fit responsibilities that the Senate, and the American public, had accepted in the past or might reasonably be expected to assume in the future.

Article X of the League posed the hardest problem. It committed members to preserving the territorial integrity and political independence of all members. Root warned that the commitment, "[i]f perpetual…would be an attempt to preserve for all time unchanged the distribution of power and territory made in accordance with views and exigencies of the Allies in the present…affairs. It would necessarily be futile.…It would [also] be mischievous. Change and growth are the law of life, and no generation can impose its will in regard to the growth of nations and the distribution of power, upon succeeding generations."

Root recognized the need for stability during Europe's postwar turmoil. He believed that the United States had a duty to help provide order and assist in reconstruction. Therefore, Root suggested accepting Article X for now, but allowing any member to withdraw after five years. Wilson, in turn, further muddied the waters by arguing that Article X "is binding in conscience only, not in law." Given Root's commitment to incremental but serious commitments, he worried that Wilson's mixture of morality and law could undermine the whole project of international law.[46]

France posed a special problem. Germany's larger population and manufacturing base loomed over the future. Paris could no longer rely on Russia to check Berlin from the east. Root's solution was direct: "If it is necessary for the security of western Europe that we should go to the support...of France...let us agree to do that particular thing plainly, so that every man and woman in the country will understand the honorable obligation we are assuming. I am in favor of that."[47]

Root's reservations aimed to preserve the Treaty and the League against the attacks of the Senate "irreconcilables." In addition to protecting the United States' freedom to act under Article X and clarifying the procedure to withdraw from the League, the reservations protected the Monroe Doctrine. Root also urged a resolution pressing the president to negotiate stronger international arbitration and legal institutions. In March 1920, a Senate majority approved the treaty with reservations similar to Root's, but President Wilson called on Democratic senators to oppose the package, and it failed the two-thirds majority by seven votes.[48]

The World Court and Diplomacy Between the Wars

Undaunted, Root wrote a series of articles and speeches pointing to ways to revive America's international law tradition. He explored a pathway between a world of alliances and a proletariat internationalism that would destroy national governments. Root remained wary of the old model of alliances because he believed they committed governments to act inflexibly without exercising judgment. International legal institutions, in contrast, offered ways to resolve controversies unemotionally. In particular, Root believed that the world needed three mutually supportive institutions. One would provide an immediate conference when a conflict or misunderstanding threatened war. A second would facilitate arbitration of controversial but not-justiciable questions. And the third would consist of a permanent court that could judge questions of legal right between nations.[49]

Root was working on the third body, a World Court, in 1920–21 when he and Hughes agreed to defer action. In February 1923, building on their success with the Washington Conference treaties in the Senate, Hughes and Root persuaded President Harding to propose U.S. membership in the new Permanent Court of International Justice. The administration proposal included four reservations to give the United States the same rights as League members who belonged to the court. Senate opponents, egged on by the Hearst press, delayed action, although both the Republican and Democratic Conventions of 1924 supported the plan. In December 1924, President Calvin Coolidge tried again, adding a fifth reservation about advisory opinions. In January 1926, the Senate finally ratified, by a vote of 76 to 17, America's bid to join the World Court. But there was one more catch. The court's other members accepted four of the U.S. reservations. But the language of the fifth reservation would enable the United States to veto any request for an advisory opinion, and the League had not yet determined whether any other state had this authority. The matter seemed an odd one for drawing a red line: Advisory opinions were not binding, and the United States would be free to disregard them. President Coolidge, however, decided the court needed to accept all five Senate reservations without question and announced, in November 1926, that he would drop the effort.

The Final Try

Root's wife was fatally ill, and his own health was slipping. Yet in early 1929, at age eighty-three, Root agreed to take one more trip to Geneva to try to resolve the fifth reservation as part of a review of the court's charter of 1920. He came up with a lawyer's formula that would enable the United States to object to the hypothetical advisory request and quit the tribunal without any negative imputation if a majority did not agree. One biographer believes the "Root formula" would have satisfied the Senate in the summer of 1929, but President Hoover, while supportive, had other priorities. In 1931, at age eighty-six, Root presented the case for almost three hours to the Senate Foreign Relations Committee. The committee still hesitated to act. When Franklin Roosevelt became president, Root tried again. But the world had changed a great deal from the 1920s. Germany and Japan had withdrawn from the League. Adolf Hitler was shredding the Versailles Treaty. Hughes's naval disarmament effort was slipping away. A disillusioned American public wanted nothing to do with foreigners. FDR failed to recognize the strength of the rising opposition in the Senate. Root made a last-minute appeal to energize the White House, but it was too late. On January 29, 1935, the Senate passed the court protocol by a vote of 52 to 36, seven votes short of the necessary two-thirds.[50]

Root died in 1937 on the eve of his ninety-second birthday. He kept looking ahead until the end. Root's last legal opinion, sent to MIT dean Vannevar Bush (in December 1936), was about MIT's future patent policy. (Vannevar Bush, the subject of chapter 12, was the father of America's application of science to policy.)[51]

International Law as an Element of U.S. Diplomacy

Elihu Root, unlike some of his contemporaries, recognized the limits of international law. He knew that not all questions could be arbitrated. He realized that a threatening power, such as Imperial Germany, had to be resisted by force.[52] Root viewed law as just one component of diplomacy. In his dealings with Japan, China, Manchuria, and Korea, the idea of spheres of influence prevailed over assertions of rights. Yet Root appreciated that national interests required calculations looking beyond short-term objectives; Root drew on ideas from the U.S. experience to experiment with new types of American internationalism. The disaster of the Great War seemed to discredit Europe's balance of power alliances. Wilson's League turned out to be an overreach—a challenge to constitutional authorities and an endless entanglement in foreign strife. International law, in contrast, could evolve with civilization's progress and public opinion.

The breakdown of global order in the 1930s dashed the progressive hopes of international law. Nazi Germany, fascist Italy, Imperial Japan, and the Communist Soviet Union portended a new age of violence and danger.

After World War II, the victorious Allies created a new United Nations and an International Court of Justice, but the Cold War froze the development of both. The principal lawyer-diplomats among the post–World War II generation steered toward a balance of power standoff with the Soviet bloc. They reflected a shift in U.S. thinking about law—toward legal realism. Nevertheless, the post–World War II leaders' defense of freedom, and development of economic and political rules among allies and partners, created new opportunities for international law and institutions.

Debating Root's Legacy

In 2006, a century after Root cofounded the American Society of International Law, the Society convened a session to debate "The Legacy of Elihu Root." Professor Anne-Marie Slaughter argued that Root's experience showed "that a durable system of international law can be established only within a community of democracies." Professor Anthony Carty responded that in fact Root believed that democracies needed international law—including codification and compulsory adjudication by apolitical judges—"as a form of self-discipline." Professor Jonathan Zasloff countered that "the central problem with Root's vision of the international order" is that "[w]ithout some kind of enforced order, law cannot develop." Without that security, Zasloff maintained that Root's cause of building an international rule of law was doomed.[53] The debate continues.

Zasloff, a legal historian, traced Root's beliefs about international law to the classical ideology that characterized the leading American legal thinkers around the turn of the twentieth century. This classical view contended that law, whether domestic or international, derived its effectiveness from popular customs and social norms, not from coercive state power. Over time, societies developed consensual mechanisms to resolve disputes, moving in effect from violence to litigation. For Root, Zasloff argues, law was a neutral, apolitical source of order that could evolve over time and meet the needs of varying social groups.

One can see how Root applied this logic internationally. He thought that conflicts among nations stemming from misperceptions and irrationalities could be channeled gradually into legal processes through the development of institutions. Yet Root always struggled to define the sanction that other states would apply to lawbreakers. He seemed to believe that public opinion, a recognition of self-interest, and, on occasion, economic sanctions or even force would sustain the legal order. Zasloff concludes that this aspiration led Root and his disciples to avoid the question of making strategic commitments to ensure global stability.[54]

Zasloff has a point. But Root worked within the practical limits of American politics. He supported TR's efforts to sustain balances of power in Asia and Europe through mediation. Root probably concluded that the U.S. Congress and public would not sustain a balance of power diplomacy involving commitments of use of force. When the foreign threat was manifest, as in World War I, Root did not shrink from military action. He supported a security guarantee for France after World War I. But Root's principal interest remained the development of international law. He worked with the tools—and aspirations—of American internationalism available to him.

American diplomacy cannot rest on power politics alone. Nor should it. Among nations with similar goals and values, international law, institutions, and regimes can foster cooperation to advance common interests. Robert Keohane has been the intellectual leader of a body of writing about regimes that share information, lower the costs of joint action, build institutional capacity, encourage common outlooks, structure incentives, and offer ways to mediate or resolve disputes. Such regimes have provided the foundations for international trade, investment, and finance since World War II. They have extended into a widening set of other activities—health, the environment, oceans, law enforcement, terrorism, development, communications, energy, and transport, to name just a few.[55]

Root also recognized another tradition of American diplomacy: that the United States was born with a larger purpose. Root referred to the country's "conscience," natural rights, and concepts of liberty and justice. Succeeding generations spoke about fundamental freedoms and human rights. Joe Nye applied the term "soft power" to the idea of changing attitudes and political culture through the attractiveness of America's beliefs and aspirations.[56] Americans prize the country's sovereignty and freedom of action, and Congress will sharply reprimand any errant official who seems too willing to constrain national prerogatives.[57] At the same time, Americans retain a "decent respect to the opinions of mankind." And the country has taken pride in helping others, especially those who strive for democratic values.

Root once said, "Cynics are always nearsighted, and often the decisive facts lie beyond their range of vision." He is quoted as adding, "Men do not fail; they give up trying." American diplomacy has had to blend this optimistic spirit with Hamilton's cold calculation: "I have thought it my duty to exhibit things as they are, not as they ought to be."[58] Striking that balance is a challenge of pragmatism.

———◆———

CHAPTER 10

Cordell Hull

Reciprocal Trade

Trade and Foreign Policy

Cordell Hull devoted his life to a big idea: that trade could lessen the risks of conflicts, even wars, and that trade could build prosperity and foreign friendships for the United States. In his memoirs, America's longest-serving secretary of state (eleven years and nine months) recounted his most prolonged and consequential fight: "I was thirty-six years old when in my maiden address in Congress I pleaded for lower tariffs and fewer trade restrictions. I was sixty-two years old when in 1934 we finally won the fight to reduce them."[1] Hull's great achievement was the Reciprocal Trade Agreements Act of 1934.

Hull acknowledged that he had first advocated tariff cuts to lower the cost of living for working people and to fight trusts and monopolies. Furthermore, if other countries had a hard time selling to Americans, they would have less ability to buy U.S. exports.

"The year 1916," Hull explained, was "a milestone in my political thinking." He began to associate unhampered trade with peace, and tariffs, barriers, and unfair competition with war. Hull "realiz[ed] that many other factors were involved," but recognized that freer trade could boost the living standards of all countries and eliminate economic dissatisfactions and jealousies that fueled conflicts.[2] Especially after witnessing the economic breakdowns of the 1920s and '30s, Hull argued that economic misery led societies to "[fall] . . . easy prey to dictators."[3]

In 1936, Hull proudly aligned his foreign policy with Jefferson's "peace, commerce, and honest friendship with all nations, entangling alliances with none."[4] Hull, like Hughes and Root, sought a U.S. role in the international order without resorting to alliances. His solution was to rediscover the earlier American tradition of connecting trade with foreign policy.

Hull understood that America's graduation to economic powerhouse required it to assume new leadership responsibilities. In 1934, Hull recalled President Wilson's warnings about the international economy right after the Great War. Wilson—and Hull—explained that the United States had become Europe's creditor. Europeans could pay their debts only if they received new private credits, transferred gold, or sold goods to the United States. Wilson had explained that neither more loans nor gold payments were possible. Therefore, for Europeans to pay their debts and buy more from the United States, Americans needed to lower barriers to imports. Hull concluded that "[w]e have learned that a prohibitive protective tariff is a gun that recoils upon ourselves." In a homespun way, Hull explained that America's domestic economic recovery in the 1930s could not succeed without an accompanying restoration of worldwide commerce. America would pay a price—one way or another—for economic failures overseas.[5]

Cordell Hull and Alfred Thayer Mahan, the naval strategist, may seem like unlikely policy companions. Yet they both shared an ardent belief that America's trade policy had to be fused with its foreign policy. They also understood that the United States could add to national influence by expanding American commerce. The exchange needed to be two-way; both men argued that protectionism was a defensive withdrawal for societies that had lost competitive spirit. America needed access to foreign ports and the highways of the sea, not colonies and defensive ramparts.

The Constitution and Politics

The connections between foreign and trade policies may seem obvious. But the two U.S. endeavors have often gone their own ways because the Constitution and domestic politics have made it difficult to unite them.

Article I of the U.S. Constitution grants the Congress authority "To regulate Commerce with foreign nations" and "To lay and collect Taxes, Duties, Imposts, and Excises." When James Madison wrote *Federalist 10* to explain how the varied American interests would thrash out differences under the new Constitution, he used trade policy as an example. From the start, Congress waged many of its fiercest domestic political battles over trade. Those clashes reflected the economic interests of different regions and producers. When presidents and their cabinets intruded on the congressional prerogative, they emerged bloodied.

Trade Policies: Revenue, Restriction, and Reciprocity

In a recent comprehensive history of U.S. trade policy, Douglas Irwin divides the American experience into three eras, each marked by Congress's principal purpose: revenue; restriction; and reciprocity. Alexander Hamilton, as we saw in the first chapter, relied almost totally on customs revenues to fund the new government and pay interest on its huge debts. In 1792, the new federal government devoted 87 percent of its revenues just to interest payments. Receipts did not cover current expenditures and interest until 1796. Hamilton advocated the neutrality policy to maintain trade in order to pay the bills.[6]

Hamilton wanted to encourage domestic manufacturing, but he preferred bounties (subsidies) to protection. As Irwin explains, Hamilton recognized that tariffs raised prices for users of goods, sheltered inefficient procedures, and encouraged smuggling. As Gerard Clarfield wrote, "The key word in Hamilton's conception was *encouragement*, not *protection*" for manufacturers.[7]

From 1790 until 1860, tariffs provided about 90 percent of federal governmental income. Congress's trade policy was the result of its revenue (and debt) policy, as determined by battles among regions and producers. The new manufacturers sought protection, and farmers generally wanted lower prices and more opportunities to export. The average tariff on dutiable imports rose from about 20 percent in the early 1800s to about 25 percent in 1820 and then to 62 percent after imposition of the Tariff Act of 1828. This Tariff of Abominations, as the name suggests, was the result of unrestrained electoral maneuvering for political favors. Much of the country reacted with dismay; South Carolina threatened to secede. The subsequent Compromise of 1833 set tariffs on a downward path to an average of about 20 percent in 1859.[8]

The Civil War ushered in Irwin's next era, one of restrictive trade policy. The North's desperate need for revenue to fight the war led Congress to raise the average dutiable tariff to about 50 percent, where it remained for most of the rest of the century. The secession of Southern states—and then the long political domination of Republicans—favored the North's industrial interests. The United States had also wracked up huge debts during the war, along with obligations to veterans. Between 1860 and 1913, customs revenues still provided about half of the government's revenues.[9]

The United States, supported by the navy, pushed to open other countries' markets, most prominently in Japan during the 1850s. But the first glimmers of revived thinking about tariffs and trade as matters of international policy appear late in the nineteenth century. James Blaine, twice secretary of state, observed that Latin Americans sold commodities to the United States but bought manufactures from Europe. Blaine wanted to bargain to lower Latin American trade barriers through reciprocity agreements. To do so, he needed Congress to grant the executive branch flexibility to adjust tariff rates through negotiation. Because almost 90 percent of Latin America's commodity exports already entered the United States without duties, the McKinley Tariff Act of 1890 granted the president authority to impose penalties and retaliatory duties on countries that would not grant concessions to U.S. exporters. In 1891–92, Blaine negotiated ten agreements, eight of which were with Latin American countries. When the Democrats took control of Congress, they reversed the policy in 1894 and abrogated the deals in favor of uniform duties. The angry Latins retaliated with higher duties on American goods. Reciprocity was not off to a good start.[10]

U.S. trade policy blundered into foreign policy, intentionally or not. In 1876, the United States had given Hawaii preferential access for sales of sugar. When the 1890 McKinley tariff eliminated all duties on sugar, Hawaii's economy plummeted; the powerful community of American planters in the islands overthrew Hawaii's monarch in 1893 and sought U.S. annexation.

The United States reimposed sugar duties in 1894, while restoring Hawaii's preference. This time, the Cuban economy, which had benefited from zero duties, tumbled. The turmoil fed the Cuban insurgency, which in turn prompted a Spanish crackdown. These events contributed to the Spanish-American War of 1898.[11]

At the turn of the twentieth century, the world economy appeared to be in the midst of a major shift. As Europe's empires expanded in Asia and Africa, Americans feared exclusion from raw materials and markets. These conditions contributed to John Hay's Open Door policy for China. Germany and France offered trade concessions to others but discriminated against the United States. The British Empire initiated an internal system of preferences. In 1897, Canada, historically an important market for the United States, began discriminating against the United States in favor of London.[12]

Trade politics at home were shifting as well. Traditionally, U.S. farmers—especially of cotton, grains, and some meats—were exporters. By the turn of the century, big U.S. manufacturers also became net exporters. Andrew Carnegie asserted that the Congress could eliminate the tariff on iron and steel without harming domestic production. But smaller producers disagreed, and the Republican Party remained devoted to protection.[13]

Nevertheless, President McKinley, the proud author of the Tariff Act of 1890, signaled the changing times. He wanted to push the new idea of reciprocity. In a speech to the Pan-American Exposition in Buffalo on September 5, 1901, McKinley declared that economic "isolation is no longer possible or desirable.... Reciprocity treaties are in harmony with the spirit of the times, measures of retaliation are not." A day later, a deranged man assassinated the president.[14]

Neither Teddy Roosevelt nor William Howard Taft took much interest in tariff policy. The party politics were too dangerous. Taft worked to enact a reciprocity agreement with Canada, but Canadians rejected the accord in a 1911 referendum.

Trade and Progressivism

Progressives pressed the trade debate in new directions. Ida Tarbell, the muckraking journalist, decried the higher prices paid by working families. She argued that tariffs imposed an unfair tax burden on consumers of shoes, clothes, food, and coal. Her colorful accounts revealed that tariffs were the grease of corrupt politics and special interests. Others contended that tariff distortions promoted monopolies and industrial concentration.[15]

Woodrow Wilson coupled the Progressives' call for fairness and reformed government with Democratic Southerners' long opposition to high tariffs. Tariffs and antitrust topped the new president's priorities in 1913. The Underwood-Simmons bill cut the average tariff on dutiable imports from about 40 to 27 percent and shifted many products to the duty-free list. Much more important for the future, the states had just ratified the Sixteenth Amendment authorizing an income tax; at the direction of the chairman of the Ways and Means Committee, Congressman Cordell Hull of Tennessee drafted provisions for a federal income tax to be added to the tariff bill. Hull handled the floor debate, too. In 1913, tariffs still provided 45 percent of federal revenues. With the new income tax, the customs' share fell to 28 percent of total revenues by 1916. After World War I, tariffs accounted for less than 5 percent of federal receipts. Without Hull's income tax, the United States would have struggled to pay for World War I. Furthermore, a lower portion of revenue from tariffs opened the possibility that the United States could cut tariffs without risking unacceptable fiscal costs.[16]

World War I and Versailles

The World War, like the Napoleonic Wars a century before, underscored the ties between America's trade—and U.S. economic influence—with conflicts overseas. The war also transformed the country's international economic standing. The volume of U.S. exports nearly doubled between 1914 and 1926, and sales of finished manufactured goods nearly tripled. Imports fell. The United States shifted from being an international debtor to a huge creditor.[17]

The second and third of Wilson's Fourteen Points of January 1918 sought freedom of the seas and "the removal, so far as possible, of all economic barriers and the establishment of an equality of trade conditions among all the nations." Yet as Wilson left for Europe in December, he said he was "not much interested in the economic subjects." He added, "I do not think that international trade questions will be directly broached by the Peace Conference."[18] Hull, in contrast, had urged the creation of "a permanent international trade congress" to "promote fair and friendly trade relations" and avoid dangers of "economic warfare."[19]

Wilson's fight with Republican senators over the League carried over to tariff policy. One of Senator Lodge's fourteen reservations avowed Congress's power to regulate trade. By 1920, the average dutiable tariff had fallen to 16 percent, the lowest level since 1792.[20]

The 1920s

The Federal Reserve tightened money in 1920, prompting a severe deflation and economic downturn. The new Republican Congress turned to its favorite remedy: higher tariffs. Their tariff bill of 1922, at 130 pages, restored higher, protectionist rates. Nevertheless, the legislation planted seeds of innovation that would grow in importance over time. Working with Secretary of State Charles Evans Hughes, Congress enacted a flexible tariff provision intended to permit the president to adjust rates based on expert calculations of "costs of production." The concept proved unworkable, but granting the executive authority over tariffs (which the Supreme Court upheld in 1928) offered an important precedent.[21]

Equally important, the 1922 Act endorsed the principle of *unconditional* most favored nation (MFN) treatment.[22] The United States had been applying its MFN obligation conditionally. A conditional MFN withheld the new trade concession unless the MFN partner offered a new (although perhaps different type of) benefit. This process led to complex national tariff schedules riddled with discrimination and exceptions.

Under unconditional MFN, all partners would gain without further action. Few people noticed the change because the United States was not negotiating many deals, and, in any event, Congress was raising tariffs, not lowering them. Cordell Hull, however, recognized the potential power of the tool. The application of unconditional MFN would not only lower barriers, but also create an international system that expanded the liberalizing gains from one-on-one bargains.[23]

While most of the U.S. economy boomed in the 1920s, farmers struggled. The agricultural Midwest demanded price supports and, failing to get them, called for tariff protection. But American agriculture, a net exporter, depended on worldwide prices determined by global supply and demand.

Domestic protection would have had little effect on worldwide farm prices for U.S. exports.

Smoot-Hawley: Protectionism and Breakdown

Nevertheless, the domestic political pressure to protect farmers led to Congress's greatest blow to the fragile international economy: the Smoot-Hawley bill, the Tariff Act of 1930. The Smoot-Hawley bill listed individual duties for almost 3,300 products. Everyone joined in a frenzy of the "old and worst type of logrolling." As the crash of October 1929 spread into a banking crisis and Depression, Congress added even higher protections. Though 1,028 economists urged President Hoover to reject the bill, he signed it anyway on June 17, 1930.[24]

The vast majority of economists now believe that monetary and financial factors were the primary causes of the depth and length of the Great Depression. The Smoot-Hawley bill compounded the problems and triggered a wave of higher tariffs and reprisals.[25]

The average U.S. tariff peaked at 59.1 percent in 1932. Between 1929 and 1932, the value of U.S. exports and imports plummeted nearly 70 percent; in terms of quantities, exports dropped 49 percent and imports fell 40 percent.[26]

Congress never seriously considered the foreign reaction to its bill. Some sixty-five foreign governments protested, but Senator Reed Smoot of Utah and his colleagues countered that "the tariff is a domestic matter.... No foreign country has a right to interfere." Professor Irwin's review of the *Congressional Record* found twenty pages of debate about the tariff on tomatoes, but few words on the international effects of Congress's handiwork.[27]

Canada, which accounted for about 20 percent of U.S. exports in 1929, retaliated firmly. By February 1932, Britain had retreated from its traditional policy of free trade to an imperial economic bloc. In 1930, 70 percent of U.S. exports to Britain had entered duty-free; that figure fell to 20 percent by the end of 1931. Together, Canada and Britain had taken more than one-third of U.S. exports.

Other countries established economic blocs based on preferences, special licenses, exchange controls, quotas, and even barter. Germany looked to southeast Europe and then national economic autarky. Japan created its Great East Asia Co-Prosperity Sphere. The volume of world trade fell 26 percent between 1929 and 1933. By the end of the 1930s, world trade had still not reached the level of 1929.[28]

The United States spent much of the 1940s and '50s attempting to clear away the international economic debris of the Tariff Act of 1930.

Smoot-Hawley had left a bad taste with the American public, but U.S. trade policy remained adrift until 1933, when Cordell Hull had his opportunity to reshape trade history.

Cordell Hull's Political Education

Hull had traveled a long road to the secretary of state's office. At age seventeen, he began the journey with a horse and buggy that he drove for a governor campaigning for election.[29] Hull's family's relative prosperity in east-central Tennessee, near the Kentucky border, enabled him to gain a reasonable education, including a year at Cumberland Law School. The young man practiced a little law, but Hull decided early on that his true avocation was politics. He entered the state legislature at twenty-one, serving two terms before captaining a company of volunteers in the Spanish-American War. Hull never saw action but learned to curse like a trooper, a trait that later surprised people accustomed to his demeanor as a chivalrous, reserved, and somewhat stiff Southern gentleman.

Hull moved on to become a state circuit judge, whose journeys around ten counties furthered his political education. Hull's political mentor, a congressman who favored low tariffs, retired in 1906, clearing Hull's path to Congress. He served in the House from 1906 to 1930, except for one defeat in the Republican landslide of 1920. Hull used the brief interregnum to build ties and a wider reputation as a diligent chairman of the Democratic National Committee. Hull had moved to the powerful Ways and Means Committee in 1911 and built a respected expertise on tariff and tax matters. In 1930, Hull won a Senate seat.

Hull had learned political patience. He was, wrote one biographer, "above all else, a survivor." He would need those traits in the trials ahead of him.[30]

In the early 1920s, while chairing the DNC, Hull reached out to Franklin Roosevelt. FDR's role as the Democratic vice presidential candidate in 1920 advanced his influence, though his polio (contracted in 1921) shadowed his political prospects. Hull recognized that the Democratic party was a coalition, reflecting regional interests, and judged FDR as a future leader. From 1926 on, the two professional politicians met regularly to compare perspectives. FDR backed Hull as a Southern nominee for vice president with Al Smith, the 1928 presidential candidate from New York.[31]

When FDR's turn came to run for president in 1932, Hull was an early backer. The Tennessean offered high-profile Southern support and served as Roosevelt's man in the Senate. James Farley, FDR's campaign manager, summarized Hull's worth to Roosevelt when the candidate most needed him: There was "no man in America, who, in the days when we needed a friend, rendered more efficient and loyal service in the preconvention days." Hull had built a mighty store of political capital.[32]

Hull Becomes Secretary of State

Following Roosevelt's landslide election, the new president had to assemble a cabinet that reflected his political coalition. Hull was never a personal friend of FDR's, but they respected each other's political acumen. And Hull was near the ideological center of the party.[33]

After twelve years out of office, and Wilson's highly personalized foreign policy for eight years before that, the Democratic stable lacked international expertise. Hull's congressional ties, standing as a Southern leader, political loyalty, and familiarity with international issues through tariff policy made him a reasonable candidate. Hull looked the part, too. In any event, FDR's first priority would be the economic crisis at home. And the supremely confident new president probably felt that he would run foreign policy anyway.

Hull did not jump at the offer to become secretary of state. In fact, he waited almost four weeks. Hull had health problems—he had just learned that he had tuberculosis—but his hesitation seems to have stemmed from doubts about New Deal economic policies, slights from some of FDR's "Brain Trusters," and uncertainty about the new president's commitment on the tariff issue. Hull's economic philosophy emphasized individualism, especially the interests of farmers and small businesspeople, not collectives, controls, and cartels. FDR had designated one of the Brain Trusters, Professor Raymond Moley, as an assistant secretary of state, and Hull learned that Moley had already schemed against his prospective secretary. After personal assurances by Roosevelt that Hull would be able to set policy at the State Department, Hull signed on.[34]

Hull was to learn the hard way that FDR liked to keep his options open and manipulated those around him without hesitation. But Hull had assets, too. He was generally acknowledged to be the most popular person in the administration after the president. He was the administration's leading Southerner and Wilsonian, and Southern seniority in Congress gave the region powerful chairmanships. Hull had earned political friends at the White House as well. And he knew how to wait for the right moment to destroy a foe who created a vulnerability.

The London Economic Conference of 1933

Hull's first major international outing was to the London Economic Conference in June 1933. British prime minister Ramsey MacDonald had visited

FDR that April to persuade the Americans to take part. MacDonald wanted to restore economic confidence—through actions on debt, currencies and monetary policies, and trade. But the London meeting turned out to be a disaster.

Hull headed the U.S. delegation, but not the American planning, which Moley sought to dominate. The delegation was an odd mixture of personalities, ideologically split and personally contentious. Hull never asserted leadership. He hoped that the president would send Congress tariff reform legislation before the adjournment of Congress's emergency session so that Hull could propose an international negotiation to cut trade barriers. The president abandoned the proposed bill while Hull was on his way to London.

Hull was left without any authority other than to talk generally about trade. The deeply depressed secretary almost resigned. The dispute within the administration was about much more than legislative priorities. The Brain Trusters of the early New Deal had a fundamental conflict with the Wilsonian internationalists. Raymond Moley, Rex Tugwell, and other FDR advisers had designed the National Industrial Recovery Act and Agricultural Adjustment Act to cut domestic production in order to raise prices. They wanted to use production controls, planning, and cartels to reduce supplies. Imports would undermine their plans for organized, "fair competition" within a self-sufficient national economy. In fact, the economy's problems were the tight money supply and lack of demand, not overproduction. But the New Dealers had the wind in their political sails.

To make matters worse, Moley decided to come to London to "save" the conference by negotiating a monetary stabilization agreement. During six days at sea, Moley savaged Hull in the press. Moley then ignored Hull and worked with the British and French on a vague monetary declaration—which FDR disavowed. The president issued a populist statement blasting the whole idea of the financial conference. His priority, the president bluntly made clear, was to cure economic ills at home. The conference erupted in outrage. MacDonald wanted to shut it down—blaming American obstructionism and FDR's gaffes.

An article the following year in *Current History* reported that Hull was "[b]eaten to a pulp in London." Yet the secretary returned with three accomplishments. He managed to hold off MacDonald's adjournment for a few weeks while dissipating some of the hostility against the United States. Hull even got the conference to record an American resolution about reducing the world's tariffs. Most important, Moley's public sniping led Hull to send the president what was in effect an ultimatum. By the end of the summer, Moley was gone.[35]

Trade Strategies

During Hull's first year, he had gained an insight about how to design his trade-negotiating strategy. He had decided that it was folly to try to repeal Smoot-Hawley or even cut tariff rates directly. In his memoirs, the former secretary recalled that originally he "had been in favor of any action or agreement that would lower tariff barriers, whether the agreement was multilateral, signed by many or all nations, whether it was regional, embracing only a few, or whether it was bilateral, embracing only two." But before and after the London conference, Hull had concluded that no country, especially the United States, would embrace a worthwhile multilateral deal. Therefore, Hull and his associates "agreed that we should try to secure the enactment of the next best method of reducing trade barriers, that is by bilateral trade agreements which embraced the most-favored-nation policy in its unconditional form—meaning a policy of nondiscrimination and equality of treatment."[36]

When I became the U.S. trade representative in 2001, I recalled Hull's experience. A number of countries had thwarted an effort to launch a new round of trade liberalization in the World Trade Organization. Many capitals were reluctant to devise new rules for sectors—such as services and technologies—that had become huge in the world economy. In the spirit of Hull, we decided on a strategy of "competitive liberalization"—negotiating multilaterally, regionally, and bilaterally. If some countries were not ready or willing, the United States would proceed with those that were. We used bilateral agreements, just as Hull had done, to build international backing for rules that we could then apply in regional and even global deals.

The Reciprocal Trade Agreements Act of 1934

In late 1933, President Roosevelt remained hesitant about pushing legislation to authorize trade negotiations. But the secretary carefully courted cabinet colleagues and members of Congress. He prepared a draft bill of only three pages.

On February 28, 1934, the president met with Hull, the vice president, key Democratic senators and congressmen, the secretary of agriculture, and a few others to consider Hull's draft. The proposal was bold—and simple. The bill would give the executive the authority, through trade agreements, to reduce (or increase) import duties from the Smoot-Hawley rates by up to 50 percent. The tariff reductions would apply to all countries with U.S. agreements by including unconditional MFN clauses. The agreements did not require approval by Congress.[37]

By structuring the bill as a congressional grant of authority to the president, the administration bypassed the Senate's role in ratifying treaties. Moreover, Congress would only need to vote once because the new power was not limited by time. This was a sweeping reach for authority.

FDR gave the go-ahead. The Democratic chairman of the Ways and Means Committee introduced the bill and moved quickly. The committee took just five days to hear from seventeen witnesses, seven of whom spoke for the administration. In moving the bill to the floor, the chairman made one significant change: The new authority would lapse after three years unless Congress extended it.[38] Unlike the New Deal shifts of congressional authority to domestic agencies, Congress wanted to keep a close watch over trade policy. For the next eighty years, presidents would have to battle with Congresses to retain trade-negotiating authority. Over time, Congress insisted on adding limits, procedures, and eventually, votes on agreements.

On March 29, 1934, the House passed the Reciprocal Trade Agreements Act (RTAA) by a vote of 274 to 111. Former Republican secretary of state Henry Stimson endorsed the bill in a national radio address. On June 4, the RTAA passed the Senate by a vote of 57 to 33.[39]

As Professor Irwin relates in his study of U.S. trade policy, "[T]he RTAA has long attracted the interest of scholars studying regime change." He concludes that "the RTAA was a pragmatic response to the circumstances of the day."[40] It eased the politics of support for trade. The face of the trade issue shifted from how high to set tariffs to agreements to lower barriers. Congressional reviews of RTAA authority would now include consumer and export interests. In addition, the executive branch had the ability to factor national security and foreign policy considerations into tariff and trade policy.

Fighting to Implement the RTAA

Secretary Hull had three years in which to establish a record of results. Within three months, the State Department announced a trade agreement with Cuba and an intention to negotiate with eleven other countries.[41]

Yet Hull first had to best another bureaucratic foe, a much more dangerous one than Moley. As Hull explained in his memoirs, "The greatest threat to the trade agreements program came not from foreign countries, not from Republicans, not from certain manufacturers or growers, but from within the Roosevelt Administration itself, in the person of George N. Peek."[42]

Peek had a base of political support in the agricultural community. He became the first administrator of the Agricultural Adjustment Act, and his plan was to buy farm surpluses and dump them overseas to prop up prices at home. After Agricultural Secretary Henry Wallace pushed Peek out,

Roosevelt appointed Peek as special adviser in foreign trade. Peek established a bureaucratic position of power outside the State Department by taking charge of the new Export-Import Bank. Hull later wrote that, "If Mr. Roosevelt had hit me between the eyes with a sledgehammer, he could not have stunned me more than by this appointment."[43]

Peek assumed that the new trade world of high tariffs, quotas, and controls on foreign exchange was not going to change. His answer was managed trade, which he would direct through "a coordinated and integrated government trading house." To get around controls on foreign exchange, Peek would make bilateral barter deals of commodities. His Ex-Im Bank could finance and even subsidize the sales.[44]

Peek considered Hull's plans to rebuild an open international trading system based on equality of treatment to be "unilateral economic disarmament." Peek wanted economic controls and state-directed trade; Hull thought governments should stop directing trade flows so that private firms and farmers could compete openly based on price and quality. Hull was trying to build a system of international rules in which both Americans and foreigners could thrive; Peek wanted to do individual deals on terms set by governments. Hull's program would take time to work because private parties would have to seize the opportunities after his agreements reduced barriers. Peek had the advantage of promising Roosevelt politically pleasing announcements of sales in the short run, and most politicians live in the short run.[45]

The struggle between Hull and Peek dominated U.S. trade policy in 1934 and early 1935, stalling the State Department's implementation of the new RTAA. Hull worked quietly to build support among his cabinet colleagues. Peek, in turn, began a campaign for the final showdown, but his eye for the best battleground failed him.

Peek pressed to trade cotton for wines from the new Nazi regime in Germany. The Germans wanted to acquire U.S. commodities without spending hard currency, liberalizing their trade policy, or ending discrimination against U.S. bondholders. The State Department pointed out the conflicts between U.S. trade and financial policies and that Germany was seeking to hoard cash to buy munitions. Peek announced a deal with Berlin anyway in November 1934. Germany would pay only 25 percent of the cotton's price in dollars; it financed the rest with German marks that the Americans could only use to buy German products.

Peek's transaction also drew Brazil into the struggle. Hull had been negotiating an agreement with Brazil to pull it away from a discriminatory transaction with Britain and toward U.S. policy. But Brazil was a major cotton exporter; if the United States practiced discriminatory, bilateral barter deals, Brazil would need to retaliate and rely on political trade transactions as well.

President Roosevelt approved Peek's barter with Germany on December 12 while Hull was away. Hull's deputy managed to get the White House to hold off announcing the decision while he informed the secretary. Although the State Department considered FDR's decision irreversible, an ailing Hull swung into action. He sent an ardent "personal and confidential" message explaining how the deal contradicted a trade policy that was both a cornerstone of U.S. foreign policy and the best way to open foreign markets for U.S. farmers. Germany had reneged on its debts and discriminated against Americans. This transaction would end up costing either the Ex-Im Bank or American farmers so that Berlin could save funds to purchase "immense armament." In effect, it subsidized German goods that would compete unfairly with American products. And Peek's project would be "almost certain to engender extreme resentment among that large section of American public which is violently opposed to the Hitler regime."

I suspect that few of FDR's colleagues had the leverage, arguments, and political cunning to best the president. Hull did. Roosevelt withdrew his approval.[46] Peek's influence waned. By the end of 1935, he was gone.

Negotiating Trade Agreements

Hull could now concentrate on his trade agreements. He proceeded expeditiously but carefully, always alert to domestic political risks. Hull's agreements sought to reduce barriers and expand the acceptance of the principles of nondiscrimination and unconditional MFN while holding public support. The United States was not negotiating free trade agreements. The negotiators looked to two principles: first, reduce barriers to products from the chief supplier, so as to limit the benefits to other MFN partners not part of the deal; and second, try to concentrate on goods that would not agitate opposition at home. Hull conceded privately that "only five percent [of his program was] economic, while the other 95 percent [was] more or less political or psychological."[47]

The United States closed its second agreement, with Brazil, in early 1935. The U.S. manganese producers objected, and Hull worried about sustaining political support.[48] But closer economic ties with Brazil paid dividends during World War II, when Brazil's friendship helped Washington secure the backing of the Americas, a base for an air bridge to Europe, and Brazilian combat troops.

The Senate's rejection of U.S. membership in the World Court in early 1935 shook Hull's confidence. Roosevelt and Hull hesitated over an agreement with Belgium and Luxembourg, but each man decided they could accept the deal if the other took responsibility. Ultimately, facing a political deadline in Belgium, the State Department's under secretary signed off while Hull was away and the president unavailable.[49]

The first deals gave the United States momentum. The State Department decided to offer countries unconditional MFN treatment for six months if they started negotiations with the United States for their own deals. By the end of 1936, the United States had signed additional agreements, in chronological order, with Haiti, Sweden, Colombia, Canada, Honduras, the Netherlands and its colonies, Switzerland, Nicaragua, Guatemala, France and its colonies, Finland, and Costa Rica.[50]

The Canadian accord was especially important. The two countries had "the largest two-way trade relationship in the world." But U.S. exports had plunged from almost $1 billion in 1929 to just over $210 million in 1933. Both Canadian Conservatives and Liberals backed the negotiation through a change of governments. Prime Minister William Lyon Mackenzie King, long a friend of North American unity, shared Hull's vision of creating an open international economic system. Hull also appreciated that a Canadian accord might help him draw London and the British Empire into his emerging trade order.[51]

As the negotiations with Canada reached the final stage, Hull seemed to shrink from the scene. He was ill and needed rest. But he also hesitated because of political risks. This time FDR reviewed the list of proposed concessions personally and scratched out a few affecting interests in important states. But once he was ready to move, FDR did so enthusiastically, calling back Hull from North Carolina for a big White House signing with Prime Minister King and the whole U.S. cabinet as witnesses on November 15, 1935. The president wanted his political secretary of state to sign and assume responsibility. To his credit, Hull stepped up to counter the critics. Two-way trade between the North American partners surged back.

War Looms: Trade with Britain and Japan

Hull's top priority was now the United Kingdom. Britain was a significant economy: During the 1920s, Britain, with Canada, had been one of the two top markets for U.S. exports. But Hull's real aim was to win London over to his plan for open international trade. Hull later wrote "that our trade agreements program could not be considered complete until the United Kingdom was inserted as the apex of the arch." For centuries, Britain reigned as the world's great trading power, first as a mercantilist with colonies ringing the globe and then as a free trader. But the Depression had forced London to become a leader of a system based on a sterling bloc, protectionism, imperial preferences, and even bilateral balancing and barter deals. The aftermath of the Great War had left both countries frustrated with one another; the war debt issue remained a bleeding wound, too. In the mid-1930s, the image of Britain for many Americans was that of a snobbish commercial rival that resented America's rise, held on to old imperial privileges, and failed to pay its obligations—not that of Winston Churchill leading a plucky democracy that stood up to fascists. Hull and others conveniently overlooked that British protectionism, a response to Smoot-Hawley, was less virulent than America's.[52]

From early 1936 until late 1938, London and Washington jousted over trade. Canada sought to help; protectionist Australia resisted. Prime Minister Neville Chamberlain and Foreign Secretary Anthony Eden could see the foreign policy benefits of closer trade ties, but the Treasury and Board of Trade struggled with economic realities. Britain had limited concessions to offer and few ways to compensate the Dominions that would lose trade to the United States. Island Britain saw clouds of war and needed to hold on to the unity of Empire and sources of supply. London could not rely on America because of Washington's restrictive neutrality laws. Hull might recognize "that the world is on fire" and that like-minded states needed to "stand together in some practical program," but America demanded commercial negotiations, not political terms.[53]

Prime Minister Chamberlain eventually concluded that an agreement "would help to educate American opinion to act more and more with us, and because I felt sure it would frighten the totalitarians. Coming at this moment, it looks like an answer to the Berlin-Rome axis." But the U.S. recession of 1937–38 further complicated a difficult negotiation. The Munich Agreement of September 1938 appeared to break the last impasse, and the United Kingdom, Canada, and the United States signed a modest deal on November 17, 1938. Within a year, Britain would be at war and would adopt severe controls on trade. After 1941, America's trade with Britain would depend on a new Lend-Lease program. Hull's successors would have to contend later with London's imperial preferences and discriminatory trade.[54]

Hull was a natural opponent of the dictatorships. His political inclinations were reinforced by his antagonism to Germany's and Italy's autarkic economic and trade policies. Yet his economic logic blinded him to the fascists' true motivations. Hull kept believing that "economic rehabilitation" would offer people "contentment" through trade rather than militarism.[55]

Japan presented a more complex case. Tokyo would have benefited from the open trading system Hull was advocating. The two economies were largely complementary. In 1935, U.S. ambassador Joseph Grew explained the causes of Japan's expansionary tendencies. Its industrialization, overpopulation, and lack of natural resources prompted the country to look outward.

But the world's markets were closing to Japan. Grew pointed out clinically that Washington could preserve its interests in the Far East for a generation or two by either "granting larger markets and opportunities" or by going to war. Grew's logic might have been expected to appeal to Hull's belief that economic expansion offered an alternative to military aggression. But Hull worried that Japan's inexpensive exports—especially of textiles, apparel, and other consumer goods—would subvert the New Deal's efforts to boost prices. He feared the domestic political reaction would doom the RTAA. So Hull urged Japan to impose "voluntary" limits on its exports. He claimed that the administration was "carrying all the load possible" to reopen international trade. Japan would have to look elsewhere for markets. It did.[56]

The Congressional Politics of Renewing the RTAA

Hull always kept his eye on the politics of renewing the RTAA. Roosevelt, buoyed by his smashing electoral victory in 1936, wanted Congress to make the negotiating authority permanent in 1937. Hull suspected, more accurately, that Congress would want to keep the renewal on a leash. The administration's rationale for the program also began to shift from boosting economic recovery to countering threats to peace. The House passed a three-year renewal by a vote of 285 to 101; the Senate leadership had to fend off potentially crippling amendments, but then supported the bill by a vote of 58 to 24.[57]

By late 1939, Hull was arguing that his trade principles and agreements should "serve as a cornerstone around which nations could rebuild commerce on liberal lines when the war ended." He decried "suicidal economic nationalism, with its Hawley-Smoot embargoes." Roosevelt liked Hull's speech. The long-suffering Hull recorded, "For the first time since 1933, I had the feeling the President was really behind me on trade agreements."[58] Some American producers, however, were fighting renewal. The political opposition in Congress increased, even though a poll showed that the modest percentage of people who knew about the RTAA were strongly supportive. The House passed a renewal in February 1940 by a vote of 218–168. A Senate amendment requiring Senate approval of future agreements (by a two-thirds vote) was defeated by only three votes, and final Senate passage carried by only five votes.[59]

The Republican Party platform of 1940 signaled a shift toward criticizing how the administration ran the RTAA program rather than advocating its termination. Nevertheless, during the renewal debate of 1943, a rash of amendments threatened to disable the RTAA authority. A compromise extended RTAA for only two years, so that Congress could reflect on postwar trade arrangements at the appropriate time. Nevertheless, the report of the Ways and Means Committee, the House body with primary jurisdiction and expertise, reflected a significant shift from a decade before. "The broad question," the report noted, was not about particular tariff rates, "but whether we as a Congress shall establish a policy which will best serve the major interests of the country as a whole and authorize a practical procedure for making such a policy effective."[60]

Agreements and Trade Policy Principles

Hull plowed ahead with more trade agreements before and after the United States entered World War II. He added Turkey, Venezuela, Argentina, Peru, Uruguay, Mexico, Iran, and Iceland to the roster, along with supplementary accords for a few countries. All told, Hull concluded thirty-one agreements with twenty-eight countries. Irwin suggests that by 1939 the average U.S. tariff on dutiable imports was just below pre–Smoot-Hawley levels. With lower barriers to U.S. producers, exports to countries with agreements rose 63 percent between 1934–35 and 1938–39. (Exports to countries without agreements rose only 32 percent.) According to Irwin, "the United States seemed to be making progress in regaining its share of world trade."[61]

More important, Hull's innovation revolutionized America's trade policy. Future presidents had the option to develop a comprehensive trade policy that they could align with foreign and economic policy objectives. The domestic political foundations for Hull's new approach were—and have remained—shaky. Congress is jealous of its prerogatives. Some members recognize the benefits of permitting the executive to frame national policies and negotiate agreements with individual countries, regions, or globally. But all members know that their politics are local and so are their economic interests.

Smoot-Hawley, the Tariff Act of 1930, lies uncomfortably dormant on the statute books. President Trump has demonstrated that a self-proclaimed "tariff man" can use executive authority to raise barriers to trade instead of lowering them.

Assessing Hull

As the United States edged closer to World War II, Hull did not grow into an effective partner for FDR. The president felt his way as he sought to awaken the American public to the danger. Hull's single-minded focus on trade missed the mark. As a war president, FDR controlled all the reins of foreign policy. Hull seemed a peripheral figure. He was worn out. Hull did note that the "political line-up followed the economic line-up." The United States did not fight with any country that had one of Hull's trade agreements, and almost all joined the United States against the Axis powers.[62]

Near the war's end, however, as the country faced the challenge of devising a postwar world, Hull resumed a modest role. He resisted Secretary of the Treasury Henry Morgenthau's plan to "pastoralize" Germany. Hull contributed to U.S. planning for the new United Nations. And he knew that postwar reconstruction depended on a revival and even expansion of his trade program.[63]

At times, Hull was idealistic and naïve, but he could also be practical and successful. Senator Paul Douglas, who taught economics at the University of Chicago and fought as a marine in the Pacific, offered his assessment in 1972: "[T]he shrewd, hillbilly free trader and militia captain from the Tennessee mountains outwitted for beneficent ends the high-priced protectionist lawyers and lobbyists of Pittsburgh and Wall Street." Douglas could have added that Hull had bested some New Dealers and even, at times, FDR.[64]

Hull's immediate successors recognized the importance of his legacy. Dean Acheson, who carried Hull's work forward, beginning with the RTAA's renewal in 1945, explained in his 1969 memoir that Hull's liberalization of international trade was "the prerequisite to peace and economic development" in the decades after World War II. He wrote that "Mr. Hull's amazing success..., a reversal of a hundred years of American policy, was due both to his stubborn persistence and to his great authority in the House of Representatives and the Senate."[65] As we will see in the next chapter, Hull's principal disciple was Will Clayton. In December 1944, the newly appointed Clayton wrote to the just-retired Hull: "The first letter I sign on State Department stationery is to you....I want to assure you that your foreign policy is so thoroughly ingrained in my system that I shall always work and fight for it."[66]

Hull's legacy is Congress's delegation of authority to the president to negotiate trade agreements in order to lower barriers and establish principles for an open trading system. Furthermore, Hull recognized that America's trading relations are a key element of U.S. foreign policy, even if he overestimated the power of trade to prevent conflicts. Hull also understood that Congress shifted authority to the executive grudgingly; protectionist pulls of local interests require U.S. trade negotiators to manage political coalitions at home carefully while striking deals internationally. Hull's imagination, pragmatic politics, and negotiations contributed a consequential idea to American diplomacy.

IV

A NEW ORDER OF AMERICAN ALLIANCES

CHAPTER 11

◆

Architects of the American Alliance System

The Turn

Over the course of three years, from 1947 to 1949, a small group of American statesmen led a dramatic shift in U.S. relations with the world: They devised an international economic and security system that has lasted through today. In doing so, these leaders created a new sense of national involvement in—and even responsibility for—problems around the globe.

This startling turn in American diplomacy was not the product of a strategic plan. But it was pragmatic, bold, and responsive to a Soviet threat to the United States and a free world. The United States officials had to deal with four pressing problems: the security of Greece and Turkey; the economic and political recovery of Europe; the future of Germany; and transatlantic security. A fifth challenge then presented itself: how to win the support of the U.S. Congress and the American public.

1945: Winning the Peace

World War II had shaken U.S. confidence in the security of a Fortress America bordered by vast oceans. The surprise attack on Pearl Harbor, with its pictures of smoking hulks of battleships, left an indelible image of national vulnerability. Strategic bombers could threaten people far beyond the frontlines. Newsreels of the atomic bomb's mushroom cloud warned of uncontrolled devastation. World War II had cost Americans 522,000 lives—among some 50 million dead around the world. Another world war would seem to threaten human existence.[1]

When General George C. Marshall, chief of staff of the U.S. Army, prepared his final report to the secretary of war in 1945, he reflected on the challenges ahead. "For probably the last time in the history of warfare those former ocean distances were a vital factor in our defense," Marshall cautioned. The general recalled that when he had analyzed prospective dangers in 1940, he could not even imagine fighting in Burmese jungles or across Pacific atolls just a few years later. Hemispheric security would no longer suffice. "We are now concerned with the peace of the entire world."[2]

Marshall was not alone. As Professor Mel Leffler, an eminent historian of the early Cold War, points out, in 1945 the Brookings Institution assembled international experts to study America's future security. Like Marshall, the study's authors focused on the need to prevent any power or coalition from controlling the vast Eurasian land mass, ranging from Europe to the Asia-Pacific. They reflected the rise of geopolitical thinking in the United States, which combined assessments of potential power—such as resources, people, industrial capacity, and technology—with an appreciation of geography, transport, and critical locations. The most important space on the map was the landmass of Eurasia, which Nazi Germany and Imperial Japan had almost conquered.

Once the military planners of the Joint Chiefs of Staff (JCS) discovered the Brookings paper, they classified it. Like the Brookings paper, the JCS concluded that the United States needed partners across the oceans. "The potential strength of the Old World [Europe, Asia, and Africa]," the JCS review concluded, "in terms of manpower and in terms of war-making capacity is enormously greater than that of [the Western Hemisphere]." The United States needed access to, and friendships with, the "rimlands" of Eurasia.[3]

Yet in late 1945, the American people felt that their sons and daughters had accomplished their mission. Americans should come home. The United States had no tradition of a large peacetime military establishment. In May 1945, the U.S. military had approximately 12.3 million people under arms; by mid-1946, demobilization had slashed U.S. forces to 1.5 million.[4] In October 1945, just 7 percent of Americans considered foreign problems to be vitally important.[5]

FDR had been a masterful war leader, but he had only vague plans for winning the peace. Like many skillful politicians, he prized flexibility and was cautious in committing to courses of action. He believed his personal charm could overcome most difficulties. The president seemed to expect that the "Four Policemen"—the United States, the Soviet Union, Great Britain, and the Republic of China—would secure postwar global cooperation while leading in their respective regions. The new United Nations might be both a symbol of and vehicle for international collective action. Although FDR's last weeks in April 1945 were darkened by brutal Soviet actions in Poland and Romania, the president held on to the hope of postwar cooperation with the USSR. So did his key military chiefs, including Generals Marshall and Dwight Eisenhower.

The American leaders knew of Stalin's and the Soviets' cruelty and secrecy. But they also were aware that the vast battles of 1941 to 1945 had devastated the USSR. Soviet air and naval power did not remotely approach that of the United States, which had waged victorious war across oceans on two fronts, not one. In any event, FDR (and Eisenhower) expected U.S. forces to be out of Europe within two years; working with the Soviets looked like a practical necessity for stabilizing the war-torn continent.[6]

Harry Truman

Roosevelt's successor, President Harry Truman of Missouri, would have been unaware of FDR's postwar plans even had they existed. In his eighty-two days as vice president, Truman had had only two meetings with FDR.[7]

Truman had served in the U.S. Senate since 1934 as a strong New Deal Democrat—of a Midwestern, more conservative stripe. His virtuoso biographer, David McCullough, wrote that "in manner, background, language, age, choice of companions, he bore no resemblance to the ardent young New Dealers." Truman was a prodigious reader of history and a skilled politician, from the grassroots to the folkways of Congress. He valued his friends and avoided making enemies when in Congress.[8]

During World War I, Truman had served as a captain in the U.S. field artillery in France. Rising out of the Pendergast political machine in Kansas City, Truman jumped from presiding judge of Jackson County (an administrative post) and middle America's assemblies—the Masons, Eagles, Elks, American Legion, and Veterans of Foreign Wars, plus even the International Acquaintance League—to the U.S. Senate in 1934. His Senate service included the Military Affairs Committee and the Military Subcommittee of the Appropriations Committee. During World War II, Truman chaired the Senate Special Committee to Investigate the National Defense Program.[9]

The "Truman committee" gave its chair experience with the vast expansion of the U.S. military. He also got to know many of the military's leaders firsthand. Senator Truman recognized General Marshall as exceptional. In an interview with the *Kansas City Star*, Senator Truman saluted the general as "the greatest living American"—even while FDR was still alive.[10]

Truman followed a dominating, heroic personality who had steadied the nation's spirit during a cataclysmic economic depression, led the country to victory around the world, and passed into martyrdom in the war's final weeks. Many Americans had little recollection of any other leader. No other American—and certainly not Harry Truman—could fill that void.

The United States in 1945–46

In late 1945 and into 1946, the new president focused on the home front, not on remaking the world. With the surrender of Japan in August 1945, Truman promptly canceled Lend-Lease aid to Britain, the Soviet Union, and France. He announced a twenty-one-point progressive economic plan for America.[11]

No one knew what to expect from the economy. In striking contrast to the rest of the world, factories in the United States—the industrial arsenal of democracy—were firing on all cylinders. Production in 1945 doubled that of 1939. Workers' incomes had doubled, too. Unemployment was at 2 percent. But people recalled the slump of 1920–21 after World War I and the terrible times of the Great Depression. Though late 1945 was a time of peerless prosperity, the country expected a hard landing.[12]

Truman was overwhelmed by the problems of an economy in transition from war to peace. The unmet needs from both wartime restrictions and the dire 1930s fed powerful demands. Shortages, especially of housing for young families, fueled inflation. Labor strikes created a sense of strife; waves of work outages rippled through every sector. At one point, more than one million workers walked off their jobs. Democratic prospects for the midterm elections in November 1946 sank—along with Truman's popularity.[13]

"The New Dark Continent"

Across the Atlantic, Europe suffered. The signs were evident even before the last battles. Assistant Secretary of War John McCloy, returning from Europe in April 1945, reported, "There is a complete economic, social, and political collapse going on in Central Europe, the extent of which is unparalleled in history unless one goes back to the collapse of the Roman Empire." The breakdown extended far beyond the economic. Then assistant secretary of state Dean Acheson, visiting Greece in December 1944, warned that "[t]he peoples of the liberated countries...are the most combustible material in the world....They are violent and restless." He foresaw "agitation," "arbitrary and absolutist controls," and the "overthrow of governments."[14]

Benn Steil, the author of the classic study of the Marshall Plan, points out that after World War I, when borders changed, people generally remained in place. After World War II, Europe was crisscrossed by tens of millions of displaced peoples, former slave laborers, released prisoners of war, and liberated but devastated Jews. Reprisals were a way of life. Much of Europe was "lawless, violent, even savage." Churchill called it "a rubble heap, a charnel house, a breeding ground of pestilence and hate." The *New York Times* declared Europe "The New Dark Continent."[15]

A Year of Learning

Harry Truman's memoir recalled his first eighteen months in office as a "Year of Decisions." More accurately, Dean Acheson called 1946 "a year of learning." The men who would advise President Truman in 1947–49 sought to comprehend shocking conditions, the remnants of foreign capabilities, and Soviet probes. They had to better understand the prospects of recent allies such as Britain and France, recent enemies such as Germany and Italy, and an ally (of convenience) that could become a foe—the USSR. Although the Cold War later divided Europe into east and west, Americans of 1945 did not yet envisage a Europe split asunder. Asia was a confusing maelstrom of civil wars and nationalist movements. Americans also had to assess the importance of and risks to Eurasia's borderlands, such as Iran, Greece, and Turkey.

The statesmen of 1947–49 knew that Woodrow Wilson had had an appealing vision, but he had lost the peace. Witnesses to the economic breakdowns of the 1920s and '30s, they believed, like Cordell Hull, that a world free of trade barriers could generate economic and political recovery. In such an economic system, the private sector, the creative engine of America's success, should be an instrument of political-economic policy. They wanted to avoid the divisive policies of economic blocs and autarky. Marshall, Acheson, Will Clayton, and their colleagues knew of the connection between economic and military power and economic and political systems.

Two other fundamental experiences influenced them: First, appeasement had failed to satisfy dictators. Second, a successful American foreign policy required congressional and public support.

Will Clayton

Will Clayton is the least known of the architects of America's new alliance policy. He never wrote a memoir, and biographers overlooked him throughout the Cold War. Students of security studies might also have been drawn more to the political-military events than to the economic underpinnings of the new systems that Clayton forged.

Clayton's memos and remarks reflect the style of a successful business executive who became a forceful policy advocate, an effective negotiator, and a driver of policy actions; they are less likely to woo scholars than George Kennan's lyrical, historical, and reflective explanations. Yet Clayton's ideas, practical understanding of economics, ability to persuade, and skill at getting results deserve attention.

Born in 1880, Will Clayton grew up in Jackson, Tennessee, when the

American South was still overcoming the devastation of the Civil War. His family lived on the financial edge. Clayton's grade school principal recommended the young man, age thirteen, to the county clerk to help with paperwork. Clayton managed to hold the job, graduate from the eighth grade, and learn shorthand and typing on the side. From 1895 on, Clayton combined work with studies of all kinds. Jackson was a transport hub, a center of regional commerce, and local businessmen recognized Clayton's skills and drive. One cotton merchant took the sixteen-year-old to New York City, where Clayton became an expert in the trade of America's largest cash crop.[16]

By 1904, Clayton launched his own firm—in Oklahoma City and later Houston—which became the world's largest cotton brokerage. Clayton mastered the whole value chain—from farming through ginning, spinning, weaving, grading, marketing, and transport—in a worldwide business extending to Europe and East Asia. This experience gave Clayton rare, practical insights into what he would call, in 1946, the "division of labor." He understood that modern economies depended not just on resources and production, but on property rights, commercial ties, finance, exchange—and confidence—to unite producers and consumers in a vibrant marketplace.[17]

In 1918, Clayton served as a "dollar-a-year man" (an executive volunteer) with the War Industries Board to assist in the distribution of cotton. After World War I, Clayton capitalized on another insight that would assist him in 1947: He recognized that European merchants wanted a say in their own future, so he organized a network of semiautonomous units across Europe, generally led by Europeans. At the same time, he pressed relentlessly for efficiencies throughout the production, processing, and distribution chain. In 1936, *Time* magazine featured Clayton in a cover story, titling him "King Cotton," reigning over a $1 billion U.S. industry, sustaining the livelihoods of some ten million Americans.[18]

Clayton could see the disastrous consequences of the Smoot-Hawley tariff of 1930. He was disappointed by FDR's New Deal market controls, but backed his friend Cordell Hull's Reciprocal Trade Agreements Act. Beginning in 1940, Clayton assisted Nelson Rockefeller's effort to integrate Latin America's economies with the United States in anticipation of a rivalry with Nazi Germany for supplies. Then Jesse Jones, one of the builders of modern Houston, persuaded Clayton to join the Reconstruction Finance Corporation to run America's wartime procurement of global commodities, waging a "warehouse war" that kept resources out of the hands of the Axis enemies. Histories of World War II usually just assume America's industrial dominance; Clayton was a key figure in the operations that supplied the inputs for success.[19]

In November 1944, with Cordell Hull's resignation as secretary of state,

FDR named Clayton as assistant secretary of state for economic affairs. Clayton was the ideal man to carry on Hull's trade work and to apply practical economic wisdom to the challenges of reconstruction and building a new international economic system.[20] Clayton's first priority was to shepherd congressional passage of the new Bretton Woods institutions: the International Monetary Fund (IMF) and International Bank for Reconstruction and Development (IBRD, or World Bank). Harry Dexter White, an assistant to Secretary of the Treasury Henry Morgenthau, had led the U.S. teams that negotiated the charters, completing the work in July 1944. By the time President Truman signed the Bretton Woods legislation on July 31, 1945, the new president had pushed Morgenthau to resign and White's influence waned. The lead role for U.S. international economic policy shifted to Clayton and the State Department.[21]

Benn Steil has emphasized the significance of the change in leadership. FDR's Treasury policies were "grounded in the belief, born of the Depression and World War II, that economic instability led to currency wars, trade wars, and ultimately military wars." Clayton, Acheson, and the State Department leadership shared that assessment. But Morgenthau and White had assumed a political context of U.S.-Soviet cooperation, a "pastoralized" Germany after economic dismantlement, a safe receding of the British Empire, and the reestablishment of global trade supported by the IMF's modest balance-of-payments financial support. Each of these assumptions proved incorrect. As Steil points out, "[t]he U.N. and IMF...had been founded to maintain peace and stability rather than manufacture it."[22] The architects at the State Department would have to come up with a novel approach.

The Loan to Britain

Will Clayton was in London in August 1945, when President Truman announced the immediate end of Lend-Lease. Clayton, who had been working on plans for a transition, had no warning. He telephoned Secretary of State Jimmy Byrnes with strong words: "I was never so close to resigning." Truman later recalled that the sharp termination was the "worst decision" of his presidency.[23]

Britain was not the potential economic rival—or partner—that U.S. policy makers had imagined. It had lost vast national wealth, investment earnings, and exports. The new Labour government's nationalization of industries discouraged domestic investment. Clayton understood that Britain needed to rally if the United States was going to build an open international economic system and avoid fragmentation into trading blocs.

Clayton managed to ease the terms of the UK's financial cutoff, and eventually the United States wrote off most of Britain's Lend-Lease debt. Clayton worked with Lord Keynes to negotiate a new U.S. loan of $3.75 billion (about $49 billion today). Clayton, who recalled the half-hearted debt restructurings after World War I, favored a bigger loan with easier financial terms in exchange for London agreeing to policy changes that would benefit Britain and international economic recovery. In essence, he outlined the logic underpinning the Marshall Plan of 1947.[24]

In 1946, Clayton had to win Congress's approval of the loan. The experience prefigured the politics of the Marshall Plan. An early Gallup poll showed 27 percent in favor of a loan to Britain—and 60 percent against. The State Department organized more than one hundred speeches on behalf of the loan between February and April 1946, and editorial and public opinion began to swing in favor. On May 10, the Senate gave its approval by a vote of 46–24.

Rising uncertainty about Soviet behavior in 1946 offered a new argument for financial assistance. In May, Massachusetts Republican congressman Christian Herter hosted a dinner for Clayton with other representatives from New England. (Herter would later serve as President Eisenhower's second secretary of state and as the first special trade representative under President Kennedy.) Clayton used the dinner to explain the loan's connection to trade, referencing interests in members' districts. But the evening discussion drifted to the dangers of Soviet expansionism. A few days later, Herter wrote Clayton: "I find the economic arguments in favor of the loan much less convincing to this group than the feeling that the loan may serve us in good stead in holding up the hand of a nation we may need badly as a friend because of impending Russian troubles." Clayton took the hint. As the debate moved into the summer, the anti-Communist argument became louder. On the afternoon of July 13, 1946, the House approved the British loan 219–155. As Gregory Fossedal summarized in his book *Our Finest Hour*, on Clayton and the Marshall Plan, "The core idea of the Truman Doctrine and the Marshall Plan—U.S. aid as a lever both to win economic reforms and to thwart communist imperialism—had met its first test in Congress and the country."[25]

General Lucius Clay and Germany

Conditions in Germany also required a reassessment of initial U.S. plans. The Carthaginian peace of the Morgenthau Plan—embodied in the military's occupation directive, JCS #1067—was starving the German people. From the start of his appointment, General Lucius Clay, the confident, assertive, and politically well-connected head of the U.S. military government in Germany, tried to change the terms of his orders. When unsuccessful, he used the directive's loopholes creatively to chart a different course for Germany.

Clay was not anti-Soviet; his greatest frustration was with the French. Most of all, he was pro-German and sensibly American. He wanted the Germans to avoid malnutrition and disease so they could rebuild their country as soon as possible. He wanted the Germans to govern themselves democratically, become "citizens of the world again," and contribute to a rebuilt Europe. Clay recognized that a vengeful U.S. policy—without a self-sustaining Germany—would end up costing Americans monstrous sums. Moreover, he did not believe a vindictive policy would suit Americans for long. Security strategy, economic realities in Germany and Europe, and a sound moral compass guided General Clay's alternative policy.[26]

Clay believed that the United States could cooperate with the Soviets in Germany. But Clay's first priority was a successful Germany. In May 1946, he halted deliveries of reparations from the American zone, a move he directed more toward Paris than Moscow. Clay believed Germany needed to produce—and survive—before it could turn over more means of livelihood to the victors.

Clay explained his action to General Eisenhower, who had succeeded Marshall as army chief of staff: "After one year of occupation, zones represent airtight territories, with almost no free exchange of commodities, persons, and ideas. Germany now consists of four small economic units... in spite of the fact that no one unit can be self-supporting.... Economic unity can be achieved only through free trade...and a common trade policy designed to serve Germany as a whole. A common financial policy is equally essential. Runaway inflation accompanied by economic paralysis may develop at any moment."[27]

Clay called for the implementation of common policies for transportation, communications, food and agriculture, industry, and foreign trade. The suffering of Germans, he warned, would choke off democracy and encourage sympathies that would defeat American objectives. Clay might have directed his cutoff of reparations at the French, but the conditions he described and actions he demanded also required a different Soviet policy toward Germany. When Marshall became secretary of state in 1947 and promptly spent six weeks in Moscow seeking a solution regarding Germany, he would draw on Clay's analysis to reach critical conclusions about Europe's future.[28]

Although Clay concentrated on Germany, his assessments led naturally to a European policy. Before the war, Germany's Ruhr accounted for 40 percent of Europe's output of hard coal; almost one-third of that German coal fueled Western Europe's production and electricity. By April 1946, Germany's coal production had not reached half its prewar levels, and exports fell even further. More of Germany's plants had survived the war than expected, but partly for lack of coal, steel output was about 14 percent of the 1938 level. Americans began to recognize that Europe could not recover without Germany, and Germany would not recover without a new policy. Britain, the masters of the Ruhr, had failed to stimulate revival. France's solution was to assume control of the Saarland. Western Europe was fragmenting into unstable domains on half rations.[29]

George Kennan and the Soviet Union

The "year of learning" included a changing U.S. assessment of the Soviet Union. On February 9, 1946, Stalin gave an "election speech" in the Bolshoi Theater. George Kennan, America's premier Sovietologist, read nothing new. Stalin's turgid Marxist-Leninist analysis warned that capitalism, which he asserted had led to conflicts in 1914 and 1939, would inevitably do so again. Therefore, the Soviet Union must prepare itself for the dangers of capitalism's violent demise.

Kennan posted a summary. Washington wanted more. The Soviets had rejected the Bretton Woods system. Soviet espionage operations in the United States and Canada sought to steal atomic secrets. Stalin seemed to be maneuvering for advantage in the Middle East. The State Department's Soviet desk asked Kennan for an "interpretive analysis."

Kennan's response, the "Long Telegram," at more than five thousand words, reiterated points he had made before: Russia's historical and geographical insecurities, dressed up with Marxist-Leninist ideology, led it to seek even larger military power and a confrontation with the capitalist West. Although the Soviets might engage in diplomatic dances, they would use Communist parties and other groups to "disrupt national self-confidence, to hamstring measures of national defense, to increase social and industrial unrest, to stimulate all forms of disunity." In sum, Kennan warned, the Soviets were "committed fanatically to the belief that... there can be no permanent modus vivendi, that it is desirable and necessary that the internal harmony of our society be disrupted, our traditional way of life destroyed, [and] the international authority of our state be broken." The Soviets were "impervious to the logic of reason," but "highly sensitive to the logic of force."

The innumerable analyses of Kennan's cable testify to its influence. Kennan's biographer, John Lewis Gaddis, writes that Kennan later viewed his telegram as a kind of "primer" to arouse the citizenry. "It hit Washington at just the right moment," said Ambassador Averell Harriman, who had just returned from Moscow. Kennan's analysis crystalized and explained confusing and worrying circumstances without hedging or hesitation. He did not offer alternatives. Kennan's logic was unstinting. He provided a unifying theme. But Kennan did not provide a plan of action. American officials were still left with messy choices about what to do in the face of particular problems. Admirers of Kennan's analysis—and of his later refinement of thinking into the doctrine of containment—would argue adamantly with one another about what the United States should actually do. That was the practical work of diplomacy that came to a head in 1947–49.[30]

Truman and the Soviet Union

President Truman struggled to reach conclusions about Soviet policy. In March 1946, Winston Churchill delivered his "Iron Curtain" speech in Fulton, Missouri. Churchill had discussed his speech with the president, who approved of and encouraged the seminal statement. But when editorials criticized Churchill's hostility to Moscow, Truman equivocated. "No comment," the president said when pressed for his opinion. While Truman's senior officials were avidly digesting Kennan's cable, the president's conflicting statements sent the real message: no U.S. policy yet.[31]

The Soviets, however, appeared to have a policy: They would take advantage of weakness. The day of Churchill's speech in Fulton, the State Department sent a note to Moscow seeking explanations for Soviet actions in Iran, Eastern Europe, and Manchuria. In the immediate aftermath of his victory over the Nazis, Stalin stood before a large map and expressed his dissatisfaction with the southern Soviet border in the Caucasus. He pointed to Iran and Turkey. Stalin wanted more territory and oil concessions. The Soviets sponsored an armed rebellion in northern Iran and blocked Iranian forces seeking to subdue it. In March 1946, the Soviets announced that they would ignore a 1942 treaty with Iran and Britain and not withdraw troops from Iran. The Red Army was only forty miles away from Tehran.

Washington signaled its interest by sending the battleship USS *Missouri* to the region, ostensibly to carry the deceased former Turkish ambassador home. The Iranian prime minister worked out a joint oil project with Moscow, and the Soviets withdrew. But the Iranian parliament rejected the oil deal, and the separatist party demanded local elections. With Secretary of State Byrnes away, Under Secretary Acheson, with Truman's approval, told the Iranians that the United States could support them, but Iran needed to take the initiative. Elections in the disputed territory, said Acheson, seemed like a mistake until Iran reestablished its authority. The Iranians reasserted control, and the separatist movement collapsed.[32]

Kennan's advice, to face Soviet tests with firmness, seemed to be correct. But Truman's defense advisers were wary of bluffing and miscalculations, especially as the U.S. military rapidly demobilized. The Joint Chiefs of Staff assessed contingency plans, looking principally to airpower and the necessary bases. British bases in the United Kingdom and the Middle East figured prominently in their calculations. The three chiefs of staff gave the go-ahead for informal and secret planning talks with the British.[33]

In August 1946, Stalin tested the West again. He demanded that Turkey concede joint control over the Dardanelles and the straits to the Mediterranean. Kennan had pointed out that the Soviets were Russians who held centuries-old beliefs about security, including sea access through these straits. At Yalta in 1945, Roosevelt and Churchill agreed, outside the formal record, to review the 1936 Montreaux Convention governing Turkey's rights. Stalin was now rewriting that convention by himself and even demanding Soviet bases.

On August 15, Acheson served as the spokesman to the president for a group of officials. He emphasized the threats to Turkey and Greece and the strategic implications for the Eastern Mediterranean, the Balkans, and the Suez Canal. The group proposed a diplomatic note that rejected any intrusion on Turkish control of the straits while offering to consider "valid criticisms" of the 1936 treaty. To back the verbal message, the group recommended sending the new supercarrier USS *Franklin D. Roosevelt* and a powerful naval task force to join the *Missouri*. After listening carefully, Truman directed the preparation of the note and orders.

General Eisenhower asked Acheson in a whisper whether they had made clear to the president that this course of action could lead to war. Before Acheson could reply, Truman asked if the general wished to say something. Acheson relayed Ike's question. As Acheson wrote in his memoir, the president, who loved maps and military history, took out a map of the Middle East and Mediterranean and asked the group to gather around his desk. Truman "then gave us a brief lecture on the strategic importance of the area and the extent to which we must be prepared to keep it free from Soviet domination."[34]

Truman liked plain speaking. But he had not yet decided on a blunt confrontation with the Soviet Union. The White House system for making policy was chaotic. The president had no National Security Council or staff to frame decisions. Even after Congress created such a mechanism in 1947, Truman did not rely on it. His personal style—delegation and decisiveness—depended heavily on the qualities of, and his relationships with, his senior officials.

In 1945–46, Truman did not yet have the team he needed. Acheson and Clayton were strong, respected figures at the State Department, but their secretary, former senator Jimmy Byrnes, was away most of the time and lost the president's confidence. He communicated poorly with his cabinet colleagues, his own department, and most important, with the president. To help with the challenges ahead, the president knew that he needed a superior secretary of state. He had one in mind: General George Marshall.

More immediate, Truman needed help thinking about the Soviet Union. In July 1946, he complained to two White House aides, Clark Clifford and George Elsey, about feeling pushed around. He directed them to prepare an accounting of Soviet compliance with past agreements. Elsey expanded the project into an assessment of U.S.-Soviet relations. Elsey and Clifford prepared a set of questions to guide an interdepartmental review, the first such examination of America's most vital foreign policy topic.

They completed their work, "American Relations with the Soviet Union," in September 1946. They did not equivocate. With almost one hundred thousand words, the report presented in detail a much more alarming, even ominous, picture than Kennan's historical and conceptual narrative. Soviet military power and preparations cast a dark and growing shadow over the world. Espionage and subversion reached everywhere. As the threat loomed larger, alternative assessments of Soviet behavior—considering Soviet weaknesses and even hesitation—vanished.

Historians cannot pinpoint the conclusions Truman drew from the Clifford-Elsey report. But after staying up much of the night to read it, the president called Clifford at home early the next morning. Truman asked how many copies existed. Ten, said Clifford. Put them under lock and key immediately, directed the president. The report was so "hot," explained Truman, that if it ever became public, the effect on his efforts to resolve the East-West conflict peacefully would be "exceedingly unfortunate." The report did not see the light of day for twenty years, until former president Truman spoke of it in an interview.[35]

The 1946 Elections

The year of learning ended with one more lesson, a political one. The Republicans swept both the Senate and House for the first time since the Depression, almost a generation before. They controlled the House 246–188 and the Senate 45–41; Republicans also won a majority of state governorships. The New Deal was sent packing. The voters' rejection of the "accidental" president, Harry Truman, seemed to recall Andrew Johnson's rapid collapse after Lincoln's death.

The fall from political grace was a shock to Democrats. J. William Fulbright, a Rhodes Scholar and promising young senator from Arkansas with an interest in foreign affairs, feared a breakdown in Washington at a moment of global crisis. Fulbright proposed that Truman appoint Senator Arthur Vandenberg of Michigan, the leading Republican voice on foreign policy, as secretary of state, and then resign, making Vandenberg president. Truman dismissed Fulbright as "Halfbright."[36]

In his memoir, Dean Acheson writes that the cabinet had a custom of meeting President Roosevelt's train on FDR's return from his many campaigns. When Truman's train pulled into Union Station the morning after the 1946 election, Acheson discovered to his horror that he was alone on the platform except for the station master and a reporter or two. The president never forgot Acheson's gesture.

Truman took Acheson with him to the White House, where the president dismissed a suggestion to recall Congress to confirm various nominations and boost Democratic Party spirits before the Republicans took charge. Acheson argued that such a partisan ploy would look terrible. The better course, urged Acheson, was to acknowledge the will of the people and pledge to cooperate fully with the new Congress. The president agreed.[37]

On New Year's Day, 1947, Truman phoned Vandenberg, the incoming chair of the Foreign Relations Committee, and Joe Martin, the new Republican Speaker of the House. Truman was encouraged by the warmth and spirit of cooperation from both men. The year 1947 would prove to be a defining moment for all of them and for American diplomacy.[38]

Arthur Vandenberg and the Senate

Arthur Vandenberg turned out to be as influential in shaping the new American alliance system as any of Truman's colleagues in the executive branch. His story helps explain the role individuals in Congress can play in framing U.S. foreign policy, a dimension often overlooked by students of statecraft.

Vandenberg has passed into historical lore as the senator who declared that the attack on Pearl Harbor "ended isolation for any realist." But as one biographer, Lawrence Kaplan, explains, Vandenberg recorded that memory with considerable hindsight; his long transition to Truman's vital ally in the Senate had been complicated. The senator was a political party leader, balancing obligations to his electorate and party colleagues, resistance to FDR and parts of the New Deal, protections of the Senate's prerogatives, personal ambition and vanity, and assessments of dramatic international shifts before, during, and after a tragic war. The man who became known as a paragon of "bipartisan" foreign policy actually preferred the term "unpartisan" so as to steer clear of political connotations—or obligations.[39]

Like Truman and Clayton, Vandenberg was a Midwesterner whose family's hard times spurred him toward achievement. He was born in 1884, forty-seven days before Truman. When Vandenberg was nine, the Panic of 1893 ruined his father's harness and leather goods business in Grand Rapids, Michigan. His "qualities of enterprise" became the fiber of a self-made man. Like Truman, Vandenberg was a self-taught historian drawn to the excitement of contributing to America's twentieth-century destiny. Vandenberg loved public speaking and enjoyed writing. In his senior year in high school, the aspiring politician won a silver medal in a state contest for a speech about the Hague Conference of 1899.[40]

At the turn of the twentieth century, Grand Rapids was a trading and transport center, similar to Truman's Kansas City and Clayton's Jackson. Forty trains a day passed through freight yards, markets, and warehouses of the city of fifty thousand. The pine logs coming down the Grand River fed the factories that made Grand Rapids America's "Furniture City."[41]

Vandenberg managed to market his writing skills into a post with the *Grand Rapids Herald*. He proved to be an energetic and wide-ranging journalist, covering everything from the police beat to the Electoral College. Vandenberg found the money for one year at the University of Michigan. In 1906, William Alden Smith, the local congressman, acquired the controlling interest in the *Herald*, a leading Republican paper in Western Michigan. When the *Herald*'s editor died, Congressman Smith appointed Vandenberg as editor in chief and general manager. The rising star was about to turn twenty-two.[42]

In the first decades of the twentieth century, regional city newspapers offered an influential public platform, like radio commentators, local TV news personalities, and social media figures did for later generations. The *Herald* was a voice on local, state, national, and even international topics— as well as running features that showed a true feel for the reading public, such as comic strips and baseball scores.

Vandenberg became a newspaper businessman and an investor. As the Republican Party moved rightward, Vandenberg's moderation blended with Midwestern nationalism and conservatism. His father's dying wish, offered during the 1912 election when TR bolted from the party, elicited a promise that Arthur would always be a Republican. Vandenberg was comfortable with Elihu Root and Charles Evans Hughes. He understood the possible benefits of Wilson's League of Nations, but sided with reservationists to safeguard constitutional powers.[43]

These formative years offer hints about Vandenberg's future contributions to American diplomacy. His mind reached across eras and events. He respected tradition and held the Constitution sacrosanct. He recognized the sweep of history, including challenges of change, but wanted to keep America—and his politics—rooted in local enterprise and sensitivities.[44]

When Congressman Smith moved to the Senate, Vandenberg kept an eye out for political opportunity. In early 1928, Michigan's governor appointed Vandenberg, age forty-four, to the seat of a senator who had died, and Vandenberg won the seat resoundingly that November. He joined the Foreign Relations Committee in 1929 and backed President Hoover's (and Elihu Root's) failed effort to join the World Court. He stayed with the cause of the court under FDR, although adding a qualifying amendment, a tool that became a specialty of the experienced senator and vote counter in later years.[45]

Vandenberg was by nature a conciliator. He preferred influence to standing outside as a critic. Like many successful legislators, Vandenberg was a practical man, not a visionary. James Reston of the *New York Times* wrote, "He tends to be indifferent to anything that he feels cannot be translated into action."[46]

Vandenberg was effective in both public halls and back rooms. He spoke powerfully, with a hearty style and colorful phrases. Vandenberg learned how to maintain his political standing within a minority party, where criticism of the president and the majority was a duty, while working as a legislator. He was reelected to the Senate in 1934, the lone Republican from an industrial state to survive the Democratic sweep.[47]

As early as 1936, Republicans mentioned Vandenberg as a possible presidential candidate. But a combination of his own practical political instincts and lack of willingness to organize the effort kept Vandenberg in check. He waited to be "anointed." But Vandenberg used too many "5 dollar" words and had a poor radio voice. The senator became a leader in protecting the Constitution—first against FDR's assault on the Supreme Court in 1937 and then the president's assertion of powers to pull the United States into war.[48]

Vandenberg served with Senator Gerald Nye's Munitions Inquiry and became a leader of the Neutrality Acts of the 1930s. He opposed the Selective Service and Lend-Lease Acts and favored tariff protection. His attacks on war profiteers stemmed from a Main Street hostility to arms manufacturers, financiers, and speculators, not a belief that the United States could ignore the world. In 1940, he wrote that "isolationism is impossible in this foreshortened world. But insulation continues to be entirely practical." He recognized that Hitler's victory posed a serious danger; the issue, he argued, was how best to insulate the United States from the prospect. Most of all,

Vandenberg believed that the evasive FDR was stretching the president's executive powers beyond recognition and dragging the United States into war. He was frustrated—trying to play the role of a leading senator of a minority party with a president who treated him dismissively. Vandenberg wanted to be a player, but he was not.[49]

During the war, Vandenberg worked well with the Democratic chair of the Foreign Relations Committee. Secretary Hull, as a former senator, tried to treat the committee respectfully, but Hull was far from FDR's inner circle and war cabinet. General Marshall was one of the few wartime leaders who made the effort to explain difficult decisions to Vandenberg and his colleagues. Vandenberg reciprocated and remembered.[50]

Vandenberg wanted to bridge the views of old Republican isolationists and the increasingly influential internationalists, such as Governor Thomas Dewey of New York, the Republican presidential nominee of 1944 and 1948. Vandenberg also sought to manage the interventions of a rising Republican star, Senator Robert Taft of Ohio. In effect, Vandenberg worked out an informal partnership with Taft, in which Vandenberg became the Senate foreign policy spokesman and Taft guided domestic policy. Without this arrangement, which the two senators strained to the limit, President Truman would never have achieved vital Republican support in 1947–49.[51]

As long as war raged, Congress—especially its stewards of foreign policy—was overshadowed by the commander in chief. As the president began to make commitments concerning the shape of the postwar world, both Democratic and Republican senators signaled their interest. Everyone recalled Woodrow Wilson's failed peace.

Negotiating the United Nations Charter

Vandenberg's service as a delegate to the San Francisco Conference (April 25–June 26, 1945), which prepared the charter of the new United Nations, sealed his conversion. The administration did not want to repeat Wilson's failure in 1919 to include senators and Republicans. FDR passed away less than two weeks before the conference convened; President Truman decided promptly to hold to the schedule and put Secretary of State Edward Stettinius, Hull's successor, in charge. Following all his frustrations with FDR, Vandenberg liked the idea that there was no "indispensable man bigger than America."

Vandenberg had worked amicably with the new president when both were senators; they were professional colleagues, not personal friends. Truman later reflected that "Vandenberg was familiar with the workings of the Senate and knew how to get results." For his part, Vandenberg suspected that

Truman would be firmer with the Soviets than Roosevelt, especially with respect to Poland. Michigan had a sizable Polish-American community.

Stettinius worked closely with Vandenberg and Tom Connally of Texas, the chair of the Foreign Relations Committee. Truman told Stettinius to make sure that the senators agreed with "every move," and the president offered both direct access to him. Vandenberg, aided by John Foster Dulles, was avid and forceful. He chaired the Committee on Regional Arrangements. Vandenberg reveled in the politics, advocacy, negotiations, and drafting of diplomacy. He was justifiably proud of translating the vague statements of the Dumbarton Oaks Conference of late 1944 into specific UN Charter language. He jousted with the Soviets and worked on the respective authorities of the Security Council and the General Assembly. Vandenberg played an important role in reconciling regional security arrangements with the important role of the Security Council. He helped develop the compromise language of Article 51 (pertaining to the right of collective self-defense) in order to permit a Western Hemispheric security group; as it turned out, that provision later provided the formula for the North Atlantic Treaty of 1949.

Senators Connally and Vandenberg presented the UN Charter treaty to their colleagues in late June 1945. On July 28, the Senate ratified their handiwork by a vote of 82–2. Not only had Wilson's failure faded into history, but the UN gained a proponent in the Senate.[52]

During 1946, Vandenberg spent 213 days at UN and Council of Foreign Ministers meetings (of the four victorious powers) in London, Paris, and New York. He was critical of Secretary of State Byrnes's concessions to the Soviets, but reconciled with Byrnes when he took a firmer line.[53] Vandenberg's Senate speech of February 27, titled "What's Russia Up to Now?" had more effect on the thinking of the general public about the Soviets than Kennan's Long Telegram.[54]

Breaking with Taft, Vandenberg managed to win seventeen Republican senators to support Clayton's loan to Britain. In November, the senator won reelection with the second largest majority of his career, which he took as an "unmistakable endorsement" of his contributions to a "united, bipartisan foreign policy." The Republicans were finally in the majority, and Vandenberg, with his ever-present cigar, was the new chair of the Senate Foreign Relations Committee.[55]

George Marshall, Dean Acheson, and the State Department

President Truman was also ready to make a fresh start. During the summer of 1946, he had asked General Eisenhower, who was about to leave on an inspection tour of the Far East, to inquire if General Marshall, then in China, would be willing to succeed Byrnes as secretary of state at some future time. Marshall replied that he would serve in any capacity the president wished. The president nominated Marshall as secretary of state on January 7, 1947.[56] Recognizing Marshall's reputation with Congress and capacity to lift foreign policy above partisanship, Truman considered Marshall to be "a wonderful ace in the hole" that the poker-playing president especially needed.[57]

As Marshall returned to Washington, Vandenberg pushed the general's confirmation through the Foreign Relations Committee without a hearing or any opposition. Asking for a suspension of the Senate rules, Vandenberg won the full Senate's approval of the new secretary the same day.

As Marshall got off the train in Union Station, an aide handed the new secretary a note with a tip from a journalist about Vandenberg's concern about Marshall's political plans. Marshall made a brief statement and asked for questions. No one asked Marshall about politics. Marshall then raised the topic directly and stated that the post was nonpolitical; he would not be involved in political matters, could not be a candidate, and could never be drafted. Marshall was being "explicit and emphatic...to terminate [the topic] once and for all."[58]

The new secretary was also decisive about running the State Department. He established a Secretariat to coordinate the paper flow and direct communications.[59] Marshall also established a new Policy Planning Staff. The new secretary understood that "line" offices, which at the State Department have been the regional bureaus, were busy with daily operations. As Acheson described, "[P]olicies acquired their own momentum and went on after the reasons that inspired them had ceased." Marshall wanted a small staff to look ahead, not to the distant future, but to extend the vision of the secretary and operating executive—to anticipate, stimulate thinking, and devise fresh approaches. He also consolidated State's intelligence and research functions into one bureau to ensure that their assessments were independent of regional bureau biases.[60]

Secretary Marshall also directed Under Secretary Acheson to run State as a de facto chief of staff. Marshall wanted Acheson to serve as the sole channel for issues requiring decision and to send each matter forward with a recommendation. Acheson recognized the drawbacks of too much centralization, and he urged the secretary to participate earlier in the decision process so that the staff could factor in his views and any presidential guidance. Acheson also suggested considering alternatives, not just recommendations. Marshall tried to adapt to Acheson's suggestions but did not like it. One of Marshall's most lasting dictums, made after listening to a debate among a group of section chiefs, was, "Gentlemen, don't fight the problem, decide it."[61]

Marshall's appointment, and his executive style, were critical given Truman's own leadership. The president granted wide authority to advisers. But he had no system to consider contrasting views coherently or to structure and integrate decision-making. Truman was decisive, but in 1945–46, no one presented the key choices to the president in an organized way or related problems to one another. Processes matter. So do a president's key people. In January 1947, the president looked to Marshall, leading a more cohesive State Department, to take the lead in framing a new foreign, security, and international economic policy. The Pentagon, including the uniformed military, was the other key voice and instrument in the executive branch; Marshall enjoyed enormous respect with them, too. The final key player was Congress, where Vandenberg was ready to be a partner.

Greece and Turkey on the Precipice

Within a month, the new team faced the first of the four decisions that redefined America's diplomacy for decades. On Friday, February 21, 1947, the British ambassador's private secretary asked if Lord Inverchapel could personally deliver "a blue piece of paper" to Secretary Marshall without delay. He was using the expression for a formal message from London. Marshall had just left for Princeton to give his first address as secretary of state. Acheson suggested that the embassy provide him a copy right away; the ambassador could fulfill his instructions by formally presenting Marshall the message face-to-face on Monday morning.

The British conveyed two papers on Greece and Turkey. Acheson recalls the documents as a "shocker," even though the State Department had been receiving a stream of scary field reports. The cable traffic had described economic chaos, rampaging guerrillas, and a Greek government on the brink of collapse.

The real news from London was that within six weeks it would halt all aid to Greece and Turkey and withdraw its forty thousand troops from Greece. Washington, the British suggested ruefully, might need to step in. Turkey was not near such a breakdown, but it could not finance its modernization and the large army that had withstood Moscow's recent threats.[62]

Clayton, who had dealt with the end of the 1946 Lend-Lease loan to Britain, was not surprised by the economic realities. "The reins of world leadership," Clayton summarized about this time, "are fast slipping from Britain's competent but very weak hands." Either the United States or Russia would pick them up, warned Clayton. If the United States stepped up, it could prevent war; if Russia took charge, Clayton foresaw war in a decade or so.[63]

Acheson informed Truman and Marshall of the British note by telephone while directing a team to "work like hell" over the weekend of February 22–23. On Saturday, Acheson assessed the facts, and he pressed for an explanation of the importance of an independent Greece and Turkey to Western Europe. He added the army and navy operations staff, and their secretaries, to the process in order to outline the needs and supplies by Monday.[64]

Acheson oversaw a final review on Sunday at home. By Monday morning, Marshall had read the papers and prepared to meet Inverchapel at 10:00 a.m. The secretary pressed Acheson on a list of issues. The under secretary could offer only preliminary judgments. Marshall was leaving for Moscow in about a week to meet with his Soviet, British, and French counterparts to discuss Germany's fate. Real, practical decisions must usually be made with partial information under severe time pressure.

The problem in Greece and Turkey was not a direct move by the Soviets. But the U.S. feared that Greek Communists, aided by Tito in Yugoslavia, would seize power in Greece and align with the Soviets. The Pentagon worried that a Soviet foothold in the Eastern Mediterranean would surround Turkey, loom over access to Middle Eastern oil and other resources, and threaten the airfields that hosted America's strategic airpower. The success would encourage Communist parties in France, Italy, and other Western European countries.

In early 1947, Communist parties in Europe had a powerful appeal, in contrast with even a few years later. Disaffected Europeans viewed the Soviets as the victor in a death struggle with the indomitable Nazi war machine. The Red Army had liberated much of the continent. Communists had fought fiercely in the resistance (once Hitler attacked the USSR). The public looked at the old political order with disdain and a dark association with Depression days. Communist Party membership soared in Europe.[65]

The Making of the Truman Doctrine

Clayton had identified the core problem: The United States needed to decide whether it would offer Europe an alternative. If so, what would be the mix of political, economic, and military factors? And would Congress and the American public back this radical "entanglement" with Europe?

The president and the army and navy secretaries supported Marshall's approach and recommendations. As the staff raced to finalize the package for Greece and Turkey, some raised the question of support for South Korea, China, and other vulnerable countries. General Eisenhower urged an expanded study so as to provide the basis of a wider request to Congress for funds. But the imperatives of time and the Congress kept the project focused for the moment on Greece and Turkey. The question of the geographic scope of America's commitment would pose practical choices very soon and for many years to come.[66]

Truman and Marshall moved fast. On February 27, just six days after Acheson received his copy of the "blue piece of paper," the president convened eight congressional leaders in the White House: four Republicans and four Democrats. Chairman Vandenberg, building future political capital with his caucus, noted to the president that Senator Taft had been mistakenly overlooked.

Marshall read a statement, as was his practice in formal settings. His text warned of "the first crisis of a series which might extend Soviet domination to Europe, the Middle East, and Asia," but his style was flat. For once, Marshall's reasoned, calm control failed to fit the circumstances.

The Republican attendees asked why the United States should step in to "[pull] British chestnuts out of the fire." The new Republican majority had committed to cutting foreign aid. They asked Congress's favorite question to administrations proposing initiatives: How much would this cost?

According to Acheson's account, he whispered to Marshall, "Is this a private fight or can anyone get into it?" Marshall asked the president if Acheson could speak. Acheson realized he had one chance to reframe the issue. The under secretary drew in Senators Vandenberg and Connally by referencing their trips to Europe with Secretary Byrnes to negotiate peace settlements with the Soviets. He explained that Moscow had devoted the last eighteen months to enveloping Iran, Turkey, Greece, and Germany, always probing for weakness. Greece was now at immediate risk of collapse. This crisis was not a matter of British chestnuts; Britain was finished. Only two great powers remained—a polarization unmatched since the contest between Rome and Carthage.

If Greece collapsed, Acheson argued, others would fall like infected apples: Iran and the east; Asia Minor, Egypt, and Africa; Europe through Italy and France. "The Soviet Union was playing one of the greatest gambles in history at minimal cost." It did not need to win each hand; even one or two would present great gains. This contest was ideological: democracy and liberty versus dictatorship and totalitarianism. Aiding Greece was not about the British or humanitarian aid. The initiative was about supporting free peoples and American national security. The United States could act boldly or lose by default.[67]

Acheson had read his audience. For men who had studied history and lived through an epic war, for men who recently had surveyed maps of armies and navies sweeping across continents and seas, Acheson's plea awoke a sense of destiny. These were hard-bitten, practical politicians. But many had followed a political calling because they believed they could make a mark on history. This was their moment.

After a long silence, Vandenberg was the first to rise to the summons. "Mr. President," he said gravely, "if you will say that to the Congress and the country, I will support you and I believe that most of the members will do the same." According to one account, Vandenberg added that Truman "would have to scare the hell out of the country." The meeting broke up without much further discussion.[68]

Vandenberg was setting a pattern that he would follow again and again over the next few years. He offered support, but with a condition—and later, amendments—that would bring along his Senate colleagues and the public. This was the politics of American diplomacy. Now Truman faced the challenge of his presidency.

Marshall headed to Moscow on March 5. Acheson guided the preparation of the plan for $400 million (about $4.6 billion today) for economic and military aid to Greece and Turkey. He also supervised the preparation of the president's speech to Congress on March 12. And Acheson prevailed upon Britain to delay the departure of troops and asked the Greek government to write a request for help. Acheson set the stage with the press, too.

Truman had heard Vandenberg's message. He wanted a speech without "hedging...hesitation, and double-talk." Kennan was concerned that strong language might provoke the Soviets; he had a practice of writing persuasive analyses and then pulling back. Clifford thought the first effort was too weak. In contrast, Marshall saw "too much rhetoric." Clayton argued that the president needed to "shock" the U.S. public into assuming world leadership; to do so, "it is only necessary for the President and the Secretary of State to tell them the truth and the whole truth." Acheson recognized that with Congress, it is sometimes necessary to make arguments "clearer than truth."[69]

Consider the context as it looked to Truman. On the day Acheson had received the British note (February 21), the president had asked Congress for $350 million of international relief funds, causing consternation among Republicans and Democrats. Former president Hoover, who had just returned from a trip to Europe to consider food needs, reported terrible conditions, but recommended that Congress should "stop, look, and listen" before rushing relief. The new Republican Congress had been elected to restore budget economy. On March 4, the Senate voted to slash the president's next budget by $4.5 billion, the House having voted for a $6 billion cut. A large group of senators and representatives met in the president's office on March 10, just two days before his speech, and they offered, in Acheson's words, "a cool and silent reception" to the administration's case, despite Vandenberg's encouragement. Truman told his daughter that he had been "worn to a frazzle" in deciding to present his request to Congress: "I knew that George Washington's spirit would be invoked against me," the president recalled later.[70]

Truman stood before a packed House chamber just after 1:00 p.m. on March 12, 1947. In a speech of just nineteen minutes, the president took the first big step toward a lasting American entanglement with Europe and the wider cause of freedom beyond America's shores.[71]

He drew a picture of Greece as a broken country, unable to recover because of want, misery, and a militant minority led by Communists. He reported the Greek government's request and acknowledged its mistakes. Then he explained Turkey's different needs and connection to order in the Middle East. The objective, stated Truman, was the "creation of conditions in which we and other nations will be able to work out a way of life free from coercion." This had been a purpose of the recent World War.

Then Truman explained that every country now faced a choice between the institutions of freedom and the ways of oppression. In a sentence that would resonate through the years as the "Truman Doctrine," the president stated: "I believe that it must be the policy of the United States to support free peoples who are resisting attempted subjugation by armed minorities or by outside pressures." The means would be primarily "economic and financial."

Next Truman drew a verbal map describing the geopolitical stakes of the challenge. He asked for $400 million through June 1948 and for authority to deploy civilian and military personnel. He compared this "investment in a world of peace and freedom" with the $341 billion the United States had spent to fight World War II. The president concluded that "Great responsibilities have been placed upon us by the swift movement of events." He expressed confidence that "Congress will face these responsibilities squarely."[72]

As Acheson described the scene, Congress gave the president a standing ovation. But, Acheson added, "[t]his was a tribute to a brave man rather than unanimous acceptance of his policy."[73]

Scholars have pored over Truman's words for seventy years, especially his Doctrine. Ironically, the sentence they target most was from a State Department draft quoting a State-War-Navy report, not a White House political sound bite. Critics have traced many U.S. tragedies over future decades— and especially Vietnam—to Truman's call. Bold presidential language can become a club for later advocates to use against those arguing for restraint.

But the critics overreach. Political leaders have to make their own pragmatic decisions, in changing contexts, about purposes, means, and public support. Indeed, in the congressional hearings that followed Truman's request, both Acheson and Clayton emphasized that policies must be judged by "the circumstances of each case."[74]

Truman had not mentioned the Soviet Union in his speech. He referred to "Communists" just once. Benn Steil properly notes that the most momentous shift in American diplomacy inaugurated by Truman's speech was the reliance on economic and financial aid as the core element of America's new entanglement with Europe and the world.[75] Alexander Hamilton, William Seward, John Hay, and Cordell Hull had recognized the vital connection between open economic diplomacy and American interests. The most lasting legacy of Truman's speech was the expectation that global leadership is intrinsic to U.S. foreign policy.[76]

Vandenberg and Aid for Greece and Turkey

A wary Congress posed lots of questions. But Senator Vandenberg pressed ahead. "[I]f we desert the President...we cease to have any influence in the world forever," he warned.[77]

Acheson admired Vandenberg's congressional skills. "One of Vandenberg's strategems was to enact publicly his conversion to a proposal....The method was to go through a period of public doubt and skepticism; then find a comparatively minor flaw in the proposal, pounce upon it and make much of it; in due course propose a change, always the Vandenberg amendment." Then the senator could offer his followers "a true doctrine," "a kind of political transubstantiation."[78]

Vandenberg invited his Senate colleagues to submit questions, and he boiled the list down to 111, which the administration promptly answered. The vital issue remaining, Vandenberg asserted, was the administration's "colossal blunder in ignoring the UN," whose Charter the senator knew well. The reality, which Clayton had experienced firsthand, was that the UN and its relief administration was incapable of the work ahead. But the American public vastly preferred handing over the Greek problem to the UN. Vandenberg drafted an amendment giving the UN a role in assessing the need for the aid. Acheson conceded. The move weakened the opposition, led by Senator Taft. The Senate passed the bill on April 23 by a vote of 67–23, with thirty-five Republicans in support, and the House approved the bill by a vote of 287–107. President Truman signed the legislation on May 22, just before taking his second step toward transforming American diplomacy.[79]

In reality, Greece was not high on Stalin's list of geopolitical or even Balkan objectives. He doubted the capabilities of the Greek Communists and expected the United States to protect its line of communications in the Mediterranean. Truman's earlier firm response in Turkey had convinced Stalin that a misstep in the region could trigger action by the United States and Britain. In Moscow, the Truman Doctrine looked like a regional countermove, perhaps even a blow against America's capitalist rival, Britain. By the summer of 1949, the newly empowered Greek government stamped out the insurgency.[80]

The Moscow Conference of 1947: The Fate of Germany and Europe

Washington had not yet recognized, however, Stalin's determination to assert Soviet rights on the central front: in Germany and the buffer zone of Central and Eastern Europe. Secretary Marshall, who landed in a snowy Moscow on March 9, 1947, as Truman was wrestling with the preparation of his speech to Congress, was about to get a frigid lesson in Stalin's strategic priorities.

The fundamental question for the Moscow meeting of the four foreign ministers in March was the future of Germany and, in particular, its reparations. The Americans and Soviets had drawn fundamentally opposite lessons from the experience after World War I. The United States, prodded by General Clay, wanted to restore the German economy to avoid having to finance its subsistence. Moreover, a captive and destitute Germany might again become a revanchist Germany. The Soviets, in contrast, believed that they had paid a perilous price for permitting German power to rise again. The Soviets wanted reparations—now—to pay for the Nazis' devastation and to keep a foot on Germany's throat while the USSR regained strength.

Neither Clay nor Marshall wanted a break with the Soviets. The Americans' practical recommendation was to permit Germans to feed themselves, unify economically and politically across the four zones, produce more, and then yield reparations. The unacceptable course would be to have American taxpayers finance Germany's life support while the Soviets (and French) squeezed away Germany's lifeblood. In that case, the U.S. military would need to garrison its German economic ward for an indefinite time. To prevent just such a result, Clay had suspended reparations the prior June and had unified a German "Bizonia" with Britain at the start of 1947.

Marshall and Clay represented America's optimism, a rare attribute in European diplomacy. "We will never democratize Germany by the mere negative process of depriving the Nazis of their positions and influence," argued the secretary.[81] The Soviets, in contrast, feared Germany, whether democratic or not.

During the course of forty-three four-hour-long sessions over five weeks, Marshall got a taste of Russian diplomacy. Foreign Minister Vyacheslav Molotov justified his reputation as "stone ass." As Marshall reflected, "In diplomacy you never can tell what a man is thinking. He smiles at you and kicks you in the stomach at the same time." Marshall found the vagueness, droning, and needling to be frustrating. He read Harold Nicolson's book on the Congress of Vienna of 1815 on the side to keep up his spirits. Marshall had come to Moscow to resolve differences and solve problems, but instead confronted a crude test of endurance and patience.[82]

Marshall had observed a decisive Stalin at the three wartime summits. He asked to see Stalin personally. They met on the night of April 15, 1947. Marshall laid out the agenda—demilitarization, reparations, and Germany's future economic and political architecture—and declared that the parties had not been making any progress. Over the course of ninety minutes with Stalin, nothing changed. The Soviets wanted to keep control over all of a prostrate Germany, serving the USSR. Stalin would avoid, at all costs, a Germany that might combine with the capitalist Americans and British.

Marshall now recognized that the obdurate Molotov was just doing his master's bidding. Stalin offered a "compromise"—a plebiscite of the German people—a chilling thought in light of the Soviets' manipulation of elections in Poland and other eastern nations.[83]

As Stalin calmly doodled wolves'-heads, he suggested that he was more optimistic than Marshall. These were "only the first skirmishes.... [A]fter people exhausted themselves, they recognized the necessity of compromise.... It was necessary to have patience."

That was a comment certain to frustrate an American diplomat who had identified a pressing problem—for both Germany and Europe—and who was urging pragmatic solutions. Marshall reported to the president that he still hoped to salvage something from the conference, perhaps an agreement on Austria. But Molotov's continued resistance convinced Marshall that Stalin would order no change.

Over thirteen months in 1945–46, Marshall had encountered the irreconcilable differences between Chinese Nationalists and Communists. He recognized the ineffectiveness of his negotiation, and he reached courageous conclusions about the limited ability of outsiders to influence and support Chiang Kai-shek.[84] Now, for the second time, Marshall recognized the limits of negotiated compromises. He was coming home. But he had reached a very different conclusion on what needed to be done to change the underlying circumstances in Europe.

The European "Patient Is Sinking"

Before he left Moscow, Marshall met his British and French colleagues. Both described the economic breakdown and political dangers in Europe, even risks of civil war. Both pleaded for U.S. assistance.

Charles "Chip" Bohlen, Marshall's translator, wrote later that "Stalin's seeming indifference to what was happening in Germany made a deep impression on Marshall. He came to the conclusion that Stalin, looking over Europe, saw the best way to advance Soviet interests was to let matters drift.... This was the kind of crisis that Communism thrived on. All the way back to Washington, Marshall talked of the importance of finding some initiative to prevent the complete breakdown of Western Europe."[85]

Marshall would later say that he had finally decided in Moscow that the United States could not negotiate with the Russians. He thought the American people had wanted him to try. Marshall said that the Economic Recovery Plan, also known as the Marshall Plan, "was an outgrowth of [my] disillusionment over the Moscow Conference." The United States was proceeding toward its second transformational decision about the nation's international role in the face of precarious problems.[86]

Marshall met with the president on April 27 to present his impressions and recommend a course of prompt action. On April 28, he spoke to the nation by radio. He described Europe's disintegration. The secretary did not call for a break with Moscow, but he warned that "[t]he patient is sinking while the doctors deliberate." He was previewing a need for a new approach: "[A]ction can not await compromise through exhaustion." Marshall closed with a request for bipartisan unity.[87]

Kennan's Paper

On April 29, Marshall summoned Kennan, who was still in transition from teaching at the National War College to becoming the first director of Policy Planning, for their first face-to-face conversation. The secretary wanted to seize the diplomatic initiative. Marshall directed Kennan to examine the question of Europe's future and recommend what Marshall should do. Kennan had two weeks. When Kennan asked if Marshall would offer any other guidance, the secretary gave his classic response: "Avoid trivia."[88]

Kennan took a little over three weeks. His first policy planning paper, which would look shockingly brief to officials today, would be his office's most influential. Having little background in economics, Kennan drew from the work of Clayton and his staff and an interagency report produced in April. But his main contribution was to define the problem and outline a barebones diplomatic strategy. He wrote that Europe's problem was "economic maladjustment which makes European society vulnerable to exploitation by any and all totalitarian movements and which Russian communism is now exploiting." Kennan's target was Europe's own breakdown, not Communism. The new plan must be "frankly stated to the American public." The aim was to make Europe "self-supporting."

In the short term, Kennan said the challenge was to identify "effective and dramatic action" that would overcome structural bottlenecks in European economies and, just as important, "serve as a catalyst for hope and confidence" by demonstrating a U.S. commitment. The long-term challenge was to revitalize European economies through a European initiative supported by the United States with appropriate "safeguards." Kennan recognized a key prerequisite that has plagued development plans for decades: The locals must own the project. In this situation, Kennan maintained, the ownership must be by a group of friendly European nations, not through isolated appeals from each country. The United States had to push Europeans to integrate their economies, an obvious idea today but a big step in 1947.

Kennan's memo made a critical geographical assumption about the definition of Europe. He never mentions Germany, but hints at its inclusion through a reference to the "Rhine Valley." The U.S. offer, he explained, should be to all of Europe, but "in such a form that the Russian satellite countries would either exclude themselves by unwillingness to accept the proposed conditions or agree to abandon the exclusive orientation of their economies." Kennan was gambling that the Soviets would isolate themselves rather than join a European recovery based on American principles of cooperation and market economics.

Kennan's closing section tried to rewrite the Truman Doctrine. He worried that the American public approached world problems through "a defensive reaction to communist pressure" rather than aiding others because of sound economic logic. He also feared the Doctrine was becoming "a blank check to give economic and military aid to any area of the world where communists show signs of being successful." His first concern revealed a stunning lack of practical political sense about how to get Congress to spend vast sums abroad. But Kennan's second point was a wise caution to policy makers who would have to wrestle with other cases once the political flames of anti-Communism were kindled.[89]

Kennan's intellectual ponderings, usually expressed through fine prose, gave him precedence with historians exploring the origins of the Marshall Plan. However, Kennan's boss, Acheson, wrote later that Clayton's punchy memos and presentations to Marshall had a more powerful effect on the secretary than Kennan's carefully structured guidance.[90] I suspect that both contributed to the decision to proceed.

Clayton's Experience

Clayton's experience with the British loan and European relief in 1946 sharpened his sense of the continent's deepening crisis. In late December, a high-pressure zone massed over the Arctic Circle. As the front rolled south and settled over northern Europe, blizzards paralyzed the region. Food and fuel supplies could not move. Production stopped. People were starving and freezing to death.

Britain was hit hardest. Snow piled as high as twenty feet. The drifts blocked railways and highways. Coal mines closed. Power shut down. Alan Bullock wrote that "British industrial production was effectively halted for three weeks—something German bombing had never been able to do." The cost to London over four months was an estimated $1 billion, almost one-third of the loan that Clayton and Keynes had expected would support Britain for five years.[91]

At the start of 1947, Clayton began meeting weekly with his staff to monitor Europe's tribulations. He asked how best to estimate regional needs as a whole, pushing the concept of continental integration. Paul Nitze developed a shorthand measure: the U.S. payments surplus, which was the amount of gold and foreign exchange Europeans had to pay the United States to balance accounts. Nitze estimated a figure of about $5 billion a year, a number that would become a rough benchmark in the months to come.[92]

Clayton was not thinking only in terms of aid. His goal was to get the engine of the European economy working again and to reengage its gears with a growing global economy. Extension of the 1945 Reciprocal Trade Agreements Act, which Clayton and Acheson had carried forward after Hull's departure, would expire in 1948. Clayton was preparing for a multilateral trade negotiation in Geneva in April 1947.[93]

Some members of the new Republican majority wanted to postpone the Geneva meeting and repeal the RTAA. Clayton refused and argued that the U.S. initiative was vital to thwart the "strangulation" of commerce by a resurgent web of national controls and discrimination. Senator Vandenberg, formerly an opponent of the RTAA, stepped in. He proposed five procedural changes, most of which the president addressed through an executive order.[94]

At Baylor University on March 6, less than a week before the president's address to Congress on Greece and Turkey, Truman presented the case for an aggressive trade agenda and U.S. economic leadership. He compared the "turning point" of 1947 with that of 1920.[95] Clayton and the State Department had contributed to the first draft of Truman's Baylor speech. Greg Fossedal unearthed an intriguing section Clayton had considered adding, but had held back. The supplemental language drew a direct connection between trade and a bolder aid program to achieve "American security and prosperity." It would have introduced Nitze's idea of a payments gap, referencing the $5 billion surplus. Acheson and Clayton probably figured that a trade, aid, and European economic recovery plan would have overloaded political circuits when the administration was rushing to make its case on Greece and Turkey. These statesmen were moving very fast, and their new secretary was just leaving for Moscow. The launch of the Marshall Plan was still three months away.[96]

Nevertheless, one can identify the strands of practical decision-making coming together. Clark Clifford revealed that Clayton met regularly with the president between January and April 1947 to report on Europe's intensifying economic crisis. Truman's memoirs point to his Baylor speech as part of his thinking about the eventual European Recovery Program. Initial criticism of Truman's plan for Greece and Turkey by Walter Lippmann, America's most influential columnist on foreign affairs, as well as by the New York Times and Washington Post, called for a wider European effort. By late March, apparently after briefings by Clayton and Nitze, the influential journalists reported an encouraging, more encompassing economic strategy in the works.[97]

A memo prepared by Clayton on March 5 offers excellent insights into the origins of the Marshall Plan. We do not know how Clayton intended to use the memo. It reads as if he was attempting to organize his own reflections amidst the rush of events. The record suggests that Clayton used this note to present a coherent argument to his colleagues and possibly also to the president. Acheson cites Clayton's powerful message as important in sparking his thinking.[98]

Clayton began with a list summarizing the world situation and peril. Russia was taking advantage of economic and political breakdowns around the world to "bor[e] from within . . . a new technique with which we have not yet learned how to cope." The United States needed to assume the role of world leader from a fading Britain. The program for Greece "only goes part of the way." Clayton expected Marshall's Moscow mission would be disappointing. When the secretary returned, the president and Marshall needed to issue a clear statement to Congress and the American people, which Clayton outlined in fifteen points. He presented America's purpose, the nature of the threat, and the need for and types of action. Clayton explained how the new World Bank could help, but why neither it nor the UN was capable of countering this threat. He addressed two likely objections and called for a joint executive-congressional effort, launched with an appropriation of $5 billion. Clayton's memo looks like a précis of the economic security argument for the Marshall Plan. Over the next two months, Clayton would travel to Europe and add up-to-date political and economic reconnaissance to help Marshall make his momentous recommendation.[99]

Creating a New Trading System

After helping Acheson with the congressional work on Greece and Turkey, Clayton left for Europe on April 10. He was launching the trade negotiation in Geneva. The president also asked Clayton to attend the first UN Economic Commission for Europe (ECE) meeting, a possible mechanism for a European recovery plan. While traveling between European capitals, Clayton could learn firsthand about conditions and the need for assistance.

Clayton saw trouble everywhere. Weak currencies, failing production, and a drop in food supplies were breaking down "the modern system of division of labor." As governments failed to cope, people hoarded goods, farmers stopped delivering food to cities, and looters roamed freely. Clayton pressed for 553 tons of grains for France, a nation with a verdant countryside. On May 9, the World Bank made its first loan, $250 million, to Paris to modernize France's steel industry, procure raw materials, and straighten out transport.[100] Clayton concluded that the UN ECE, which included the Soviet Union and its satellites, could not operate as the vehicle for a recovery plan.

Then trouble in Washington threatened Clayton's trade initiative in Geneva. The negotiation on the proposed General Agreement on Tariffs and Trade had started well. Working off U.S. efforts, the negotiations drew many of the new multilateral rules from Hull's reciprocal trade agreements. Then the parties turned to offers to cut tariffs. In a demonstration of leadership and good faith, Clayton opened with U.S. offers. But the product-by-product negotiations began to stalemate.[101]

The new Republican Congress was legislating a 50 percent tariff on wool imports. Trade in wool—along with a few other commodities—would determine the fate of the new multilateral negotiations. Australia depended heavily on wool exports to America; an increased rate would lead America's recent Pacific ally to walk out, forcing Britain, as leader of the Commonwealth, to withdraw as well. Without access to British markets, Europeans would pull back. Clayton decided he had to return to the United States to persuade the president to block the higher wool tariff.[102]

The Making of the Marshall Plan

On May 19, just as Kennan was drafting his policy planning paper, Clayton returned and began working on a memo to complement his first effort of March 5. Acheson received Clayton's memo on May 27 and scheduled a meeting with Marshall the following day to discuss the Clayton and Kennan memos. Acheson wrote that "Will Clayton was one of the most powerful and persuasive advocates to whom I have listened. Both qualities came from his command of the subject and depth of his conviction."[103]

Clayton's May 27 memo presented a strong case. He opened by drawing an important distinction between "the physical destruction" of Europe, which Americans had understood, and "the effects of economic dislocation on production—nationalization of industries, drastic land reform, severance of long-standing commercial ties, disappearance of private commercial firms through death or loss of capital." As a result, "we grossly underestimated the destruction to the European economy by war...."

"The political position," he continued, "reflects the economic." Countries lurched from crisis to crisis as people starved, and farmers fed grain to cattle instead of selling it. "The modern system of division of labor has almost broken down in Europe."

Then Clayton offered data to the secretary, who demanded facts. He summarized payment deficits, including key components such as coal, grains, and shipping services. "Without further prompt and substantial aid from the United States," Clayton maintained, "economic, social, and political disintegration will overwhelm Europe." The costs would be awful for peace, security, and the U.S. economy.

Clayton called for an annual grant—not a loan—of $6 to $7 billion worth of goods for three years. The grant would support a European plan, which the UK, France, and Italy should lead in preparing. Europe needed an economic federation, not an economy "divided into many small watertight compartments as it is today." Other countries, especially farm and commodity producers, could contribute. But they had to avoid another UN Relief Administration. "The United States must run this show," Clayton concluded.[104]

According to Acheson, Clayton added illustrative detail at the meeting of May 28 with Marshall. The secretary concluded that the United States could not "sit back and do nothing." His principal concern was whether to address all of Europe or only the Western states. The working suggestion was to make the Soviets responsible for dividing Europe through Moscow's obstruction; Kennan proposed responding to any Soviet interest by calling for donations of Russian commodities.[105]

Marshall's Speech at Harvard

Marshall thought he could use a brief commencement address at Harvard on June 5 to plant the seeds of his ideas. He planned to speak only about ten minutes. Chip Bohlen, whose direct writing style suited Marshall's voice, prepared a draft from Kennan's and Clayton's memos. Marshall recalled that he also asked Kennan to prepare a version, and the secretary said he'd integrated the two drafts along with his own thoughts. Marshall was still rewriting on his way to Boston on June 4.[106] A fascinating side-by-side comparison of Clayton's May 27 memo (800 words and 10 main points) with Marshall's speech of June 5 (1,200 words and 8 main points) shows a close overlap.[107]

Truman knew about the work at the State Department to develop an aid plan for Europe. But in an amazing oversight, which Marshall later acknowledged, the secretary never showed the president an advance draft of his speech. In any event, Truman saw the benefit of having Secretary Marshall out front. "Anything going up [to Capitol Hill] bearing my name will quiver a couple of times, turn belly up and die," Truman told Clark Clifford. From the start, the president had an eye on counting Republican votes.[108]

Marshall might not have expected to make much news. His speech at Harvard would have seemed serious to the audience but not stirring. In highlighting Europe's plight, the secretary explained the nature of the continent's economic dislocation and the remedy of "breaking the vicious cycle and restoring the confidence." He focused on the need for countries to consider "Europe as a whole," hinting at Clayton's push for federation.

In two famous lines, Marshall announced, "Our policy is directed not against any country or doctrine but against hunger, poverty, desperation, and chaos. Its purpose should be the revival of a working economy in the world so as to permit the emergence of political and social conditions in which free institutions can exist." This was a positive formulation, linked to America's beliefs. Yet the crowd reacted more to Marshall's warning that countries blocking recovery would get no help, and that the United States would oppose those seeking to profit from the perpetuation of human misery.

Marshall closed with the diplomatic message urged by Kennan and Clayton: that "[t]he initiative...must come from Europe" because "[t]his is the business of the Europeans." Marshall wanted the Europeans to own the plan, both to unify economically and to assume responsibility for their own future.[109]

The U.S. press barely took notice of what would become an epic statement of American diplomacy. But Acheson knew how to make a dry speech into

a practical foreign policy initiative. Working through British correspondents in Washington, he primed them to alert British foreign secretary Ernie
Bevin. Acheson pointed out that Marshall would be inviting Europeans to
propose a cooperative design for recovery, backed by American aid. Bevin
got the message. He said the BBC account was "like a lifeline to a dying man.
It seemed to bring hope where there was none." He sent word to the State
Department that he was "taking the initiative" and racing to Paris to work
with the French. In Moscow, the Soviets also paid attention. The United
States had surprised them. The full diplomatic implications were far from
clear.[110]

Indeed, the U.S. plan looked vague to Americans, too. Six weeks after
Marshall's speech, Kennan complained, "Marshall 'plan,' we have no plan."[111]
U.S. officials had identified and defined a problem. They had announced
general principles of a possibly far-reaching response. Now they—and most
of all, the Europeans—had to come up with practical steps to make it work.

Wool Tariffs and the General Agreement on Tariffs and Trade (GATT)

Clayton was heading back to Europe to assist. But before departing he had
to keep the U.S. trade initiative alive. The House had passed the wool tariff
legislation 151–65 in May, and Congress was about to send the president a
highly protectionist bill. On June 19, Truman gave the secretary of agriculture and Clayton fifteen minutes each to make their respective case. The
agriculture secretary scoffed at the trade impasse in Geneva and warned
the president of the loss of support in up to seven wool-producing states in
the 1948 election. Clayton pointed to the connection of trade to America's
long-term interest in the international economy and urged an opportunity
to work for success in Geneva. The next day, the president told Clayton that
he would veto the wool bill and even gave Clayton authority to offer a 25 percent cut in the wool tariff. Years later, Clayton called the president's decision
"the greatest act of political courage I have ever witnessed." The Australians
grumbled about wanting a deeper tariff cut, but the negotiations started
moving again.[112]

Over the summer of 1947, Clayton served as Truman's ambassador to
Europe on the Marshall Plan while seeking to close the GATT negotiations
in Geneva. Once again, the British were immovable on any effort to remove
imperial trade preferences, even with the promise of Marshall Plan aid and
despite Clayton's efforts to offer creative transitions. The UK had adapted to
the U.S. protectionism of Smoot-Hawley. Once countries—and their interest groups—invest in alternatives to open trading systems, the cost of prying

them back toward freer trade can be very high politically. At one point in August, Clayton was ready to leave the British out of the new multilateral trading system. But the president had too many other priorities with Britain in 1947, and the United States agreed to launch GATT even with Britain's imperial preferences.[113]

This first multilateral trading round, with twenty-three participants, proved that cooperation on trade liberalization was possible. The parties cut tariffs on forty-five thousand items, covering about half of world trade. The process stimulated world trade even as economies were struggling to recover and remove foreign exchange controls. Some in Congress complained about a trade "giveaway," but the new trade diplomacy helped unleash unparalleled economic growth in the United States and the world for decades. The engine of the American economy that eventually overwhelmed the USSR relied on a trading system imagined by Hull and Clayton.[114]

For Clayton, the launch of the GATT dovetailed with his mission to prod the Europeans to develop their Marshall Plan proposal. His economic diplomacy interconnected trade liberalization, the revival of Europe's internal "division of labor," European economic integration, stable money, and U.S. aid. But the two principal capitals—London and Paris—balked at core elements. The British Labour Party government wanted a planned economy with controls directing markets. In Paris, Clayton had to push the understandably resentful and fearful French to accept Germany's economic recovery and integration with the rest of Europe.

The Soviets Respond to Marshall's Proposal

London and Paris did agree, however, on an approach to the Soviets. Bevin and French foreign minister Georges Bidault invited Molotov to Paris to discuss Marshall's proposal. Molotov, guided by Marxist principles, suspected the Americans were facing another crisis of capitalism; this explained America's imperialistic move to dominate Europe's economy. The Soviets were willing to request assistance as part of a package with others, but would never permit foreigners to assess Soviet resources and requirements or join in a coordinated project led by Washington.

Soviet spies had penetrated the British government, including the embassy in Washington. Assembling various reports, Soviet intelligence sent Stalin an "urgent" report. The nefarious Western plan, the spymasters argued, would block the Soviets' consolidation of control in Eastern Europe. The capitalists were scheming to draw Germany into their fold as well and would cut off Soviet reparations from current German production.

Stalin sent new instructions to Molotov, who became "completely uncompromising" according to Bevin. After five sessions, Molotov walked out. As Averell Harriman said later, Molotov "could have killed the Marshall Plan by joining it." But as Kennan had surmised, the Soviets "must decline or else enter into an arrangement that would mean an ending of the Iron Curtain." Unfortunately, the Soviets had the power to pull back their satellite states, too. The Marshall Plan, designed to counter economic crisis, triggered a Soviet decision to divide Europe—with its ensuing forty-year-long security confrontation.[115]

The Birthing Pains of a New Europe

On July 12, 1947, the foreign and trade ministers of sixteen nations met in Paris to plan a new Western European economy, backed by American aid. As Benn Steil described, "[I]n this magnificent hall consecrated to the glories of the French empire, Europe's top diplomats assembled to plea for aid from a former British colony."[116] The proud states of Europe started to debate ideas about European integration that few would have contemplated seriously before Marshall issued his invitation.

For the next two months, the birthing pains of a new Europe were starkly evident. Clayton tried to keep the conference on track. He pushed for a payments union, a customs union, open trade, and greater reliance on markets over state planning. In 1947, the governments of European states were not ready for these innovations. But Clayton's ideas would eventually become cornerstones of today's European Union.

As the summer dragged on, Washington grew worried. After hours and hours of talk, the emerging results looked like a long compendium of national wish lists, billed to Washington. As is often the case in diplomacy, the critics in the capital focused on their overseas representation, over which they had control, instead of the foreign politics, which were beyond Washington's reach. The State Department decided Clayton was pushing his ideas too hard, although at the same time Washington determined more "friendly aid" from the United States was necessary to bring the Europeans to closure.

Kennan believed that Europe's political weakness limited Europeans' ability to act boldly. Rather than giving the Americans more leverage, a feeble Europe could take only limited steps. The U.S. strategic judgment in the summer of 1947 was not to make the perfect the enemy of the good. Washington needed to keep the momentum going for Europe's economic recovery and for more open trade. It would have to fix unresolved and frustrating problems in the future.

The State Department opted for a process instead of the well-organized plan that it had hoped Europe would deliver. On September 22, the

Europeans delivered two volumes totaling 690 pages to Secretary Marshall. The Europeans recognized the political nature of the exercise. They committed to production targets and assumed responsibility for internal financial stability. They nodded in the direction of European economic cooperation. Rather than present a "shopping list," the countries agreed to work, individually and together, on structural problems. They recognized the need for private investment, complemented by World Bank financing. The appendix on Germany reflected conflicting opinions, but at least the rest of Europe recognized that Germany was an integral part of the puzzle they were trying to solve. The drafters of the report also acknowledged that their effort would be ongoing, and they agreed to supplementary work and the creation of an organization to review progress.[117]

The existence of a European Union today grew in part out of the European political outlook stirred by the Marshall Plan project. The Dutch delegate Ernst van der Beugel observed later that the Paris conference served as "the primary school for many ... who would play a major role on the postwar European scene, with additional loyalties to a broader entity than their own government."[118]

The Americans recognized that Europeans had taken a first, crucial step. The administration would decide what to submit to Congress, which would decide whether to foot the bill. Then the U.S. government needed to develop a mechanism to coordinate with Europeans to deliver the aid. In the interim, the administration needed to work with Congress to keep Europeans—and hope—alive.

Vandenberg and the Marshall Plan

Action on Marshall's plan now shifted to Congress—and principally to Senator Vandenberg. Years later, Marshall said "Vandenberg ... was just the whole show when we got to the actual [working out] of the thing." Without the senator's leadership, "the plan would not have succeeded. I feel that he has never received full credit for his monumental efforts ..., and that his name should have been associated with it." Marshall knew how to enlist Vandenberg; as early as May, Marshall had explained to Vandenberg that the administration would need his help on a big assistance effort in months to come. They met privately twice a week at the Blair House across from the White House.[119]

Vandenberg carefully balanced the roles of both critic and advocate in order to sway skeptics. He separated the financial request from the State Department's budget and control. Even with the secretary's high standing, Congress suspected that his department represented foreigners, not

Americans. A big foreign aid program looked like a worldwide, New Deal WPA to fund socialism.

Vandenberg persuaded President Truman to appoint three bipartisan committees of leading figures to advise on the need for the aid and the domestic effects. He worked with the people who wrote the committees' reports to emphasize the theme of self-help and to recommend improvements.[120]

Vandenberg urged Under Secretary of State Robert Lovett—Acheson's successor and a Republican—to organize business support, including top-level witnesses for congressional hearings. Agricultural, labor, veteran, and religious groups joined in.[121]

The Truman administration organized a huge effort to win support and votes. The secretary of state made a cross-country speaking tour. "I worked on that as hard as though I was running for the Senate or the presidency," Marshall recalled. "That's the thing I take pride in, putting the damned thing over." As in any campaign, the nature of the advocacy adapted to fit the audience. Opposition to the Soviet Union and to the spread of Communism sharpened. The threat was no longer only "hunger, poverty, desperation, and chaos," but the survival of independent European nations and even America's own way of life. The message, however framed, resonated. Seven Cub Scouts from Troop 232 in Bethesda, Maryland, visited Marshall to explain their plan to raise money to feed eight European boys.[122]

The best advocates turned out to be members of Congress themselves. Between August and November 1947, more than two hundred congresspersons traveled to Europe. The most notable mission was led by Republican congressman Christian Herter, who had helped Will Clayton make the case for the loan to Britain. The eighteen representatives, including just-elected Richard Nixon, spent forty-five days in Europe and prepared an 883-page report. They were witnesses to both sinking economies and the rising reach of Communism.

By November 1947, the Marshall Plan had gained strong support. The administration named it the European *Recovery* Plan (ERP) to distinguish this aid from the past run of requests to keep Europeans afloat. But first the administration had to win one more stopgap measure to sustain France, Italy, and Austria while Congress deliberated on the ERP. This would be a test vote. When Senator Taft and others tried to cut the amount, Vandenberg countered that they were "throwing a 15-foot rope to a man who is drowning 20 feet from shore." The Senate stood by Vandenberg and Truman with a vote of 83–6. The final bill for $522 million (about $6.01 billion today) passed on December 15. The administration sent up the follow-on ERP legislation on December 19.[123]

From January 8 to February 3, 1948, Chairman Vandenberg heard ninety-five witnesses in the Foreign Relations Committee, producing a record of 1,466 pages. The House of Representatives, which has the power of the purse, heard even more. Vandenberg, always with an ear to his colleagues' concerns, masterfully posed questions whose answers he could use to win votes. He crafted language for the bill that looked vague or superfluous to the untrained eye. But as Vandenberg told a colleague, "Just leave those words in. I can tell nineteen different Senators...who are worried about something—'your problem is taken care of by that clause in the bill.'"[124] But the main theme was one that all senators had to treat seriously: war and peace.

Vandenberg had three cards left to play. First, Congress could seek "consideration" from Europe, just as the United States acquired bases from Britain in exchange for Lend-Lease aid in 1941. The State Department had to gain promises of access to strategic raw materials and for closer military cooperation.

Second, Vandenberg needed someone other than "foreign service bureaucrats" to run a multi-billion-dollar operation. But Marshall would not accept "two secretaries of state." Vandenberg compromised on an independent agency, the Economic Cooperation Administration (ECA), to run operations, subject to the State Department's policy guidance. Vandenberg insisted that the director come from the business world, a step that reassured Taft and other Republicans. Vandenberg also persuaded the president to select Paul Hoffman, the president of the Studebaker Corporation. Truman and Hoffman made Averell Harriman the ECA representative in Europe.

Third, Vandenberg had to sort out the budgeting. Congress is highly protective of its financial prerogatives. In 1947, total federal spending amounted to $34.5 billion. Marshall sought authorization of $17 billion over four years. Vandenberg accepted the overall amount, but thought Congress was more likely to accept a process of multiple tranches. He settled on $5.3 billion over twelve months.[125]

On March 1, 1948, Vandenberg rose before his colleagues and a crowded Senate gallery. Vandenberg now had a bill with the unanimous support of his committee. The old newspaper editor had written, rewritten, and typed his nine-thousand-word speech himself. He was a powerful orator in the old Senate style.[126] Vandenberg made the case for America's self-interest. "The iron curtain must not come to the rims of the Atlantic either by aggression or default." This vote "can be the turning point in history for 100 years to come." (He turned out to be right for at least seventy.)[127]

According to Benn Steil, the polls showed that 80 percent of Americans had now heard of the Marshall Plan. Favorable opinion far outpaced unfavorable, 57 to 18 percent.[128] Current events also served as an alarming reminder of recent history: The Soviet-directed coup in Czechoslovakia that February and March offered stunning evidence of the peril. A decade before, Britain and France had sacrificed Czech independence in a forlorn effort to appease the Nazis. Stalin was also pressing the intrepid Finns to submit to a defense pact.[129]

Shortly after midnight on March 14, 1948, the Senate passed, by a vote of 69–17, a one-year ERP authorization of $5.3 billion. Vandenberg had carried along thirty of his Republican colleagues, including Taft. The president pressed for House action before the Italian elections in mid-April, because the Communist Party there offered a serious challenge.

On April 2, the House passed the final conference report 318–75, with the Senate acting by voice vote. The president signed the Marshall Plan into law on April 3, 1948.[130] It had been ten arduous months from Marshall's speech at Harvard until the passage of the ERP. The first sign of a political turn came two weeks later, when the centrist Italian coalition bested the Communists by a considerable margin and even won an absolute majority in the Chamber of Deputies.[131]

The rush of events had led to a series of responses that reversed 150 years of American foreign policy tradition toward Europe and the world. But more problems loomed immediately ahead. Within two months, the Republican chairman of the House Appropriations Committee cut ECA funding by 25 percent. Vandenberg, who had worked diligently to bring along his Republican colleagues, took the unusual step of asking to address the Senate appropriators. He overturned both congressional comity and Republican unity to attack the "cynical reversal" of a major national policy decision. "I beg of you," he pleaded, "for the sake of hopes by which free men live, that you give the ECA a fair chance." The Senate restored the money and prevailed in the conference committee. Battles in Congress often have to be rewon multiple times.[132]

Benn Steil concludes that the United States eventually contributed $14.2 billion (in 1952 dollars) to the sixteen Marshall Plan countries between 1948 and 1952. In today's dollars, the four years of Marshall aid was worth $138 billion. (The amount was 1.1 percent of U.S. GDP; the same proportion over four recent years would be $800 billion or more.) The United States had made a huge investment in an entangling transatlantic partnership.[133]

Vandenberg's leadership in 1947–48 eroded any prospects he had for the Republican presidential nomination. He had earned respect, but his partnership with Truman and Marshall was no basis for a partisan campaign. In any event, his duties as a statesman in Congress were not yet completed.

The Role of Germany in Europe

The third critical diplomatic decision after World War II concerned the fate of Germany. By 1948, the German problem had changed—from conquering an enemy to supporting a potential partner, one that could become the keystone of an integrated and secure Europe. Germany would become the central front—the *Schwerpunkt*, in Clausewitzian strategic terms—during the Cold War. This realization guided U.S. policy in 1989–90 as well, when President George H. W. Bush and Secretary Baker embraced Germany as America's principal partner in creating "a Europe whole and free." The origins of America's strategy toward Germany for a half century trace to the decisions of 1948.[134]

After sorting through the rubble of the Third Reich, the victors discovered that about 80 percent of Germany's industrial capacity remained intact. The country had a greater stock of machine tools, much of it new, than before the war. The great bombing raids had demolished urban housing and key transportation facilities. With repairs of bottlenecks, the availability of inputs, and a return to a functioning monetary system, Germany could power its own recovery and contribute mightily to Europe's.[135]

The United States knew that Germany would have to be part of Europe's recovery. In July 1947, within a month of his Harvard speech, Marshall agreed with the secretaries of the army and the navy "that Germany must cooperate fully in any effective European plan, and that the economic revival in Europe depends in considerable part on a recovery in German production." The State and War Departments sent a new directive to General Clay in Germany: "[A]n orderly and prosperous Europe requires the contributions of a stable and productive Germany." The Morgenthau plan for a pastoral Germany was a distant memory. The plan now was to ensure food supplies, boost German production, draw France into a three-way zone, and connect Germany with America's recovery plan for Europe.[136]

But Germany's potential also posed a problem. The Moscow Conference in 1947 revealed Stalin's priority to strip Germany bare. The Paris Conference on the Marshall Plan showed the tension between gaining Germany's economic help and reviving Teutonic economic mastery. The faltering coal mines in Germany's Ruhr highlighted the price of uncertainty: If workers could not get enough food, they could not excavate coal. Germans failed to show up for work. Even if miners worked, there were few goods for them to buy.[137] Occupying armies make poor business managers. The Americans were frustrated that the British were testing the Labour Government's socialism on Germany's mines. Marshall and Clayton told Bevin that they "regarded the British management of the Ruhr coal problem as pathetic."[138]

The real problem, however, was France's fears. France was importing vast amounts of coal and grain from the United States. The French wanted German coal, but just for themselves and without reviving German steelmaking and chemical production. Bidault, Jean Monnet, and Robert Schuman, the French fathers of economic recovery and European integration, had little room for political maneuvering, assaulted by the Communist left and the Gaullist right. It became increasingly clear that France needed security assurances as well as aid; the French now feared the Soviets as well as the Germans. When U.S. admiral Richard Conolly summarized his discussions with the French late in 1947, he reported, "What is worrying French officials is SECURITY." They see "colossal ground forces to the eastward." If the United States precipitated a conflict with Moscow over Germany, the Soviets might subsume German resources and technology and turn on France.[139]

Yet Paris had to choose. The Americans "hinted" that France's share of Marshall Plan aid might depend on cooperation over Germany. On March 5, 1948, the United States, the UK, and France issued a bold communique in London. The "London Program" coordinated the economic policies of the Anglo-American Bizonia with France's zone, incorporated the western zones of Germany into the Marshall Plan, and created a West German government.[140]

The same day, Washington received a top secret cable from General Clay warning of "a subtle change in Soviet attitude" over the past few weeks. Then he dropped his "bombshell": The general—who had thought the Soviets were unlikely to resort to war—said war might now "come with dramatic suddenness." The effect on Washington was stunning. The Air Force checked on the timing of moving atomic bombs closer to the USSR. Joseph and Stuart Alsop wrote that the postwar atmosphere had chilled to "a prewar atmosphere."[141]

The Marshall Plan, which began as an economic response to security risks, was triggering calls for a military complement. But a peacetime security alliance would be a true revolution in U.S. policy toward Europe.[142]

A New Deutschmark and the Berlin Blockade

During March and April, Stalin ordered his forces to begin interfering with the Western powers' transportation to Berlin. He did not want a full blockade yet. He maneuvered to divide the United States, Britain, and France and frighten them from proceeding with the London Program for West Germany.[143]

Germany still did not have a workable postwar currency. The Soviets inflated the printing of the first occupation marks, ruining those bills. Clay's experts recommended the creation of a new Deutschmark in 1946, but the Soviets would not agree to U.S. control of the printing plates. By 1948, western Germany's inflation was surging—at roughly 10 percent a month—reminding Germans of Weimar's collapse. This battle over currency would precipitate a crisis over Berlin and a forty-two-year division of Germany.

The Western powers announced that they would introduce the new Deutschmark on June 20, though not yet in Berlin. The Soviets began blocking road traffic and inspecting trains. June 24, 1948, would turn out to be the critical day. The Soviets introduced their own Ostmark. The Soviets began to choke the city with a full blockade of rail, highway, and water traffic. President Truman learned of the Soviet challenge just as the Republicans chose Governor Thomas Dewey as their nominee for the November election.

The Berlin Airlift

The Americans, British, and French had one route left to Berlin: the air. The Americans began flying in supplies, and the president ordered a full-scale airlift, but no one expected that they could meet the needs of the city.[144]

The Berlin Airlift has been extolled as a demonstration of American resolve and technical capability. The reality is that the Americans and their partners were uncertain, even doubtful. They thought the airlift would be, at best, a short-term expedient while they figured out what to do. Clay wanted to challenge the Soviets with an armed convoy. In September, the president reviewed options, including nuclear strikes. The CIA concluded that the circumstances made the Western position in the city "untenable in the long run."[145]

Stalin wanted even more: to derail the meeting on September 1 of the West German Parliamentary Council—sixty-four elected representatives, with Konrad Adenauer of the Christian Democratic Union as president—to begin drafting a new constitution for West Germany. Stalin had decided to push the Western powers out of Berlin.

The men in charge—West and East—overlooked two factors. First, the Berliners showed courageous resistance. More than three hundred thousand Berliners cheered the city leaders near the Brandenburg Gate as they lashed into the Soviets. As in 1961 and 1989, Berliners became a political force in their own right. The Americans and other Western powers admired Berliners' tenacity on the front line of freedom—and recognized they would pay a price for failing to support such valor.

The second oversight was of Major General William Tunner, who became the commander of the airlift in late July. He was an unusual airman. In an era of bomber and fighter pilots, Tunner was devoted to mastering transport and logistics. He was the epitome of the pragmatic American problem solver. Based on time-and-motion studies of scientific management, the general changed procedures. He boosted daily deliveries from 2,226 tons in July to more than 3,800 tons in August and almost 4,600 tons in September. Planes were landing every four minutes and averaged three flights a day. Ground crews serviced the planes around the clock. The French added a new Berlin airport at Tegel to expand landing capacity.[146]

Truman had to decide whether to double down his bet on Tunner, Clay, and the Berliners. The Berlin Airlift had already absorbed half of the available air fleet. Air Force Chief of Staff Hoyt Vandenberg (a nephew whom the senator had assisted with a nomination to West Point) warned of dangers to American airpower globally. Winter was coming, reducing hours of daylight, increasing bad-weather days, and requiring more coal. Truman ordered navy planes to join the peaceful air armada and procured new planes to replace old ones. The British put their planes under Tunner's command. Clay was able to increase Berliners' food rations to 2,000 calories per day, less than the average for Americans (3,300) but above the supplies elsewhere in Germany. By October, 84 percent of West Berliners were confident the Americans would supply their city by air—and 95 percent wanted the Yanks to stay.[147]

As the 1948 election approached, two of Truman's speechwriters wanted to show the voters that he was a man of peace. In early October, they convinced the president that he should send a special envoy to Stalin to test the possibility of a "deal." Truman asked Supreme Court Chief Justice Fred Vinson to serve as the envoy to discuss "the moral relationship" between the countries, not negotiate about Berlin. When Marshall, in Paris, learned of the gambit, he was furious at the madness of the idea. The United States was succeeding in Berlin and West Germany. In doing so, it was building the confidence of Britain, France, and the other states in the West. Stalin could never yield Eastern Europe. He would relent in Berlin only if the United States showed staying power. Marshall embodied the art of alliance management just as the United States was entering a new era of alliance diplomacy.

Truman had been swayed by election positioning. According to his biographer McCullough, the president dropped the scheme after Marshall objected. Jonathon Daniels, an old Truman friend dating back to World War I and now a speechwriter and confidant, warned the president that the mission was the last, best chance to be reelected. But Truman demurred.[148]

Reelection and a New Secretary of State

On November 2, 1948, Truman managed one of the greatest political upsets in presidential history. The Democrats regained control of both Houses of Congress. Secretary Marshall had made clear that he would step down after the election. A few days after the election, the press printed a rumor that the president would ask Vandenberg to succeed Marshall. We do not know if Truman floated the prospect. The idea must have been tempting to the former chairman, now back in the minority. But knowing of Truman's practice to announce appointments before asking, Vandenberg preempted the possibility with a statement. Truman had run hard against the "do nothing, good for nothing" Republican Congress. By keeping his Republican ties in the Senate, Vandenberg reasoned, he could contribute more to a bipartisan foreign policy.[149]

The president asked Dean Acheson to become the new secretary of state. The nomination was shadowed by Acheson's connections to Alger Hiss, who was under suspicion of spying for the Soviets. Vandenberg helpfully drafted a statement for Acheson to use to stress his anti-Communism—and to offer a cover for senators' votes.[150]

Acheson faced difficult decisions quickly. By March, General Tunner had proven that his airlift could best the German winter. The record average daily tonnage rose to 7,850 tons in April. The coal deliveries beat the target by 50 percent. In an overwhelming display of logistical power in one day, Tunner arranged an air train of almost 13,000 tons of coal, with almost 1,400 planes, landing almost every minute over twenty-four hours.[151]

The Soviets began to feel the strain of the Western powers' counterblockade of shipments east: coal, steel, and food. Acheson expanded the embargo by banning freight shipments across the Western zones to all the Soviet satellites.[152]

The Soviets signaled the possibility of a mutual end to restriction on trade and communications, but they also maneuvered to delay the formation of the new Federal Republic of Germany. Acheson held firm. On May 4, the United States, Britain, and France agreed with the Soviets to end the blockades on May 12. A passenger train from Western Germany arrived in Berlin at 5:11 a.m. on March 12. Berliners celebrated. Berlin, the capital of the Third Reich, was now freedom's city.[153]

Acheson and the German Question

Acheson still had to answer the German question. He had not been part of the diplomacy of the London Program for Germany. George Kennan was having cold feet about U.S. policy toward Germany. He had written a paper for Marshall proposing to withdraw foreign armies, end military governments, and establish an independent and neutral German government. When Acheson took over, he was "initially intrigued by Kennan's case." He doubted that foreign powers could occupy Germany indefinitely. The new secretary said he would wait for Kennan to return from a trip to Germany to decide.[154]

While Kennan was traveling, his opponents—General Clay, others in the State Department, the Defense Department, and the Joint Chiefs—were busy. Acheson would be meeting his British, French, and Soviet counterparts at the end of May.

On May 12, James Reston published a front-page story in the *New York Times*. The headline read, "Big 3 Would Withdraw to Ports in the North Under Proposals. French Would Go Home." The British and French were both blindsided and shocked. The West Germans objected, too. Acheson abandoned Kennan's plan in an off-the-record briefing on May 18. With a touch of irony, the Soviet general in command of East Germany dismissed Kennan's plan, too: "[T]he Germans hate us. It is necessary that we retain our forces in Germany."[155]

The difference between Acheson and Kennan as diplomats is revealing. After Acheson's death, Kennan lamented that Acheson "was basically a Washington lawyer, not a diplomat." Benn Steil astutely explains Kennan's complaint: "Like Kennan, Acheson had a fine mind, but a practical one, not a ruminative or emotional one. Confronted with a problem, he would insist that if you can't *do* anything about it, just stop *thinking* about it," recalled his daughter Mary. 'Get on with something!' "[156]

Kennan was bipartisan in his aspersions. He decried "catering to Senatorial opinion in instances when one might better have attempted to educate the protagonists to a more enlightened and effective view." He thought that Vandenberg and his ilk did not deserve "admiring applause every time they could be persuaded by the State Department to do something sensible." It is difficult to imagine Kennan trying to win votes.[157]

On May 8, 1949, the Parliamentary Council in Bonn approved "the Basic Law," a nonthreatening term for a new West German constitution. The Western powers accepted the Basic Law on May 12, and the trizonal German Länder (states) promptly ratified the constitution so it could come into force on May 23.[158]

The Vandenberg Resolution and Transatlantic Security

Acheson and Vandenberg had one more step ahead: the creation of a transatlantic security alliance, the ultimate "entangling" treaty. As the Truman administration pursued its plans for Europe and Germany, leading figures recognized two more problems. First, Western Europeans in general, and France in particular, could not rehabilitate and revive Germany without a security assurance against a renewal of German power. Second, the hostile Soviet response to Germany's recovery and division threatened both the Germans and the rest of the continent. Logic pushed toward the idea of a U.S. military alliance with Europe, but political tradition and Congress's dislike of ceding war powers argued against the prospect.

Britain, France, and the Benelux countries took the first step by creating a Western Union Defense Organization on March 17, 1948. But the new group's mission was to cooperate on "measures of mutual assistance in the event of a renewal of German aggression."[159] After the coup in Prague in 1948, Secretary Marshall agreed with Bevin to begin secret discussions about "an Atlantic security system." The original idea was to consider North American military support to the new Western Union in the event of a Soviet attack. Late in March, the United States, Britain, and Canada began planning talks on "the possibilities of a military ERP." The president authorized private contacts with Congress.[160]

Early in 1948, Vandenberg invited Under Secretary of State Lovett to come by his apartment in the evenings to brainstorm over cocktails. Lovett would bring a "sheaf of telegrams" to review events around the world. They pondered the question of supporting regional security arrangements in Europe in the face of Soviet obstructionism in the UN. Vandenberg did not want the debate over an alliance to interfere with action on and early funding of the Marshall Plan. Yet he recognized the need to start laying a foundation in the Senate for a European security arrangement, especially given the Berlin blockade and the formation of the new Western Union Defense Organization.[161]

Vandenberg and Lovett brought in their staffs to start drafting a Senate resolution. Vandenberg, the old editor, was unhappy with the length. He typed, and revised, a simple but pointed page. He drew on his experience with the drafting of the UN Charter and the precedent of a regional security arrangement, the Rio Treaty of 1947 for the Western Hemisphere. He deftly respected the Constitution, Congress's authority to declare war, and Article 51 of the UN Charter, which authorized individual or collective self-defense. Vandenberg charted a course within the UN, but outside the reach of the Soviet veto.

He introduced "the Vandenberg Resolution" to the Foreign Relations Committee in May. His colleagues scrutinized the six paragraphs in three long, closed-door sessions. Vandenberg explained the parallels with the Marshall Plan: European self-help and American self-interest. Unlike in

1919, there would be no doubt about preserving Congress's constitutional right to commit U.S. forces to war.

On May 19, 1948, the committee approved Vandenberg's resolution unanimously. As president pro tempore of the Senate, Vandenberg scheduled a full Senate vote on June 11. Vandenberg explained his resolution as a plan for "practical American cooperation" given European circumstances. With a nod to the great triumvirate, he pointed out how his approach never stepped "outside the United Nations Charter...the Constitution of the United States...[or] the final authority of the Congress." The Senate endorsed Vandenberg's resolution 64–6.[162]

Dean Acheson, whose sharp-tongued memoirs reveal his frustrations with Congress, praised Vandenberg for recognizing the importance of the word "advice" in the constitutional phrase "with the advice and consent of the Senate." Acheson wrote that "by getting the Senate to give advice in advance of negotiation he got it to accept responsibility in advance of giving its consent to ratification. Equally important, he got the Senate to give good advice."[163]

The North Atlantic Treaty

Vandenberg's resolution gave Marshall and the State Department political authorization to begin a negotiating process that challenged one of America's oldest diplomatic traditions. During the rest of 1948, the administration strained to find an approach to collective self-defense that matched Europe's needs with Congress's willingness to assume obligations and pay the bill for military assistance along with economic aid.

American diplomacy had to be sensitive to European history and current politics, especially in France. Schuman and Bidault had won a narrow legislative victory in June 1948, and France's posture on Germany depended on security assurances.[164] Marshall had to ease the way for the French to come to terms with a difficult choice: To get Marshall aid, Paris had to accept the U.S. plan for European integration, including Germany. The Americans gradually removed French alternatives, such as reliance on reparations and underpriced German goods or holding on to German territory. After World War I, the Americans had gone home. Washington had to commit to stay this time if it wanted to fashion a different Western Europe and German policy.[165]

When Acheson succeeded Marshall as secretary of state in 1949, he began dual track negotiations on a North Atlantic Treaty with the potential allies and Congress. Vandenberg, now in the minority, was the administration's most able guide in assessing what the Senate would accept.

They had to determine what nations to include, the nature of the obligations, what action would trigger a response, whether it would be automatic, and the role of Congress in deciding on military action. As Acheson later wrote, Vandenberg sought to balance the need for a specific commitment to deter the Soviets with keeping faith with the Constitution and senators whose votes might depend on a more general pledge.

Vandenberg turned to a congressional favorite—referencing its prior actions as justifications for new ones. He drew the phrase "an attack on one is an attack on all" from the recently ratified Rio Treaty for the Americas. He referenced joint and several measures to restore peace and security from the UN's Article 51. Acheson added two phrases—one to please Congress and the other to reassure the Europeans. The "measures" would involve "such action as each deems necessary," a clause that enabled Congress to have a later say, yet the measure "includ[ed] the use of armed force" to demonstrate seriousness of purpose to allies. Vandenberg added a pledge for alliance members to provide "continuous and effective self-help" as a marker for sharing burdens in the future. Most important, Vandenberg assured his colleagues that the treaty was not an automatic commitment to go to war.

On April 4, 1949, a year and a day after the president had signed the Marshall Plan into law, the foreign ministers of ten European states and Canada joined Acheson in signing the North Atlantic Treaty. When the Foreign Relations Committee held hearings, Vandenberg sought to broaden Republican support; he arranged for two colleagues not on the committee to attend hearings and question witnesses. He worked with Acheson on an exchange to clarify that the Senate would need to consent to any new NATO member. The Senate consented to the North Atlantic Treaty on July 24, 1949, by a vote of 82–13. Republicans backed Vandenberg 32–11.[166]

With no apparent sense of irony, a State Department white paper described the treaty as the "most important step in American foreign policy since the promulgation of the Monroe Doctrine"—which John Quincy Adams had drafted to keep the United States *out* of Europe's squabbles.[167] More honestly, the State Department's John Hickerson, who had worked tirelessly on the new transatlantic bond, said, "I don't care whether entangling alliances have been considered worse than original sin since George Washington."[168] Hickerson confused Jefferson's language with Washington's, but otherwise understood that the United States was taking a huge, historic step to address a modern problem. Acheson would soon add that "neutralism," another long-standing American doctrine, "is a shortcut to suicide."[169]

Vandenberg helped overcome the old loathing of alliances by redefining the idea behind the term. He said "the North Atlantic Pact is *fundamentally* of an entirely different character" from "a 'military alliance' in the historic pattern." The pact was primarily a diplomatic tie, not a military league. He called the NATO agreement "the greatest war deterrent ever devised." The aging and now ailing senior senator probably best liked the honor bestowed on the Vandenberg Resolution by a younger colleague who called it the "Magna Carta of new hope for freedom in a Communist-assaulted world."[170]

By early 1950, Vandenberg's bipartisan approach to foreign policy was breaking down under the pressures of the Communists' victory in China and Senator Joseph McCarthy's charges. On April 18, 1951, Vandenberg died of cancer. Yet one of Vandenberg's final political protégés was a new congressman from Grand Rapids, who defeated an isolationist incumbent in the primary race. The new representative was Gerald Ford.[171]

The true test of NATO would come through events and perceptions in Europe. *Time* magazine captured the United States position: "Europe can't fully recover until the sickle is removed from its throat." Benn Steil records that French prime minister Henri Queuille emphasized that France had "taken dangerous steps to bring about a freer and more effective economy in Europe," while cultivating "a friendly attitude toward Germany which it had been very difficult to persuade the French people to endorse." Yet France did well, too. The Marshall Plan and NATO offered a much better combination than the Dawes Plan for German debt and the Locarno Treaty after World War I. Lord Ismay, NATO's first secretary general, offered the most pithy summary of NATO's purpose: "to keep the Russians out, the Americans in, and the Germans down."[172]

Konrad Adenauer would devote the rest of his days to creating a new Franco-German partnership. But he recognized that he operated within a framework of American diplomacy. The new transatlantic framework offered visionary Europeans—such as Monnet, Schuman, and later Jacques Delors and Helmut Kohl—an opportunity to advance ideas for European communities that eventually led to the European Union of today.[173]

Countless other problems lay ahead. The new NATO's military arm, led by General Eisenhower, would have only fourteen divisions, two of which were American. Soviet bloc forces were twelve times larger. The issue of Berlin was not resolved. As we will see, NATO would need to rely on a nuclear deterrent and careful alliance diplomacy through the very end of the Cold War.[174]

◆

CHAPTER 12

Vannevar Bush

Inventor of the Future

Three Big Ideas

In July 1945, as Americans were turning from the imperatives of war to the uncertainties of peace, Dr. Vannevar Bush advanced three ideas that shaped the nation's security for the rest of the century. He wrote two as designs for the future, although for very different audiences. The third involved an immense blast in New Mexico.

Bush titled his first paper "Science, the Endless Frontier." It was a thirty-four-page introduction to dry committee reports published by the Government Printing Office. The papers—and Bush's introduction—responded to an inquiry from the late President Roosevelt (prompted by Bush) about lessons learned from scientific-governmental cooperation during wartime.[1]

As Bush recalled many years later, in late 1944 FDR had called Bush into his office to ask, "What's going to happen to science after the war?" Bush replied, "It's going to fall flat on its face." Roosevelt countered, "What are we going to do about it?" To which Bush answered, "We better do something damn quick."[2]

Bush's public paper was the start of a big "something." His title invoked the quintessential American image of pioneers. He called for governmental funding of basic research in peacetime—in partnership with universities and industry—to discover "a largely unexplored hinterland" of science. For well over a century, Americans had defined their frontiers in geographical terms. For many foreign policy experts, the fashion of geopolitics trained diplomatic eyes on continental heartlands, rimlands, and maritime states. Bush offered another perspective on power and influence: "Scientific progress is one essential key to our security as a nation, to our better health, to more jobs, to a higher standard of living, and to our cultural progress."[3]

Bush urged the creation of a new National Research Foundation (NRF) as an independent agency outside the federal government to encourage "freedom of inquiry." The NRF, guided by an expert board and small staff, would direct contracts and grants to "colleges, universities, and research institutes, in both medicine and the natural sciences."[4]

Bush's call to action eventually led to the creation of the National Science Foundation. More important, his initiative—and the success of his wartime work—led to the construction of a military-industrial-academic network that gave the United States an unmatched technological edge in world affairs.

Bush's second publication that summer of 1945 was an article in the July edition of the *Atlantic* titled "As We May Think." Bush described a machine of the future, a "memex," to "give man access to and command the inherited knowledge of the ages." In stark contrast with Bush's idea of an organized public-private research and development complex, the memex would empower individuals through a desktop screen that opened a portal to a universe of information. Bush's visionary machine would be a personalized aid to memory, a gateway for research, and a device to help automate thought through a "trail" of mental associations. He even imagined what became known as file sharing and hypertext links. At a time when the world had only begun to consider the possibilities of huge computers—much less smaller ones—Bush was anticipating a new era of information technology accessible to the public.[5]

As Walter Isaacson explained in his book *The Innovators*, a number of the revolutionary creators of personal computers traced their inspiration to Bush and his article. In 1945, Douglas Engelbart shipped out to the Philippines as a young navy radar technician as the war was ending. He recalled rummaging through a Red Cross library in a thatched hut on stilts on Leyte Island, where Engelbart discovered an illustrated *Life* magazine reprint of Bush's article. "The whole concept of helping people work and think that way just excited me," Engelbart remembered years later. After his navy service, Engelbart earned an engineering degree and then a doctorate in computer science. In 1962, he wrote a far-reaching paper on "Augmenting Human Intellect," in which he explained the possibilities of human-computer symbiosis; he credited Bush's memex machine for the seed of his idea. Engelbart even wrote Bush a fan letter seventeen years after the older man had published his concept for the machine. J. C. R. Licklider of the Defense Department's Advanced Research Projects Agency (then ARPA and today DARPA)—whose funding was another legacy of Bush's initiatives—gave Engelbart a grant to launch the Augmentation Research Center at the Stanford Research Institute. As Isaacson concluded, "It became another example of how government funding of speculative research eventually paid off hundreds of times over in practical applications."[6]

Bush had been working on the third idea for four years. On July 16, 1945, Bush and Dr. James Conant—Harvard's president, a distinguished chemist, and Bush's deputy for the Manhattan Project—peered through a dark glass across the sands of New Mexico ten miles from Ground Zero to witness the first atomic blast.[7] July 1945 became the first month in a new calendar of the atomic age.

Long before, in October 1941, FDR had asked Bush if an atomic bomb could be built and, if so, at what cost. In March 1942, as U.S. forces were still reeling from the initial Japanese onslaught across the Pacific, and Nazi Germany marched victoriously across Europe, Bush had written the president, "Present opinion indicates that successful use is possible, and that this would be very important and might be determining in the war effort. It is also true that if the enemy arrived at results first it would be an exceedingly serious matter." In August 1942, Bush had endorsed a crash program to develop the A-bomb.[8]

Technological Innovation and Diplomacy

Ben Franklin, scientist and inventor, used the brilliance of his Enlightenment reputation to light his standing as a novel kind of diplomat from a new type of nation. More than 150 years later, Vannevar Bush, scientist and inventor, recognized that technological innovation could create a new type of military and political power. Jerome Wiesner, president of MIT and science adviser to President Kennedy, observed that in the twentieth century, "[n]o American has had greater influence on the growth of science and technology than Vannevar Bush." *Time* magazine, in a 1944 cover story, simply labeled Bush "General of Physics."[9]

Jefferson, "the Futurist" and a patron of science, recognized America's potential to combine exploration, science, and freedom of thought to create a new type of American society and power. Bush's story highlights that U.S. diplomacy in the twentieth century built upon the strength of American society, and especially the national capacity to combine freedom with invention. Bush recognized the complementary but different roles of the federal government, industry, a free and independent scientific community, and private entrepreneurs. In the Cold War competition for technological superiority, Bush created a model of innovation that eclipsed the Soviets' "governmental-statist" system.

In the twenty-first century, America's exploration of Bush's "Endless Frontier" will become even more important to the international standing of the United States. We are likely to see a new competition between models of innovation, this time between the United States and China.[10]

Bush: Engineer, Inventor, and Public Entrepreneur

Bush's principal biographer, G. Pascal Zachary, wrote that Bush "was a pragmatist who thought that knowledge arose from a physical encounter with a stubborn reality." Bush descended from a family of Yankee sea captains, particularly whalers, who inspired the inventor's sense of adventure, self-reliance, and salty style of charismatic and autocratic leadership.[11]

Vannevar, named after his father's Dutch-American friend, was born in 1890. He grew up in an era of invention—gas-powered cars, airplanes, X-rays for medicine, commercial motion pictures—and the expanding technologies of telephony, the phonograph, electricity, and the radio. Bush combined a high aptitude for math with a tinker's spirit. He liked to shape things with his hands. The mathematician Norbert Wiener later described Bush as "one of the greatest apparatus men that America has ever seen—he thinks with his hands as well as his brain."[12]

Bush's attributes and interests drew him toward engineering. Zachary explains that Bush's idea of an engineer was a "pragmatic polymath." Bush described the engineer as "not primarily a physicist, or a businessman, or an inventor but [someone] who would acquire some of the skills and knowledge of each of these and be capable of successfully developing and applying new devices on the grand scale." After some false starts learning the psychology of human behavior, Bush figured out how to direct people as well as things.[13]

Bush forged a moral code that matched his zeal for engineering enterprise. He prized meritocracies. He wanted society to respect expertise. At the same time, Bush believed scientists could serve a democratic society if their freedom and independence could be assured. Democratic liberty created a place for mavericks, and mavericks, in turn, could spark progress in liberal societies. Bush moved beyond invention, and even engineering, to create a model of "public entrepreneurship" that would challenge, prod, and invigorate industrial-age bureaucracies. As Bush tried to marry science to public purposes, he fought to create institutions that served both the scientific spirit and the public mission.[14]

Bush had a quirky combination of "braininess and folksiness" that appealed to the media. He wrote for *Popular Mechanics* as well as esteemed journals, and he played the role of patriotic inventor on Edward R. Murrow's TV show. In government, he displayed a critical "make-things-happen" quality: "If I have any doubt as to whether I am supposed to do a job or not, I do it, and if someone socks me, I lay off."[15]

As a sophomore at Tufts, Bush stepped into teaching a class for an ailing math instructor. He discovered that he could earn a master's as well as a bachelor's degree in four years if he could manage the course load. To save time, Bush read the textbook for a course and took the final test without attending a single classroom lecture. On the last day of 1912, as Bush was about to graduate, the U.S. government awarded him his first patent for a "profile tracer," a surveying device that combined a crude calculator with a mechanical recording device. For Bush, patents represented an inventor's tie with the creative spirit of America's founding generation; after all, the Founders had even included patent rights in the Constitution. In the 1930s, Elihu Root wrote his last legal opinion to help Bush, then a dean at MIT, with the problem of intellectual property.[16]

Bush completed his doctoral dissertation in electrical engineering at MIT in less than a year. His adviser demanded that Bush "increase the scope" of his work without explaining why. Bush appealed to the departmental chairman and won. He was a fearless advocate as well as a scientist.[17]

Bush taught at Tufts and began learning about new technologies through industrial research. During World War I, Bush developed a device to help detect German U-boats but was thwarted by the navy bureaucracy. Bush pocketed the lesson "how not to fight a war." He also recognized that modern war was much more than a contest of arms and armies. War "is a great engineering undertaking," declared the president of Tufts, a Bush mentor.[18]

Bush joined MIT's faculty in 1919 just as the university began to embrace an industrial mission and funding. Electrification was remaking American business and society. Autos, manufacturing methods, and machines seized the public imagination. Bush was fascinated by radio and cofounded Raytheon to build new tubes that made radios into a mass-market industry.[19]

Bush kept inventing. His "differential analyzer" solved equations mechanically. It was an analog computer, relying on gears, shafts, and motors to create "a physical model of abstract mathematical relationships." Bush never sought a patent and encouraged others to improve on his big machine. During World War II, Bush's invention guided the development of ballistic tables for artillery.[20]

In 1932, Bush became MIT's dean of engineering and vice president, just as the country's faith in technological progress plummeted. The shock of the Great Depression shook the very foundations of industrial capitalism. People cried that they needed jobs, not machines. FDR's New Deal heralded an age of economic collectivism, not entrepreneurial individualism. Funds for science dried up.

Bush kept tinkering, inventing, and receiving patents, whose proceeds he granted to MIT. He moved from electronics to solar power, a more efficient gas engine, and an idea for automated dialing for Bell Labs. Bush was particularly intrigued with the automatic retrieval—and computation— of masses of material, whether microfilm, fingerprints, or documents. In the mid-1930s, at the request of the navy's new Communications Security Group, Bush explained how his "Comparator" machine could help automate the cracking of Japanese codes—which, after various refinements in 1940–41, it did.[21]

Technology and War

As fascism marched with militarism in the 1930s, Bush began to speak out about defense preparedness. He was especially troubled by the U.S. military's lack of interest in the changing technology of war.[22] The mood in Congress, symbolized by the Nye hearings (in which Senator Vandenberg took part), assailed the "merchants of death" who had allegedly pushed America into the Great War. The U.S. military was not much better; they treated scientists and engineers as a lower caste of hired help.

Bush found two vital allies. Dr. James Conant, president of Harvard, was recognized as a "science statesman." Frank Jewett, chief of AT&T's Bell Labs, guided the nation's leading industrial research facility. With Jewett's support, Bush became chair of the Division of Engineering and Industrial Research of the National Research Council. In December 1937, Bush pushed the idea that this group could help forge links among scientists, engineers, industry, and the military in a "time of stress and emergency."[23]

Bush was exploring a radical idea for the time. The United States did not have a science policy. The federal government had sponsored utilitarian research in a few fields, such as agriculture and weather. The scientific community and universities relied on support from the great foundations, such as Carnegie and Rockefeller, and was wary of the political control that might be the price of federal patronage. Industrial labs focused on commercial applications. The Army and Navy Departments, steeped in tradition, embraced change only after facing brutal realities in wartime. Bush feared that the technologies of modern warfare would overwhelm America's haphazard approach to scientific research before the U.S. system could adapt. As America edged closer to battle, Bush stated his case boldly: "It is being realized with a thud that the world is probably going to be ruled by those who know how, in the fullest sense, to apply science."[24]

On January 1, 1939, Bush left MIT for a new platform: He became president of the Carnegie Institution of Washington, "a top-drawer patron of science in America." In addition to a sizable endowment, research budget, laboratories, and an observatory, the Carnegie post gave Bush a respected foothold in Washington. Bush also gained personal access to influential trustees, including FDR's uncle.[25]

Bush was promptly appointed to the National Advisory Committee for

Aeronautics (NACA). NACA suggested a possible model of a government agency and lab that drew on independent civilian expertise. The drama of modern airpower spurred a willingness to think differently. Bush learned how to work with generals; he was fortunate that General Henry "Hap" Arnold, leader of the Army Air Force, welcomed cooperation with scientists and engineers. Bush had his first experience testifying before Congress, too, which was a disaster. But he learned.[26]

Bush "tried to see the world through a soldier's eyes." He helped the military fix its problems, favoring practice over theory. He gave answers in the plain language of a man who understood tools and equipment. Bush's extraordinary reach across the scientific-technology communities— combined with his unique intellectual range—enabled him to check promptly across universities and industry to answer questions.[27]

Bush was not intimidated by gold braid. To the contrary, he concluded that senior officers lacked the imagination to integrate new technologies into novel systems. The problem of air defense, Bush recognized, needed to combine information from radar with better methods of shooting down planes, whether by other planes or antiaircraft fire, in a seamless network.[28] Britain's triumph in the 1940 Battle of Britain relied on just such a system.

By 1940, Bush was making headway with the military. He also won the favor of Henry Stimson, the former Republican secretary of state and war whom FDR was about ready to recall to service to lead the War Department. Stimson was intrigued by technology. Yet Bush needed to enlist the scientists, too. The National Academy of Sciences had been slow in responding to army requests; university life did not naturally adapt to mobilization for war. No one in the academy anticipated a senior governmental push—or funding—to muster science and technology to arms.[29]

Creating a Defense Research Committee

Dr. Conant, an ardent internationalist and promoter of ties with Britain, recognized Bush's unique skills and position in Washington. Frank Jewett of Bell Labs, the first industrialist elected to the presidency of the National Academy of Sciences, also lauded Bush. Their support was critical for Bush's next step: the creation of a National Defense Research Committee (NDRC) that would unite scientists with the military in a common mission.

Bush recognized that two elements were still missing: money and authorization from the top. "I knew that you couldn't get anything done...unless you organized under the wing of the President."[30] It took a man who had contested his dissertation adviser to try a run at the president to create a whole new organization for defense research.

In May 1940, Bush asked his Carnegie trustee, Frederic Delano, to arrange a meeting with the president. Delano was an excellent emissary. The president's uncle was a successful businessman, respected for his wide-ranging interests, friendships, and experience with resource planning. Delano gave Steve Early in the White House a one-page memo describing the need to connect fundamental research to modern warfare through the NDRC. Berlin's blitzkrieg across Western Europe that very month illustrated the stakes and new means of battle. Even as the United States ramped up the quantity of arms produced, Bush was arguing that quality would be decisive.

In early June, Bush connected with Harry Hopkins, FDR's close assistant. Hopkins could read that Bush was knowledgeable, focused, and terse—with the temperament of a sea captain. As Zachary described the encounter, Bush shared "a short memo describing his plan for a coordinating committee, responsible to the President, that would contract with universities and industrial labs to perform research at the behest of the Army and Navy." Hopkins recognized that Bush had the qualities and drive to mobilize America's technologists for war. He arranged for Bush to see the president on June 12, two days before the Wehrmacht marched into Paris.[31]

FDR was in the midst of a reelection campaign for an unprecedented third term. He was juggling resistance to war in Congress, a wary and anxious public, and the necessity of building America's military might. The president balanced neutrality with a lean toward embattled Britain, which might not survive. The U.S. military priority appeared to be production over invention, and FDR had neither a background in science nor advisers on technology. Nevertheless, the president was a master improviser who was willing to shake up old orders during times of crisis.

Accompanied by Hopkins, Bush gave the president one page with a six-point outline of his plan to muster America's technologists to the modern missions of the army and navy. The NDRC would include experts from the War, Navy, and Commerce Departments, the National Academy of Sciences, and the science and engineering fraternities, all serving without pay. The committee would support research—not industrial development or manufacturing—of devices of warfare in educational, scientific, and industrial labs. The research would supplement and aid, not replace, military activities.

Bush was prepared to answer a host of questions. Instead, in less than fifteen minutes, Roosevelt engaged in a little conversation and wrote "O.K.—FDR" on Bush's paper. The two very different men were off to a remarkable relationship. Two days later, on June 14, the president announced that Vannevar Bush would chair the new NDRC.[32]

Bush was well aware that FDR often changed his mind about who would be in charge of a project and that presidential grants of authority could vanish quickly. While still serving as Carnegie's president, Bush recruited Conant, Jewett, a physicist from Caltech, the patent commissioner, the navy's chief research admiral, and an army brigadier. He met with General George Marshall, Admiral Harold Stark, and General Arnold of the Army Air Force to seek lists of research projects. And he moved fast to show results.

Bush's new weapon was the government contract. His version was fast, flexible, and targeted. His "federalism by contract" enabled Bush to create a national research network without building bureaucracy, creating new government labs, hiring scientific cadres as government employees, and disrupting researchers' existing work and facilities. Bush was inventing a new governance model instead of machines. His system relied on elite expertise, shielded from politics. It operated outside of standard rules, civil service habits, and even the military chain of command. The potential conflicts would be deemed unacceptable today. People would fear Bush's power as too far-reaching. But in 1940, FDR wanted to enlist Bush's unique network, and he trusted Bush's judgment. In mid-1941, the president transformed the NDRC into the Office of Scientific Research and Development (OSRD) supported by congressional appropriations instead of the president's "emergency funds." FDR added a Committee on Medical Research, too.[33]

Bush knew that he had to work effectively with the military. But he wanted the process to be a creative one, not just filling orders from technically unsophisticated officers. Bush had the advantage of independent (and even presidential) authority and funding. Stimson was an ally, too. But Bush had to beat back a bureaucratic attack from an admiral heading the Naval Research Laboratory. He also had to keep a close rein over OSRD's research agenda. The question he demanded of all projects was, "Will it help win a war; *this* war?"[34]

OSRD produced results. It developed radio-proximity fuses, enabling shells to detonate at points where they would most damage targets. The invention required electrical innovation, extraordinary miniaturization, and ruggedness. Only the United States used these fuses in battle, and they were an important part of the defenses against Germany's V-1 missiles in 1944. OSRD's official historian ranked the proximity fuse as one of the three or four most important inventions of the war.[35] Building on British inventions, Bush sponsored a central radar lab at MIT that innovated microwave capabilities to meet a range of military needs, including automated tracing of targets and identification of surfaced U-boats.

The Battle of the Atlantic

The Battle of the Atlantic provides a superb example of how a cycle of technological advances could be integrated with strategy and tactics to win a campaign. In early 1943, the Allies were losing more than one hundred ships a month to U-boat wolfpacks that massed to sink supply flotillas. If the United States could not secure the Atlantic highway, the Nazis could destroy troop transports carrying the American army to Britain. Admiral Ernest King, the chief of naval operations, was wedded to a defensive plan relying on convoys with escorts.

Bush believed that technology created the possibility of an offensive strategy to detect submarines and guide attacks from sea and sky. Stimson tried to take on antisubmarine operations, but King resisted. An exasperated Bush wrote a six-page letter to the admiral making the case that rapidly advancing technologies, combined with changing tactics, would make the U-boat war a life-and-death struggle between integrated scientific and military strategies.

King conceded a trial effort commanded by Rear Admiral Francis Low. By May 1943, Admiral Low led a new fleet, the Tenth, but without any ships; Low's fleet was armed instead with information, statistical analysis, and new organizational means to find, track and sink U-boats. Search planes used radar to identify submarines when they surfaced. With the help of feedback loops, scouting aviators learned that people actually paid attention to the data in their reports, which were the feedstock for a new type of statistical analysis called operations research. Flight crews reported technical glitches that were then overcome. The Tenth Fleet devised search patterns to increase probabilities of discovering U-boats. Stations along the east coast recorded daily radio intercepts as U-boats reported to headquarters in high-speed bursts. With the help of an IBM data processing machine, civilians analyzed reams of information on sightings, shipping, intercepts, and attacks every twenty-four hours. The Allies integrated this new information with customized naval and air task forces to make the Atlantic into a killing ground for U-boats. In April and May 1943, the Allies sank forty-five German submarines. In the face of irreplaceable losses of boats and crews, Admiral Karl Doenitz, Hitler's U-boat commander, withdrew his submarines from the North Atlantic. Doenitz later complained that Germany lost its sole offensive naval weapon, not because of "superior tactics or strategy," but due to "superiority in the field of science." Bush had recognized the scientific-strategy-tactics interconnection just in time. By the summer of 1943, the Atlantic was safe for the Allies' logistical bridge.[36]

Medicines and Missiles

In his 1945 "Endless Frontier" report, Bush recalled the medical war against wounds and disease. Penicillin, insecticides, better vaccines, surgical advances, and antimalarial techniques drastically lowered military mortality rates. He pointed out that the army's death rate from disease was cut from 14.1 per thousand in World War I to 0.6 per thousand in World War II.[37]

The wartime record demonstrated, however, as Bush acknowledged, that the United States' technological race with Germany was a near-run thing. Germany's V-1 and V-2 rockets highlighted the power of ballistic missiles, which the United States had not made a priority. The Allies had no effective counter to the V-2, first fired in September 1944, other than bombing and overrunning the launch sites. If the Nazis had had the V-2 a year earlier, General Eisenhower's build-up in Britain for D-Day would have turned into a nightmare. German aircraft engines were also better than American models, as were Japanese torpedoes for much of the war.[38]

Building the Atomic Bomb

The greatest venture was the atomic bomb. After being warned by Albert Einstein and other immigrant physicists of the danger in 1939, FDR had established a "uranium committee," but it was stumbling. In 1940–41, as Bush was trying to demonstrate that the new NDRC-OSRD could produce practical results in a matter of months, he thought at first that the prospect of a nuclear fission bomb seemed remote and likely to swallow all the funds. Ernest Lawrence, a Nobel laureate in physics, pressed Bush to act anyway. By the summer of 1941, Bush began to map an approach for a political decision. The work of British scientists convinced Bush that a bomb could be made. Enrico Fermi provided a memo with engineering data that helped Bush understand the economic challenges as well as the physics. Finally, Bush had to calculate the risk that the Germans would succeed first. As Bush explained to Jewett, the skeptical president of the National Academy of Sciences, "Now in times of peace the things we are talking about would be almost absurd." Research and engineering work would need to proceed at the same time.[39]

At FDR's suggestion, Bush turned to Vice President Henry Wallace to discuss the competing concerns about an atomic weapon. Wallace, an inventor of hybrid corn, was the only member of the cabinet with a scientist's knowledge of technology. Bush and Wallace met the president on October 9, 1941. According to Bush's recollection, FDR directed the preparations for a bomb should be "expedited . . . in every way possible," but told Bush to return to the president before taking "definite steps." In addition to the president and Wallace, Bush was to involve only Stimson, Marshall, and Conant. They agreed that any "broader program" that might lead to building atomic bombs would necessitate a new organization. For money, the president decided to create the country's first "black" or secret weapons budget, hidden in the funding for the Army Corps of Engineers.[40]

Bush relied on Conant to oversee the nuclear work. Together, they decided, on December 6, 1941—the eve of the Japanese attack on Pearl Harbor—to ask the army to run the project. But Bush still assumed responsibility for the link with the president. On March 9, 1942, he advised Roosevelt to proceed with an army program. He estimated completion by 1944. Two days later, the president told Bush to push ahead in absolute secrecy, with time of the essence.

In August 1942, Bush advocated making the atomic effort a crash, top-priority program. In September, Colonel Leslie Groves, who had just completed building the massive new Pentagon, became chief of a new "Manhattan Engineering District" project. Bush became head of a three-person committee that would serve as a "board of directors," with Conant guiding day-to-day issues.[41]

In *Danger and Survival*, the classic study of the first fifty years of the atomic bomb, McGeorge Bundy concluded that Bush was the "indispensable man" in the U.S. program. Bush understood the science, the engineering, and FDR's Washington. Bush also had a direct relationship with the president—and Roosevelt's trust.[42]

Bush did not engage in debates about the goals of atomic research. Some scientists viewed Bush as a mere engineer, unable to understand the policy implications. In any event, the requirements of wartime secrecy limited opportunities for discussion. Bush and Conant had a difficult job to do under incredible pressures. As Richard Hewlett and Oscar Anderson Jr., historians of the Atomic Energy Commission, later wrote, the two men "had to navigate between the Scylla and Charybdis of pessimism and soaring optimism. They had to set a course by the Pole Star of fact."[43]

Bush believed that building the bomb was a political decision for the president to make. As McGeorge Bundy later wrote, American presidents bear "intimate and inescapable responsibility" as the "chief political officer[s] for nuclear policy." That remains true today.[44]

Bush did advise on the international implications of atomic policy. In late 1944, Bush and Conant presented Stimson with principles that might avoid an arms race. They knew America's advantage would be temporary. But FDR seemed unwilling or incapable of engaging on the topic of future conflict—he was struggling to finish this one.[45]

The Future of Science—and Global Competition

As the prospect for victory brightened late in 1944, Bush had other priorities to discuss with the president: the future of science in America and of technology's contribution to the country's security. According to Bush's biographer Zachary, Bush focused on two postwar challenges. First, the U.S. military had now embraced technology but lacked the intellectual discipline to curb its appetites. Bush feared duplicative projects by the services and costly, wasted efforts. He wanted civilian technologists to lead the development of a research agenda with the military, as he had done during the war.

Second, Bush wanted the country to invest in basic research, the "seed corn" of future technologies. He understood that scientific experimentation needed the freedom to test ideas without considering immediate utilitarian purposes. Neither the military nor industry had the patience—or vision—to back pure scientific research.

Bush's plans reflected a linear model of innovation that began with scientific knowledge, translated into engineering practice, and led to practical products and processes. He could probably see that in reality the stages of this progression blurred into a network of feedback loops among theory, applied research, testing, refinements, new discoveries, and new processes and tools. Yet he would have had difficulty explaining that circuitous pattern of innovation. Bush knew that the pressures of war had squeezed out blue sky research and experimentation that was fundamental to creating new knowledge. Bush anticipated a new global competition of power, premised significantly on technologies, and he wanted the United States to invest in all the components to establish an innovative edge.[46]

Bush drafted a letter in Roosevelt's name that was addressed to Bush; he wanted the president to ask OSRD to evaluate the lessons of its experience. Harry Hopkins offered sound advice: Keep the letter to two pages; do not make claims about the past that will divert into arguments with others; and suggest an idea without arguing for a government project. Sam Rosenman, FDR's speechwriter, polished the redraft.

On November 17, 1944, shortly after winning his fourth term, the president sent "his" letter to Bush. As Zachary notes, the letter became "Holy Writ" among America's scientific elite. Bush reprinted the letter in the front of his "Endless Frontier" report.[47]

The letter asked for Bush's recommendations on four points. Bush was to suggest civilian "spinoffs" from wartime military research. Then he was to recommend how to continue "the war of science against disease." Next came the heart of the matter: "What can the Government do now and in the future to aid research activities by public and private organizations," considering the roles and relations of public and private research? Finally, Bush was to opine on "discovering and developing scientific talent in America's youth."[48]

Bush formed committees to address each topic. Bush guided their work, although the medical committee revealed an independent streak and called for a separate foundation for medical research.

Bush recognized that his introductory essay would make or break the report. He understood that wartime technologies, rapid in development and startling in life-and-death applications, had stirred the public imagination. Very soon, the atomic bomb would add shock and awe. The laments during the Depression about technology destroying jobs were changing into admiration of scientists as navigators of the future.

"The Endless Frontier": A New Model of Governance

Bush had tried out the idea of science as the new frontier in a 1937 speech to fellow engineers. Now he would use "Science, the Endless Frontier" to make the public case for a National Research Foundation (NRF), established by Congress, responsible to the president but run by scientists, to build America's scientific capital.[49]

Bush stated boldly, "We have no national policy for science." Not only would Bush create one, but he devised a new public-private governance model. The Bush approach encouraged "freedom of inquiry and that healthy competitive scientific spirit," while serving public purposes. The NRF would fund basic research for medicine, the natural sciences, and national defense. It would also support scientific education and the dissemination and exchange of knowledge, including internationally. Bush even added a special patent policy, a long-standing interest for the inventor.[50]

Bush's proposal sought to address a complex of issues that would bedevil Americans for the rest of the twentieth century and beyond. Bush was proposing more than a science policy. The Progressive Era had encouraged reliance on experts in society—and a belief that knowledge would lead to progress. The wave had crested in the 1920s, and the Depression challenged both the old order and faith. World War II had revived interest in technology and America's can-do spirit. For all the fearsome capabilities of the Axis powers, America's rearmament, invention, and industrial might had overwhelmed its enemies. But there was another model. The Soviet Union's amazing revival from self-inflicted destruction and Hitler's invasion demonstrated awesome strength.

Now the forces of the United States and the Soviet Union stretched across Eurasia and the world. Bush understood that victory—and America's future power—depended on governmental organization and industrial resourcefulness as well as technology. As Walter Millis noted a few years later, "The centralized modern state had developed into an incomparable instrument for waging war."[51]

But which modern state system would prove superior? Bush expected that scientists—and expertise—would determine the answer. He wanted to find ways in which scientists could contribute, and become principal advisers for political leaders, without losing the independence and creativity that was the essence of the scientific craft. He was suspicious of big institutions, detested bureaucracy, and abhorred the dullness of mass mediocrity. So he tried, in Zachary's words, to invent a way to "[marry] the intellectual resources of an ascendant community of technologists to the bureaucratic imperatives of a security-obsessed state."[52]

The American press applauded the release of "The Endless Frontier" in July 1945.[53] Bush's skillful writing offered touchstones for most everyone: exploration and frontiers; military advantage and security; government activism and private enterprise; health and education; and prosperity and freedom. But the accolades turned out to be the high watermark of his adventure.

Systems of Science and Policy

The military was ready with an alternative. It had embraced Bush's spirit of technological warfare, and some officers even recognized that the services needed to attract civilian skills instead of command them. The Army Air Force had been the quickest to draw on scientific analytical expertise. After the war, the Air Force wanted to pursue rocketry, a field that Bush considered more expensive than useful. The Air Force sponsored its own think tank, Project RAND (for research and development). In 1946, RAND released a farsighted report about the capabilities of rockets to launch satellites that could orbit the earth. In addition to the espionage and scientific value of satellites, the study predicted that a man-made vehicle circling the globe "would inflame the imagination of mankind, and would probably produce repercussions in the world comparable to the explosion of the atomic bomb."[54]

The navy argued that its innovation in ship design, engines, submarines, and aircraft carriers warranted ranking as America's senior engineering service. But the army had run the Manhattan Project, and Bush's OSRD had been in the forefront of radar. Bush's call to close down OSRD—which he hoped would prod politicians to act on his idea of a research foundation—spurred the navy to create its own Office of Naval Research.[55]

In 1946, Army Chief of Staff Eisenhower issued five principles for developing a "military-industrial-academic complex"—ironically, a network that he would later decry. The general called for civilian assistance in planning as well as weapons production. He recognized the need to assure freedom of research. R&D responsibilities should be separate from procurement, purchase, and distribution. Ike even directed an integrated approach by civilians and the military, and suggested considering utilizing "industrial and technological resources as *organic parts* of our military structure in time of emergency."[56]

The military services had to face postwar budget realities. Bush's idea for a research organization could not compete with the services' fierce rivalry for resources and standing. Technology had graduated from the service shops of 1939 to a practical symbol of military superiority in 1946.

The National Security Act of 1947, which created the National Security Council and the Central Intelligence Agency, mandated a Research and Development Board to advise the new secretary of defense. Bush hoped to become the first secretary of defense, but Truman never considered him. Bush opted instead to head the Pentagon's new Research and Development Board, but the weak powers of the post and the secretary doomed Bush's efforts to rationalize military research.[57]

Bush faced a challenge from a totally different quarter. The New Dealers were social engineers. The war had ended the Depression, but Progressives feared a return to mass unemployment. They wanted scientists, engineers, and planners to turn their skills from the arts of destruction to the social science challenges of economic management, housing, education, and hunger. Bush thought these "do-gooders" would pervert research with politics, statist economic policies, and populist policy fads. He warned that they failed to understand the distinction between basic and applied research. They wanted to undermine patent incentives. And their funding allocations would reflect geographical favoritism instead of expert judgments of quality.

After five years at the apex of scientific power, Bush faced rivalries within the scientific community. Other senior figures chafed at Bush's authority and recalled his slights. He had been a hard charger, operating with FDR's imprimatur. With FDR's death, Bush had to establish a relationship with a very different president.

Moreover, a younger generation of scientists, who had struggled to gain a foothold during the Depression, looked upon federal funding as a lifeline, not as a risky embrace. If the government and military showed a willingness to accommodate scientists' creative spirit of experimentation, these younger stars saw no reason to return to the hierarchies and limits of the prewar, elite order.[58]

Bush made political missteps. After the exigencies of war, Congress reasserted its prerogatives under a new president. Senator Harley Kilgore of West Virginia, a New Deal liberal and friend of Truman's, had a hopeful, earthy interest in using scientific research to solve all of America's ills. He thought big business and cartels blocked social innovation. Kilgore championed a National Science Foundation and reached out to Bush for help. Bush and other scientists worried about Kilgore's direction. But the senator majored in persistence if not science.

Bush probably could have worked out a compromise with Kilgore in the summer of 1945, but instead he tried to circumvent the senator. Not surprisingly, the legislation stalled. Kilgore and Bush reconciled in 1946, and Congress passed a bill for a National Science Foundation in 1947. Truman vetoed it, objecting to the absence of the president's direct authority to appoint the NSF's head. The more fundamental problem seemed to be Truman's dislike of Bush's aggressive advocacy and promotion of experts to senior government posts.[59]

Don Price, an eminent scholar on science policy and one of the founders of public policy studies, recalled Truman's attitude as "Don't let the specialists have the last word." Truman "wanted experts on tap, but not on top." As international policy problems became more technically complex—whether in arms control, the environment, economics, energy, disease, or a host of other topics—the challenge of reconciling the views represented by Truman and Bush has become a constant of policy making.[60]

By 1950, Congress and the president agreed on a bill for the National Science Foundation. It was a pale version of Bush's proposal in "The Endless Frontier." The military unit was gone. So was the medical group. James Hershberg, Conant's biographer, concluded, "Rather than subsuming federal science policy under a single agency, as [Bush] originally envisioned, the NSF only added yet another contestant to an already crowded field." Bush and Conant agreed that the military had requisitioned the research agenda. Bruce Smith, a historian of U.S. science policy, observed that while Bush and Kilgore battled over the structure of the NSF, the government's research system evolved toward a model neither wanted, with large, mission-oriented agencies in charge.[61]

Questions of Nuclear Policy

The Truman administration established the predicates for future U.S. nuclear policy. Bush first met the new president shortly after FDR's death, when Truman asked for a briefing on the Manhattan Project. Admiral William Leahy, the long-time Roosevelt aide with the title of the chief of staff to the commander in chief, sat in. After Bush explained the science of the atom bomb, Leahy concluded, "This is the biggest fool thing we have ever done. The bomb will never go off, and I speak as an expert in explosives." Bush's bias against military judgments about technology could only have been strengthened.[62]

Truman relied heavily on Stimson for advice about the new weapon. The secretary of war explained that the bomb would be ready to be used against Japan by August 1. He also cautioned that the A-bomb could obliterate civilization. Nuclear policy had "[become] a primary question of our foreign relations." Based on Stimson's recommendation, Truman authorized him to chair a small advisory group to consider atomic policy issues. Stimson included Bush on the eight-person Interim Committee.

The committee recommended using the bomb against Japan without a warning or demonstration, which the group figured would prove ineffective. Committee members were wary of sharing much information at the time with the USSR, noting that even Britain did not have the blueprints. General Groves guessed that the Soviets would need twenty years to build an atomic bomb; Bush predicted three to four years.[63]

Bush's biographer Zachary noted that the brutality of the Pacific War inured Bush and others to the terrible destructive power of the bomb. Compared to the firebombing of Tokyo and the death toll of an invasion, Bush expected the bomb would save lives. Zachary points to two other factors influencing Bush's expectations about the future diplomacy of weapons of mass destruction. Bush had observed that the use of chemical weapons in World War I had led to restraints on their use in World War II; he now hypothesized that the use of the atomic bomb would lead to demands for controls in the future. "Deterrence arose from fear of the known, not the unknown," he said. Furthermore, in the new age of awesome arms that Bush helped introduce, he was even more worried about biological weapons. He restricted work on biological agents to defensive precautions.[64]

Bush had become an outrider in a shadowy, frightening new land of weaponry that could wipe out humankind. There were no rules or even norms. Whether the scourge was nuclear, chemical, biological, or digital, American diplomacy would have to struggle with novel challenges of proliferation, deterrence, limits and inspections, testing, resilience, countermeasures, prevention, and even preemption.

In September 1945, after the world had witnessed the devastating effects of atomic weaponry, Truman invited memos from a select group about sharing atomic information, especially with the Soviets. Bush advocated testing the possibility of international controls, largely because he knew the knowledge behind the bomb would not remain secret for long. The Soviets almost certainly would have developed a weapon regardless of U.S. diplomacy. But

Bush's memo is interesting for its forecast of the military and diplomatic challenges of nuclear weapons.

Bush saw few possibilities for defense, other than extraordinary steps to disperse and move industries and people underground to improve prospects for survival. Rockets would make "interception" "highly difficult." Weapons would become more destructive and less expensive.[65]

Yet Bush raised the question of whether there would be "powder in the gun, for it could not be drawn." He was posing the problem, as military historian Russell Weigley would later describe, of whether the United States could use atomic weapons in combat to achieve the traditional ends of war and statecraft. U.S. diplomacy had used force to achieve political ends, but those ends had not included exterminating other countries. Moreover, warfare that produced mutual annihilation would be senseless.

Bush's observations suggested that concepts of military—and diplomatic—strategy would need to change. Weigley points out how strategies of deterrence assumed new preeminence in American policy. As Bush had predicted, the advance of technology would move civilians into roles that complemented traditional military planning and preparations. In the 1950s, civilians such as Bernard Brodie and a young Henry Kissinger would play leading parts in shaping nuclear strategy. That shift then led to new debates about the connections between conventional and nuclear strategies.[66]

Technology, Security, and Democracy

After leaving government in 1948, Bush wanted to offer his ideas about technology, security, and democracy. In 1949, he published *Modern Arms and Free Men: A Discussion of the Role of Science in Preserving Democracy*. His timing was superb. The news was slipping out about the Soviets' first test of an atomic bomb. The Book of the Month Club gave Bush top billing, and *Life* published two long excerpts.

Bush's book tried to counter the high anxieties of the early Cold War and "the frenzy over Russia's atomic test by reminding Americans that their nation's true edge was its commitment to individual freedom and an open society." One of his "chief conclusions" was that "the democratic process is itself an asset." Yet after the unity of wartime, the fractures of American society reappeared. The shock of the Korean War in 1950, and the frustrations of the Korean campaign and stalemate, left Americans unhappy. The U.S. military, the pride of a victorious nation in 1945, looked unprepared just five years later. The country also recognized that it needed quality conventional forces as well as nuclear weapons.[67]

Bush's message about the importance of rational planning and the inevitability of human progress was drowned out by a political search for internal enemies. In late 1953, the anti-Communist Red Scare turned on Robert Oppenheimer, the scientific chief of the Manhattan Project. Bush was a political conservative, and he understood the need for security against subversion. Yet he viewed the witch hunt against Oppenheimer as settling scores because of the scientist's opposition to the hydrogen bomb. Bush recognized McCarthyism's danger to his efforts to build a partnership between researchers of independent minds and the government.

On April 23, 1954, in the face of Senator McCarthy's recent attack on a government conspiracy against the H-bomb, Bush let loose a torrent of outrage at a closed hearing of the Atomic Energy Commission, which was considering Oppenheimer's security clearance. He put himself on the line, defending the right—and vital need—for free people to express strong opinions. The AEC stripped Oppenheimer's clearance anyway, by a vote of 2–1. Bush took his defense public in a powerful *New York Times* op-ed.[68]

President Dwight Eisenhower thought Truman's responses to the postwar challenges lacked coherence and a steady hand. Ike, like Bush, recognized the importance of America's values in the twilight struggle against the Soviets and Communism. Eisenhower valued scientific expertise, too, and appointed the first science adviser to the president. From 1953 to 1961, federal support for R&D grew 14 percent annually in constant (inflation-adjusted) dollars. But President Eisenhower countered his opponents and maneuvered his policies with a deft "hidden hand" instead of through Bush's blunt resistance.[69]

Eisenhower's political-military strategy prioritized fiscal discipline and military restraint. The defense budget had reached 70 percent of federal spending. The former general's "New Look" defense posture threatened nuclear "massive retaliation," which Bush considered too risky.[70]

Eventually, the Berlin-Cuban Missile Crisis of 1962, as related in the next chapter, jolted the United States and the Soviets into considering measures of nuclear arms control. During the 1960s, '70s, and '80s, nuclear and other arms control negotiations assumed a prominent place in American diplomacy.

Nuclear and missile diplomacy remains at the heart of American foreign policy. Today, the problems concern Russia, China, North Korea, Iran, Pakistan, and other potential nuclear states. Relations with key allies depend on U.S. deterrence policies. American diplomacy also has to consider the foreign policy challenges of other technological innovations, such as digital, environmental, oceanic, biologic, chemical, space, and others all along the "Endless Frontier." In 1949, Congress passed an Export Control Act, beginning a long debate about the security risks of transferring U.S. technologies abroad that continues to this day.[71] Today's tensions with China trace in part to a competition over innovation, and technological espionage and theft.

Science and Technology Policy

U.S. diplomacy in the civilian areas of science and technology has rarely garnered the high-level attention devoted to security studies or even international economics. Yet the debates over pandemics, climate change, and other environmental topics suggest these dimensions of foreign policy will grow in importance. Bush inspired a huge government investment in science, but he failed to establish a guidance system led by the country's technological elite. Bush was skeptical of Kennedy's goal of putting a man on the moon; he considered the venture more spectacle than productive innovation. Bush's priorities ran to alternative energy sources, food, and materials. Even so, Bush's approach to the research and development of the atomic bomb became a model for other "big science" projects.[72]

In the 1960s and '70s, research became more politicized and subject to interest-group advocacy. JFK's dramatic space program was followed by LBJ's drive for expert-led social change and Nixon's search for the cure for cancer. Research funding became congressional pork. Bush's idea of targeted government contracts for basic research degenerated into bureaucratic contracting, extraordinarily long development schedules for new weapons, and industrial dependence on military contracts. Furthermore, the overselling of technology—and the failure of experts in Vietnam and with a sluggish economy—led to a backlash. Environmentalists challenged the costs of industrial growth and the narrow perspectives of scientists. The science establishment looked like an elite bastion of unaccountable privilege and power, not open to minorities and women.[73]

Other critics questioned Bush's inattention to industrial innovation in the "Endless Frontier." Harvey Brooks, a scholar of science and policy, recounts, "The implicit message . . . seemed to be that technology was essentially the application of leading-edge science and that, if the country created and sustained a first-class science establishment based primarily in the universities, new technology for national security, economic growth, job creation, and social welfare would be generated almost automatically."[74] But a revived Europe and Japan created more competition. As U.S. corporations failed to adapt, America's commercial technology faltered. To regain their competitive edge, U.S. companies modified Bush's linear model of research into loops of unceasing improvement through experimentation, trials, and feedback.

The Personal Computer Revolution

Looking back over more than seventy years, Bush's third innovation in July 1945—in addition to "Science, the Endless Frontier" and the atomic bomb—warrants special attention. His "As We May Think" article—with his hypothetical memex machine—planted the seed for inventions that countered the ossification of centralized systems. At first, America's computer revolution produced bigger and bigger mainframes, designed for large institutions, not individuals. But Bush always wanted to close the gap between machines and people. He understood the problems of information overload. He imagined a desktop information, memory, processing, and interconnecting machine that empowered individuals.

Bush never made the transition from the analog to digital worlds. He preferred wrenches and machines with gears to code and devices with software. The inventors of personal computers—people such as Douglas Engelbart, J. C. Licklider, and Theodore Nelson—embraced Bush anyway. They increased the acceptability of their radical ideas by tracing a provenance to Bush, the elder statesman of science. Fred Terman, a doctoral student of Bush's who became Stanford's dean of engineering and then provost, created an industrial park that later became known as Silicon Valley. Bush's vision even acquired a counterculture tinge as the digital pioneers took on the established order that Bush thought had bogged down.[75]

Innovation Policy and Global Competition

In his book *The Innovators*, Walter Issacson reminds us that inventors expand ideas across generations.[76] Future American power—and diplomacy—depends on promoting a scientific-technological-economic system, a nonlinear innovative ecosystem, that prizes creativity, collaboration, learning, incentives, and entrepreneurialism. In addition to a diplomacy of geopolitics and geoeconomics, the United States needs to create conditions that foster the nation's capacities on the frontiers of science.

Ben Franklin represents the old model of the gentleman scientist and inventor of independent means; advances proceeded linearly—and slowly. By the turn of the twentieth century, inventors such as Thomas Edison or the Wright brothers received support from governments that became "first customers"; government purchases reduced risks for innovators in an era without venture capital funds. Bush added two key components to the U.S. model of innovation: First, he achieved government funding earlier in the technology life cycle—for basic research before proof of concept and proto-typing; and second, he established a connection with university research. Today, scholars refer to this university-industry-governmental system as the Triple Helix concept of innovation for a "knowledge society"; they contrast it with the "industry-government dyad in the Industrial Society."[77]

The Cold War became a competition between Bush's ideas—and the Triple Helix system—with the Soviet Union's state-directed model. Enter-prises in the USSR did not have the flexibility to reallocate resources freely, which Joseph Schumpeter identified as vital for entrepreneurship. Soviet universities lacked the academic freedom essential for research that changes paradigms of thought.

The Chinese innovation model relies on government direction of uni-versity research and—to a substantial degree—industrial investment. Japan adopted a similar approach decades earlier. The government-guided model assists with development strategies to catch up to technologically advanced societies. As countries approach technological frontiers, however, central-ized guidance might not prove as adaptable to uncertainties and transfor-mations as the self-organizing dynamic of the Triple Helix. In any event, the United States must invest in a healthy ecosystem for innovation and entre-preneurship to compete successfully.

American diplomacy should promote complementary international sys-tems. Those regimes and networks should be imbued with Bush's principles of science and policy. Cooperative efforts among states should draw on scientific research and encourage ongoing assessments. Actions to address problems should rely on incentives, markets, innovation, and transnational private actors instead of centralized state controls. Policy systems should be flexible, leaving room for innovation.

In 1991–92, those concepts guided my approach when I supervised the U.S. delegation that negotiated the 1992 United Nations Framework Con-vention on Climate Change. All modestly successful efforts to fill in the Framework, including the Paris Agreement of 2016, have relied on those pragmatic premises. And the 1992 treaty has been the only climate change agreement ratified by the U.S. Senate.[78]

As Bush's biographer Zachary concluded, "Bush never claimed to be a prophet. He had an engineer's respect for failure, and the unanticipated opportunities arising from failure." When Bush died in 1974 at age eighty-four, the *New York Times* called him "the paradigm of the engineer—a man who got things done."[79] As Harvey Brooks concluded, Bush got an exceptionally big thing done: "[W]hat is remarkable about the post–World War II research system is continuity.... [D]espite much debate—and cries of alarm from the scientific community, it appears that the basic outline of the 'social contract' proposal in Bush's famous report... have remained more or less intact, and are still broadly accepted by public and politicians."[80] Bush is the scientific godfather for an American diplomacy that leverages perpetual technological change.

⬥

CHAPTER 13

John F. Kennedy

The Crisis Manager

June 1963: *"Ich bin ein Berliner"*

President John F. Kennedy had not even been sure he should come to Berlin. This was only his second presidential trip to Europe, and the president's national security adviser, McGeorge Bundy, had been concerned that the visit might affront Soviet premier Nikita Khrushchev. Kennedy was worried about a comparison with President Charles de Gaulle's tour of Germany late in 1962. The French president, speaking in German, had sought to convince West Germans that they should rely more on France than America.[1]

President Kennedy arrived on June 26, 1963, the fifteenth anniversary of the launch of the 1948 Berlin Airlift. Richard Smyser, a young U.S. diplomat who served in the Berlin mission when Kennedy arrived, recounted that the president was "unprepared for the overwhelming waves of humanity" that engulfed his motorcade from the moment he left Tegel airport. The whole city seemed to turn out. Berliners stood five to ten deep. Some had climbed trees, lampposts, traffic lights, construction cranes—anything—for a view. West Berliners cheered themselves hoarse, threw flowers, and reached out to touch the young American president. "Ken-ne-dy!" they shouted. For the first time, JFK saw Berliners in human, not diplomatic, terms. And he perceived Berlin not as a chip to be bargained but as a city and its people.[2]

The president handed his draft speech to Major General James Polk, the American military commandant in Berlin, asking, "You think this is any good?" After skimming the platitudes and stilted assurances to Berliners, Polk answered, "This is terrible, Mr. President." "I agree," said Kennedy.[3]

The president stopped briefly at the recently built Wall to peer into East Berlin. He saw only armed East German guards, except for a few intrepid women waving cautiously while dodging the watch of the East German police. Yet this brief view revealed the great disparity between lives in the East and the West. The president looked grim.[4]

Kennedy took a short break in Mayor Willy Brandt's suite before making his remarks at City Hall. Acting on his political instincts, Kennedy threw away most of his speech cards and quickly wrote on others. The president decided to add two short sentences in German. Kennedy did not feel comfortable with other languages, but he wanted to say something directly to Berliners. He wrote the sentences phonetically, in red ink, and practiced them with two interpreters.[5]

When the president spoke that June day, he rarely glanced at his remaining cards. Kennedy recalled from his student days that ancient Romans would proclaim their pride by declaring, "I am a citizen of Rome." As he stood before a half million Berliners crowded in the square, the president realized that the proudest boast anyone could make was to claim citizenship with Berlin. "*Ich bin ein Berliner*," he called out. The crowd erupted. He repeated the pledge, and thanked his interpreter for the better pronunciation. The Germans cheered and cheered—and would not stop. The cool man who knew how to excite a crowd was moved, but also a bit disturbed by the Germans' emotion. Kennedy observed that if he had cried out, "March to the Wall—tear it down," the Berliners would have done so.[6]

Afterward, Bundy said to Kennedy, "I think you went a little too far." Years later, Jacqueline Kennedy complained in jest that it seemed unfair that her husband's most famous words were in a foreign tongue.[7]

The visit—and the speech—had a momentous effect on President Kennedy. For the first time, he recognized West Berlin as "an asset, not a liability, in the wider struggle for Europe." Berlin—and the freedom it represented—stood at the core of the Atlantic Alliance. Americans, who had fought a fierce war with Germans not long before, could draw a lesson from Thucydides. As the Greek historian wrote in the fifth century BC, we "acquir[e] our friends by conferring not by receiving favors."[8]

Just two days after Kennedy's speech, the Soviet leader Nikita Khrushchev came to East Berlin to celebrate East German leader Walter Ulbricht's seventieth birthday. Speaking before the City Hall in East Berlin, Khrushchev called out, "*Ich liebe die Mauer.*" I love the Wall. But Berliners did not.[9]

The Berlin Crisis of 1961–63

The Berlin Crisis of 1961–63 dominated Kennedy's presidency more than any other single issue. It tested him. It molded him. The Berlin Crisis—which became the Cuban Missile Crisis as well—was the first attempt to use the blunt threat of war between nuclear powers to force a solution to an international problem. Khrushchev had chosen Berlin as the spot to brandish the threat of his nuclear arsenal to intimidate the West. Kennedy genuinely feared the risk of nuclear war. Kenneth O'Donnell, the president's long-time aide, later wrote that Kennedy felt "trapped" by Berlin. O'Donnell found that JFK scratched the word "Berlin" over and over on a yellow pad he kept on the cabinet table during White House meetings.[10]

Kennedy and his team had not started well. Their initial focus was on Moscow, not Germany. Reflecting on the "lessons" of 1914, the "New Frontiersmen" were anxious about miscalculations that could escalate to nuclear Armageddon. Prime Minister Harold Macmillan of Britain, America's wartime ally, pushed this view, too. After two world wars against Germany, the Anglo-Americans asked whether they could risk the nuclear destruction of their own countries in order to defend the surrounded former capital of their wartime enemy.

1960: The Cold War Competition

JFK had boldly waged his 1960 election campaign against Vice President Richard Nixon on the issue of Cold War security. Neither Kennedy nor Nixon spent much time on other topics. To question the foreign policy legacy of the outgoing president, the respected former general Dwight Eisenhower, the youthful Kennedy needed a fresh message of activism: The forty-two-year-old challenger argued that the country had lapsed into "eight years of drugged and fitful sleep" while world events had raced ahead. Kennedy warned that history might judge "that these were the days when the tide began to run out for the United States . . . and the Communist tide began to pour in."[11]

Events seemed to back Kennedy's claim. In 1957, Moscow had beaten Washington in the first leg of the space race by sending its Sputnik satellite into orbit. Americans shivered at the apparent loss of technological superiority. Candidate Kennedy warned of a "missile gap" that suggested, wrongly, that the United States had even lost the edge in the nuclear arsenal that America had invented. Recently retired general Maxwell Taylor, a Kennedy friend, wrote a book with the warning that Eisenhower's fiscal frugality had starved the military of the men, material, and modern capabilities needed to withstand the monstrous Soviet forces. President Eisenhower had scrapped a visit to Japan because of anti-American riots. Even the economic foundations of America's power seemed rickety: In Paul Samuelson's 1961 edition of his ubiquitous *Economics* textbook, the MIT professor explained that Soviet growth rates "have been considerably greater than ours"; he included a graph that projected that the gap between the U.S. market and the Soviet planned economy could disappear.[12]

Kennedy also pointed to America's failure to compete in the Third World, a fast-expanding arena. The old capitals of Europe were conceding the independence of former colonies. In 1960 alone, eighteen new states—including sixteen in Africa—joined the United Nations. Wars of national liberation assailed regimes that tried to hold back the new wave. Vice President Nixon's visit to Latin America prompted violence, demonstrating vividly that the United States was falling behind even in its home hemisphere. A recent revolution turned Cuba Communist. Guided by anti-Communist economic thinkers such as Walt Rostow, the can-do Kennedy men embraced a modernization theory that mapped enterprising courses for both nation building and counterinsurgency.[13]

When Kennedy accepted the nomination at the Democratic Convention in 1960, he rallied Americans toward a "New Frontier." Like Vannevar Bush, JFK embraced the frontiers of science and added the exploration of space. He wanted to revive America's revolutionary spirit and, drawing from Rostow, "get the country moving again."[14]

Crisis Managers

In contrast with the supposed complacency of the Eisenhower years, Kennedy stoked a sense of crisis. He demanded a new spirit; his favorite word seemed to be "vigor." His youthful team reinforced JFK's message of national impatience. Robert S. McNamara, the new secretary of defense, warned that it was better to make "the wrong decision...than no decision at all." Many years later, Arthur Schlesinger Jr., Kennedy's White House historian, recalled that "activism" was the "besetting sin of the New Frontier." The Kennedys, he said, were "improvisers," "not planners." They were "impatient with systems." Paul Nitze, who observed presidential administrations over five decades, concluded that the Kennedy style created "a perpetual state of reaction to one crisis after another rather than [an administration] working toward long-term goals." The historian Thomas Paterson rued that "'Crisis Management' became celebrated codewords of the Kennedy team, which seemed to thrive on the opportunities."[15]

Kennedy's narrow election victory did not dampen the new president's ardor for boundless change. He devoted his entire inaugural address to a "revolution" in America's global exertions—led by "a new generation of Americans" who would "[defend] freedom in its hour of maximum danger." In a brief, rapid trumpet call, Kennedy sounded the charge east and west, north and south, to huts and villages and the depths of oceans, "pay[ing] any price, bear[ing] any burden, meet[ing] any hardship, support[ing] any friend, oppos[ing] any foe to assure the survival and success of liberty."[16]

Even today, Kennedy's words inspire. I heard their echo in President

George W. Bush's second inaugural in 2005, which proffered his Freedom Agenda. As the U.S. trade representative, about to become deputy secretary of state, I listened from a seat on the Capitol portico. I was moved by the president's summons for a foreign policy infused with fundamental values, but I took a deep breath as I reflected on the challenges ahead. Kennedy's urging in 1961 would have been electric. JFK was just starting out, with the vitality of a first presidential term and a fresh team, amidst a national climate of optimism. But I wonder if his appointees also reflected on means, ends, and methods. Activist diplomacy, which I favor, benefits from lots of questions and practical planning.

President Kennedy combined his national call to arms and freedom with an offer to negotiate with adversaries, especially over "the dark powers of destruction unleashed by science." He hoped for neither an "uncertain balance of terror" nor "a new balance of power, but a new world of law, where the strong are just and the weak secure and the peace preserved."[17] Elihu Root would have smiled, Woodrow Wilson would have applauded, and Teddy Roosevelt would have been both skeptical and envious.

The day before his inauguration, Kennedy met President Eisenhower. At its best, the peaceful passage of political power in the United States, including the transition preparations, recognizes both worthy past labors and hope for future endeavors. Eisenhower, a master of outward geniality, revealed to the new team the cold calculation that propelled him to the top in war and peace. He warned his successor of the risks of war around the globe, including in Cuba, Berlin, and Laos. Activism had encountered cunning experience; Bobby Kennedy, JFK's younger brother, soon to be attorney general, left with a queasy feeling about Ike's calm assessments of nuclear diplomacy on the precipice.[18]

The First Crisis in Cuba

President Kennedy's first crisis blew up from Cuba, the strategic significance of which both TR and Elihu Root had been well aware. Fidel Castro's revolutionary victory on January 1, 1959, followed by Soviet courtship, prompted the CIA to plan a counterrevolutionary invasion. Eisenhower had pressed for preparations while imposing limits and conditions, leaving the decision to act to his successor. JFK seemed uncertain about the scheme, but felt pressured by time, his prior criticism of Eisenhower's and Nixon's inactivity, and a bias toward boldness. So he gave the go-ahead.

On April 17, 1961, 1,400 Cuban exiles floundered while attempting a landing at the Bay of Pigs. The disastrous venture never had a serious chance of success; the president and his close advisers had not done their homework.

As one presidential aide explained, "Nobody in the White House wanted to be soft." As the dreadful news poured in, the CIA and navy pressed Kennedy to authorize U.S. air strikes; he refused to send Americans to war and risk escalation elsewhere, including Berlin. The president accepted responsibility and later fired the CIA leaders.[19]

Kennedy learned lessons. Eisenhower offered the president public support when JFK was struggling, but before doing so imposed an instruction: "Mr. President," the general asked, "before you approved this plan did you have everybody in front of you debating the thing so that you could get the pros and cons yourself and then make the decision?" Kennedy admitted he had not. Activism requires inventive but careful staff work.[20]

A Crisis in Vienna

Kennedy's second crisis arose in Vienna. The president had wanted an early meeting with Khrushchev, although after the Bay of Pigs fiasco he worried that the Soviets, sensing weakness, would demand too much. JFK, like many American leaders, thought that he had a reasonable message that his adversary would understand if only Kennedy could meet Khrushchev face-to-face. In fact, Kennedy and Khrushchev had totally different agendas and contrasting ways of communicating. Kennedy wanted to reduce the risks of nuclear war by conveying reasonableness, but with firm resolve. Khrushchev wanted to solve his Berlin problem by pushing the Western allies out; his method, from the Soviet experience, was to corner, bully, and threaten his opponent. Khrushchev was willing to improve relations if Kennedy conceded Berlin. Khrushchev perceived Kennedy's back-channel messages as a sign of weakness, because he figured that the president could not directly face an aggressive militant U.S. faction. The old Communist thought the president was young, inept, inexperienced, too weak to follow through in Cuba, and likely to yield under pressure—"a boy in short pants."[21]

This time Kennedy prepared thoroughly, but he got bad advice. George Kennan told the president that Khrushchev would be cautious. Ambassador Llewellyn Thompson in Moscow, who later would offer astute counsel, thought Khrushchev wanted a positive encounter. The CIA briefed the president similarly.[22] Especially for summits with adversaries, presidents should prepare both by planning their messages and approach and by considering how to respond to various types of behavior. American politicians who reach the top are confident in their interpersonal skills and instincts. When Americans meet leaders from dissimilar systems of power, they need to be ready to play by a variety of rules.

From the start of the Vienna Summit on June 3, Khrushchev over-whelmed Kennedy. As Lawrence Freedman wrote, the Soviet idea of a "sum-mit was not so much a means of rising above the cold war but of fighting it." Khrushchev started with an ideological debate. Kennedy, steeped in the history of 1914 and destructive wars of miscalculation, tried to explain the need for checks on escalation. But Stalin-era Soviets did not reach the top by debating risks of mistakes or reasoning how to solve thorny problems. Those qualities showed weakness to the Soviets of 1961. Kennedy reported that Khrushchev went "berserk," yelling "Miscalculation! Miscalculation! Miscalculation!... You ought to take that word and bury it in cold storage and never use it again! I'm sick of it!"[23]

Khrushchev knew what he wanted: Berlin. He revived a threat he had made to Eisenhower—to sign a separate peace treaty with East Germany, which would challenge allied rights in Berlin and the existence of a free West Berlin. Ever since the Berlin Airlift, the city had become a symbol of Amer-ica's backbone. Kennedy countered firmly. The United States was in Berlin because it had fought its way across Europe, Kennedy argued, not because of "someone's sufferance." An America that abandoned Berlin could not be counted upon to defend Western Europe, which was vital to U.S. national security. "We cannot accept that." Kennedy distinguished Laos, where he was willing to accommodate rival forces in a neutral government.[24]

Khrushchev apparently shocked Kennedy by rejoining, "[L]et the war be better now, before the emergence of new, even more terrible means of warfare"—although both delegations left that blast out of their transcripts. It was up to the Americans, Khrushchev added, "to choose peace or war." Kennedy closed by warning of "a cold winter."[25]

The president had begun to recognize that the reasoned diplomacy he preferred could be built only upon a foundation of fortitude, backed by power. JFK worried that he might not have made his resolve clear to Khru-shchev. Returning home through London, Kennedy related his impressions to Prime Minister Macmillan. The savvy British veteran recorded, "The President was completely overwhelmed by the ruthlessness and barbarity of the Russian Chairman. It reminded me in a way of Lord Halifax or Neville Chamberlain trying to hold a conversation with Herr Hitler."[26] The young president was on the verge of a crisis of confidence with his allies as well.

Before leaving Vienna, the Soviets gave the Americans a paper demand-ing concessions in Berlin in "no more than six months." Moscow published its ultimatum on June 10. The heat was on, and Kennedy now "thought about little else."[27]

Preparing for a Berlin Crisis

The president enlisted Dean Acheson to help with contingency planning for Berlin. The former secretary of state returned to the fundamentals of early–Cold War diplomacy: demonstrate determination by mobilizing America's strengths, in conjunction with allies, while preparing, but not scaring, the U.S. public. Acheson foresaw a test of wills. He doubted that negotiations with Moscow would settle differences, but in any event he knew that Kennedy needed to operate from a position of credible power. Some of the president's advisers objected to Acheson's lack of a "political" element that reached out to the Soviets; they wanted ways to meet Khrushchev's complaints through negotiated accommodations.

The president accepted most of Acheson's premises but wanted to preserve room for maneuver. He decided to signal determination, strengthen his hand, and muster public support—while avoiding a confrontation that slipped beyond a point of no return. After the experience of the Bay of Pigs and Vienna, Kennedy wanted to retain control over key decisions and preserve the flexibility to combine stalwart resistance with bargaining.[28]

Kennedy spoke to Americans, Soviets, and the world through a television address on July 25. The president stated a clear U.S. policy: "We cannot and will not permit the communists to drive us out of Berlin, either gradually or by force." He explained who was the aggressor: "[I]f war begins, it will have begun in Moscow, not Berlin." To back up the U.S. position, the president called for six new army divisions, emergency airlift capabilities, authority to triple draft calls and mobilize reserves, and an expanded program of civil defense; by preparing fallout shelters, JFK was signaling that even nuclear options were on the table. The president secured his public support, too. According to a Gallup poll, 85 percent of Americans were willing to risk war to hold the line in Berlin. Congress voted overwhelmingly to fund the military expansion.[29]

Kennedy's speech combined strength with a willingness to explore diplomatic avenues. He even included a hint. Kennedy referred to West Berlin as the U.S. vital interest, not the Four-Power Agreement of 1945 that encompassed all of the old German capital. West Berlin became the watchword in the president's other remarks and diplomatic messages; this was no slip by a speechwriter.[30]

Kennedy sensed that Khrushchev, for all his belligerence, might be hiding a weakness: The lifeblood of East Germany was exiting through Berlin. Soviet threats worsened that problem. In July, thirty thousand East Germans fled to camps in West Berlin, the largest monthly number since the Soviet crackdown in 1953. Ulbricht warned Moscow that "if the present situation of open borders remains, collapse is inevitable." When presidents are under pressure (and their aides rally to show strength), it is hard for presidents to pause to consider their foes' frustrations. Kennedy could do so and even stretched further—by assessing both Khrushchev's problem and offering a distinction that the Soviets might use to solve it. In doing so, however, Kennedy created a new problem that he had not yet fully grasped: whether Berlin, West Germany, and the Western alliance could survive the blow to morale of any perceived retreat from the defense of U.S. rights to all of Berlin.[31]

The Berlin Wall

Shortly after midnight on August 13, Soviet forces ringed Berlin, while the East German police stopped subways and built a barbed wire barrier along the boundary with West Berlin. On August 19, the East Germans started to build a Wall that would divide Berlin for twenty-eight years. Ulbricht had wanted to squeeze the Western allies out and close air corridors so that Berliners, East and West, could not flee. The Wall was his fallback. Khrushchev insisted on acting quickly, keeping the East German public quiet and not provoking the West.[32]

The Americans and their allies were surprised—and anxious. They had not seriously contemplated a wall and had not prepared for it. Berliners might explode in protests as they had done in 1953. The Soviets and East Germans might take a second step to seal off the city. Washington decided to signal calm to downplay thoughts of imminent war. JFK went sailing—then issued a mild statement; he did not rush back to the White House to make it. Privately he told O'Donnell, "[A] wall is a hell of a lot better than a war." Highly attuned to public imagery, Kennedy thought that the Soviets and East Germans looked terrible: They were creating an ugly, visible, and concrete reminder of Communist oppression.

The cool response from Washington contrasted with the feelings in Berlin. Berliners and other Germans were outraged. They felt betrayed. Neither East nor West Berliners ever accepted that Wall. Berliners would die resisting it. Berliners would eventually tear it down.[33]

Early in the administration, Acheson had cautioned Kennedy to focus on Germany, not Moscow. He urged that America concentrate on the German government and people. Reinforcing this view, Henry Kissinger, then a professor advising the White House, had recommended that Kennedy press the rights of self-determination and unification for all Germans. Smyser concluded that the Kennedy team "wanted to use diplomacy to improve relations with Moscow and to fend off Khrushchev's threats," whereas Kissinger believed "diplomacy should primarily reinforce the Western alliance."[34]

The allies were divided. Macmillan maneuvered toward a compromise on Berlin. De Gaulle might not have minded if Kennedy stumbled, thus showing the Germans that Europeans could not rely on Americans. And Adenauer spoke cautiously, wary of a break with his allies and suspecting a Khrushchev plot to depose him in coming elections.[35]

Edward R. Murrow, the veteran wartime correspondent and Kennedy friend, happened to be in Berlin on August 13. He commented to a colleague, "I wonder if the President realizes the seriousness of the situation." Murrow, who was then director of the U.S. Information Agency, wrote JFK a cable warning of a political and diplomatic disaster. He feared a break in confidence that could wreck the alliance, not only in Berlin but in Germany, Europe, and beyond. "What is in danger of being destroyed here is that perishable quality called hope," Murrow concluded.[36]

Investment in West Berlin plummeted. Young people began to leave. Mayor Willy Brandt wrote the president that a "second act" would surely follow the first. "Berlin would be like a ghetto, which has not only lost its function as a refuge of freedom and symbol of hope for reunification, but which would also be severed from the free part of Germany. Instead of a flight to Berlin, we might then experience flight from Berlin." He urged U.S. signals to restore confidence. Kennedy was irked by the criticism—as well as by the political risks posed by Brandt's letter—but recognized the implications. Khrushchev had isolated West Berlin. He still wanted to push the Americans out. Kennedy began to worry, in the words of the head of the U.S. mission in Berlin, that "the Soviets, having taken such a big slice of salami and successfully digested it…, may be expected to snatch further pieces greedily."[37]

Marguerite Higgins—a veteran war correspondent, visitor to Germany, and friend of the Kennedys—met the president in the Oval Office to express her concerns. JFK shared Mayor Brandt's letter and his frustration. Higgins offered Kennedy a precious gift for presidents: honest, even if unwelcome, advice. "I must tell you frankly," she replied, "the suspicion is growing that you're going to sell out the West Berliners." Higgins urged Kennedy to ask retired General Lucius Clay, the hero of the Berlin Airlift, to go to Berlin. (She had already checked if Clay would be willing to do so.) Higgins suggested sending Vice President Lyndon Johnson, too.[38]

General Clay Returns to Berlin

Kennedy asked Clay to return to Berlin as the president's "Personal Representative." Clay was a close friend of former president Eisenhower and had played a key role in persuading Ike to return from Europe to run for president in 1952. The strong-willed Clay had a reputation for independent action. Kennedy took a political risk in appointing him. Kennedy's advisers were concerned that Clay might become "another MacArthur"—the imperious general whom President Truman had to fire for insubordination during the Korean War. Kennedy's men had repeatedly warned the president that any confrontation with Moscow could escalate to nuclear war.[39]

Clay treated the president respectfully and made clear privately that he would take no action that would add to the president's problems. Yet Clay brought a fresh viewpoint to Berlin: As Smyser wrote, "Clay believed that Ulbricht wanted the Wall not only to encircle West Berlin but to neutralize it and ultimately take it over."[40] Clay set out to shift Kennedy's thinking from that of his advisers.

Clay believed Germans might choose neutrality if disappointed with the United States and the West. He wanted to bolster their courage and commitment. Clay suspected that measured firmness would deter the Soviets, whom he distinguished from the East Germans. Clay wanted Moscow to keep a firm grip on the German Communists; Clay thought the East Germans were risking dangerous confrontation and challenging both Soviet and American control of Berlin.

Clay recommended the prompt dispatch to Berlin of a battle group of 1,500 men via the Autobahn; Vice President Lyndon Johnson joined Clay to welcome the reinforcements when they arrived in West Berlin on August 20, within a week of the border closure. A nervous Kennedy tracked the convoy every twenty minutes as it edged across East Germany toward the city. Despite objections from Prime Minister Macmillan and the U.S. military, Clay instituted convoys and patrols of the Autobahn. Clay also insisted on patrols of sector borders in Berlin.[41]

When an East German fled to the isolated village of Steinstücken, the East German police threatened to seize him. The little hamlet was administratively part of West Berlin but separated from it by one hundred meters. The U.S. Army ignored Clay's request to send troops to the enclave. Clay flew over in his personal helicopter and spent about an hour reassuring the villagers. The East German guards pointed their weapons at the helicopter but dared not fire. Upon his return, Clay asked for weekly helicopter visits to show the U.S. presence and to fly out refugees.[42]

Clay assumed risks that Kennedy approved after the fact; Kennedy almost

certainly would not have authorized them in advance. But Clay was calculating hazards with a purpose. He wanted to challenge infringements,
especially by East Germans, of basic U.S. rights. He did not bother with all
harassment. Clay said that he refused to be bound by the constraints of an
"escalation theory" that precluded U.S. reactions to East German probes.
Passivity, Clay believed, would lead "to the continuing erosion of an already
eroded position." Instead, he chose to signal that East German aggression
created risks for the Soviets. He ordered the construction of a replica section
of the Wall in a secluded location in West Berlin so that U.S. military engineers could experiment with ways to break it down. When the U.S. European Commander learned of Clay's practice sessions, he ordered a stop and
dismantlement of the target wall. But Soviet intelligence had already sent
photos to Moscow. Washington was in the dark.[43]

The Crisis at Checkpoint Charlie

Clay's game of chess on the Berlin board concluded with the placement of
tank pieces at Checkpoint Charlie in late October. American officials had the
right to travel all around Berlin in vehicles without showing identification;
East German guards had no jurisdiction over them. Ulbricht wanted to show
West Berliners that he could cow an impotent United States. Without checking with Moscow, the East Germans insisted that allied civilians show pass-
ports to enter East Berlin. British and French officials complied. Under Clay's
direction, the Americans responded by adding armed escorts and driving
cars back and forth past East German guards. When the East Germans tried
to block them, the Americans demanded the presence of a Soviet officer—to
emphasize which powers were really in charge.

On the morning of October 25, two U.S. soldiers dressed as civilians
tested the rules at Checkpoint Charlie. East German guards stopped them,
demanding identification. The Americans insisted on seeing a Soviet official. This time, the new Soviet political adviser came personally—and said
the Americans had to obey East German regulations. Ulbricht had forced
Khrushchev to back him.

Clay brought up tanks, which stood watch as squads of U.S. soldiers
escorted cars in and out of the checkpoint, and East Germans jumped out of
the way. The Soviet military commandant, an old hand called out of retire-
ment like Clay, had fought his way into Berlin in 1945. He noted that some
U.S. tanks had bulldozer blades, raising the prospect of an advance right
through the heart of East Berlin—the location of ministries and even the
Soviet embassy. On October 27, the Soviets brought up their own tanks,
but only in numbers to match the Americans. The Soviets had two aims:

to prevent an advance by the Americans, and to keep a watch on the East Germans. The Soviet marshal placed one of his officers in control of the checkpoint, although the Soviets tried futilely to cover up their insignias and pretend they were Germans.

Clay recognized that the Soviets were exerting control. An American car again forced the East Germans to leap aside. When U.S. tanks rolled up right to the dividing line between East and West, Soviet tanks moved up as well. As afternoon passed into evening, searchlights glared and photographers recorded this one point-blank standoff of U.S. and Soviet tanks during the Cold War. Clay issued a press release: "The fiction of an East German stoppage is now destroyed."

Back in Washington, Kennedy's advisers wanted Clay to back off. From London, Macmillan ranted about Clay. The president wanted to speak to the old general personally before deciding. The two men spoke by phone on October 27 at about 6:00 p.m. in Washington, midnight in Berlin. Surrounded by staff, the president leaned back in his chair and put his feet on his desk to show he was comfortably in charge. Clay reassured the president that the drama was under control, in large part because the Soviets, who did not trust Ulbricht, had taken charge. The president told Clay, "Don't lose your nerves." Clay replied that he was fine, but "we're worried...whether people in Washington were losing theirs." The president assured him: "I've got a lot of people here that have, but I haven't." In fact, Kennedy was not relying totally on Clay. His brother Robert had begun a back-channel negotiation to pull back the tanks. At 10:30 in the morning in Berlin on October 28, the Soviet tanks began to withdraw; the American armor pulled back within a half hour.

Clay had accomplished important objectives. Berliners' morale jumped; they were regaining the confidence in America that poured out during Kennedy's visit in June 1963. The U.S. garrison found a greater sense of purpose following the confrontation. After the collapse in the Bay of Pigs and the unsettling story in Vienna, the world, including nervous allies, saw pictures of America's armored resolve.

Clay had respected his Soviet military counterparts during his first tour of occupation duty in Germany right after World War II; he read the Soviet unwillingness, sixteen years after fighting their way to Berlin, to turn their fates over to East Germans. Khrushchev later put Ulbricht in his place. If the Soviets decided on confrontation, they wanted to be in charge. The sovereignty of East Germany did not extend to challenging, on its own, the occupying powers.[44]

Yet Clay paid a price in Washington, where (as Secretary Baker often told me) one does not win battles with the White House staff. Kennedy did not like to lose—or to appear to Americans as losing, so he probably valued Clay's results if not his methods. The president, interested in hearing multiple views, kept an open channel to Clay. But Kennedy's principal advisers wanted no more risks of miscalculation. Some foolishly criticized Clay to Soviets in Washington. Secretary of State Dean Rusk ordered a halt to civilian probes with armed escorts into East Berlin; U.S. civilian officials were to stop traveling to the East except for one unarmed car a day.[45]

Clay left Berlin in May 1962. By then the crisis atmosphere had eased, and the post-Wall flight had stopped. Clay had even managed to encourage General Motors and other U.S. firms to open offices and invest in Berlin. Robert Kennedy had visited, and Clay urged him to persuade the president to come. Clay could justifiably say to the seven hundred thousand Berliners who came to say good-bye that he had done his job. He claimed his heart would remain with Berlin and he would return if ever needed.[46]

The Future of Berlin and Germany

In less than a year in office, Kennedy had learned much about questioning assumptions, encouraging internal debate while remaining in control, preparing public support, sending signals to Moscow, using back-channel diplomacy, and maintaining "off-ramps" in nuclear confrontations. The president observed that the Soviets were also wary of escalations. Kennedy still needed to learn more about negotiating from strength and guiding alliance politics. He needed the experience—because Khrushchev was not finished with Berlin.[47]

Kennedy's team knew that the Berlin pot would continue to boil. After the East Germans constructed the Wall and then the showdown in the autumn, the Americans had little room to negotiate with the Soviets about the city. Americans now recognized the fragility of Berliners' confidence; mistaken signals could prompt an exodus that would hollow out Berlin. The administration's solution was to expand its offers to encompass issues concerning the two Germanies and the unfinished work of the postwar settlement.

After over a decade of Cold War in Europe, Kennedy and his advisers wanted to negotiate a new status quo. Rusk proposed concessions on points the Soviets had pressed for years—and which Truman and Eisenhower had rejected—such as the sovereignty of East Germany, defining German frontiers, nuclear prohibitions for both Germanies, and a nonaggression pact between the alliances. He even floated the idea of an international access authority, including East Germany, that would control transport into West Berlin. For Europeans and especially Germans, these were not just diplomatic niceties. The United States seemed ready to concede the legality of two

German states, one without freedom, and to give up on the idea of reunification. The United States was offering to concede major points to preserve rights it already had. Soviet Foreign Minister Andrei Gromyko's fear of agreeing to anything kept Americans from yielding too much.[48]

Kennedy and Rusk kept relinquishing positions to the Soviets. The secretary of state prepared a "principles paper" that presented the bag of concessions and added more, including the idea of joint West-East German commissions. Smyser, who served in Berlin during these years, termed this proposal "smorgasbord diplomacy"—a tableful of offers from which Khrushchev could select. To make the choices more appealing, Rusk used language from Soviet texts and discussions. He passed an informal draft to Gromyko in March without sharing it with the Germans and French. The allies got to see the "final" version in April. London was enthusiastic. French officials objected harshly, pointing out the absence of references to free elections, reunification, and the democratic principles that distinguished West Germany from the East. The French warned that Washington risked an explosive and dangerous reaction from Bonn; not only were the Americans ignoring the political foundations of the new Federal Republic of Germany, but they presumed to negotiate the fate of the Germans over their heads. For his part, de Gaulle might have been pleased that Washington was pushing Adenauer toward Paris, its only reliable friend.

The State Department gave the West Germans only twenty-four—later extended to forty-eight—hours to respond to the paper. Adenauer exploded. He was sure that the new U.S. "principles" threatened Berlin, West Germany, European security, and the Federal Republic's membership in the Western alliance. Kennedy's youthful team seemed unaware that it was picking up Soviet ideas from the 1950s to neutralize Germany—while leaving East Germany under Soviet control. The old German chancellor wanted the Kennedy men, noted for their brainpower, to factor in experience—and a better sense of history. The principles paper promptly leaked to the German press and the *New York Times*. Adenauer denied the leak, but Kennedy erupted. The U.S. public reaction doomed Kennedy's and Rusk's overture to the Soviets. Americans saw no reason to yield to an East German dictatorship and Soviet bullying. They inundated the White House mailroom with black "Chamberlain" umbrellas, a reminder of Britain's (and Kennedy's father's) appeasement of Hitler in the 1930s.[49]

Kennedy's activism in the face of Soviet immovability revealed a weakness of diplomacy that is too impatient to "solve" problems: The Americans were negotiating with themselves; as the Soviets sat intractably, the United States kept trying to offer more. Even worse, the concessions gained nothing but Khrushchev's contempt because the single-minded Soviet leader wanted Berlin, not a negotiated European settlement. Ernest May and Philip Zelikow, in their study of the Berlin-Cuba Crisis based on Kennedy's taped conversations, concluded that "Khrushchev acted more from instinct than calculation."[50] The Soviet premier scented weakness in Kennedy, in part because of the zealous search for U.S. compromise before the administration had demonstrated that it could firmly say no. I have been highlighting stories that show the timing of initiatives is vital; this account points out that knowing when to hold back—when *not* to act—is critical, too.

Khrushchev's Plan

In March 1962, Khrushchev sent Kennedy a private message arguing that Berlin should be a demilitarized free city. In July, the Soviet premier followed up with a precise proposal to replace Western troops in Berlin with a UN police force that would be phased out after a future peace treaty settled German affairs for good. West Berlin would be a free city, without any tie to West Germany. Then NATO and the Warsaw Pact could cut forces in central Europe and conclude a nonaggression pact. Khrushchev invited Kennedy to come to the USSR to crown the achievement with a signing event. Kennedy rejected the proposal and repeated that keeping U.S. forces in Berlin was a vital U.S. interest, but he tried to keep a door open to discussions. JFK suggested focusing on "practical" measures and avoiding topics unacceptable to one another.[51]

In late September, Khrushchev switched tack, suggesting that he would help Kennedy by putting German questions on ice until after the U.S. congressional elections in mid-November. Formal diplomacy paused. But warning lights began flashing. In September, Khrushchev called in Stewart Udall, the U.S. secretary of the interior, who was visiting Moscow. Khrushchev demanded that U.S. forces leave Berlin. He would wait until after the November elections. But then Kennedy would have to choose: "go to war or sign a peace treaty." Unlike in the past, Khrushchev added, "now we can swat your ass." The Soviet premier said he would put Kennedy in a position where the United States had to act. Showing his disdain, the old Communist postured that the president "has understanding, but what he does not yet have is courage." As for Adenauer and de Gaulle, "they will get wise in a hurry," for "war in this day and age means no Paris and no France." Khrushchev delivered a similar message to the West German ambassador, hinting that he was prepared to force West Berlin to become a free city. With the gusto of a man in control, the Soviet leader added that "Kennedy is waiting to be pushed to the brink—agreement or war? Of course, he will not want war; he will concede." In October, Gromyko delivered a matching, but less blunt, message directly to the president about the "rotten tooth" of West Berlin, "which must be pulled out."[52]

The Cuban Missile Crisis

In October, the threats to Berlin came to a head in an unusual spot—the Caribbean Sea. Although at one time historians studied the Cuban Missile Crisis as a separate event, many now suspect that Khrushchev viewed Berlin as a key, maybe even the major, objective of the plan to put intermediate-range nuclear missiles in Cuba.[53] Soviet diplomacy demonstrated that the United States needs to keep in mind its traditional priority of continental security, including the nation's southern flank, and to recognize the new connections between North America and the projection of power globally.

Khrushchev planned to come to the United Nations in November 1962 to settle Berlin after installing the missiles in Cuba. Once he could announce their presence, Khrushchev wanted to position his UN plan for Berlin as a "compromise" to avoid escalation. The Soviets did not need nuclear missiles to defend Cuba; their purpose was to threaten the United States and to push Kennedy to back down. In preparation for the autumn showdown, the Soviets built fuel pipelines across East Germany and deployed large forces on the border with West Germany. They made no effort to camouflage these moves. The massive show of force would add to the threat, forcing Germans and the other Western allies to "get wise in a hurry," in Khrushchev's words.[54]

About this time, the president gained additional intelligence on the strategic balance of power. In 1960, JFK had argued that the United States was on the short end of a "missile gap" with the Soviets; by October 1962, the president knew without doubt that there was indeed a missile gap, but that America was far ahead. Satellite images and spies confirmed the assessment from U-2 aerial photographs that the United States held an enormous lead in intercontinental capabilities; the Soviets had far fewer intercontinental ballistic missiles (ICBMs) than expected earlier, and Moscow even had problems with the first-generation ICBMs it had deployed. More important than the disparity in the numbers, a U.S. National Intelligence Estimate concluded that the U.S. "second strike" capability was at least as extensive "as the Soviets [could] deliver by striking first." In October 1962, the president authorized the deputy secretary of defense to make a dry presentation of the numbers of U.S. missiles, strategic bombers, and missile submarines—adding up to a strategic imbalance favoring the United States. To help Moscow get the message, Washington ordered briefings of NATO allies, with pictures, that Soviet intelligence would certainly report.[55]

When the CIA discovered the Soviets' nuclear missiles in Cuba in mid-October, it recognized Moscow's maneuver to shift the strategic balance. A National Intelligence Estimate concluded that if the Soviets successfully deployed these nuclear weapons Moscow "would probably estimate lower risks in pressing the US hard in other confrontations, such as Berlin." Studying Soviet records decades later, May and Zelikow concluded that while Khrushchev and his colleagues "care[d] a great deal about Cuba, the thought of deterring a U.S. invasion figured only incidentally in their discussions about the missile deployments. Calculations about the strategic nuclear balance were much more in evidence. Berlin was an omnipresent and dominating concern."[56]

Cuba and Berlin

In 1958 and 1961, Khrushchev had let the deadlines for his ultimatums on Berlin slip away. The East Germans wanted Moscow to show a stiffer spine. In March 1962, new Soviet ambassador Anatoly Dobrynin met with Premier Khrushchev before assuming his post in Washington. "Germany and Berlin overshadowed everything," recalled Dobrynin. Khrushchev claimed the Americans were "particularly arrogant" about their nuclear deterrent, and it was "high time their long arms were cut shorter." May and Zelikow wrap up their book on the Cuban crisis by stating, "We believe, with [U.S. Ambassador to the USSR] Thompson and the experts in London, that the key to Khrushchev's strategy for Berlin in 1962 was missiles in Cuba."[57]

The president recognized from the start the multiple connections between the missiles in Cuba and Berlin. In his first speech alerting the American public to the Soviet missiles, the president warned Moscow not to make a hostile move against Berlin. On October 19, Kennedy told the Joint Chiefs that a U.S. attack on Cuba would offer an excuse for a Soviet takeover of West Berlin. But a U.S. failure to act would also embolden a Soviet move on Berlin. He emphasized, "Our problem is not merely Cuba but it is also Berlin. And when we recognize the importance of Berlin to Europe, and recognize the importance of our allies to us, that's what has made this thing be a dilemma." As Lawrence Freedman concluded, Kennedy "saw Cuba as an extension of the Berlin crisis, with a move against the city an almost inevitable consequence of any action he took." Berliners immediately understood what events in Cuba meant for them. They cheered JFK. Berliners said they knew "Kennedy was fighting *their* battle as much as his own."[58]

There are excellent accounts of Kennedy's skillful diplomacy in forcing Khrushchev to withdraw his missiles.[59] The president took advantage of Soviet overreach in a theater where the United States enjoyed military dominance. He applied firm demands and measured steps—backed by sufficient military power, coordinated with allies, and supported by the public—all focused on his core objective. He gave Khrushchev time and opportunity to avoid escalation, especially to nuclear weapons, while "keep[ing] the heat on." The "quarantine-blockade" committed the United States to action while providing a pause for his opponent to weigh consequences. Kennedy gave Khrushchev an escape hatch and used a private channel to offer a concession. Khrushchev made no move to add a showdown in Berlin to the danger in Cuba, although a deputy foreign minister suggested an attack on Berlin as a diversion. Kennedy asked General Clay to head to Berlin if the Soviets began a blockade.[60]

The subsequent Soviet retreat from Cuba changed the course of the Berlin Crisis. The United States and its allies showed the strength of firm responses to aggressive moves—the approach that General Clay had sought to apply in Berlin. Khrushchev's bluster now lacked credibility. Harassment in Berlin continued, but it became more careful and less assertive.[61]

A Thaw in the Cold War

Having finally earned a reputation for strength, Kennedy could pursue his preferred course to ease Cold War tensions, especially the risk of nuclear war. In June 1963, Washington and Moscow agreed to establish a hotline for rapid communications during emergencies. In August 1963, the United States and the Soviet Union signed the Limited Test Ban Treaty, which prohibited nuclear explosions in the atmosphere. The accord, while not militarily significant, nevertheless represented the first U.S.-Soviet effort to control arms.[62]

Some students of the Cold War believe that the dangers of the Berlin and Cuban crisis became the point of departure for a new path in East-West relations. The combination of determination, deterrence, and discussion that developed out of the 1961–63 experience eventually led to the dramatic days of 1989–90. The future of Berlin, Germany, and Europe would be determined by another generation in another era. The line from which the Western allies would work would be the Wall—not the Elbe, the Rhine, or the English Channel. Around the world, Berlin and Berliners would stand for freedom.[63]

Back in Berlin on June 26, 1963, President Kennedy delivered a second speech, a more sober policy address, at the Free University. He stressed the importance of negotiations. He spoke of German unification, but warned that it would require patience, be "neither quick nor easy," and that others would "need to see their own true interests better than they do today."[64] Twenty-seven years later, Kennedy would be proven correct.

Securing Frontiers in the Cold War

We now know how the Cold War ended. From this distance in time, it is hard to imagine the fears of that tense, prolonged standoff. In 1947–49, the United States had decided, in an initial rushed reaction, to build an alliance system that bound American security to territories across the Atlantic and Pacific. The violent stalemate of the Korean War of 1950–53 demonstrated the high cost and difficulty of that new diplomacy. American presidents had to determine how best to secure far-flung frontiers over decades. Dwight Eisenhower wanted the U.S. public to concentrate on building the economy and returning to normality after the Depression, World War II, fears of a Europe in crisis, and the Korean War. Eisenhower expected a protracted struggle with the Soviet Union; the country faced "a long-term responsibility," "not a temporary emergency." America needed endurance to prevail. He used covert operations to wage the Cold War in secondary theaters and brandished nuclear superiority to hold the line for core interests, but Eisenhower avoided new, full-scale military commitments. Not one U.S. soldier died in conflict during his eight years.[65]

John F. Kennedy, like Eisenhower, inherited an extensive American alliance system that, for the first time in U.S. history, posted vast U.S. forces, fleets, and air flotillas around the globe. In 1963, the United States had 275 major bases in thirty-one nations and well over one million military-related personnel stationed abroad.[66] Unlike Eisenhower, Kennedy faced a Soviet Union armed with increasing numbers of nuclear missiles that could blast much of America into a wasteland. No wonder that Kennedy wanted both to assure robust deterrence and to prevent miscalculation by either side. Accidents happen. People miss signals. Leaders in capitals as well as combatants on the front lines can overreact or even panic.[67]

Assessing Kennedy's Diplomacy: Germany, Activism, and Crisis Management

The story of Kennedy's Cold War diplomacy offers three insights. First, Kennedy and his advisers initially concentrated on Moscow, whereas Marshall and particularly Acheson made U.S. allies their strategic priority. The early Cold Warriors concluded that negotiations with the Soviets would be either fruitless or impossible until after the United States had built the transatlantic coalition into a partnership of economic, political, and military power— sustained, over a long struggle, by democratic public opinion and purpose.

Kennedy's impatience led him to look for bargains with Khrushchev. At first, Kennedy viewed Berlin like a hostage—one that prevented any diplomatic initiative to lessen nuclear tensions. Acheson and Clay, in contrast, argued that steadfast support for Berlin and West Germany secured the transatlantic alliance, which was the cornerstone of America's strength in the Cold War. Over time, Kennedy, more than his advisers, came to recognize Berlin as an asset—a vibrant outpost of freedom that starkly illustrated the failures of Communism. Berlin reminded everyone of America's willingness to stand guard over Europe's security. The divided city also created an emotional and practical bond with the Federal Republic of Germany, the country in central Europe that would determine the fate of the Cold War.

Ironically, this difference of strategic perspectives arose again as the Cold War came to a close in 1989–90. As chapter 17 will relate, President George H. W. Bush lined up strongly with Chancellor Helmut Kohl to achieve democratic Germany's peaceful unification within NATO and the then European Community. Prime Minister Margaret Thatcher of Britain hesitated, in part because she did not want to cause trouble for President Mikhail Gorbachev and feared the power of a united Germany. At first, President Francois Mitterrand of France also disliked the prospect of unification. After Germany's unification, President Bill Clinton's adviser on Russia, Strobe Talbott, criticized Bush and Secretary Baker for being "primarily concerned with shoring up their fellow conservative Helmut Kohl and thus staying on the good side of a vital ally"; Talbott argued the "disruptive consequences of quick unification" weakened Gorbachev.[68] At that time, Talbott ranked helping Gorbachev above keeping alliance commitments and securing a democratic Germany as a partner within the transatlantic security system.

The United States should never take its partnership with Germany for granted. By reason of its size, economic power, and geography, Germany will play a decisive role in Europe's future, as it has in Europe's past. Having earned a special relationship with Germany over the decades of the Cold War, and especially through the successful closing chapter, Washington would be foolish to ignore the consequences of a lasting break.

Kennedy—like Bush and Baker decades later—also recognized the importance of Berliners and Germans to their diplomacy. Berliners refused to be pawns of powerful statesmen. In 1948–49 and 1961–62, Berliners defied tyrants on freedom's front line; abandoning them would have been an incalculable loss. In 1989–90, Berliners and other Germans, East and West, sparked the diplomacy of unification. The United States and the Federal Republic used their momentum to propel a democratic takeover, not a merger of one free and one totalitarian state.

The second insight concerns JFK's diplomatic activism. I admire his drive to be "on offense" so as to set the terms of debates and reshape calculations. The bureaucratic inclination of most governments, including the large U.S.

departments, is just to react. Leaders have to struggle to change the status quo and rethink conventional approaches. Acheson had made this point in defining the role of policy planning. Moreover, Kennedy displayed the skill of democratic leadership by carefully courting U.S. public support.

Nevertheless, Kennedy learned that impulsive activism or poorly considered actions are perilous. The effective activist needs to study the history of an issue, challenge assumptions, and consider the steps likely to flow from the first move. It helps to understand how others perceive the problem. When dealing with adversaries, the activist should know the other side's experience, mind-set, and even political culture. Kennedy grew in office—from acting rashly to weighing choices carefully.

Kennedy's active intellect worked creatively to solve problems. He wanted to maintain "exit ramps" for himself; he also considered ways for Khrushchev to back down without breaking down. Most international relationships necessitate some ongoing coexistence, so high-level diplomacy and negotiation usually require achieving objectives while still expecting future rounds. The United States can destroy an opponent only on rare occasions, and even when it does so—whether in Germany or Japan in World War II or in Iraq, Afghanistan, and Libya more recently—American officials must pay close attention to what might arise from the ashes.

As an activist negotiator, Kennedy had to learn when to hold back. Because he was willing to negotiate—and pressed for creative solutions—Kennedy also had to show that he could draw a firm line and be willing to walk away. Especially in regions where power overshadows reason—most notably in the Middle East—pragmatism requires demonstrations of strength. Pragmatists look for solutions, but sometimes the time is not ripe. Then one has to step back and consider changing the context—whether of power or perception.

Third, the Kennedy style veered too readily toward crises. His bright, confident, and energetic band became enamored, even stimulated, by crisis management. After the climax in Cuba, the Kennedy team offered the *Saturday Evening Post* a self-congratulatory (and inaccurate) insider account. Robert McNamara, who came out particularly well in the story, offered a summation of the new statesmanship: "There is no longer any such thing as strategy," intoned the powerful secretary of defense, "only crisis management."[69]

Management by crisis can fail to consider how pressing problems relate to longer-term, strategic interests. On November 21, 1963, the evening before the president left for a campaign visit to Dallas, he spoke with Michael Forrestal, his NSC staffer on Vietnam who was headed to Cambodia. Kennedy seemed tired and wanted to muse a bit. "You know when you come back I want you to come and see me," JFK told Forrestal, "because we have to start to plan for what we are going to do now in South Vietnam. I want to start a complete and very profound review of how we got into this country, and what we thought we were doing, and what we now think we can do. I even want to think about whether or not we should be there." The activist, can-do president had aged into the analytical, more reflective statesman. For Kennedy and Vietnam, time ran out. When Forrestal arrived in Saigon later the next night, he learned that Lee Harvey Oswald had killed Kennedy. JFK had left the crisis of Vietnam unresolved.[70]

CHAPTER 14

Lyndon Johnson

Learning from Defeat

Calling for Help

In May 1964, President Lyndon Johnson was rolling up political successes. After the shocking assassination of President Kennedy the previous November, Johnson had skillfully redirected the nation toward fulfilling the martyred leader's congressional agenda. LBJ had capably assumed the mantle of trustee for the country's lost captain.

Johnson had been a masterful majority leader of the Senate during the 1950s. He knew how to manipulate the levers of power in Washington, especially in the Congress. In January 1964, he called for a war on poverty and began mobilizing his social service vanguard through the Economic Opportunity Act. In February, the president steered JFK's stalled tax bill to passage. That same month, the House passed LBJ's far-reaching Civil Rights Act, and by May the president was maneuvering to end the Senate debate on the bill; early in June, Johnson overcame a filibuster on civil rights legislation for the first time in the Senate's history. LBJ's string of successes positioned him to win the presidency in November in his own right. Then Johnson could press ahead with his life's work—the creation of a Great Society that would be the fulfillment of FDR's unfinished New Deal and Truman's sidetracked Fair Deal. LBJ knew that wars had thwarted the domestic dreams of his Democratic predecessors.

In May 1964, however, troublesome news about Vietnam interrupted the president's legislative parade. French president Charles de Gaulle had called for negotiations to "neutralize" Vietnam and Southeast Asia. Walter Lippmann, America's premier foreign affairs columnist, then stirred the political pot. After a contentious visit on May 21 with McGeorge Bundy, the president's inherited national security adviser, Lippmann criticized the Johnson administration's Vietnam policy. The United States had "no credible policy for winning the war or for ending it," wrote Lippmann. "There is no light at the end of the tunnel." In LBJ's circle of Washington power, Lippmann's opinion mattered.[1]

On May 24, the president met with the Executive Committee of his National Security Council to discuss Vietnam, Laos, and Cambodia. Secretary of Defense Robert McNamara stated bluntly that "the situation is going to hell. We are continuing to lose." The war cabinet urged "selected and carefully graduated military force against North Vietnam." The sole question was whether to act now or wait.[2]

On May 25, Bundy sent Johnson a proposal for military escalation in Vietnam. Bundy's haphazard mix of ideas reflected more fervor than analysis. He added that Secretary of State Dean Rusk and McNamara agreed with the paper and that "there is more thinking on these topics than this particular paper shows."[3] The national security adviser was carelessly recommending an American war.

Late on the morning of May 27, LBJ placed three quick phone calls to discuss Vietnam. First, the president called UN ambassador Adlai Stevenson, probably because LBJ knew Stevenson would counsel against expanding the fight; Stevenson, the Democratic standard-bearer in two presidential elections and voice of the party's liberal wing, could be expected to counter the views of the president's hard-liners. Next, LBJ called his old friend and mentor, Senator Richard Russell of Georgia, chairman of the Armed Services Committee. Russell deemed Vietnam to be "the damn worst mess I ever saw." The senator thought South Vietnam's leaders were not stepping up to their responsibilities. He worried about sliding into a major war, including with China. The American public was not prepared to send in troops, warned the senator. Russell wanted the United States to get out of Vietnam, but he did not know how to do so. After the assassination of President Ngo Dinh Diem in November 1963, no one seemed fully in charge in Saigon. Russell suggested finding a new South Vietnamese leader who would ask the United States to leave.

LBJ complained to Russell that he was under pressure from his advisers, as well as Republicans, to put more military chips on the table. He worried about treaty obligations and a "domino effect" from a loss in Vietnam that would lead a row of Southeast Asian countries to fall to Communism. The choice seemed to be to get in or get out, said LBJ. In a bid for sympathy and support, the president speculated that he would be impeached if he pulled out of Vietnam. Johnson griped about the U.S. ambassador in Saigon, Henry Cabot Lodge, a former Republican senator and Nixon's running mate in 1960, whom Johnson suspected would return to run for president later in 1964. Johnson and Russell both doubted that bombing North Vietnam would break Hanoi's will. And Johnson said that the idea of sending a sergeant who served as his valet, a father of six, to Vietnam "makes the chills run up my back....I just haven't got the nerve to do it, and I don't see any other way out of it."

The president then promptly called Bundy:

I'll tell you the more that I stayed awake last night thinking of this thing...I don't know what in the hell—it looks to me like we're getting into another Korea. It just worries the hell out of me. I don't see what we can ever hope to get out of there with, once we're committed. I believe that the Chinese Communists are coming into it. I don't think we can fight them ten thousand miles away from home....I just don't think it's worth fighting for and I don't think we can get out. It's just the biggest damned mess I ever saw.

Bundy acknowledged the gravity of the decision. The two men speculated who else might offer advice. Bundy turned to briefing the president on how to escalate, not whether to do so. LBJ closed by returning to Lippmann's views and wondering what the columnist would recommend. Later that day, Bundy arranged for the president to meet Lippmann, McNamara, and Under Secretary of State George Ball to discuss Vietnam.[4]

The exchanges of May 27 encapsulate most of the topics debated by President Johnson and his advisers in 1964 and early 1965. These were the critical months when they decided to turn the Vietnam conflict into an American war. Historians have to be careful, however, in taking any of Johnson's discussions, even private ones, at face value. The master politician's conversations were always maneuvers to send messages, curry favor, create appearances, and pin down statements of others for future use—as well as just to gain information. In the calls of May 27, Johnson was probably genuinely soliciting views, while using Stevenson to cover his liberal flank and counter his war cabinet, lining up Russell's support if the president decided to escalate, and pushing Bundy, as a representative of the Kennedy clique, to test his advisers' resolve to fight.[5]

LBJ

Lyndon Johnson was no warmonger. He had no political desire or need to become a war leader. He was not even optimistic about the course he eventually chose. Unlike JFK, Johnson did not find foreign policy particularly interesting; he wanted to become America's greatest domestic president. Nevertheless, he made the key decisions to begin a massive bombing campaign against North Vietnam and committed U.S. forces to an ever-expanding, drawn-out battle on the ground.[6]

Joe Califano worked at LBJ's side day and night for almost four years as domestic and economic policy adviser, after four years of stewardship with Robert McNamara. Califano's insights on Johnson are rich and candid:

> The Lyndon Johnson I worked with was brave and brutal, compassionate and cruel, incredibly intelligent and infuriatingly insensitive, with a shrewd and uncanny instinct for the jugular of his allies and adversaries. He could be altruistic and petty, caring and crude, generous and petulant, bluntly and calculatingly devious—all within the same few minutes....
>
> Once he made up his mind, his determination to succeed usually ran over or around whoever and whatever got in his way. He used his prodigious energy...—as others, allies and adversaries alike, slumped in exhaustion—to mount a social revolution and to control everyone and everything around him. He gave new meaning to the word Machiavellian, as he gave new hope to the disadvantaged.[7]

To reach the pinnacle of American politics, presidents must have extraordinary qualities—good and bad. To understand how U.S. diplomacy is actually made, we need to comprehend the behavior of these political leaders in the context of their times. The story of the Vietnam War is in large part a political history.

Deciding on War

The Vietnam War tore the United States apart. More than fifty-eight thousand American names are etched on the Vietnam Memorial. Some 1.5 to 3 million Vietnamese died. The wounds of war left deep scars in individuals and the national psychology.[8]

Historians have written much about the war, including assessments of the U.S. decisions in 1964–65.[9] This tale of tragedy and defeat offers a cautionary study for American diplomacy. Hindsight sharpens our perception of mistakes. Over the course of decades, Southeast Asian states did not fall like dominoes to Communist aggression. An authoritarian Communist regime rules all of Vietnam today, though the Vietnamese eventually rebuilt ties with the United States. After observing the successes of their Asian neighbors, the government in Hanoi transformed the economy by turning to markets and private initiatives. As a counterweight to Vietnam's historical nemesis, China, Hanoi has even sought limited security ties with its former American enemy. The U.S. decision to wage a costly, divisive, long, and ultimately failed war in Vietnam probably becomes increasingly incomprehensible to younger generations.

How could Johnson, McNamara, Bundy, Rusk, Maxwell Taylor, and others fail so terribly? These were intelligent, experienced people who thought they were making sensible choices in perplexing circumstances. They did not. Why?

At the close of the best study of the decisions of 1964–65, *Choosing War*, Fredrik Logevall explains that decisions on when and how to *disengage* from conflicts are "exceedingly important for historians as well as the policymakers of tomorrow." In considering post–Cold War diplomacy, the historian John Prados claims, "[t]here is wisdom too in knowing when to stop.... [S]trategies for holding out amid uncertainty without damaging escalation; for defusing local crises by bluff and maneuver; for disengaging from crises by walking away—these are concepts that could be of enormous value."[10]

After years of long wars in Afghanistan and Iraq, and calls for U.S. interventions around the world, the questions of whether and how to engage, with what means, for what ends, at what costs, and for how long are important for choices today. This story suggests topics to consider—and questions to ask—in choosing to fight a war. We have one advantage that LBJ and his advisers lacked: a costly lesson that U.S. military power alone may fail to achieve the nation's foreign policy aims.

Was There Really a Choice?

Many early critics of the U.S. war in Vietnam, including former American officials, maintained that there was never a *real* choice whether or not to go to war: For example, Les Gelb and Richard Betts argued that the course was predetermined. They stressed prior U.S. commitments and America's concern for credibility, which were reinforced by bureaucratic assumptions and practices and backed by the "Cold War consensus" of American public opinion; the key actors subscribed to the same ideology and failed to consider alternative views.[11]

The war cabinet of the Johnson administration assumed America could not disengage from Vietnam. Professor Logevall believes, nevertheless, that Johnson had the flexibility to decide. A number of senators, including prominent leaders and committee chairs, wanted to exit. In early 1965, Johnson's new vice president, Hubert Humphrey, wrote two cogent memos making the political cases against escalation. Major media opinion argued against widening the war. The public probably did not have a definite view. Key allies opposed escalation and refused to join in, although Australia urged action and offered support. U.S. partners in East Asia were lukewarm, although South Korea sent troops. Most important, the South Vietnamese leadership was fractured, and the war-weary Vietnamese public was reluctant to fight. The South Vietnamese viewed Americans suspiciously. U.S. intelligence reports noted Hanoi's resolve, Saigon's pessimism, and Washington's long odds of transforming the picture on its own. Republicans and some powerful media voices would have decried Johnson's retreat, which would have wounded the president's popularity. A Communist success might have spread in ways that the United States could not foresee, but knowledgeable people minimized domino effects. Local conditions usually determine local outcomes. In sum, an artful politician such as Johnson might have avoided escalating the war, although he risked looking weak.[12]

President Eisenhower, who understood life-and-death decisions of men and nations, wrote his assessment in his diary after LBJ announced that he would not seek reelection in 1968. "[T]he President is at war with himself and while trying vigorously to defend [his] actions...and urging the nation to pursue [his] purposes regardless of costs, he wants to be excused from the burden of office to which he was elected."[13] Harsh but believable.

David Halberstam's 1972 bestseller, *The Best and the Brightest*, offered another popular thesis. Halberstam, a *New York Times* correspondent who had argued in 1964 for a greater U.S. commitment, contended in his book that Johnson's smart and smug advisers led the president into a "quagmire." Halberstam's account suited the antiestablishment mood of the early 1970s. Nevertheless, the records reveal that Johnson was at the heart of his own agonizing story. The very hands-on president knew what he was doing and how he was failing.[14]

LBJ Defers a Decision

Prior to the election in November 1964, LBJ wanted to dodge making decisions on Vietnam. The hidden purpose of his phone calls and meetings in late May 1964 was to demonstrate attention without taking further action.

As early as February 20, 1964, the president instructed his secretary of defense how to speak publicly about Vietnam. He told McNamara to begin with the U.S. commitment to Vietnamese freedom. America could send in the Marines, but U.S. troops would soon be bogged down in a war. Then, LBJ continued, explain that the country could take the course of appeasement and pull out. That would not do. The right option was for Americans to train and advise the Vietnamese how to defend themselves. That was the way the United States had helped Greece and Turkey to halt the spread of Communism. Throughout the year, LBJ kept reminding his circle to "maintain the status quo." In March 1964, when the Joint Chiefs pressed for preparations to attack and blockade North Vietnam, the president instructed them that he was a "trustee" until he or someone else won an election. Neither

Congress nor America's mothers were ready to "go with us in a war." When Walt Rostow, director of policy planning at the State Department and later LBJ's stalwart national security adviser, began, in Johnson's words, "raising hell about having a little war in North Vietnam," the president told Rostow to clam up. "[T]he President doesn't know the position of the administration," said Johnson bluntly, "so *you* can't know it."[15]

As the year went on and conditions in South Vietnam worsened, the president focused on two concerns. First, he did not want to be the first president to lose a war, to "[turn] tail," and "[give] up the Pacific." He pressed McNamara for a general who "can give us some military plans for winning the war." LBJ was not yet ready to move, but he could see that "[w]e're losing." Second, he needed to ease out Ambassador Lodge, a potential political foe, from Saigon without creating electoral vulnerability. Johnson would need a successor for Lodge, too, perhaps a proconsul to run the politico-military operation in Vietnam, like Lucius Clay had done in Germany and Berlin.[16]

The Gulf of Tonkin Resolution

In early August, the president seized an opportunity for which he had been preparing. North Vietnamese torpedo boats attacked (but did not harm) a U.S. destroyer. The ship had been near the North Vietnamese coast conducting electronic surveillance while the South Vietnamese undertook covert operations nearby. The president recognized that the apparent connection between the ship and the coastal attack might have prompted the North Vietnamese strike. Nevertheless, LBJ ordered a reinforced U.S. naval patrol back to the area. The navy reported a second night attack, although murky conditions raised doubts about what had really happened. In later years, McNamara decided that no attack had actually taken place, and he ascribed the confusion to poor visibility and mistaken sonar soundings. The North Vietnamese always denied the second assault. In 2005–06, the U.S. National Security Agency released an internal review that had concluded that multiple errors contributed to the mistaken report of a second attack.[17]

LBJ was not of a mind to investigate carefully. Two months earlier, with the civil rights bill pending in the Senate, Bundy had recommended congressional authorization for use of force against North Vietnam—but he acknowledged the sensitive timing. Johnson had waited then; now he could move.

On the morning of August 4, before even receiving news of the alleged second attack, the president had ordered Bundy to ready the draft resolution on use of force. When Bundy suggested taking time to think about the step, LBJ shot back, "I didn't ask you what you *thought*, I told you what to *do*." The president told McNamara to prepare a retaliatory attack in case

North Vietnam tried another foray at sea. By late morning on August 4, when Washington received the confused report of the second night attack in the Gulf of Tonkin, LBJ was ready. He knew that McNamara would stand by the account of two attacks. At 6:15 p.m., after a brief meeting of the National Security Council, the president ordered sixty-four sorties by navy planes against North Vietnamese patrol boat bases and oil facilities. At 6:45 p.m., the president met congressional leaders to present his request for legislative authorization. At 8:01 p.m., in the midst of Johnson's final preparations, the FBI alerted him that it had found the bodies of three missing civil rights workers in Mississippi; LBJ thought to ask the Bureau to notify the families before the announcement of the discovery. At 9:02 p.m., Johnson checked with his congressional liaison about the effects of U.S. bombing and the military authorization request on the administration's antipoverty bill, which was at a critical stage. At 9:15 p.m., McNamara called to alert the president to a slight delay in the launch of the U.S. strike; Johnson hesitated about making a televised statement, but McNamara pointed out that the news of action should come from the president. At 10:06 p.m., Johnson reached Senator Barry Goldwater, his opponent in the upcoming presidential election, to read the statement LBJ would soon deliver to the nation. LBJ added some detail about the navy's targets for Goldwater, drawing him in. Goldwater replied, "Like always, Americans will stick together." The president gave his televised statement at 11:36 p.m., explaining, "We seek no wider war." On August 7, the Senate passed Johnson's Tonkin Gulf resolution by a vote of 88–2, and ten absent senators offered public endorsements. The House vote was 416–0.[18]

Johnson had neutralized Vietnam as a political issue in November. He appeared resolute without looking militant. Goldwater's calls for more military action just made the Republican appear dangerous. On the campaign trail, Johnson asserted that, "[w]e don't want our American boys to do the fighting for Asian boys... [t]o get involved with 700 million people and get tied down in a land war in Asia." Bundy worried that the president's political rhetoric could be turned against him if the administration later took the military actions that seemed necessary.[19]

During President Johnson's first eleven months in office, he had managed Vietnam superbly—as a domestic political issue. He had avoided dramatic new actions. In August, the president had won sweeping congressional authority for a bigger fight if he chose. In November, Johnson won the presidency in his own right with a landslide 60 percent of the popular vote. His electoral coattails gave the Democrats overwhelming majorities in Congress. LBJ prized political power and flexibility. He now seemed to have both. But Vietnam was still "a mess."

What Went Wrong?

Over the next six months, the president, advised by his war cabinet, made fateful decisions. Six factors dominated their thinking and the results:

1. The power of recent history
2. Credibility
3. Presidential experience and psychology
4. America's faith in its military power
5. Combining military power and diplomacy
6. The failure of advisers

These factors offer cautions for future U.S. diplomacy.

1. The Power of Recent History

Momentous events offer analogies, often poorly compared, to warn of dangers and guide success. The names of places and arguments serve as mental-shorthand references to the past. The invocation of recent history is often a political exercise, not an effective use of the past to understand current problems.

Most of the Americans deciding about Vietnam came of age in the 1930s. For them, the words "appeasement" and "Munich" signaled mistaken, wishful, and weak accommodations that fed the ambitions of brutal men; they had watched as assaults in the 1930s on seemingly unimportant, faraway places had signaled the first moves in a contest for global domination. They were the men who were called upon to reverse and then destroy the tyrants who took advantage of appeasement.[20]

No sooner had America's younger leaders succeeded in World War II than they faced a Cold War, a new type of struggle among blocs and even within countries. Communism appeared even more threatening than the fascism of the 1930s. For the first time in its history, the United States committed to—and led—alliances. Schoolbooks diagrammed an array of security partnerships—the North Atlantic Treaty Organization, the Southeast Asian Treaty Organization, the Central Treaty Organization, plus bilateral alliances—that intersected in the United States. These security organizations reflected almost twenty years of efforts in Washington to apply Kennan's powerful but ill-defined idea of containment.

The leaders of the new American alliances considered the extent of U.S. commitments case by case. The Kennedy men—who were now Johnson's men—had stood up to threats in other divided places: Berlin, Germany, and Korea. They had been part of JFK's commitment to South Vietnam, which by 1963 amounted to about sixteen thousand men and expenditures of about a million dollars a day. The notion of retreat was foreign to these successful leaders. They had witnessed the U.S. temptation to pull back to "Fortress America" after World War I, and the terrible price the country and the world had paid for that withdrawal.

In 1954, President Eisenhower had offered a corollary to the containment doctrine; he applied his domino theory to Vietnam and Southeast Asia. The Communists wanted to seize the grain basket and resources of Southeast Asia. The expansion of Communism threatened the nearby archipelago states, too, raising the question of Japan's and Korea's future in a Communist Asia. Nevertheless, in June 1964, the CIA produced a major study that became known as the "Death of the Domino Theory." The CIA recognized that the fall of Vietnam would damage U.S. prestige and credibility "profoundly," and other states in the region would seek to accommodate the Communists. Nevertheless, the agency stated, "We do not believe that the loss of South Vietnam and Laos would be followed by the rapid, successive communization of the other states of the Far East," with the possible exception of Cambodia. Bundy was aware of the CIA's estimate but did not rely upon it. Policy debates about what to do in the short term are often dominated by fears of worst-case scenarios. Many years later, Bundy recalled that "for LBJ the domino theory was really a matter of domestic politics." General Eisenhower had pronounced the theory—even though he had not taken military steps based on the idea. According to Bundy, "No serious contender for political office [could] propose letting go of Vietnam."[21]

For LBJ, all recent history was political history, and he had drawn his own lessons. No president could look soft on Communism and survive politically. He told Doris Kearns Goodwin, "I knew that Harry Truman and Dean Acheson had lost their effectiveness from the day that the communists took over in China. I believed that the loss of China had played a large role in the rise of Joe McCarthy. And I knew that all these problems, taken together, were chickenshit compared to what might happen if we lost Vietnam." Later historians might differ with Johnson's interpretation of the past, but at the time he was not willing to assume the political risks.[22]

The U.S. decision-makers also had fresh reference in the Korean experience. They applied it in different ways, however, demonstrating the malleability of analogies. Korea was an unpopular, stalemated war. Eisenhower believed that his threat of nuclear escalation had led to a Korean settlement in 1953. LBJ worried about China's intervention. Bundy focused on the American public's willingness to fight in Korea for three years, with the loss of some thirty-five thousand U.S. combatants, for "a hard choice, but incontestably right both in morals and politics." In 1961, JFK, the man no longer at the table, had offered a more critical comparison with Korea. Kennedy had differentiated the clear North Korean aggression and the UN support in Korea from the case of Vietnam. Someone should also have noticed that the geography of the Korean peninsula favored U.S. military capacities and its ultimate defensive strategy.[23]

Johnson's war cabinet reflected the afterglow of the U.S. military's victory in World War II and their own successful crisis management in Berlin and Cuba. Even though post–World War II surveys questioned the effectiveness of U.S. strategic bombing, modern U.S. air power looked extremely potent. Air attacks offered sharp, violent signals that could be used as part of "coercive diplomacy," which was a hot topic of security studies in the 1960s. The Washington warriors faced uncertainties and had "no quick solution," but Johnson recalled that after Pearl Harbor no one knew the length of the U.S. road to victory.[24] These men's experiences led them to hope for and expect the best, and certainly not to assume the United States would lose. None looked to the dismal French experience in Vietnam for warnings or guidance.

The Johnson administration would have benefited from a look back further in history. Alfred Thayer Mahan had outlined, based on his study of maritime history and geography, a Pacific strategy for the United States. The extended U.S. security perimeter, according to Mahan, should not reach beyond the islands of the western Pacific. After World War II, Japan became a keystone in that maritime perimeter. Americans could conceive of Korea as a continental outpost given the history of security for Japan in Northeast Asia, about which the United States had learned when TR mediated the Russo-Japanese War. As Michael Green points out, "the real objective of U.S. grand strategy in the Pacific [was] the prevention of a hostile hegemon from dominating the region."

In contrast, Vietnam looked like the gateway to a land war in Asia, which Mahan had warned against. In 1961, when retired general Douglas MacArthur visited Washington to discuss Vietnam with President Kennedy, Robert Kennedy recalled MacArthur saying that they "would be foolish to fight on the Asiatic continent and that the future of Southeast Asia should be determined at the diplomatic table."[25]

The Johnson administration also ignored recent economic history. The Marshall Plan had recognized (in the spirit of Alexander Hamilton and in contrast to the 1930s) that economic recovery was the prerequisite for European security. By 1960, Japan's economic success provided a model for other countries in Asia; U.S. trade policies had offered Japan a nonmilitary path to prosperity and power. In 1962, a Japanese economist predicted a "flying geese theory" that Japan's example of economic modernization could trigger a new regional growth dynamic. South Korea and countries in Southeast Asia were beginning to move toward the export-led growth that fueled the "East Asian Economic Miracle."

Senator Mike Mansfield complemented this regional economic perspective with his recognition that Asian nationalism could support U.S. strategic interests. Mansfield foresaw Vietnamese resistance to China's hegemony. India, which suffered a border conflict with China in 1962, might also have assisted in a strategic security objective of buying time for Southeast Asia's economic and political rise. Vietnam might fall to Hanoi's Communists, but the larger U.S. interest was regional. Economic development—combined with the management of intraregional rivalries in a local balance of power—offered a strategic alternative to the domino theory. Teddy Roosevelt would have grasped the logic, as he had done in Northeast Asia sixty years earlier. But the Johnson administration failed to appreciate that history and the economic-security connection.[26]

2. Credibility

Powerful states influence others through reputation and psychology as much as by actions. Far-flung regimes pose too many issues, every day, to monitor and control. The guardians of order need to rely on self-regulation, backed by their willingness to carry out promises and threats. Kissinger argues strongly for the importance of keeping commitments: "Credibility for a state plays the role of character for a human being."[27]

The U.S. alliance system prompted a procession of questions about credibility. Other states wanted to know if they could rely on the United States. America wanted others to assume risks and pay costs that served mutual interests. In his May 1964 phone calls, Johnson referred to treaty obligations, but he also asked what others would contribute. Years later, Bundy wrote that the "cardinal" principle of the U.S. intervention in Vietnam was for America "*not* to be a Paper Tiger. Not to have it thought that when we commit ourselves we really mean no major risk." Even skeptics of escalation, such as George Kennan in 1966, maintained that U.S. "prestige" tilted the balance toward U.S. action in Vietnam.[28]

On the other hand, when officials hear the word "credibility" used to justify actions, they would be wise to press for a fuller explanation. Credibility can become an excuse for acting even when reason fails. Credibility became a crutch in Vietnam.

Assistant Secretary of Defense John MacNaughton explained the stretched logic of credibility in September 1964. His "good doctor" thesis made the case for escalation even in the face of pessimism and prospects of defeat. Even failure "would...demonstrat[e] U.S. willingness to go to the mat [and] tend to bolster allied confidence in the U.S. as an ally." An escalation "would demonstrate that the U.S. was a 'good doctor' willing to keep promises, be tough, take risks, get bloodied, and hurt the enemy badly."[29]

Others adapted MacNaughton's argument of sacrifice. In February 1965, Bundy pressed for military action to show resolve. He could not estimate the odds of success. "[E]ven if it fails, the policy will be worth it. At a minimum, it will damp down the charge that we did not do all we could have done, and this charge will be important in many countries, including our own." International credibility was blurring into domestic political credibility. By March, Bundy was more blunt: "Questions: in terms of U.S. politics which is better: to 'lose' now or to 'lose' after committing 100,000 men? Tentative answer: the latter."[30]

Under Secretary George Ball, arguing against escalation and for withdrawal, had to counter his colleagues' arguments about credibility. Ball faced the issue head on: Knowing when to cut losses would win more respect than sinking into a bottomless quagmire, he stated. He observed that America's Asian partners—Japan, Thailand, and the Philippines—lacked enthusiasm for deeper U.S. involvement. Allies in Europe discouraged it. Neutrals would welcome a political settlement and a U.S. exit. The Soviets and Chinese would not respect American power more if the United States became bogged down in a long, costly, and indecisive war—or worse, a drawn-out defeat. The first responsibility, Ball stressed, was for the South Vietnamese government to demonstrate its cohesive commitment to fight and carry its public along. Ball's case looks logical in hindsight, but he was not able to address Johnson's own credibility.[31]

Johnson viewed all choices through his personal political lens. In the near term, the president's standing at home would suffer a blow if he acknowledged defeat and the Communists won. LBJ recalled vividly the effects on Truman of the "loss" of China. Throughout the 1950s, Johnson had watched how the label of "soft on Communism" had dragged down the Democratic Party and his colleagues. At a minimum, the charge of "cutting and running" would distract from LBJ's drive—and dream—to overcome America's domestic ills. No U.S. president had lost a war. As Mike Green points out, "there was no precedent to suggest complete failure was a possible scenario." For Johnson, credibility in Vietnam meant political and even personal survival.[32]

3. Presidential Experience and Psychology

Some historians refer to Vietnam as McNamara's war, but as Fred Logevall points out, Johnson loomed over Vietnam policy.[33] LBJ brought the mentality of a shrewd Senate majority leader to the presidency. Senate leaders have less direct authority than Speakers in the House of Representatives. Senators have more freedom to act independently because of their longer terms and Senate rules. An effective leader in the Senate must continually assemble shifting coalitions. The leader must know the interests, strengths, and weaknesses of ninety-nine other people. The leader's skill is persuasion—not issuing orders. The leader's reputation for solving problems, usually through negotiation, is a key source of power.[34]

As president, Johnson continued to build coalitions for his policies. He was always counting votes. He did not like dissent. LBJ pressed his advisers for internal consensus, instead of encouraging debate to sharpen the choices. He was uncomfortable with open discussions that might slip away from his guiding hand. After the Bay of Pigs, Kennedy had used debates to gain information and insight, while relying on Bobby Kennedy and others to keep the range of options open for decision. In late 1961, JFK had overruled a push by McNamara, Bundy, Rusk, and Taylor to escalate in Vietnam.

Johnson's deliberations have a feel of stage management. They look prearranged and circumscribed. Bundy cautioned Gordon Goldstein, who wrote an insightful book on Bundy, about the perils of tracing decisions solely through the written record or even LBJ's taped conversations: "The real state of play, Bundy often reminded [Goldstein], could not be discerned by the documentary record alone. He advised [Goldstein] to be wary of the 'paper trail way of missing the political point.'"[35]

Johnson directed his mastery of coalitions—internal and external—toward immediate issues. George Reedy, LBJ's assistant of many years, said Johnson "could think but not reflect; devise ingenious schemes for achieving goals but not ponder the validity of the goals; outguess his fellow human beings in playing the game of one-upsmanship without realizing that the game may not be worth playing."[36]

Busy presidents often do not have time to listen to "context" or complex discussions of factors in play; being "long-winded" or "too intellectual" is a political dismissal to a policy adviser. A practical adviser has to get to the point quickly by defining a problem and a solution. It helps to be good-natured and entertaining, too. Yet the pressured White House environment risks overreliance on the type of immediate political calculations that won the presidency in the first place. Johnson failed to recognize that his great strengths were also his vulnerabilities.

LBJ's diplomacy, in turn, became a type of political haggling with foreigners. Johnson did not care to learn about political motivations in other countries; he kept judging them according to familiar American models. LBJ once joked, while making a point, that "[f]oreigners are not like the folks I am used to."[37]

Johnson relied on consensus politics to decide on military strategy. In July 1965, the president arranged a back channel (through Deputy Secretary of Defense Cyrus Vance and McNamara, who was in Saigon) to bargain with General William Westmoreland on the number of battalions the general would accept. Bundy later complained that historians reviewing the written records assumed that the president was weighing McNamara's recommendation for escalation against Under Secretary of State George Ball's resistance. In fact, Bundy recalled, Johnson "was trying to work out how to get a decision that he had already worked out *with* McNamara, in a way that would maximize everybody's sense that they had been consulted."[38]

Johnson's critical decisions about Vietnam in late 1964 and early 1965 look like maneuvers to assemble a legislative package. He identified the course of least resistance around which his advisers, the generals, and Congress could assemble. Johnson thought he was acting incrementally and preserving future flexibility, a strong preference of all politicians. In fact, LBJ's short-term calculations deepened the country's commitment to a long-term course. The president did not want a serious debate about possible outcomes, costs, and dangers that might leak and interfere with Johnson's political plan for 1965.[39]

Once Johnson determined that he needed a military answer to stave off defeat in Vietnam, he worked his advisers to produce a solution to the political—instead of the foreign policy—problem. The day before his election in November, the president created an NSC working group to study "immediately and intensively" the options for Vietnam. Johnson wanted a consensus on how to win the war or at least prevent defeat. He doubted the effectiveness of air strikes. Even as the working group developed escalation options late in 1964, the president urged Ambassador Taylor (who had moved from chairman of the Joint Chiefs to ambassador to South Vietnam in July 1964) to work with General Westmoreland to recommend a campaign by U.S. ground forces. Taylor could not conceive of defeat, but he worried about the numbers necessary to fight a counterinsurgency and the poor prospects for success. He opposed the introduction of U.S. ground troops. By January 1965, Bundy and McNamara presented the "Fork in the Road" Memorandum to press LBJ to decide whether to escalate militarily or negotiate some settlement. In a huge lapse of analysis, they did not address the specific military steps or how they would achieve diplomatic outcomes.

Following the president's own method, Bundy and McNamara were offering a political plan, not a military and foreign policy strategy.

In February, the Viet Cong killed nine Americans and wounded 137 more in an assault on a South Vietnamese headquarters at Pleiku. Bundy and others argued for a swift bombing retaliation. Johnson had set the stage, whether he had fully recognized it or not, for U.S. air strikes from Vietnamese bases. Before long, the U.S. military decided it needed troops to defend the bases. They called in the Marines. Before long, the Marines needed to patrol beyond perimeters. Patrols became offensive ground actions. Within a month of the Marines' arrival, the Pentagon committed the 173rd Airborne Brigade.[40] By the summer of 1965, the president's major review focused on troop levels—and whether to call up reserves or National Guard units. He still did not have a military-diplomatic strategy.

Johnson now owned the war. He felt trapped. Johnson suspected that if he had failed to step up, Robert Kennedy would have criticized his weakness. Eisenhower hovered, too, with his warning that once the United States entered a war, it must win.

Johnson's psychology included noble aims. He believed that America was a force for good in Vietnam, without the motives of the old colonial powers. The United States had no desire for imperialistic economic advantage. To the contrary, if the Vietnamese could live in peace, Johnson would bring the New Deal to them. In a speech at Johns Hopkins University in April 1965, the president offered a Johnson-style development program for the North, including a plan for food, water, and power along the Mekong River based on the experience of FDR's Tennessee Valley Authority.[41]

The president shuddered at the thought that Vietnam would divert his political energies from his Great Society legislation. Johnson, the political calculator, figured he had about two years in which he could dominate Congress. Congress took up his landmark voting rights and Medicare bills in 1965. He could not afford to lose votes or public focus because of a retreat in Vietnam.

In 2008, the journal *Diplomatic History* published a vibrant debate about Vietnam and the Great Society. Francis Bator, a Harvard professor who had worked for Johnson as Bundy's deputy, launched the exchange. Bator's thesis was that "Johnson believed—and he knew how to count votes—that had he backed away in Vietnam in 1965, there would have been no Great Society.... It would have been stillborn in Congress." Eminent commentators offered both support and criticism.[42] Whether or not Bator was correct, and whether or not the cost was worth the Great Society, the implication for American diplomacy is that presidents have to juggle international actions with complex domestic and political calculations—and balance both institutional and personal interests and responsibilities.

Johnson opted for "guns and butter." He chose not to prepare the American public for war. He tried to deny the risks to the economy. He did not mobilize the nation's resources or call up reserves. He did not seek a congressional resolution to clarify his course; he did not even offer a prime-time address to explain the purpose. The president, as a master of power in Washington, thought he could rationalize the war as an incremental continuation of past policies. He judged, rightly, that Americans would rally around their president and the troops once soldiers were bloodied in combat. He judged, wrongly, that American power would somehow prevail.[43] Johnson had set up a collapse of his own credibility when his war dragged on endlessly.

4. America's Faith in Its Military Power

Americans have respected successful military leaders from the earliest days of the republic. Americans also expect to win wars. They have not, however, always respected their military. The triumph of World War II created a new esteem for U.S. warriors. The Cold War added a need, for the first time, for a large standing military, with dedicated men and women guarding the ramparts of freedom in all corners of the world. The military's self-critical effort to rebuild its professionalism and effectiveness after Vietnam, based upon a volunteer force, has earned even more admiration.

Yet success and effectiveness can create a temptation for American foreign policy. Civilian leaders may overestimate what military power can accomplish. In 1964–65, the decision to deploy U.S. combat troops became a touchstone of political will. The very presence of American fighters was supposed to boost morale in South Vietnam and demonstrate America's strength of purpose.

America's military had overcome daunting dangers in 1941–45. Subsequently, the Korean War had turned into a frustrating stalemate, but America's fighting record showed resilience, adaptability, boldness—and devastating firepower. The unsatisfactory result was accompanied by a strain of thought—as there always is when militaries fall short—that the blame rested with tepid civilian leaders.

Militaries have to believe they will prevail. They know they will have to adapt to the uncertainties of the enemy and the battlefield. These qualities, combined with personal experience over decades, imbued the U.S. military of 1964–65 with an indomitable spirit, even hubris. As Bundy reflected decades later, "No one asks...what kind of war it will be and what kind of losses must be expected. The military of 1965 are almost trained *not* to ask such (cowardly?) questions." The military leaders were not the only ones who went to war without scrutinizing objectives, means, costs, and even the geographical constraints. Bundy's memos reflect much uncertainty about the effectiveness of U.S. ground troops, even as he advised the president about options for various numbers of troops; when he could not explain the military objective, he fell back to the logic of trying and testing. He just assumed U.S. forces would prevail if the country made an effort such as the one in Korea.[44]

In 1964–65, both civilians and generals lapsed into a strategy of attrition. The U.S. military was prepared for battles and mobility, but not for counterinsurgency warfare. Overwhelming U.S. airpower was supposed to destroy enemy forces, demolish supply lines, and break the determination of the leaders and public in the north. Americans respected the tenacity of their Vietnamese enemies while somehow doubting the Vietnamese will to fight and endure.

Since Vietnam, U.S. generals and admirals are more likely to ask questions about military objectives and the means to achieve them. They encourage civilian leaders to explain how military accomplishments serve foreign policy purposes. They seek to point out that America's military power, while overawing, cannot alone achieve many goals.

As a rising officer with a sterling record in combat, H. R. McMaster accused the Joint Chiefs of Staff during the Vietnam War of a "Dereliction of Duty" for their failure to express their views forthrightly to the president and their preoccupation with narrower service perspectives.[45] One might counter that the Joint Chiefs—who argued for greater attacks against North Vietnam—were wrong, but not derelict. LBJ, as commander in chief, decided on the military strategy. After serving as President Trump's national security adviser, McMaster has a better sense of the complexities of civil-military relations at the highest level.

Ironically, the lessons learned by the U.S. military after Vietnam, and its professionalism, made U.S. military power look like a potential answer to many subsequent diplomatic problems. President Ronald Reagan's deployment in Grenada, and especially President George H. W. Bush's decisions in Panama and to liberate Kuwait, demonstrated the effectiveness of U.S. military force. But these were limited operations with defined objectives. The twenty-nine years since 1991 have demonstrated the difficulty of deciding whether and how U.S. military strength can contribute to U.S. diplomacy.

5. Combining Military Power and Diplomacy

Ben Franklin used the American victory at Saratoga to push the French to agree to the United States' first alliance. The success at Yorktown helped Franklin to negotiate peace with Britain. Thomas Jefferson staged the threat of American militia marching on New Orleans to urge Napoleon to sell Louisiana. Lincoln, on the other hand, negotiated a resolution to the *Trent* crisis with Britain because he wanted only one war at a time. Seward held the Union Army in check on the border with Mexico as leverage to force a French withdrawal. Teddy Roosevelt sent the Great White Fleet around the world to intimidate would-be foes; he also mediated diplomatic resolutions between competing and even warring great powers. TR recognized the limits of military power. The alliance builders of 1947–49 combined U.S. economic strength, backed by a security commitment, to put Western Europe on the road to a safe recovery. Dwight Eisenhower relied on nuclear deterrence to establish a crude balance in the Cold War. And John Kennedy marshaled the U.S. military to help him negotiate in Berlin and Cuba.

In Vietnam, however, the Johnson administration deluded itself that U.S. military power could supplant the need for a diplomatic solution. The United States would either win militarily or, at a minimum, strengthen America's hand in later negotiations to achieve some ill-defined settlement.

The story of 1964–65 leaves an important actor backstage: Secretary of State Dean Rusk, the country's chief diplomat, was not interested in negotiations or fashioning options for settlements. He believed that the U.S. military had to turn around the war before he gave serious thought to diplomatic outcomes. Rusk had also observed how the battles between Truman's secretaries of state and defense had weakened the administration; he was an ardent believer in team play. Moreover, his boss, the president, viewed diplomacy as a sign of weakness to be avoided, unless Hanoi accepted U.S. terms. Bundy's voluminous memos never seriously examined how U.S. military power, or the threat of its use in late 1964 and early 1965, could be used as negotiating leverage.[46]

Americans have been prone to hand the policy baton to the War and Defense Departments at times of war. Woodrow Wilson turned the fighting of World War I over to General John Pershing with little consideration of how the 1918 armistice would lead to a successful peace. FDR sidelined his State Department in World War II and had only vague ideas of what would follow victory. Truman, to his sorrow, let General MacArthur drive toward the Yalu River border with China, prompting Beijing's intervention and two more years of war; no one discussed the possibility of a halt along a defensible line well north of the Thirty-Eighth Parallel but south of the Yalu River border with China that would have left a crippled North Korean regime as a small buffer with China.

Diplomatic negotiations depend on incentives, including through the use of force. Kissinger observed that "[t]he prevalent view within the American body politic sees military force and diplomacy as distinct, in essence separate, phases of action. Military action is viewed as occasionally creating the conditions for negotiations, but once negotiations begin, they are seen as propelled by their own internal logic." He explained that even the Congress of Vienna of 1815, "long considered the model diplomatic conference," required a threat of war to achieve a long-lasting settlement.[47]

I observed the shift from diplomacy to war during the first Gulf War. Even with Secretary Baker's skill at assembling a thirty-four-nation coalition against Saddam Hussein's invasion of Kuwait, and Baker's close friendship with President Bush, once the armies assembled and flags unfurled, attention veered toward victory and away from what was to follow. In 1990–91, however, President Bush was determined to wage a limited war to eject Iraq out of Kuwait. Baker moved to build upon a coalition triumph and a reshaping of the security landscape by launching a peace process between Israel and Arab states. But even that skilled foreign policy team had not fully considered what the outcome should be for Iraq and regional security. Indeed, the challenges for statecraft after the first Gulf War extended much further. When someone asked the chief of staff of the Indian army about the conclusions he drew from the 1991 Gulf War, the general replied: Don't fight the United States—unless you have weapons of mass destruction. The overwhelming success of U.S. conventional forces in the first Gulf War expanded the interest of possible foes in acquiring weapons of mass destruction and missiles to deliver them. Victories, even overwhelming ones, do not automatically produce the best diplomatic outcomes.

In determining U.S. policy toward Vietnam in 1964–65, no one analyzed whether the threat of escalation could help produce an acceptable, if unsatisfactory, settlement. In October 1964, Under Secretary of State George Ball outlined possible political solutions. He first suggested a ceasefire, which could be followed by local settlements in the South, an uneasy coalition in Saigon, and an international conference to welcome a neutral South Vietnam.[48]

Bill Bundy (assistant secretary of state for East Asia and Mac's brother), generally concurred with Ball's outlook for Vietnam and assessment of regional implications. But Bundy thought a U.S. escalation would strengthen America's position. To the contrary, once Washington took over the war the United States reduced its flexibility to disengage and hardened Hanoi's resolve to win on its terms.[49]

Early on, in 1963 and 1964, it appears that some in Hanoi wanted to avoid U.S. escalation. The North would not shrink from a fight, but key figures wanted to avoid the resulting carnage.[50] In December 1963, the Party Central Committee stated internally that it was willing to consider a longer "step-by-step" process of "complex forms and methods" to overcome the

Saigon regime over a period of uncertain length. The Saigon government, shaken by recent coups, appeared weak, but Hanoi wanted to avoid a full-fledged war with the Americans.

In the spring of 1964, the United States asked a Canadian emissary to convey a message to Hanoi. He met North Vietnam's premier twice. The premier signaled a willingness to work on a face-saving exit for Washington. But Washington communicated an ultimatum, not an interest in settlement. U.S. "coercive diplomacy" threatened escalation and demanded that Hanoi stop supporting the National Liberation Front in the South; no one considered using the military threat to negotiate a U.S. departure. Logevall recounts that through January and February 1965, the North Vietnamese "sen[t] out signals that they were willing to enter talks, the primary aim of which would be to gain an American withdrawal from the conflict." After the United States began systematic air strikes in February 1965, Hanoi hardened its position. Johnson had escalated to solve a political problem, and he figured that a show of strength would assist future bargaining with Hanoi. He miscalculated terribly. By the middle of 1965, the president was asking his advisers, "How do we extricate ourselves?" Send in more men, his advisers urged, and then negotiate. By the end of 1965, the United States had 180,000 troops on the ground in Vietnam. But no one had considered how to combine military power with diplomacy.[51]

6. The Failure of Advisers

President Johnson made the critical decisions of 1964–65. Nevertheless, his advisers served him and the country poorly. Tom Wicker summed up LBJ's counselors on Vietnam policy: "He would look around him and see in Bob McNamara that it was technologically feasible, in McGeorge Bundy that it was intellectually respectable, and in Dean Rusk that it was historically necessary."[52] What was missing?

The team around a president matters. Most advisers want to ease the president's burdens. They look for ways to offer support and encouragement. These are good motives, but White House air filters have not yet cleared the atmosphere of sycophancy. No one, including a president, wants to hear bad news. In the rushed, impatient environment of the West Wing, there is little time to ease an executive toward a course that is resisted. People who relay unwelcome information pay a price. Opponents might tag critics as negative, soft, defeatist, or even disloyal; at a minimum, naysayers run out of personal capital. Advisers who disagree with the president might hold their tongues out of deference to a chief executive who won office through an election. (I was continually struck that people who promised to convey difficult messages to presidents folded once they were actually in the Oval Office.) As a practical matter, advisers have to pick their shots. Presidents, in turn, look to trusted colleagues or friends. If the president's prior life did not introduce him to fair-minded, knowledgeable people with good judgment, the risks in the White House increase.

Johnson's advisers in 1964 were Kennedy men who were trying to build relationships with a new, very different type of leader. U.S. presidents do not have equals, but they need peers. It may be too much to expect, but such peers should be most concerned with helping the president make the best decisions and achieving good results—instead of maximizing the adviser's power. Seward, Hay, Root, Hughes, Marshall, Acheson, Shultz, Scowcroft, and Baker all played such a role.

Bundy's role as national security adviser was especially vital for Johnson, who had no chief of staff.[53] National security advisers and chiefs of staff are among the few people who see the president frequently and privately. They can judge moods, assess the timing to raise issues, and suggest involving others. They are best positioned to push presidents to reconsider. On Vietnam, Bundy adjusted his advice to fit LBJ's biases. He avoided uncomfortable conclusions. Gordon Goldstein, who spent many hours with Bundy in later years trying to figure out what had happened, concluded that Bundy "was disinclined to challenge the prevailing consensus, particularly if it enjoyed the President's support." Bundy considered his own role as "that of the staff officer who knows the big decision is made and is working to help in its execution." Yet if Bundy would not force difficult questions, who else could be expected to do so?[54]

The national security adviser might have started with the five topics above—probing the assumptions of recent history, checking the merits of defending "credibility," offsetting the weaknesses of presidential psychology, challenging the effectiveness of U.S. military power, and insisting on synchronizing military and diplomatic actions. JFK, unlike Rusk, had been able to distinguish the strategic differences between the defense of Berlin and that of Saigon;[55] Bundy never raised that question, much less offered a Mahanian assessment of America's maritime strategy in the Pacific and the limits of core U.S. security interests on Asia's continent. Bundy's processes ruled out a disengagement option because, as he said, "I didn't see any way of leaving Vietnam alone and simply getting out in 1965."[56] General Taylor also could not conceive of a U.S. withdrawal. Ironically, Taylor's experience with Korea had led him to conclude "that the United States should never again fight a land war in Asia, at least without nuclear weapons."[57] Neither Bundy nor Taylor, the key men in Washington and Saigon, forced an assessment of whether the preservation of a non-Communist South Vietnam was vital, whether the United States could achieve that objective, what troops and costs would be necessary to try, and whether and how the United States might pursue alternatives, even if unappealing. Johnson especially valued McNamara's opinion. McNamara's calculations about the prospects for South Vietnam were looking bleak as early as March 1964. He also did not identify serious U.S. security interests in Vietnam. His hawkishness seemed to stem from loyalty to the president, who had made clear that he would not accept defeat.[58]

Johnson's advisers failed to challenge the president's assumptions—either because they shared them, lacked imagination, or were bound by loyalty. If the president's advisers had decided differently, they could have used four techniques to pry open the process. First, the national security adviser could have widened the debate. The CIA kept writing warnings. In June 1964, for example, a CIA estimate described South Vietnam's dismal outlook and Saigon's ineffective moves to counter the guerrillas; the agency "doubt[ed] that victory [could] be won" and urged "some kind of negotiated settlement." The U.S. embassy in Saigon, including Taylor's deputy, kept filing gloomy reports. The Joint Chiefs conducted war games in April and September 1964, both of which warned that U.S. bombing of North Vietnam would provoke stiffer resistance, fail to hurt the Viet Cong in the South, and in fact lead the North to reinforce the southern guerrillas.[59]

In October 1964, Under Secretary of State George Ball prepared a trenchant sixty-four-page memo arguing against escalation and for a path to settlement. Mac Bundy later claimed he had forwarded the paper to the president during the final weeks of Johnson's reelection campaign—when LBJ was unlikely to be reading long memos. Bundy—and the president—seemed to treat Ball as an internal "devil's advocate" to show critics (and perhaps future historians) that the process weighed a range of options.[60] Assistant Secretary of State Bill Bundy's reply to Ball, which agreed with many of the under secretary's findings, could have been used by his brother Mac Bundy to sharpen the focus of disputes.

In February 1965, as the president appeared ready to take the critical steps toward military escalation, Hubert Humphrey, the new vice president, sent two thoughtful memos arguing against a wider war. Humphrey based his case on domestic politics, not international implications. "It's always hard to cut losses," Humphrey recognized, but he suggested 1965 was "the year of minimum political risk." He warned of the uncertain public support and the political trouble to come. Johnson was livid; he probably thought his vice president was papering the record. Johnson froze his vice president out of Vietnam policy.[61] Bundy, as national security adviser, could have recruited the vice president to work with Senators Richard Russell, chairman of the

Armed Services Committee; William Fulbright, chairman of the Foreign Relations Committee; and Mike Mansfield, the majority leader and an old Asia hand. Bundy could have offered the senators CIA briefings and asked for their help in giving LBJ a way out. He could also have drawn out McNamara's and Taylor's doubts.

Second, Bundy would have needed to change the face of the debate. Rather than make the decision a question of U.S. political will, Bundy could have pressed whether Saigon had the will, unity of purpose, and commitment to carry the South Vietnamese to war. South Korea had fought for its freedom; would South Vietnam?

Third, Bundy, as manager of the process, could have added to the substantive scope of the debate. He could have directed work on possible settlements and diplomatic approaches, in combination with plans to escalate. If Rusk remained passive, Ball and Bill Bundy could have examined the ideas of some of the allies—such as Britain, Canada, France, and Australia—which had knowledgeable officials in Vietnam.

Finally, Mac Bundy might have offered Johnson practical alternatives—*political* as well as policy choices. CIA Director John McCone, a respected conservative, could have briefed former president Eisenhower and key senators, preparing the way for their political help. Instead, McCone resigned in frustration in April 1965. Johnson's Democratic friends in the Senate could have helped devise a political exit strategy premised on Saigon's failures. Russell's idea of getting the South Vietnamese to ask the United States to leave was worth pursuing; during most of this period, Washington worried that the revolving door of leaders in Saigon feared a big U.S. presence because America's shadow had already darkened their weak political legitimacy. Taylor—as a successful general, friend of the Kennedys, and man on the scene—could have offered political, military, and diplomatic cover for a withdrawal. McNamara could have prepared plans to protect Thailand, the Philippines, and other frontline states while advancing their economic prospects. Mac Bundy should also have had some fresh diplomatic initiatives in his pocket—as Nixon and Kissinger would do—to draw Washington's attention elsewhere. A prudent withdrawal—with a negotiated time period during which Saigon could rally or not—would have enabled the president to direct his energies toward the Great Society.

Bundy would have had to work informally to bring the pieces together through the processes he supervised. The ingredients were available. Bundy's greatest problem would have been convincing the president to let his advisers range more widely in an effort to help protect him. Instead, Bundy circumscribed the circle and narrowed the debate about premises and options. The sum of his strategy was to "[presume] the ascending application of

military force would deprive the insurgency of victory and that the ensuing
stalemate and its associated costs would eventually compel the Vietnamese
Communists to compromise their objectives." But this was just an unex-
amined assumption.[62] Between October 1964, before LBJ's election, and the
February decision to bomb the North after the Pleiku attack, Bundy did not
organize one NSC meeting. He sat in the cockpit of a plane on autopilot
to war.

A Failure of Pragmatic Politics

In 1964–65, President Johnson faced a strategic problem about Vietnam. He
needed to decide whether America's doctrine of containment—as operation-
alized through the nation's new network of alliances—required Washington
to save South Vietnam from determined enemies within and without. Johnson treated the problem as a political question. He concentrated on the costs
to his domestic power in the near term. LBJ overestimated the capacity of
U.S. military power to solve diplomatic problems. He failed to connect military actions to diplomacy. He never examined Vietnam as part of a regional
strategy. This is not to say that the United States should have ruled out all
threats and interventions in Vietnam and the region. Pragmatic diplomacy
is an art, not an algorithm that operates according to fixed formulae.

Johnson's principal advisers relied on the ad hoc methods of crisis management that they had learned with JFK—but without JFK's skeptical questions and ability to take problems apart to test assumptions and possibilities.
Kennedy achieved a personal detachment that helped him calculate coldly.
Secretary of State Baker seemed to have a similar ability. These men might
have appeared outgoing, but they appraised and acted bloodlessly. Baker
used to joke, with more than a hint of seriousness, "I want you to know that
I'll stick with you as absolutely long as I can." In contrast, every encounter
and every problem seemed hot and personal to LBJ.

Crisis management methods pulled Johnson's advisers toward immediate
maneuvers without consideration of how various outcomes short of victory
might meet U.S. interests. They narrowed responses to the problem instead
of facing up to uncomfortable questions about long-term purposes, realistic
objectives, and means to achieve ends. They permitted the president's political inclinations to dominate. Ironically and tragically, this most political of
U.S. presidents failed to recognize that the American public would abandon
a costly war fought just for credibility. Johnson's war turned out to be the
opposite of practical—it descended into senseless sacrifice.

———◆———

CHAPTER 15

Richard Nixon and Henry Kissinger

American Realpolitik

The Week That Changed the World

On February 17, 1972, President Richard Nixon left Andrews Air Force Base for the first leg of his long trip to China. As Air Force One took off, he still did not know if he would meet with Chairman Mao Tse-tung, the legendary Communist leader of China.[1]

Nixon, the ardent anti-Communist, had prepared with care. For months, he had enthused about the historic nature of his journey. He would be the first president to visit China while in office. China had always evoked fascination and contradictions for Americans, who had fought with—and against—the Chinese over the previous thirty years. Americans had viewed China as a great commercial bounty and as a hopeless economic prospect; they had tried to convert the Chinese to Christianity and modernization, and been stung by Chinese rejection. For more than two decades after Mao's Communists ordained a revolutionary regime, the United States had refused even to recognize the People's Republic of China. Nixon told the press that his adventure would be "like going to the moon."[2]

Nixon wanted to be at his best when he arrived in China. He rested in Hawaii and then stopped in Guam, bases along America's Pacific perimeter that were legacies of Nixon's turn-of-the-century predecessor, William McKinley. The president practiced using chopsticks. From Guam, Nixon flew to Shanghai for a quick breakfast. A Chinese navigator and radio operator came on board the plane; the Americans had grudgingly agreed, after considerable negotiation, to permit the Chinese to help guide Air Force One to Beijing.[3]

Nixon arrived at the Chinese capital at 11:30 a.m. on February 21, a cold and hazy day. The timing permitted evening TV news coverage in the United States. Nixon descended the stairs alone, greeted by China's premier,

Chou En-lai. Nixon extended his hand to Chou. Cameras clicked. Once the president and premier got into a car to drive into the city, Chou commented, "Your handshake came over the vastest ocean in the world—twenty-five years of no communication." Both men recognized the historic symbolism: In 1954, at a Geneva Conference on Vietnam and Korea, Secretary of State John Foster Dulles had ignored Chou's outstretched hand. Diplomacy communicates through gestures, and symbolism has significance. In 1954, Chou sought to offer the United States a settlement of outstanding differences, but Dulles snubbed him. In 1972, the United States showed respect and again opened a door to China, in the spirit of John Hay.[4]

China, in turn, was signaling a cautious greeting to a great power. The countries would meet as equals. At the airport, the two nations' flags hung side by side. Nixon merited a welcome party of about twenty-five officials and an honor guard, but no crowd. A Chinese banner at the terminal denounced imperialists and capitalists. The welcome took fifteen minutes, a brief courtesy for a land that counted its history in millennia. Chou added a personal touch as Henry Kissinger followed the president. "Ah, old friend," said the premier to the president's national security adviser, who had spent many hours with Chou on two previous visits to prepare Nixon's mission. In decades to come, "old friend" would serve as the Chinese recognition of foreigners who had earned reciprocal regard.[5]

As Nixon arrived, Mao got ready. The ailing autocrat had his first shave and haircut in months. He put on a new suit and shoes, necessary in part because Mao was bloated. The seventy-eight-year-old revolutionary had a weak heart, high blood pressure, fluid in his lungs, and swollen legs. Strokes had impaired his speech. The chairman distrusted his doctors, but finally agreed to basic treatment so he could greet the American president respectably. Mao's doctors had co-opted oxygen tanks and a respirator that the American advance team had sent ahead in case Nixon needed emergency help. The Chinese hid the equipment in Mao's bedroom.[6]

Nixon's visit excited Mao. He had received progress reports as Air Force One neared. Mao sought to see the president right away, but Chou persuaded him to let Nixon first settle in to the Diaoyutai guest villa. By 2:30 p.m., the impatient Mao urged Chou to bring Nixon to the secluded Zhongnanhai red-walled compound, near the Forbidden City, where the top Communist Party leadership lived. Many of the buildings in the aloof quarter dated to China's last empire; very few foreigners or Chinese entered the lakes, groves, and walled houses of the Communist court of China. Chou relayed the chairman's summons to Kissinger, who claimed that he remained outwardly cool while feeling both energized and relieved. The meeting with Mao would signal to the world and the Chinese people that the "Great Helmsman" welcomed this new day.[7]

As Nixon entered Mao's study, an assistant helped China's chairman to his feet. The host shuffled toward the president and shook Nixon's hand warmly for a long time. Chinese photographers, the only ones permitted, captured the moment. Both men knew that the photo would flash around the world.[8]

After the two leaders sat down, in chairs arranged in an arc according to Chinese style, Nixon tried to discuss relations between the countries and the international context; he sought to build a relationship based on worldviews. The president emphasized that what mattered was a country's policies toward the United States and the world, not "a nation's internal political philosophy." Mao deflected specifics about other countries—"all those troublesome problems"—to Chou, saying that he preferred "philosophical questions." Nixon flattered Mao by referring to his essays and poetry. Mao dismissed his scribblings—even though his Little Red Book of sayings had passed for life-and-death doctrine during the Cultural Revolution. Mao commented that Nixon's volume, *Six Crises*, "is not a bad book." Kissinger interjected that he had directed his students at Harvard to read Mao's works; in turn, both leaders teased the national security adviser. Chou sat quietly, except for laughing at some of Mao's self-deprecating comments.[9]

Mao used indirect and even humorous comments to make brief points on the USSR, Japan, South Korea, and especially Taiwan, the outpost of his life-long foe, Chiang Kai-shek. The old Communist said he "voted" for Nixon and liked rightists. Nixon replied that in America, "those on the right can do what those on the left can only talk about," and Kissinger chimed in that "[t]hose on the left are pro-Soviet."[10]

The exchange, scheduled for fifteen minutes, ran an hour, although the translation permitted about thirty minutes of talk. Chou kept looking at his watch, and Mao asked if they had covered enough for the day. In closing, Nixon wanted the chairman to know that the president was a man who kept his word. As Mao walked slowly to see Nixon to the door, China's leader revealed that he had not been feeling well.[11]

Margaret MacMillan, the author of the revealing *Nixon in China*, termed the conversation "curiously inconclusive…with Nixon trying to lay the groundwork for future talks and Mao meandering about." Some, especially Kissinger and his notetaking aide, Winston Lord, later read great meaning into Mao's enigmatic comments. Nixon felt the awe of the moment as well. As the Americans reread their notes of the meeting, they discovered a "many-layered design of allegories, directness, and hidden meaning." Perhaps so. Mao spoke indirectly about Taiwan to signal that the island's situation was for the Chinese to settle and need not interfere with the opening to the United States. "We can do without them for the time being and let it come after 100 years." I sense that some of the later exaggerations of meaning stemmed from the drama of meeting a historical figure at a turning point of diplomacy—and to enhancing the status of the witnesses.[12]

The real message was the fact of the meeting: Both parties were willing to set aside sharp differences to explore a new relationship. The Americans conceived of Mao as a strategist who recognized the possibilities of their opening and received them warmly. Nixon saw his own reflection in a leader who could "seize the hour and seize the day" "when an opportunity comes." After Nixon departed, Mao told his doctor that he liked the forthright Nixon, "no beating around the bush," like the leftists, "who say one thing and mean another." Mao respected Nixon's direct assessment of the benefits to America of better relations with China. In 1974, Mao told British prime minister Edward Heath that Nixon "knows what he stands for, as well as what he wants, and has the strength of mind to get it." But Mao was not moved by Kissinger's charm and sparkling intellect. He found Kissinger "just a funny little man. He is shuddering all over with nerves every time he comes to see me."[13]

Nixon concluded that his visit "was the week that changed the world."[14] He was right. Indeed, the turn he began still shakes the world. People around the globe will continue to ask whether the two great powers of the Pacific can work together.

History and Realpolitik

Both sides approached one another cautiously. Each presumed that *it* was the center of the world. China believed it was the nucleus of world revolution, an energizing fusion of Marxism and nationalism. The United States was the leader of the free world and the agent of global capitalism. The Western protector of legitimate order wanted to discuss philosophy and interests with the Eastern insurgent who urged sweeping change.

Moreover, history shadowed their bold enterprise. The American fascination with China, dating at least to the voyage of Robert Morris's *Empress of China* in 1784, had swung between friendship and hostility over two centuries. China treasured its old civilization; the United States expounded a new one. American merchants had dreamed of open doors to China's markets while missionaries sought to save Chinese souls. John Hay and Teddy Roosevelt had resisted China's dismemberment by colonial powers, and Charles Evans Hughes had tried to help China secure its sovereignty. In effect, Americans had always wanted to keep China whole while converting the Chinese—to Christianity, commerce, or republicanism. When the Chinese spurned America's goodwill, the United States responded with hostility. In

1972, the two countries attempted to overcome two decades of isolation and suspicion. Both Nixon and Mao, each of whom had courted political dangers throughout their careers, were gambling.[15]

Nixon was a risk taker. He founded his political career on ardent anti-Communism, building political capital that he decided to spend on an opening to Red China. He also played for large geopolitical—even historic—stakes. The president believed that America's era of extraordinary dominance after World War II could not last. The long, painful war in Vietnam added to the trial of transition because Nixon feared the debacle would shrink Americans inward, breeding a new American isolationism. At the same time, Soviet power seemed to be expanding. A revived U.S. relationship with China, Nixon calculated, might usher in a new era of multipolarity, in which agile U.S. diplomacy could maneuver among rivals to build a new order of peace among the great powers. No one fully understood China's potential. Nixon hazarded a trip to an ideological foe would increase America's options to strike a new international balance of power.[16]

Nixon later wrote that the notes he prepared for his meetings in China emphasized his confidence that America's superior system would prevail against China's competing ideology. Nixon wanted the Chinese to appreciate, despite the domestic turmoil of the late 1960s, that "our system is not coming apart at the seams." Nevertheless, neither Nixon nor Kissinger relied on their upbeat arguments; whether to court the Chinese or out of doubts about the extent of future U.S. power, Nixon referenced U.S. limitations as he explored a new modus operandi with China. The difference in tone—and underlying assumptions—between Nixon's realpolitik and Ronald Reagan's revivalism is striking, as I will relate in the next chapter.[17]

Mao, the revolutionary who had battled his way to the top of hundreds of millions across all of China, pursued a life of risk, too. After Kissinger's first day in China, Mao ordered Chou to issue a statement with one of the chairman's cherished themes: "[A]ll under the heaven is in great chaos." Mao believed that a world in turmoil produced historic change. He governed through disruptive change—including a Great Leap Forward and the Cultural Revolution.[18]

Mao matched his Marxist ideology with Chinese practicality. He recognized China's dangerous isolation, external enemies, and internal debility after the Cultural Revolution. The Soviet invasion of Czechoslovakia in 1968, justified by Leonid Brezhnev with a doctrine about the right to intervene in wayward socialist states, unnerved the Chinese. Military clashes along the Soviet-Chinese frontier in the summer of 1969 sharpened Mao's sense of danger. The Chinese had even heard rumors of a possible Soviet surgical strike against China's nuclear program. Mao, like the emperors from

China's past, could play distant barbarians off against the Middle Kingdom's encircling neighbors—the Soviet Union, of course, but also Japan and India. An impoverished China needed economic help, although it could not ask for it.[19]

Powerful leaders prize survival and success over ideological consistency. In May 1969, Chairman Mao published an article titled "People of the World, Unite and Defeat the U.S. Aggressors and All Their Running Dogs." As Kissinger observed, when Mao looked to the United States as part of a global equilibrium, he "dismissed his own anti-imperialist pronouncements as 'empty cannons.'" The Americans differed from Russians, Mao told his doctor, because "[t]he United States [had] never occupied Chinese territory."[20]

Kissinger had alerted Nixon that Chinese diplomacy began by specifying principles; once the Chinese had clarified the tenets of the big picture, they could be flexible about tactics. Chinese scholars have made the same point to me. Americans, in contrast, are accustomed to moving straight to ideas to solve problems. They suspect that the Chinese preference is too conceptual, a waste of time, or a diversion from the hard task of hammering out actions.[21]

After the opening session, Nixon enjoyed the challenge of presenting his strategic principles to Chou, recognizing that Mao would read an account of the exchange. The president explained why he wanted, over time, to normalize relations with China. Nixon recognized that differences over Taiwan were an irritant, but he sought a peaceful resolution. He wanted China to know that the United States was serious, reliable, and a necessary counterweight to aggressive nations such as India, and of course, the Soviet Union. Nixon hoped that Japan would not again turn militarist, but the U.S. presence served as a brake on the possibility. Nixon also pointed to the political opposition he faced at home—from the right that supported Taiwan, the left that did not want to disturb the Soviets, and a bureaucracy wedded to the status quo. The president drew a geopolitical design that explained why the U.S. role in the Asia-Pacific contributed to stability, reduced dangers of confrontation, and restrained the USSR. He explained that he would run political risks because of his belief in principles—and in openness to China.[22]

Nixon and Kissinger repeatedly assured Chinese leaders that the United States would not collude with the USSR, or any other country, to hurt China. To demonstrate their commitment, the Americans turned over highly secret information about Soviet military capacity, including that along the border with China. Kissinger offered to provide more details if the Chinese requested them. They did. He would also share closely held information about U.S. discussions with the Soviets, including on nuclear arms control.

Nixon and Kissinger, in turn, wanted China to press Hanoi to reach an accommodation in Vietnam. The Americans understood that they could not bargain bluntly for assistance. They needed China to perceive a positive role for the United States in the region, which the continued bloodletting in Vietnam undermined. Similarly, the two countries would not brusquely present a common front against the USSR; they would instead rely on their relationship to create uncertainty in Moscow, deter hostile Soviet acts, and pressure the USSR to compete for cooperation. To use a favorite Kissinger term, "ambiguity" would suggest latent power and ability to maneuver. These were the methods of realpolitik. As Kissinger explained, "[T]he practical issues [of overcoming differences] would be resolved as a consequence of Sino-American rapprochement, not chart the path toward it."[23]

Realpolitik is also about positioning, appearances, and the suggestion of power behind a hidden curtain of status and standing. Nixon's visit to China spoke through symbolism as well as strategic exchange. The president and his staff understood the power of the media, especially television, in an era when only a few channels shaped public opinion. Nixon needed to excite people with the drama and mystery of the visit in order to help overcome U.S. constituencies that objected to China. He also understood that the photos would mark his place in history.

The Chinese, fine artists of propaganda, were stunned by the details of U.S. media planning. The White House advance team directed Air Force One to land at a particular location, with just the right angle for photos of the president's walk down the stairs to meet Chou and the receiving line; leaving nothing to chance, the Americans marked the measured runway with paint. Chou was skeptical about Nixon's image building. "The image of a man depends on his own deeds.... We do not believe that any world leader can be self-styled."[24] Kissinger, a mandarin from a different culture, nevertheless shared some of Chou's frustration, decrying "the monomaniacal obsession of the Nixon White House with public relations."[25] But neither had to run for reelection.

Nixon's publicity was actually a means to a much larger end. As Kissinger later wrote, the president's "primary aim was to regain the American initiative in foreign policy." The two masters of realpolitik "could not have encountered a group of interlocutors more receptive to Nixon's style of diplomacy than the Chinese leaders."[26]

Kissinger to China

Henry Kissinger traveled twice to Beijing to prepare the way for the president's visit. The two countries—without formal relations and with a legacy of miscommunication—had had difficulties signaling an interest in open-ing a discussion. By the spring of 1971, however, Premier Chou had sent an invitation, through the Pakistanis, for a U.S. emissary's visit as a prelude to a presidential trip. Although Chou had highlighted the U.S. withdrawal from Taiwan as the first question for discussion, he had added that each side could freely raise "the principal issue of concern to it." Nixon and Kissinger recognized that Beijing was offering a wide-ranging discussion about issues, not just a debate over Taiwan.[27]

The Chinese agreed to keep the mission secret, although they did not know why the Americans insisted on concealment. Nixon had multiple motives. He loved the drama—and a bold fait accompli would throw off opponents at home. The president and Kissinger also distrusted their own bureaucracy, which could pose obstacles, leak the news, and slow the pro-cess. They feared that public speculation would limit maneuvering room, and the criticism could prompt the Chinese to pull back before they had understood Nixon's aims. The Chinese suggested a public announcement after the talks had begun.[28]

Now—fifty years later—it is hard to imagine the uncertainties of Kis-singer's mission. He expected the Chinese to be tough negotiators. He readied for China's demand that the United States pull out forces from Tai-wan. He prepared eighty pages of notes about U.S. positions across a range of topics, in addition to his briefing papers. But Kissinger recognized that he also held high cards. The Chinese wanted recognition as a great power, and a presidential visit would supply "spectacular proof."[29]

Kissinger had a few foreign service officers from the State Department on his staff, but he cut the State and Defense Departments out of his secret mis-sion. Neither he nor Nixon knew that the navy had sent a stenographer-clerk to help with NSC paperwork, and the dutiful yeoman made copies of NSC documents and forwarded them to his Pentagon masters.[30]

Kissinger arrived at a military airport in Beijing a little after noon on July 9. The Chinese whisked Kissinger off to the Diaoyutai guest compound, where Chou began their seventeen hours of talks over the next forty-eight hours. On the ride from the airport, a Chinese official reminded the Ameri-cans of Dulles's rebuff of Chou's handshake in 1954. This time, Kissinger offered his hand to Chou, and Chinese cameras recorded the reversal of history for later release. The Americans certainly now knew that Chinese diplomacy valued dignity and expected mutual respect.

The two men talked until almost midnight. The Chinese offered Kis-singer the opportunity to open, which they suggest to guests in China (and also to their hosts when abroad). A diplomat usually wants to hear first what his or her counterpart will propose—or reveal, assume, or giveaway. In this case, Kissinger wanted to set the strategic stage. He wanted to avoid "a shopping list of mutual irritations."

Kissinger once explained, in a different context, his essentials of diplomacy: "Knowledge of what I am trying to do. Knowledge of the subject. Knowledge of the history and psychology of the people I am dealing with. And some human rapport... To have some human relations with the people I am negotiating with. This takes some rough edges off, [although they] won't make concessions they wouldn't otherwise make."[31]

Kissinger flattered Chou and China; over the two days, both men charmed one another. Kissinger found Chou's intellect, deftness, cunning grace, and discipline entrancing. Chou was already a figure from history in 1972, a survivor, and Kissinger's genuine admiration is understandable. Yet the American emissary had serious messages. Kissinger began by respecting China's national pride. "We come together on the basis of equality," he said. China's "achievements, tradition, ideology, and strength" entitled it to an equal role on all matters affecting the peace of Asia and the world. They need not argue about superior ideology; history would decide. Chou agreed that "[a]ll things must be done in a reciprocal manner" between equals and that agreement on fundamentals needed to precede work on particular problems.[32]

Kissinger wanted to explain his president's worldview. He later wrote that he and Chou "spent hours together essentially giving shape to intangibles of mutual understanding." Nixon differed from his presidential predecessors, Kissinger confided. U.S. dominance was "undesirable," having drawn the country into "every struggle at every point of the world at any point in time." America's "missionary tendencies" led it to pursue costly and nonessential causes. Nixon, in contrast, would act "on the realities of the present and not on the dreams of the past."[33]

Kissinger shared his world-weary but wiser perspective of realpolitik—he looked beyond a settlement in Vietnam and a reduction of the U.S. military in Taiwan. Kissinger realized that currents in the region were flowing against the United States and its allies. He affirmed that "we will not stand in the way of basic evolution," and "we are not proposing a treaty to stop history." Many problems, he surmised, would take care of themselves or otherwise fade with historical realities.[34]

I imagine that Kissinger attempted to show that the powerful United States was not a threat to China or to a wider peace. He knew that mutual suspicions were high. After all, Kissinger still needed to secure the president's visit and a positive reception. He had to put aside two problems—Taiwan and Vietnam—that were "insolvable in the short term."[35] And by signaling that Nixon would not further dissipate American strength, Kissinger laid a foundation for assuring China that the United States could be relied on to focus power and attention where it mattered. Nevertheless, I cringe a bit at Kissinger's fatalistic tone about America. Rather than relying so much on Nixon's and Kissinger's skills in guiding a waning power, I would have preferred more realism than realpolitik: U.S. diplomats can recall, without bravado, America's record of resiliency, latent energies and capacities, and potent ability to reinvent itself economically and technologically. In fact, a measured tone conveys practical strength. I believe the U.S. message should always be that it is a good friend and a fearsome enemy.

Chou's fundamental issue was Taiwan. To ensure that the Americans grasped the message, Chou met Kissinger on the second day in the Fujian Room of the Great Hall of the People, named after the province across the strait from Taiwan. No doubt under Mao's instructions, Chou surprised his guests with a harsh statement before returning to his courteous style. "There is chaos under heaven," said Chou, picking up Mao's favorite phrase. He complained about the two superpowers, U.S. provocateurs in Taiwan and Indochina, and Japanese militarism. Probably to show the Americans—and his own people—that China did not fear the Soviets, the Americans, or anyone else, Chou touted the strength of a "people's war" in the event of foreign invasion. Most important, Taiwan was fundamental to a recognition of the People's Republic, not an isolated issue. There could not be two Chinas. Nixon must address the issue or not come.[36]

Kissinger pushed back courteously. He reminded his host that the Chinese had suggested Nixon visit—so Beijing could decide on timing. But the two countries had many issues to solve, and a visit would signal that the parties would be able to do so. Normal relations would follow inevitably. Kissinger said that he had already spoken of U.S. plans to withdraw forces from Taiwan. He went so far as to suggest that the U.S. defense of the island had been a historical mistake. Relying on his favorite formulation, Kissinger claimed, "Maybe history can take care of events." He likely raised Beijing's expectations on Taiwan, especially in light of the almost half century that has followed.[37]

Kissinger reported that he sought to avoid a confrontation over differences with what he described as "Chinese Communist liturgy." Chou returned to a pointed but diplomatic debate about Asian issues: Indochina, Southeast Asia, Japan, Korea, the conflict between India and Pakistan, and of course the Soviet Union. The Chinese did not want to seem eager for U.S. assistance against Moscow, but they touched on their shared interest subtly. Kissinger told the Chinese that America's greatest present concern was to end the war in Vietnam. He sought to persuade the Chinese that an honorable peace—one that upheld America's commitments—was in China's interest because the U.S. reputation for reliability could benefit Beijing. The two vastly different countries and leaders shared information and perspectives to build trust. As Kissinger later recorded, they had to bridge "two decades of mutual ignorance." They had "to establish enough confidence to turn a first meeting into a process."[38]

Kissinger's courtship included a disparaging assessment of U.S. allies. He said Washington had been "extremely naïve" about Japan, building up an economic rival that someday could be a military threat. Kissinger hoped that China would see U.S. ties with Japan as constraining on Tokyo's possible militarism, but Chou replied that America's allies "will be chased off the stage of history by their own peoples." Kissinger also declaimed a U.S. interest in keeping troops in South Korea, another problem, he anticipated, that would "take care of itself." His signal on Taiwan was that America's reliability was the key issue, not a preference for a particular political outcome.[39] I appreciate Kissinger's need to build bonds after twenty years of venomous exchanges, but I think in this instance he weakened America's hand by treating Japan and South Korea dismissively. Kissinger, the strategist of European realpolitik, overlooked America's Mahanian strategy of securing a maritime perimeter in the Asia-Pacific from which Washington could work with a realistic appreciation of its alliance and market power.[40]

The discussions between Chou and Kissinger still had to produce one concrete result: the announcement of President Nixon's visit to China. Given that the diplomacy centered on symbolism, the phrasing of the four-hundred-word statement assumed great significance. The Chinese wanted to say that Nixon had asked for an invitation so that he could settle the issue of Taiwan as a step toward normalizing relations. The Americans could not accept Nixon as a supplicant, nor such a narrow agenda. The Chinese delayed a resolution until an hour before Kissinger had to leave, in part because of a need to consult Mao, who had gone to bed, and Chou's duty of hosting North Koreans during the evening. The statement eventually agreed that "knowing of President Nixon's expressed desire to visit the People's Republic of China," China had invited him to seek the normalization of relations and to exchange views on matters of concern on both sides. "President Nixon accepted the invitation with pleasure." The two sides agreed to release the announcement on the evening of July 15 (U.S. time). As Kissinger flew away, he sent the president the codeword of success, "Eureka," and rushed to California to brief Nixon.[41]

On July 15, the president read the agreed text as part of a seven-minute speech that he recorded at a TV studio in Burbank. Nixon explained that the new relationship with China was "a journey for peace, not directed at any other nation." But of course it was. Moscow got the message of the new "triangular diplomacy" of American realpolitik.[42]

Kissinger wrote the president a twenty-seven-page report on his discussions in Beijing. He appealed to Nixon's desire for a legacy by stating, "We have laid the groundwork for you and Mao to turn a page in history." The "enormous shock waves around the world" could make "a revolution"—if the Americans could "master this process." But Kissinger warned against "illusions." "Profound differences and years of isolation yawn between us and the Chinese . . . [a]nd they will prove implacable foes if our relations turn sour." The Chinese Communists were "deeply ideological, close to fanatic in the intensity of their beliefs." Kissinger recognized that the opening could "panic the Soviet Union," "shake Japan" loose from its U.S. "moorings," "cause a violent upheaval in Taiwan," and increase India's "already substantial hostility." Yet Kissinger was hopeful about a Sino-American rapprochement. The Chinese "concentrated on essentials; they eschewed invective and haggling," in contrast with thuggish Russians, who ignored concepts and "batter[ed] away . . . with a dogged persistence designed to wear down . . . rather than persuade."[43]

Nixon and Kissinger perceived the great potential of a carefully crafted realpolitik policy toward China. The North Vietnamese might worry about the support of their allies. The Soviets would want to clear away obstacles to a summit with Nixon and to better relations with Washington. Even America's allies would recognize that U.S. support had to be earned, not taken for granted. The American public would observe that the White House was capable of agile world leadership. And the electorate could see the wartime president as a man of peace.

Not all Americans were enamored. California governor Ronald Reagan signed a public declaration of unhappiness with Nixon's policies of détente toward Russia and China. Kissinger met with conservative leaders to assuage their concerns. Nixon, he argued, faced the practical realities of limits with Congress, Vietnam, and other powers. The president was maneuvering adroitly: conceding nothing not already lost and using dexterous diplomacy to play off foes—at home and abroad—against one another. The critics, in turn, wondered why the U.S. president did not just make a straightforward case for what the U.S. needed in order to regain military—and, presumably, economic—superiority. Realpolitik looked slippery—and perhaps even like a sellout. By the end of the decade, détente, rapprochement, and realpolitik—all foreign words—would fade from fashion.[44]

The Shanghai Communique

Kissinger returned to Beijing publicly on October 20 to prepare a joint communique that the countries would release at the end of the president's visit.

He spent some twenty-five hours talking through world events and history with Chou over the course of five days.[45]

Communiques are standard tools of diplomacy. Staffs commonly negotiate them in advance, sometimes identifying a limited number of key differences for the principals to resolve. Communiques usually include general statements of goodwill and purpose, unsurprising language of agreement, and fuzzy phrases about differences. Readers with keen eyes will examine sentences carefully for shifts in wording. Occasionally, the document will highlight a real breakthrough or a bold proposal. Though seemingly commonplace or even clichéd, communiques can sometimes offer frameworks for follow-up work or reference points on a path toward future action.

Kissinger gave the Chinese a bland and long draft. Mao loathed it. The Americans wanted to pay homage to peace and security; Mao demanded revolution for the oppressed. Having received his marching orders, Chou confronted Kissinger. The reality, he argued, was that the two countries had significant differences. They should recognize them honestly. Turning Kissinger's historical masterpiece against him, Chou said the Americans were acting like Metternich after the Napoleonic Wars by trying to suppress revolution and sustain an old order. The Americans, reminded Chou, had once been revolutionaries; they should appreciate that a generation of peace must be based on turmoil that reflected hopes for the future, not a restoration of an old, contemptible system. The Chinese presented their idea of a communique. Their draft stated their revolutionary sentiments, overall approach, and views on major issues, leaving space for the United States to present its views on the same topics.

The stage was set for master diplomatic craftsmen to prepare a historical document. The process could easily have gone awry. Kissinger later explained that after he overcame his surprise, he warmed to the different structure and approach. "I began to see that the very novelty of the approach might resolve our perplexities." Each side could explore common ground while protecting themselves against attacks from their domestic hard-liners. The first task was to refine the language so that they could signal differences without provocation. As Kissinger said, the president could not come twelve thousand miles to release a document embodying "the sharpest possible formulations against United States policy."[46]

The discussions over differences then became a laboratory for diplomatic exploration. At one point, Kissinger recounted, he "offered to trade an offensive phrase in the Chinese draft for something in the American draft version to which [Chou] might object." "We will never get anywhere this way," Chou objected. "If you can convince me why our phrase is offensive, I will give it to you." Kissinger explained that Chou was acting out of long-term priorities, not goodwill. China needed to build confidence; "scoring debating points would have been against its interests." As the discussions continued, Kissinger also hinted that on some sensitive topics, especially Taiwan, Nixon could do more than he could now say, especially after the 1972 election.[47]

Within an intense twenty-four hours, Chou and Kissinger drafted a new type of communique. "[M]ore than half of it was devoted to stating conflicting views of the two sides on ideology, international affairs, Vietnam, and Taiwan.... In a curious way," Kissinger continued, "the catalogue of disagreements conferred greater significance on those subjects on which the two sides agreed." They knew that capitals around the world would scrutinize this communique carefully. The United States and China would proceed with normalization of relations, "in the interest of all countries." China and the United States would "reduce the danger of international military conflict." Neither would seek regional hegemony, and each would oppose efforts of others to do so. Neither would negotiate on behalf of third parties, nor enter into agreements with the other directed at other states. Kissinger the historian compared his handiwork in forming a "tacit alliance to block Soviet expansionism in Asia to the Entente Cordiale between Britain and France in 1904" (which TR helped preserve in the first Moroccan Crisis).[48]

The debate over language on Taiwan proved most difficult. Kissinger recalled a U.S. phrase from the 1950s that impressed Chou: "The United States acknowledges that all Chinese on either side of the Taiwan Straits maintain there is but one China. The United States does not challenge that position." The United States understood that Beijing had stated it did not intend to use force to resolve the question of which government would control "one China," although the Communists have never renounced the option. The work on the draft communique was not yet complete, but as Chou said good-bye to a departing Kissinger, he spoke in English for the first time: "Come back soon for the joy of talking."[49]

Indeed, during the week of Nixon's visit in February, Chou, Kissinger, and their colleagues had to finish their work on the communique during late-night and early-morning sessions. They still had to resolve differences over Mao's call for revolution and three other issues: trade and exchanges, the recent war between India and Pakistan, and Taiwan.[50]

The drafters captured revolutionary fervor as "important changes and great upheavals." They handled common views and variations on policies in South Asia by including shared phrases in separate sections. The references to trade and exchanges turned out to be ironic in light of subsequent events. China was wary about foreigners coming to China and had little interest in trade and tourism. Kissinger explained that "sentimental public pressure" necessitated positive language, but trade would be "infinitesimal" and exchanges "will not change objective realities." As Kissinger has admitted, his feel for economics has been a weak spot. Nixon and Kissinger had lost touch with the American tradition of shaping international ties through trade and private entrepreneurialism.[51]

Disputes over the wording on Taiwan, not surprisingly, lingered the longest. As Kissinger said frankly to Chou, "The trouble is that we disagree, not that we don't understand each other." The Chinese wanted firm dates for the United States to withdraw its troops and for Taiwan to accept Beijing's rule. Nixon offered verbal assurances about "one China," gradually reducing U.S. forces, keeping Japan out of Taiwan, and not supporting Taiwanese independence. The final text used Kissinger's earlier formulation about "One China," affirmed interest in "a peaceful settlement," and pledged to reduce forces and installations "progressively" on the way to the "ultimate objective of... withdrawal." Almost fifty years on, U.S. forces have long gone, but the Taiwan Relations Act commits the United States to types of support, and Beijing is still waiting to resolve the Taiwan question.[52]

Near the very end of the president's week-long trip, Kissinger shared the supposedly final communique with Secretary of State William Rogers and the State Department experts. Now Kissinger paid the price for his secret, close-hold drafting process. State's East Asia hands raised concerns, especially about a reference to U.S. defense commitments to Japan and South Korea but not Taiwan. They feared China and the world might interpret Taiwan's exclusion as turning a blind eye to hostile action. The experts recalled Secretary of State Acheson's failure in 1950 to mention South Korea as part of the U.S. defense perimeter shortly before North Korea attacked. In his memoirs, Kissinger found the State Department's complaint to be trivial mischief making. Kissinger had to return, deeply apologetic, to his Chinese counterparts. They exploded. China did not really need the communique, the officials objected. The Chinese negotiators had already cleared the communique with Mao. Now the Americans not only wanted changes, but the alterations concerned Taiwan. Eventually, the two sides reached another compromise that watered down U.S. references to Japan and South Korea so as not to single out Taiwan. By way of penalty, the Chinese insisted on another word change to heighten America's moral obligation not to seek "hegemony" in the Asia-Pacific.[53]

Such closing dramas are not unusual in drafting negotiations. When they occur, exhausted negotiators need to stay disciplined, with an eye on the main objective, and remain creative in solving problems. On the other hand, drafters who gain a reputation for seeking last-minute advantage, especially if without good explanation, lose the credibility essential to dealmaking.

The United States and China issued the communique in Shanghai on the afternoon of Sunday, February 27. The president left China the following day. Kissinger held a press conference for the exhausted corps of U.S. journalists who had accompanied the president. He alerted his Chinse counterparts in advance to the answers he would give on expected questions, especially on Taiwan. (Kissinger had a good sense for what to expect, especially because he had suggested questions to reporters.) The week of news certainly registered at home. Gallup recorded public awareness of Nixon's trip at 98 percent, the highest in Gallup's history.[54]

In the years that followed, Kissinger received justifiable praise for his work on the Shanghai Communique. His writings invested the script with special standing as an example of realpolitik. Kissinger stated that the Communique "provide[d] a road map for Sino-American relations for the next decade." Within a year, he recounted, the language of understanding used by the two countries became "both more explicit and more global." "Sino-American relations...moved from strident hostility and isolation to *de facto* alliance against the pre-eminent threat." Note how Kissinger's use of the word "alliance" is much closer to the nineteenth-century usage to which America had long objected than to the mid-twentieth-century security, economic, and political partnerships that the United States forged with Europe and then Asia. The United States' mid-twentieth-century partnerships may be closer to Seward's concept of loose economic, political, and even confederal ties, based on the post–Civil War respect for a union of states. Kissinger's de facto alliance with China was part of "a framework that reflected each nation's willingness to support the other where national interests coincided." Nixon and Kissinger's "new structure of peace" depended on calculations of self-interest, not shared beliefs.[55]

Realpolitik views alliances instrumentally, not as long-lasting partnerships based on shared economic and political values that underpin common security interests. American diplomacy has included elements of realpolitik from its earliest days—as demonstrated by the maneuvers of Washington, Hamilton, Jefferson, Monroe, and John Quincy Adams in earlier chapters. On occasion, Americans revel in the advantageous maneuvers, as they did with Nixon and Kissinger. But other schools of American thought about relations with the world have intruded insistently. Ironically, Kissinger's preference for achieving order through rebalancing international equilibria has proven unstable because of Washington's need to accommodate additional American political and diplomatic traditions.

America and the World in 1969

Richard Nixon was the fifth of nine Cold War Presidents. When he assumed office in January 1969, the United States and the Soviet Union were facing off with thirty-seven thousand nuclear weapons having the explosive power of a million Hiroshima blasts. Nixon recognized that war with either the USSR or China would amount to "national suicide." He longed to realize Woodrow Wilson's dream of ending "big" wars among the great powers. Nixon wanted his legacy to be a structure for "permanent peace."[56]

Yet Richard Nixon became a war president from his first day in office. H. R. Haldeman, the White House chief of staff, noted in an oral history, "Don't ever—no matter what facet of the Nixon presidency you consider— don't ever lose sight of Vietnam as the overriding factor in the first Nixon term. It overshadowed everything, all the time, in every discussion, in every decision, in every opportunity, and every problem." Nixon, who had served as Eisenhower's understudy, seemed at first to think he could draw on the general's tactics in Korea to end the war in Vietnam quickly. But the new president misread his North Vietnamese opponent, Soviet and Chinese relations, the lack of South Vietnamese resolve, and, most important, the willingness of the American public to escalate (much less to threaten nuclear weapons). Nevertheless, Nixon knew he had to cut U.S. troop numbers quickly, and he did; during the first half of 1969, the United States suffered almost half the casualties incurred during all of Nixon's presidency.[57]

Nixon led a badly divided country. As Kissinger reflected, "American idealism...had defeated itself with its own weapons.... [B]oth sides in the debate over Vietnam perceived their goals in terms of moral absolutes and never found a means of bridging the gulf between them." Nixon had to lead a retreat, a most dangerous maneuver in war and diplomacy. The U.S. public "wanted the war to end and America not to capitulate," said Kissinger. After the U.S. invasion in Cambodia in 1970, Kissinger told a columnist, "The trick...is to stage a great retreat and emerge the other end still a great power reasonably cohesive at home."[58]

The president recognized that Vietnam was both a tragedy on its own terms and an obstacle to his strategic plans. Vietnam constrained America's ability to focus on the East-West competition, take advantage of tensions between Beijing and Moscow, and address perils in the unsettled Mideast after the 1967 war between Israel and the Arabs. Nixon worried that the public's frustrations over Vietnam might pull Americans inward toward a new isolationism and passivity.[59]

As Americans stepped back, the Soviets looked like they were on the march. Having overcome the nuclear and missile deficit of the early 1960s,

Moscow was building an atomic arsenal second to none. The Red Navy added flotillas and posed new risks to America's maritime passage to Europe and Asia. The invasion of Czechoslovakia, and the invocation of the Brezhnev Doctrine, demonstrated Moscow's steely resolve to hold on to its empire and discipline wayward Communist regimes. The Soviets were pouring arms into Middle Eastern states that they hoped would support Moscow's play for influence in the Mediterranean and the energy hub of the world.

Kissinger perceived a dangerous combination in Moscow. Lacking "a strong central point of decision making" since Stalin, the dull, blundering leaders of the 1970s might be tempted to throw their powerful military into aggressive and destabilizing adventures. Communism had lost its ideological appeal. Some socialist states were showing nationalist and independent tendencies. Moscow was willing to rely on brute force to enforce unity.[60]

The shrinking U.S. military was stretched. Between 1969 and 1972, Washington cut its forces from 3.4 million to 2.3 million, the lowest level since before the Korean War. In addition to the Vietnam drawdown, the United States reduced its forces in Japan and Korea by one-third and in the Philippines by half. Nixon's new "doctrine" of 1969 looked to allies to supply manpower for their own defense. The new nuclear doctrine was "sufficiency," no longer "superiority," in support of a "stable deterrence." As Robert Osgood and later Michael Green concluded, Nixon's new grand strategy required *"military retrenchment without political disengagement."*[61]

America was becoming cost-conscious. Washington had run budget deficits in every year but one since 1962. LBJ's "guns and butter" policy strained the economy, stoking inflation and weakening the U.S. dollar. Europe and Japan, although military allies, had become robust economic competitors. By the time of his visit to China, Nixon would have to devalue the dollar and break the Bretton Woods system of fixed exchange rates, further fueling inflation and threatening the trade and investment regime that had complemented the American alliance system for more than twenty years.

Hamilton had sketched a realistic U.S. foreign policy as a complement to the creation of American economic power. Nixon and Kissinger aimed to reorder the international system of power politics to suit what they had accepted as a decline in relative U.S. economic power.

The Precepts of Nixon's and Kissinger's Realpolitik

President Nixon, like Kennedy, viewed himself as a foreign policy president. He had traveled far and wide when out of office, meeting leaders and experts, probing for insights, and preparing for a second chance at the top rung. Foreign Service officers recalled Nixon's "tremendous intellectual curiosity";

one added that Nixon was "the best informed on foreign affairs of all the luminaries who visited."[62]

The incoming president combined intellectual groundwork with an assumption about how superior nations make a historical mark: Nixon told Kissinger that "nations must have great ideas or they cease to be great." He explained to Haldeman that the United States risked going "down the drain of a great power." His political instincts alerted him to the longer-term danger of the calamity in Vietnam. The president would not "fall into [the] dry rot of just managing the chaos better." "Only if we act greatly in meeting our responsibilities abroad will we remain a great Nation," concluded Nixon.[63]

Nixon sensed the currents of the era; his leadership challenge was to "give history a nudge." To do so, he had to make "bold decisions," "take risks, be exciting," and even "go for broke." Especially in American democracy, and given the national woe, Nixon thought he had "to electrify people." Half measures would never do. "Competence and willpower" would become diplomatic assets. "Audacity" would inspire political support. The price of such leadership throughout history, Nixon reflected, was loneliness and lack of understanding by the established guardians of old orders. One had to turn the tables on opponents.[64]

In early 1968, Nixon told Theodore White, the political journalist and China hand, "If I am elected President, the first thing I'll do is get in touch with Red China." Over the next generation, no one could run the world without working with China. Maybe, Nixon speculated, he could "play Russia and China off against each other." After his election in November 1968, Nixon met with Kissinger to discuss the world and the post of national security adviser. The newly elected leader included one of his ruminations—the need to revisit policy toward the People's Republic of China.

Kissinger had undertaken two extensive field trips to Vietnam to gather intelligence for the Johnson administration. But he was a Europeanist by background and profession, with concentration on the Soviet Union and nuclear arms. In February 1969, shortly after assuming office, the new president sent Kissinger a memo directing him to determine how to reach out to Beijing. Kissinger told Alexander Haig, his military aide, "Our leader has taken leave of reality. He has just ordered me to make the flight of fancy to come true." In the summer, Haldeman reminded Kissinger that the president really wanted to visit China during his first term: "Fat chance," replied the national security specialist.[65]

Kissinger learned to work with his boss's bias for boldness, adding his own disposition toward maneuver, ambiguity, and nuance. Kissinger preferred acting as a "strategic negotiator" within a framework of explicit and implicit power that he would painstakingly construct. He recognized that

Nixon's instinct was always to "play for all the marbles." Their realpolitik policies reflected a blend of their impulses.[66]

Nixon's first inaugural in 1969 sounded a very different note from JFK's trumpeting address only eight years before. Nixon urged Americans to rise above divisions to support "an era of negotiation" instead of "a period of confrontation."[67]

Nevertheless, Nixon, the bold leader, wanted to achieve much more than just an accommodation to trying circumstances. The president believed he could refashion the new map of power into a lasting peace among great nations. He tried to explain that America's loss of domination could be constructive; this was not a fashionable idea in American politics. Kissinger points to a quote from Nixon's interview with *Time* in early 1972: "It is when one nation becomes infinitely more powerful in relation to its potential competitors that the danger of war arises....I think it will be a safer world and a better world if we have a strong, healthy United States, Europe, Soviet Union, China, Japan, each balancing the other...[creating] an even balance."[68]

Nixon's call for a balance of power has a more optimistic ring than Kissinger's explanations of complexity. The president believed the United States was a force for good; Kissinger would never have denied that, but he was skeptical about moral claims in international relations. Kissinger understood the difference, stating that the president relied on Wilsonian rhetoric to present a "sustainable role for an idealistic America." Nixon wanted to appeal to Wilson's "internationalism and belief in America's indispensability." "Wilsonianism and *Realpolitik* would merge," wrote Kissinger years later.[69]

Kissinger's approach paralleled Nixon's, but with subtle differences. His dissertation and founding book, *A World Restored*, promotes the idea that the European balance of power was a safeguard against aggression; Americans, in contrast, viewed Europe's threatening alliances as a prelude to conflict. Kissinger noted that the nineteenth-century Concert of Europe sought stability, not perfection. Friction and maneuver were necessary components of fluid, shifting equilibria of power. So was agile diplomacy. He recognized the need, on occasion, for bold moves against conventional wisdom. The challenge, according to Kissinger, was to seek stability amidst perpetual change. The system must avoid revolutions that could overthrow the established order. Niall Ferguson, Kissinger's worthy biographer, titled his subject provocatively as *The Idealist* in part because Kissinger wanted to avoid devastating breakdowns in international society.[70]

Both Nixon and Kissinger perceived linkages among issues and states. This represented a long journey from McNamara's bluster that crisis management had supplanted strategy. The two men connected the dots of policies that others viewed as individual problems; indeed, some criticized Nixon's and Kissinger's proclivity to treat local conflicts principally as maneuvers by pawns on the great power, East-West chessboard. Kissinger termed his integrative outlook a "seamless web of reality." Within this web, powers were likely to have conflicts and relationships simultaneously.[71]

In 1968, Kissinger assessed America's position in an essay. "In the forties and fifties, we offered remedies; in the late sixties and in the seventies our role will have to be to contribute to a structure that will foster the initiative of others." Others needed to share burdens. Statesmen needed to recognize linkages among overlapping relations. More pointed, after "a decade of almost continuous decline," Kissinger believed the United States was "living off capital" and could not recover its old dominance. Later in 1969, he told the press, "[W]e have run out of [the] particular vision" of the Marshall Plan era. Other parties, with greater self-confidence, were playing greater roles. "Communism is no longer monolithic." We "face the problem of helping to build international relations on a basis which may be less unilaterally American."[72]

According to Kissinger's lessons of history, the transition to multipolarity would be better for the United States as well as the world—if the United States could manage and understand the shift. Counterweights "would discipline our occasional impetuosity and...modify our penchant for abstract and 'final' solutions." U.S. diplomacy could rely on "maneuver, originality, and imagination" to fashion "a new period of creativity."[73]

Kissinger's argument—and rationalization—was founded in part on his objections to the U.S. foreign policy traditions that he had deduced from years of study. The professor-practitioner battled what he judged to be "American folklore." Kissinger thought America had mistakenly imbued its interactions with the world with moral principles and righteousness. The legends constrained U.S. flexibility. U.S. officials applied legalisms instead of calculations of power. They sought ad hoc, technical solutions instead of structures and equilibria. They were sentimental instead of scheming. According to Kissinger, these myths of American exceptionalism had rigidified containment into either a strict theology or a psychiatric search for misunderstandings.[74]

Kissinger wanted to educate Americans about the complexity of the world. His principal reference points were European history. He vastly oversimplified and even parodied the multiple strands of thought and experience that had created America's diplomatic traditions. Kissinger underestimated America's capacity for renewal—and new types of dominance and leadership—in part because he did not grasp America's economic traditions.

But Kissinger was framing an important argument, which unsurprisingly included overstatement. His realpolitik ideas contributed to the American diplomatic pantheon.[75]

Kissinger warned that the world could be a savage place. U.S. efforts after World War II had created large reaches of the world that might be governed through assumptions of affinity, cooperation, and even rules. But hostility is not an aberration in the world. Kissinger reminded that security and stability should not be taken for granted. Skilled diplomacy necessitates complex calculations about use of force and economic power. Moreover, whether with partners or foes, Kissinger argued that negotiation is "about trading concessions." Only in "fantasy negotiations" would Americans find all the concessions made by the other side.[76]

Robert Dallek, author of a joint biography on Nixon and Kissinger, concluded that Kissinger "never changed his mind about the primacy of order over justice or abstract moral good." Kissinger's words about Nixon's perception also applied to himself: "Peace and harmony were not the natural order of things, but temporary oases in a perilous world where stability could only be preserved by vigilant effort." Upon returning from Nixon's trip to China, Kissinger reported, "We gave up a total preponderance of power . . . we are now in the position that every other nation has been throughout history. We need wisdom and judgment in order to survive, and we cannot simply rely on assumed moral superiority and overwhelming productive capacity."[77]

Triangular Diplomacy

Nixon's opening to China converted the bilateral superpower standoff into "triangular diplomacy," with the Americans seeking the apex of the triad. As Kissinger explained in his *Diplomacy*, "so long as China had more to fear from the Soviet Union than it did from the United States, China's self-interest would compel it to cooperate with the United States." Nixon "had no conceivable interest in placing the United States unambiguously on either side of the conflict between China and the Soviet Union. America's bargaining position would be strongest when America was closer to *both* communist giants than either was to the other."[78]

Kissinger's historical reference point was European realpolitik. He had explained the logic in a 1968 essay reviewing Bismarck's approach to European multipolarity: "If Prussia managed to create a maximum of options for itself" by remaining "closer to any of the contending parties than they were to each other," then "it would be able to utilize its artificial isolation to sell its cooperation to the highest bidder."[79]

Triangular diplomacy required "agility," said Kissinger. "We had somehow not to flex our own muscles, but, as in judo, to use the weight of an adversary to propel him in the desired direction." He dismissed the simplistic reference to a "China card," which suggested taking an action with Beijing that aggravated Moscow, thereby producing an opportunity to bargain. "[O]ur view was that... the triangular relationship was in itself a form of pressure on each of them." Washington informed each side what it was doing with the other. "[T]hat created its own pressures, but we added no threat." The openness improved the confidence of each with the United States, while Washington pursued détente with Moscow and rapprochement with Beijing. Nixon and Kissinger wanted a "structural improvement" with the two Communist powers that was valuable with each separately, with both together, and as an asset with third parties in other conflicts. This multidimensional quality of triangular diplomacy helps explain Kissinger's otherwise Delphic statement that "[t]he essence of foreign policy is precisely the ability to accumulate nuances in pursuit of long-range goals."[80]

To serve as more than diplomatic artistry, the "nuance" and "ambiguity" of Nixon and Kissinger's realpolitik needed to serve strategic objectives. First, they wanted to prevent nuclear war. Second, the administration wanted to "[restrain] Soviet expansion and manag[e] Cold War conflicts to American advantage." And third, Nixon sought to construct a more stable "structure of peace" among the great powers.[81]

The "State of the World" Reports: An Education in Realpolitik

Nixon and Kissinger sought to educate Americans about realpolitik even as they were conducting diplomacy. They aimed for more than political support; the plan was to break bad historical habits and teach the country why Americans needed to think differently about foreign policy.

Each year, President Nixon sent Congress an "Annual Report on United States Foreign Policy." They became known as "State of the World" reports that complemented the president's State of the Union address. Kissinger and his NSC staff prepared these lengthy statements. He later wrote, "[F]or the student of the period they constitute the best road map for the foreign policy of the Nixon era." He also bemoaned the fact that "many journalists and foreign leaders" overlooked the concepts and hints in the reports because of the habit of focusing instead on the "news" of "day-to-day... diplomatic exchanges." The first report of February 1970 is the best.[82]

Kissinger summarized "the basic theme" of the reports: "that American foreign policy would... be geared to an analysis of the national interest, and that America would engage itself for political causes rather than the exegesis of legal principles."[83] Indeed, the first report is an instruction in realpolitik as of 1970. It declared an end to the "postwar period in international relations." The study outlined the components of a "framework for a durable peace." "The Nixon Doctrine" would be the cornerstone, presenting the mutual obligations of "partnership." The administration wanted to redefine the early Cold War "commitments" from a set of U.S. obligations to a discussion of how allies and friends would define and interpret their responsibilities for one another. A key message said, "Our interests must shape our commitments, rather than the other way around." The phrases may appear bland, but consider the difference with LBJ's mistake of letting commitments in Vietnam overwhelm a U.S. calculation of interests. The very idea of a cohesive foreign policy report—trying to relate discussions of regional, economic, and scientific policies to a strategic whole—represented a fundamental break with JFK's style of crisis management. One of Nixon's implicit messages about his strategy was "no more Vietnams."[84]

Realpolitik and the American Experience

The president and his national security adviser took pride in their challenge to America's foreign policy past. They were outsiders. As Margaret MacMillan observed, "Even historians who disapprove of psycho-history find themselves tempted irresistibly with Richard Nixon."[85]

The two men's plan to revolutionize American diplomacy accorded with their distrust of the establishment. They disdained the liberal enthusiasms that had led America into the Vietnam quagmire. Dallek, their biographer, concluded that both were "self-serving characters with grandiose dreams of recasting world affairs" with "a relaxed view of scruples." That description might apply to many of their historical peers as well. Nevertheless, Nixon and Kissinger's boldness in shifting strategy sharply reinforced their desire to keep control in the hands of the White House. The very methods of realpolitik lent themselves to "constant intrigue and manipulation." Another biographer, Walter Isaacson, wrote, "They both had a penchant for secrecy, a distaste for sharing credit with others, and a romantic view of themselves as loners." Both yearned for historical recognition and were insecure about criticism.[86]

These traits were the seeds of vulnerabilities, especially for the president. They undermined the public's faith in the transplant of European realpolitik to the field of American diplomatic tradition. Nevertheless, it took root. Kissinger deployed self-deprecation, brilliance, charm, amazing persistence, and many good books to counter critics. Like Churchill, Kissinger expected to fare well in history because he would write it.

Kissinger recognized only one other American president, Teddy Roosevelt, as a foreign policy model. He wrote that TR, like Nixon, looked to a "balance of power to produce stability, and considered a strong America essential to the global equilibrium."[87] I have recounted Roosevelt's recognition of the need for balance in Asia and Europe and his skill at mediation to restore balance. TR also wanted to maximize U.S. power in the wider North American region; the continent was the nation's base for projecting strength. Yet TR blended his foreign policy realism with a belief in America's republican purpose and a sense of national honor, as had John Quincy Adams. Roosevelt was even willing to look for ways to promote the rule of law internationally when conditions permitted. His realism and balance of power diplomacy were part of a richer amalgam of U.S. experience and ideas.

Furthermore, Kissinger overreached when he wrote that none of Nixon's twentieth-century predecessors, other than Roosevelt, "had treated American idealism as one factor among many, or the future in terms of permanent engagement as opposed to specific crusades with fixed terminal points."[88] Truman, Eisenhower, and Kennedy offer counterexamples. FDR recognized the imperatives of power politics. Even during the 1920s and '30s, pragmatic statesmen worked within their domestic political limits to offer systemic U.S. international leadership—before the creation of America's new era of alliances after World War II.

Assessment

At the end of Nixon's visit to China, the Shanghai Revolutionary Committee arranged for the president to tour the Shanghai Industrial Exhibition. He used a magnifying glass to see the engraving of a Mao poem on a tiny piece of ivory. Chou had explained the well-known verse to Nixon days earlier. Plum blossoms attained their sublime splendor, explained Chou, just as they are about to fall; similarly, the initiators of great events may not survive to delight in the outcomes. "You may not be there to see [the] success" of the restored ties between the United States and China, cautioned the experienced premier. Kissinger scoffed. In a little more than two years, Nixon resigned in disgrace.[89]

The Americans hoped that their opening to China—and the new leverage with Moscow—would help America extricate itself from Vietnam with honor. China urged Hanoi to let the South Vietnamese president take part in a provisional coalition, reasoning that Hanoi could do what it wanted once the Americans left Vietnam. The North Vietnamese saw Nixon's visit as a sign of Beijing's priorities; they charged Beijing with "betrayal." Chinese arms shipments to North Vietnam appeared to increase (still a subject of debate) as Chou moved to reassure them. The Soviets also competed with China to show support for their Communist comrades in the North. Nevertheless, when Nixon thwarted the massive North Vietnamese offensive of 1972 with devastating airpower, neither Beijing nor Moscow exacted a price, and the U.S. domestic response was not as explosive as after the U.S. assault into Cambodia in 1970. Washington's primary problems were North Vietnamese military power, Hanoi's resolve to complete the takeover of the country, and Saigon's inability to resist on its own. Triangular diplomacy could not overcome the facts on the ground in Vietnam and the United States. As Michael Green aptly summarized, the "contradictions between [Nixon's policy] of *predictable* withdrawal and *unpredictable* use of force" were unsustainable on the political home front.[90]

Realpolitik's primary target was the Soviet Union. The effects were mixed. Kissinger's first visit to Beijing moved Moscow to resolve impediments to a Nixon-Brezhnev summit, which took place in Moscow in May 1972, after Nixon's trip to China. Nixon and Brezhnev signed the SALT I nuclear arms control agreement and agreed on an approach to lessen confrontation in Europe. Brezhnev feared China, but his eyes and interests were focused westward. The Soviet economy had begun to stagnate, and Moscow hoped that Western grain, equipment, and consumer goods—along with the more normal trade ties—could raise Soviet living standards. Brezhnev also worried about West Germany's rising power. The Soviets wanted to resolve open questions about post–World War II borders in Europe, including East Germany's. Georgy Arbatov, Moscow's leading expert on America, reflected that the Soviets' needs to settle tensions over Berlin and to secure East Germany were more important motivations to reach terms than was triangular diplomacy.[91]

Kissinger quickly grasped the opportunity in Berlin and Germany. The United States now had a West German ally, Chancellor Willy Brandt, formerly the mayor of West Berlin, who wanted to ease tensions with East Germans, Eastern Europe, and Moscow through a new "Ostpolitik." The Americans' realpolitik created opportunities for astute allies. In 1971, the Western allies finally reached an accord with the Soviets and East Germans on Berlin—an accord that lasted until 1989–90.[92]

The White House asserted that its willingness to link issues prompted greater Soviet cooperation. Despite rough U.S. rhetoric, it appears that Nixon pulled back from confrontations with Moscow that could have disrupted the traditional agenda. The Soviets continued to seek inroads around the world and did not ease off public blasts against the United States and its allies. Nixon did not want to lose the domestic political benefits of looking statesmanlike, attending summits, controlling nuclear arms, and appearing as a man of peace. The drama of realpolitik, for a time, could rebut critics at home. A few years later, Ronald Reagan pursued a very different approach toward the Soviets.[93]

U.S. allies in the Pacific had more difficulty adjusting to realpolitik and the opening to China. Economic competition and conflicts exacerbated the tension of the strategic shift. Japan's economy posed a challenge to U.S. producers. The old Bretton Woods currency exchange rates were out-of-date. Nixon applied the boldness of realpolitik to economic arrangements without the finesse and nuance that Kissinger infused into traditional foreign policy. Nixon looked to his treasury secretary, former Texas governor John Connally, to lead on international economics. Connally, an LBJ protégé, succinctly expressed his economic realpolitik: "Foreigners are out to screw us ... our job is to screw them first."[94]

Reopening the door to China would stand as an achievement in its own right. Dallek wrote that Kissinger viewed "the developing friendship with China as a second only to Great Britain." Kissinger was fascinated by his discussions with Mao and Chou—and the attention the Chinese bestowed upon him. Given China's size, history, and potential—combined with the swings in Sino-American ties—Kissinger's interest is understandable. Nevertheless, the normalization of relations foretold in the Shanghai Communique stalled with Nixon's resignation and Mao's death. The two sides opened liaison offices, with future president George H. W. Bush serving in Beijing. President Jimmy Carter completed the recognition of China in 1979 and terminated formal diplomatic ties with Taiwan. Congress, upset by Carter's methods, passed the Taiwan Relations Act of 1979 to institute a new type of relationship and security support for the island.[95]

Realpolitik also ranked as a diplomatic achievement in the accounting of "intangibles," to employ a Kissingerian term. Nixon had regained the initiative for the United States. Indeed, he earned a lasting aphorism: "Only Nixon could go to China." The president frequently compared his trip to China with going to the moon. In fact, America's successful landing of a man on the moon in 1969 and Nixon's visit to China in 1972 both symbolized that the troubled United States could innovate and create new, even unexpected, opportunities.[96]

Nixon understood the power of pictures to reshape public opinion. Kissinger tried speeches—including a series of "heartland" addresses in cities across America—to explain the administration's foreign policy. He discussed thoughtfully the defense of freedom, pursuit of peace, humanitarian purposes, and the risks of congressional restrictions on executive flexibility. Yet one can see the challenge of grafting the branch of realpolitik onto America's foreign policy tree when reading Kissinger: "The issue is whether we have the courage to face complexity and the inner conviction to deal with ambiguity." Explanations of "structure" and "nuance" compete poorly with Americans' historic sense of serving a larger purpose.[97]

Robert Dallek stripped away the rhetoric to conclude that Nixon and Kissinger used détente as a realistic adaptation of containment and as a complement to deterrence. They prevented a nuclear war or major Soviet victories at a time when U.S. foreign policy was struggling.[98]

Kissinger, as secretary of state, also combined his insights from realpolitik with tenacious negotiations in a masterpiece of diplomacy: He realigned security relations in the Middle East after the 1973 war between Israel and many of its Arab neighbors, effectively pushing his Soviet competition out of the region. The secretary brought about a durable truce between Egypt and Israel that laid the foundation for a historic peace treaty. Kissinger demonstrated to the Arab states that successful negotiations depended on Washington, not Moscow. And he pushed to end an OPEC oil embargo and rework America's diplomatic approach to energy security.[99]

In 1976, when Governor Ronald Reagan challenged President Gerald Ford for the Republican nomination, he called for "superiority" instead of détente. "The evidence mounts that we are Number Two in a world where it's dangerous, if not fatal, to be second best." Détente had not stymied aggressive Soviet moves in missiles and military power, Asia, and Africa. Nor had Moscow's rhetoric signaled much of an acceptance of a new balance of power. The Soviet Union looked like an unreliable partner, and Americans wondered whether the policies of détente had weakened the West's defenses and resolve.[100]

Nixon's and Kissinger's failure to enhance America's economic power— or to recognize its usefulness in adding new pieces to the chessboard, or perhaps even in designing an alternative board—left them looking like skillful managers of America's decline. The ideas of Hamilton, Lincoln, Seward, Hull, Clayton, and Vannevar Bush could have helped them.

Kissinger later recognized in frustration that he had been unable to build a sustainable foreign policy consensus. Critics from the left and right, he observed painfully, promoted ideologies and human rights over geopolitics and negotiations. As Stephen Sestanovich observed, "Kissinger's version of the story [was] a contest between prudent centrism and America's irresponsible extremes." Yet Kissinger's vulnerability, Sestanovich concluded, stemmed from the secretary of state's inability to "keep the center with him." After eight years at the pinnacle of power, Kissinger's weakness understandably reflected the accumulations of enemies, mistakes, envy, and honest differences.[101] The realpolitik of Nixon and Kissinger also needed a complementary blend of ideas from other American diplomatic traditions.

◆

CHAPTER 16

Ronald Reagan

The Revivalist

The Journey to Westminster

President Ronald Reagan arrived at the Royal Gallery in London's Palace of Westminster around noon on June 8, 1982. Earlier that warm summer day, the president had toured the grounds of Windsor Great Park on horseback with Queen Elizabeth II. Reagan had originally hoped to speak at Parliament's Westminster Hall, but the Labour Party and others blocked the president from that venue. Prime Minister Margaret Thatcher expressed her strong personal interest in the president's speaking despite the snub, and Reagan acceded to her wishes.[1]

The Royal Gallery honors Britain's warrior kings and queens with imposing statues, stained glass windows, and two enormous paintings of the victories at Trafalgar and Waterloo during the Napoleonic Wars. A block of wood from the jetty of the daring British evacuation at Dunkirk in 1940 rests in front of a glass memorial commemorating the 408 members of the House of Lords who died in service during the two World Wars. The setting fit the moment, because on that very day the queen's forces were far off in the Falklands in the closing stages of a bold campaign to recapture the islands from Argentine invaders.[2]

Yet Reagan's message at Westminster was neither regal nor militant. Instead, the president wanted to exalt democracy and peace. His staff welcomed the site at Westminster because of a different historical connection: In 1946, Winston Churchill gave his "Iron Curtain" speech, signaling the start of the Cold War, at Westminster College in Fulton, Missouri. Almost forty years later, Reagan wanted to tell this audience of Churchill's heirs at Britain's Westminster how the Cold War should end.[3]

Reagan stopped in Britain in the midst of a ten-day trip to Europe, his first as president. He had already met the Polish pope John Paul in the Vatican and worked through a difficult G-7 economic summit at Versailles.[4] In reality, preparation for this speech had begun much earlier—not only Reagan's many years of personal commitment to the power of liberty and free markets through decades of Cold War, but back to the first days of America's diplomatic history. In the opening of this book, I related how, in 1774, Ben Franklin had endured the Privy Council's ridicule in Whitehall, not far from Westminster, turning a proud Englishman into a patriotic American. In the beginning of his speech, President Reagan referenced Franklin's foe, His Royal Majesty King George III, but said he had accepted Prime Minister Margaret Thatcher's counsel "to let bygones be bygones."[5]

Reagan's moment at Westminster was not auspicious. The early summer of 1982 felt like a low point of the Cold War. The mood at the G-7 economic summit in France reflected the sorrows of a global economy that had grown very little between 1977 and 1982. The U.S. recession, which had begun in August 1981, would not bottom out until November 1982. The economic maladies weakened public support for governments in the West. The bad times and sour moods shook national resolve, prompting people to ask why the West bothered to wage the Cold War. The G-7 Summit included a fractious debate between the United States and its European allies, and especially Britain, over U.S. plans to sanction companies helping to build a Soviet-European pipeline for oil and gas. The Americans wanted to block the pipeline because of the Communist crackdown in Poland.[6]

Large crowds in Europe and the United States marched for peace and a "nuclear freeze" to halt the arms race. Reagan had to maintain European and U.S. support for the deployment of intermediate-range Pershing and cruise missiles to counter the recent introduction of much more numerous Soviet arms. The United States and its NATO allies had agreed on a "dual track" diplomacy of building up missiles to persuade the Soviets to negotiate down. The Reagan administration wanted to eliminate all these missiles, a goal that many arms control wizards viewed skeptically. European publics protested the introduction of the U.S. missiles, and NATO capitals struggled to keep their commitments.[7]

The president would be speaking to three audiences—Americans, Europeans, and Soviets—who ranged from worried and doubtful to hostile. The deep U.S. recession threatened public support for Reagan's large boost to the defense budget. Americans and Europeans feared that Reagan risked war. Critics thought the older president was an out-of-touch actor who did not grasp foreign policy complexities; Richard Pipes, on the NSC staff, recognized that the English elite regarded Reagan as "a mere simpleton." The Soviets looked for every opportunity to dash Western resolve, split the United States from Europe, and halt the arrival of the U.S. missiles.[8]

The *Times* of London had warned that the president's visit was "one of the most important journeys undertaken by an American President in years." Reagan understood the stakes. He later wrote, with his typical clarity, that he knew he had to address the "concern among several of our European allies, who had their hands full with the nuclear freeze movement, which was being fired up by demagogues depicting me as a shoot-from-the-hip cowboy aching to pull out my nuclear six-shooter and bring on doomsday."[9]

Almost all of the Labour Party parliamentarians boycotted Reagan's speech. Nevertheless, the president benefited from a proper setting. The speaker of the House and the lord chancellor, in long robes and wigs, stood beside him. Five Beefeater guards, with scarlet uniforms and halberds, stood behind. The BBC carried the speech live to one of its largest audiences, as did the morning news shows in America. Margaret Thatcher was impressed that the president spoke freely without notes; the prime minister had not realized that the transparent barriers near the podium were the screens of a teleprompter (a device invented in Britain), not security shields. (She adapted quickly, and Reagan gave her a teleprompter of her own.) Reagan's address was unlike JFK's impromptu remarks in Berlin; the president had planned, rewritten, and edited the speech with great care.[10]

The Speech at Westminster

Reagan opened with a trip report, leading to his arrival "at home…in your house," "democracy's shrine." One of his two key themes was a shared Anglo-American dedication to the institutions of freedom. He contrasted the homes of liberty with the Berlin Wall, a "dreadful gray gash." He saluted Solidarity's resistance to oppression in Poland, "at the center of European civilization."

The president recalled with optimism the Churchillian challenge of the age—the contest between the "not-at-all-fragile flower" of democracy and totalitarianism. He acknowledged great threats, including that of global nuclear war and even extinction. The president committed to work for peace through negotiations to reduce nuclear forces, not just control them.

Then Reagan connected his two themes of democracy and peace by warning that state dictatorship, armed with the most dangerous weapons, threatened human freedom internally and externally. He did not believe "that Soviet Russia desires war," but instead that it hungered for "the fruits of war and the indefinite expansion of [Soviet] power and doctrines." The "mission" of the West at this "turning point" was "to preserve freedom as well as peace."

Reagan, like Churchill, offered a vision. He flipped Karl Marx's revolutionary dialectic on its head. "[T]he home of Marxist-Leninism, the

Soviet Union," faced a crisis. History was turning against those who denied "human freedom and dignity." The Soviet Union could not feed its own people. The refugees of the world were fleeing Communism. Totalitarians confronted "an uprising of the intellect and will." And freedom offered more than political power. "[N]ew schools of economics" in America, Britain, and France, which rejected arbitrary state power and collectivism, were freeing "human impulses" to lead better lives.

Britain, the president flattered his hosts, contributed "the great civilized ideas: individual liberty, representative government, and the rule of law under God." Reagan argued that these ideas now had universal appeal. He reached back across the Atlantic to talk about Central America, a faraway place to his audience. To connect with the listeners, the president drew on a favorite method: He told them stories about women and the elderly risking their lives to vote. Then he strengthened the bond by praising British warriors in the even-more-distant South Atlantic, "fight[ing] for a cause," against armed aggression, not "for mere real estate."

Democracy's flower, while not delicate, needed "cultivating," explained Reagan. Democracy's friends should not stand aside just because a totalitarian state had acquired nuclear weapons. After all, the USSR's chairman, Leonid Brezhnev, had stressed that "the competition of ideas and systems must continue" and found a rivalry of beliefs "entirely consistent with relaxation of tensions and peace." The president's ideological offensive would not just prod dictatorships at the periphery. Even "[t]he Soviet Union itself is not immune to [the] reality" of "explosions against repression." Reagan assured his audience that he recognized the need to "be cautious about forcing the pace of change," and explained that he did not expect an "instant transformation." Nevertheless, the democratic states should "declare our ultimate objectives."

The president added practical steps to his principled summons. He wanted "to foster the infrastructure of democracy"—a free press, unions, political parties, and universities—working through political foundations, the public and private sectors, and the Council of Europe.[11]

Reagan reversed Leon Trotsky's Marxist liturgy about the inevitable triumph of Communism over capitalism by prophesying that "the march of freedom and democracy...will leave Marxism-Leninism on the ash-heap of history." NATO's military strength and bold proposals to cut and eliminate nuclear arms were prerequisites, the president asserted. But the "ultimate determinant [would be] a test of wills and ideas, a trial of spiritual resolve."

Reagan closed with a historical hymn to Anglo-American, and especially

British, resolve. Britons knew about rallying hope to overcome evil during the darkest hours. Britain, "the cradle of self-government," with "the Mother of Parliaments," understood the spiritual power of democracy. At this generation's moment of "emergency," Reagan knew that Britons would not shrink in the face of aggressive adversaries.

The president's vision proved far more clear-eyed than any of his listeners expected. In one respect, though, he erred, because Reagan claimed that "the task I've set forth will long outlive our own generation." In fact, the Cold War ended peaceably within a decade. From the longer perspective of American diplomacy, however, Reagan was correct that his charge to infuse freedom and democracy into U.S. foreign policy would outlive any one generation.[12]

A New Message and Policy

Reagan had once told his aide Richard Allen that his approach to the Cold War was simple and direct: "We win and they lose." In his first presidential press conference in 1981, Reagan explained that "détente's been a one-way street," because the Soviets had reserved "the right to commit any crime, to lie, to cheat" in order to "further their cause." In that first year of his presidency, Reagan did not deliver an address that explained how the United States would win the Cold War. In May 1982, Reagan used a speech at Eureka College, his alma mater, to present the principles of a strategy that his administration had recently framed in National Security Decision Document (NSDD) 32. The key theme of the Eureka address was "peace through strength." Reagan wanted a dialogue with Brezhnev, but only as part of a military buildup that restored balance, technology controls, true arms reductions, and a changed dynamic in regional conflicts. Brezhnev's dismissive reply left Reagan cold.[13]

In the Westminster speech, the president worked with speechwriter Tony Dolan, plus many editors, to set out a fuller vision of his Cold War strategy. They drew ideas from Tom Reed and Richard Pipes on the NSC staff. Reagan worked hard on drafts to convey his own thoughts. A wonderful book on the speech by Robert Rowland and John Jones concluded that the president wrote or edited at least 33.5 out of 59 paragraphs of the Westminster address.[14] Dolan recognized that the president's contribution was even greater because he and his fellow speechwriters drew Reagan's "idiom and ideas" from more than thirty years of the president's own writings. Lou Cannon, a journalist and later biographer who had covered Reagan from the Californian's earliest days as a politician, concluded that "Reagan's message had been much the same when Dolan was a toddler and Reagan was writing his own speeches on three-by-five cards." Reagan added the "ash-heap" reference but sought to distinguish ideological principles from national rivalries. He also stressed that ideological conflict need not lead to war. Reagan detested the Soviet Union, yet at the same time he wanted to avoid any misstep that could lead to a nuclear catastrophe. Cannon later wrote that Reagan's Westminster speech revealed "the blend of principle and pragmatism that was the hallmark of Reagan's dealings with the Soviet Union."[15]

Reagan's White House, especially in his first term, witnessed great battles over speeches to shape policy. The writers often wanted to sharpen edges, while the senior staff sought to avoid scary language. Another notable Reagan biographer, Steven Hayward, discovered that Dolan's early draft described the USSR as an "evil empire," only to have Communications Director David Gergen excise the label before the president reviewed the copy. But Dolan tried again, successfully, the next year.[16]

Even with the help of many contributors, the message of the Westminster speech was unmistakably Reagan's. The détente of Nixon and Kissinger was out. The president would not accept what Cold War historian John Gaddis described as "for the foreseeable future, the world as it was." The watchwords of containment through détente—stability, mutual deterrence, coexistence, long-term sustainability—were replaced by new terms: transformational democratic change, deep cuts to and even abolition of weapons, dynamic shifts, and crusades and victory.[17]

The president wanted a fresh type of diplomacy to work toward his new objectives. He expanded the range of competition to include a debate about ideas, including the fight for human rights that President Jimmy Carter had begun. Rather than compromise, Reagan wanted the Soviets to accept democratic political principles. The president did not just want to "win"; he wanted to *convert* his former foe to his ideology.[18]

Reagan's sword of liberty had a double-edged blade. Political freedom offered a moral advantage. Economic freedom provided the national might to advance the ideas. As Cannon later wrote, the Westminster speech encapsulated Reagan's belief that the Cold War was "a contest of ideas and economics as much as a competition in military prowess." As Professor Gaddis concluded, Reagan perceived "that the Soviet Union had lost its ideological appeal, that it was losing whatever economic strength it once had, and that its survival as a superpower could no longer be taken for granted. Why not hasten the disintegration?"[19]

Reactions

The early reviews of Reagan's speech were less than enthusiastic. The president's delivery won praise, but most commentators seemed guided by their image of the American leader. The UK press was unimpressed. Reagan's tone sounded "hard line." His view was "oversimplified." Even those who admired the rhetoric, such as the conservative *Times* of London, questioned the lack of specific proposals. It seemed "irrelevant" to crises enflaming the world. The best that papers of the left could offer was "mediocre" and "unmemorable."[20]

Most American news coverage lined up with media preconceptions. The *New York Times* headline proclaimed: "President Urges Global Crusade for Democracy: Revives Flavor of the 1950s." The actor-president had achieved "more stagecraft than statecraft." Harsher critics thought the president was "reckless," "hostile," and "crude." TV commentaries ranged from "Vintage Reagan" and "old stuff" to "naïve." Lou Cannon, the national reporter who knew Reagan best, was the lonely voice who recognized that Reagan "was committed to a battle of ideas, not weapons." Yet Cannon also thought that "Reagan seemed to be debating with himself," an intriguing insight that would play out in the years ahead. Many Americans simply did not believe Reagan meant what he said, and a few conservatives feared that he did. The skeptical Cold Warriors worried that Reagan did not appreciate Moscow's military potency and thought the president was too willing to limit arms.[21]

Prime Minister Thatcher embraced the "magnificent speech" as "a triumph." She was responding to more than the messenger she so admired. As a conviction politician who understood the power of ideas, the prime minister drew a connection between the "unfinished work" that Lincoln had addressed at Gettysburg and the "unfinished work" that Reagan had just heralded at Westminster. Thatcher added to her text, by hand, an observation from General Eisenhower: "One truth must rule all we think and all we do. The unity of all who dwell in freedom is their only sure defense."[22]

Reagan had an audience in Moscow, too. Soviet officialdom erupted. TASS and *Izvestiya* unleashed a harsh, even insulting response. In the words of John Gaddis, "No American President had ever before talked like this, and the effects were profoundly unsettling in Moscow." Reagan smiled and said, "So we touched a nerve." He had tried to speak to the Soviet people, and thought he had drawn their attention. The president had sensed their desire for change. After Reagan's final trip to Russia as president in 1988, John Patrick Diggins could see how Russians respected and even trusted Reagan. "[T]he more Reagan criticized communism, the more the Russian people listened."[23]

Early analyses and histories of the Reagan presidency followed the patterns of the news coverage. Most ignored the Westminster speech. Historians struggle to understand the connections of speeches to policy, especially if the rhetoric is thin on practical prescriptions. Rowland and Jones, who are professors of communications, offer an appealing analogy between Reagan's reference to the Parliament as "the lengthening shadow of a man" and the "lengthening shadow" of the Westminster speech over time. With distance, one can see that Reagan expressed his "entire, [successful] Cold War strategy" at Westminster, including its rhetorical dimension. His words "show[ed] both the Soviets and the free world that the Soviets could not intimidate the United States and could not win an arms race." The speech offered "the fullest roadmap to Reagan's vision" for achieving the "dualistic" aims of peace and democracy. Cannon agreed. Reagan knew what he was doing; he declared in 1989 that Westminster was "one of the most important speeches I gave as President." The former president believed that he had more than rallied the United States and its allies. "I think our honesty," said Reagan, "helped the Soviets face up to their own weaknesses and uncertain future."[24]

Speeches and Policy

H. W. Brands opens his story of Reagan's life with an account of "the speech." In 1964, in the closing days of Senator Barry Goldwater's doomed presidential run against LBJ, the Republicans asked Ronald Reagan, a former actor and TV host, to deliver a thirty-minute televised speech before a few hundred supporters. After a slow start, Reagan hit his stride. By the end, the newcomer to politics had electrified his audience in living rooms around America. LBJ buried Goldwater in a landslide, but Reagan ascended to new political heights. Forever after, Reagan's supporters spoke of "the speech" in the awed tones of a great awakening. At the close of his biography, Professor Brands explained that "few presidents paid closer personal attention to what went into their speeches than Reagan."[25]

Reagan had in fact been mastering the art of blending communications, ideas, and policies since his time in Hollywood in the late 1940s and 1950s. As a union leader with the Screen Actors Guild, Reagan viewed Communism as part of a perpetual battle between good and evil. Democracy, he argued, was the strongest weapon of the forces of light and freedom. He never favored outlawing Communism. Reagan believed that the democracies could win the Cold War, not just stave off tyranny; indeed, if the United States and its allies held their resolve, the Soviets would eventually recognize the superiority of free societies and modify their diabolical system.[26]

For two decades preceding his presidency, Reagan thought and wrote about America's political and policy problems. Between 1954 and 1962, he spoke to the employees of General Electric's 135 plants around America. After Reagan's governorship of California (1967–75), he agreed to produce five-minute radio commentaries, five days a week. About 50 million people listened to these pieces every day. The former governor passed up an opportunity for a twice-a-week TV commentary because he thought the visual audience would tire of him. On radio, the only medium would be his voice and the only message would be his words. He wrote the scripts himself. Reagan's security-advance man recalled that Reagan "was constantly writing"—on planes, during car rides to his ranch, at home on weekends. Reagan wrote to the allotted time. For speeches, he developed a card system and shorthand so his remarks seemed to flow naturally and he could connect with the audience.[27]

Reagan thought through problems—and how to express his beliefs—as he drafted radio scripts and speeches. Years later, Bud McFarlane, one of the president's many national security advisers, told then secretary of state George Shultz that McFarlane could not grasp how Reagan "knows so little and accomplishes so much." The answer seems to be that Reagan combined focus with conviction. Reagan's writing honed both. Then he tested his messages with audiences, again and again.[28]

Reagan was optimistic. He flattered his countrymen. He held out a faith in an "idealistic nationalism" supported by the appeal of free markets and personal freedom. His prepresidential tone was antagonistic but aspirational, as fits a leader in opposition. But his voice remained soothing.[29]

The stark titles of some of Reagan's radio commentaries from 1975 to 1979 provide a feel for the foundation stones for his later policies as president: "Two Worlds"; "Communism, the Disease"; "America's Strength"; and "Peace." He characterized his enemy as a false ideology, not the Russian people; he believed Russians were like Americans, but were victims of their own totalitarian government. For Reagan, unlike for Nixon and Kissinger, peace would not be the product of a balance between equal powers. Because the two political systems were antithetical, the choice was between "power dominance and submission."[30]

After Reagan became president, the world knew him as "the Great Communicator." The late Richard Darman, who oversaw the president's in and out boxes as deputy to the chief of staff and staff secretary, once told me that in fact Reagan was "the Great Editor." George Shultz remembered the president's "intense interest and fondness for the spoken word." Shultz recalled sharing a draft speech with Reagan, who declared the paper "perfectly satisfactory." After a pause, the president explained that "if I were giving that speech, it would be different." When Shultz pressed, Reagan explained that Shultz's speech had been written to be read, whereas he sought to "talk to people...and that's different." To help Shultz understand, Reagan turned to a page at random, made four or five edits, and added a caret in the margin with the word "story." Shultz could see how Reagan the editor had created a totally different tone. Reagan the president knew how to touch his audience.[31]

Reagan was not just a skilled actor speaking lines. H. W. Brands wrote that "Reagan wasn't acting when he spoke; his rhetorical power rested on his wholehearted belief in all the wonderful things he said about the United States and the American people." Shultz traced Reagan's strength as a communicator to the president's "ability to work an issue in his mind and to find its essence, and by his depth of conviction."[32]

Reagan's thinking emphasized ideas and imagination. His biographer Hayward appreciated that Reagan formed insights through discovery, not deduction. Brands wrote that the president was an "idea man, a purveyor of big principles." Those principles both inspired Reagan's Cold War statecraft and guided his domestic policies. The president left the details to others.[33]

Reagan enlivened his messages through stories, anecdotes, and humor. His stories drew memorable "word pictures" in his listeners' minds. His explanations offered "analysis by anecdote." And the president eased difficult moments through the "disarming power of humor."[34]

In combination, Reagan's speeches and style made him a master of setting policy directions and mobilizing support. Brands, who also wrote about FDR, concluded that Reagan "was the most persuasive political speaker since Roosevelt, combining conviction, focus, and humor." On top of that art, Reagan was an attractive and often underestimated political leader. Lou Cannon recalled how in the mid-1960s Reagan's opponents had belittled the former actor who was just beginning in politics. After meeting Reagan in 1965, Cannon said that he "couldn't understand why anyone would want to run against such a self-assured and friendly man."[35]

Policy Fundamentals

In a quiet moment during the 1980 presidential campaign, Stuart Spencer, a savvy political strategist, asked Reagan why he wanted to be president. "To end the Cold War," replied the candidate. "How?" asked Spencer. "I'm not sure, but there has got to be a way," Reagan asserted. Détente, according to its architects, necessitated a subtle diplomacy that combined balance and containment. When, in the 1970s, the Soviet Union had continued its expansionism, President Carter struggled to fuse confrontation with détente. Reagan eschewed this subtlety and complexity. In a prepresidential letter, he explained to a friend, "I have long believed that our search for complex answers to many of our problems is, in truth, an effort to avoid obvious, simple answers because, though simple, they are hard."[36]

President Reagan wanted to both undermine and engage the USSR. He thought that the American economy, if freed to prosper, could win the technology race; the weak Soviet economy could not keep up. Then, if the Red Army had to retreat from Eastern Europe, the citizens of those countries would choose independent paths. And he trusted the American people would back a big buildup of arms if U.S. leaders demonstrated a preference for cooperation with Moscow. Ultimately, Reagan wanted to eliminate Communism and abolish nuclear weapons. Along the way, the president's aims might appear to conflict with one another, but Reagan, ever optimistic, was not interested in tradeoffs. As James Graham Wilson explains in his study of the end of the Cold War, Reagan's approach to the policy fundamentals relied heavily on the support of Secretary of State George Shultz to improvise the execution. James Baker played an analogous role in domestic economic policy in the first term and with tax policy and the international economy in the second.[37]

The outlook for America in January 1981 looked bleak. In 1975, *Time* magazine had asked, "Can Capitalism Survive?" and conditions had worsened since. Oil price shocks and stagflation led to high unemployment and inflation. The debacle in Vietnam preceded reversals in Afghanistan, Iran, and Central America. Revelations from the CIA shook Americans' confidence in their institutions—and even their sense of moral purpose. The Soviets seemed ascendant. In the decade after Nixon's and Kissinger's SALT treaty, Moscow had out-built the United States in land- and sea-based ICBMs by a factor of four to one. The Soviets had installed new SS-20 intermediate-range rockets in Europe to overawe the NATO allies. In December 1981, the Polish Communist military had suppressed the Solidarity movement, signaling that the Soviets had no intention of loosening their hold over their empire. Even the weak developing countries of the Third World confronted the United States with a host of economic demands that were supposed to constitute a new international economic order. A favorite theme of public intellectuals—not for the last time—was "America's decline."[38]

The first step in Reagan's revival had to be to rebuild America's confidence. "The key to [his] success, like that to [Franklin] Roosevelt's, was his ability to restore Americans' faith in their country." The Reagan formula was simple. Political liberty and economic freedom were companions; together they unleashed individual and national creativity, energy, and industry. Reagan declared the U.S. economy, with the right policies, was "one of the great wonders of the world." He also sensed "profound transformation" globally with the technology of the information age. "Free markets, low tax rates, free trade" were the "weapons of peace we must deploy in the struggle to win a future of liberty for mankind." Economic strength was also entwined with peace. In 1982, the president wrote in a letter, "I've known four wars in my lifetime. None of them came about because we were too strong."[39]

Reagan looked to five fundamentals of policy to revive Americans' spirits and set the country on the right path. The president's speeches, including the address at Westminster, rallied people to the cause and explained his policy purposes.

First, the president had to unleash America's economic potential. In a speech in December 1978, Reagan had explained that a "successful strategy" needed to "include political, economic, and military and psychological measures." "Too often," he added, "we focus purely on the military aspect." Alexander Hamilton would have been delighted. Once in office, the president had to establish practical priorities. In January 1981, White House Chief of Staff James Baker advised the new president that the "one hundred day plan [has] three priorities and those . . . are economic recovery, economic recovery, and economic recovery." The tools were tax and spending cuts, deregulation, and monetary policies to subdue inflation.[40]

Second, Reagan wanted to build U.S. military strength. He believed America could afford an arms race, while the Soviet Union could not. Moreover, America's new weaponry would take advantage of the country's technological superiority. Reagan's peacetime military expansion, the largest in history, emphasized quality *and* quantity. President Carter had actually begun the increase, so that by 1985 the Department of Defense budget was almost double that of 1980. In strategic terms, Reagan viewed military power as "the cement which makes national power effective in the diplomatic arena."[41]

Third, operating from the high ground of military strength, the president would try to negotiate reductions in the most dangerous arms. He especially wanted to eliminate nuclear weapons. Reagan believed that the arms race was a symptom of the Cold War, not its cause—he did not expect that arms negotiations alone would end the conflict or improve bilateral relations. Just as Charles Evans Hughes had tried to connect naval arms reductions to the security politics of East Asia, Reagan wanted to situate the nuclear and missile arms race in the larger context of the Cold War. But Reagan, unlike Hughes, had much more budgetary leverage. "If they want an arms race," the president said in 1983, the Soviets would have to "break their backs to keep up." Reagan believed that the United States had fallen behind the Soviets after the SALT deals. He would build up to negotiate down. While negotiators often hold their bargaining strategies close, Reagan expressed his plan baldly—to persuade both opponents and supporters that he was serious.[42]

The president found nuclear weapons particularly abhorrent. He was troubled by a Pentagon briefing in 1983 on SIOP, the Single Integrated Operational Plan for all-out nuclear war. He found the deterrence logic of "mutually assured destruction" (MAD) to be deeply disturbing, and he struggled to escape its grasp. As Reagan said repeatedly, including at his first meeting with Soviet president Mikhail Gorbachev in Geneva in 1985, "a nuclear war cannot be won and must never be fought." The administration's early proposal to eliminate all U.S. and Soviet intermediate-range missiles, as part of the dual-track deployment and negotiation, suited Reagan's logic. Some later analysts believe that proposal was the seed of Reagan's subsequent move to abolish nuclear arms. Holding to the zero-for-zero principle, the president rejected an early informal effort that would drastically reduce, but not eliminate, intermediate-range missiles.[43]

Reagan's fourth fundamental policy was the promotion of freedom and democracy and delegitimizing Soviet Communism as a system, the ideas at the heart of the Westminster speech. The administration's expression of this policy evolved. At first, the president lifted the banner of democratization as a means of attacking Communism's failings. He combined that critique with calls for economic freedom and open societies. As part of this contest in his first term, Reagan accepted Jeanne Kirkpatrick's distinction between friendly authoritarian states, which might permit evolutionary political reforms, and Communist totalitarians, which Kirkpatrick argued would never yield.[44]

In his second term, Reagan, with Shultz's encouragement, expanded his policy of democratization and moved beyond Kirkpatrick's categories. The American people, he stated in early 1986, would "oppose tyranny in whatever form, whether of the left or the right." The United States edged away from supporting authoritarian leaders in the Philippines, South Korea, Chile, and South Africa, while easing those countries' democratic transitions.[45]

Fifth, Reagan believed Americans needed an "insurance policy" against nuclear weapons. Even as he fought to achieve a dream of doing away with both MAD and nuclear weapons, the practical Reagan wanted some protection. He did not know what type of shield his Strategic Defense Initiative (SDI) would eventually provide.[46] At times, Reagan recognized that even just the prospect of an eventual defense against missiles added to Soviet fears about America's technological edge and the cost of keeping up; yet the president also offered to share the results of U.S. inventiveness with Moscow. The president's commitment to the principle of finding a technological solution to nuclear defense was so strong that he could not conceive of limiting SDI's field-testing through negotiation, even as part of an exchange to eliminate strategic nuclear weapons with the Soviets. George Shultz recalled that SDI was a "bargaining chip" that forced Gorbachev to offer great concessions, but that the United States could never actually trade away the SDI chip. SDI had to remain in play as a threat and an incentive. Reagan would never yield his hope that American ingenuity could produce a vital shield for U.S. security.[47]

The president believed his role was to hold fast to these policy fundamentals. He could articulate them better than anyone else. He promoted principles through stories—historical and current. He knew how to negotiate based on his principles while not giving any away. H. W. Brands wrote that Reagan's greatest strength was his ability to focus; the president's message never changed, although details varied.[48]

Reagan was not a hands-on executive. His messages and policy fundamentals left considerable room for debate and internal conflict. He rarely intervened to clarify his guidance. The president relied on others to resolve the conflicts, which persisted as long as his advisers held to strong, even antagonistic, views. One could argue that the president benefited from hearing a range of views. But the ongoing internal battles increased risks of missteps, contradictions, and stumbles from one crisis to the next.[49]

The Complementary Shultz

Secretary of State George Shultz titled his memoir *Turmoil and Triumph*.[50] The accounts of the tumult within the Reagan administration certainly warrant the first word, and the results, for Shultz and the country, justify the second. James Graham Wilson's rendition of the extraordinary Reagan-Shultz partnership details why the secretary was the valuable complement to Reagan's diplomacy. Shultz later observed that Reagan had "an ability to break through the entrenched thinking of the moment to support his vision of a better future, a spontaneous, natural ability to articulate the nation's most deeply rooted values and aspirations, and a readiness to stand by his vision regardless of pressure, scorn, or setback."[51]

An effective secretary of state needs to understand his or her president, as Shultz did, in order to follow the boss's direction while helping; that aid should include tactfully offsetting the president's weaknesses. Shultz admired Reagan. The two men shared ideas and humor. The secretary won the president's trust. The solid Shultz absorbed the blows of critics, and the resilient Shultz bounced back. Most important, the secretary recognized and encouraged Reagan's impulse to put principles into practice through face-to-face encounters.[52]

Shultz later recalled that the president "loved negotiations, and he and I would exchange stories drawn from our common experiences in the arena of labor relations." The secretary had also been struck upon assuming office in the middle of 1982 by a comment from his friend Helmut Schmidt, then chancellor of West Germany: "The situation is dangerous; there is no human contact." Shultz resolved to create the context in which the president could meet senior Soviets and eventually negotiate. Reagan went on to attend five summits with Gorbachev, the most encounters between leaders of the super-powers during the Cold War.[53]

Shultz shared Reagan's optimism about America's free enterprise engine. With a doctorate in industrial economics from MIT, the secretary had an interest in the market transformations of the information age. He believed all economies, with the right policies, had the capacity to change. That included the Soviet Union. As Gorbachev began to experiment with pere-stroika, his economic restructuring, Shultz offered tutorials to Soviet leaders on the world economy, why the USSR was falling further behind, and what they needed to do to fix things. He projected America's self-confidence along with sensible advice. A colleague termed Shultz's instruction "psychological warfare."[54]

Shultz favored broad-based engagement with the Soviets on an agenda that reflected U.S. interests and values. This approach conflicted with the designs of Defense Secretary Caspar Weinberger, NSC Adviser Bill Clark, and CIA Director William Casey. They worried, mistakenly, that face-to-face contact might trigger the romantic Reagan to yield America's advantage. The defense hawks also feared that a relaxation of tensions might undermine Congress's and the public's willingness to invest in the military.

Shultz's engagement with the Soviets dropped the linkage favored by Nixon, Kissinger, and Reagan's first secretary of state, Alexander Haig. By early 1984, Shultz had won the ability to maneuver within a four-part framework of human rights, regional conflicts, arms control, and bilateral ties. He also secured vital alignment between the State Department and the NSC through the appointment of Jack Matlock, a Foreign Service officer and Soviet specialist, as Richard Pipes's successor on the NSC staff. Most impor-tant, he had Nancy Reagan, the president's wife, on his side.[55]

Shultz viewed longer-term strategies through an economic lens, which suited Reagan's fundamental beliefs about economic liberty, trade, and cooperation. Both men recognized the importance of North America. In launching his presidential campaign in late 1979, Reagan had maintained,

"[T]he key to our own future security may lie in both Mexico and Canada becoming much stronger countries than they are today....It is time we stopped thinking of our nearest neighbors as foreigners." When the landmark U.S.-Canada FTA negotiations floundered in 1987, I recall that Shultz urged then secretary of the treasury Baker to step in and take over the negotiations, which Baker concluded in 1988.[56]

Rhetorical Diplomacy

As Shultz was building his relationship with Reagan in 1983, the president continued to use speeches to fashion his Soviet diplomacy. On March 8, the president seized the opportunity at the close of an address to the National Association of Evangelicals to denounce the Soviet Union as an "evil empire." The audience in Orlando, Florida, was domestic, and listeners might have been surprised to hear the pivot from a discussion of abortion, prayer in the public schools, and the Ten Commandments to explanations of arms control. But the churches' embrace of the nuclear freeze movement troubled Reagan. He wanted to denounce the idea that the superpowers were morally equivalent and the corollary that a nuclear freeze offered a peaceful solution because both sides were "equally at fault." He explained that the notion of a freeze was "a very dangerous fraud." Closing with a theme from Westminster, Reagan cautioned that the world struggle was a trial of moral will and faith, not of bombs and rockets.

The president later claimed that he employed the phrase "evil empire" "with malice aforethought." Because the speech in Orlando was supposed to be "domestic," the White House staff had not included the State Department and NSC as reviewers of the draft. Tony Dolan, once thwarted, inserted "evil empire" again. David Gergen, who had scratched out the phrase in 1982, backed down when he learned that the president wanted to include the blast. Shultz later wrote that he was unaware of the president's plan to use the language, which "had not been planned or developed through any careful or systematic process." The secretary felt he had lost a skirmish against those in the administration who wanted to block presidential outreach to the Soviets. Shultz encouraged the president to present his case to the Soviets directly.[57]

On March 23, the president did so—but in an unexpected way. Still frustrated by the political momentum of the nuclear freeze movement, Reagan spoke to the nation on television. He asked the public to contact Congress to support his arms buildup. And he went further. Reagan recalled the national commitment of the Manhattan Project, which (with the help of Vannevar Bush) produced the first nuclear weapons. "What if free people could live secure in the knowledge that their security did not rest upon the threat of instant U.S. retaliation to deter a Soviet attack, that we could intercept and destroy strategic ballistic missiles before they reached our own soil or that of our allies?" The president urged the scientific community to invent a device to defend rather than avenge. He had just launched the SDI.[58]

Shultz recognized that Reagan's rhetorical diplomacy against the nuclear freeze and the moral equivalency of the superpowers—and for missile defense—still left room for Reagan's personal diplomacy. On April 6, 1983, the president noted in his diary that "[s]ome of the NSC staff are too hard line and don't think any approach should be made to the Soviets. I think I am hard line and will never appease but I do want to try and let them see there is a better world if they'll show *by deed* they want to get along with the free world."[59]

By January 1984, Reagan was ready to use a speech to send another signal. Tensions had become dangerously taut by late 1983. The Soviets had walked out of the arms control negotiations in Geneva. They had shot down a civilian Korean airliner that had strayed accidentally into Soviet airspace. A NATO exercise appeared to stimulate high anxiety in Moscow about a preemptive U.S. nuclear attack. Reagan received word of rising Soviet fears that increased everyone's sense of risk. The media toyed with comparisons to the dystopian world of George Orwell's novel *1984*.

On the other hand, NATO was deploying its intermediate-range missiles successfully. The U.S. defense buildup was well on its way, and further support depended on offering peace signals. A quick U.S. invasion of Grenada in the Caribbean had ended the threat of a Cuban outpost and freed grateful U.S. medical students. Reagan's popularity was rising. The year 1984 was an election year, too, and Reagan, Nancy, and his political advisers wanted to emphasize the president's commitment to peace as well as strength.[60]

On January 16, the president delivered in the East Room of the White House a televised "Address to the Nation and Other Countries on United States–Soviet Relations." Reagan believed he had to battle Soviet propaganda with his own voice. The president used the convening of a European disarmament conference in Stockholm the following day as his hook, and he spoke in the morning so that European viewers could watch during the day. Reagan proclaimed success in halting America's decline, promoting economic recovery, rebuilding defenses, solidifying alliances, and defending democratic values—which taken together had strengthened deterrence. Deterrence made the world safer—but it was not enough. The president wanted a serious and constructive dialogue with the Soviets in the cause of peace. He offered a search for mutual interests in regional conflicts, arms reductions, and better working relations "built on deeds, not words." The latter included "the rights of individual citizens." He was foreshadowing the four-part agenda that would frame U.S.-Soviet relations for the rest of his presidency.[61]

The president closed with a favorite technique. He introduced a figurative "Ivan and Anya" to a "Jim and Sally." He explored the similarities in their lives and families, jobs and interests, fears and hopes. Reagan wanted to look beyond "differences in governmental structure and philosophy" to pursue the common interests in peace. He was showing respect to the Soviet people, even as he challenged their government.[62]

Reagan had long wanted to meet his Soviet counterparts. He had written personal letters to the three Soviet leaders who had preceded Gorbachev— Leonid Brezhnev, Yuri Andropov, and Konstantin Chernenko—although he had been disappointed by their stolid replies. He could not make progress, he used to joke, "if they keep dying on me." The rise of Gorbachev in early 1985 changed the dynamic. Even as Reagan built his relationship with the younger Soviet president, the U.S. president's rhetorical diplomacy continued to frame U.S. strategy. In June 1987, Reagan stood before the Brandenburg Gate in Berlin and declared, "Mr. Gorbachev, tear down this wall!" The president's secretary of state, national security adviser, and most senior White House staff argued vigorously to cut the line. They worried that the president would look foolish, embarrass West German chancellor Helmut Kohl, anger Gorbachev, and stir up false hope in East Germany. The president told Ken Duberstein, deputy White House chief of staff, "[I]t stays in." Reagan was urging Gorbachev to prove that the Soviet leader was committed to reform. The president's speech in Berlin continued the strategy he had laid out at Westminster. Nor was the line just a one-off sound bite. The president repeated the phrase in a televised speech to the nation, used it with Republican senators, deployed it in remarks to a "Captive Nations" conference, and recalled the demand fourteen more times before he left office. While the East Germans reinforced the barrier, U.S. intelligence picked up reports that Moscow was urging East Berlin to ease restrictions on movement through the wall.[63]

Even in May 1988, during the president's last official visit to the Soviet Union, he was, according to Steve Sestanovich, "an affable if provocative guest." Reagan remained on the ideological offensive. His speech at Moscow State University, Gorbachev's alma mater, returned to the themes of Westminster, customized for a Russian audience. Standing beneath a large statue of Lenin, he welcomed a revolution—but not that of 1917. He connected the "technological or information revolution" to "freedom of thought, freedom of information, freedom of communication." He forecast that entrepreneurs, not government planners, would be explorers of the future.

The president surveyed the march of democracy around the globe and encouraged the students of Moscow to join in. Russians could sign up through churches, courts, union halls, legislatures, and the marketplace. He was "speak[ing] to the true greatness of the heart and soul of your land."

Reagan's Moscow speech praised the U.S.-Soviet progress on arms control. But as in 1982, he wanted to subject arms to a higher cause: "an inward music—the irresistible power of unarmed truth." And he recalled the history that "Americans [sought] always to make friends of old antagonists." The revivalist who had dismissed declinism in America would not rest until he converted his erstwhile foe as well.[64]

Yet Reagan the personal diplomat adapted to work with his counterpart. The Soviets had resented the epithet "evil empire" for five years. They bridled at Reagan's persistent assault on the immorality of Communism. In the weeks before the Moscow Summit, Gorbachev and Ambassador Anatoly Dobrynin sent messages urging the president not to embarrass the Soviet leader. When a U.S. reporter in Moscow's Red Square asked Reagan, who was standing next to Gorbachev, whether the president still thought the USSR was an evil empire, Reagan hesitated. And then he said "No." Asked why, the president replied, "I was talking about another time in another era."[65]

Reagan the Negotiator

Historians and other analysts of Reagan's diplomacy are uncomfortable relying too heavily on the president's speeches, even though the words turned out to be prescient. They seek to connect the messages to specific policy actions. The missing link, especially for America's Soviet policy, is Reagan's personal diplomacy, and especially his abilities as a negotiator.[66]

George Shultz understood this dimension of Reagan's leadership. The president wanted to close the distance with his adversaries. Reagan recounted that "I tried to use the old actor's technique of empathy to imagine the world as seen through another's eyes and try to help my audience see it through my eyes." He sought to understand Gorbachev's concerns. Reagan also exuded personal warmth. But Reagan's empathy, understanding, and even kindness did not lead him to yield. He did not like giving in or even compromising. He preferred to keep the pressure on his foes. With the Soviets especially, Reagan resisted "split-the-difference" accommodation. "We're in no hurry," he would remind his national security team.[67]

Shultz started the process of personal contact by bringing Soviet ambassador Dobrynin to the White House for a two-hour chat with Reagan on February 15, 1983. Dobrynin had worked in Washington for twenty years and was fun and facile. Reagan enjoyed the to-and-fro. The president asked the Soviets to permit seven Pentecostal Christians living in the U.S. embassy basement to leave the compound safely and eventually the USSR; if Moscow went along, Reagan said he would not grandstand. Dobrynin had to push General Secretary Andropov, but the Soviets permitted the Pentecostals to leave quietly for Israel within four months; Reagan quietly approved a grain sale, and both sides started to build trust.[68]

More than a year later, on March 5, 1984—after the "evil empire" and "SDI" speeches, and after Andropov's death—Reagan told his advisers that he wanted a summit with Konstantin Chernenko, the new Kremlin leader. The ill Chernenko, who would die within a year, responded ploddingly to the president's overture. Nevertheless, Reagan met the stiff, dogmatic, and long-surviving Soviet foreign minister, Andrei Gromyko, in September 1984; the optimistic president came away from the stilted exchange believing that he still could bring the Soviets around. After Reagan's landslide reelection in November, Moscow agreed to return to the arms negotiations with the ultimate goal of eliminating nuclear weapons.[69]

On March 11, 1985, the same day Gorbachev succeeded the deceased Chernenko, the president wrote to propose a summit. This time, the Soviet leader was ready to move ahead. In July, he kicked Gromyko upstairs to a ceremonial post and installed the open-minded, intelligent Eduard Shevardnadze, the party secretary of Georgia, as foreign minister to help develop "new thinking." Reagan and Gorbachev agreed to meet in Geneva, Switzerland, in November 1985.[70]

Reagan began what his NSC staff called "Soviet Union 101." Jack Matlock prepared twenty-one papers of about eight to ten pages each on the country's history and the psychology of Russians. He humanized Russians, explained their pride and insecurities, and softened the impression that people's lives were guided by Marxist-Leninist ideology. The empathetic Reagan became an avid student of the Russian character. He supplemented his "coursework" with tutorials by Suzanne Massie, a writer of popular histories about czarist Russia. Massie talked about the "Russian soul," which she believed had survived the twentieth-century intervention of the Soviet man. Reagan liked the distinction. He wanted to free the Russians from Soviet oppression.[71]

The president drew on this education to dictate four pages of notes about how he assessed Gorbachev. He summarized his counterpart's aims and constraints. Reagan also focused his key messages. If the two countries could not agree on arms reductions, there would be "no alternative except an arms race." He would make clear to Gorbachev that there was "no way we will allow them to win such a race." The United States could outspend them forever. The president knew that democracy imposed public constraints—but he would push them to the limit to win the Cold War on his terms.[72]

Amidst the symbolism of the superpower summit, the two leaders jousted over strategic arms, SDI, military buildups, regional conflicts, and human rights. Sometimes the president seemed to be making points to an audience that was not in the room. Gorbachev evidenced frustration with Reagan's confident assertions, which were seemingly impervious to argument. He thought Reagan was a "political dinosaur." The Soviet seemed eager to get down to business without looking overeager, so Gorbachev assumed an intellectually superior and pushy role. Gorbachev was not the only negotiator to become cross with Reagan when the president just repeated his beliefs in a friendly, yet detached and firm manner.[73]

Reagan seemed to operate at a different level, and he returned home more upbeat. He felt he had communicated his core points and that he would eventually persuade his counterpart. His diplomacy did not rely on reasoning one's way toward compromises. Reagan's method depended on building trust, and the president thought he had made a start. He later said, "Gorbachev was tough and convinced communism was superior to capitalism, but after almost five years I'd finally met a Soviet leader I could talk to." Reagan had invited Gorbachev to continue their conversation in the United States in 1986, and the Soviet leader proposed a reciprocal visit to the USSR in 1987.[74]

Reagan perceived progress after Geneva, even though most of his advisers disagreed. Now the president was leading the way toward working with the Soviets, pulling his colleagues along. When the Soviets tried to seize the communications high ground two months after Geneva by proposing the abolition of nuclear weapons by 2000, U.S. officials wanted to swat the plan aside as propaganda. Reagan differed. He suggested that the United States embrace the goals and urged work on the details. "Why wait until the end of the century?" he teased Shultz.[75]

But fate and other decisions set their own course. In April, the nuclear reactor at Chernobyl exploded, and the Soviet bureaucracy added to the fallout with a foolish, failed coverup. Gorbachev was both embarrassed and shaken. A sharp fall in world oil prices hit the Soviet budget hard. Reagan kept up the pressure while welcoming dialogue. The United States withdrew from Carter's signed but never ratified SALT II treaty. Washington proceeded with the huge MX rocket in the United States and intermediate-range missiles in Europe. Reagan approved more nuclear tests and kept faith with the SDI. Late in 1985, the genial president had signaled his steely resolve to his National Security Council: "We *want* peace. They *need* peace."[76]

During the course of 1986, CIA assessments stressed that Soviet capabilities were increasing and their intentions remained threatening. Secretary

Weinberger and CIA Director Bill Casey added pessimistic drumbeats to the CIA analysts' warnings, in part to prod Congress to keep up military spending as budget deficit disciplines posed constraints.[77]

In May, Shultz pushed the president to break the grip of the growing deadlock in U.S.-Soviet relations. He pointed to the political risks to good U.S. allies in Britain and West Germany if the United States stood pat. That summer, President Francois Mitterrand of France encouraged Gorbachev to keep trying with Reagan, whose common sense and intuition the French leader respected. The American "is not an automaton. He is a human being." In September, Gorbachev proposed a meeting without much advance preparation. Reagan agreed. They met in Reykjavik, Iceland, in October.[78]

The dramatic meeting at Reykjavik has been the subject of extensive accounts and analyses.[79] The days and nights typify Reagan the negotiator. Gorbachev arrived feeling that world opinion supported his bold, new directions. He decided to tempt and test Reagan with unimagined arms control concessions and initiatives. Gorbachev doubted that Reagan would agree, but either way the younger Soviet leader would be setting the agenda, gaining international goodwill, and priming a historic arms control agenda with the next American president. But Gorbachev departed Iceland empty-handed, with his concessions left on the table. He told the media, "We are not withdrawing our proposals." Before long, the ground the Soviets had ceded would form the basis for follow-on negotiations. As Shultz later observed, "We had seen the Soviets' bottom line."

Reagan pocketed Gorbachev's willingness to eliminate all U.S. and Soviet intermediate-range missiles. The president moved along a path from cutting strategic offensive weapons in half, to eliminating all ballistic missiles, then doing away with all strategic weapons, and on to abolishing all nuclear weapons. But he refused to cede freedom to test SDI, his "insurance policy" against a revival of nuclear weapons after they had been destroyed. The president repeatedly compared SDI to a purely defensive "gas mask."

My reading of Reagan's arguments to Gorbachev suggests another strong interest. He had given his word to the American people that he would not abandon the promise of defense against strategic missiles. The most successful presidents have an intuitive feel for when abandoning a promise will break their bond with the American public. Reagan told Gorbachev that to yield on SDI "will definitely hurt me badly at home." He asked the Soviet for the "personal favor" of "one word" to permit SDI tests outside laboratories. Gorbachev replied that the point was not one word, but a principle. For an instant, Reagan hesitated. He passed a note to Shultz: "Am I wrong?" Shultz whispered, "No, you are right."

When Gorbachev reported to the Politburo on the Reykjavik meeting, he still sounded as if he and the USSR held an ideological and global propaganda edge. He explained the struggle with a class enemy and its personal representatives, "who exhibited extreme primitivism, a caveman outlook, and intellectual impotence." But the general secretary concluded that the larger problem was a U.S. misreading of the Soviet system: "It is the belief that the U.S. might exhaust us economically via an arms race, create obstacles for me and the entire Soviet leadership, undermine its plans for resolving economic and social problems and thereby provoke popular discontent." As he went on to explain to a visiting U.S. legislative delegation, the Reagan administration "believes the Soviet Union is in a corner and can be squeezed"; it is "waiting for us to drown."[80] He was correct.

Gorbachev's intellectual hubris had crashed on the rock of Reagan's simple but powerful conviction. Gorbachev should have taken Reagan's speech at Westminster seriously. The president wanted to discuss and persuade, and he was willing to consider Gorbachev's concerns. But Reagan also knew that America had the far stronger leverage, and he would not compromise his fundamental principles. Moreover, Reagan *would* squeeze the Soviets—to help free the Russian people while shining a light on the failures of the Soviet system.

At the same time, the hardheaded American leader was a romantic—some would say visionary—about reducing and even eliminating nuclear arms. Margaret Thatcher, Reagan's closest ally, reminded him firmly that America's nuclear deterrent was critical to the defense of Europe and transatlantic security, especially given the Soviet dominance of conventional armies. It is hard to understand how Reagan's abolition of U.S. and Soviet nuclear weapons would have worked out. Other countries would still have had nuclear missiles and even more states could have developed them. No issue better symbolizes Reagan's intuitive approach to transforming the world.[81]

As it turned out, Gorbachev's eagerness to abolish nuclear weapons led him to decouple the items left on the Reykjavik table in order to close deals and lessen his country's burdens. By early 1987, the Soviets agreed to proceed with the elimination of intermediate-range missiles even as the START negotiations continued. Throughout the year, Moscow gave way on a series of other demands involving missiles in Asia, a type of shorter-range missile, and token restrictions on SDI research. The United States pressed on regional conflicts, including a Soviet withdrawal in Afghanistan and removal of Moscow's military aid to Nicaragua. Eventually, the Soviets would even drop the connection between START and SDI, enabling Secretary Baker to close the START deal in 1991.[82]

At the third Reagan-Gorbachev summit, held in Washington in December

1987, the leaders signed the Intermediate-Range Nuclear Forces (INF) Treaty, eliminating a whole class of U.S. and Soviet missiles. Reagan focused next on the 50 percent reductions of START. Gorbachev backed away from battling SDI, but sought a U.S. commitment not to withdraw from the ABM treaty, a possibility the Americans had considered in Iceland. But now the United States resisted. Reagan would not limit SDI in any way. Gorbachev complained about Reagan's Berlin speech, and the president treated the rebuke as part of a good-natured debate. Gorbachev won public acclaim, especially with crowds in Washington. Reagan smiled and gathered all the policy chips on the table, pushed for more, and held his ideological ground.[83]

The pattern continued through Reagan's trip to Moscow in late May 1988, when the president delivered his Moscow State University speech. Neither side expected major progress on arms control in the waning months of Reagan's presidency. Nevertheless, Reagan's journey was the first presidential visit to the USSR in fifteen years, since the Nixon-Brezhnev summit of 1973. Gorbachev was looking for public diplomacy support for his internal and international transformations. At their first one-on-one session on May 29, Gorbachev proposed a joint political statement that referenced equality of states, not interfering in internal affairs, and the freedom of countries to choose their own sociopolitical systems. Amazingly, Gorbachev sought a U.S. blessing for the USSR's equal standing and legitimacy. Reagan said he would take a look. Then he pulled out a list of human rights cases. A frustrated Gorbachev said that he wanted to help the United States with its problems of poverty and racial discrimination. Reagan then turned to religious freedom, saying he was raising the issue privately to avoid embarrassment because Gorbachev must know of this Soviet failing. At the end of the visit, in the final plenary session, Gorbachev pushed and cajoled, seeking his political statement. Reagan sympathized, but said no. Reagan the negotiator had worked assiduously to prevent war, and even to abolish nuclear weapons, but he would never hold back in the competition of ideas.[84]

Stephen Sestanovich observed that Reagan's "genuine liking for Gorbachev misled fellow conservatives as to the nature of his strategy, just as it has confused historians ever since." Reagan's "affability masked the reach of his ambition." But Gorbachev, who shared Reagan's competitive streak, understood. The Soviet Union could not keep up. In contrast to his confidence after Reykjavik, by the end of 1987 Gorbachev told his Politburo colleagues that they needed a new direction because "[w]e have no choice. We are ... at the end of our tether."[85]

Reagan's Diplomacy: The Battle of Ideas from a Position of Strength

President Reagan waged the Cold War as a battle of ideas. His empathy for Gorbachev and the Russians never diverted him from pursuing his ideological vision to victory. John Gaddis admired Reagan's "ability to see beyond complexity to simplicity." The president believed he could break the "psychological stalemate"..."by exploiting Soviet weaknesses and asserting western strength. His preferred weapon was public oratory." Reagan recognized the importance of military weapons but used them with great care. He avoided direct military clashes with the Soviets. Instead, the president used his arms buildup as part of his rhetorical offensive.[86]

Martin Anderson, a long-time policy aide, maintained that Reagan had a "grand strategy," "never fully articulated," but "simple...elegant and quite radical." Reagan believed a nuclear war could not be won. The deterrence of MAD was immoral. He pursued arms control through serious reductions. The Soviet Union was an "evil empire" that could not be trusted. And the U.S. market economy was much more powerful than the Soviets' central planning. Reagan would prevent nuclear war while persuading the Soviets that they could not win and that change was in their own interest. "Reagan was convinced," concluded Anderson, "that [the Soviets] would act in their own best interests, that the Soviets would always do the right thing if they had to. He believed the trick was in getting them to recognize what was in their best interests, and demonstrating clearly to them that they had no other alternatives."[87]

Reagan had written out his plan: "[I]n an all out race our system is stronger, and eventually the enemy gives up the race as a hopeless cause. Then a noble nation believing in peace extends the hand of friendship and says there is room in the world for both of us." The final "win" would be a conversion of the erstwhile foe: "The more we focus attention on internal Soviet repression...the better chance that over the years Soviet society will lose its cruelty and secrecy. Peace could then be assured not only because the Soviets fear our deterrent, but because they no longer wish to blot out all who oppose them at home and abroad."[88]

John Diggins considered Reagan "a political romantic impatient with the status quo." But he was more than a romantic. Reagan's ideology directed his attention to practical Soviet weaknesses, especially the absence of democracy and a free economy. H. W. Brands concluded that "Reagan's political practice was flexible pragmatism." Secretary Shultz encouraged Reagan's inclination to meet his principal foreign policy opponents and to negotiate, creating opportunities for practical outcomes. White House chief of staff and later secretary of the treasury Baker played a similar role on economic issues. Both men, with shrewd political sense and negotiating skills, appreciated Reagan's unusual abilities and how they could best complement those abilities. They both respected Reagan's fundamental principles and knew when and how to check with the president as they negotiated on his behalf.[89]

Reagan had a sense of history and of his place within America's story. In rereading his speeches, I am struck by how he viewed—and explained—his ideas within a much longer stream of the American experience. His words are moving. The ideas are inspiring. The stories carry the listeners along with a sense of down-home humor, as from a grandfather.

I am impressed by Reagan's commitment to his convictions, despite fierce criticism and dark days, and his decency in not permitting even sharp differences to slip into spite. I hope that his optimism will always be a part of American diplomacy. There need to be ways to connect Reagan's strengths to operating methods less prone to lead to dangerous conflicts and breakdowns.

Reagan's successes were historic.[90] One also has a sense that he had that quality that Napoleon most esteemed in his generals: good fortune. I am not sure that his diplomacy would have produced similar achievements in other times and places. Even during the era of Reagan, the president stumbled badly in the wider Middle East, which ignored his rhetoric and turned administration interventions into fiascos. Reagan needed top-level talent, such as George Shultz, James Baker, and Howard Baker, to stay on top of day-to-day operations. When overzealous and blindered NSC staff undertook covert operations in Iran and Nicaragua—and the NSC adviser and White House chief of staff failed to supervise within the law and common sense—the Iran-Contra scandal almost overwhelmed Reagan and his presidency.

In considering policies for the future, Reagan's foreign policy principles align well with the diplomatic traditions I have identified. U.S. policy should always hold to the nation's founding ideals even as leaders work pragmatically on the problems of the day. Reagan was committed to a vision of North America. He recognized the critical foundation of economic strength and the connectivity of trade to American interests and ideas of freedom. He respected the two-way bonds of alliance partners, even as he was willing, as a leader, to challenge obsolete assumptions. Reagan understood the need to ground his policies with public support and to work with Congress. And he believed in much larger purposes for America in the world.

V

AN END AND A BEGINNING

◆

CHAPTER 17

George H. W. Bush

Alliance Leader

A Lesson About Alliance Leadership

Late in the evening of May 29, 1989, during President George H. W. Bush's first NATO summit meeting in Brussels, I sat behind Secretary Baker during a debate among foreign ministers over the draft NATO communique. The day had started well. Only a week before, President Bush had proposed a bold plan to his NATO allies: an offer both to cut drastically and equalize the armies facing off in the heart of Europe. Bush's plan moved beyond Reagan's nuclear arms control agenda; the former vice president, having taken office only four months earlier, wanted to challenge Gorbachev to pull out and cut back the ground armies that truly divided Europe.

Bush's proposal had an ancillary benefit for U.S. relations with Germany. The elimination of intermediate-range missiles through the 1987 INF treaty left only short-range nuclear forces (SNF) in Europe. NATO officials wanted to modernize those missiles. But as the German political leader Volker Rühe quipped, "The shorter the missiles, the deader the Germans." Therefore, Germans wanted to negotiate SNF reductions and postpone the introduction of new missiles.

Margaret Thatcher suspected the Germans wanted to eliminate all SNF missiles. If so, Europe would be effectively denuclearized. The Soviets still had vastly predominant conventional forces, and NATO strategy had relied on nuclear forces for deterrence. Thatcher and other allies warned that if the U.S. nuclear deterrent were decoupled from Europe's, someday Americans would wonder why they alone should be at risk of a nuclear exchange to defend Europe.

Bush's proposal lessened the need for nuclear deterrence. If the Soviet-led Warsaw Pact no longer had a powerful advantage in conventional forces—indeed, if the two sides were equal—then NATO could deemphasize nuclear defense. In any event, the United States wanted to maintain some SNF. Bush,

Baker, and Brent Scowcroft, the president's national security adviser, recognized, however, that their German ally stood on the political front line. Gorbachev was stirring hopes for an end to the Cold War. The Americans did not want Germans to perceive NATO as an obstacle. Bush—a competitive man—did not like being compared detrimentally with the dynamic Soviet leader. Bush's proposal challenged Gorbachev to match words with deeds on the central front of the Cold War.

My job on the afternoon of May 29 was to negotiate a NATO declaration with representatives of the other fifteen NATO countries. By early evening, when we turned our draft over to the foreign ministers, I was pleased. The draft communique welcomed and embodied the president's plan. We had not agreed on the SNF language, but the United States would have been comfortable with any one of the three "bracketed" possibilities. Moreover, as the new, and much younger, man at the oval NATO table, I had been able to achieve our aims relatively amicably. In contrast, Sir Michael Alexander, the United Kingdom's ambassador to NATO and formerly an assistant to Prime Minister Margaret Thatcher, had aggravated many people. Alexander sat to my immediate right. I was aware of the fire he attracted as the group worked on the draft text.

As the ministers' debate over the unresolved text stretched well into the night and early morning, I became increasingly troubled. Alexander, sitting behind British foreign secretary Geoffrey Howe, jumped up regularly to whisper into Howe's ear. Howe would then object about what seemed to be a peripheral point. Howe looked uncomfortable; he was known to have differences with Thatcher, and he now seemed to be following Alexander's directions.

My greatest surprise was that Baker would speak up to support Howe each time the Briton made a point. I thought my boss was dissipating the goodwill of the other allies for no purpose. We did not need to join in Howe's demands. I asked Baker why he kept seconding Howe's quibbles.

Baker's reply was an instruction in alliance leadership. He said, "I watched Margaret Thatcher wrap Ronald Reagan around her little finger for years. Sometime late tonight or early tomorrow morning, my friend George Bush will have to decide who's running the alliance, him or her. When that moment comes, I want to make it as easy as possible for him to say, 'Margaret, Jim stood with Geoffrey every step of the way. We now have to decide. And I decide...'"

I was thinking only about the negotiation within the room, while Baker was planning steps ahead. Not long after I spoke with him, Baker walked toward the other side of the table, where the Germans sat. Foreign Minister Hans-Dietrich Genscher, the shrewd and experienced leader of the Free

Democratic Party and Chancellor Kohl's coalition partner, stood up and walked toward Baker. The calls to speak from the rest of the table quieted; the United States and Germany were the heavyweights that night.

Genscher squinted at Baker warily. Baker said with a friendly tone, "Hans-Dietrich, I think Geoffrey is in a tight spot; we have to help him." Genscher's smile beamed, and he quickly replied with a laugh, "Ach ja, that terrible woman!" Genscher, a masterful politician and diplomat, immediately understood that Baker was not his protagonist. Genscher saw that Baker was negotiating at multiple levels at once.

The heads of government approved the ministers' work the following day, May 30. The language authorizing a new SNF negotiation delayed that step until after NATO and the Warsaw Pact had begun to implement agreed cuts in conventional forces. Moreover, the SNF negotiations would seek a partial reduction, in line with U.S. objectives. The heads of government in Brussels and people throughout Europe recognized that Bush was the leader of the alliance at a critical time. The president traveled on to Germany for a visit to Chancellor Kohl's home state of Rheinland-Pfalz, where Bush gave a landmark speech. His theme was that the United States and Germany should become "Partners in Leadership." His vision was for "a Europe whole and free."[1]

The story of how Bush developed his proposals for the NATO summit—and then built on them throughout 1989—explains his approach to America's allies in ending the Cold War.

Bush and Baker

By background, outlook, temperament, and personal style, President Bush was a natural alliance leader. His family imbued him with a sense of duty and service to country and the less fortunate. From a few days before his nineteenth birthday, when Bush became the youngest U.S. Navy pilot, through his years as Ronald Reagan's loyal vice president, he experienced an age of American global leadership. He was knowledgeable about foreign policy, which he loved, but he led as much through instinct as analysis. As he explained in his speech to the Republican Convention when accepting the presidential nomination in 1988, Bush's life journey had been a progression of missions to accept and accomplish.[2]

George Bush was a genuine gentleman, with a sincere personal decency that set him apart from the vast majority of political leaders. He was empathetic, gracious, and warm. Bush was also "prudent"—to use a favorite word of his—and careful, sometimes to his political detriment in mass market democratic politics. Yet Bush was fiercely competitive, too. He was restless.

He sought action—whether through racing a boat and "speed golf," seeking out people, or achieving goals. A proud man operated behind the courtesies. A number of close associates were told, "If you're so smart, how come I'm the one who's president?"[3]

Bush's eight years as vice president, including many miles of travel around the world on President Reagan's behalf, gave the new president an incredible international network. He had served as CIA director, U.S. ambassador to the United Nations, and U.S. representative to China before it received full diplomatic recognition. The American vice president is, however, an understudy who inevitably appears, at best, as a number two, not the person in charge. With his election, President Bush had to establish his own style of leadership, for his country and the alliances it guided.

President Bush's stewardship reflected his upbringing and personal manner. He was less comfortable with the set speeches that Reagan used skillfully. Bush liked direct, informal outreach to other leaders, with plenty of phone calls and personal notes. The president flattered other leaders with attention. He asked lots of questions. He sought their opinions. I recall being the notetaker for a one-on-one meeting between President Bush and President Francois Mitterrand on the island of St. Martin in mid-December 1989. The Berlin Wall had just fallen, and huge questions about the future of Germany and Europe loomed. Bush arranged separate meetings with Thatcher in Bermuda and with Mitterrand to stay in close personal contact—and to nudge them toward U.S. preferences. After a small group meeting with Mitterrand to discuss breaking events in Europe, Bush added the one-on-one with the French president. Bush opened by commenting on Mitterrand's knowledge of the Middle East and asking for the French leader's views. Some forty-five minutes later, as my hand stiffened from rapid writing, the president of France concluded. Bush had only interjected a few compliments and affirmations. As we got up to depart, I puzzled why the president had not offered points from the U.S. perspective; my direct boss, Secretary Baker, certainly would have found openings to state his case. As I watched a delighted Mitterrand walk away, however, I appreciated Bush's style. We had already made our priority points about Germany, NATO, Europe, and the Soviet Union. The president wanted to use the one-on-one session to stroke his colleague's sense of importance. As Mitterrand flew home, he would be boosted by the American president's solicitousness, interest, and touch of respect. Bush probably filed away a few recollections of his partner's perspectives on the Middle East, too.

President Bush and Secretary Baker shared an extraordinary and yet a complex bond. Not since Thomas Jefferson and James Madison had a president and a secretary of state combined talents to create such a productive partnership, although the two pairs reflected different attributes. The Bush-Baker friendship grew out of decades of personal achievement and sorrows, companionship and competition, and common interests and differences. At times, their underlying trust, respect, and protection for one another created the appearance of older and younger brothers. They shared stories, humor, and a fierce, but disciplined, drive to succeed. Each was self-confident but not arrogant, and they knew how to draw the best from each other. Bush, the president, was the primary figure, and in public Baker always treated his friend—and the office of the president—respectfully. Sometimes, privately, Baker reflected frustration with Bush's judgment or behavior. But then Baker was back to work. He was the lawyer-counselor, combining political insights, a mastery of strategy and details, unmatched negotiating skills, and a drive to get things done. Both were men of action, and they recognized that their combination offered powerful but practical American leadership—exercised with restraint, which created an aura of even more strength in reserve.

The new team had an opportunity to communicate the nature of their partnership within a few days of Bush's inauguration. Henry Kissinger had suggested to the president-elect that Kissinger could speak to Gorbachev about arranging a secret U.S.-Soviet channel. The former secretary of state was heading to Moscow in January for a previously scheduled conference. Kissinger, established as a wise man of American foreign policy, had written publicly about the need to develop a new East-West political structure in Europe. Bush agreed to Kissinger's outreach. In Moscow, Kissinger suggested to Gorbachev that Brent Scowcroft, Bush's national security adviser (and former deputy to Kissinger), could speak for Bush and the United States. An intrigued Gorbachev proposed former ambassador to the United States Anatoly Dobrynin, Kissinger's old counterpart, for the tightly held Soviet channel. Kissinger promptly reported in writing to the White House on January 21. A couple of days later, Gorbachev called to congratulate the new president. Bush said he would meet Kissinger to hear his report in person. Then the president explained that the channel for U.S.-Soviet contacts would be through James Baker. Baker would first consult with America's NATO allies. The president hoped Baker would build the close working bond with Soviet Foreign Minister Shevardnadze that Shultz had enjoyed. "Jim Baker was very close to [me]," underscored Bush.[4]

The World in January 1989

In January 1989, both the western and eastern boundary lands of Eurasia were in flux, and the vast space in between, ruled principally by the Soviet

Union, roiled with uncertainties. Reflecting his historical perspective, Kissinger had warned that when empires yielded control, they unleashed forces within and without.[5] In early 1989, statesmen and women were peering ahead, but few could anticipate what was to come. Naturally, some clung harder to the foundations they knew.

In December 1988, Gorbachev had spoken to the United Nations in New York about his arms control aspirations. As he closed out his time with Reagan and met President-elect Bush, the Soviet leader wanted to prod a faster pace for negotiations. Even though Reagan had wanted to complete his historic nuclear accord, the START negotiations had been bogged down for years over technically complex matters—especially regarding cruise missiles and bombers—in addition to the unresolved connection to SDI. The chemical weapons talks confronted complex questions of verification. And the new Conventional Forces in Europe (CFE) talks involved a staggering array of topics debated by delegations from twenty-three NATO and Warsaw Pact states.

As a public figure, Gorbachev both stimulated and unsettled. Europeans were impressed by his bold moves and vibrant personality; their leaders admired the Soviet's political initiatives but wondered what he would unleash, whether he would succeed, and what they should do. The American political class was wary. Before Secretary-designate Baker's confirmation, I recall sitting in on his courtesy calls on senators. Even liberal Democrats cautioned that Reagan's romanticism might have led the retiring president to embrace Gorbachev too unreservedly; the Bush administration, they suggested, needed to calculate America's positioning carefully. A National Intelligence Estimate (NIE) from April 1989 typified the caution. The NIE concluded that the USSR would "remain the West's principal adversary" for the foreseeable future.[6] The intelligence community interpreted Gorbachev's moves as a way to shift the nature of competition, focusing more on political and economic topics. The new tactics might weaken the cohesion of NATO states, undermine military resolve, and stir public sympathies that would be more likely to concede to Moscow.

The West faced other risks as well. Gorbachev's reforms might strengthen the Soviet economy and ease access to advanced technologies without changing Soviet plans to threaten and dominate Europe. Alternatively, Gorbachev might fail and be replaced by hard-liners. In the past, any relaxation of Moscow's iron grip had prompted calls for more freedoms across the Soviet bloc, and the old order had cracked down brutally.

Eastern Europe posed the biggest risks. The Polish Solidarity movement kept pressing for greater openness and even legalization after the Communist military's suppression in 1981. In Hungary, the ruling Socialist Workers'

Party experimented with market and even political reforms. Dissenters in other Warsaw Pact states called for glasnost (openness) for their countries, but rigid Communist leaders in East Berlin and Prague resisted both Gorbachev and their own peoples. Earlier in the Cold War, modest moves toward liberalization in Poland, Hungary, and Czechoslovakia had ended terribly.

Western Europe had its own agenda. Washington sought to understand the implications of Europe's deeper political, economic, and monetary integration for the transatlantic partnership and the world economy. The European Community had signed the Single European Act in 1986, and European Commission president Jacques Delors was advancing an EC92 plan to create a single market, supported by a European Monetary System and eventually a European Monetary Union. Americans worried that the Europeans would combine deeper internal integration with higher external barriers to trade with the United States; hefty EC subsidies to agriculture, quotas, and regulations had already frustrated America's farmers and ranchers, and U.S. agriculture offered vital support for U.S. efforts to open trade and resist protectionism. In 1986, the Reagan administration had pushed to launch a new Uruguay Round of global trade negotiations in the GATT, the international body that embodied Cordell Hull's principles. Washington feared that EC92 would subvert the Uruguay Round and international trade.

Even though Gorbachev and Europe seized most of the headlines, the rest of the world agitated for change as well. Throughout the 1980s, Latin America had struggled through debt crises and to implement economic reforms that were the price of new funding packages. In late 1988, Mexico was the first country to negotiate, with the help of Washington, partial debt forgiveness. Other Latin countries were soon knocking at the door. The United States and Canada had approved their landmark free trade agreement (FTA) late in 1988. Mexico, and later others, began speculating whether free trade with the United States could catalyze growth strategies that would draw investment, help pay debts, and assist Latins to compete with East Asians and, soon, Eastern Europeans.

Across the Pacific, economies in Southeast Asia studied the East Asian Economic Miracles of Japan, South Korea, Taiwan, Hong Kong, and Singapore. Export-led growth beckoned—if developed economy markets remained open and local officials could manage exchange rates and internal reforms. Yet Japanese and South Korean trade protectionism and surpluses threatened American public support for the trading system upon which East Asian growth depended.

A new and much larger dragon awoke in China. A decade after Deng Xiaoping had begun to open China to the world, younger Chinese wanted to speed up those reforms. Incomes were improving, but inflation rose rapidly. Corruption ran rampant. Gorbachev challenged old Communist controls in the USSR. A new generation in China demanded political reforms—and some senior Communist officials, Deng's inheritors but not Deng himself, seemed sympathetic.

As the new Bush administration surveyed the panorama of transformation, perhaps even revolution, one place on the map drew the most attention: West Germany. Since the time of the Marshall Plan, America's strategy for the revival and integration of Western Europe depended on cooperation with the Federal Republic of Germany (FRG). The repeated crises in Berlin had symbolized, in stark human terms, the American commitment to German freedom. NATO's mission depended on both the defense of the FRG and the troops of the Bundeswehr, the German military that served as part of the allied integrated command. West Germany would be the political Schwerpunkt (center of gravity), to use Carl von Clausewitz's strategic term, for ending the Cold War.

Gorbachev's overtures had a special appeal to West Germans. His opening to the West seemed to confirm the wisdom of Bonn's Ostpolitik strategy to lessen tensions across a divided Europe. Many Germans hoped that more active political and economic ties could ease fears on both sides. Historically, Germans had considered themselves a Central European country, looking both East and West. During the Cold War, Germany locked its fate to the West; some Germans now wanted to rebalance relations with the East. Germans remained drawn to Russia, even after brutal wars. There were ties of migrations, empires, business, and, after World War II, guilt. Gorbachev fascinated them. Germans dared to hope that Gorbachev's openness would loosen the stifling controls in East Germany, so that fellow Germans, often family members, could live better lives.

In the event of war between NATO and the Warsaw Pact, West and East Germany would likely explode into a nuclear wasteland. Gorbachev called for peace and more arms control. The idea of modernizing the SNF missiles, as NATO had agreed to do, repelled the German public. And the governing coalition, led by Chancellor Kohl and Foreign Minister Genscher, faced elections by the end of 1990.

Bush's Agenda

From the start, President Bush decided to be an alliance president. The approach suited his personal style and experience. His reading of the political, security, and economic landscape also argued for solidifying his international political base before engaging Gorbachev. Bush wanted to hear from his counterparts directly and to build the personal ties that would enable him to call other leaders on short notice.

The president's conversations with his close advisers, especially Baker and Scowcroft, reinforced his inclinations. Baker had worked with many of the alliance leaders as White House chief of staff and then treasury secretary. Scowcroft's national security career had emphasized alliance management, and his personal style was curmudgeonly but consultative. The new secretary of defense, Richard Cheney, was also familiar with alliance networks from his service with President Gerald Ford, interest in security issues, and the U.S. military's Cold War culture of combined operations with allies. During the recent presidential campaign, Bush had pledged that his new secretary of state would promptly visit all fifteen NATO allies. Baker began that trip when he and the president visited Ottawa on February 10, 1989. Baker then raced to meet presidents, prime ministers, chancellors, and ministers of all fifteen allies within eight days.

The Ottawa meeting with Prime Minister Brian Mulroney, Foreign Minister Joe Clark, and Mulroney's chief of staff, Derek Burney, reinforced President Bush's initial ideas. Mulroney, a good friend, spoke in plain terms. Gorbachev had captured the public imagination in the alliance's political backyard, and the president needed to take the initiative, perhaps with a trip to Eastern Europe. Bush outlined his thinking. The United States had to consult with allies, "take the offensive, to save the Alliance, not just be seen as reacting to yet another [Gorbachev] move." Perhaps "get in there in his end zone," in Eastern Europe. The prudent Bush did not want to set off a revolution; he did not want to see Soviet tanks rolling down the streets of Budapest and Warsaw. Nevertheless, the United States could signal its support for human rights, freedom, and democracy. America could explore constructive cooperation with more open regimes in the East.

When asked about alliance priorities beyond Eastern Europe, Bush listed three. He needed to solidify the alliance, with a special eye on Germany. He would move ahead with the USSR, including with arms control initiatives. And the United States needed to work with the EC so that EC92 did not turn protectionist. (I recall the president's worry that the year for completing economic integration through EC92 would also be his reelection year.)[7]

Bush was competing with Gorbachev. But he would do so on his own terms. The president intended to move promptly, after he and Baker did their homework with allies, drew out differences among friends, and secured the ability to move in concert through NATO. The Americans had to keep the West Germans on their side. Bush knew that he needed initiatives to compete with Gorbachev. His moves should test Gorbachev's seriousness and willingness to change policies toward Eastern Europe, military confrontation, and even the Soviet system itself. Scowcroft, his deputy Bob Gates, and Cheney were more cautious than Bush. They were prone to wait to see what Gorbachev would do—and whether he would succeed. Baker, in contrast, read his presidential friend's desire to go on offense. Baker's method was to frame the context for maneuver and negotiation. Baker wanted to get things done. Though the administration could not know whether Gorbachev would survive (and in fact Baker had his doubts), as long as Gorbachev was around Baker thought the United States should move to "add things to our basket."[8]

The White House mapped out plans for travel to Western and Eastern Europe to promote the president's agenda. Yet an event intervened—and provided opportunities. Emperor Hirohito of Japan had died on January 7, 1989, and Tokyo scheduled the funeral for February 24. The president, who had fought against Japan as a young navy pilot, decided to attend the funeral of Japan's controversial wartime leader and show respect to a vital Pacific ally. Moreover, the trip gave Bush an opportunity for a quick "working visit" to Beijing; meetings in China would be both a homecoming for the former U.S. liaison and an occasion to consult with the Chinese before Gorbachev visited Beijing.

At the president's meeting with Deng (I was able to sit in), Bush asked the lively, diminutive chief about the Soviet Union. Deng began his reply with a baffling story of silkworms and the mulberry leaf. As Deng held up his hand, fingers outstretched, he explained that China was like the mulberry leaf. Russia had eaten out portions of China's lands over the centuries, just like silkworms devoured the edges of a leaf. He pointed to the spaces between his fingers. Until China had restored its leaf to full size, it would never be comfortable with its hungry Soviet neighbor, concluded Deng.[9]

Baker on Point

Bush would rely on Baker to push his agenda, starting with America's allies. The hopscotch through NATO capitals in early February served a number of practical purposes, as Baker discussed in his memoir. Baker recognized that the personal contacts would be of benefit in negotiations to come. He needed to hear his counterparts' views directly and privately. Baker stopped in each capital because he thought that smaller countries would be more disposed to support American ideas—"if they felt we were taking consultations with them seriously." Indeed, the Netherlands' foreign minister, Hans van den Brock, planted a seed in Baker's mind about the knotty SNF problem: He suggested that perhaps German political sensitivities could be addressed by combining an arms control plan with modernization. Finally, Baker knew that his friend the president read intelligence assessments avidly, but placed the greatest stock on insights from personal contacts.[10]

Shrewd diplomats employ their external networks to influence internal debates. (This is true for executive-congressional relations, too.) A timely reference to the views or actions of an outside actor, especially a respected or powerful one, can often tilt discussions within a government. Good information can be a source of power.

Baker fed the president's interest in personal intelligence with his one-page "Night Note" to the president every evening. Each night, especially when traveling, Dennis Ross (director of policy planning) or I would draft the one-page report with a personal flavor of the day's meetings. The president would receive them with his CIA briefing the following morning. Even when in the United States, I worked with the State Department's executive secretariat to prepare a Night Note of a few paragraphs on meetings or events.[11] Margaret Tutwiler, the assistant secretary of public affairs, stayed in constant touch with Marlin Fitzwater and the White House Press Office; she had been working with both Bush and Baker since Bush's 1980 campaign.

Right after Baker's return from Europe, he headed to Asia with the president. Then Baker was off to Vienna for a meeting of the thirty-five-nation Commission on Security and Cooperation in Europe, and his first session with Shevardnadze. At the main event, the United States promised to remove the last of its chemical weapons from Germany, reiterated U.S. support for a convention to ban all chemical weapons, and announced a project with Australia to draw private industry into the effort. But Baker drew his primary impressions from his bilateral meetings. The Polish and Hungarian foreign ministers spoke about movements of radical, even revolutionary, political change. Both said the Soviets seemed supportive. The Eastern Europeans did not want the Americans to be absent. The Polish and Hungarian reformers recognized that they risked backlash and needed U.S. help to maneuver and consolidate their democratic gains.[12]

Shevardnadze met Baker on March 9 at the residence of the U.S. ambassador, the same spot in Vienna where Kennedy had hosted Khrushchev in 1961. But the tone almost three decades later was entirely different. Shevardnadze wanted rapid progress reducing conventional weapons. The Soviets had signaled readiness to cut tanks, armored personnel carriers, and artillery. They wanted Americans to negotiate aircraft, helicopters, and numbers of troops. Shevardnadze's most important message in his one-on-one with Baker went far beyond arms control. He sought to explain perestroika. He wanted Baker to understand the internal dynamics of a "revolution" in the Soviet state and society, a revolution that would only gain momentum. Shevardnadze believed that the USSR's "new political thinking" would make it a "reliable partner" for the

West. Baker stressed that the president supported perestroika. Shevardnadze said he wanted to discuss the Soviet Union's internal transformation in much greater detail with Baker in future meetings. It was impossible to listen to this exchange, and to meet Shevardnadze, without recognizing that Gorbachev and Shevardnadze were barreling along toward drastic change.[13]

Baker met with President Bush the following day, March 8, for one of their regular, twice-weekly, informal get-togethers. Baker relayed that events in Eastern Europe were speeding ahead. The United States needed plans to support reformers economically and to accelerate political liberalization. He urged Bush to visit Poland and Hungary soon.

Although he conveyed Shevardnadze's urgency, Baker sensed that the Soviets lacked a plan. They were searching and scrambling. The United States might have an opportunity to supply the substance of vague concepts such as "New Thinking." U.S. initiatives could steer Soviet and Eastern European actions. On the other hand, a reluctant United States would enable the Soviets to set the agenda, even if Moscow was uncertain of the implications of its rushed activities. Bush needed his own initiatives—very soon.[14]

Coincidentally, Scowcroft had sent the president a memo just a few days before warning against "early and dramatic proposals." The NSC adviser had commissioned an interagency "Strategic Review" a few weeks before. The idea was for the new administration to step back to consider how the president could put his own imprint on policy. Baker decided the work was neither "strategic" nor a serious "review." The bureaucracy and holdover officials were most likely to restate past positions with, at best, modest revisions; most of Bush's new appointees were not yet confirmed by the Senate. Baker's team just monitored the papers churned out by the process to be sure they did not constrain freedom of action. The more creative members of the NSC staff also recognized the work as a "vague and unfocused" "restatement." Baker later termed it "mush."[15]

Gorbachev and the Soviet Union provoked different reactions among the president's top advisers. Bush consulted Soviet specialists who debated whether perestroika was a "breathing space," after which the Soviets would strengthen competition, or a fundamental shift, "socialism with a human face"—like the Czechoslovak reformers of 1968. Baker concluded the debate was "academic theology." In the spring of 1989, both arguments had their strengths and weaknesses. "What mattered to me were what actions we could take in the face of these two different possibilities, in order to maximize our diplomatic gains while minimizing risks." Baker argued for activism. He thought Gorbachev's success depended overwhelmingly on factors within the Soviet Union. Baker wanted Gorbachev to succeed, but he expected U.S. efforts could only affect prospects "on the margins." Internationally, however, the United States could help frame the hard choices the Soviets would face—with positive and negative incentives. The United States might encourage USSR moves that would serve mutual interests.

To lead allies and the Soviets, the United States needed to shape the context—quickly. "In international politics, as in domestic politics, a sitting target is usually the easiest target," Baker explained. In contrast, Scowcroft and Cheney leaned toward "status quo plus": bide time and wait for Gorbachev to offer concessions. Their approach risked Gorbachev splitting the alliance and missing opportunities to challenge the Soviets to accept dramatic changes.[16]

Diplomatic activists do not, however, enjoy the luxury of working on one issue at a time. On March 2 and 3, before leaving for Vienna, Baker presented Republicans and Democrats in the House and Senate a plan to deal with the Sandinistas in Nicaragua as part of a request to Congress to supply humanitarian, not military, assistance to the Contra resistance. The existing aid would run out at the end of March. Baker's approach built upon principles developed by Central American leaders, organized by Costa Rica. He wanted to push the Nicaraguans to offer free elections while pressing the Soviets to cut military aid to Managua. In Vienna, Baker urged Shevardnadze to do so.

Baker had mused out loud with me that he might be able to employ his relations with Congress to give the president an early win. Bush was elected with both houses of Congress controlled by the opposition party. Many Democrats liked and, more important, trusted Baker and Bush. Nevertheless, it took twenty-two days of grueling shuttle diplomacy throughout March with the Senate and House, Democrats and Republicans, to reach a deal on Nicaragua.[17]

On March 30, 1989, Bush, Baker, and a small group of colleagues met informally to brainstorm about events in Europe. Scowcroft tried out proposals to pry Soviet forces out of Central and Eastern Europe. As a good national security adviser, he also likely recognized the president's interest in recommendations that could seize the initiative. Scowcroft suggested withdrawing all Soviet and American forces from Central Europe. Baker tried the idea of pulling out tanks. The Department of Defense and Joint Chiefs were in shock; Bush's senior team was exploring bold, even radical, ideas. During April, Americans and Europeans flew back and forth across the Atlantic, exchanging views about transatlantic security; this was a serious consultative process, as Bush and Baker had imagined.[18]

Baker had one more significant trip before the president left for Europe and the NATO summit. On May 10, Baker flew to Moscow for his first visit to the Soviet Union. He needed to reassure Gorbachev and Shevardnadze that the United States supported their reform efforts, despite Secretary Cheney's recent comment that Gorbachev would "ultimately fail." Baker also wanted to lessen attention to arms control despite strong media interest. He urged more intensive work on regional issues (including Central America and Afghanistan) and transnational topics such as nonproliferation, counter-terrorism, and the environment. He wanted the discussion of security to look beyond numbers of weapons systems.

Baker's exchanges with Shevardnadze deepened his understanding of the Soviet outlook on Eastern Europe. He also agreed to resume START negotiations in Geneva; the new lead U.S. negotiator, Richard Burt, formerly U.S. ambassador to West Germany, had earned a reputation as a smart, hard-driving problem solver who understood the strategic stakes.

Over a dinner at the Shevardnadze apartment with their wives, Baker gained a keener sense of his hosts' attachments to their Georgian homeland and the fissures of nationality in the Soviet Union. In early April, Soviet troops had forcefully suppressed an uprising in Tbilisi, Georgia, leaving twenty protestors dead. Shevardnadze's wife sounded much more Georgian than Soviet.

Baker's session with Gorbachev in the Kremlin led to a different kind of insight. Gorbachev strode into the room, bursting with energy and conveying a sense of impatient command. He made clear that he knew the Western press and suggested he knew how to work them. The Soviet leader wanted to leave no doubt about the momentum behind perestroika and his belief that the two powers needed to progress toward a constructive relationship. Gorbachev wanted regular meetings with Bush. He pushed for results in the START and CFE negotiations without wasting time.

Near the end of the encounter, Gorbachev announced that the Soviets would withdraw five hundred tactical nuclear weapons from Eastern Europe. If the United States was willing to engage, the Soviets might be willing to pull out all tactical nuclear weapons from Eastern Europe by 1991. He added mischievously that "we in Europe" feel this is an "urgent problem." Gorbachev was well aware of the NATO debates about SNF. He also knew that the Soviets had already modernized their short-range missiles, which outnumbered the Americans' launchers 1,400 to 88. Baker pushed back with numbers about the conventional and missile imbalances, while adding that he understood the "political appeal" of what Gorbachev was doing. By the time Baker left the Kremlin to fly to Brussels for a briefing of NATO allies, the Soviets had released Gorbachev's proposal to the press. The media played up the Soviet surprise.[19]

Baker did not like being played by the Soviets. But he was disciplined, accepted the cold reality of Gorbachev's maneuver for advantage, and drew the important conclusion. President Bush had about two weeks to come up with a bold proposal for the NATO summit. In June, Gorbachev would visit Europe—no doubt with a surprise for Bush like the one he had delivered to Baker. If the president could not lead imaginatively at NATO, Baker later wrote, he "risked being upstaged diplomatically by Gorbachev." Baker also filed away a political assessment. While Gorbachev could play to crowds abroad, his domestic audience seemed less enthusiastic. Gorbachev relied on distant applause to maintain his standing in the Soviet Union. The best democratic leaders, Baker knew, solidified their base at home to ensure resiliency in the face of setbacks.[20]

Bush's Plan

The SNF issue kept festering in German politics, further threatening the prospects for a successful NATO summit. The NATO defense ministers had agreed in late April to postpone the SNF modernization decision until after 1990. But German politics demanded more. A press leak from Bonn reported that the coalition government wanted East-West SNF negotiations immediately. Bush called Kohl to register his displeasure with the Germans fixing positions in public without preserving the flexibility to work out a solution in NATO. Thatcher was really irritated. Kohl pleaded the complexities of coalition government. In a second call, Kohl asked Bush to send an emissary. After Baker's visit to Moscow, Bob Gates, Scowcroft's deputy, and I diverted to Bonn to see if we could reach an understanding on SNF. We had good discussions—but no good results. A few days after Baker returned, the president gave a speech at Texas A&M University about how to move "Beyond Containment" with the Soviet Union. The press criticized the speech for its lack of specific proposals.[21]

Bush knew that he faced a potential breakdown at the NATO summit at the end of the month. His impatience, no doubt reinforced by Baker, led the president to pressure Secretary Cheney and the Defense Department to come up with a serious plan to cut conventional forces in Europe. Baker and Scowcroft recognized that the issue of armies in Europe should be joined with the questions of modernizing and negotiating SNF weapons. A vast reduction—and equalization—of conventional forces would lessen the need for deterrence through SNF missiles. A major withdrawal of the Red Army from Central and Eastern Europe would send an unmistakable political signal to reformers pushing for democratization and independence. Moreover, a future Soviet leader would not be able to easily reverse the cuts and withdrawals. Smaller conventional forces could help Gorbachev lower his crushing military budget and lessen the militarization of Soviet society. The Americans also recognized that large U.S. forces and maneuvers, particularly in Germany, led to tensions with civilians; a smaller U.S. foot-print would be more sustainable. The big diplomatic premise was the idea that the allies could defer *both* SNF modernization and negotiation while the CFE negotiations changed the military landscape.[22]

Like many fine diplomatic strategies, the Baker-Scowcroft idea needed to be bolstered by practical steps that highlighted the content and com-mitment. First, the United States had to demonstrate that the CFE negotia-tions could produce results soon. Second, the Americans needed a dramatic CFE proposal that outlined the shape of a deal. Robert Blackwill and Philip Zelikow of the NSC staff, who had experience with arcane conventional arms control, were already working on a proposal.[23]

Bush decided to negotiate parity (at lower levels) in tanks, artillery, and armored vehicles—as well as in combat planes and helicopters, which were NATO's strength. The president proposed a common ceiling of troops in Europe at 275,000. The United States would cut its existing forces by about 15 percent from the present deployment of about 320,000. The Soviets would need to send home more than half of their larger number of divisions in Eastern Europe. The United States also called for rapid action, with negotia-tions over six months to a year and full implementation of the cuts by 1992 or 1993.

Secretary Cheney and the Defense Department pushed back hard. They argued that these proposals would shock other NATO capitals; Cheney feared the effect would "unhinge the Alliance," not solidify it. But Cheney was a good friend of Baker's and Scowcroft's and respectful of the president. That team worked out differences quietly and effectively. On the other hand, William Crowe, chairman of the Joint Chiefs, resisted fiercely what he con-sidered to be PR moves. Bush listened but overruled him. "I want this done," he said. "Don't keep telling me why it can't be done. Tell me how it can be done."[24]

By mid-May 1989, Bush had a bold plan. But he had to win the agreement of NATO's leaders quickly. They were used to incremental diplomacy. The president quietly dispatched Deputy Secretary of State Larry Eagleburger and NSC Deputy Bob Gates to visit key capitals to explain the U.S. ideas. To be sure the Europeans knew that they spoke for him, Bush called leaders per-sonally in advance. Kohl was overjoyed. Mitterrand, who was visiting Bush in Maine, approved. Thatcher was displeased—and let the envoys know of her unhappiness in no uncertain terms. On his way to Brussels, including in Rome, the president kept promoting his plan. Most allies were pleased—and relieved.[25]

These were the events that led to my work on the NATO communique on May 29 and Baker's maneuvering and negotiations later that night. We finished the sixty-five long paragraphs around 2:00 a.m. During the evening dinner of heads of government, Prime Minister Thatcher had pressed the president about not negotiating SNF missiles. "We must not give in on this," she reminded Bush. "You're not going to give in, are you?" she added. On two occasions during the long night session, Baker called the president to report on the situation. Baker might have been on point, but he made sure his boss would be ready to sign on when the deal was done.

By the morning of May 30, when the leaders met to pass on the communique, Thatcher sounded enthusiastic. Bush thought she was motivated in part by wanting to appear in agreement with the United States. Baker had crafted a deal, ensured the president was comfortable, and enabled Thatcher's representatives to report that they had squeezed every last ounce out of the negotiation.[26]

Gorbachev and Shevardnadze responded positively to NATO's proposals. NATO and the Warsaw Pact resolved the basic structure of the CFE negotiations right away. The parties signed the treaty the following year. It was the most extensive and far-reaching arms control agreement ever completed. The SNF issue faded away, overtaken by events still to come in 1989–90.

Commentators at the time and afterward rarely observed the shift of priority from Reagan's negotiations over nuclear arms to Bush's attention to conventional forces. (Baker worked through the complex START details as well, and both sides signed the START treaty in July 1991.) But the Bush-Baker logic for ending the Cold War had concentrated on the "central front" of U.S.-Soviet standoff: the Red Army's occupation and control of Central and Eastern Europe. The division of Europe was at the heart of the Cold War. To end the Cold War, the United States and its NATO allies had to heal that breach. The natural next steps of the strategy would lead to the lands of Eastern Europe—and even East Germany.

The president's visit to Bonn and Mainz after the NATO summit gave him an opportunity to explain his strategic themes and deepen personal bonds that would be invaluable in coming months.[27] Chancellor Kohl hosted the president on a Rhine cruise and visit to his home state, which had important local elections in June. Bush's speech in Mainz explained his approach to the end of the Cold War with, as Scowcroft later wrote, "a German accent." The president presented proposals to overcome history's divide, to achieve a "Europe whole and free." Bush embraced the emerging liberties in Eastern Europe. He highlighted NATO's recent decisive steps on reducing arms. Bush recognized the importance of European integration and countering environmental degradation. He supported Gorbachev's glasnost. Indeed, Bush called for glasnost for East Berlin. To face all these challenges, the transatlantic president prodded Germans to become America's "Partner in

Leadership." Some Germans were flattered; others felt cautious about standing out. Either way, the president was preparing German thinking for cooperation on vital issues just over the horizon.[28]

The United States, which a month before looked to Europeans as behind the times, now was in the vanguard, urging its allies to think big. Indeed, in the middle of May, President Bush had given an interview welcoming the idea of German unification. His overture freed Germans to pursue their dream—if circumstances permitted. Scowcroft's memoir relates that some of us had included a reference to unification in the Mainz speech, but he had deleted it. We managed to keep in a phrase about "self-determination for all of Germany and all of Eastern Europe." By the end of the year the word "unification" would be back in play.[29]

Bush Moves East

After President Bush solidified the alliance in May, he was ready to take the competition to Gorbachev's "end zone" in Eastern Europe. Bush was fascinated by the rapid and startling turn of events behind the old Iron Curtain. As vice president, Bush had visited Poland in 1987 and Hungary in 1983. I recall that the president had listed Eastern Europe on a one-page, hand-typed list of priorities that he had given Baker during the transition.

In early 1989, Eastern Europe was in flux. In Poland, in March and April, the roundtable negotiations agreed on parliamentary elections in June. Solidarity won overwhelmingly. But the transition arrangement had reserved seats in the Parliament for the Communists. The government, still nominally headed by General Wojciech Jaruzelski, was in disarray. In Hungary, also in June, a group of reformers in Hungary's ruling Socialist Workers' Party moved toward multiparty, free elections in March 1990. The Hungarian government also started to remove barbed wire on the border with Austria, unintentionally opening up what would become a massive escape valve for East Germans later in the summer of 1989.[30]

Bush was eager to meet the key actors in Poland and Hungary. In Moscow in May, Baker had explained to Shevardnadze that the president planned to visit the two countries in July, before the G-7 economic summit in Paris. Shevardnadze encouraged the trip, saying that more routine contacts between East and West would be constructive. Since that time, however, on the night of June 3–4, right on the heels of the president's successful work at NATO, the Chinese Communist Party had demonstrated—with tanks in Tiananmen Square—the limits of dissent. Gorbachev had refused to denounce the "Chinese solution." Bush was walking a fine line: encouraging the movements toward freedom in Eastern Europe while avoiding actions that might provoke forces that wanted to reverse—or crush—the movements toward democracy and liberation.[31]

The president arrived in Warsaw late on the warm evening of July 9. Early the next morning I went to the state guesthouse where Secretary Baker stayed. As I sat in a small waiting room before meeting Baker, I spied a revealing picture on the wall: a painting of a Polish lancer chasing off a Russian Cossack. That seemed interesting artwork for the official government quarters.

In Poland, Bush interspersed symbolic events with discussions about the country's political process and economic needs. He laid wreaths at the tomb of the unknown soldier and a memorial to Polish Jews in World War II. The president met Jaruzelski and Solidarity leader Lech Walesa. He lunched with Solidarity, Communist, and Catholic figures. And he spoke to the Sejm, the new national assembly. Bush listened, offered support for a historic moment, and, in an understated way, offered practical advice about the transition. The president knew that Poland's economic problems ran deep, and the country's towering debts cast a dark shadow over the restructuring of the economy just ahead. The main role for the president, now as an economic alliance leader, would be to work with the G-7, the IMF, the World Bank, and especially the European Community to organize substantial support for a process that would sustain Poland for years.[32]

The next day the president visited Lech Walesa at his modest home on the fringes of Gdansk, the port city that was Solidarity's birthplace. Then Bush went to speak at the shipyard. This was the president's only large public event in Poland; he did not want settings where crowds could overreact; the White House figured that Walesa and Solidarity could manage its hometown holiday. I recall being stunned by the vast crush of enthusiastic, emotional, and yet orderly people. Thousands lined the street leading to the Solidarity workers' monument in the square. The crowds overflowed everywhere—even climbing towering shipyard cranes festooned with flags. About 250,000 people had shown up. Walesa kept repeating, "Oh my God, oh my God" in English. I could see that even the prudent Bush was bowled over with emotion. Bush spoke of Poland's destiny and dreams, of Polish courage, and of Polish pride. He later modestly wrote that the "crowd would have cheered anything."[33]

On July 11, Bush landed in Budapest. A thunderstorm delayed his landing, and by the time the president arrived in Kossuth Square another huge crowd stood rain-soaked but still spirited. They waited patiently amidst more rain while Hungary's president droned through a fifteen-minute introduction. Bush shook off an umbrella, stepped to the microphone, tore up his speech cards, and said a few words. (Having worked on the lost speech, I at first felt bad that the world would not read his fuller message—but Bush had better understood that moment. As he would say, that was why he was president.) Bush's brief remarks did not rise to the inspiring levels of JFK's rewrite at the Berlin Wall, but the crowd loved the president and all that he stood for. Seeing a wet, elderly woman looking cold near the podium, Bush instinctively took off his raincoat, stepped down, and wrapped the coat around the grandmotherly figure. The crowd roared its approval. As the moment passed, the gentlemanly Bush recalled that the coat belonged to a Secret Service agent; Bush apologized and later gave the man a new coat.[34]

The next day the president met with Communist reformers and opposition figures and gave a thoughtful speech at Karl Marx University. He promised exchanges, trade openings, the Peace Corps, and an enterprise fund to boost the emerging private sector. The Hungarians seemed to have a better grasp than the Poles of the fundamentals of a market economy. (At the evening dinner, I asked a Hungarian professor from Karl Marx University how he had learned about free markets. He replied that he had studied agricultural economics years ago, and his textbooks were from a U.S. land-grant university in the Midwest.)[35]

The president journeyed on to Paris for the economic summit hosted by President Mitterrand. For the two hundredth anniversary of Bastille Day, Mitterrand had organized a grand military parade, including high-speed armored vehicles carrying the names of the nation's momentous victories. As a host with a sense of history, Mitterrand wanted to celebrate France's global reach; he invited leaders from Africa and other former territories, aiming to encourage a new development agenda.

The White House agreed that Bush would attend the parade in exchange for Mitterrand refocusing the G-7 agenda on Eastern Europe. Bush had arrived from Poland and Hungary with his personal observations. The United States and West Germany pressed the transatlantic nations for a constructive response to events in Eastern Europe. The G-7 agreed to ease and reschedule Poland's debt, most of which was owed to European banks. Forty years after the Marshall Plan, the Americans wanted the Western Europeans to pay the costs of reform for Eastern Europe. Baker, a former treasury secretary with a practical eye for combining financial aid with market reforms, recognized that some entity needed to coordinate the two. In exchange for agreement on a conference to connect aid and debt plans with structural economic changes, Baker worked out a plan for a "G-24" organized by the European Commission. This work also led to the creation of a new European Bank for Reconstruction and Development. The roles for Europe won Mitterrand's support. The new process would work closely with the IMF and World Bank on macroeconomic, institutional, and private-sector reforms.

As Brent Scowcroft recalls in his memoir, the U.S. press wanted more presidential leadership and less consultation. I recall thinking that the critics missed the strategic point. The United States wanted the integrated states of Western Europe to assume more responsibility for a "Europe whole and free." Not only would U.S. diplomacy save dollars while achieving American ends, but the EC-led process might naturally open the way for a "wider" European Community (soon to be European Union) including Central and Eastern European states. In addition to helping countries that we hoped would become new democracies, if the Eastern states joined the European Community they would likely become voices for strong U.S.-EC ties. The United States was in fact demonstrating effective alliance and coalition leadership—on security, political, and economic topics—by sharing responsibilities and costs to achieve common ends and build new arrangements.[36]

Before Bush left Paris, he joined Mitterrand at the Élysée Palace for an informal conversation. Bush talked about Eastern Europe. He wanted to hear Mitterrand's views of Gorbachev. The French leader relayed Gorbachev's sense of direction, mounting problems, fears, and fatigue. Bush suggested it might be time for him to meet Gorbachev. Mitterrand encouraged Bush. Even if the Americans and Soviets had not wrapped up arms control deals, they needed to talk. Gorbachev was "nervous," said Mitterrand. The Soviet leader wanted to build a personal relationship with Bush. Mitterrand still expected firm limits from Moscow on Eastern Europe. But just waiting for perestroika to fail would make things worse.

Bush returned to the American embassy in Paris and sat with Baker and Scowcroft out on a garden terrace. The president told his friends that he wanted to meet Gorbachev. The next stop would be a summit in Malta in December amidst stormy seas.[37]

An Alliance Leader

The conventional historical wisdom about President Bush at the end of the Cold War is that the new administration "paused" for much of 1989 as Bush considered what to do. According to these accounts, a prudent Bush hesitated until the opening of the Berlin Wall forced action and the Malta summit triggered a flurry of diplomacy.[38]

As my story shows, the belief in a pause is seriously mistaken. The misunderstanding is important because it obscures insights into Bush's alliance diplomacy. Bush did shift course from Reagan—but not to hit the brakes in East-West diplomacy. Bush decided to solidify alliance ties first before engaging Gorbachev. In particular, the president had to strengthen the alignment with West Germany, especially by overcoming the SNF conflict that he had inherited; in doing so, Bush proposed a U.S.-German partnership that would prove invaluable by the end of 1989.

Bush also needed to unify NATO around his style of consultative—but sometimes bold—leadership. His CFE proposal did so, especially when combined with the deft handling of the SNF dispute.

The president's partnership with Western Europe extended to welcoming the European Community's deeper integration, as long as it would support, and certainly not limit, the expansion of global trade. Bush also recognized that an economically stronger EC would be both a magnet—and source of support—for Eastern Europe.

President Bush used the first part of 1989 to spur on—prudently—the transformation of Eastern Europe. He was competing with Gorbachev—while trying not to threaten him. Bush acquired diplomatic leverage, not to trade but instead to build the momentum of events. He was securing relationships that could be of help in the days soon to come. On the home front, Baker and Larry Eagleburger organized a legislative package authorizing a range of new assistance programs for the Central and Eastern European states. Congress passed this Support for East European Democracy (SEED) Act by November.[39]

The president's jam-packed agenda during his first six months belies the idea of a pause. One also needs to add in important trips to Japan and China and Baker's achievement of an accord on Nicaragua and Central America. Especially considering the time taken to appoint and confirm a new top tier of officials, few new administrations have accomplished so much by July.

When the Iron Curtain cracked open, and the gates through the Berlin Wall swung clear, the president held to his strategy of alliance leadership. He kept his focus on Germany—and on securing a united Germany within NATO and within an integrated European Union. Students of Russia ponder the "Russian Question." Bush was alert to addressing the "German Question" first. The future of a unified, democratic Germany was fundamental to Western, Central, and Eastern Europe—as well as to transatlantic ties. An effective policy toward Russia required U.S.-European alignment. Bush had inherited, and personally embodied, the strategic logic of the American founders of the alliance system of 1947–49.

Some commentators ask whether Bush could have done more to "save" Gorbachev, or whether Bush's emphasis on helping Kohl and Germany with unification as a priority was misguided.[40] In Bush's worldview, the U.S. commitment to its allies—and particularly to West Germany—took precedence over Moscow. Not only had the United States given its word to Germany and other allies over the years, but U.S. interests would be better served by preserving a partnership with its democratic allies in Europe. They would help the United States with the USSR, Eastern Europe, and the world economy. America's European partnership could also be the cornerstone of the free world's architecture in dealing with challenges to come.

The question of whether a U.S. administration should make NATO and Western Europe or the USSR its policy priority was not new. I have related how JFK, over the inclinations of his advisers, came to recognize the vital place West Berlin, West Germany, and NATO held over finding some new condominium with Moscow. Reagan reached out to Gorbachev, but only after first consolidating alliance agreement on the critical East-West issues of the early 1980s. These were realistic—but not quite realpolitik—assessments of U.S. strength premised on both the power of the transatlantic allies and the bonds of free societies.

Bush's belief in the U.S. role in encouraging liberty also shaped his Europe-first strategy. In late 1988 and early 1989, Kissinger and others speculated about high-level, quiet negotiations over a new East-West political-security structure for Europe. After critics suspected a "new Yalta," the trial balloons deflated quickly.[41] Bush wanted a "Europe whole and free," not a rearranged balance of power with two rivals again establishing a cordon sanitaire.

Bush and Baker wanted Gorbachev to succeed, but they were practical men who recognized the challenges of internal political and economic reform. They believed that Gorbachev's success depended principally on the Soviet leader's own choices. They encouraged Gorbachev to embrace a comprehensive restructuring that had a greater likelihood of success, for example, Grigory Yavlinsky's "500 Day Plan." But Gorbachev continually backed away from the economic reforms he would have to make. The tragedy of Gorbachev—as Baker sensed early in evaluating Moscow's "New Thinking" in foreign policy—was that the last leader of the USSR knew what he did not like and had a vague vision of what he would like to achieve, but lacked the content to fill in the space in between.[42]

A New World Order?

On the night of January 13, 1991, on the eve of ordering U.S. and coalition forces into battle in the first Gulf War, George Bush wrote in his diary of his anguish. He had to decide whether to step back "or to move forward . . . [to] help establish a New World Order." His speculation about world order probably stemmed from his conversations with Brent Scowcroft, who likely channeled Kissinger's fascination with the topic.[43]

Bush was uncomfortable with intellectual debates about concepts. He probably thought such disputes were too theoretical—or a way of putting on cerebral airs. The president viewed his role as making decisions—based on consultations, study, experience, instinct, and a sense of duty to his country. He also believed he knew how to lead and draw the best from others—including principally Baker, yet also Scowcroft, Cheney, General Colin Powell, and the teams that aided them.

Nevertheless, Bush, the alliance leader, worked his way toward an American role in a changing world order after the peaceful end of the Cold War. The Bush-Baker diplomacy of the Gulf War coalition offered another example of the president's method of leadership. Bush's ending of the war after the liberation of Kuwait underscored his restrained use of power and resolve to hold to the terms of the coalition mission. Similarly, Baker's drive to convene face-to-face peace talks between Israel and Arabs typified his activist ambition to use the momentum of success and power "to get things done."[44]

Bush's decision to negotiate a North American Free Trade Agreement (NAFTA) with Mexico and Canada added another component to world order. The president viewed NAFTA as both an economic and a foreign policy venture. He wanted to strengthen the United States and its neighbors economically and, in doing so, deepen the political partnership on the continent. A more competitive United States, working within a larger North America, would also have greater global influence.

Just as the president had urged European Commission president Delors to fit EC92 integration within a more open global economy, Bush wanted to link NAFTA to the Uruguay Round of GATT. The United States used the prospect of NAFTA to urge economies around the globe, and especially the EC, to close the GATT deal. Bush was practicing a competition in trade liberalization. In the waning months of his administration, Bush's trade and agricultural negotiators reached agreement with the EC on the knotty issues of farm subsidies and access. President Clinton picked up on the Bush administration's work, reached terms with 116 other economies in 1994, and agreed on a new World Trade Organization (WTO).

Baker had helped launch the Asia-Pacific Economic Cooperation group in 1989. As treasury secretary, he had recognized the importance of the fast-growing Asia-Pacific region. He had experimented with economic coordination in the G-7 and pondered the idea of a group of Asia-Pacific finance ministers. As the Cold War drew to a close, Baker sought to build an economic network of trade and investment across the Pacific that would complement the U.S. bilateral security alliances. He aimed to promote transpacific ties while turning American eyes toward the economic and political potential of East Asia. Subsequently, President Clinton promoted the meetings of ministers into a summit of leaders.

Bush and Baker assembled, piece by piece, a new post–Cold War architecture for U.S. political, economic, and security ties. A more integrated North America would have multiple connections with Europe, East Asia, and the Persian Gulf. Working from this geopolitical and economic foundation, the United States would seek to deepen engagements with Russia, China, India, Latin America, and, someday, Africa. The United States would work with the UN system, regional organizations, and multilateral economic institutions to preserve basic security, expand opportunity, and share responsibilities and costs. The president used international groups and institutions to extend America's power, not to cede it. Bush had in mind a world order with the United States as a nucleus of intersecting networks—not a hierarchical, unipolar, or balance of power system. Under Bush's style of leadership, the United States would be consultative and careful—and also active and agile.

The brief U.S. economic recession of 1990–91 collapsed Bush's support at home. He lost backing in his own party after breaking his 1988 pledge not to raise taxes; he had done so to reach a budget deal that disciplined spending and contributed to a united U.S. posture leading up to the Gulf War.

In mid-August 1992, Baker returned to the White House as chief of staff, and I followed as deputy chief. We discovered that messages recalling Bush's foreign policy success were counterproductive; people complained that if the president could lead around the world, why wouldn't he take care of them at home? I prepared a second-term economic plan for the president, the "Agenda for American Renewal," which combined programs to help citizens adjust to change with negotiations to open markets for Americans abroad. The aim was to connect Bush's believable international leadership with a complementary proposal to help Americans adapt to disruptions.[45]

I am not sure that Bush ever internalized the message. We did not have much time. And after forty years of Cold War, twelve years of Republican presidents, and the worries of the recession, American voters wanted change.

American diplomacy would change, too. But Bush's successors struggled to offer steady, successful direction.

———◆———

CHAPTER 18

Five Traditions of American Diplomacy

Searching for Doctrines

On August 18, 1993, Tony Lake, President Clinton's national security adviser, assembled a small group in his West Wing office to brainstorm about a problem. Clinton's foreign policy was off to a rocky start, and Lake sought an overarching term that could offer guidance after the end of the Cold War. He launched what became known as the "Kennan Sweepstakes," the search for a successor to the doctrine of containment. Jeremy Rosner, working closely with Lake, began drafting a "grand strategy" paper to encompass the concept of "enlargement." On September 21, Lake tried out the idea in a speech at Johns Hopkins School of Advanced International Studies titled "From Containment to Enlargement." The new U.S. strategy, explained Lake, was to enlarge "the world's free community of market democracies"; the president embraced "democratic enlargement" a week later in his address to the UN General Assembly. The phrase never seemed to win acceptance. In Clinton's second term, he added the idea that America is "the indispensable nation."[1]

After the attacks of September 11, 2001, President George W. Bush declared a "Global War on Terror," which he complemented in his second term with a "Freedom Agenda." President Barack Obama, reflecting a mood of retrenchment, turned to "don't do stupid stuff" and a reliance on the "arc of history." President Donald Trump revived "America First." Scholars took up the post–Cold War challenge by launching new studies of "grand strategies."[2] They debated concepts such as hegemony, primacy, offshore balancing, realism (including classical, neo, and democratic variants), liberal internationalism, multilateralism, and many others.

My stories suggest that a different approach to American diplomacy may be more useful. The concepts from international relations and doctrines help frame debates, but they do not offer policy makers guidance about what to do. The pragmatic practitioners of American diplomacy have had to solve problems in the context of their times. They considered strategic reference points—about geography, economics, power, and politics—but prized flexibility, adaptability, and trying what might work. Indeed, doctrinal labels—such as neutrality, no entangling alliances, the domino theory, and even containment—at times became constraining, or at least misleading, instead of useful. Moreover, as Secretary Baker reflected in his memoir, "Almost every achievement contains within its success the seeds of a future problem."[3] The guiding doctrine from one era may impede creative thinking about what to do next.

Based on the American experience, I have identified five traditions to consider in shaping strategies. Taken together, they offer a framework for thinking about America's role in the world.

The North American Base

Geopolitical strategists, even those who are American, are preoccupied with Eurasia; their discussions of heartlands and rimlands concentrate on Europe and East Asia. More recently, strategists have debated access points to Eurasia through the Middle East, the Persian Gulf, and South and Southeast Asia. They consider the rising role of India. The prospect of China's Belt and Road project captures their attention because it may reopen Eurasia's internal land route and increase Chinese influence.

Geopolitical thinkers treat North America as one region on the distant periphery of Eurasia. In similar fashion, strategists view South America and Africa as sources of resources and, increasingly for Africa, as a driver of population growth and migration.

The American diplomatic tradition, in contrast, begins with North America. The United States battled and bargained with the British, French, Spanish, and Russian empires, as well as with indigenous peoples, to dominate its home continent. In later years, the United States competed with Canada and Mexico for territory. And the United States wanted to make the Caribbean basin into an American sea.

Such domination was not foreordained. No other state achieved hegemony in Europe, East and Central Asia, the Middle East, or South America. Nor were the territorial boundaries of the United States set by geographical barriers. For example, after the U.S.-Mexican War of 1846–48, President James Polk wanted to acquire more lands in northern Mexico and Baja California. His negotiator in Mexico City, Nicholas Trist, ignored the president's recall in order to conclude a treaty that Trist believed would permit the United States to limit Mexico's humiliation and thereby restore relations over time. Similarly—for a brief moment—the people of British Columbia, with Seward's encouragement, considered joining the United States and connecting the northwestern states with Alaska.[4]

By the opening of the twentieth century, U.S. territorial borders appeared settled, but not relations with neighbors. The Mexican Revolution demonstrated that weak neighbors, not just strong ones, could pose security dangers. The United States veered toward a second war with Mexico in 1916. Germany's offer to Mexico in 1917 to cooperate in conquering the U.S. Southwest showed that Europeans could still threaten the U.S. homeland.

Over the decades that followed, Americans turned their attentions further afield. Yet FDR intended his Good Neighbor Policy to help secure the southern flank of the United States against Nazi adventures. Cordell Hull and Will Clayton employed trade and commodity purchases to ward off German influence in South America.

During the Cold War, the prospect of Soviet missiles in Cuba precipitated America's most dangerous nuclear showdown. Cuba supported Communist insurgencies in Central and South America. Today, the crisis of the authoritarian regime in Venezuela, backed by Cuba, threatens security across the Caribbean basin.

States around the Caribbean have faced transnational threats—especially organized crime and drug trafficking. Criminal groups connect with transnational terrorist causes. The Clinton and George W. Bush administrations worked closely with Congress over many years to support Plan Colombia, helping to save Colombian democracy. One of the United States' major foreign policy challenges today—a wave of immigrants and asylum seekers from Guatemala, Honduras, and El Salvador—stems from violence, crime and corruption, weak governments, and economic fragility in the small states of Central America.

The Bush administration negotiated NAFTA in 1991–92 because it recognized that Mexico faced a historic political and economic transformation. The ruling PRI party, in power for decades, had created a corporatist state during the twentieth century. The institutions of Mexican society—unions, the media, businesses, universities, schools, the courts and police, the military—fit within a hierarchy controlled by the PRI, and ultimately by the president of Mexico. But in the 1980s, that old political structure began to break down, raising the question of the future of Mexico. Corruption and organized networks of violence and crime permeated the old order and were poised to infect any new one.

President Carlos Salinas understood that Mexico had to compete in a changing global economy, yet investors looked instead to the new market economies of Central and Eastern Europe. Mexico was left to stumble through debt crises, with falling oil production and prices.

NAFTA was always more than a trade agreement. It offered a framework within which the United States and Canada could support Mexico's democratization, opening of civil society, and economic growth. The Bush administration envisaged NAFTA as the cornerstone for deeper cooperation across many issues—immigration and workforce, the environment, and economic and foreign policies. Just as Seward had foreseen in the nineteenth century, the "gravity" of the United States could draw a Mexico in transition closer to U.S. democracy, institutions, and civil society.

The potential trading ties of North America might help all three partners. Many years before, Cordell Hull had recognized that Canada was the United States' most important trading association; his deals with Canada were at the heart of his plans for reviving the global trading system. In 1988, the United States and Canada completed a comprehensive, modern FTA. A reforming Mexico could make the twosome into a continental economy. As Mexico's income rose, Mexicans would both buy and supply more to the United States and Canada. All three economies, with deeper integration, would be stronger competitors globally.

For reasons of history, the United States, Canada, and Mexico are each highly protective of their independence and sovereignty. Therefore, NAFTA created a model of economic integration that respected national sensitivities. The NAFTA approach contrasted with the European Union's plan for "shared sovereignty."

I saw the resulting changes in behavior firsthand. Canadians and Americans had been security allies throughout the twentieth century, but deeper economic integration through the U.S.-Canada FTA and then NAFTA drew the societies even closer. Through the 1980s, Mexican foreign policy had often highlighted its national independence by opposing U.S. positions; by the time I became U.S. trade representative in 2001, my closest partners on global trade issues were my Canadian and Mexican colleagues. Cooperation on other international economic policies, foreign policies, intelligence, and environmental topics deepened enormously.

In the twenty-first century, the United States should view North America as its continental base. A stronger base will help the United States to extend its power globally. Our vision should be of three democracies of 500 million people; an integrated infrastructure that fosters interconnected and highly competitive manufacturing, agriculture, services, resource development, technology, and innovation; a shared, more skilled and educated workforce (while respecting different citizenships) that prospers through investment in human capital; energy self-sufficiency and even exports; a common natural bounty of air, water, lands, biodiversity, wildlife and migratory species; partnerships on international economic and foreign policies; close security cooperation on regional threats of all kinds; and closer links when dealing with the rest of the world, focusing first on challenges in our own hemisphere.

A North American power with those attributes and size compares well with China and India. Mexico and Canada should be natural partners when facing the regional topics of today—such as instability in Central America and Venezuela, immigration, natural disasters, climate change, and the Arctic.

Over two hundred years, the nature of U.S. priorities for North America has changed, but North America will remain our immediate neighborhood. U.S. global diplomacy depends on having a healthy and friendly neighborhood.

Trade, Transnationalism, and Technology

From the earliest days of independence, Americans viewed trade as an expression of liberty. The Founders thought that new rules for trade could create a changed international system; they did not see trade solely as an economic efficiency. After all, the American Revolution arose out of protests against London's controls and taxes on trade. London and other centers of empire had extended trade through conquest and maintained domination through imperial monopolies. Americans wanted to end Europe's attempts to possess their wealth through exclusive arrangements.[5]

In 1776, Congress ranked trade at the top of its agenda. John Adams took charge of drafting the "Treaty Plan of 1776," a template for commercial agreements. Adams's model attacked mercantilism. His key principle was "national treatment," an even more audacious demand than recognition as a most favored nation (MFN). With national treatment, "U.S. merchants and ships [if not goods] would receive the same standing in foreign countries as their own domestic merchants and ships."[6] In 1778, Franklin employed the model agreement in the negotiation with France, establishing one of the United States' first two treaties.

The Americans moved with the vanguard of new thinking about political economy. They were influenced by Adam Smith's *The Wealth of Nations*, published in 1776. Smith argued that all parties would gain from trade; commerce was not a zero-sum transaction. Ben Franklin stated in 1781 that "I find myself rather inclined to adopt that modern [opinion], which supposes it is best for every Country to leave its Trade entirely free from Encumbrances." Thomas Jefferson wrote, "I think all the world would gain by setting commerce at perfect liberty"; he maintained that trade restrictions served private, not public, interests.[7]

Smith's theory of free trade acknowledged exceptions for reasons of

national defense and, in specific circumstances, to retaliate to achieve reciprocal treatment. As a practical matter, the United States required customs
duties to raise revenue; the Americans sought primarily to eliminate colonial preferences and discrimination.

The Americans also aimed at a bigger target: They wanted to change the
international political and economic order. In 1785, John Adams stated this
motivation explicitly in a letter to John Jay, the secretary for foreign affairs
for the Confederation Congress. Adams declared he wanted "a *Reformation*, a Kind of *Protestantism*, in the Commercial System of the World."[8] The
American plan would supplant imperial mercantilism with the freedom of
independent states to trade as they chose.

During 1785, Adams and Jefferson were in the midst of a two-year assignment to negotiate the new U.S.-style trade treaties. But under the Articles
of Confederation, they had no leverage to negotiate. James Madison wrote
years later that the need to regulate foreign commerce became a primary and
powerful impulse to draft the Constitution.[9]

Once the new Constitution was ratified, Hamilton used the regulation of
trade and customs revenues to breathe life into his new economic system.
Contrary to claims of later apologists for protectionism, Hamilton disliked
high, protective tariffs. He favored bounties (subsidies) to spur new manufacturing industries, or modest additional tariffs only for a limited time.[10]

The Founders expected that trade would be the new nation's principal
foreign policy.[11] America encouraged transnational ties, and private parties' participation, from the start. A fair trading system required contracts,
respect for private property, letters of credit, and the rule of law. Individual
rights edged into human rights.

Jefferson mistakenly believed that he could translate America's trade
power into a weapon of foreign policy. In 1807–09, frustrated by British and
French seizures of U.S. ships and sailors during the Napoleonic Wars, he
embargoed all U.S. maritime exports. The policy hurt America much more
than the Europeans. Over two centuries, Americans continued to experiment with sanctions—of trade and, more recently, of finance—to weaken
adversaries or at least signal displeasure short of going to war.[12]

America's interest in trade encouraged the development of the navy. The
attacks of the Barbary pirates on U.S. merchant ships in the Mediterranean
prompted Presidents Washington and Adams to commission six heavy
frigates; Jefferson deployed them in the Mediterranean instead of paying
tribute.[13] The navy, in turn, assisted in opening new markets, most notably
Japan. Dreams of a potentially vast trade with China drew American merchants and then a host of other transnational actors: missionaries; educators; doctors and nurses; soldiers of fortune; engineers, miners, and railway

builders; and adventurers of all types. Hay's Open Door was as American in concept as Adams's Treaty Plan of 1776.

Wilson based his defense of neutrality in World War I on America's right to trade. After the war, American officials recognized the interconnections among Germany's reparations, foreign debts to the United States, and debtors' abilities to earn dollars by exporting to the United States. But domestic politics blocked the development of a comprehensive package solution. Charles Dawes and Owen Young patched together debt and reparations rescheduling as a stopgap.[14] The protectionism of the Great Depression paralyzed recovery and created support for the autarkic economics of national socialism in Europe and Japan's Great East Asia Co-Prosperity Sphere. Americans had to relearn hard lessons about the connections of economics and security.

Hull's trade agreements, backed (tentatively) by Congress, began the long process of reviving the international trading system. The core principles in Hull's agreements—nondiscrimination, unconditional MFN, and shifting from quantitative barriers to tariffs—became the basis for the GATT and, later, the WTO.

After World War II, Clayton drew lessons from the economic failures of the interwar decades—and incorporated Hull's principles—to create an international economic system of recovery, growth, and development. The economic designs of Marshall, Clayton, and Acheson complemented the new U.S. alliance order.

In East Asia, the post–World War II open trading system enabled Japan to pursue the path to economic strength and democratic stability that it had considered, but abandoned, in the 1920s. South Korea, Taiwan, and economies in Southeast Asia followed similar courses of export-led growth.

America's reliance on private initiative and independent experimentation created an encouraging environment for technological innovation. Vannevar Bush applied a lesson from America's technological advantage in World War II to the postwar era: He urged an ongoing federal government investment in basic science—in cooperation with universities and business—to explore an endless frontier of science and technology. His Triple Helix model relied on the innovation of America's private sectors. America's scientific culture and transnational system proved far superior to the Soviet Union's closed model of national planning.

At various junctures, often amidst shocks, the United States forced adaptations of the system of international trade, finance, and technology. After World War II, the U.S. dollar served as the principal reserve currency. In the 1970s, the United States abandoned the Bretton Woods system of fixed exchange rates, launching in its stead a floating (and sometimes pegged) exchange rate system. The rise of OPEC in the 1970s compelled the United States to experiment with approaches to energy security. More recently, technological, market, and environmental innovations have again transformed energy and environmental politics.

The United States adapted the economic system, often fitfully, to assist with development. The United States and other developed nations offered trade preferences to developing economies. Banks in the United States and other international financial centers channeled petrodollars from oil-producing states to developing countries, whose large borrowings led to debt and exchange rate crises. The U.S. Treasury and other finance ministries turned to the public multilateral financial institutions—especially the IMF and World Bank—for help in managing these economic breakdowns.

Over decades, Washington led in devising new rules for trade, investment, and technology. The old trade in manufactured goods expanded to agriculture, services, intellectual property protections, investment, and dispute settlement. Using bilateral FTAs and regional agreements, the United States demonstrated the usefulness of new rules on anticorruption, transparency, border procedures, information technology standards, the environment, and core labor standards. Today the international economy has to devise rules for the use, privacy, security, storage, and transfer of data.

As the U.S. economy struggled to adapt to changes in international trade and the economy, public and then congressional support for openness waned. Exchange rate gyrations and manipulations caused pain for workers in many industries. Some developing countries became powerful competitive threats. Americans complained of a lack of reciprocity. U.S. programs to help people adapt to change have fallen far short.

The United States is in the midst of reassessing the country's global connectivity. Historically, America's openness—to goods, capital, people, and ideas—has given the United States an advantage. Competition compelled the United States to recognize its mistakes and fix them. Yet there are periods when the pace of change or other fears have led the United States to pull back.

Today, the forces of globalization and fragmentation pull in different directions, creating political tension. Challenges of security, technology, disease, migration, the environment, and financial and information flows are likely to increase, not decrease. At the same time, people demand reassurance. The U.S. Triple Helix and entrepreneurial model of science and technology faces a challenge from China's state-directed system. Americans will need to decide again what type of international trade, technology, and economic system they want. The spirit of 1776 looked to liberty, reformation, innovation, and opportunity. So did the flexible design of the past seventy years. A breakdown or repudiation of the inherited system of economics and security will prove costly and dangerous.

Alliances and Order

For 150 years, the United States associated alliance politics with Europe's empires, mercantilism, and wars. The new American nation valued independence—and the freedom to explore modern ways to reorder ties among states and peoples. America's strong sense of sovereignty precluded committing to the security of others, especially for any extended period of time.

In 1947–49, the United States shifted sharply. It became the leader of an alliance network that overshadowed all prior alliances. In doing so, the United States rewrote the meaning of alliances, and it has continually adapted the concept through practical applications.

With Europe and Canada, the United States built a regional political-security alliance, supported by an organization, NATO, and even an integrated military command. The U.S. security guarantee included a willingness to back military defense with nuclear deterrence. The United States sponsored other regional alliances—SEATO and CENTO—but without the political and military mutuality of NATO.

In the Asia-Pacific, U.S. alliance policy took the form of spokes in a wheel—a set of bilateral defense commitments between Washington and partners in East Asia without obligation by the Asian counterpart to come to America's defense. The United States used its treaties with South Korea, Taiwan, and Japan to constrain as well as defend. After recognizing the People's Republic of China in 1978 (as of January 1, 1979), the United States terminated its alliance with Taiwan, but Congress substituted defense commitments through the Taiwan Relations Act. With Australia and New Zealand, the United States established mutual security ties.

In the Western Hemisphere, the Rio Treaty of 1947, which provided the precedent for the North Atlantic Alliance, evolved into a loose understanding without a security organization.

The United States created a range of implied security commitments, primarily in the Middle East and Persian Gulf. For example, Israel retains full freedom to defend itself as it sees fit, although it expects that the United States will protect its existence. Various Arab states host U.S. bases, work with American forces, share intelligence, and look to U.S. protection.

During the Cold War, these alliances and partnerships gave the United States points of access around the perimeter of Eurasia. After the Cold War, the United States looked to many of its allies as associates in a democratic zone of peace. The United States enlarged NATO to include the new democracies of Central and Eastern Europe. It asked its allies for support—and even troops—as part of coalitions fighting post–Cold War threats. After the attacks of 9/11, NATO allies and other partners joined U.S. forces fighting in Afghanistan. Military interoperability, training, planning, use of intelligence, and shared logistics became valuable assets for U.S. forces. Allies and partners offered the United States valuable bases and ports for America's global positioning.

Almost all these allies and partners participated in the international market economy that the United States helped build, finance, and expand. The U.S. economy presented a magnetic pull, as Hamilton and later Seward had hoped it would many years before. The United States drew closer to its partners through a complex web of economic interconnections. America and its allies shared an interest in preserving that system—including its assurances about sources of energy, maritime and air routes, and security.

Thirty years after the end of the Cold War, changing perspectives and assumptions buffer the U.S.-led alliance network. Economic competition strains cooperation, although that problem is not new. Allies face changing threats, such as cyberattacks, and varying perceptions of dangers. Internal politics make it harder for some capitals to accept U.S. leadership—and demands. Absent recognition of a blunt threat to U.S. interests, Americans may balk at protecting countries with different political systems or uneven records of friendship and reliability. Washington wants its allies to share burdens more evenly. This tension is also not new: The Nixon Doctrine of fifty years ago called on allies to step up to regional security responsibilities.

The United States must determine its commitment to this alliance system in the future. Without American attention and encouragement, the processes and habits of alliance consultation, compromise, and cooperation will unravel. The U.S.-led system has relied on an extraordinary feature: trust. The United States could press difficult demands and quarrel with its partners, but other countries ultimately relied on a blend of U.S. goodwill and self-interest.

If the United States abandons its own alliance order, America will remain a potent security and economic force. But its political role—and the nature of its influence—will change tremendously. The world order would look more like the Great Power competition of 1900. The United States, China, and India would likely participate as the principal, big nation-states, wielding economic, military, and political influence. The European Union would weigh in with economic power, and perhaps political standing, yet today's European militaries have limited scope, and weak political integration keeps the EU from forging a strategic perspective. Britain's post-Brexit power is a question mark. Russia, by reason of geography, cyber, energy, and military capacity, would be a factor. Japan could have influence; its future strategy depends greatly on its relations with the United States—and China.

Such a multipolar system could seek security stability through balancing coalitions. Economic and other relations would likely look more transactional and be less reliant on agreed rules. Medium- and smaller-sized nations would probably be pulled closer to larger powers' spheres of influence. Those powers might insist on economic arrangements that primarily serve the interests of the regional hegemon.

Without its alliance network, the United States might return to the types of international arrangements it promoted during America's first 150 years. Ties of trade, finance, and technological innovation would loom large. A strong North American base, free of dangers, would be important. The United States might seek partnerships among republics. U.S. leaders with the right skills, like Teddy Roosevelt's, might play mediating roles in other regions. Nixon's and Kissinger's methods of realpolitik might have a revival in the hands of a deft president.

Adapting to a new international order without the U.S. alliance network would pose major challenges for American diplomacy; no president and Congress should abandon the system out of ignorance. Americans need to understand the historical importance of—and reasons for—their alliance and economic network.

The wisest course would be for the United States to adapt and update the alliance order. The United States modified its alliances—and the roles of international economic institutions and trading systems—after the end of the Cold War. America might prune security commitments; it should not make promises it cannot or will not keep.

The principal U.S. allies in Europe and the Asia-Pacific could complement U.S. diplomacy, especially if Washington remembers the skills of alliance leadership demonstrated by George H. W. Bush. The United States should, over time, add to its weight through a new North American partnership and alliance. Washington could draw upon examples I have outlined to build new networks of influence—short of alliances—with India and partners in Asia, Latin America, and Africa. The United States should stress economic and technological linkages, ties among republics, regional security arrangements with associated arms limits, legal bodies to help resolve disputes, and timely mediation. An older European-style realism—or even realpolitik—fits uneasily within the traditions of American statecraft. But a pragmatic American realism—drawing on both the republican and power principles of John Quincy Adams, updated to meet today's circumstances—would offer an attractive contribution to the future world order.

Public and Congressional Support

U.S. diplomacy depends on the court of public opinion, not on court politics or the plans of strategists. The most successful American statesmen could read—and shape—the public will.

Franklin maintained political allies in the Continental Congress to strengthen his effectiveness in France. He emphasized his republican bona fides to retain the confidence of his political audience at home, and he used republican ideas to win over Enlightenment audiences in Europe. Franklin also relied on his practical feel for power politics to gain France's financial and military aid and to strike an excellent deal for independence.

Hamilton won critical votes in Congress to establish the economic foundations for the new United States. But public sentiment blocked his rapprochement with Britain.

Jefferson both used and deflected public feeling to purchase Louisiana. Napoleon's representatives judged that the British or Americans might seize New Orleans, and congressional acts to raise troops caught Napoleon's eye. To gain time to negotiate a continent's worth of real estate, Jefferson sent Monroe, a man trusted by Westerners, to Paris.

Madison, Jefferson's protégé, moved with public opinion toward war instead of a peaceful settlement. His declaration of war in 1812 stressed Britain's violations of neutral rights and maritime offenses. But Madison's backers were "War Hawks" in the west and south who wanted to destroy Native Americans on the frontier and to seize Canada. "Mr. Madison's war" was handicapped by the lack of political support in New England and New York, poor military preparation, and weak finances. The charter of Hamilton's national bank had expired, and Congress had shelved Hamilton's plans to organize an effective army. The United States eked out a draw—and a peace treaty that restored the prewar status quo. Americans believed they were destined to rule the continent, but their means were not aligned with their aspirations.

John Quincy Adams struggled to understand the politics of the expanding democratic franchise in the United States. Unlike his political foe, General Andrew Jackson, Adams did not have the common touch. Nor could Adams count congressional votes like his onetime adversary and eventual colleague, Henry Clay. Nevertheless, Adams's diplomatic commitment to independent U.S. action matched his countrymen's attitudes. He understood a public mood that wanted to keep European politics out of North—and even South—America, while preserving the freedom of the United States to expand. He waved the flag of republican pride. At the same time, Adams wanted Americans to steer clear of Europe's conflicts—to avoid temptations to take on threats beyond U.S. horizons. Adams's appeal took hold of Americans' minds. They combined his idea about protecting the distinctive hemisphere with their expansionist drive; his cautions about Europe planted an aversion to U.S. involvement with Europe's security.

President Polk's bold plans for continental expansion clashed with mounting northern fears about adding slave states. Both John Quincy Adams and a new congressman from Illinois, Abraham Lincoln, opposed the U.S.-Mexican War of 1846–48.

In the *Trent* affair, Lincoln and Seward navigated around war with Britain and public outrage. They chose a pragmatic course of one war at a time and devised a public explanation that drew from early American principles about maritime rights. Seward used diplomatic messages and the press to state his case. He recognized that with time, initial popular calls for action can lose fervor. The shrewd statesman needs not only a sense of timing on when to act internationally but a feel for the right moment to ask for support at home.

Lincoln and Seward learned that the United States could shape foreign public opinion. They started to include international public diplomacy in their calculations. They appreciated the changing democratic politics and antislavery attitude in Britain.

John Hay crafted his Open Door initiative with British help, but he insisted on an American stamp of ownership. He recognized that U.S. opinion can be influenced by national, ethnic, or religious connections overseas.

Even as Teddy Roosevelt mediated conflicts in Asia and Europe, he kept an eye on public biases and congressional wariness about U.S. involvement. Anti-Japanese and anti-Chinese hostility and violence embarrassed him; Russian pogroms offended him. He conducted his Moroccan mediation behind the scenes to avoid Senate critics. Yet Roosevelt would never simply acquiesce to public constraints; he fought to educate: TR viewed the Great White Fleet as a call to greatness for Americans.

Woodrow Wilson exhibited sensitivity to public opinion. For three stressful years, he worked to reconcile long-held American beliefs that collided with one another: He had to stay out of Europe's war while defending the rights of neutrals at sea. Wilson's popularity in the election of 1916 depended on keeping the country out of war; he had to fight one of the major political battles of his life in order to prepare the United States for the possibility of war.

When Wilson finally determined on war, he rallied his cause around America's diplomatic traditions. He redefined neutrality as an agenda to rewrite the rules of international politics. He said that he was applying the ideas of the Monroe Doctrine to the world. Wilson still rejected old-style alliances, but he pledged to create a new type of collective security. At first, Wilson's vision was wildly popular, at home and abroad.

Wilson's hopes could not withstand traditional security imperatives abroad and the Senate's strong sense of its constitutional prerogatives. Wilson could probably have won Senate ratification of the Versailles Treaty and the League of Nations. He should have included senators in his delegation—as Charles Evans Hughes did a few years later—or at least added people who could influence his Republican opponents.

Root's reservations offered Wilson a path to ratify the treaty and participate in the League. Wilson chose instead to take his case to the American public, as he had done successfully before. This time, Wilson stumbled—and failed. On the last, critical vote, Wilson blocked passage by urging Democrats to reject the compromise reservations.

When Hughes became secretary of state in 1921, he recognized that he had to reestablish the executive branch's leadership in foreign policy. The Senate, having frustrated a president, wanted to control future policy. Hughes drew upon a public movement for naval disarmament to reset the agenda. He devised a strategy that combined the public's interest with a national interest in negotiating security arrangements in East Asia. To strengthen the likelihood of success—including the Senate ratification of treaties—Hughes allied with key senators of both parties. He understood the terms he needed to win Senate votes.

Hughes's close colleague, Root, also understood how to combine longer-term visions with near-term political needs. Root and Hughes were artful negotiators, working simultaneously with domestic and international audiences. Root believed legal systems—the development of both rules and peaceful means to resolve disputes—developed incrementally. He had a sense of direction—and patience. Root understood how modest achievements could build experience and confidence while broadening public support. He did not let the perfect become the enemy of the good. But public and especially Senate sensitivities about U.S. sovereignty limited the country's commitment to international legal restrictions—as it has to this day.

Hull used his standing in FDR's Democratic Party coalition as well as his congressional ties to best administration rivals who advocated barter and managed trade. The secretary won congressional authority to launch negotiations that both lowered barriers to trade and established principles that would underpin a more open trading system. But Hull and his allies had to fend off—or conciliate—protectionist interests. Congress's constitutional authority over trade and its constituent economic interests have always pulled U.S. policy away from free trade. Votes in later years extending the executive branch's negotiating authority required a strong political push. American trade negotiators must mobilize the support of exporters and avoid a coalescence of protectionist factions. At times, leaders like Marshall and Clayton have successfully explained how trade contributes to much larger economic, financial, and security goals for America.

Franklin Roosevelt faced the enormous political task of preparing Depression America for a second World War. Public disappointment with the results of World War I created a resistance to involvement. In 1937, FDR's Quarantine Speech tried to prod Americans to consider ways to work with peace-minded countries to oppose aggressors and "bandit countries." But when Roosevelt could not explain what he had in mind, the public feared the United States would be pulled randomly into overseas disasters. FDR retreated to a more familiar combination of neutrality declarations, supplies and credits to friends, and economic sanctions against foes. The Japanese attack on Pearl Harbor, and the foolish German decision to declare war against the United States, forced the United States' hand.[15]

After victory in battle, Truman, Marshall, Acheson, Clayton, and Lovett had to mobilize support for the new alliance order of 1947–49. The Truman administration counted on the leadership and skill of Senator Vandenberg. Vandenberg saw his challenge as assembling congressional coalitions—especially with the support of his Republican colleagues. Over the course of the forty-year Cold War, Vandenberg's example inspired a small number of successors from both parties. The United States is not likely to sustain a successful foreign policy without such members of Congress, working in league with executive branch officials such as Root, Hughes, and Baker, who knew how to assemble congressional coalitions.

Eisenhower worried that the American public would not maintain the high political and emotional tempo of the early Cold War. He returned to Hamilton's principle about the importance of national economic strength. Eisenhower conducted a planning exercise, the "Solarium" project, that tried to establish priorities. He organized a national security process to systematize responses to the inevitable intrusion of unexpected events.

Kennedy thought Eisenhower's approach had made Americans too complacent; he sought to inspire his countrymen to assume greater challenges. When Kennedy faced crises in Berlin and Cuba, he carefully mobilized the country to back his positions. As JFK grew uncomfortable with risks of nuclear disaster, he started to speak to the nation about controlling these doomsday weapons, beginning with limits on testing.

Johnson lost his presidency because he was afraid the public would reject him if he abandoned the war against Communists in Vietnam. LBJ could never face the challenge of explaining to Americans that the country would be wiser to retreat, even to accept defeat. Instead, he escalated and hoped for a negotiated peace.

Nixon and Kissinger had the miserable task of extricating America from a bloody, costly, and ultimately failed venture. Nixon worried that the experience would lead Americans to withdraw from responsibilities around the world. He and Kissinger substituted a realpolitik policy of maneuver and balance, which they hoped would both reposition a wounded nation to counter its foes and educate Americans about the necessities of unadorned power politics.

Americans admired the achievements of Nixon and Kissinger; they respected their diplomatic skills. But Congress, which had already turned on LBJ, lost trust. The public grew uncomfortable with realpolitik; some objected to the disconnect from America's values, others rejected détente's accommodations with the Soviets, and many did not like the idea that the United States was just one of a number of countries in a multipolar world. Nixon and Kissinger struggled unsuccessfully to build public support for their diplomatic strategy.

Jimmy Carter tried to recast U.S. foreign policy with doses of human rights, and he struggled to adjust to a flurry of upheavals around the world. Circumstances contributed to an image of weakness. Stagflation and an energy crisis added to the nation's sense of gloom.

Reagan told Americans that they could rise above the difficulties of the present. He flattered the public by recalling a courageous past and promising a better future. He believed that he could combine economic recovery with military revitalization. With a new foundation, Reagan raised the flags of freedom and democracy in an ideological contest with the Soviet Union. At the same time, Reagan steered away from direct military confrontation with the USSR. He understood the incalculable risks of military conflicts and stated repeatedly that no country could win a nuclear war.

George H. W. Bush used America's sense of revival, and its multiple strengths, to lead the North Atlantic Alliance in the closing act of the Cold War in Europe. He organized an unprecedented coalition, authorized by the UN Security Council, to reverse the first major aggression after the end of the Cold War. He started to build a post–Cold War architecture for U.S. leadership. His countrymen admired Bush's foreign policy skill. But they wanted his attention directed toward domestic priorities, especially during an economic recession. And they turned Bush out of office.

Without the perils of World War II and then the Cold War, the United States would never have stepped forward to lead the world, especially by deploying military power around the globe. The devastation of Europe and Asia propelled America to financial and manufacturing dominance. At the same time, confronting fascism and then Communism sharpened America's standing as the leader of a free world.

After the end of the Cold War, observers wondered whether the United States would continue to lead. In fact, the American-led alliance order started to adapt to a wider range of challenges. September 11, 2001 shocked Americans. But long, unsatisfactory, and costly wars—combined with a painful financial and economic crisis—prompted many Americans to pull back.

The United States remains at the heart of the alliance and economic networks it created. Those alliances and networks are wearing thin. They will continue to operate, even in diminished form, out of a combination of self-interest and institutional momentum. Americans today are more likely than those living before World War II to recognize their global interconnectedness. Many are proud of their country and believe it should continue to play a positive role. The shape of America's future international engagement will depend on political leadership—and events.

America's Purpose

From the beginning, Americans imagined that the country came into being to serve a larger purpose. The story of national origin contributed to this sense of a providential cause. Like the biblical story of Moses and the Israelites that early Americans knew well, the settlers undertook hazardous journeys to a new land. Those who followed believed they were building a New World.

The thirteen American colonies expanded a heritage of representative government into a cause of liberty and independence. By the late eighteenth century, Americans saw themselves as the practical practitioners of the Enlightenment. After the Revolution and independence, the citizens of the United States understood that they were participating in an experiment of self-government.

The American purpose reached further than expanding the country's territory, population, and economic strength: The nation was supposed to stand for ideas—put into practice by men and women. As the country's power grew, and the people's ideas changed, so did America's purposes.

At first, the new republic simply had to survive in a world of empires. Monarchies feared that America's revolutionary beliefs in liberty and self-government would threaten the divine order of kings. Early American transnationalism made individuals—not just states—into agents of change. As revolutionary republicanism caught fire in France and leapt to colonies in Latin America, the flames threatened to ignite factionalism within the United States.

With difficulty, the first leaders of the United States fashioned a practical compromise: In the words of John Quincy Adams, Americans would be "well wishers of liberty" to all, but "champions only of their own." The United

States embraced neutrality to limit the risk of internal division; it eluded foreign conflicts that could doom the American experiment. The United States also made a historic choice about how it would enlarge: through adding coequal states with republican governments. But expansion included another fateful compromise—the extension of slavery in Southern states and the extermination, banishment, or absorption of Native Americans.

The U.S. constitutional order assumed that power flowed from citizens to a government of limited powers. In contrast to European systems, where legitimacy and authority flowed from the top and through the power of the state, Americans relied on individual and community initiatives. The new U.S. government tried to help open doors abroad for Americans' peaceful pursuits. The new American diplomacy expected merchants, sea captains, missionaries, mechanics, and fortune hunters to lead in creating a new transnational order.

Some Americans wanted to greet republicans from foreign lands more warmly. Henry Clay compared the envoys of the new republics of Latin America with Ben Franklin during the American Revolution. At a minimum, Clay wanted to embrace fellow republicans through commerce. He hoped fellow republican states would become partners in developing a new international order of independent states with respect for neutral rights. But divisions of religion, race, and culture checked moves toward an "American System" that spanned the hemisphere.

Lincoln explained the global implications of the U.S. Civil War in his Gettysburg Address. The Civil War tested whether the United States, or any nation "conceived in liberty" and "dedicated to the proposition that all men are created equal" "can long endure." Americans waged their Civil War for a cause very different from the contemporaneous Taiping Rebellion in China or wars of German unification.

A republican union could offer a model for confederations among states. In 1867, Canada formed a confederation of provinces. The United Mexican States (the formal name of Mexico) re-won their independence by expelling a European pretender. The United States expanded its Union by buying territories. The force of U.S. ideas and economy became magnets for other independent states seeking association.

The United States believed it had shown how a republic could establish a nationalism based on ideas, not on bloodlines and ethnicities. World War I forced the question of what type of international order would arise out of the destruction of empires. Wilson declared America wanted "to make the world safe for democracy." The United States was not yet pressing other states to become democracies, but it wanted to protect those peoples who had chosen democracy.

Americans believed that the rule of law was the prerequisite for and companion of democracies; the United States sought to encourage respect for international law and to experiment with practical ventures to build legal regimes. With time, America's stand for individual rights combined with its respect for international law to catalyze movements for international human rights.

In World War II, FDR presented an uplifting vision of the peace to be won. The Anglo-American Atlantic Charter of 1941 announced principles for security, trade, self-government, freedoms, and a structure of peace. FDR's Four Freedoms included speech and worship, and freedom from want and fear.

After the war, the United States revived its vanquished enemies as democracies, safeguarded by U.S. power and enriched through a new economic order. The United States returned, sometimes fitfully, to its anticolonial origins to support the sovereignty of independent states arising from old empires: It provided public goods of security, trade, and opportunities for development. Relying on its transnational qualities, the United States also purveyed soft power through culture, education, networks, technology, and ideas.

During the Cold War, America became the leader of the free world—a role it assumed with a mixture of self-interest, calculation, and idealism. After the Cold War, Americans felt different pulls of purpose.

Some countries objected to America's self-assumed role, and others just wanted to be left alone. Some Americans wanted to retreat—to focus on purposes at home, shed burdens, and counter national hubris. A new movement argued that internationalism and transnationalism conflicted with America's nationalism. Americans have long been sensitive to impositions on their own national freedom of action.

Nevertheless, Americans never viewed nationalism and internationalism as antithetical. The founding generation of Americans assumed that their republic served a larger purpose in the world. Restless Americans believed they could promote new and better international orders. Even when the United States has enjoyed dominant power, it did not rest contentedly with the status quo. It has even continually challenged the international system that it helped build. The U.S. experience reflects an ability to adapt pragmatically to a welcome dynamism.

A narrowly defined U.S. nationalism will fail to inspire American diplomacy. It will stunt America's true power. The United States does not exist just to be another listing in the UN directory. The deepest tradition of U.S. diplomacy has been to advance America's ideas.

From Traditions to Today

Four Presidents

Historians have only begun to sift through the presidencies of the past twenty-five years. Political battles still dominate the interpretations of their foreign policies.

Neither Bill Clinton nor George Bush, successful governors, expected to become foreign policy presidents. But events compelled both to define new American roles in a changed world order. Ironically, both two-term presidents worked within the framework sketched by the one-term George H. W. Bush. While most historians treat George H. W. Bush as the careful steward of the closing chapter of the Cold War, in fact Bush also pointed toward transformations in North America, trade, alliances, nuclear arms reductions, and even climate change. His initial efforts with a more integrated European Union, Central and Eastern Europe, Russia, the Persian Gulf and Mideast, the Americas, China, Japan, the rapidly growing economies of the Asia-Pacific, and regional hotspots—from Somalia to North Korea—shaped the diplomatic landscape for his two successors. His budget deal previewed Clinton's package and almost two decades of strong economic growth. Recent and fierce partisan debates to the contrary, I suspect that historians will recognize that the diplomacy of the two Bushes and Clinton had much in common, especially when compared to their successors.

Barack Obama said that he respected George H. W. Bush's diplomacy, but Obama steered toward a less assertive retrenchment—in contrast with Bush's guiding hand and prudent alliance leadership. After the long wars in Iraq and Afghanistan, and amidst the uncertainties of a global financial crisis, Obama's caution and capacity for national self-criticism were understandable. His skepticism led him to reach out to old foes, such as Russia, Iran, and Cuba. Yet Obama was not comfortable combining his diplomatic adjustment with a redesigned role for the United States. He never warmed to the idea of a special American purpose in the world.

By chance, I was the one American with President Obama during his first discussion with the principal group of foreign leaders. UK prime minister Gordon Brown had convened a G-20 summit in London in early April 2009; Brown was trying to organize a collective response by the world's major economies to the still-spreading financial crisis.[1] The summit opened with a working dinner attended only by the heads of government and the leaders of the IMF, UN, and World Bank. Brown asked Obama to lead off. The president seemed hesitant and discursive; he sounded informed, but knowing of Obama's intelligence and speaking skill, I had hoped that the president would take the opportunity to define the challenge, build confidence by explaining what the United States would do, or at least align strongly with Brown's energetic efforts. Nevertheless, I recognized that Obama was newly elected and had to navigate with sizable egos who had no shortage of complaints about the United States. As the dinner ended, I encouraged the president. Obama replied that he had not wanted to start the discussion, but Brown had told him that the United States had to open. I affirmed that. "Mr. President, you really did have to speak first; the others will look to you to set the stage." President Obama always treated me graciously, and I watched him handle subsequent international economic issues tactfully and effectively. He was popular overseas, but his natural reserve contributed to a perception of diffidence—in contrast with the leadership styles of the Bushes and Clinton, even recognizing their considerable differences.

Historians may eventually view Obama's diplomatic reticence as a precursor to Donald Trump's blunt reversal. Trump stresses his breaks with the past—including with the American-led order of alliances, trade, and economic networks. Trump favors transactional dealmaking over the diplomacy of ongoing partnerships.

I will close with a quick look at U.S. policy over the past decades through the lens of the five traditions.

North America

George H. W. Bush completed the NAFTA negotiation, but Bill Clinton had to pass the agreement; to do so, he organized a bipartisan political push. Clinton then supported Mexico through the 1994 financial crisis and its democratic transition. Clinton initiated a Summit of the Americas—with the vision of a wholly democratic hemisphere—and launched a negotiation for a Free Trade Area of the Americas. The president's rhetoric outran his practical policy steps, but Clinton was an ardent advocate of the hemispheric vision.

George W. Bush's first foreign trip as president was to Mexico. He worked with both North American partners to improve border cooperation and deep trading ties. In his second term, even with wartime preoccupations, Bush launched a Security and Prosperity Partnership of North America to connect local governments and business groups to national projects for transportation, financial services, the environment, and intelligence sharing. The president also assisted trade, development, and democracy in Central America, in part through cooperation with Mexico. Bush pressed Congress to pass immigration reform—to no avail and with disruptive long-term consequences.[2]

Barack Obama never recognized the strategic potential of North America, although he maintained neighborly ties. NAFTA had become politically unpopular in the president's party, so the administration would not mention NAFTA and gave up making the public case; it is hard to win a debate in which only one side argues. Obama's appointees scaled back Bush's project to build trilateral institutional ties. However, as President Felipe Calderon of Mexico targeted the country's networks of organized crime and drugs—and tried to reform courts and the police—Obama offered quiet and important assistance. Vice President Joe Biden led an effort to thwart state breakdown and criminal capture of governments in Central America. But as the U.S. economy's recovery strengthened, the surge of illegal immigration and asylum seekers dominated regional relations.

Donald Trump made a wall with Mexico into a signature political issue. He pointed to Mexicans and Central Americans as dangers and threatened them. The administration does not view a healthy Mexican economy as a North American asset. Nonetheless, after twenty-five years of deeper continental integration, the three societies have built resilient bonds that have withstood Trump's call to end NAFTA and Mexican president Andrés Manuel López Obrador's past opposition. The renegotiated U.S.-Mexico-Canada Agreement (USMCA) leaves most of NAFTA in place, modernizes a few features, adds some restrictions, and incorporates labor and environmental provisions. Unfortunately, the USMCA will end after sixteen years unless extended. Americans will likely need to relearn that a healthy, strong home continent offers the best foundation for U.S. global policy.

Trade, Transnationalism, and Technology

In November 1992, after George H. W. Bush's electoral defeat, his administration reached a critical agreement on agriculture with the European Commission in the global GATT trade negotiations. The Clinton administration picked up the baton and, in 1994, completed the Uruguay Round with more than one hundred other economies, transforming the GATT into the new World Trade Organization (WTO). Clinton adroitly used the passage of

NAFTA in 1993 and the convening of the first Asia-Pacific Economic Cooperation summit to imply that the United States would pursue regional trade liberalization if the Europeans and others balked at a global deal.

These trade accomplishments supported the Clinton-Lake vision of enlarging the world market economy. By the end of the 1990s, advances in information technologies, combined with more open trade and capital markets, spurred opportunities—and risks—of a greater globalization.

Yet Clinton faced growing political resistance to trade, especially in his own party, and he slowed his initial momentum. His team focused on overcoming Japanese protectionism and then on bringing China into the new WTO. In the late 1990s, Clinton's Treasury team engaged in financial rescue operations with emerging markets across East Asia, Latin America, and Russia. Congress failed to extend the president's trade negotiating authority, and Clinton's effort to launch a new WTO trade round collapsed amidst antiglobalization protests in Seattle.

In 2001, George W. Bush directed me to revitalize the trade agenda; even after the attacks of September 11, the president emphasized how open trade and economic freedom complemented his drive to thwart, in his words, "isolationism, protectionism, and nativism."[3] His administration regained congressional authority to negotiate and pursued a strategy of competitive liberalization, working globally, regionally, and with individual countries. Bush completed free trade agreements with seventeen countries, finished the accession of China and Taiwan into the WTO, expanded the African Growth and Opportunity Act (first signed by President Clinton), and launched (but did not complete) new global and transpacific trade deals.

Obama, in contrast with Clinton and Bush, pulled back on trade during his first term. Unlike FDR and Hull, Obama missed an opportunity to connect trade openness with world economic recovery after a devastating recession; instead, Obama's first trade representative dismissed the very idea of negotiating agreements. As the financial crisis shook the world's lending systems, the Federal Reserve quietly used dollar swap agreements to stabilize other markets, a sober reminder of the importance of the U.S. dollar, even in the Eurozone. As president of the World Bank, I worked with my friend Pascal Lamy, head of the WTO, to persuade financial regulators and bankers to not choke off trade finance to developing economies.

Beginning in 2013, Obama's new trade team promoted Bush's Trans-Pacific Partnership (TPP), a region-wide accord with eleven other economies (six of which already had FTAs with the United States). In 2015, the Republican Congress cleared the way for a vote, but the administration could not close the deal in time.

Trump withdrew the United States from the TPP. He proudly proclaimed that he was a protectionist, "a tariff man." For Trump, trade protectionism and hostility to immigration were signals to his political base that he rejected past policies. Trump thought he could cut U.S. trade deficits; he did not care about framing international rules for cutting-edge sectors such as services, technology, and data. No other U.S. president since Herbert Hoover has wholeheartedly embraced protectionism; the terms of Trump's deals have more in common with the managed trade of George Peek in the 1930s than Cordell Hull's strategy.

Alliances and Order

During the negotiations for German unification, George H. W. Bush began transitioning NATO to a post–Cold War role of guaranteeing transatlantic security, including for Central and Eastern Europe. Clinton and George W. Bush added new members to the east. When the Europeans were unable to end the bloody wars following the breakup of Yugoslavia, the Clinton administration used NATO's airpower to force the negotiation of a fractious peace. France rejoined NATO's military arm. After the attack of September 11, NATO invoked for the first time the collective defensive response of Article 5—Vandenberg's handiwork—to help the United States fight in Afghanistan.

Nevertheless, NATO's cohesion and sense of purpose weakened. When the United States opened a pathway to membership for Georgia and Ukraine, Russia seized some of their territory. France, Germany, and others resisted George W. Bush's attack on Iraq, creating bitter feelings. Europeans slashed defense spending, although revived anxieties about Russia are prompting reconsideration. NATO has been slowly preparing for new threats, such as Russia's hybrid tactics or cyberattacks. NATO has to consider how it would respond to Russian intimidation along NATO's eastern frontier, especially in the Baltic states. Turkey's interests have focused increasingly on the lands of its Ottoman past instead of future Euro-Atlantic ties.

Disputes among NATO allies are not new. In the past, however, Washington assumed responsibility for devising accommodations. Trump, in contrast, has signaled his ambivalence about NATO. He views Europe primarily as an economic rival. He seems more comfortable with authoritarian leaders than democratic ones.

The breakup of the USSR and Russia's painful transition to a postimperial state inevitably posed dangers. Clinton, Bush, and Obama each tried to forge a constructive relationship with Russia, but Moscow felt disrespected. Russia wanted the status of an equal, not a junior partner. Putin has marshaled Russia's strengths—nuclear weapons, energy, cyber, and specialized military forces—to reposition Russia in its traditional role as a Eurasian power, maneuvering between East and West. His Russia gains influence when America's Atlantic and Pacific alliance ties weaken and confidence in democracy falters. Putin prefers a diplomacy of great power manipulation and a world that looks more like 1900 than 2000. But as in 1900, Russia's leadership transition is uncertain.

America's post–Cold War presidents have recognized that Russia's nuclear arsenal poses a unique challenge. They have tried to limit the risks of stolen or sold materials and negotiated smaller stockpiles. U.S.-Russian nuclear diplomacy provides a basis for cooperation to prevent nuclear proliferation. The most recent U.S.-Russian nuclear arms limitation expires in 2021, and the Trump administration has not been interested in an extension.

The Bushes, Clinton, and Obama worked to transform U.S. Pacific alliances into a mutually supportive network. To do so, they needed to expand Japan's role and relationships. George W. Bush deepened intelligence ties. Clinton, Bush, and Obama encouraged Tokyo to assume more mutual responsibilities with U.S. forces. While Japan has built ties with Australia, India, and ASEAN countries, Tokyo and Seoul have not been able to resolve past animosities. A nuclear North Korea, with an insecure regime, poses hazards to both. The stories in this book warn that trouble in Northeast Asia reverberates much further. Trump's skepticism about U.S. alliance obligations and protectionism has added to Asian anxieties, especially as China's power overshadows the region. We should not be surprised that America's uncertain partners will be quietly preparing alternatives to the U.S.-led order; their options range from accommodating China to developing nuclear deterrents of their own.

George W. Bush took a major strategic step by accepting India as a legitimate nuclear power. For decades, U.S. policy viewed India through the prism of its conflict with Pakistan. Bush conceived of India as a potential partner—in security, economics, and as a democracy—in Eurasia and even global diplomacy; he "dehyphenated" the relationship from Pakistan. Obama's "Af-Pak" diplomacy risked reviving the old Indo-Pak logic, but his administration eventually returned to Bush's strategy. India is understandably preoccupied with economic development, including through relations with China. Trump's narrow trade mind-set has led to higher barriers with India, and he has irritated Delhi by offering to mediate with Pakistan.

From the perspective of 2020, China's rise poses the most significant change in the world order. George H. W. Bush labored to maintain ties with China following the crackdowns in 1989. After failing to impose human rights conditions, Clinton resumed the long-standing U.S. effort to integrate China into the world economy while encouraging cooperation in other areas; Clinton's team also hoped to shape Chinese behavior through stronger alliance ties with Japan, a web of multilateral relations, and the presence of the U.S. Navy in the Western Pacific.

In 2005, when serving as deputy secretary of state, I gave a speech that recognized the steps China had taken to integrate into the international system: its membership in the WTO, the IMF, the World Bank, and the UN Security Council and participation in pacts ranging from ozone depletion to nuclear weapons. China had benefited enormously from the U.S.-led international order. I urged China to move from "membership" to becoming a "responsible stakeholder" in the international system.[4]

The speech reflected the work of a strategic dialogue the Bush administration initiated with China in 2005. We discussed longer-term perspectives—in some detail—looking beyond the agenda of the moment. After I left the State Department, Secretary of the Treasury Hank Paulson launched a Strategic Economic Dialogue, and the first-term Obama team conducted a high-level economic and diplomatic exchange, although the Obama administration appeared to shift from strategic discussions to working through a list of issues. In Obama's second term, the process withered, and the United States lost close contact with developments in China, just as President Xi Jinping began charting new directions. Gaps in perceptions—and frustrations—grew.

Trump has focused on the U.S. trade deficit with China, using tariffs to prod negotiations and decouple economic ties. The United States proceeds alone, not in concert with allies. There are no strategic discussions about how the two biggest powers will cooperate, compete, or contest the future regional and world orders.

In the Mideast and Persian Gulf, Clinton extended Baker's push for Israeli-Arab peace negotiations with some success. But Clinton could not bridge the suspicions and differences between Israel and the Palestinians. At first George W. Bush stepped back, but he too reached for a two-state solution. A frustrated Obama withdrew, especially after revolts within Arab states threw the old order into turmoil.

Clinton struggled with Saddam Hussein's revival and circumvention of sanctions. Fears about terrorists with weapons of mass destruction grew in the 1990s. After the shock of September 11, Bush determined that he would not risk Saddam developing such weapons. The president faced a rash of dire warnings about attacks that would cause mass casualties; with the passage of time, it is hard to reimagine the intensity of the fears of more attacks on the U.S. homeland. The president needed intelligence advisers who were willing to stand against the tide and explain carefully the uncertainties about Iraq's weapons programs. In 1964–65, none of LBJ's close advisers could conceive of withdrawal as a serious alternative to escalation; in 2002–03, none of Bush's key lieutenants would make the case for relying on deterrence over preemption. No one knows what would have happened if the sanctions regime shriveled and Saddam acquired weapons of mass destruction. President Bush wagered his presidency on a war, and wars are always the most unpredictable and unstable elements of statecraft.

After the early combat and collapse of the Afghan and Iraqi regimes, Bush's advisers seemed of two minds about what would follow; the poor planning reflected a lack of clear direction. One group eschewed nation building and wanted to exit quickly; another sought to work with Afghans and Iraqis to build democratic states. By the time I shifted to the State Department in early 2005, this debate still reverberated. In the president's second term, he doubled down with his Freedom Agenda. In 2007, Bush adapted his political-military strategy in Iraq with a troop surge and counterinsurgency plan, in cooperation with tribal leaders, to reverse sectarian violence and Al Qaeda's chokehold.

Obama wanted to get out of both Iraq and Afghanistan. He thought the United States was overextended, especially in the midst of a financial crisis. Obama had opposed the Iraq war from the start, unlike most of his Democratic opponents. He knew the American public was weary of long wars with high human and financial costs. Trump's rhetoric is bellicose, but he also wants to avoid overseas commitments and military action.

Obama and Trump diverge, however, on Iran. Obama negotiated a deal to limit the risks of Iranian nuclear breakout, though—unlike Charles Evans Hughes—Obama did not match his arms control aim with a regional security strategy. Instead, he hoped lower tensions would lead to more cooperative behavior. Trump pounced on this weakness, opting for more intense economic pressure on Iran. He might have chosen to keep Obama's deal and pushed with allies to constrain Iranian missiles and adventurism. But one of Trump's political principles is to break with his predecessors. Trump's approach necessitates closer ties with Saudi Arabia and the smaller states in the Persian Gulf region. As a result, more than twenty-five years after George H. W. Bush's liberation of Kuwait, the United States remains deeply enmeshed in the regional security order even without formal alliance ties.

Since the end of the Cold War, U.S. participation beyond the geopolitical and economic realms has been sporadic. George H. W. Bush negotiated and ratified America's one climate change treaty, a framework accord calling for national action plans and scientific feedback loops. That framework continues to provide the foundation for UN efforts today.[5] Clinton overreached by agreeing to the Kyoto Climate Protocol of 1997, which established a centralized model of obligations that applied only to developed countries; the Senate expressed disapproval, 95–0.[6] In his second term, George W. Bush recognized that carbon emissions and absorption depended principally on agreement among a group of large developed and developing economies, but he came to this too late to accomplish anything. In 2015, Obama returned to George H. W. Bush's framework model by agreeing to collective national political commitments in Paris; Trump withdrew from that accord.

George W. Bush pressed innovative systems to protect global health, especially in sub-Saharan Africa. The president's Emergency Action Plan for AIDS Relief became the largest international health initiative to combat a specific disease, and Bush's malaria plan turbocharged the global effort to counter one of the world's most debilitating diseases.

Developments in science, health, and technology will necessitate new international regimes to encourage cooperative action and counter threats. Influenzas and contagious diseases such as SARS and the more recent coronavirus will require the type of initiative and precautions that Bush prioritized and Obama used against Ebola. Cybersecurity—and even warfare—also looms in the future. The "rules" for potential conflict are murky, just as they were for nuclear weapons when Vannevar Bush first contemplated how the atomic bomb would change diplomacy and war.

The current U.S. transactional diplomacy, relying on threats and uncertainties to increase leverage in making one-off deals, leaves the United States ill prepared.

Public and Congressional Support

After George H. W. Bush led a thirty-four-nation coalition to victory in the first Gulf War in March 1991, his public approval soared to 89 percent—higher than Truman after V-E Day in 1945 and above the peaks for Eisenhower, Kennedy, Johnson, Nixon, Ford, Carter, and Reagan.[7] But the U.S. economy had begun to turn down in October 1990, with a recession running through mid-1991 and a painfully slow recovery in 1992. In part to avoid a budget crisis as the nation was going to war, Bush had broken his campaign pledge not to raise taxes. In early 1992, Patrick Buchanan challenged Bush in the primaries with an isolationist "America First" message, highlighting the president's vulnerability. Ross Perot jumped in with populist complaints. Bill Clinton—whose tagline was "It's the economy, stupid"—won with 43 percent of the popular vote.

Clinton's foreign policy stumbled at first, with setbacks in Somalia, Haiti, Rwanda, and the Balkans; he seemed uncertain whether the American public would back military interventions where U.S. interests appeared more humanitarian than strategic. Yet Clinton won a budget deal that built on Bush's, passed NAFTA and the new WTO agreement, and prospered with a strong economy through the 1990s. Although Clinton lost control of Congress in 1994, he gained backing from key Republicans for his enlargement of NATO and roles as a peacemaker, including in the Balkans, Mideast, and

Northern Ireland. The administration's global financial firefighting in the late '90s could rely heavily on the resources of the IMF and World Bank without large congressional commitments. Clinton rode a wave of unparalleled U.S. power; his critics argued that he dissipated a rare opportunity to redefine an international system to America's long-term advantage.

George W. Bush became a war president. But he had to wage a new type of conflict against confusing enemies. At first, Americans rallied around their president. But as victory—or even success—became harder to define, Bush's support ebbed. The president knew he was fighting a long war, and long wars challenge democracies. He emphasized that the United States respected Islam as a peaceful religion. Bush worked to keep faith with America's internationalist traditions—with North America, immigration, trade, humanitarian relief, and international economics. Like Woodrow Wilson, he wanted to make the world safe for democracy; like Wilson, Bush triggered deep public disappointment when costly realities fell far short of his aspirations. The American public grew weary of war and worldwide responsibilities, but did not abandon either until the global financial and economic crisis of 2008.

Obama had to counter the crash. He also faced the fury—at home and abroad—of charges that America's hubris created the problem. Political divisions deepened. By temperament, Obama was the leader of a hopeful political movement, not a legislative negotiator. The U.S. economic recovery was distressingly slow. America's historic partner, the European Union, struggled to master the weaknesses of its currency zone, but it no longer accepted American advice. In his second term, Obama sought to address social injustices instead of the economic agenda he had inherited. Neither Obama nor Bush could fashion a compromise on immigration.

By 2016, the American public seemed exhausted—and frustrated—by the succession of twenty-first-century disappointments. Long wars, a financial collapse and sluggish recovery, many foreign complaints, and a loss of control of borders eroded America's confidence in managing its own house, much less the world. The context was ripe for punching back, blaming others, and experimenting with a new direction.

America's Purpose

The Bushes and Clinton believed that the United States should keep working toward something approaching the "New American Era" that Charles Thomson heralded in 1782. Obama, reflecting public disillusionment, was more cautious and less ambitious. Trump is unpredictable and haphazard; he believes he can use America's power to make deals, though as I write, it is not clear what his dealmaking will accomplish. Trump believes in personal politics, not in building institutions and relations that serve larger purposes.

I suspect that America's capacities to shape the future world order are greater than either Trump or many of his critics believe. Alexander Hamilton understood the potential power of the U.S. financial system and economy; Jefferson and John Quincy Adams recognized that a continental United States offered unmatched advantages. Seward, Reagan, the Bushes, and Clinton perceived that North America presented an opportunity to build an even broader foundation. Lincoln knew that the republican Union represented an ongoing experiment in self-government that could reach far beyond America's shores.

During the 1920s and '30s, Americans became disenchanted with the world. The public learned, through the world's most devastating war, that the United States could not afford to withdraw from the world. In the 1970s, Americans were uncertain about their prospects. Nixon and Kissinger knew the United States could not just "come home," so they instituted a worldwide scheme of maneuver, balancing, and dramatic diplomatic intervention. But they accepted the expectations of decline. They underestimated the innovative capacity that Vannevar Bush had fostered and the revival that Reagan believed was possible.

Future U.S. presidents can draw on all these experiences. They can recall Teddy Roosevelt's skill at mediation and balancing powers. They need to respect the appeal of Wilson's aspirations. And they should understand the benefits—and mutual responsibilities—of the system of alliances and economic relations first established in 1947–49. In addition to devising the country's foreign policies, presidents need to educate the public about America's role in the world.

I expect America's leaders and citizens will continue to pursue these challenges pragmatically—trying what works. As Tocqueville observed almost two centuries ago, "[T]he greatness of America lies not in being more enlightened than any other nation, but rather in her ability to repair her faults."[8]

Acknowledgments

My wife, Sherry, has studied, researched, and written about American diplomatic history with me since we first met forty-six years ago. As an editor and author, counselor and partner, she deserves more respect and appreciation than I can ever give. Thank you.

Daniel Chardell assisted skillfully and diligently with research, sources, edits, notes, advice, and good spirit over three years while working on his doctorate in history at Harvard. I look forward to following his future scholarship, academic excellence, and interest in "applied history."

Breyana Lehman made this book possible by typing and reworking, always with incredible care and accuracy, even while keeping the Washington office of the Brunswick Group running smoothly. Her sense of responsibility has amazed me, and my thanks are deepfelt. During the early stages of this project, Sharada Strasmore and Vivian Tran helped as well.

I am exceptionally grateful to Graham Allison, who encouraged me in countless ways. He sponsored the work—then prodded, questioned, reviewed many drafts, sent memos of advice, and organized a seminar of faculty and graduate students at Harvard to read and comment on my manuscripts. Anyone who knows Graham recognizes his unmatched energy and enthusiasm; from both I have benefited greatly. His venture to spur contributions of "applied history" is leading a new generation of researchers and practitioners to relate the past to future challenges.

Graham's seminar for my book depended on the generosity and patience of a dedicated assembly of professors, senior Fellows, and rising scholars. All of them kindly read draft chapters and offered thoughtful advice. I owe much to Anne Karalekas (who will soon produce a biography on Robert Lovett), Fred Logevall, Erez Manela, Joe Nye, Meghan O'Sullivan, and Arne Westad; also, Graham's Fellows of the future—including Yakov Feygin, Julian Gewirtz, Arjun Kapur, Jason Kelly, Brandon Mendoza, Aroop Mukharji, Benjamin Rhode, Calder Walton, and Justin Winokur—offered excellent insights and critiques. The invaluable Simone O'Hanlon kept the grand enterprise on track!

Philip Zelikow, one of the country's leading diplomatic historians, and a former colleague, has been a pillar of this project from the start. Phil guided me to sources. He read drafts. We enjoyed long discussions about our work. Phil organized a faculty seminar at the University of Virginia across historical specialties so that I could test first concepts. The notes for this book reveal the incredible range of Phil's own published work. I am delighted to add that there is more to come from such a gifted and inquiring scholar.

I am also indebted to the Nitze School of Advanced International Studies (SAIS) at Johns Hopkins University. Deans Vali Nasr and Eliot Cohen kindly offered me access to the Mason Library at SAIS. Director Sheila Thalhimer, Josh McDonald, and their colleagues were of unfailing good-natured assistance as we hunted for books and other source materials; they were exceedingly patient as I relearned library research skills after years away. SAIS is also the home of the new Henry Kissinger Center for Global Affairs, guided by Professor and Director Frank Gavin; Frank arranged a dinner with scholars to discuss my plans and a videoconference to discuss a chapter with a consortium of faculty and graduate students from various universities. Frank's encouragement of scholars to contribute to policy debates dovetails with the premise for this book.

I appreciate that Professor John Lewis Gaddis of Yale, a great and inspiring historian, took the time to read and offer comments on my précis for this book.

John Deutch of MIT urged me to include international technology policy, which led to my chapter on Vannevar Bush and the vital roles of science and innovation systems in foreign policy. I believe this dimension of power and diplomacy will only grow in importance.

Twenty years ago, I first had the idea for a book on U.S. diplomatic history. At that time, Ernest May, then and perhaps always the dean of the field, wisely urged me to look beyond secretaries of state. May also recommended the assistance of an accomplished doctoral candidate, Alexis Albion. Alexis is a superb historian; I discovered many years later the usefulness of the primary materials she assembled for me. Fortunately, I was able to again benefit from Alexis's skills as a colleague at the World Bank.

Marin Strmecki and the Smith-Richardson Foundation gave me a grant in the late 1990s when I began the long road that led to this book. Twelve or more years of public service intervened; I can only thank Marin and Smith-Richardson profusely for their exceptional patience. I also owe thanks, and apologies, to Robert Gallucci, then dean of the Georgetown School of Foreign Service, who permitted me to borrow many books, for too long, on his library account.

As I turned research into chapters, many friends helped by offering comments on drafts or answering questions: Richard Burt; Bruce Ferguson; Niall Ferguson; Jeff Garten; Gordon Goldstein; Lord Charles Powell; Chris Schroeder; and Ambassador Michael Thawley. Professor Will Inboden of the University of Texas invited me to present three chapters to the Clements Center Seminar on History and Statecraft, where I enjoyed the interaction with an inspiring group of Fellows. Dung Huynh and Jaehan Park enlisted to read other chapters, and their follow-up notes, along with Will's, led to useful refinements. Sad to say, Matt Niemeyer, a close friend and colleague for many years, who cheered me on as I began, died young and is not here to see the finished work. Matt loved to read biographies and narrative histories. I kept him in mind as a reader while writing.

I am deeply grateful that Sean Desmond and the skilled editorial team at Twelve—Bob Castillo, Rachel Kambury, and copyeditor Mark Steven Long—have been willing to back a new author with good guidance, editorial direction, and careful attention to details. I have appreciated their professionalism and friendly partnership. I am indebted to agent and bibliophile Andrew Wylie for showing me how to propose a book and for introducing me to Sean and Twelve.

Because this book combines history with my personal assessments, I also owe a great deal to the leaders and colleagues who helped me learn the practice and promise of diplomacy and foreign policy, economic policy, development, and bureaucratic, national, and international politics—whether in the U.S. government, at the World Bank, or through the experiences of other countries. Some of their names appear in the text or notes, but many more were in mind as I wrote.

In particular, my respect for and debt to James A. Baker III runs throughout these pages. It was my great good fortune to work with Secretary Baker, watch him in action, and contribute to historic events as part of his team. Whatever ideas or points I could contribute, Baker always improved them.

The nature of this work, as explained in the Introduction, relies on the research and findings of generations of true scholars studying events over a span of 240 years. I tried to compare varying views, adding primary source research where I thought it helpful; I also supplemented the work of others with my insights and judgments. But this book rests upon the studies of many, many others.

The best way I can recognize the spirit of historical inquiry of so many persons of learning is by thanking Sherry's and my first professor of diplomatic history, James A. Field Jr. Field's writing still sparkles and his scholarship has stood the test of time. But he was a teacher, too—a master of just the right details, Professor Field brought history alive, pushed his students to question assumptions, taught them how to mine sources, and lightened the whole experience with dry wit.

While many others helped in many ways, the responsibility for the final work is mine alone.

Notes

Introduction. America's First Diplomat

1. R. M. Bache, "Franklin's Ceremonial Coat," *Pennsylvania Magazine of History and Biography* 23 (1899), 444–52, quote on 450. Cited in Walter Isaacson, *Benjamin Franklin: An American Life* (New York: Simon & Schuster, 2003), 345, 552.

2. Edmund Burke, "Edmund Burke, Esq., Letter to the Marquis of Rockingham," February 2, 1774, in *Letters of Edmund Burke: A Selection*, ed. Harold J. Laski (London: Humphrey Milford, Oxford University Press, 1922), 180. Quoted in Lord Edmond Fitzmaurice, *Life of William, Earl of Shelburne*, vol. 1, *1737–1776* (London: Macmillan and Co., 1912). "Extract of a Letter from London, [19 February 1774]," in *The Papers of Benjamin Franklin*, vol. 21, *January 1, 1774–March 22, 1775*, ed. William B. Wilcox (New Haven: Yale University Press, 1978), 112.

3. Isaacson, *Franklin*, 347; Don Cook, *The Long Fuse* (New York: Atlantic Monthly Press, 1995), 286–88; Stacy Schiff, *A Great Improvisation: Franklin, France, and the Birth of America* (New York: Henry Holt, 2005), 128–33 (more skeptical of the forty-two-hour delivery).

4. See "Franklin's 'Hints' or Terms for a Durable Union [between 4 and 6 December 1774]," *Papers of Benjamin Franklin*, vol. 21, 365–68.

5. Schiff, *Great Improvisation*, 409.

6. Gordon S. Wood, *The Americanization of Benjamin Franklin* (New York: Penguin, 2004), 195, 277, quoting Franklin letter to Robert R. Livingston. For the original letter, see Doc. 1426, "To Robert R. Livingston," July 22, 1783, in *The Writings of Benjamin Franklin*, vol. 9, *1783–1788*, ed. Albert Henry Smyth (New York: Macmillan Company, 1907), 62.

7. Schiff, *Great Improvisation*, 294.

8. Both quotes from Schiff, *Great Improvisation*, 324, 338 (emphasis in original).

9. Richard B. Morris, *The Peacemakers: The Great Powers and American Independence* (New York: Harper & Row, 1965), 386–87.

10. Schiff, *Great Improvisation*, 412.

11. Quoted in Schiff, *Great Improvisation*, 295. For the original, see Franklin to Morris, March 7, 1782, in *The Revolutionary Diplomatic Correspondence of the United States*, vol. 5, ed. Francis Wharton (Washington, DC: Government Printing Office, 1889), 228.

12. Morris, *Peacemakers*, 438–39, 548. For the original, see Franklin to Laurens, May 25, 1782, in *The Works of Benjamin Franklin*, vol. 9, ed. Jared Sparks (Boston: Hilliard, Gray, and Co., 1840), 290–291.

13. For discussions of Franklin's negotiations in Paris, see Schiff, *Great Improvisation*; Morris, *Peacemakers*, 192–99, 248–313, 334–85; Isaacson, *Benjamin Franklin*, 324–429; Wood, *Americanization of Benjamin Franklin*, 169–200; Cook, *Long Fuse*, 360–73; Gerald Stourzh, *Benjamin Franklin and American Foreign Policy* (Chicago: University of Chicago Press, 1969), 123–79. See also Andrew Stockley, *Britain and France at the Birth of America: The European Powers and the Peace Negotiations of 1782–1783* (University of Exeter Press, 2001), 5–73, for a focus on Anglo-French negotiations and the European balance of power, which downplays the American dimensions and "luck."

14. Henry Kissinger, *Diplomacy* (New York: Simon & Schuster, 1994), 36.

15. George F. Kennan, *American Diplomacy*, 60th ann. rev. & exp. ed. (Chicago: University of Chicago Press, 2012), 99–102, 109.

16. Walter McDougall, *Promised Land, Crusader State: The American Encounter with the World Since 1776* (Boston: Houghton Mifflin, 1997).

17. William Appleman Williams, *The Tragedy of American Diplomacy*, 50th ann. ed. (New York: W. W. Norton & Co., 2009 [c1959]).

18. John Lewis Gaddis, *The United States and the Origins of the Cold War, 1941–1947* (New York: Columbia University Press, 1972), vii; idem., "The Emerging Post-Revisionist Synthesis on the Origins of the Cold War," *Diplomatic History* 7, no. 3 (July 1983), 175.

19. The four schools of thought coursing through American foreign policy that Mead identifies are the Hamiltonians, dedicated to security via trade and economic prosperity; the Wilsonians, champions of democracy abroad; the Jeffersonians, guardians of democracy at home and skeptics of entangling alliances; and the Jacksonians, caretakers of the physical security of the nation. See Walter Russell Mead, *Special Providence: American Foreign Policy and How It Changed the World* (New York: Alfred A. Knopf, 2001).

20. David Milne, *Worldmaking: The Art and Science of American Diplomacy* (New York: Farrar, Straus and Giroux, 2015).

21. See Jennifer Ratner-Rosenhagen, *The Ideas That Made America: A Brief History* (New York: Oxford University Press, 2019), 103–8; William James, *Pragmatism: A New Name for Some Old Ways of Thinking: Popular Lectures on Philosophy* (Cambridge, MA: Riverside Press, 1907).

22. For a comprehensive reflection on the historiography of American diplomacy, see Jerald Combs, *American Diplomatic History: Two Centuries of Changing Interpretations* (Berkeley: University of California Press, 1983).

23. Henry Kissinger, *A World Restored: Europe After Napoleon* (New York: Grosset & Dunlap, 1964), 331.

24. Ernest R. May and Richard E. Neustadt, *Thinking in Time: The Uses of History for Decision-Makers* (New York: Free Press, 1986), 263.

25. Fredrik Logevall and Kenneth Osgood, "Why Did We Stop Teaching Political History?" *New York Times*, August 29, 2016. For insight into this debate, see Daniel Bessner and Fredrik Logevall, "Recentering the United States in the Historiography of American Foreign Relations," *Texas National Security Review* 3, no. 2 (Spring 2020), https://protect-us.mimecast.com/s/rV4AC5yw1yfWv4DJFzAOSh?domain=tnsr.org/; Hal Brands and Francis J. Gavin, "The Historical Profession is Committing Slow-Motion Suicide," December 10, 2018, *War on the Rocks*, https://warontherocks.com/2018/12/the-historical-profession-is-committing-slow-motion-suicide/.

26. James A. Field Jr., *America and the Mediterranean World, 1776–1882* (Princeton, NJ: Princeton University Press, 1969), 3, 4.

Chapter 1. Alexander Hamilton: Architect of American Power

1. See G. W. Parke Custis, *Recollections and Private Memoirs of Washington* (New York: Derby & Jackson, 1860), 349. Forrest McDonald questions Custis's account in *Alexander Hamilton: A Biography* (New York: Norton, 1982), 128. See also Charles Rappleye, *Robert Morris: Financier of the American Revolution* (New York: Simon & Schuster, 2010), 454. On Morris's services, see Ron Chernow, *Alexander Hamilton* (New York: Penguin Press, 2004), 155. On Hamilton becoming George Washington's aide, see Willard Sterne Randall, *Alexander Hamilton: A Life* (New York: HarperCollins, 2003), 122.

2. Rappleye, *Robert Morris*, 454.

3. For the original letters, see "From Alexander Hamilton to Robert Morris, [30 April 1781]," in *The Papers of Alexander Hamilton*, vol. 2, *1779–1781*, ed. Harold C. Syrett (New York: Columbia University Press, 1961), 604–35; "From Alexander Hamilton to James Duane, [3 September 1780]," in ibid., 400–418; "From Alexander Hamilton to—, [December–March 1779–1780]," in ibid., 236–51. On the significance of Hamilton's proposals, see Chernow, *Alexander Hamilton*, 156; Randall, *Alexander Hamilton*, 231; McDonald, *Alexander Hamilton*, 40.

4. For the original letter, see "From Alexander Hamilton to Lieutenant Colonel John Laurens, [12 September 1780]," in *Papers of Alexander Hamilton*, vol. 2, 426–28. See Randall, *Alexander Hamilton*, 231.

5. See "From Alexander Hamilton to Robert Morris, [30 April 1781]," in *Papers of Alexander Hamilton*, vol. 2, 604–35.

6. Chernow, *Alexander Hamilton*, 138.

7. See especially *Federalist* numbers 11–36 in *The Papers of Alexander Hamilton*, vol. 4, *January 1787–May 1788*, ed. Harold C. Syrett (New York: Columbia University Press, 1962), 339–490. On Hamilton's contributions to the *Federalist* papers, see Chernow, *Alexander Hamilton*, 254–55.

8. McDonald, *Alexander Hamilton*, 156–61. On the Pitts, see John Lamberton Harper, *American Machiavelli: Alexander Hamilton and the Origins of U.S. Foreign Policy* (New York: Cambridge University Press, 2004), 271.

9. For the original, see "Eulogy on Nathanael Greene, [4 July 1789]," in *The Papers of Alexander Hamilton*, vol. 5, *June 1788–November 1789*, ed. Harold C. Syrett (New York: Columbia University Press, 1962), 345–59. See also Harper, *American Machiavelli*, 145.

10. McDonald, *Alexander Hamilton*, 35 (emphasis in original).

11. McDonald, *Alexander Hamilton*, 135.

12. "From Alexander Hamilton to Robert Morris, [30 April 1781]," in *Papers of Alexander Hamilton*, vol. 2, 604–35. For insights on Hamilton's vision of finance, see McDonald, *Alexander Hamilton*, 143–210; Chernow, *Alexander Hamilton*, 291–304; Randall, *Alexander Hamilton*, 373–403; Harper, *American Machiavelli*, 46–48.

13. McDonald, *Alexander Hamilton*, 164.

14. See, for example, the work of historian and editor of Thomas Jefferson's papers Julian P. Boyd, *Number 7: Alexander Hamilton's Secret Attempts to Control American Foreign Policy* (Princeton, NJ: Princeton University Press, 1964). For critical assessments of Boyd, see Harper, *American Machiavelli*, 74–75; Chernow, *Alexander Hamilton*, 393–95.

15. Chernow, *Alexander Hamilton*, 295.

16. See the concluding chapter in Harper, *American Machiavelli*, especially at 273, 275.

17. Chernow, *Alexander Hamilton*, 393.

18. Later Hamilton had similar exchanges with the first British minister, George Hammond, who arrived late in 1791. See "Conversation with George Beckwith," October 1789, in *Papers of Alexander Hamilton*, vol. 5, 482–90. See Chernow, *Alexander Hamilton*, 294–95, 394; Harper, *American Machiavelli*, 49–50, 75–82, 93–96.

19. Harper, *American Machiavelli*, 49, 156.

20. For the original, see "Remarks on the Treaty of Amity Commerce and Navigation Lately Made Between the United States and Great Britain [9–11 July 1795]," in *The Papers of Alexander Hamilton*, vol. 18, *January 1795–July 1795*, ed. Harold C. Syrett (New York: Columbia University Press, 1973), 404–54. See Chernow, *Alexander Hamilton*, 392, 460, 461; Harper, *American Machiavelli*, 158.

21. On "peace with pro-British bias," see Harper, *American Machiavelli*, 273. On the "prison" of past treaties with France, see ibid., 104. On steering clear of foreign connections, see ibid., 84. For the original, see "Enclosure: Answers to Questions Proposed by the President of the United States to the Secretary of the Treasury [15 September 1790]," in *The Papers of Alexander Hamilton*, vol. 7, *September 1790–January 1791*, ed. Harold C. Syrett (New York: Columbia University Press, 1963), 37–57.

22. Harper, *American Machiavelli*, 169. For "impassioned pragmatism," see Chernow, *Alexander Hamilton*, 442.

23. On creating an army, see Harper, *American Machiavelli*, 231–37; Chernow, *Alexander Hamilton*, 556–57. For Hamilton's designs on Spain, see Chernow, *Alexander Hamilton*, 566–68.

24. Lest later generations forget Washington's wisdom, for years Congress read the address aloud on Washington's birthday. Chernow, *Alexander Hamilton*, 505–9. See also Harper, *American Machiavelli*, 177. On the origins and impact of the address, see Felix Gilbert, *To the Farewell Address: Ideas of Early American Foreign Policy* (Princeton, NJ: Princeton University Press, 1961).

25. See Harper, *American Machiavelli*, 83, 165. For the original, see "The Defence No. V [5 August 1795]," in *The Papers of Alexander Hamilton*, vol. 19, *July 1795–December 1795*, ed. Harold C. Syrett (New York: Columbia University Press, 1973), 88–97.

26. For the original letters, see "From Alexander Hamilton to Oliver Wolcott, Junior, 6 June [1797]," in *The Papers of Alexander Hamilton*, vol. 21, *April 1797–July 1798*, ed. Harold C. Syrett (New York: Columbia University Press, 1974), 98–101; "From Alexander Hamilton to William Loughton Smith, 5 April 1797," in ibid., 20–21. See Chernow, *Alexander Hamilton*, 546–47.

27. See Harper, *American Machiavelli*, 79, 181. For the originals, see "To George Washington from Alexander Hamilton, 15–22 July 1790," in *The Papers of George Washington*, vol. 6, *1 July 1790–30 November 1790*, ed. Mark A. Mastromarino (Charlottesville, VA: University Press of Virginia, 1996), 78–83; "From Alexander Hamilton to George Washington [5 November 1796]," in *The Papers of Alexander Hamilton*, vol. 20, *January 1796–March 1797*, ed. Harold C. Syrett (New York: Columbia University Press, 1974), 374–75. For "candor, goodwill, and good sense," see McDonald, *Alexander Hamilton*, 269.

28. James Thomas Flexner, *The Young Hamilton: A Biography* (Boston: Little, Brown, 1978), 449.

29. Harper, *American Machiavelli*, 56.

30. For Hamilton and Talleyrand, see Allan McLane Hamilton and Willard Sterne Randall, *The Intimate Life of Alexander Hamilton* (New York: Skyhorse Publishing, 2016), 75, 195; Chernow, *Alexander Hamilton*, 465–66, 548–49.

31. Charles Maurice de Talleyrand-Périgord, *Memoirs of the Prince de Talleyrand*, vol. 1, ed. Duc de Broglie, trans. Raphael Ledos de Beaufort (London: Griffith Farran Okeden and Welsh, 1891), 185.

Chapter 2. Thomas Jefferson: The Futurist

1. For Jefferson's Notes on Coinage, see the documents contained in *The Papers of Thomas Jefferson*, vol. 7, *2 March 1784–25 February 1785*, ed. Julian P. Boyd (Princeton, NJ: Princeton University Press, 1953), 150–203. Congress adopted Jefferson's decimal system in 1785. See Willard Sterne Randall, *Thomas Jefferson: A Life* (New York: Henry Holt and Company, 1993), 361. On the thirty-one reports, see Dumas Malone, *Thomas Jefferson: The Virginian* (Charlottesville, VA: University of Virginia Press, 1948), 411.

2. Randall, *Thomas Jefferson*, 362.

3. For the Report of the Committee appointed to prepare a plan for the temporary government of western territory, see *The Papers of Thomas Jefferson*, vol. 6, *21 May 1781–1 March 1784*, ed. Julian P. Boyd (Princeton, NJ: Princeton University Press, 1962), 603–12.

4. Randall, *Thomas Jefferson*, 362; Malone, *Jefferson the Virginian*, 412–13; Noble E. Cunningham Jr., *In Pursuit of Reason: The Life of Thomas Jefferson* (Baton Rouge, LA: Louisiana State University Press, 1987), 85–86; Jon Meacham, *Thomas Jefferson: The Art of Power* (New York: Random House, 2012), 173; John Ferling, *Jefferson and Hamilton: The Rivalry That Forged a Nation* (New York: Bloomsbury Press, 2013), 148–49.

5. "Jefferson's Observations on DéMeunier's Manuscript, 22 June 1786," in *The Papers of Thomas Jefferson*, vol. 10, *22 June–31 December 1786*, ed. Julian P. Boyd (Princeton, NJ: Princeton University Press, 1954), 58. On Jefferson's decision to no longer press the slavery issue, see Meacham, *Thomas Jefferson*, 174.

6. Joseph Ellis, *His Excellency: George Washington* (New York: Alfred A. Knopf, 2004), 212. For the original source, see "Enclosure, 15 June 1789," in *The Papers of George Washington: Presidential Series*, vol. 2, *1 April 1789–15 June 1789*, ed. Dorothy Twohig (Charlottesville, VA: University Press of Virginia, 1987), 490–95. For the struggle to develop and implement a policy for western lands under the Articles of Confederation, see George William Van Cleve, *We Have Not a Government* (Chicago: University of Chicago Press, 2017), 639–60. The classic account on the Northwest Ordinance is Peter S. Onuf, *Statehood and Union: A History of the Northwest Ordinance* (Bloomington: Indiana University Press, 1987). For a view of the Ordinance as an agreement reflecting internal divisions and geopolitical rivalries, see Jay Sexton, *A Nation Forged by Crisis* (New York: Basic Books, 2018), 49–51.

7. See David Hendrickson, *Peace Pact: The Lost World of the American Founding* (Lawrence, KS: University Press of Kansas, 2003); idem., *Union, Nation, or Empire: The American Debate over International Relations* (Lawrence, KS: University Press of Kansas, 2009); Elizabeth Cobbs Hoffman, *American Umpire* (Cambridge, MA: Harvard University Press, 2013).

8. Charles A. Cerami, *Jefferson's Great Gamble: The Remarkable Story of Jefferson, Napoleon and the Men Behind the Louisiana Purchase* (Naperville, IL: Sourcebooks, 2003), 5.

9. Cerami, *Jefferson's Great Gamble*, 11, 40; Alexander De Conde, *This Affair of Louisiana* (New York: Charles Scribner's Sons, 1976), 27, 28, 95, 105.

10. Napoleon would actually have been called Bonaparte at this time, because he was not yet emperor; I use his more common name in history. De Conde, *This Affair of Louisiana*, 86, 87, 91, 92; Jon Kukla, *A Wilderness So Immense: The Louisiana Purchase and the Destiny of America* (New York: Knopf, 2003), 204.

11. Cerami, *Jefferson's Great Gamble*, 32–33, 35–36.

12. Cerami, *Jefferson's Great Gamble*, 37, 41, 42; De Conde, *This Affair of Louisiana*, 91, 107, 111; Kukla, *Wilderness So Immense*, 216, 225–26.

13. Cerami, *Jefferson's Great Gamble*, 24, 32; De Conde, *This Affair of Louisiana*, 98.

14. De Conde, *This Affair of Louisiana*, 73, 113; Cerami, *Jefferson's Great Gamble*, 57.

15. Sainte Dominique was the name of the western part of the island of Hispaniola until 1804, when it became the Republic of Haiti. Spain ruled the eastern part, which today is the Dominican Republic. Both countries will play roles in later chapters. De Conde, *This Affair of Louisiana*, 98–102; Cerami, *Jefferson's Great Gamble*, 45–54.

16. De Conde, *This Affair of Louisiana*, 99–103. Piero Gleijeses questions De Conde's reference to American aid to Haiti, but he acknowledges that American merchants traded with the Haitian rebels. See Piero Gleijeses, "Napoleon, Jefferson, and the Louisiana Purchase," *International History Review* 39, no. 2 (2017), 241–42.

17. De Conde, *This Affair of Louisiana*, 102–4; Cerami, *Jefferson's Great Gamble*, 43, 68–69.

18. De Conde, *This Affair of Louisiana*, 113, 116–17; Cerami, *Jefferson's Great Gamble*, 57–59, 66.

19. Livingston's imagination ranged even more widely. He later financed Robert Fulton's steamboat experiments, opening a new age of navigation. And in 1809, he published an "Essay on Sheep." Kukla, *Wilderness So Immense*, 235–38.

20. For a discussion of Livingston and his diplomatic style, see Cerami, *Jefferson's Great Gamble*, 74–90; Kukla, *Wilderness So Immense*, 239–45. Livingston's perspective is also offered in Frank Brecher, *Negotiating the Louisiana Purchase: Robert Livingston's Mission to France, 1801–1804* (Jefferson, NC: McFarland & Co., 2006). Brecher also includes an English translation of Livingston's memo to Napoleon on colonies.

21. De Conde, *This Affair of Louisiana*, 112; Cerami, *Jefferson's Great Gamble*, 118.

22. Cerami, *Jefferson's Great Gamble*, 118–19; De Conde, *This Affair of Louisiana*, 117.

23. Ultimately, one of the businessmen, Eleuthère Irénée, founded a successful company producing gunpowder.

24. Cerami, *Jefferson's Great Gamble*, 134–40; De Conde, *This Affair of Louisiana*, 114–15, 130.

25. Cerami, *Jefferson's Great Gamble*, 139.

26. Cerami, *Jefferson's Great Gamble*, 142–43.

27. See Edward Channing, *The Jeffersonian System, 1801–1811* (New York: Cooper Square, 1968), 60–72; De Conde, *This Affair of Louisiana*, 119–22; Cerami, *Jefferson's Great Gamble*, 123–25.

28. De Conde, *This Affair of Louisiana*, 121–22.

29. De Conde, *This Affair of Louisiana*, 124.

30. De Conde, *This Affair of Louisiana*, 127–29, 132–34; Cerami, *Jefferson's Great Gamble*, 124–27.

31. Monroe served as Washington's minister to revolutionary France from 1794 to 1796. Though he was charged with maintaining neutrality toward Britain and France, Monroe's statements suggested strong U.S. sympathy for France. After America signed the Jay Treaty with Great Britain, American relations with France soured, prompting Washington to recall Monroe from Paris. Monroe would go on to be elected governor of Virginia in 1799.

32. For the original letter, see "From Thomas Jefferson to Thomas Mann Randolph, 17 January 1803," in *The Papers of Thomas Jefferson*, vol. 39, *13 November 1802–3 March 1803*, ed. Barbara B. Oberg (Princeton, NJ: Princeton University Press, 2012), 341. See De Conde, *This Affair of Louisiana*, 135.

33. On a possible alliance with Britain, see Cerami, *Jefferson's Great Gamble*, 144, 165. Robert W. Tucker and David C. Hendrickson, in *Empire of Liberty* (New York: Oxford University Press, 1990), 110–16, are skeptical that Jefferson was ever serious about an alliance with Britain. On the British chargé's recommendation, see De Conde, *This Affair of Louisiana*, 135.

34. "From Thomas Jefferson to the Senate and the House of Representatives, 18 January 1803," in *Papers of Thomas Jefferson*, vol. 39, 350–354. See De Conde, *This Affair of Louisiana*, 136–37. For an overview of the Lewis and Clark expedition, see, among others, Stephen E. Ambrose, *Undaunted Courage: Meriwether Lewis, Thomas Jefferson, and the Opening of the American West* (New York: Simon & Schuster, 1996).

35. De Conde, *This Affair of Louisiana*, 136; Tucker and Hendrickson, *Empire of Liberty*, 117–22.

36. Cerami, *Jefferson's Great Gamble*, 181; De Conde, *This Affair of Louisiana*, 136. For government outlays, see U.S. Bureau of the Census, *The Statistical History of the United States, from Colonial Times to the Present* (New York: Basic Books, 1976), 1115. (Of the $9.4 million, $4.4 million were for interest on the public debt.)

37. De Conde, *This Affair of Louisiana*, 151.

38. Cerami, *Jefferson's Great Gamble*, 123.

39. De Conde, *This Affair of Louisiana*, 141.

40. Cerami, *Jefferson's Great Gamble*, 126–28; De Conde, *This Affair of Louisiana*, 140, 157; Kukla, *Wilderness So Immense*, 267–68.

41. De Conde, *This Affair of Louisiana*, 142.

42. De Conde, *This Affair of Louisiana*, 153–54.

43. The French historian was Marie Joseph Louis Adolphe Thiers. See chapter 9 of De Conde, *This Affair of Louisiana*, especially 157–58.

44. De Conde, *This Affair of Louisiana*, 162–64; Cerami, *Jefferson's Great Gamble*, 92–94, 163–64; Kukla, *Wilderness So Immense*, 255–56 on Livingston's influence. Marbois is the source of accounts of discussions with Napoleon.

45. Cerami, *Jefferson's Great Gamble*, 165–66; De Conde, *This Affair of Louisiana*, 163.

46. See De Conde, *This Affair of Louisiana*, on France's verbal commitment (95) and then in writing (105).

47. De Conde, *This Affair of Louisiana*, 164–65.

48. France had wanted to acquire the Floridas, but Spain refused to offer them, given their importance to the Gulf Coast. See De Conde, *This Affair of Louisiana*, 169.

49. Cerami, *Jefferson's Great Gamble*, 180.

50. For a discussion of Monroe's decision, see Cerami, *Jefferson's Great Gamble*, 192–200.

51. For discussions of bargaining over price, see Cerami, *Jefferson's Great Gamble*, 202–5; De Conde, *This Affair of Louisiana*, 167–72. For size, see Cerami, *Jefferson's Great Gamble*, 258; Monticello, "The Louisiana Purchase," https://www.monticello.org/thomas-jefferson/louisiana-lewis-clark/the-louisiana-purchase/.

52. For a discussion of the arguments on constitutionality, see De Conde, *This Affair of Louisiana*, 178, 180–85; Cerami, *Jefferson's Great Gamble*, 208–12.

53. Quoted in De Conde, *This Affair of Louisiana*, 191.

54. Cerami, *Jefferson's Great Gamble*, 214–15.

55. Cerami, *Jefferson's Great Gamble*, 223, 239.

56. Prime Minister Henry Addington later requested that Barings halt payments, but Hope continued them with Barings' quiet support. De Conde, *This Affair of Louisiana*, 172, 173; Andrew Roberts, *Napoleon* (New York: Viking, 2014), 325–26.

57. De Conde, *This Affair of Louisiana*, 124. In a more recent historical review, Gleijeses concludes that Jefferson played "no role." See Gleijeses, "Napoleon, Jefferson, and the Louisiana Purchase," 237. I think that this conclusion underappreciates the roles of patience, promoting a conducive context, use of careful threats, and timing in this diplomacy. The Federalists had called for prompt military action (which likely would have appealed to Hamilton); another possibility was a president who responded with diffidence and inaction.

58. Tucker and Hendrickson, *Empire of Liberty*, 125.

59. Cobbs Hoffman, *American Umpire*, 90.

60. Henry Adams, *History of the United States of America During the First Administration of Thomas Jefferson*, vol. 2 (New York: Charles Scribner's Sons, 1921), 48–49.

Chapter 3. John Quincy Adams and Henry Clay: American Realism and the American System

1. Ernest May, *The Making of the Monroe Doctrine* (Cambridge, MA: Belknap Press of Harvard University Press, 1975), 1.

2. James Traub, *John Quincy Adams: Militant Spirit* (New York: Basic Books, 2016), 203; Samuel Flagg Bemis, *John Quincy Adams and the Foundations of American Foreign Policy* (Westport, CT: Greenwood Press, 1949), 231.

3. See Kissinger, *World Restored*.

4. For the circumstances of Canning's proposal, see May, *Making of the Monroe Doctrine*, 1–4; Dexter Perkins, *A History of the Monroe Doctrine* (Boston: Little, Brown, 1955), 36–38; Jay Sexton, *The Monroe Doctrine: Empire and Nation in Nineteenth-Century America* (New York: Hill and Wang, 2011), 49–51.

5. For naval comparisons, see May, *Making of the Monroe Doctrine*, 4.

6. For the international comparison, see May, *Making of the Monroe Doctrine*, 11.

7. May, *Making of the Monroe Doctrine*, 6. For the original, see "Mr. Rush to Mr. John Quincy Adams," August 23, 1823, no. 323, in *The Clayton-Bulwer Treaty and the Monroe Doctrine: A Letter from the Secretary of State to the Minister of the United States at London* (Washington, DC: Government Printing Office, 1882), 36.

8. For Canning's policy of cabinet maneuvers, see May, *Making of the Monroe Doctrine*, 122–28.

9. May, *Making of the Monroe Doctrine*, 190–91.

10. For Alexander and Russia, see May, *Making of the Monroe Doctrine*, 66–85. For the ukase and Russia in North America, see ibid., 79–80. For the population size, see ibid., 66. For geographic references, see Traub, *John Quincy Adams*, 276–77.

11. For JQA's discussions with Baron de Tuyll, see May, *Making of the Monroe Doctrine*, 194–96; Traub, *John Quincy Adams*, 276–77.

12. For Greece, including references to U.S. public opinion and the press, see May, *Making of the Monroe Doctrine*, 9–10.

13. For the background on Monroe, see May, *Making of the Monroe Doctrine*, 12–24. See also the Monroe biography by Harry Ammon, *James Monroe: The Quest for National Identity* (New York: McGraw-Hill, 1971).

14. For Monroe's principles, see May, *Making of the Monroe Doctrine*, 21. For the original Monroe quote, see Monroe to Thomas Jefferson, January 11, 1807, in *The Writings of James Monroe*, vol. 5, *1807–1816*, ed. Stanislaus Murray Hamilton (New York: G. P. Putnam's Sons, 1901), 2.

15. On JQA, see the biography by Traub, *John Quincy Adams*. See also Samuel Flagg Bemis's two landmark studies, *John Quincy Adams and the Foundations of American Foreign Policy* (New York: Knopf, 1950) and

John Quincy Adams and the Union (New York: Knopf, 1956). For the diary quote, see JQA, *Memoirs of John Quincy Adams*, vol. 4, ed. Charles Francis Adams (Philadelphia: J. B. Lippincott & Co., 1875), 388.

16. Quoted in Bemis, *John Quincy Adams and the Foundations of American Foreign Policy*, 243.

17. Quoted in Traub, *John Quincy Adams*, 69, 78.

18. Quoted in Perkins, *Monroe Doctrine*, 29. For the original, see JQA, *Memoirs of John Quincy Adams*, vol. 4, 438.

19. Stratford Canning was Britain's minister to the United States and cousin of Foreign Secretary George Canning.

20. Quoted in Traub, *John Quincy Adams*, 261–62. For the original, see JQA, *Memoirs of John Quincy Adams*, vol. 5, ed. Charles Francis Adams (Philadelphia: J. B. Lippincott & Co., 1875), 252.

21. Traub, *John Quincy Adams*, 229.

22. Traub, *John Quincy Adams*, 231.

23. Traub, *John Quincy Adams*, 261.

24. JQA, *The Writings of John Quincy Adams*, vol. 7, *1820–1823*, ed. Worthington Chauncey Ford (New York: Macmillan Company, 1917), 469.

25. On JQA's commercial diplomacy, see Traub, *John Quincy Adams*, 261; Norman Graebner, "John Quincy Adams," in *American Statesmen: Secretaries of State from John Jay to Colin Powell*, ed. Edward S. Mihalkanin (Westport, CT: Greenwood Press, 2004), 23.

26. Traub, *John Quincy Adams*, 239.

27. See May, *Making of the Monroe Doctrine*, x, xi, 35–36. For a differing view, see Traub, *John Quincy Adams*, 270.

28. On British bullying, see Traub, *John Quincy Adams*, 261. On condescension and arrogance, see Perkins, *Monroe Doctrine*, 39. JQA quoted in May, *Making of the Monroe Doctrine*, 28. For the original JQA quote, see JQA, *The Writings of John Quincy Adams*, vol. 1, *1779–1796*, ed. Worthington Chauncey Ford (New York: Macmillan Company, 1913), 478.

29. Quoted in May, *Making of the Monroe Doctrine*, 28. For the original, see JQA, *The Writings of John Quincy Adams*, vol. 3, *1801–1810*, ed. Worthington Chauncey Ford (New York: Macmillan Company, 1914), 300. Charles Edel's *Nation Builder* uses a grand strategy framework to relate Adams's life and service. See Edel, *Nation Builder: John Quincy Adams and the Grand Strategy of the Republic* (Cambridge, MA: Harvard University Press, 2014).

30. On the July 4 speech, see Traub, *John Quincy Adams*, 256–59. For the original text of the speech, see JQA, *An Address Delivered at the Request of a Committee of the Citizens of Washington; on the Occasion of Reading the Declaration of Independence on the Fourth of July, 1821* (Washington, DC: Davis and Force, 1821).

31. On Clay, see Robert V. Remini, *Henry Clay: Statesman for the Union* (New York: W. W. Norton, 1991); David S. and Jeanne T. Heidler, *Henry Clay: The Essential American* (New York: Random House, 2010). See also May, *Making of the Monroe Doctrine*, 50–57. Quotes from Remini, *Henry Clay*, 155. For the original, see *Annals of Congress*, 15th Congress, 1st Session (Washington, D.C.: Gales and Seaton, 1854), 401–4.

32. Quoted in Traub, *John Quincy Adams*, 250. For the original, see Louisa Catherine Adams, *A Traveled First Lady: Writings of Louisa Catherine Adams*, ed. Margaret A. Hogan and C. James Taylor (Cambridge, MA: Belknap Press of Harvard University Press, 2014), 252.

33. For Clay's political strategy, see May, *Making of the Monroe Doctrine*, 173–81.

34. On Clay's speech, see Remini, *Henry Clay*, 174–75. For the original speech, see Henry Clay, *The Life, Correspondence, and Speeches of Henry Clay*, vol. 5, ed. Calvin Colton (New York: A. S. Barnes & Co., 1857), 243.

35. On Clay's speech at Lexington, see May, *Making of the Monroe Doctrine*, 180. For the original speech, see Henry Clay, *The Life, Correspondence, and Speeches of Henry Clay*, vol. 1, ed. Calvin Colton (New York: A. S. Barnes & Co., 1857), 241.

36. Traub, *John Quincy Adams*, 258–59.

37. May, *Making of the Monroe Doctrine*, 191, 197.

38. For JQA discussions with de Tuyll see May, *Making of the Monroe Doctrine*, 196, 199; Traub, *John Quincy Adams*, 276–77, 279; Perkins, *Monroe Doctrine*, 40.

39. On the cabinet meeting discussion, see May, *Making of the Monroe Doctrine*, 198–200; Traub, *John Quincy Adams*, 279–80; Perkins, *Monroe Doctrine*, 41–42.

40. May, *Making of the Monroe Doctrine*, 200–208; Traub, *John Quincy Adams*, 280–81.

41. May, *Making of the Monroe Doctrine*, 204, 208–10.

42. May, *Making of the Monroe Doctrine*, 210.

43. For Monroe's draft and debate, see May, *Making of the Monroe Doctrine*, 211–18; Perkins, *Monroe Doctrine*, 43–44; Traub, *John Quincy Adams*, 281–82.

44. For Wirt, see May, *Making of the Monroe Doctrine*, 220–21; Traub, *John Quincy Adams*, 285; Sexton, *Monroe Doctrine*, 61.

45. On the length and context of Monroe's message, see Sexton, *Monroe Doctrine*, 47–48. On the text, including the less noted opening and closing paragraphs, see ibid., 53–62. On "open diplomacy," see Perkins, *Monroe Doctrine*, 62. On JQA's anticolonialism, see Traub, *John Quincy Adams*, 285.

46. May, *Making of the Monroe Doctrine*, 219–28. For Monroe's letter to Jefferson, see Monroe to Jefferson, December 4, 1823, in *The Writings of James Monroe*, vol. 6, *1817–1823*, ed. Stanislaus Murray Hamilton (New York: G. P. Putnam's Sons, 1903), 342–45.

47. For Canning's reaction and response, see May, *Making of the Monroe Doctrine*, 240–44; Sexton, *Monroe Doctrine*, 65–66.

48. Quoted in Perkins, *Monroe Doctrine*, 56–57.

49. Perkins, *Monroe Doctrine*, 57–58.

50. Quoted in Remini, *Henry Clay*, 221–22. For the original, see JQA, *Memoirs of John Quincy Adams*, vol. 6, ed. Charles Francis Adams (Philadelphia: J. B. Lippincott & Co., 1875), 224.

51. Cobbs Hoffman, *American Umpire*, 105; Perkins, *Monroe Doctrine*, 4, 387–89.

52. Traub, *John Quincy Adams*, 286.

53. Traub, *John Quincy Adams*, 286.

54. See the essays by Root and Hughes in *The Monroe Doctrine: Its Modern Significance*, ed. Donald Marquand Dozer (New York: Knopf, 1965), 51, 87, respectively.

55. Ammon, *James Monroe*, 491.

56. Sexton, *Monroe Doctrine*, 61.

57. On Bolivar, see Kinley Brauer, "Henry Clay," in Mihalkanin, *American Statesmen*, 129. On the U.S. invitation to the Panama Congress, see Remini, *Henry Clay*, 285; Perkins, *Monroe Doctrine*, 71; Sexton, *Monroe Doctrine*, 74; Heidler and Heidler, *Henry Clay*, 194; Traub, *John Quincy Adams*, 342.

58. On Clay's instructions, see Remini, *Henry Clay*, 297–300. For the original text of the instructions, see Clay to Richard C. Andersen Jr. and John Sargeant, May 8, 1826, in *The Papers of Henry Clay*, vol. 5, ed. James F. Hopkins and Mary W. M. Hargreaves (Lexington, KY: University Press of Kentucky, 1984), 313–344.

59. Remini, *Henry Clay*, 297–300.

60. Remini, *Henry Clay*, 287–97. On the popularity of the Panama Congress, see Traub, *John Quincy Adams*, 345; Sexton, *Monroe Doctrine*, 75–80; Heidler and Heidler, *Henry Clay*, 195.

61. Remini, *Henry Clay*, 300–301.

62. Traub, *John Quincy Adams*, 259–60.

63. For an account of Adams's "Grand Strategy of the Republic," see Edel, *Nation Builder*, especially at 2, 4, 8, 61, 62.

Chapter 4. Abraham Lincoln and William Seward: Pragmatic Unionists

1. Kevin Peraino, *Lincoln in the World: The Making of a Statesman and the Dawn of American Power* (New York: Crown Publishers, 2013), 66–68; Dean Mahin, *One War at a Time: The International Dimensions of the American Civil War* (Washington, DC: Brassey's, 1999), 7; Walter Stahr, *Seward: Lincoln's Indispensable Man* (New York: Simon & Schuster, 2012), 269–73; Glyndon Van Deusen, *William Henry Seward* (New York: Oxford University Press, 1967), 282–84 (emphasis in original).

2. Peraino, *Lincoln in the World*, 116–17.

3. See, most important, Peraino, *Lincoln in the World*; Mahin, *One War at a Time*; Howard Jones, *Blue and Gray Diplomacy: A History of Union and Confederate Foreign Relations* (Chapel Hill, NC: University of North Carolina Press, 2010).

4. According to Stahr, the "best evidence" that Lincoln said "one war at a time" is found in the *Norfolk (MA) County Journal*, which printed on December 28, 1861, that Lincoln "never spoke a wiser word than when he said 'one war at a time.'" Moreover, the *New York Times* reported on April 29, 1865, that Seward's policy was based on "the President's famous motto: 'one war at a time.'" See Stahr, *Seward*, 323, 618–619fn81. Stahr suggests that Mahin provides no citation for the title of his book, *One War at a Time*, though Mahin does quote Lincoln writing "one trouble at a time" with regard to Mexico (233).

5. For perspectives on the international order in flux, see D. P. Crook, *Diplomacy During the American Civil War* (New York: Wiley, 1975), 2–11, 185; Peraino, *Lincoln in the World*, 7, 65, 69, 174; Norman Graebner, "Northern Diplomacy and European Neutrality," in *Why the North Won the Civil War*, ed. David Herbert Donald (Baton Rouge, LA: Louisiana State University Press, 1960), 55–56.

6. On the "scramble for America" and Palmerston, see Crook, *Diplomacy*, 2–3. For the original, see Lord Palmerston to Lord Clarendon, December 31, 1857, in Kenneth Bourne, *The Foreign Policy of Victorian England, 1830–1902* (Oxford: Clarendon, 1970), 334. For the economic data, see Crook, *Diplomacy*, 8–12, 109; Amanda Foreman, *A World on Fire: An Epic History of Two Nations Divided* (London: Allen Lane, 2010), 9, 64; Mahin, *One War at a Time*, 83–87.

7. Crook, *Diplomacy*, 8.

8. For Confederate perspective, including "King Cotton," see Crook, *Diplomacy*, 8–16. For implicit embargo, see Mahin, *One War at a Time*, 21.

9. Foreman, *World on Fire*, 26–27.

10. Doris Kearns Goodwin, *Team of Rivals: The Political Genius of Abraham Lincoln* (New York: Simon & Schuster, 2005).

11. For Russell, see John Taylor, *William Henry Seward: Lincoln's Right Hand* (Washington, DC: Potomac Books, 1991), 144–45. For the physical description of Seward, see Van Deusen, *Seward*, 225. See also Stahr, *Seward*, 213.

12. Mahin, *One War at a Time*, 258.

13. See Peraino, *Lincoln in the World*, 71, 75, 101; George Herring, *From Colony to Superpower: U.S. Foreign Relations since 1776* (New York: Oxford University Press, 2008), 255.

14. For concerns about the Buchanan administration, see Peraino, *Lincoln in the World*, 96–97. On Seward's three points, see Van Deusen, *Seward*, 293.

15. On British attitudes, the Cornwallis comparison, and *Times* of London quote, see Mahin, *One War at a Time*, 24–25.

16. On the blockade decision, see Peraino, *Lincoln in the World*, 114–15, 121 (including Lincoln's quote); Mahin, *One War at a Time*, 44–45; Crook, *Diplomacy*, 27–29.

17. For Britain's neutrality proclamation, see Crook, *Diplomacy*, 32–37; Mahin, *One War at a Time*, 42–49; Peraino, *Lincoln in the World*, 114–15 (including Seward's quote); Stahr, *Seward*, 292–95; Van Deusen, *Seward*; Graebner, "Northern Diplomacy," 60.

18. For the U.S. reaction, see Mahin, *One War at a Time*, 46–51; Crook, *Diplomacy*, 40; Stahr, *Seward*, 291; Peraino, *Lincoln in the World*, 114–15; Van Deusen, *Seward*, 301; Graebner, "Northern Diplomacy," 61.

19. On the *Trent* incident, see Norman Ferris, *The Trent Affair: A Diplomatic Crisis* (Knoxville, TN: University of Tennessee Press, 1977); Mahin, *One War at a Time*, 58 on; Stahr, *Seward*, 307 on; Crook, *Diplomacy*, 43 on; Jones, *Blue and Gray Diplomacy*, 83 on.

20. In 1906, Mason's daughter revealed that the Confederate envoys had asked the British officer in charge of the mails to lock up their papers and deliver them to a Confederate commissioner, which he later did. These papers were clearly contraband under the queen's proclamation, although the facts were not known for almost fifty years. See Mahin, *One War at a Time*, 60.

21. On "white elephants," see Mahin, *One War at a Time*, 62; Peraino, *Lincoln in the World*, 125.

22. On "999 out of 1,000," see Peraino, *Lincoln in the World*, 125.

23. Palmerston quoted in Peraino, *Lincoln in the World*, 129.

24. Palmerston quoted in Peraino, *Lincoln in the World*, 129.

25. Palmerston quoted in Peraino, *Lincoln in the World*, 137.

26. Foreman, *World on Fire*, 181–82, 188; Stahr, *Seward*, 313–14.

27. The tale was probably based on a misunderstanding of a bad joke by the teasing Seward, but now the maladroit behavior was taken as a prophecy. Seward had also once jibed that the Canadian provinces would make "excellent states."

28. Stahr, *Seward*, 316–17.

29. Peraino, *Lincoln in the World*, 162–63; Foreman, *World on Fire*, 190.

30. Stahr, *Seward*, 312.

31. Mahin, *One War at a Time*, 75.

32. Stahr, *Seward*, 316.

33. Peraino, *Lincoln in the World*, 157.

34. For the text of Seward's proposal, see Mr. Seward to Lord Lyons, December 26, 1861, in *The Works of William H. Seward*, vol. 5, ed. George Baker (Boston: Houghton, Mifflin and Company, 1884), 295–311.

35. Peraino, *Lincoln in the World*, 161; Stahr, *Seward*, 320–21.

36. Mahin, *One War at a Time*, 81.

37. See Peraino, *Lincoln in the World*, 159–60.
38. On the slave trade treaty, see Peraino, *Lincoln in the World*, 168–69. For data on slaves transported to Cuba, see Stahr, *Seward*, 337–38. On recognition of Haiti and Liberia, see ibid., 335–36.
39. On the cotton market, see Mahin, *One War at a Time*, 86–94; Crook, *Diplomacy*, 72–79. On the French foreign minister, see Mahin, *One War at a Time*, 96–97; Graebner, "Northern Diplomacy," 68; Crook, *Diplomacy*, 81. On the Commons debate, see ibid., 83–84. On Russia, see Stahr, *Seward*, 347–52. On Poland, see ibid., 364–65. On British and French textiles, see Peraino, *Lincoln in the World*, 204–5.
40. On Seward's guidance, see Mahin, *One War at a Time*, 126.
41. On the British reaction, see Crook, *Diplomacy*, 95–97. On "servile insurrection," the Indian Mutiny, and "trash," see Mahin, *One War at a Time*, 131–33.
42. At an Aspen seminar that I helped organize in 1995, Sir Michael Howard, the eminent British military historian, used the example of European intervention in the U.S. Civil War to caution well-meaning Americans to weigh carefully the consequences of trying to stop warring parties from finishing their battles. Sometimes peace requires one side to win, or both sides to fight until they decide more killing is futile. Michael Howard, "Managing Conflict: Lessons from the Past," in *Managing Conflict in the Post–Cold War World: The Role of Intervention*, Aspen Institute (Queenstown, MD: Aspen Institute, 1996), 3.
43. Crook, *Diplomacy*, 91–93; Mahin, *One War at a Time*, 130.
44. Crook, *Diplomacy*, 93–105; Mahin, *One War at a Time*, 133–38.
45. On mass meetings, see Crook, *Diplomacy*, 123. On Lincoln's letter and U.S. payments, see Peraino, *Lincoln in the World*, 216–17. On British support and the letter to Manchester, see Foreman, *World on Fire*, 394–95.
46. Foreman, *World on Fire*, 319.
47. See, e.g., Kori Schake, *Safe Passage: The Transition from British to American Hegemony* (Cambridge, MA: Harvard University Press, 2017), 84–117. Lord Chancellor quoted in Foreman, *World on Fire*, 212.
48. Crook, *Diplomacy*, 167; Mahin, *One War at a Time*, 142–60, 174 on; Rodney P. Carlisle, *Civil War and Reconstruction* (New York: Facts on File, 2008), 174 on loss of the merchant fleet.
49. On *Alabama* arbitration, see Mahin, *One War at a Time*, 286.
50. On Mexico, see Crook, *Diplomacy*, 155 on; Mahin, *One War at a Time*, 106 on.
51. On the importance of the Union as a model of international relations, see David Hendrickson, *Union, Nation, or Empire: The American Debate over International Relations, 1789–1941* (Lawrence, KS: University Press of Kansas, 2009).
52. Seward quoted in Peraino, *Lincoln in the World*, 70–71. On Asia trade, see Stahr, *Seward*, 502.
53. Stahr, *Seward*, 453–54.
54. The poor Russian minister was stuck with a bill of more than $9,000 when he used an international telegraph, a new tool of diplomacy, to seek St. Petersburg's rapid approval of the treaty before the Senate recessed. Stahr, *Seward*, 482–91, including telegraph bill at 485.
55. Stahr, *Seward*, 497–500.
56. Seward drafted the treaty with Anson Burlingame, who had served as U.S. envoy to China during the Civil War. Burlingame had resigned his post in order to negotiate on behalf of the Qing empire. The novel treaty he negotiated with Seward banned discrimination against Chinese workers in the United States and enabled Chinese immigrants to become U.S. citizens. Article 7 committed the United States to welcome Chinese at any educational institution under control of the U.S. government, an intriguing innovation that initiated a student and intellectual Sino-American exchange that continues through today. Although the United States would later reverse some of the treaty's terms, especially its opening of immigration, the sovereignty and most-favored nation trade provisions previewed John Hay's "Open Door" policy at the end of the century. For Seward as an Asia strategist and the "Far West," see Michael Green, *By More Than Providence: Grand Strategy and American Power in the Asia Pacific Since 1783* (New York: Columbia University Press, 2017), 56–61, 77. On Midway and the navy report to Congress, see Stahr, *Seward*, 494. On Hawaii, see ibid., 500. For the U.S.-China treaty terms, see John Pomfret, *The Beautiful Country and the Middle Kingdom: America and China, 1776 to the Present* (New York: Henry Holt and Company, 2016), 65.
57. President Grant would later annex the Dominican Republic, but the Senate rejected his treaty. Stahr, *Seward*, 494–96, 519–20.
58. On Panama, see Stahr, *Seward*, 523–24. On Greenland and Iceland, see ibid., 516.
59. Lincoln quoted in Peraino, *Lincoln in the World*, 2.
60. Lincoln quoted in Mahin, *One War at a Time*, 216.
61. On Lincoln's speeches, see Peraino, *Lincoln in the World*, 279, 282. See Abraham Lincoln, "Response to a

Serenade," November 10, 1864, in *The Collected Works of Abraham Lincoln*, vol. 8, ed. Roy P. Basler (New Brunswick, NJ: Rutgers University Press, 1953), 101; idem., "Second Inaugural Address of Abraham Lincoln," March 4, 1865, The Avalon Project: Documents in Law, History, and Diplomacy, Yale University, http://avalon.law.yale.edu/19th_century/lincoln2.asp.

62. Fulbright quoted in Peraino, *Lincoln in the World*, 299.

Chapter 5. John Hay: The Open Door

1. John Taliaferro, *All the Great Prizes: The Life of John Hay, from Lincoln to Roosevelt* (New York: Simon & Schuster, 2013), 359–60.

2. Taliaferro, *All the Great Prizes*, 362–66; Green, *By More Than Providence*, 94–95; Pomfret, *Beautiful Country*, 106; Robert W. Merry, *President McKinley: Architect of the American Century* (New York: Simon & Schuster, 2017), 417.

3. Taliaferro, *All the Great Prizes*, 330. For the original letter, see Hay to Roosevelt, July 27, 1898, in *The Life and Letters of John Hay*, vol. 2, ed. William Roscoe Thayer (Boston: Houghton Mifflin Company, 1915), 337.

4. Howard K. Beale, *Theodore Roosevelt and the Rise of America to World Power* (New York: Collier Books, 1962), 38. For background on Mr. Dooley, see Warren Zimmermann, *First Great Triumph: How Five Americans Made Their Country a World Power* (New York: Farrar, Straus and Giroux, 2002), 352.

5. Beale, *Theodore Roosevelt*, 226–29. See Brooks Adams, *America's Economic Supremacy* (New York: Macmillan Company, 1900).

6. On Mahan's views, see Green, *By More Than Providence*, 80–85. See Alfred Thayer Mahan, *The Influence of Sea Power Upon History, 1660–1783* (Boston: Little, Brown and Company, 1890). For "debated and debatable," see idem., *The Problem of Asia and Its Effect upon International Policies* (Boston: Little, Brown, 1900). For Mahan's views on tariffs and "moral influence," see "The United States Looking Outward," *Atlantic Monthly*, vol. 66 (December 1890), 816–24. This article was subsequently reproduced with slight modifications as the first chapter in *The Interest of America in Sea Power, Present and Future* (Boston: Little, Brown and Company, 1897).

7. Beale, *Theodore Roosevelt*, 226–29. See Mahan, *Problem of Asia*.

8. Eugene Trani, *The Treaty of Portsmouth: An Adventure in American Diplomacy* (Lexington, KY: University of Kentucky Press, 1969), 24–25.

9. Beale, *Theodore Roosevelt*, 31–32.

10. Hollington K. Tong, "China's Conditions at the Peace Conference," *Millard's Review of the Far East* 4, no. 9 (April 27, 1918), 305. Variations of this statement are widely cited. See, among others, Parker Thomas Moon, *Imperialism and World Politics* (New York: Macmillan Company, 1926), 321.

11. Quoted in Zimmermann, *First Great Triumph*, 446. For the original, see Hay to Paul Dana, March 16, 1899, in *Life and Letters of John Hay*, vol. 2, 241.

12. See Thomas Pakenham, *The Scramble for Africa: 1876–1912* (New York: Random House, 1991).

13. S. C. M. Paine, *The Sino-Japanese War of 1894–1895: Perceptions, Power, and Primacy* (Cambridge: Cambridge University Press, 2002), 2.

14. On Japan's acquisitions, see Merry, *McKinley*, 415.

15. For data on China in the nineteenth century, see Merry, *McKinley*, 414–15. For two superb accounts of the Qing dynasty's last century, including the Taiping Civil War, see Stephen R. Platt's *Imperial Twilight: The Opium War and the End of China's Last Golden Age* (New York: Knopf, 2018) and his earlier *Autumn in the Heavenly Kingdom: China, the West, and the Epic Story of the Taiping Civil War* (New York: Knopf, 2012).

16. Quoted in Merry, *McKinley*, 416.

17. On the *Empress of China*, early U.S. trade, and "Jackal Diplomacy," see Green, *By More Than Providence*, 22, 24. More broadly, see Arthur Power Dudden, *The American Pacific: From the Old China Trade to the Present* (New York: Oxford University Press, 1992); Foster Rhea Dulles, *The Old China Trade* (Cambridge, MA: Riverside, 1930); idem., *China and America: The Story of Their Relations Since 1784* (Princeton, NJ: Princeton University Press, 1946), 1–17.

18. For data on U.S.-China trade, see Zimmermann, *First Great Triumph*, 446; Taliaferro, *All the Great Prizes*, 354. On cotton and other exports and Hong Kong, see Pomfret, *Beautiful Country*, 106. On U.S. export growth to Asia, see Merry, *McKinley*, 414.

19. On missionaries, see Green, *By More Than Providence*, 93. Pearl S. Buck, raised in China by missionary parents, was the first American woman to win the Nobel Prize for Literature (in 1938). Her book *The Good*

Earth, a bestseller in 1931–32, received the Pulitzer Prize in 1932, and Hollywood later made the tale into a movie viewed by millions.

20. Green, *By More Than Providence*, 80; Zimmermann, *First Great Triumph*, 7.

21. The United States had sent only ministers abroad, instead of ambassadors, until 1893, signaling a note of republican reserve about monarchical ambassadors. Zimmermann, *First Great Triumph*, 50.

22. Quoted in Taliaferro, *All the Great Prizes*, 335. For the original source, see *Life and Letters of John Hay*, vol. 2, 181.

23. Taliaferro, *All the Great Prizes*, 336.

24. Zimmermann, *First Great Triumph*, 82.

25. On telephones, electricity, and the size of the State Department, see Taliaferro, *All the Great Prizes*, 335–36.

26. Born in Philadelphia, raised in France, Rockhill had graduated from Saint-Cyr, the French military academy, and then served two years in Algeria as an officer in the French Foreign Legion. His interest in Buddhism led to studies of Sanskrit, Chinese, and Tibetan. Appointed to the American legation in Beijing, the intrepid diplomat took two treks across China to the Himalayas. He also served in St. Petersburg and Constantinople, and ran a ranch in New Mexico. At six foot four, with red hair and an extravagant mustache, Rockhill fit his State Department nickname, "Big Chief." For Rockhill's background, see Pomfret, *Beautiful Country*, 105–7; Taliaferro, *All the Great Prizes*, 326; Green, *By More Than Providence*, 94. See also Paul Varg, *Open Door Diplomat: The Life of W. W. Rockhill* (Urbana, IL: University of Illinois Press, 1952); Peter Stanley, "The Making of an American Sinologist: William W. Rockhill and the Open Door," *Perspectives in American History* 11 (January 1977), 419–62.

27. On Rockhill's appointment, see Taliaferro, *All the Great Prizes*, 349.

28. Pomfret, *Beautiful Country*, 107–8.

29. Taliaferro, *All the Great Prizes*, 357; Merry, *McKinley*, 416–17. For the original letter, see Hay to Paul Dana, March 16, 1899, in *Life and Letters of John Hay*, vol. 2, 241.

30. Taliaferro, *All the Great Prizes*, 357–58; Merry, *McKinley*, 417.

31. Taliaferro, *All the Great Prizes*, 358. For the original source of the Schurman quotes, see "Dr. Schurman Talks of China: How to Insure the Integrity of That Empire Is the Great Question in the Orient," *New York Times*, August 16, 1899, 7.

32. Taliaferro, *All the Great Prizes*, 359.

33. For the Boxer Rebellion and the second Open Door note, including all information and quotes from the above paragraphs, see Taliaferro, *All the Great Prizes*, 376–85; Pomfret, *Beautiful Country*, 108–13 (including Rockhill quotes at start and end); Merry, *McKinley*, 419–28. For a detailed study of Hay's diplomacy and the domestic and international contexts in which the Open Door notes were formulated, see Betty Talbert, "The Evolution of John Hay's China Policy" (PhD diss., University of North Carolina, 1974).

34. On the settlement, see Taliaferro, *All the Great Prizes*, 385–89 (including Hay persuading McKinley to keep troops in place); Pomfret, *Beautiful Country*, 114–16, 122–24 (including use of indemnity for education and Tsinghua); Merry, *McKinley*, 428–30 (for McKinley quote on friendship with China and Hay persuading the president not to withdraw troops).

35. On Rockhill's economic agenda like today, exclusion of Chinese and "yellow peril," Chinese protest, and TR quote, see Pomfret, *Beautiful Country*, 115–19.

36. Quoted in Taliaferro, *All the Great Prizes*, 386–87; Pomfret, *Beautiful Country*, 120. For the original letter, see Hay to Alvey A. Adee, September 14, 1900, in Alfred L. P. Dennis, *Adventures in American Diplomacy, 1896–1906* (New York: E. P. Dutton & Company, 1928), 258.

37. Root quoted in Pomfret, *Beautiful Country*, 111.

38. Green, *By More Than Providence*, 107; Alfred Thayer Mahan, *The Interest of America in International Conditions* (Boston: Little, Brown, 1910), 178–83.

39. The Roosevelt letter to Taft is reproduced in part in A. Whitney Griswold, *The Far Eastern Policy of the United States* (New York: Harcourt, Brace and Company, 1938), 132.

40. See chapter 8. For the implications of the Open Door notes and their later role in U.S. diplomacy, see also Green, *By More Than Providence*, 95, 121, 139, 149.

41. Kennan, *American Diplomacy*, 39.

42. Williams, *Tragedy of American Diplomacy*, 50.

43. For the percentage of U.S. exports to China, see Green, *By More Than Providence*, 103.

44. Adam Tooze, *The Deluge: The Great War, America, and the Remaking of the Global Order, 1916–1931* (New York: Viking, 2014), 15–16.

Chapter 6. Theodore Roosevelt: Balancer of Power

1. Tyler Dennett, *Roosevelt and the Russo-Japanese War: A Critical Study of American Policy in Eastern Asia in 1902-5* (Garden City, NY: Doubleday, Page & Company, 1925), 150; John Albert White, *The Diplomacy of the Russo-Japanese War* (Princeton, NJ: Princeton University Press, 1964), 148–50.

2. Raymond A. Esthus, *Double Eagle and Rising Sun: The Russians and Japanese at Portsmouth in 1905* (Durham, NC: Duke University Press, 1988), 1.

3. Raymond A. Esthus, *Theodore Roosevelt and the International Rivalries* (Waltham, MA: Ginn-Blaisdell, 1970), 25 (hereafter *TR*); Trani, *Treaty of Portsmouth*, 27–29.

4. On the terms of Anglo-Japanese alliance, see Esthus, *TR*, 26. On the Korean "neutral zone," see ibid., 27. The Korean king had fled to the Russian legation after the Japanese killed the queen. See Seung-Young Kim, "Russo-Japanese Rivalry Over Korean Buffer at the Beginning of the 20th Century and Its Implications," *Diplomacy and Statecraft* 16, no. 4 (December 2005), 619–50.

5. Trani, *Treaty of Portsmouth*, 7, 8.

6. Beale, *Theodore Roosevelt*, 177–81; Trani, *Treaty of Portsmouth*, 8–9, 15; Esthus, *TR*, 26.

7. Quoted in Esthus, *TR*, 26. For the original correspondence, see TR to Cecil Spring-Rice, March 19, 1904, in *The Letters of Theodore Roosevelt*, vol. 4, ed. Elting E. Morison (Cambridge, MA: Harvard University Press, 1951), 760.

8. For "two thousand years," see John Milton Cooper, *The Warrior and the Priest: Woodrow Wilson and Theodore Roosevelt* (Cambridge, MA: Belknap Press of Harvard University Press, 1983), 34; for "degenerative materialism," see ibid., 36; John Blum, "Theodore Roosevelt: The Years of Decision," in *Letters of Theodore Roosevelt*, vol. 2, ed. Elting E. Morison (Cambridge, MA: Harvard University Press, 1951), 1491.

9. H. W. Brands, "Theodore Roosevelt: America's First Strategic Thinker," in *Artists of Power: Theodore Roosevelt, Woodrow Wilson, and Their Enduring Impact on U.S. Foreign Policy*, eds. William N. Tilchin and Charles E. Neu (Westport, CT: Praeger Security International, 2006), 39. For the original, see TR to Cecil Spring-Rice, August 13, 1897, in *Letters of Theodore Roosevelt*, vol. 1, ed. Elting E. Morison (Cambridge, MA: Harvard University Press, 1951), 644–49.

10. Beale, *Theodore Roosevelt*, 240–41; Trani, *Treaty of Portsmouth*, 39, 48–49.

11. See TR to Cecil Spring-Rice, March 19, 1904, in *Letters of Theodore Roosevelt*, vol. 4, 759–61. See also Trani, *Treaty of Portsmouth*, 33.

12. Esthus, *Double Eagle*, 16; Trani, *Treaty of Portsmouth*, 31–34.

13. Beale, *Theodore Roosevelt*, 234, 243; Esthus, *Double Eagle*, 16.

14. Green, *By More Than Providence*, 98.

15. Ailing John Hay would die on July 1, 1905. The president would be the sole navigator of the statecraft to come.

16. Trani, *Treaty of Portsmouth*, 41–43; Beale, *Theodore Roosevelt*, 245–46.

17. Trani, *Treaty of Portsmouth*, 46–47.

18. On Japanese views, see Esthus, *Double Eagle*, 18–20.

19. Trani, *Treaty of Portsmouth*, 51–52. On Mukden and its aftermath, see Esthus, *Double Eagle*, 24–25.

20. Trani, *Treaty of Portsmouth*, 25.

21. Quoted in Beale, *Theodore Roosevelt*, 246; Trani, *Treaty of Portsmouth*, 53. For the original correspondence, see TR to Hay, April 2, 1905, in *Letters of Theodore Roosevelt*, vol. 4, 1158.

22. Trani, *Treaty of Portsmouth*, 54–55; Esthus, *Double Eagle*, 29–36.

23. On the battle and TR's response, see Esthus, *Double Eagle*, 37–38. On the Japanese battle flag, see Trani, *Treaty of Portsmouth*, 56.

24. Esthus, *Double Eagle*, 40–41; Beale, *Theodore Roosevelt*, 245–46. For the original memorandum, see Tower to Roosevelt, June 9, 1905, in Dennett, *Roosevelt and the Russo-Japanese War*, 218–19.

25. Esthus, *Double Eagle*, 40–42; Beale, *Theodore Roosevelt*, 246–248; Trani, *Treaty of Portsmouth*, 56–58.

26. Esthus, *Double Eagle*, 44–46; Beale, *Theodore Roosevelt*, 250–51; Trani, *Treaty of Portsmouth*, 59–60.

27. Esthus, *Double Eagle*, 46.

28. TR to Henry Cabot Lodge, June 16, 1906, in *Letters of Theodore Roosevelt*, vol. 4, 1230, 1232. Russian "corruption" cited in Esthus, *Double Eagle*, 47; "lying" quoted in Trani, *Treaty of Portsmouth*, 65.

29. TR to Henry Cabot Lodge, June 16, 1906, in *Letters of Theodore Roosevelt*, vol. 4, 1230. See Trani, *Treaty of Portsmouth*, 63.

30. On Japanese instructions, see Esthus, *Double Eagle*, 58–59.

31. For citations of Nicholas in the original Russian, see Esthus, *Double Eagle*, 63 (fn22 and fn23).

32. Quoted in Esthus, *Double Eagle*, 57. For the original correspondence, see TR to Whitelaw Reid, June 30, 1905, in *Letters of Theodore Roosevelt*, vol. 4, 1258 (emphasis in original).

33. For an excellent account of Witte's perspective, see Francis W. Wcislo, *Tales of Imperial Russia: The Life and Times of Sergei Witte, 1849–1915* (New York: Oxford University Press, 2011), especially 179–214.

34. Quoted in Esthus, *Double Eagle*, 72. TR to William Howard Taft, July 29, 1905, in *Letters of Theodore Roosevelt*, vol. 4, 1290.

35. For references to Witte's Russian memoirs, see Trani, *Treaty of Portsmouth*, 16. On Witte's strategy, see also Wcislo, *Tales of Imperial Russia*.

36. On the railroad story, see Esthus, *Double Eagle*, 77.

37. On Japanese demands, see Esthus, *Double Eagle*, 82–83.

38. On Witte and Russian response, see Esthus, *Double Eagle*, 84–91; Trani, *Treaty of Portsmouth*, 130–33; Beale, *Theodore Roosevelt*, 256–58.

39. On negotiations from August 15 to the end of the conference, see Esthus, *Double Eagle*, 101–67. Japanese press cited in ibid., 167. See also Trani, *Treaty of Portsmouth*, 136–55.

40. TR to William Howard Taft, April 20, 1905, in *Letters of Theodore Roosevelt*, vol. 4, 1162.

41. TR to Cecil Arthur Spring-Rice, May 13, 1905, in *Letters of Theodore Roosevelt*, vol. 4, 1178.

42. For a discussion of Morocco and Algeciras, see Serge Ricard, "Foreign Policy Making in the White House: Rooseveltian-Style Personal Diplomacy," in Tilchin and Neu, *Artists of Power*, 17–22; Eugene Anderson, *The First Moroccan Crisis, 1904–1906* (Chicago: University of Chicago Press, 1930); Beale, *Theodore Roosevelt*, 306–34. For the reference to Sternberg's mistake, see Ricard, "Foreign Policy Making in the White House," 30fn59; Beale, *Theodore Roosevelt*, 378–80. For the reference to historians' question about TR's role in winning French acceptance to the conference, see Ricard, "Foreign Policy Making," 20 (and his difference with Beale's interpretation).

43. See Xu Qiyu, *Fragile Rise: Grand Strategy and the Fate of Imperial Germany, 1871–1914* (Cambridge, MA: The MIT Press, 2017), 173–85; A. J. P. Taylor, *The Struggle for Mastery in Europe* (New York: Oxford University Press, 1954), 441; Winston Churchill, *The World Crisis: 1911–1918*, abridged and rev. ed. (New York: Free Press, 2005), 19.

44. Trani, *Treaty of Portsmouth*, 2.

45. See Trani, *Treaty of Portsmouth*, 156–57.

46. Quoted in Beale, *Theodore Roosevelt*, 333.

47. William Tilchin, a student of Roosevelt's diplomacy, identified the five core principles of TR's "Big Stick" foreign policy. In addition to military might, as expressed through the U.S. Navy, Roosevelt relied on "act[ing] justly toward other nations," never bluffing, "strik[ing] only if prepared to strike hard," and "allow[ing] an honorable adversary to save face in defeat." William N. Tilchin, "Setting the Foundation: Theodore Roosevelt and the Construction of an Anglo-American Special Relationship," in Tilchin and Neu, *Artists of Power*, 63fn19.

48. Cooper, *Warrior*, 65.

49. By way of comparison, Japan had thirteen comparable ships built or under construction in 1907. For data on U.S. battleships, see Herring, *From Colony to Superpower*, 349. For number of Japanese battleships, see Green, *By More Than Providence*, 101.

50. Quoted in Cooper, *Warrior*, 112. For the original, see Theodore Roosevelt, *An Autobiography* (New York: Charles Scribner's Sons, 1920), 549.

Chapter 7. Woodrow Wilson: The Political Scientist Abroad

1. For the full text of Wilson's speech before Congress, see "President Wilson's Declaration of War Message to Congress, April 2, 1917," Records of the United States Senate, Record Group 46, National Archives. For Tumulty's recollections, see J. P. Tumulty, *Woodrow Wilson As I Know Him* (Garden City, NY: Doubleday, Page & Company, 1921), 256–59. For descriptions of April 2, 1917, see Robert Ferrell, *Woodrow Wilson and World War I, 1917–1921* (New York: Harper & Row, 1985), 1–3; A. Scott Berg, *Wilson* (New York: G. P. Putnam's Sons, 2013), 433–38; John Milton Cooper, *Woodrow Wilson: A Biography* (New York: Alfred A. Knopf, 2009), 385–88. For Cooper's observation on Wilson's use of the passive voice, see Cooper, "Making a Case for Wilson," in *Reconsidering Woodrow Wilson: Progressivism, Internationalism, War, and Peace*, ed. John Milton Cooper (Washington, DC: Woodrow Wilson Center Press; Baltimore: Johns Hopkins University Press, 2008), 21. On the Diet of Worms, see Cooper, *Warrior*, 321–23. See also Trygve Throntveit, *Power*

Without Victory: Woodrow Wilson and the American Internationalist Experiment (Chicago: University of Chicago Press, 2017), 217–18.

2. Berg, *Wilson*, 393; Tooze, *Deluge*, 44.

3. On the U.S. population and share of immigrants, see Ferrell, *Woodrow Wilson*, 3.

4. On the size of the U.S. army and ammunition, see Ferrell, *Woodrow Wilson*, 14.

5. Cooper, *Wilson*, 395; Throntveit, *Power Without Victory*, 244.

6. For Wilson's reactive, tactical approach, see especially John A. Thompson, "More Tactics Than Strategy: Woodrow Wilson and World War I, 1914–1919," in Tilchin and Neu, *Artists of Power*, 95–115.

7. Quoted in Thompson, "More Tactics Than Strategy," 115fn55. For the original correspondence, see Wilson to Edith Galt, August 18, 1915, in *The Papers of Woodrow Wilson*, vol. 34, ed. Arthur S. Link (Princeton, NJ: Princeton University Press, 1980), 241.

8. Quoted in Philip Zelikow, *The Road Less Traveled: The Secret Struggle to End the Great War* (New York: Public Affairs, forthcoming in Spring 2021), cited here as "The Curious End of Neutrality," unpublished article (December 2018), 37n62. For the original, see "An Interview by Ida Minerva Tarbell," October 3, 1916, in *The Papers of Woodrow Wilson*, vol. 38, ed. Arthur S. Link (Princeton, NJ: Princeton University Press, 1982), 327–28.

9. For this interpretation, see Thompson, "More Tactics Than Strategy." For Wilson's failure "in the middle range in coordinating diplomacy," see Cooper, *Warrior*, 296–97.

10. "Irony of fate" is much quoted. See, e.g., Arthur S. Link, *Wilson the Diplomatist: A Look at His Major Foreign Policies* (Baltimore: Johns Hopkins University Press, 1957), 5; John Milton Cooper, "Whose League of Nations? Theodore Roosevelt, Woodrow Wilson, and World Order," in Tilchin and Neu, *Artists of Power*, 163–64. For the text of Wilson's first inaugural speech, see "An Inaugural Address," March 4, 1913, in *The Papers of Woodrow Wilson*, vol. 27, ed. Arthur S. Link (Princeton, NJ: Princeton University Press, 1978). See also Berg, *Wilson*, 427.

11. The Wilson administration prepared a legislative program in advance, the first presidency to do so. On Wilson's domestic accomplishments, see Cooper, "Making a Case for Wilson," 10–13. Wilson's record with African-Americans was, however, a serious step backward.

12. On Wilson's role with Congress, see Cooper, "Making a Case for Wilson," 17–18. For the analogy on overcoming the balance of power in U.S. and international politics, see Lloyd E. Ambrosius, *Wilsonianism: Woodrow Wilson and His Legacy in American Foreign Relations* (New York: Palgrave Macmillan, 2002), 27–28.

13. For "lessons learned" in Mexico, see Cooper, "Making a Case for Wilson," 13–14. On the "profound revolution" and comparison to the French Revolution, see ibid., 23n4. For Wilson's statement on "a profound revolution," see *The Papers of Woodrow Wilson*, vol. 50, ed. Arthur S. Link (Princeton, NJ: Princeton University Press, 1985), 748.

14. For the reference to his wife's bedside, see Berg, *Wilson*, 334. For the quote to his friend, see ibid., 336.

15. On the first, traditional response of neutrality, see Lloyd E. Ambrosius, *Wilsonian Statecraft: Theory and Practice of Liberal Internationalism During World War I* (Denver, CO: Rowman & Littlefield Publishers, 1991), 35–36; Cooper, *Warrior*, 272–73; idem., *Wilson*, 263 for quotes and concern about domestic strife. For the original, see Wilson, "Message to Congress," 63rd Congress, 2nd Session, Senate Doc. 566 (Washington, DC: Government Printing Office, 1914), 3–4.

16. For the comment to his brother-in-law, see Cooper, *Warrior*, 274–75.

17. Berg, *Wilson*, 338. Wilson's concern over "a military nation" quoted in Thompson, "More Tactics Than Strategy," 98. For the original source, see "From the Diary of Colonel House," August 30, 1914, in *The Papers of Woodrow Wilson*, vol. 30, ed. Arthur S. Link (Princeton, NJ: Princeton University Press, 1979), 462.

18. By September, Roosevelt wrote an article calling for an "efficient world league for the peace of righteousness," two years before Wilson first publicly supported the idea of such a body. But Roosevelt's commitment to a league to safeguard security would prove inconsistent. For TR's views, see Cooper, *Warrior*, 276–80. For "militant idealism," see ibid., 327.

19. Cooper, *Wilson*, 263–64 for economic effects; Berg, *Wilson*, 340–41, including NYSE.

20. Cooper, *Wilson*, 270 for the ship purchase bill; Berg, *Wilson*, 341–42.

21. Cooper, *Warrior*, 274 for the Wilson quote.

22. Thompson, "More Tactics Than Strategy," 107 for Wilson's comments to Page on dealing with British blockade. See Arthur S. Link, *Woodrow Wilson: Revolution, War, and Peace* (Arlington Heights, IL: AHM

Publishing Corp., 1979), 32–35 for a detailed description of British tactics regarding the blockade. See also Cooper, *Wilson*, 265–66.

23. Cooper, *Wilson*, 264–65; Berg, *Wilson*, 243.

24. Cooper, *Wilson*, 269, 273.

25. Berg, *Wilson*, 350–51. House's point was analogous to the one Britain's secretary of war, Sir George Cornewall Lewis, made to Prime Minister Palmerston in late 1862.

26. Ambrosius, *Wilsonian Statecraft*, 37; Cooper, *Warrior*, 275; Berg, *Wilson*, 350–51; Cooper, *Wilson*, 275–76 on the interview.

27. Cooper, *Warrior*, 293-94; Cooper, *Wilson*, 267, 276-277; Berg, *Wilson*, 353-54.

28. Cooper, *Wilson*, 275 for U-boat data.

29. Cooper, *Wilson*, 277–78 for quotes on the Wilson-Bryan debate.

30. Cooper, *Wilson*, 278 for the use of the "America first" motto in April 1915 and its meaning. See Berg, *Wilson*, for further discussion of the term in June 1916.

31. Background on Edith Galt from Berg, *Wilson*, 355–58.

32. Americans of that era would recall May 7 in the way later generations would remember December 7, 1941, or September 11, 2001. During the 1920s, Mark Sullivan, a journalist conducting interviews for a popular book titled *Our Times*, discovered that Americans recalled where they had been when they learned about the disaster, the events of the day, and what they thought and felt. For Mark Sullivan, see Cooper, *Wilson*, 285; and idem., *Warrior*, 288–89. Sullivan's *Our Times* was published in six volumes between 1926 and 1935. See Mark Sullivan, *Our Times: The United States, 1900–1925* (New York: C. Scribner's Sons, 1926–35).

33. For TR and House quotes, see Berg, *Wilson*, 362–63. For original sources, see Theodore Roosevelt, "Murder on the High Seas," May 9, 1915; House to Wilson, May 9, 1915, in *The Intimate Papers of Colonel House*, vol. 1, ed. Charles Seymour (Boston: Houghton Mifflin Company, 1926), 434.

34. Berg, *Wilson*, 363 for German advertisements.

35. Cooper, *Wilson*, 285 for newspaper editors' "poll."

36. Cooper, *Wilson*, 286. For the original, see Wilson to W. J. Bryan, June 7, 1915, in *The Papers of Woodrow Wilson*, vol. 33, ed. Arthur S. Link (Princeton, NJ: Princeton University Press, 1980), 349.

37. For WW's diplomatic steps, see Cooper, *Wilson*, 286–89.

38. See Berg, *Wilson*, 368 for Bryan quote. For a discussion of Bryan's resignation, see Cooper, *Wilson*, 290–94.

39. See Cooper, *Wilson*, 291 on the message from two senior congressional Democrats.

40. For Lansing, see Eugene Trani, "Robert Lansing (1864–1928)," in Mihalkanin, *American Statesmen*, 314–24. For WW's decision, see Cooper, *Wilson*, 294–95.

41. See Cooper, *Wilson*, 297–98 for directions to the navy and army, and first proposals.

42. See Cooper, *Wilson*, 300–301, 303–4 for the handling of *Arabic* incident; Berg, *Wilson*, 369.

43. Cooper, *Wilson*, 308–9; Berg, *Wilson*, 386–89, including reference to "national safety" and "national dignity."

44. See Cooper, *Warrior*, 299 for the quote about "sounding too much like Roosevelt." Cooper, *Wilson*, 312–14 on the defeat of congressional resolutions.

45. See Cooper, *Wilson*, 310–12 on army-navy bills.

46. See Cooper, *Wilson*, 315–18 on the House-Grey Memorandum; Berg, *Wilson*, 385. Ambrosius's *Wilsonian Statecraft* has an extensive description of House's instructions, his approach, how House exceeded instructions, and the results. See Cooper, *Warrior*, 293–94 on House's "characteristic deviousness." In addition to the *Sussex* incident, the United States veered toward war with Mexico in 1916. After Pancho Villa attacked the border town of Columbus, New Mexico, on March 9, the president sent General John Pershing into Mexico on a punitive expedition. Eventually, the two countries agreed on a mediation commission. When the Democrats' campaign materials in the 1916 election proclaimed, "He kept us out of war," they referred more often to Mexico than to Europe. See Cooper, *Wilson*, 319–22.

47. For the *Sussex* crisis, see Cooper, *Wilson*, 323–25; Berg, *Wilson*, 395–96; Ambrosius, *Wilsonian Statecraft*, 68–70.

48. See Cooper, *Wilson*, 326 for WW's quote. For the original source, see "President on Defenses: In Speech to Anti-Militarists He Says Force Must Back Up Opinion," *New York Times*, May 9, 1916, 1.

49. For LEP and Decoration Day speeches, WW quotes, and the connection to Fourteen Points, the League of Nations, and the Democratic platform, see Cooper, *Wilson*, 326–28; idem., *Warrior*, 301–2; Ambrosius, *Wilsonian Statecraft*, 71–73.

50. See Cooper, *Wilson*, 336–38, 346–47 for background on C. E. Hughes, Republican divisions, and the campaign; 338 for "Animated Feather Duster" and "Whiskered Wilson"; 347 for North Dakota farmer. For more on Hughes's background, see chapter 8.

51. For troubles with Britain and the WW quote, see Cooper, *Wilson*, 342–43; Berg, *Wilson*, 418.

52. See Cooper, *Wilson*, 334 for "peace, preparedness, and progressivism."

53. For election results and information on key states, see Cooper, *Wilson*, 358–59.

54. For Wilson's letter, see Ray Stannard Baker, *Woodrow Wilson: Life and Letters*, vol. 6, *Facing War: 1915–1917* (New York: Charles Scribner's, 1937), 365. For background on the "peace offensive," see Cooper, *Wilson*, 363–65; Berg, *Wilson*, 417–20; Ambrosius, *Wilsonian Statecraft*, 75–77. See also Zelikow, "Curious End of Neutrality," 48n88.

55. See, e.g., Link, *Wilson the Diplomatist*, 60, 73–83; idem., *Woodrow Wilson: Revolution, War, and Peace*, 58–59; Ambrosius, *Wilsonian Statecraft*, 77–79.

56. See Zelikow, "Curious End of Neutrality."

57. Zelikow, "Curious End of Neutrality," 10.

58. See Zelikow, "Curious End of Neutrality," 20–32. See especially ibid., 28fns47–48.

59. See Zelikow, "Curious End of Neutrality," 30–31 and 55fn104 for Bernstorff reaching beyond instructions. See ibid., 26–27 and 50 on Belgium's sovereignty and neutrality. For the message from the U.S. embassy in Berlin, see ibid., 67–68fns131–32. Other scholars have provided differing views on Germany's plans for Belgium. Link, for example, argues Germany wanted to keep Belgium as a "vassal." See ibid., 31fn54 for a reply.

60. For Zelikow on Great Britain's willingness to find a compromise solution, see Zelikow, "Curious End of Neutrality," 37–47. See especially "Memorandum by Lord Lansdowne Respecting Peace Settlement," cited in ibid., 45–47fns83–84.

61. See Zelikow, "Curious End of Neutrality," 48, 31fn54.

62. See Zelikow, "Curious End of Neutrality," 9, 12, 15, 43fn77 for Keynes's quote; see Cooper, *Wilson*, 364 for more on the Federal Reserve move.

63. See Zelikow, "Curious End of Neutrality," 65–67 for the watered-down note and Lansing. See also Cooper, *Wilson*, 365–66; Berg, *Wilson*, 418–20.

64. For House-Bernstorff and Bernstorff's quote, see Zelikow, "Curious End of Neutrality," 67. For Lloyd George, see ibid., 68–69.

65. For Wilson's "Peace Without Victory" speech, see Cooper, *Warrior*, 312–15, including quotes and TR's reaction. See also, Ambrosius, *Wilsonian Statecraft*, 80–81; Cooper, *Wilson*, 369–73; Berg, *Wilson*, 421–23; Zelikow, "Curious End of Neutrality," 69, including British quote on "little official attention." For the full text of the "Peace Without Victory" speech, see Wilson, "An Address to the Senate," January 22, 1917, in *The Papers of Woodrow Wilson*, vol. 40, ed. Arthur S. Link (Princeton, NJ: Princeton University Press, 1983), 533–39.

66. Zelikow, "Curious End of Neutrality," 69, including Bethmann's quote and the U.S. ambassador to Germany in fn139. On German military assessment, see Cooper, *Wilson*, 373; Zelikow, "Curious End of Neutrality," 69.

67. See Cooper, *Wilson*, 375–76 on "yellow races" and the address to Congress. See also Ambrosius, *Wilsonian Statecraft*, 83.

68. For the Zimmermann telegram, see Cooper, *Wilson*, 378; Ambrosius, *Wilsonian Statecraft*, 84–85.

69. Wilson called upon the Senate to change its rules to enable the chamber to cut off debate, prompting the creation of the Senate's cloture procedure. For filibuster (and new rule of cloture) see Cooper, *Wilson*, 378–80.

70. See Cooper, *Wilson*, 380–83 on second inaugural, steps toward war, illness, and interview with quotes.

71. See Hendrickson, *Union, Nation or Empire*, 306–8 for the role of neutrality in international order and the shift from the "old" to "new" concept of neutrality. See also Brooke Blower, "From Isolationism to Neutrality: A New Framework for Understanding American Political Culture, 1919–1941," *Diplomatic History* 38, no. 2 (2014).

72. Hendrickson, *Union, Nation, or Empire*, 306–8.

73. Sigmund Freud and William C. Bullitt, *Thomas Woodrow Wilson, Twenty-Eighth President of the United States: A Psychological Study* (Boston: Houghton, Mifflin, 1966).

74. See, e.g., Ambrosius, *Wilsonianism*; Tony Smith, *America's Mission: The United States and the Worldwide Struggle for Democracy in the Twentieth Century* (Princeton, NJ: Princeton University Press, 1994), xv.

75. Cooper, "Making a Case for Wilson," 21.

76. Arthur S. Link, "The Higher Realism of Woodrow Wilson," *Journal of Presbyterian History* 41, no. 1 (March 1963), 1–13; Ernest May, *The World War and American Isolation: 1914–1917* (Cambridge, MA: Harvard University Press, 1959), 437; Francis Gavin, "The Wilsonian Legacy in the Twentieth Century," *Orbis* 41, no. 4 (Autumn 1997), 632; David Halberstam, *The Best and the Brightest* (New York: Random House, 1972), 56. More broadly, see Martin Walker, "Woodrow Wilson and the Cold War: 'Tear Down This Wall, Mr. Gorbachev,' " in Cooper, *Reconsidering Woodrow Wilson*, 279, 282.

77. See Throntveit, *Power Without Victory*, though WW did not consider himself to be a "pragmatist" (see 10). See also idem., " 'Common Counsel': Woodrow Wilson's Pragmatic Progressivism," in Cooper, *Reconsidering Woodrow Wilson*, 25.

78. Kissinger, *Diplomacy*, 55; see Thomas J. Knock, "Kennan Versus Wilson," and Kennan, "Comments," in John Milton Cooper Jr., and Charles E. Neu, eds., *The Wilson Era: Essays in Honor of Arthur S. Link* (Arlington Heights, IL: Harlan Davidson, 1991), 330.

79. McDougall, *Promised Land, Crusader State*, 146.

80. Ambrosius, *Wilsonian Statecraft*, xii–xvi (quotes at xv and xvi).

81. Walker, "Woodrow Wilson and the Cold War," 296.

82. Again, this insight draws from and seeks to build on Thompson's essay, "More Tactics Than Strategy," 95–110.

83. Zelikow also makes this critique of Wilson's foreign policy process and the U.S. government's lack of staffing (compared to London and even Berlin) in "Curious End of Neutrality," 2, 34–37.

84. Zelikow, "Curious End of Neutrality," 2.

85. For Keynes's observation, see Cooper, *Wilson*, 373.

86. Walker, "Woodrow Wilson and the Cold War," 296. Also, see chapter 9 for the option, devised by Elihu Root, of Senate ratification of the Versailles Treaty with reservations.

Chapter 8. Charles Evans Hughes: Arms Control and the Washington Conference

1. Roger Dingman, *Power in the Pacific: The Origins of Naval Arms Limitation, 1914–1922* (Chicago: University of Chicago Press, 1976), 196. For the original source, see *London Times*, November 12, 1921. For other descriptions of the opening, see Erik Goldstein, ed., *The Washington Conference, 1921–22: Naval Rivalry, East Asian Stability and the Road to Pearl Harbor* (Newbury Park, UK: F. Cass, 1994), 26–28; Margot Louria, *Triumph and Downfall: America's Pursuit of Peace and Prosperity, 1921–1933* (Westport, CT: Greenwood Press, 2001), 47–49; Merlo Pusey, *Charles Evans Hughes*, vol. 2 (New York: Macmillan, 1951), 466–73; Tooze, *Deluge*, 396–97.

2. For Curzon's suggestion, see Louria, *Triumph*, 41. For H. G. Wells, see ibid., 48. For the original source, see H. G. Wells, *Washington and the Riddle of Peace* (New York: Macmillan, 1922), 68.

3. Goldstein, *Washington Conference*, 27.

4. Pusey, *Hughes*, 467.

5. Pusey, *Hughes*, 467. For Harding's address, see Warren G. Harding, "Address of the President of the United States at the Opening of the Conference on Limitation of Armament at Washington, November 12, 1921" (Washington, DC: Government Printing Office, 1921).

6. For an account of the secrecy of Hughes's speech, see Pusey, *Hughes*, 464–65.

7. For the full text of the address, see Charles Evans Hughes, *Address of Charles E. Hughes, Secretary of State of the United States and American Commissioner to the Conference on Limitation of Armament, on Assuming the Duties of Presiding Officer at the Conference, Washington, D.C., November 12, 1921* (Washington, DC: Government Printing Office, 1921). For context and audience reaction during delivery, see Pusey, *Hughes*, 467–71; Louria, *Triumph*, 48–49; Dingman, *Power in the Pacific*, 197.

8. Pusey, *Hughes*, 471–72; William Allen White, *Autobiography* (New York: Macmillan, 1946), 600.

9. For the British admiral and *Manchester Guardian*, see Pusey, *Hughes*, 470–71. For the original source, see H. W. Nevinson, *Manchester Guardian Weekly*, November 18, 1921, 384. For Roosevelt's diary observation on the British reaction, see Goldstein, *Washington Conference*, 27–28.

10. See Pusey, *Hughes*, 473 for the Japanese wire cost and 472 for Ring Lardner. For the *NYT* coverage, see Dingman, *Power in the Pacific*, 197.

11. For the assessment of Hughes's risk, see Pusey, *Hughes*, 464.

12. For Balfour's quote and background on the British assessment, see Dingman, *Power in the Pacific*, 198–99. More generally, Dingman discusses the bureaucratic-political debates within Britain, Japan, and the United States.

13. The Götterdämmerung of the fearsome German battle fleet had not, however, been in combat with its British foe. The kaiser's officers followed orders to sail their surrendered ships to Scotland to be divided among their enemies, but then they flooded their fleet, which sank to the bottom of Scapa Flow. On Britain's stopping construction and savings, see Tooze, *Deluge*, 398; Dingman, *Power in the Pacific*, 200.

14. On the Japanese statement and internal debates, see Dingman, *Power in the Pacific*, 201–3; Tooze, *Deluge*, 398–99.

15. See the text of the Washington Naval Treaty in Appendix 1 in Emily Goldman, *Sunken Treaties: Naval Arms Control Between the Wars* (University Park, PA: Pennsylvania State University Press, 1994), 274 on. For Senate ratifications and votes, see Charles Evans Hughes, *The Autobiographical Notes of Charles Evans Hughes*, ed. David J. Danelski and Joseph S. Tulchin (Cambridge, MA: Harvard University Press, 1973), 245. For overall votes, see Goldstein, *Washington Conference*, 133.

16. See the treaties and declarations reprinted as appendices in Goldman, *Sunken Treaties*, beginning at 273. A list of the treaties can also be found in Richard Morris, ed., *Encyclopedia of American History*, bicentennial ed. (New York: Harper & Row, 1976), 379. See also the sources cited in note 15 above. Lodge quoted in Pusey, *Hughes*, 499.

17. "How Hughes Measures Up with the 'Veteran Diplomats,'" *Literary Digest* 71, no. 12 (December 17, 1921), 38–39, quoting Harold Phelps Stokes.

18. For an assessment of the achievements and weaknesses of the Washington Conference, see Goldstein, *Washington Conference*, 134–37.

19. *Times* of London quoted in Pusey, *Hughes*, 411. For the original, see *Times* (London), March 3, 1921. For the *Current Opinion* assessment, see *Current Opinion* 70 (April 1921), 440–443. British ambassador quoted in Hughes, *Autobiographical Notes*, 214–15.

20. See Louria, *Triumph*, 19. See also *World's Work* 41 (April 1921), 529–530; Hughes, *Autobiographical Notes*, 209 (citing Hughes's review in 1924).

21. For the Penrose quote, see *Literary Digest* 68 (March 5, 1921), 12.

22. Pusey, *Hughes*, 441–42.

23. Debt-creditor data from Hughes, *Autobiographical Notes*, 253; see Louria, *Triumph*, 3 for comments on U.S. economic capacity; Goldstein, *Washington Conference*, 126 on recession; Dingman, *Power in the Pacific*, 146 for economic data on 1920–21.

24. See Louria, *Triumph*, 9–10.

25. For France's position, see Goldstein, *Washington Conference*, 192 on. See also Tooze, *Deluge*, 401 for France's priorities.

26. See Goldstein, *Washington Conference*, 4–6 and 29 for Britain and Lloyd George's politics, 61 for Dominions; Dingman, *Power in the Pacific*, 112 (within chapter at 105–21) and 162–63.

27. On Japan, see Louria, *Triumph*, 38–40; Goldman, *Sunken Treaties*, 35–36, 59–68; Tooze, *Deluge*, 399. For almost half of the budget on military, see Pusey, *Hughes*, 454; Louria, *Triumph*, 138.

28. See Louria, *Triumph*, 12–33 on poison gas. On the Spanish influenza, see Niall P. A. S. Johnson and Juergen Mueller, "Updating the Accounts: Global Mortality of the 1918–1920 'Spanish' Influenza," *Bulletin of the History of Medicine* 76, no. 1 (Spring 2002).

29. See Louria, *Triumph*, 10 for discrediting of classical diplomacy.

30. See Dingman, *Power in the Pacific*, 17–33 on "trident tarnished" and internal British debates.

31. See Goldstein, *Washington Conference*, 39 for Britain's global and regional policies.

32. See Dingman, *Power in the Pacific*, 97–104; Green, *By More Than Providence*, 131–36 on War Plan Orange.

33. See Dingman, *Power in the Pacific*, 116–21. On parity not the same as equality, see Goldstein, *Washington Conference*, 277.

34. See Dingman, *Power in the Pacific*, 48–63 ("probable enemy number one" at 60), 122–23 for 1920 building program. See Tooze, *Deluge*, 399, and Thomas H. Buckley, *The United States and the Washington Conference, 1921–1922* (Knoxville, TN: University of Tennessee, 1970), 59.

35. See Louria, *Triumph*, 60–61 for the Japanese view of Manchuria. See also Goldman, *Sunken Treaties*, 63.

36. See Dingman, *Power in the Pacific*, 88 on the results of the Paris treaty.

37. See Dingman, *Power in the Pacific*, 143.

38. Dingman, *Power in the Pacific*, 143–46.

39. *Literary Digest* 68 (March 5, 1921), 12, including *New York Times* quote; see Hughes, *Autobiographical Notes*, xvii for the editors' quotes.

40. See Louria, *Triumph*, 17 for part of the description. See Hughes, *Autobiographical Notes*, xii for the quote and his humorous side.
41. See Hughes, *Autobiographical Notes*, xxviii and xxix for the Jackson-Frankfurter story and Frankfurter quote.
42. The secretary had a deep interest in administration, too. He helped enact the Rogers Act of 1924, which reorganized the State Department and created the foundation for the modern Foreign Service. See Hughes, *Autobiographical Notes*, xxii, xxiv, xxv for quotes and 203 for the Rogers Act; Louria, *Triumph*, 19 for press briefings and 83 for the Rogers Act; Dexter Perkins, *Charles Evans Hughes and American Democratic Statesmanship* (Boston: Little, Brown, 1956), 96 on Hughes's administrative abilities and the Rogers Act.
43. Hughes, *Autobiographical Notes*, 201–2.
44. Hughes, *Autobiographical Notes*, 199.
45. On Hughes's suggestion, see Pusey, *Hughes*, 455, citing *New York Times*, May 4, 1921; see also Dingman, *Power in the Pacific*, 148–51 on Harding-Borah ("merchants of death" at 150); Louria, *Triumph*, 25–27.
46. Louria, *Triumph*, 26; Pusey, *Hughes*, 455.
47. On the Geddes meeting, see Dingman, *Power in the Pacific*, 149–50; Louria, *Triumph*, 34–35; Tooze, *Deluge*, 395.
48. See Dingman, *Power in the Pacific*, 152 (on invites) and 169–71 (on imperial conference); Pusey, *Hughes*, 455–58; Hughes, *Autobiographical Notes*, 242–43; Louria, *Triumph*, 35–36; Goldstein, *Washington Conference*, 15–17.
49. See Dingman, *Power in the Pacific*, 153 on Borah and Lodge, including "Pandora's Box" and 154 on preliminary conference, 172 and 176 on Ireland; Louria, *Triumph*, 37–41; Pusey, *Hughes*, 457–59.
50. See Goldstein, *Washington Conference*, 19 for Chamberlain and *Spectator* quotes, citing "The Washington Conference," *Spectator*, November 19, 1921, 657–58.
51. See Goldstein, *Washington Conference*, 21–26 for Balfour's appointment, planning, and instructions; Dingman, *Power in the Pacific*, 173–77.
52. On Japan, see Dingman, *Power in the Pacific*, 178–95, including on Admiral Kato's role; Louria, *Triumph*, 40 for Hughes's assurance to Shidehara and Japan's agreement to attend; Pusey, *Hughes*, 459 about Hughes being assured Japan would accept.
53. See Goldstein, *Washington Conference*, 192–200; Louria, *Triumph*, 41, including French as an official language.
54. See Goldstein, *Washington Conference*, 249–65; Tooze, *Deluge*, 402–7 on China's predicament.
55. See Pusey, *Hughes*, 457–58 on distrust of European diplomacy and conversation with Geddes, citing "Memorandum by the Secretary of State of a Conversation with the British Ambassador (Geddes)," September 20, 1921, in *Papers Relating to the Foreign Relations of the United States*, 1921, vol. 1, Doc. 88.
56. See Louria, *Triumph*, 41–42 on Hughes's conference organization.
57. See Louria, *Triumph*, 42, 46 on U.S. delegation; Hughes, *Autobiographical Notes*, 240, 247; Pusey, *Hughes*, 459–60 on Harding's uncertainty about Root.
58. Author's interview with Ambassador Richard Burt, September 5, 2019.
59. For Hughes's development of the U.S. proposal, see Hughes, *Autobiographical Notes*, 241–46, including quote from Philip C. Jessup; *Elihu Root*, vol. 2 (New York: Dodd, Mead & Company, 1938), 449 on senators' view on future appropriations for naval building and fortifications, and also devising "yardstick"; Louria, *Triumph*, 43–47 for work with the navy; Pusey, *Hughes*, 460–65.
60. See Pusey, *Hughes*, 474–75 on conference organization, press briefings, and Hughes's chairmanship.
61. The difference in American and British calculations relates to the percentage of supplies, ammunition, and fuel to include within tonnage limits, as well as Britain's concerns about its vulnerability to future innovations in naval warfare. The Americans calculated that 35,000 legend tons were about 37,000 U.S. tons. See "Memorandum by the Secretary to the British Empire Delegation of a Conversation at the Department of State, December 15, 1921," *Papers Relating to the Foreign Relations of the United States*, 1922, vol. 1 (Washington, DC: U.S. Government Printing Office, 1938), 122–25.
62. Pusey, *Hughes*, 476–81, including Kato's proposal, delegation view on fortifications, and Balfour-Hughes cooperation on battleship adjustments. See Dingman, *Power in the Pacific*, 187–95 for Japanese view on ratios and 201–7 on treaty negotiations, including reference to intercepting cables at 203. See Hughes, *Autobiographical Notes*, 246–47 on fortifications. Goldman, *Sunken Treaties*, 121–30.
63. Roosevelt returned to France as a general landing at Utah Beach on D-Day in 1944; he died in France of a heart attack on July 12, 1944.

64. See Louria, *Triumph*, 53–55 on France, including France's logic, sense of insult, exchange with Roosevelt, loss of wine and champagne, and Briand's decision. See also Pusey, *Hughes*, 481–84. For details on internal French debates, see Goldstein, *Washington Conference*, 200–212.

65. See Pusey, *Hughes*, 484–86 for other ships, including saving the *Saratoga* and *Lexington*.

66. See the treaty in relation to the use of submarines and noxious gases in warfare, reproduced in the appendix in Goldman, *Sunken Treaties*.

67. See Pusey, *Hughes*, 468, 488 on Hughes's oversight of treaty drafting and the French and English texts.

68. For the Four-Power Pact, see Pusey, *Hughes*, 491–500, including Hughes's drafting, no use of "alliance," Lodge's presentation to the convention, and the Senate's reservation. See also Louria, *Triumph*, 57–58. For British Empire considerations, see Goldstein, *Washington Conference*, 74–78.

69. See Goldstein, *Washington Conference*, 249–65 for China's place at the conference, effects of weakness, British hopes for "rehabilitation," Japan's interests, China's ten principles, preparation of the Nine-Power Treaty, and other results on tariffs, post offices, and other matters. See Goldstein, *Washington Conference*, 67 for the "Singapore strategy." See also Pusey, *Hughes*, 501–3 and the connection to U.S. Open Door policies. See Louria, *Triumph*, 57–62 including Open Door, Manchuria, railroads, customs, and radio frequencies. Tooze has a good summary, including British reference to "patriotic grandstanding" and greater commitments to China than in the past, but "lost opportunity" in *Deluge*, 402–6. See also Wunsz King, *China at the Washington Conference, 1921–1922* (New York: St. John's University Press, 1963), 38–39. See Goldman, *Sunken Treaties*, 9 on the three principles of the Nine-Power Treaty and 132–37 on "bridging" conflicting interests.

70. On U.S.-British mediation of Sino-Japanese bilateral negotiations on Shantung and Manchuria, see Pusey, *Hughes*, 503–6, including U.S. public attitude, Hughes pushing Japan, Chinese students besieging diplomats, and thirty-six meetings. See Louria, *Triumph*, 59–62, especially on Japan's view on treaty rights from Portsmouth and Manchuria, and withdrawal from Shantung.

71. See sources cited in notes 69 and 70, especially Tooze, *Deluge*; Goldman, *Sunken Treaties*; David Armstrong, "China's Place in the New Pacific Order," in Goldstein, *Washington Conference*, including reference to historians' views at 264.

72. See Akira Iriye, *After Imperialism: The Search for a New Order in the Far East, 1921–1931* (Cambridge, MA: Harvard University Press, 1965).

73. On Anglo-American tensions, "perfidious" Britain, and British "insurance policy," see Goldstein, *Washington Conference*, 30, 127–28.

74. See Iriye, *After Imperialism*, 3 on "economic foreign policy," 9 and 26 on Japan's exports to the U.S. and capital flows. See Tooze, *Deluge*, 401 on New York City not matching London's earlier influence.

75. See Ernest May, foreword to Goldstein, *Washington Conference*.

76. For an impressive early effort, see Adam Tooze, *Crashed: How a Decade of Financial Crises Changed the World* (New York: Viking, 2018).

77. See Goldstein, *Washington Conference*, 135 for $350 million annual navy budgets; Hughes, *Autobiographical Notes*, 246–47 for later spending on fortifications; Goldstein, *Washington Conference*, 149 on development of new naval tactics; Green, *By More Than Providence*, 141–43, including reference to Nimitz thesis at 141; Tooze, *Deluge*, 401 on USN deployment of task forces.

78. See Hughes's address to the American Historical Association, "Some Aspects of Our Foreign Policy," in *Annual Report of the American Historical Association for the Year 1922*, vol. 1 (Washington, DC: Government Printing Office, 1926), 251–269.

79. See Goldstein, *Washington Conference*, 136 on "sacred ratios" and 137–44 on later conferences.

80. See May foreword in Goldstein, *Washington Conference*, for changing interpretations of the Washington Conference. See also Harold and Margaret Sprout, *Toward a New Order of Sea Power: American Naval Policy and the World Scene, 1918–1922* (Princeton, NJ: Princeton University Press, 1940). Goldstein's essays offer wider international perspectives. Goldman, *Sunken Treaties*, 3–32, examines, from an arms control viewpoint, the use of the Washington Conference experience to "[shatter] the arms control orthodoxy" of the Cold War.

81. See Goldman, *Sunken Treaties*, 3–8.

82. See Dingman, *Power in the Pacific*, xii on "process"; Green, *By More Than Providence*, 137 on treaties as "one instrument."

83. Author's interview with Ambassador Burt, September 5, 2019. For an example of a combined regional security–arms control approach in Northeast Asia today, see Robert B. Zoellick, "How to Negotiate with Kim Jong Un," *Wall Street Journal*, February 24, 2019, A17.

Chapter 9. Elihu Root: International Law

1. Governments had created the Permanent Court of Arbitration at the Hague Conference of 1899. In accordance with the treaty ratified by the Senate in 1900, U.S. presidents had nominated four Americans for the arbitration roster. Therefore, the League's secretary general sent the letters to Root and his three colleagues through the State Department. However, after the Senate's defeat of U.S. membership in the League in 1920, the State Department ignored communications from the League. In effect, the missives to Root and his colleagues ended up unanswered in a "dead letter" bin in the State Department. Root had learned of the missing letters in August and had written to Hughes to find the lost mail. Hughes promptly discovered the invitations and forwarded them. Then Root and his three copanelists had to figure out what to do. Root decided to visit Secretary Hughes in Washington. For the story of the letters, see Jessup, *Root*, vol. 2, 425–26; Richard Leopold, *Elihu Root and the Conservative Tradition* (Boston: Little, Brown, 1954), 155–56; Pusey, *Hughes*, 595–97.

2. For Root and the World Court in 1919–20, see Jessup, *Root*, vol. 2, 418–22; Leopold, *Root*, 143–44.

3. For U.S. public support of the World Court, see Perkins, *Charles Evans Hughes*, 89.

4. For de Vattel, see Cobbs Hoffman, *American Umpire*, 181. For the original source, see Emer de Vattel, *The Law of Nations: Or, Principles of the Law of Nature, Applied to the Conduct and Affairs of Nations and Sovereigns*, trans. Joseph Chitty (Philadelphia: T. & J. W. Johnson, 1844), 277.

5. For Bentham, see Cobbs Hoffman, *American Umpire*, 181–82. For the original source, see Bentham's "Plan for a Universal and Perpetual Peace," in *The Works of Jeremy Bentham*, vol. 2, ed. John Bowring (Edinburgh: William Tait, 1839), 546–60.

6. On the law of nations as the "mother of multilateral norms," see Hendrickson, *Union, Nation, or Empire*, 9.

7. For Webster and the idea of international relations for U.S. policy, see Hendrickson, *Union, Nation, or Empire*, 9. For the original, see Daniel Webster, "The Revolution in Greece," in *The Speeches and Orations of Daniel Webster* (Boston: Little, Brown and Company, 1914), 66.

8. For TR, see Cobbs Hoffman, *American Umpire*, 198–99; Hendrickson, *Union, Nation, or Empire*, 295–96. For the original address, see Theodore Roosevelt, "International Peace," reprinted in *Advocate of Peace* 72, no. 6 (June 1910), 146–47.

9. Readers will also recall from chapter 4 the role of international law—and honor—in the dispute over the *Trent* that almost led to Britain's declaration of war in 1861. On the *Alabama* claims and first involvement of foreign judges, see Cobbs Hoffman, *American Umpire*, 135. A decade or so later, the United States accepted a Paris tribunal's ruling in favor of Canadian hunters of Alaskan fur seals. See ibid., 184.

10. Cobbs Hoffman, *American Umpire*, 184; Arthur C. F. Beales, *The History of Peace: A Short Account of the Organised Movements for International Peace* (London: G. Bell, 1931), 190–91.

11. On Olney's treaties, see Leopold, *Root*, 57.

12. For Suttner, including influence on the czar, analogy to *Uncle Tom's Cabin*, and Nobel Prize, see Cobbs Hoffman, *American Umpire*, 186–87. For the original work, see Bertha von Suttner, *Lay Down Your Arms: The Autobiography of Martha von Tilling*, trans. T. Holmes (London: Longmans, Green & Co., 1894).

13. Cobbs Hoffman, *American Umpire*, 187–89.

14. For Root and the First Hague Conference work on arbitration, see Jessup, *Root*, vol. 2, 75–79. For Benjamin Harrison, see Cobbs Hoffman, *American Umpire*, 189.

15. Cobbs Hoffman, *American Umpire*, 190.

16. For the Alaskan boundary commission, including on Lord Alverstone's ruling, see Jessup, *Elihu Root*, vol. 1 (New York: Dodd, Mead, 1938), 389–401; Zimmermann, *First Great Triumph*, 451–52.

17. On Hay's arbitration treaties, exceptions, and Senate reservations, see Jessup, *Root*, vol. 2, 79–80.

18. Walter Isaacson and Evan Thomas, *The Wise Men: Six Friends and the World They Made: Acheson, Bohlen, Harriman, Kennan, Lovett, McCloy* (New York: Simon & Schuster, 1986), 28.

19. For Root's early years, see Jessup, *Root*, vol. 1; Zimmermann, *First Great Triumph*, 123–48; Leopold, *Root*, 172–189. Grandfather at Concord Bridge from Jessup, *Root*, vol. 1, 3. Bar Associations introduction from Zimmermann, *First Great Triumph*, 128. Hamilton Commencement speech from ibid., 134. For legal training, "scientific" case methods, and Root's classical legal ideology, see Jonathan Zasloff, "Law and the Shaping of American Foreign Policy: From the Gilded Age to the New Era," *NYU Law Review* 78 (2003), 239. Lodge quote from Jessup, *Root*, vol. 1, 453.

20. See Jessup, *Root*, vol. 1, 183 for quote and income. See Zimmermann, *First Great Triumph*, 144 and 488 for his views on post–Civil War amendments and defense of underdogs.

21. TR quotes from Jessup, *Root*, vol. 1, 453; Leopold, *Root*, 72.

22. "Above all things" quote from Zimmermann, *First Great Triumph*, 146. For the original source, see Root, "The Monroe Doctrine: Address at the Ninety-Ninth Annual Banquet of the New England Society of New York," December 22, 1904, in Elihu Root, *Miscellaneous Addresses*, eds. Robert Bacon and James Brown Scott (Cambridge, MA: Harvard University Press, 1917), 272.

23. Jessup, *Root*, vol. 1, 215, citing Elihu Root, *Addresses on Government and Citizenship*, ed. Robert Bacon and James Brown Scott (Cambridge, MA: Harvard University Press, 1916), 503–4. Root turned out to be much more than a colonial administrator. Scandals and infighting stemming from the recent war wracked the army. The army's organization was suited to a frontier constabulary, not the modern age. Upon the recommendation of officers who had studied Germany's successful system, Root replaced the old arrangement of independent bureaus with a chief of staff structure, including rotations between line and staff assignments. He established a new War College as the capstone of a military education system that taught special service skills, planning, and strategy. Root also began the process of building a national reserve force out of the old state militias. After World War I, one of Root's most accomplished successors as secretary of war, Newton Baker, stated that the success of the vastly expanded American army in the Great War rested on the foundation of Root's reorganization. Jessup, *Root*, vol. 1, 240.

24. Quoted in Jessup, *Root*, vol. 1, 219.

25. See Jessup, *Root*, vol. 1, 346–48, citing *Annual Report of the Secretary of War*, pt. 1, vol. 1 (Washington, DC: Government Printing Office, 1899), 24.

26. For Root's policy toward the Philippines, see Jessup, *Root*, vol. 1, 329–71, including instructions to Taft, and the commission and rights of Filipinos; Zasloff, "Law and the Shaping of American Foreign Policy," 291–99; Zimmermann, *First Great Triumph*, 386–95 and 403–17. Quote from Jessup, *Root*, vol. 1, 348, citing Arthur Wallace Dunn, *From Harrison to Harding: A Personal Narrative, Covering a Third of a Century, 1888–1921*, vol. 1 (New York: G. P. Putnam's Sons, 1922), 257.

27. Despite weighing about 325 pounds, Taft ranged across the archipelago in heat and humidity to check conditions personally. The solicitous Root once asked about Taft's health after an illness. Taft replied that his recovery had enabled him to take a long trip on horseback into the mountains. Root promptly cabled back, "Fine. How's the horse?" Quoted in Jessup, *Root*, vol. 1, 363.

28. The Platt Amendment also stipulated that Cuba would sell or lease naval stations to the United States. Accordingly, the United States acquired a lease without a termination date for a naval base on the eastern end of Cuba—at Guantanamo Bay. The effects of Root's careful legal work persist to the present. See James Brown Scott, "Elihu Root: An Appreciation," *Proceedings of the American Society of International Law at Its Annual Meeting (1921-1969)*, vol. 31, April 29–May 1, 1937 (Washington, DC: American Society of International Law, 1937), 4–6. See also Zasloff, "Law and the Shaping of American Foreign Policy," 288–90. Quote on the kaiser from Jessup, *Root*, vol. 1, 314. Ibid., 326 for Guantanamo.

29. In 2001, when I served as U.S. trade representative, the Brazilian foreign minister Celso Lafer gave me a quotation from Root as an expression of the ties we hoped to build. Diplomacy seeks to build upon the work of predecessors. See Zimmermann, *First Great Triumph*, 473 (including "Good Neighbor"); Jessup, *Root*, vol. 1, 563 on "Good Neighbor"; Leopold, *Root*, 63–67 on Root and Latin America.

30. See Zasloff, "Law and the Shaping of American Foreign Policy," 305–8, citing Elihu Root, "The Hague Peace Conferences, Address in Opening the National Arbitration and Peace Congress, in the City of New York (April 15, 1907)," in Elihu Root, *Addresses on International Subjects*, eds. Robert Bacon and James Brown Scott (Cambridge, MA: Harvard University Press, 1916), 130–31.

31. For the Second Hague Conference, see Jessup, *Root*, vol. 2, 67–82 (see 75–76 for quote from Instructions); Leopold, *Root*, 54–57; Scott, "Elihu Root," 9, 33.

32. Jessup, *Root*, vol. 2, 79–81, 267.

33. The Central American Court lasted until 1917, when the Wilson Administration undermined the venture. Jessup, *Root*, vol. 1, 500–514; Scott, "Elihu Root," 10–11 (including quote and cite about first international court with continuing functions). When I was the U.S. trade representative under President George W. Bush, I negotiated a free trade agreement with the five Central American states and the Dominican Republic to support their economic integration and development. Today, the Central Americans need U.S. support for governance and anticorruption and against organized crime and drug trafficking.

34. In anticipation, Root directed that the Pan American Union building (today the headquarters for the Organization of American States) in Washington include the Canadian coat of arms with those of other American republics. Jessup, *Root*, vol. 2, 99.

35. See Jessup, *Root*, vol. 2, 83–99 and 284 for partnership with Canada, including Newfoundland arbitration.

36. See Scott, "Elihu Root," 25–30, including quotes, citing 49 Cong. Rec. 1822–1824 (1913), and 51 Cong. Rec. 8955 (1914).

37. Scott, "Elihu Root," 8; Robert B. Strassler, ed., *The Landmark Thucydides: A Comprehensive Guide to the Peloponnesian War* (New York: Free Press, 1996), 351–53.

38. See Jessup, *Root*, vol. 2, 374–76. See Leopold, *Root*, 53 for the list of contributions.

39. See Jessup, *Root*, vol. 2, 310–12, including his 1870 experience and blaming Germany; Zimmermann, *First Great Triumph*, 129 on Dresden.

40. Jessup, *Root*, vol. 2, 313, including quotes.

41. See Leopold, *Root*, 98.

42. See Jessup, *Root*, vol. 2, 313 on the new political order. Oscar Straus quoted in Cobbs Hoffman, *American Umpire*, 197. For the original source, see Oscar Straus, "Rebuilding the Foundations of International Peace," *New York Times Current History*, vol. 4 (New York: New York Times Company, 1917), 908.

43. Elihu Root, "The Outlook for International Law," Presidential Address at the Ninth Annual Meeting of the American Society of International Law, Washington, December 28, 1915, in *Addresses on International Subjects*, 393–94.

44. Scott, "Elihu Root," 13–14, citing "Minutes of the Meeting of the Executive Council: April 27, 1918," *Proceedings of the American Society of International Law at the Meetings of Its Executive Council*, vol. 12/13, April 27, 1918, and April 17, 1919 (Washington, DC: American Society of International Law, 1919), 17–18.

45. Jessup, *Root*, vol. 2, 376; Leopold, *Root*, 129–30.

46. See Leopold, *Root*, 122–27, 133–43 including development of reservations policy at 138; Jessup, *Root*, vol. 2, 383–409 including quote on Article X at 392–93, obligation to Europe, and five-year term at 393; Zasloff, "Law and the Shaping of American Foreign Policy," 342–56 including international law critique at 342–45 and Wilson quote at 353, citing Thomas J. Knock, *To End All Wars: Woodrow Wilson and the Quest for a New World Order* (Princeton, NJ: Princeton University Press, 1992), 259.

47. On France, see Jessup, *Root*, vol. 2, 401–2 (including quote); Zasloff, "Law and the Shaping of American Foreign Policy," 356–61.

48. Leopold, *Root*, 141–43; Jessup, *Root*, vol. 2, 407–8.

49. See Elihu Root, "The 'Great War' and International Law," Presidential Address at the Fifteenth Annual Meeting of the American Society of International Law, April 27, 1921, in *Advocate of Peace Through Justice* 83, no. 6 (June 1921), 225–30; idem., "Steps Toward Preserving Peace," *Foreign Affairs* 3, no. 3 (April 1925), 351–57; idem., "The Codification of International Law," Report Submitted to the 23rd Conference on the Interparliamentary Union, Washington, DC, October 3, 1925, reprinted in *American Journal of International Law* 19, no. 4 (October 1925), 675–84.

50. For Root's efforts to get the Senate to ratify the World Court protocol, see Jessup, *Root*, vol. 2, 428–44; Leopold, *Root*, 162–68.

51. For Root's opinion to Vannevar Bush, see Jessup, *Root*, vol. 2, 472–73, citing Root to Dean Vannevar Bush, December 22, 1936, and Bush to Jessup, August 16, 1937.

52. In this regard, Root diverged from: the Taft-Knox Arbitration treaties; Taft's view that arbitration would have prevented wars in 1812, 1846, and 1898; and the Kellogg-Briand "Peace Pact." See Hendrickson, *Union, Nation, or Empire*, 296.

53. See Charles N. Brower et al., "The Legacy of Elihu Root," *Proceedings of the Annual Meeting (American Society of International Law)*, vol. 100, March 29–April 1, 2006, all quotes within.

54. See Zasloff, "Law and the Shaping of American Foreign Policy."

55. See, e.g., Robert Keohane, *After Hegemony: Cooperation and Discord in the World Political Economy* (Princeton, NJ: Princeton University Press, 1984) and, with Joseph S. Nye, *Power and Interdependence: World Politics in Transition* (Boston: Little, Brown, 1977). See also Richard Steinberg and Jonathan Zasloff, "Power and International Law," *American Journal of International Law* 100, no. 1 (January 2006), 64–87 for a helpful categorization and description of the changing intellectual movements in international law over the century. Steinberg and Zasloff would probably treat my point as a "hybrid between realism and rationalist institutionalism" (76).

56. See, e.g., Joseph S. Nye, "Soft Power," *Foreign Policy*, no. 80 (Autumn 1990), 153–71; idem., *Soft Power: The Means to Success in World Politics* (New York: PublicAffairs, 2004).

57. See Jack Goldsmith and Eric Posner, *The Limits of International Law* (New York: Oxford University Press, 2005) for a view of the limited benefits of international laws. See John Bolton, "Should We Take Global Governance Seriously?" *Chicago Journal of International Law* 1, no. 2 (2000) for the view protective of national sovereignty.

58. Cobbs Hoffman, *American Umpire*, 218, citing *Conference on the Limitation of Armament, Washington, November 12, 1912–February 6, 1922* (Washington, DC: U.S. Government Printing Office, 1922), 268. Hamilton quoted in "Legacy of Elihu Root," 216. For the original source, see "From Alexander Hamilton to Robert Morris," August 13, 1782, *The Papers of Alexander Hamilton*, vol. 3, *1782–1786*, ed. Harold C. Syrett (New York: Columbia University Press, 1962), 132–43.

Chapter 10. Cordell Hull: Reciprocal Trade

1. Cordell Hull, *The Memoirs of Cordell Hull*, vol. 1 (New York: Macmillan Company, 1948), 352.

2. Hull, *Memoirs*, 81.

3. Hull, *Memoirs*, 364.

4. Cordell Hull, "The World Waits," September 15, 1936, in *Vital Speeches of the Day* 2, no. 26 (October 1, 1936), 794–7.

5. Cordell Hull, "International Trade," November 1, 1934, in *Vital Speeches of the Day* 1, no. 4 (November 19, 1934), 107–11.

6. For data on 1792, see Douglas Irwin, *Clashing over Commerce: A History of U.S. Trade Policy* (Chicago: University of Chicago Press, 2017), 79.

7. Irwin, *Clashing over Commerce*, 86, also citing Gerard Clarfield, "Protecting the Frontiers: Defense Policy and the Tariff Question in the First Washington Administration," *William and Mary Quarterly* 32, no. 3 (July 1975), 443–64 (emphases in original).

8. See Irwin, *Clashing over Commerce*, 7, 154 for data.

9. Irwin, *Clashing over Commerce*, 7–8.

10. Irwin, *Clashing over Commerce*, 303–5.

11. Irwin, *Clashing over Commerce*, 297.

12. Irwin, *Clashing over Commerce*, 306.

13. Irwin, *Clashing over Commerce*, 316.

14. Irwin, *Clashing over Commerce*, 309–10. For McKinley's speech at the Pan-American Exposition, see William McKinley, *Last Speech of William McKinley, Delivered at the Pan-American Exposition at Buffalo, September 5, 1901* (Washington, DC: Government Printing Office, 1904).

15. Irwin, *Clashing over Commerce*, 312–14.

16. Irwin, *Clashing over Commerce*, 338–39. For Hull's role, see Hull, *Memoirs*, 80–81; Michael Butler, *Cautious Visionary: Cordell Hull and Trade Reform, 1933–1937* (Kent, OH: Kent State University Press, 1998), 3.

17. The U.S. share of world manufacturing output grew from 36 percent in 1913 to 42 percent in 1926–29. See Irwin, *Clashing over Commerce*, 340, 344 for data.

18. See Irwin, *Clashing over Commerce*, 344–45 for quotes, citing William Diamond, *The Economic Thought of Woodrow Wilson* (Baltimore: Johns Hopkins University Press, 1943), 183. For Wilson's Fourteen Points, see "President Woodrow Wilson's Fourteen Points," January 8, 1918, Avalon Project, Yale University, http://avalon.law.yale.edu/20th_century/wilson14.asp.

19. Hull, *Memoirs*, 82.

20. Some of the decline could be traced to Congress's use of specific duty amounts (rather than a percentage of the price) for some goods; with wartime inflation, those specific duties shrank as a percentage of the higher prices of the imports. Irwin, *Clashing over Commerce*, 346–47. For Lodge's reservations, see "Senator Henry Cabot Lodge's Personal Copy of His 'Reservations' of the Treaty of Versailles" (1919), Records Relating to Treaties with Foreign Countries, 1789–2000, Record Group 46: Records of the U.S. Senate, 1789–2015, National Archives Catalog, https://catalog.archives.gov/id/5678178.

21. Irwin, *Clashing over Commerce*, 356–59.

22. The MFN concept, dating back to the bilateral Treaties of Utrecht in 1713, is that if a country grants a trade privilege to another country, it will provide the same benefit to all other countries it has recognized as most favored nations. Franklin's Treaty of Amity and Commerce with France in 1778 included an MFN provision. Cobbs Hoffman, *American Umpire*, 92.

23. Irwin, *Clashing over Commerce*, 365.

24. See Irwin, *Clashing over Commerce*, 371–410 on Smoot-Hawley, including 3,300 products at 388; "logrolling" quote at 375 from House Democratic Minority Report, drafted by Hull, citing H.R. Rep. No. 7-71 (1929), 11; 1,028 economists at 386.

25. Since 1930, Congress has never again tried to prescribe a full schedule of duties. Indeed, the Tariff Act of 1930 remains on the statute books, although actual rates have been lowered through decades of negotiations under authority Congress granted to the executive. Irwin, *Clashing over Commerce*, 397. See, e.g., Milton Friedman and Anna J. Schwartz, *A Monetary History of the United States* (Princeton, NJ: Princeton University Press, 1963); Price Fishback, "U.S. Monetary and Fiscal Policy in the 1930s," in *The Great Depression of the 1930s: Lessons for Today*, eds. Nicholas Crafts and Peter Fearon (New York: Oxford University Press, 2013).

26. See Irwin, *Clashing over Commerce*, 390, 394 for data.

27. Irwin, *Clashing over Commerce*, 401. For Smoot's quote, see 71 Cong. Rec. 3537–3575 (1929) (the quote itself is at 3548).

28. Irwin, *Clashing over Commerce*, 401–8.

29. William Hard, "Mr. Hull Persists," *Current History* 40 (April 1934), 14–19.

30. For Hull's background, see Butler, *Cautious Visionary*, 1–14; Irwin F. Gellman, *Secret Affairs: Franklin Roosevelt, Cordell Hull, and Sumner Welles* (Baltimore: Johns Hopkins University Press, 1995), 23–29, 31 for quote on "a survivor"; Hull, *Memoirs*; Donald Drummond, "Cordell Hull," in *An Uncertain Tradition: American Secretaries of State in the Twentieth Century*, ed. Norman Graebner (New York: McGraw-Hill, 1961), 184.

31. Butler, *Cautious Visionary*, 4–5.

32. See Butler, *Cautious Visionary*, 6 for Farley quote, citing Frank Freidel interview with James A. Farley, Frank Freidel Interview File, Franklin D. Roosevelt Presidential Library, Hyde Park, New York.

33. Gellman, *Secret Affairs*, 29, 31.

34. See Gellman, *Secret Affairs*, 32 for TB; for delay and Moley, see Butler, *Cautious Visionary*, 19–20.

35. See Butler, *Cautious Visionary*, 28–81 for London conference; Gellman, *Secret Affairs*, 38–41; Hard, "Mr. Hull Persists," 16.

36. Hull, *Memoirs*, 356, 358, including quotes.

37. Hull, *Memoirs*, 357–61.

38. Irwin, *Clashing Over Commerce*, 425–26.

39. Butler, *Cautious Visionary*, 95–96.

40. Irwin, *Clashing over Commerce*, 431.

41. Irwin, *Clashing over Commerce*, 433.

42. Hull, *Memoirs*, 370.

43. Julius Pratt, *Cordell Hull, 1933–44*, vol. 12 of *The American Secretaries of State and Their Diplomacy*, eds. Samuel Flagg Bemis and Robert H. Ferrell (New York: Cooper Square, 1964), 117–19. Hull quote from Hull, *Memoirs*, 370.

44. Butler, *Cautious Visionary*, 100–101, including "trading house" quote from Peek at 101.

45. See Butler, *Cautious Visionary*, 97–120; Pratt, *Hull*, 117 for "unilateral economic disarmament."

46. See Butler, *Cautious Visionary*, 97–120; Hull, *Memoirs*, 371–74, including quote of note to FDR.

47. Pratt, *Hull*, 115; Irwin, *Clashing over Commerce*, 447, citing Stewart Patrick, *Best Laid Plans: The Origins of American Multilateralism and the Dawn of the Cold War* (Lanham, MD: Rowman & Littlefield, 2009), 124.

48. See Pratt, *Hull*, 120 on manganese; Butler, *Cautious Visionary*, 123.

49. Butler, *Cautious Visionary*, 124–26.

50. See Butler, *Cautious Visionary*, 127, 183 (for list of agreements through 1938).

51. See Butler, *Cautious Visionary*, 130–36 for Canada.

52. See Butler, *Cautious Visionary*, 129, 137–55 for Britain. Hull quote from Hull, *Memoirs*, 519–20.

53. See Butler, *Cautious Visionary*, 137–55. Hull quote from "Memorandum of Conversation, by the Assistant Secretary of State (Sayre)," November 16, 1937, *Foreign Relations of the United States: Diplomatic Papers, 1937, The British Commonwealth, Europe, Near East and Africa*, vol. 2, Document 58.

54. Chamberlain quoted in Irwin, *Clashing over Commerce*, 438, 439, citing Arthur W. Schatz, "The Anglo-American Trade Agreement and Cordell Hull's Search for Peace, 1936–1938," *Journal of American History* 55, no. 1 (June 1970), 100. For Munich connection, see Pratt, *Hull*, 128, 294–300; Whitney H. Shepardson and William Scroggs, *The United States in World Affairs, 1938* (New York: Harper & Brothers, 1938), 190–99.

55. See Butler, *Cautious Visionary*, 155–58 (quotes at 158) on Germany and Italy.
56. See Butler, *Cautious Visionary*, 159–61 on Japan, citing "The Ambassador in Japan (Grew) to the Secretary of State," February 6, 1935, *Foreign Relations of the United States: Diplomatic Papers*, 1935, Far East, vol. 3, 833.
57. Butler, *Cautious Visionary*, 171–74 (election), 179–80; Irwin, *Clashing over Commerce*, 443–46.
58. Hull, *Memoirs*, 746–47.
59. See Irwin, *Clashing over Commerce*, 448 for reference to Gallup poll, 449 for amendment and votes.
60. See Irwin, *Clashing over Commerce*, 450 for Republican platform, 452–54 on 1943 vote, 454 on Ways and Means Report, citing H.R. Rep. No. 403-78 (1948), 10.
61. See Irwin, *Clashing over Commerce*, 440 for list of agreements, data and quote at 439, 441.
62. See Hull, *Memoirs*, 365 for quote. See Drummond, "Cordell Hull," 184, 196–203 on Hull's limited role.
63. See Drummond, "Cordell Hull," 203, 206–8 on postwar planning and the creation of the UN.
64. Irwin, *Clashing over Commerce*, 26, citing Paul Douglas, *In the Fullness of Time: The Memoirs of Paul H. Douglas* (New York: Harcourt Brace Jovanovich, 1972), 476.
65. Irwin, *Clashing over Commerce*, 422–23, citing Dean Acheson, *Present at the Creation: My Years in the State Department* (New York: W. W. Norton, 1969), 9–10.
66. Clayton quote in Irwin, *Clashing over Commerce*, 464, citing Gregory A. Fossedal, *Our Finest Hour: Will Clayton, the Marshall Plan, and the Triumph of Democracy* (Stanford, CA: Hoover Institution Press, 1993), 136.

Chapter 11. Architects of the American Alliance System

1. See Melvyn P. Leffler, *A Preponderance of Power: National Security, the Truman Administration, and the Cold War* (Stanford, CA: Stanford University Press, 1992), 1 for 50 million; Benn Steil, *The Marshall Plan: Dawn of the Cold War* (New York: Simon & Schuster, 2018), 2 for 522,000.
2. Forrest C. Pogue, *George Marshall*, vol. 4, *Statesman, 1945-1959* (New York: Viking Press, 1987), 159, citing George C. Marshall, *The Winning of the War in Europe and the Pacific: Biennial Report of the Chief of Staff of the United States Army, July 1, 1943 to June 30, 1945, to the Secretary of War* (Washington, DC: War Department, 1945), 118.
3. Leffler, *Preponderance of Power*, 11, citing JCS 1769/1, "United States Assistance to Other Countries from the Standpoint of National Security," April 29, 1947.
4. See R. Alton Lee, "The Army 'Mutiny' of 1946," *Journal of American History* 53, no. 3 (December 1966), 557; Joseph T. Glatthaar, *The American Military: A Concise History* (New York: Oxford University Press, 2018), 89.
5. Leffler, *Preponderance of Power*, 106.
6. Leffler, *Preponderance of Power*, 25.
7. Lawrence Haas, *Harry and Arthur: Truman, Vandenberg, and the Partnership That Created the Free World* (Lincoln, NE: Potomac Books, 2016), 50.
8. David McCullough, *Truman* (New York: Simon & Schuster, 1992), 219.
9. McCullough, *Truman*, 191, 258.
10. Alexander De Conde, "George Catlett Marshall," in Graebner, *Uncertain Tradition*, 247.
11. Steil, *Marshall Plan*, 20.
12. McCullough, *Truman*, 469.
13. McCullough, *Truman*, 470, 480–81, 492–93; Leffler, *Preponderance of Power*, 44, 46.
14. Steil, *Marshall Plan*, 18–19; Leffler, *Preponderance of Power*, 63, citing Memo for the President by John J. McCloy, April 26, 1945; "Assistant Secretary of State (Acheson) to Mr. Harry L. Hopkins, Special Assistant to President Roosevelt," December 26, 1944, *Foreign Relations of the United States: Diplomatic Papers, 1945*, General: Political and Economic Matters, vol. 2, Doc. 438.
15. Quoted in Steil, *Marshall Plan*, 15–17.
16. Fossedal, *Our Finest Hour*, 16–25.
17. Fossedal, *Our Finest Hour*, 26–36.
18. Fossedal, *Our Finest Hour*, 12, 25, 36–38; Steil, *Marshall Plan*, 51.
19. See Fossedal, *Our Finest Hour*, 60–61 on trade and 65–82 on procurement.
20. Fossedal, *Our Finest Hour*, 108–9. In 1946, President Truman promoted Clayton to under secretary.
21. Benn Steil, *The Battle of Bretton Woods: John Maynard Keynes, Harry Dexter White, and the Making of a New World Order* (Princeton, NJ: Princeton University Press, 2013), 255–60; Fossedal, *Our Finest Hour*, 137–45.
22. Steil, *Bretton Woods*, 11.

23. Fossedal, *Our Finest Hour*, 182–83.

24. Fossedal, *Our Finest Hour*, 184–91. Britain made its final repayments in 2006. See Finlo Rohrer, "What's a Little Debt Between Friends?" BBC News, May 10, 2006, http://news.bbc.co.uk/2/hi/uk_news/maga zine/4757181.stm.

25. Fossedal, *Our Finest Hour*, 192–99 (his quote at 198).

26. Jean Edward Smith, *Lucius D. Clay: An American Life* (New York: Henry Holt, 1990), 356 on, including Clay quote at 356.

27. See Smith, *Clay*, 350–52 for quote.

28. Smith, *Clay*, 352.

29. Leffler, *Preponderance of Power*, 116–21.

30. For discussion of Kennan and the Long Telegram, see John Lewis Gaddis, *George F. Kennan: An American Life* (New York: Penguin Press, 2011), 216–28; Steil, *Marshall Plan*, 28–31; Pogue, *Marshall*, 155–56; Leffler, *Preponderance of Power*, 108–10. For the original text of the Long Telegram, see "Telegram, George Kennan to George Marshall," February 22, 1946, Wilson Center Digital Archive, https://digitalarchive.wilsoncen ter.org/document/116178.pdf.

31. McCullough, *Truman*, 486–90.

32. Acheson, *Present at the Creation*, 197–98; Leffler, *Preponderance of Power*, 110–11; Steil, *Marshall Plan*, 23–25.

33. Leffler, *Preponderance of Power*, 110–14; Steil, *Marshall Plan*, 24.

34. Acheson, *Present at the Creation*, 195–96.

35. Leffler, *Preponderance of Power*, 130–38 (including story); McCullough, *Truman*, 543–45; see Haas, *Harry and Arthur*, 115 for reference to twenty years.

36. McCullough, *Truman*, 523.

37. Acheson, *Present at the Creation*, 200.

38. McCullough, *Truman*, 530.

39. Lawrence Kaplan, *The Conversion of Senator Arthur H. Vandenberg: From Isolation to International Engagement* (Lexington, KY: University Press of Kentucky, 2015), 87 (citing Vandenberg's papers) and 169.

40. See Haas, *Harry and Arthur*, 2 for forty-seven days; Kaplan, *Conversion*, 1–3 (citing James Reston in 1948 on "qualities of enterprise"); and Hendrik Meijer, *Arthur Vandenberg: The Man in the Middle of the American Century* (Chicago: University of Chicago Press, 2017), 4–6, 70, 119.

41. Meijer, *Vandenberg*, 4.

42. Meijer, *Vandenberg*, 6–9; Kaplan, *Conversion*, 2–4.

43. Kaplan, *Conversion*, 3–4, 8, 11–14; Meijer, *Vandenberg*, 16.

44. Vandenberg believed that Alexander Hamilton represented a superior mix of nationalism, conservativism, and progressivism. The activist editor, a rapid writer, published in the 1920s two biographies of Hamilton. In 1926, G.P. Putnam's Sons published Vandenberg's epic history of the United States, *The Trail of a Tradition*. Kaplan, *Conversion*, 17–19.

45. Kaplan, *Conversion*, 21–23, 25–27.

46. See Haas, *Harry and Arthur*, 26 for Reston quote.

47. Vandenberg coined "hitch-hiked" and the "New Ordeal," and popularized "fiddle faddle." Meijer, *Vandenberg*, 70, 119; Kaplan, *Conversion*, 30–34.

48. Kaplan, *Conversion*, 35–39; Haas, *Harry and Arthur*, 22.

49. Kaplan, *Conversion*, 42, 66, 74.

50. See Kaplan, *Conversion*, 87 on Hull and 90 on Marshall.

51. Kaplan, *Conversion*, 97–98.

52. Kaplan, *Conversion*, 125–45; see Haas, *Harry and Arthur*, 23 for Truman quote, 35–36 for "indispensable man," and 60 for Truman's directive on "every move."

53. Kaplan, *Conversion*, 145–50.

54. Haas, *Harry and Arthur*, 101.

55. Kaplan, *Conversion*, 160–61, 164, 167.

56. Acheson, *Present at the Creation*, 192–93.

57. See Mark A. Stoler, *George C. Marshall: Soldier-Statesman of the American Century* (Boston: Twayne Publishers, 1989), 154 for Truman quote.

58. Pogue, *Marshall*, 144–45.

59. Any member of the State Department over the past fifty years would marvel how the various viewpoints and requests for action could have been managed and assessed without such a function. Over the years, U.S. foreign policy came to encompass a vast number of activities and interests, many assigned by Congress, and the State Department's ramshackle matrix organization expanded even further. Modern secretaries have had to decide how to make the Secretariat work for them and not just "the building," as the Foreign Service calls the sprawling network of diplomatic offices. Acheson, *Present at the Creation*, 213–15; Pogue, *Marshall*, 146–51.

60. Acheson, who was the first under secretary to work with the Policy Planning team, and later served as secretary in his own right, explained why the Policy Planning role is extremely difficult to perform. He wrote that planning heads are lured into becoming either an operating arm of the secretary, who might be frustrated by departmental inertia, or "encyclopedists" who amass analyses of every area and country but fail to make a difference. I would add a third risk, especially for academicians who become planning directors: writing public reports that exhibit intellectual cohesion, but have no effect on practical decisions. Historians need to assess carefully which papers really matter to the decision-makers. Acheson, *Present at the Creation*, 214–15. At a similar moment of upheaval in Europe and the international system, Secretary Baker asked me to oversee two of Marshall's innovations: the Policy Planning Staff and the Executive Secretariat. I was supposed to help integrate the "here and now" with the "future" without being bogged down by bureaucratic duties. Secretary Baker's director of Policy Planning, my colleague and friend Dennis Ross, did a superb job prodding fresh policy thinking in the spirit of Marshall's creation.

61. Pogue, *Marshall*, 147–48 (citing interview with Acheson). I often recalled Marshall's wisdom in various executive roles. My variation, after listening to extended accounts of factors, frustrations, and uncertainties has been: "What is the question you would like me to address? And what do you recommend?" Pogue, *Marshall*, 148; Acheson, *Present at the Creation*, 216.

62. Acheson, *Present at the Creation*, 217–18; Pogue, *Marshall*, 161–63; Steil, *Marshall Plan*, 22, 32–34; Leffler, *Preponderance of Power*, 142–44; McCullough, *Truman*, 541–42.

63. Leffler, *Preponderance of Power*, 143; Steil, *Marshall Plan*, 51. For the original source, see "Memorandum on the Creation of a National Council of Defense," in William Clayton, *Selected Papers of Will Clayton*, ed. Frederick J. Dobney (Baltimore: Johns Hopkins Press, 1971), 198–99.

64. See note 62. "Work like hell" quote in Steil, *Marshall Plan*, 32.

65. Leffler, *Preponderance of Power*, 7.

66. Steil, *Marshall Plan*, 33.

67. Acheson, *Present at the Creation*, 219; Steil, *Marshall Plan*, 35–36; Pogue, *Marshall*, 164–65; Kaplan, *Conversion*, 184–85.

68. See Acheson, *Present at the Creation*, 219; Steil, *Marshall Plan*, 36.

69. Acheson, *Present at the Creation*, 221–22; Steil, *Marshall Plan*, 37–41; see Fossedal, *Our Finest Hour*, 209 on Clayton.

70. Acheson, *Present at the Creation*, 221–22; Steil, *Marshall Plan*, 39, 43.

71. Steil, *Marshall Plan*, 43.

72. See "Special Message to the Congress on Greece and Turkey: The Truman Doctrine," March 12, 1947, in *Public Papers of the Presidents of the United States: Harry S. Truman, 1947*, vol. 3 (Washington, DC: Government Printing Office, 1963), 176–80.

73. Acheson, *Present at the Creation*, 223.

74. See Pogue, *Marshall*, 167 for origin of the phrase; Acheson, *Present at the Creation*, 225; Fossedal, *Our Finest Hour*, 208.

75. Steil, *Marshall Plan*, 89–91.

76. Haas, *Harry and Arthur*, 152–53.

77. Leffler, *Preponderance of Power*, 146.

78. Acheson, *Present at the Creation*, 223.

79. Kaplan, *Conversion*, 184–91; Acheson, *Present at the Creation*, 223–25; Steil, *Marshall Plan*, 49 (on the American public's preference for the UN).

80. Steil, *Marshall Plan*, 46–48.

81. Steil, *Marshall Plan*, 60.

82. Pogue, *Marshall*, 177 (forty-three meetings); Stoler, *Marshall*, 161 ("stone ass"); De Conde, "Marshall," 252 ("In diplomacy…"); see Steil, *Marshall Plan*, 71 on *Congress of Vienna* book.

83. Steil, *Marshall Plan*, 82.

84. For a recent account of Marshall's efforts in China, see Daniel Kurtz-Phelan, *The China Mission: George Marshall's Unfinished War, 1945–1947* (New York: W. W. Norton and Company, 2018).

85. Pogue, *Marshall*, 194–96, citing Charles E. Bohlen, *Witness to History, 1929–1969* (New York: W. W. Norton, 1973), 263.

86. Pogue, *Marshall*, at 196; see Steil, *Marshall Plan*, 85 for quote. For the original source of the quote, see "Editorial Note," *Foreign Relations of the United States*, 1947, British Commonwealth; Europe, vol. 3, Doc. 133 (hereafter *FRUS*).

87. Steil, *Marshall Plan*, 86.

88. Gaddis, *Kennan*, 265.

89. Gaddis, *Kennan*, 266–67.

90. As a matter of diplomatic practice and advocacy, I prefer the multidimensional Clayton: He combined on-the-ground observations with practical economic explanations. Moreover, the fingerprints of his team show up everywhere. Acheson, *Present at the Creation*, 231.

91. Fossedal, *Our Finest Hour*, 203, citing Alan Bullock, *Ernest Bevin: Foreign Secretary, 1945–1951* (New York: W. W. Norton, 1983), 361; McCullough, *Truman*, 540.

92. Fossedal, *Our Finest Hour*, 215.

93. Irwin, *Clashing over Commerce*, 475–77; Fossedal, *Our Finest Hour*, 201–2.

94. Irwin, *Clashing over Commerce*, 477.

95. Fossedal, *Our Finest Hour*, 213.

96. Fossedal, *Our Finest Hour*, 213–14.

97. Fossedal, *Our Finest Hour*, 210, 211, and 213, citing Joseph M. Jones, *The Fifteen Weeks* (New York: Viking, 1955), 226–28.

98. Acheson, *Present at the Creation*, 227.

99. Acheson, *Present at the Creation*, 227.

100. Fossedal, *Our Finest Hour*, 222–26; see Leffler, *Preponderance of Power*, 157 for World Bank loan.

101. Irwin, *Clashing over Commerce*, 48.

102. Fossedal, *Our Finest Hour*, 222–25; Irwin, *Clashing over Commerce*, 478–82.

103. Acheson, *Present at the Creation*, 231.

104. "Memorandum by the Under Secretary of State for Economic Affairs (Clayton)," *FRUS*, 1947, British Commonwealth; Europe, vol. 3, Doc. 136.

105. Acheson, *Present at the Creation*, 231.

106. Steil, *Marshall Plan*, 110.

107. Fossedal, *Our Finest Hour*, 228–29, citing "May 27 and June 5: A Comparison of William Clayton's Memorandum and George Marshall's Speech," Alexis de Tocqueville Institution, December 20, 1989, adapted from Ross J. Pritchard, "William L. Clayton" (PhD diss., Fletcher School of Law and Diplomacy, 1955), 296–98.

108. Steil, *Marshall Plan*, 111.

109. For Marshall's speech, see "The Marshall Plan Speech," June 5, 1947, George C. Marshall Foundation, https://www.marshallfoundation.org/marshall/the-marshall-plan/marshall-plan-speech/.

110. Isaacson and Thomas, *Wise Men*, 413; Steil, *Marshall Plan*, 111–15.

111. Fossedal, *Our Finest Hour*, 235.

112. Irwin, *Clashing over Commerce*, 481, citing William Clayton, "GATT, the Marshall Plan, and OECD," *Political Science Quarterly* 78, no. 4 (December 1963), 499.

113. Fossedal, *Our Finest Hour*, 248–51.

114. Irwin, *Clashing over Commerce*, 483–89.

115. Steil, *Marshall Plan*, 123–31, including "crisis of capitalism" at 123, "Soviet spies" at 127, Stalin's new instructions at 127–28, Kennan quote at 109, citing Kennan interview with Harry B. Price, February 19, 1953, Folder: "January–June, 1953," Box 1, Oral History Interview File, Price Papers, Truman Library.

116. Steil, *Marshall Plan*, 147.

117. Steil, *Marshall Plan*, 147–75, including Kennan at 169–71.

118. Steil, *Marshall Plan*, 174, citing Ernst Hans van der Beugel, *From Marshall Aid to Atlantic Partnership: European Integration as a Concern of American Foreign Policy* (New York: Elsevier, 1966), 72.

119. Pogue, *Marshall*, 238, citing author's interview with Marshall, November 19, 1956; Steil, *Marshall Plan*, 249, citing Marshall interviews with Price, October 30, 1952, reproduced in Harry B. Price, *The Marshall Plan and Its Meaning* (Ithaca, NY: Cornell University Press, 1955), 65; Kaplan, *Conversion*, 194; see Haas, *Harry and Arthur*, 174 on Vandenberg.

120. Steil, *Marshall Plan*, 194–97.

121. The administration also had to pay close attention to the Democratic minority in Congress. When an executive branch of one party has to work with a congressional majority of the other party, the administration's friends in the minority can easily feel overlooked. Acheson warned Marshall of this risk after meeting Democratic senators shortly before the Harvard speech. Kaplan, *Conversion*, 198; Steil, *Marshall Plan*, 200. See "Memorandum by the Under Secretary of State (Acheson) to the Secretary of State," May 28, 1947, *FRUS*, British Commonwealth; Europe, vol. 3, Doc. 137.

122. McCullough, *Truman*, 565; Stoler, *Marshall*, 165, citing Larry I. Bland, ed. *George C. Marshall Interviews and Reminiscences for Forrest C. Pogue*, 3rd ed., Tape 18, Recorded November 19, 1956 (Lexington, VA: George C. Marshall Foundation, 1996), 527; Steil, *Marshall Plan*, 189; see Pogue, *Marshall*, 247 for Cub Scouts.

123. Steil, *Marshall Plan*, 213, 222; Kaplan, *Conversion*, 198.

124. Kaplan, *Conversion*, 200; Steil, *Marshall Plan*, 230; see Meijer, *Vandenberg*, 308 for Vandenberg quote.

125. Kaplan, *Conversion*, 200; Steil, *Marshall Plan*, 226, 260; see Haas, *Harry and Arthur*, 160 for $34.5 billion budget.

126. Steil, *Marshall Plan*, 247, citing Francis Wilcox and Thorsten Kalijarvi, interview with Harry B. Price, August 8, 1952, Folder: "August–December 1952," Box 1, Oral History Interview File, Price Papers, Truman Library.

127. Steil, *Marshall Plan*, 248, citing 94 Cong. Rec. 1915–20 (1948).

128. Steil, *Marshall Plan*, 249, citing Gallup poll, March 3, 1948.

129. Steil, *Marshall Plan*, 250.

130. Steil, *Marshall Plan*, 258–61.

131. Steil, *Marshall Plan*, 261.

132. Kaplan, *Conversion*, 201; Pogue, *Marshall*, 253–54.

133. Steil, *Marshall Plan*, 342, including figures for amounts.

134. Steil, *Marshall Plan*, 356 also makes this point about Germany through the end of the Cold War.

135. Steil, *Marshall Plan*, 81, 357.

136. Leffler, *Preponderance of Power*, 156, citing Meeting of the Secretaries of State, War, and Navy, July 3, 1947, RG 107, Patterson Papers, Safe File, Box 3, National Archives; Department of State, *A Decade of American Foreign Policy: Basic Documents, 1941–1949*, rev. ed. (Washington, DC: U.S. Government Printing Office, 1985), 331.

137. Leffler, *Preponderance of Power*, 151–55.

138. See "Memorandum of Conversation, by the Under Secretary of State for Economic Affairs (Clayton)," June 20, 1947, *FRUS*, 1947, Council of Foreign Ministers; Germany and Austria, vol. 2, Doc. 374.

139. Leffler, *Preponderance of Power*, 187, 197–98, 211–15 (Conolly quote at 202).

140. Steil, *Marshall Plan*, 249, citing "The Ambassador in the United Kingdom (Douglas) to the Secretary of State," March 1, 1948, *FRUS*, 1948, Germany and Austria, vol. 2, Doc. 72.

141. McCullough, *Truman*, 603.

142. Steil, *Marshall Plan*, 252.

143. Steil, *Marshall Plan*, 253–55.

144. Steil, *Marshall Plan*, 269–74; McCullough, *Truman*, 630; Smith, *Clay*, 462–93.

145. Steil, *Marshall Plan*, 286, citing CIA 8-48, August 19, 1948, Folder: "NSC Meeting 18," Box 178, National Security Council—Meetings File, Subject File, President's Secretary's Files, Truman Papers, Truman Library.

146. Steil, *Marshall Plan*, 292, 302; McCullough, *Truman*, 647.

147. McCullough, *Truman*, 648; Steil, *Marshall Plan*, 293, 302.

148. McCullough, *Truman*, 685–87.

149. Meijer, *Vandenberg*, 333–34; Steil, *Marshall Plan*, 301–2.

150. Haas, *Harry and Arthur*, 254–55.

151. Steil, *Marshall Plan*, 324.

152. Steil, *Marshall Plan*, 312.

153. Steil, *Marshall Plan*, 324.

154. Gaddis, *Kennan*, 329–30; Steil, *Marshall Plan*, 326.

155. Gaddis, *Kennan*, 349; Steil, *Marshall Plan*, 327–28.

156. See Gaddis, *Kennan*, 339 for Kennan quote; Steil, *Marshall Plan*, 328, citing Gaddis, *Kennan*, 369–70.

157. Pogue, *Marshall*, 323; see Gaddis, *Kennan*, 321 for quotes.
158. The drafters had included two special articles for contingencies. Article 23 authorized other parts of Germany to accept the Basic Law and the new Federal Republic of Germany. The Saarland used this provision to join the FRG in 1957 when France ended its military occupation. Article 146 anticipated the possibility of "all German" elections to a national assembly to negotiate a new constitution for a unified Germany. In 1989–90, after the opening of the Berlin Wall, my U.S. colleagues and I researched these forty-year-old provisions, as did our West German partners. We agreed that Germany's unification should be through Article 23, which preserved the West German system of government as well as the international obligations the FRG had accumulated over the years. German unification of the five eastern Länder and Berlin would be a takeover, not a merger. Secretary Acheson was in fact way ahead of us. In May 1949, he bluntly stated that the United States would "go ahead with the establishment of a Western German government, come hell or high water. Any unification must be on the basis of the Bonn constitution." The agreement on Germany's unification in 1990 eliminated Article 23, as Secretary Baker had urged the West Germans to do privately. See Philip Zelikow and Condoleezza Rice, *Germany Unified and Europe Transformed: A Study in Statecraft* (Cambridge, MA: Harvard University Press, 1995), 201–2, 230–31; Steil, *Marshall Plan*, 330.
159. Steil, *Marshall Plan*, 251. More than forty years later, when Europeans debated creating a European group within NATO, I asked a German colleague if the Western European Union (the renamed Western Union after West Germany and Italy became members in 1954) could handle the role. "Never," he replied. He pointed out that the WEU had been directed against the Germans, and they had later only grudgingly accepted its existence. Countries' early mental associations with organizations can taint diplomatic usefulness for a long time.
160. Steil, *Marshall Plan*, 250, 253; Leffler, *Preponderance of Power*, 218.
161. By the end of 1947, the Soviets had used their veto to block an action about two dozen times. Haas, *Harry and Arthur*, 193, 230; Pogue, *Marshall*, 323; Meijer, *Vandenberg*, 312–18.
162. Meijer, *Vandenberg*, 313–17.
163. Acheson, *Present at the Creation*, 266.
164. Leffler, *Preponderance of Power*, 215.
165. Steil, *Marshall Plan*, 356.
166. Acheson, *Present at the Creation*, 276–86; Haas, *Harry and Arthur*, 257–73; Meijer, *Vandenberg*, 337.
167. Kaplan, *Conversion*, 224.
168. Steil, *Marshall Plan*, 320.
169. Leffler, *Preponderance of Power*, 17, citing Acheson Testimony, February 16, 1951, U.S. Senate, Committee on Armed Services and Committee on Foreign Relations, *Assignment of Ground Forces of the United States to Duty in the European Area*, 82nd Cong., 1st sess., 1951, 78.
170. Haas, *Harry and Arthur*, 267–73; Kaplan, *Conversion*, 219–26 (North Atlantic Pact quote at 225, emphasis in original); Steil, *Marshall Plan*, 319 (quote on "greatest war deterrent"); Meijer, *Vandenberg*, 343 for "Magna Carta."
171. Haas, *Harry and Arthur*, 276–77; see Meijer, *Vandenberg*, 334 on Gerald Ford.
172. See Steil, *Marshall Plan*, 320–21 for quotes.
173. Steil, *Marshall Plan*, 320–21; Meijer, *Vandenberg*, 343.
174. Steil, *Marshall Plan*, 320–21; Meijer, *Vandenberg*, 343.

Chapter 12. Vannevar Bush: Inventor of the Future

1. Vannevar Bush, "Science, the Endless Frontier: A Report to the President by Vannevar Bush, Director of the Office of Scientific Research and Development, July 1945" (Washington, DC: United States Government Printing Office, 1945). The following citations refer to the 1960 version of the report reprinted under the title "Science, the Endless Frontier: A Report to the President on a Program for Postwar Scientific Research" (Washington, DC: National Science Foundation, 1960).
2. Quoted in G. Pascal Zachary, *Endless Frontier: Vannevar Bush, Engineer of the American Century* (New York: The Free Press, 1997), 218. For the original, see "At 80, Scientist Bush Looks Back at Eventful Years," *Boston Globe*, September 20, 1970 (Boston Globe Library).
3. Bush, "Science," 2.
4. Bush, "Science," 9, 12.
5. Walter Isaacson, *The Innovators* (New York: Simon & Schuster, 2014), 263–64; Zachary, *Endless Frontier*, 261–75.
6. Isaacson, *Innovators*, 272–76.

7. Zachary, *Endless Frontier*, 279.

8. Bush quoted in Zachary, *Endless Frontier*, 197.

9. Isaacson, *Innovators*, at 217, 219; Zachary, *Endless Frontier*, 4. See Jerome B. Wiesner, "Vannevar Bush," in National Academy of the Sciences of the United States of America, *Biographical Memoirs*, vol. 50 (Washington, DC: National Academy of Sciences, 1979), 89.

10. Bruce L. R. Smith, *American Science Policy Since World War II* (Washington, DC: Brookings Institution, 1990), 3–6 places Bush in the larger context of science policy development. Smith notes three phases, with Bush's work critical to the first phase.

11. Zachary, *Endless Frontier*, 8, 23; Isaacson, *Innovators*, 218.

12. Zachary, *Endless Frontier*, 8, 21–22. For the original Wiener quote, see Norbert Wiener, *I Am a Mathematician: The Later Life of a Prodigy* (Cambridge, MA: MIT Press, 1964), 112.

13. See Zachary, *Endless Frontier*, 4 (for quotes) and 28 (organizing people).

14. See Zachary, *Endless Frontier*, 8 (moral code) and 149 ("public entrepreneur" phrase of Eugene Lewis).

15. When I was the U.S. trade representative—leading a small, entrepreneurial agency that had to coordinate with many others—my guidance to colleagues was, "Just keep pressing until someone says no, and then we'll figure out what to do next." Zachary, *Endless Frontier*, 4, 5, 90 (Bush quote at 5).

16. Zachary, *Endless Frontier*, 23–28. See chapter 9.

17. Zachary, *Endless Frontier*, 31–32.

18. See Zachary, *Endless Frontier*, 38 for Bush and Bumpus quotes.

19. See Zachary, *Endless Frontier*, 40 (MIT) and 44–45 (Raytheon).

20. See Zachary, *Endless Frontier*, 52 (quote) and 270 (WWII use).

21. Zachary, *Endless Frontier*, 77, 270–71.

22. Zachary, *Endless Frontier*, 80.

23. Zachary, *Endless Frontier*, 79, 81–82 (quotes).

24. See Zachary, *Endless Frontier*, 89, 420 (for quote from Bush letter to Eric Hodgins); Smith, *American Science Policy*, 17–28 for early U.S. experience.

25. Zachary, *Endless Frontier*, 83.

26. Zachary, *Endless Frontier*, 99 (Congress) and 102 (Arnold).

27. Zachary, *Endless Frontier*, 97 (quotes).

28. Zachary, *Endless Frontier*, 96–97.

29. Zachary, *Endless Frontier*, 104–5.

30. See Zachary, *Endless Frontier*, 108 for quote.

31. Zachary, *Endless Frontier*, 110–11.

32. Zachary, *Endless Frontier*, 112.

33. Zachary, *Endless Frontier*, 114, 115 ("federalism by contract"), 129 (OSRD).

34. Zachary, *Endless Frontier*, 124–28, 131 (quote, emphasis in original).

35. Zachary, *Endless Frontier*, 123, 174 (for reference to OSRD's historian).

36. Zachary, *Endless Frontier*, 168–70 (Bush quote), 171 (Doentiz), 173.

37. Bush, "Endless Frontier," 5.

38. Zachary, *Endless Frontier*, 177–78.

39. Zachary, *Endless Frontier*, 190–96, Bush quote at 198.

40. Zachary, *Endless Frontier*, 197, including quotes.

41. Zachary, *Endless Frontier*, 198–202.

42. McGeorge Bundy, *Danger and Survival* (New York: Random House, 1988) 39–51, 69–70, 105–7 ("indispensable" at 39).

43. Zachary, *Endless Frontier*, 209; Richard G. Hewlett and Oscar E. Anderson Jr., *A History of the United States Atomic Energy Commission*, vol. 1, *The New World, 1939–1946* (University Park, PA: Pennsylvania State University Press, 1962), 52.

44. Zachary, *Endless Frontier*, 208; Bundy, *Danger and Survival*, 46.

45. Zachary, *Endless Frontier*, 201–17.

46. Zachary, *Endless Frontier*, 218–19.

47. Zachary, *Endless Frontier*, 219–20.

48. See FDR's letter of November 17, 1944, reprinted in Bush, "Endless Frontier," 3–4.

49. Zachary, *Endless Frontier*, 222–23.

50. Bush, "Endless Frontier," 12 ("freedom of inquiry"), 38 (patent policy).

51. Zachary, *Endless Frontier*, 225; Walter Millis, *Arms and Men: A Study in American Military History* (New York: Putnam, 1956), 302.

52. Zachary, *Endless Frontier*, 8.

53. On the media response to the report, see Zachary, *Endless Frontier*, 257–59. For example, the *Washington Post* deemed the report a "thorough, careful plan for putting the needed push of the Federal Government behind our scientific progress and yet keeping our science independent of Government control." See Marquis Childs, "Washington Calling: 'Science, the Endless Frontier,'" *Washington Post*, July 20, 1945, 8.

54. "Preliminary Design of an Experimental World-Circling Spaceship" (May 2, 1946), 2, RAND Corporation, https://www.rand.org/content/dam/rand/pubs/special_memoranda/2006/SM11827part1.pdf.

55. Zachary, *Endless Frontier*, 231.

56. Zachary, *Endless Frontier*, 315. See National Security Agency, "Scientific and Technological Resources as Military Assets," memorandum from General Eisenhower, April 30, 1946, https://www.nsa.gov/Portals/70/documents/news-features/declassified-documents/friedman-documents/reports-research/FOLDER_065/41701309074063.pdf (emphasis in original).

57. Zachary, *Endless Frontier*, 334–35.

58. Zachary, *Endless Frontier*, 231–35.

59. Zachary, *Endless Frontier*, 232, 254, 332–33; Smith, *American Science Policy*, 52.

60. Zachary, *Endless Frontier*, 333.

61. Zachary, *Endless Frontier*, 369; James G. Hershberg, *James B. Conant: Harvard to Hiroshima and the Making of the Nuclear Age* (Stanford, CA: Stanford University Press, 1993), 560; Smith, *American Science Policy*, 48–49. According to Smith, by the mid-1960s, NSF accounted for less than 2 percent of the federal R&D budget and a bit less than 15 percent of all support for basic research (51).

62. Leahy quoted in Zachary, *Endless Frontier*, 242. For the original, see Harry S. Truman, *Memoirs by Harry S. Truman*, vol. 1, *Year of Decisions* (New York: Signet Books, 1965), 21.

63. Zachary, *Endless Frontier*, 242–44.

64. Zachary, *Endless Frontier*, 244–45.

65. Zachary, *Endless Frontier*, 292–94.

66. Russell Frank Weigley, *The American Way of War: A History of United States Military Strategy and Policy* (Bloomington, IN: Indiana University Press, 1977), 365–68; Zachary, *Endless Frontier*, 340.

67. Zachary, *Endless Frontier*, 361; Vannevar Bush, *Modern Arms and Free Men: A Discussion of the Role of Science in Preserving Democracy* (New York: Simon & Schuster, 1949), 2–3.

68. Zachary, *Endless Frontier*, 354–55; Oppenheimer account from ibid., 374–77. For the *NYT* op-ed, see Vannevar Bush, "If We Alienate Our Scientists," *New York Times*, June 13, 1954.

69. Smith, *American Science Policy*, 38–39.

70. See Zachary, *Endless Frontier*, 367, including 70 percent.

71. See Smith, *American Science Policy*, 69–70 on technology export controls.

72. Zachary, *Endless Frontier*, 383 (Bush's interests), 390–91 (space rockets), and 407 ("big science" model).

73. Zachary, *Endless Frontier*, 390–91, 395–96; Smith, *American Science Policy*, 71–72.

74. Zachary, *Endless Frontier*, 396; Smith, *American Science Policy*, 85; Harvey Brooks, "What Is the National Science Agenda, and How Did It Come About?" *American Scientist*, September–October 1987, 513.

75. Isaacson, *Innovators*, 156 (Terman connection), 263–64 (computer development), 474–75 (connections among inventors).

76. Isaacson, *Innovators*, 480.

77. For discussion of the "Triple Helix" concept, see "The Triple Helix Concept," Triple Helix Research Group, Stanford University, https://triplehelix.stanford.edu/3helix_concept. For the ideas on historical and competitive models of innovation, I relied on suggestions from Bruce W. Ferguson, a technologist, an entrepreneur, and an educator.

78. The United States ratified the United Nations Framework Convention on Climate Change with the advice and consent of the Senate in 1992. On developing regimes for climate change, see, e.g., Robert O. Keohane and David G. Victor, "The Regime Complex for Climate Change," *Perspectives on Politics* 9, no. 1 (March 2011).

79. See Zachary, *Endless Frontier*, 401–8 for quote. For the original obituary, see "Dr. Vannevar Bush Is Dead at 84," *New York Times*, June 30, 1974, 1.

80. Smith, *American Science Policy*, 109; Harvey Brooks, "The Changing Structure of the U.S. Research System:

A Historical Perspective on the Current Situation and Future Issues and Prospects," in Harvey Brooks and Roland W. Schmitt, *Current Science and Technology Policy Issues, Two Perspectives: Papers Presented at a Science Policy Seminar Series Organized by the Graduate Program in Science, Technology, and Public Policy, School of International Affairs, George Washington University* (Washington, DC: George Washington University, 1985), 17–18.

Chapter 13. John F. Kennedy: The Crisis Manager

1. W. R. Smyser, *Kennedy and the Berlin Wall: "A Hell of a Lot Better Than a War"* (Lanham, MD: Rowman & Littlefield Publishers, 2009), 3–4. See also Frederick Kempe, *Berlin 1961: Kennedy, Khrushchev, and the Most Dangerous Place on Earth* (New York: G. P. Putnam's Sons, 2011), including day-by-day accounts.

2. Smyser, *Kennedy*, 4–5, 218–19, 221.

3. Smyser, *Kennedy*, 1–2.

4. Smyser, *Kennedy*, 4.

5. Smyser, *Kennedy*, 5, 221.

6. Smyser, *Kennedy*, 221–24. Smyser also explains the reason why JFK said *"ein Berliner"* instead of just *"Berliner."* Over the years, the myth has spread that Kennedy mistakenly used slang to refer to himself as a jelly doughnut. In fact, the two interpreters argued for *"ein Berliner"* because use of *"Berliner"* alone would mean Kennedy had been born in Berlin. They figured that no one would mistake the president for a doughnut. See Thomas Paterson, *Kennedy's Quest for Victory: American Foreign Policy, 1961–1963* (New York: Oxford University Press, 1989), 54.

7. Smyser, *Kennedy*, 5 (Mrs. Kennedy), 226 (Bundy).

8. Smyser, *Kennedy*, 228. See Thucydides, *Peloponnesian War*, Greek Texts & Translations, University of Chicago, http://perseus.uchicago.edu/perseus-cgi/citequery3.pl?dbname=GreekFeb2011&getid=1&query=Thuc.%202.41.1.

9. Smyser, *Kennedy*, 232.

10. Smyser, *Kennedy*, xiii, 81. See also Kenneth P. O'Donnell and David F. Powers with Joe McCarthy, *"Johnny, We Hardly Knew Ye": Memories of John Fitzgerald Kennedy* (New York: Pocket Books, 1973), 354.

11. Stephen Sestanovich, *Maximalist: America in the World from Truman to Obama* (New York: Vintage Books, 2014), 94 (including quotes). See also Ernest May and Philip Zelikow, *The Kennedy Tapes: Inside the White House During the Cuban Missile Crisis*, concise ed. (New York: W. W. Norton, 2002), xxxviii.

12. See Campbell Craig and Fredrik Logevall, *America's Cold War: The Politics of Insecurity* (Cambridge, MA: Belknap Press of Harvard University Press, 2012), 178; Maxwell Taylor, *The Uncertain Trumpet* (New York: Harper, 1960); Paul A. Samuelson, *Economics: An Introductory Analysis*, 5th ed. (New York: McGraw-Hill, 1961), 829–30.

13. Lawrence Freedman, *Kennedy's Wars: Berlin, Cuba, Laos, and Vietnam* (New York: Oxford University Press, 2000), 27–31; Sestanovich, *Maximalist*, 103; David Milne, *America's Rasputin: Walt Rostow and the Vietnam War* (New York: Hill and Wang, 2008), 74; Craig and Logevall, *America's Cold War*, 224. On modernization theory, see, most important, Michael Latham, *Modernization as Ideology: American Social Science and "Nation Building" in the Kennedy Era* (Chapel Hill, NC: University of North Carolina Press, 2006); idem., *The Right Kind of Revolution: Modernization, Development, and U.S. Foreign Policy from the Cold War to the Present* (Ithaca, NY: Cornell University Press, 2011); David Ekbladh, *The Great American Mission: Modernization and the Construction of an American World Order* (Princeton, NJ: Princeton University Press, 2010).

14. Milne, *America's Rasputin*, 70.

15. On "vigor," see Sestanovich, *Maximalist*, 95–96; on the "crisis" atmosphere, see Freedman, *Kennedy's Wars*, 9; McNamara quoted in Deborah Shapley, *Promise and Power: The Life and Times of Robert McNamara* (Boston: Little, Brown and Company, 1993), 103; Arthur Schlesinger Jr., "A Biographer's Perspective," in *The Kennedy Presidency: Seventeen Intimate Perspectives of John F. Kennedy*, ed. Kenneth W. Thompson (Lanham, MD: University Press of America, 1985), 22–23; Paul Nitze, *From Hiroshima to Glasnost: At the Center of Decision—A Memoir* (New York: Grove Weidenfeld, 1989), 251–52; Paterson, *Kennedy's Quest for Victory*, 7, 8.

16. John F. Kennedy, "Inaugural Address of John F. Kennedy," January 20, 1961, Avalon Project, Yale University, http://avalon.law.yale.edu/20th_century/kennedy.asp.

17. Kennedy, "Inaugural Address."

18. May and Zelikow, *Kennedy Tapes*, xl.

19. On the Bay of Pigs, see Freedman, *Kennedy's Wars*, 123–46; May and Zelikow, *Kennedy Tapes*, xl–xlii; Sestanovich, *Maximalist*, 87–88, 97; Paterson, *Kennedy's Quest for Victory*, 14–15. Kennedy aide quoted in Hugh Sidey, *John F. Kennedy, President* (New York: Atheneum, 1964), 127.

20. May and Zelikow, *Kennedy Tapes*, xliv.

21. May and Zelikow, *Kennedy Tapes*, xlv–xlvi; Freedman, *Kennedy's Wars*, 54–56; Smyser, *Kennedy*, 57–72, 202.

22. May and Zelikow, *Kennedy Tapes*, xlv–xlvi; Freedman, *Kennedy's Wars*, 51, 54–57; Smyser, *Kennedy*, 57–64.

23. Freedman, *Kennedy's Wars*, 56; Smyser, *Kennedy*, 65. For Kennedy's account of the meeting with Khrushchev, see O'Donnell and Powers, *"Johnny,"* 195.

24. Sestanovich, *Maximalist*, 98–99; May and Zelikow, *Kennedy Tapes*, xlvi; Freedman, *Kennedy's Wars*, 56–57.

25. Freedman, *Kennedy's Wars*, 57. For a discussion of the possibly unrecorded exchange, see Smyser, *Kennedy*, 71–72.

26. May and Zelikow, *Kennedy Tapes*, xlvi.

27. Freedman, *Kennedy's Wars*, 64; Honoré Marc Catudal, *Kennedy and the Berlin Wall Crisis: A Case Study in U.S. Decision Making* (Berlin: Berlin-Verlag, 1980), 150; Arthur M. Schlesinger Jr., *A Thousand Days: John F. Kennedy in the White House* (Boston: Houghton Mifflin, 1965), 352.

28. For Acheson's proposals and JFK's choices, see Freedman, *Kennedy's Wars*, 68–71.

29. For JFK's address and the poll, see Freedman, *Kennedy's Wars*, 71; May and Zelikow, *Kennedy Tapes*, xlvii. For details of JFK's proposal, see Sestanovich, *Maximalist*, 99–100. For the full text of JFK's address, see "Radio and Television Report to the American People on the Berlin Crisis," July 25, 1961, *John F. Kennedy: Containing the Public Messages, Speeches, and Statements of the President, January 20 to December 31, 1961* (Washington, DC: Government Printing Office, 1962), 533–540.

30. May and Zelikow, *Kennedy Tapes*, xlvii; Freedman, *Kennedy's Wars*, 71.

31. See Freedman, *Kennedy's Wars*, 72 (for refugee numbers) and 75 (recognizing Khrushchev's problem).

32. For a detailed account on the construction of the wall, see Kempe, *Berlin 1961*, 324–71; Freedman, *Kennedy's Wars*, 73–75.

33. Kempe, *Berlin 1961*, 341–42, 359–60, 371–80; Freedman, *Kennedy's Wars*, 76–77; Smyser, *Kennedy*, 104–6.

34. Smyser, *Kennedy*, 35–38.

35. See Freedman, *Kennedy's Wars*, 77 on Adenauer; Smyser, *Kennedy*, 43–52 on Macmillan, de Gaulle, and Adenauer.

36. Smyser, *Kennedy*, 115–16; Peter Wyden, *Wall* (New York: Simon & Schuster, 1989), 166. For Murrow's assessment, see "Telegram from the Mission at Berlin to the Department of State," August 16, 1961, *FRUS*, 1961–1963, vol. 14, Berlin Crisis, 1961–1962, Doc. 114.

37. Freedman, *Kennedy's Wars*, 77; Kempe, *Berlin 1961*, 376–80. For Brandt's letter to JFK, see "Telegram from the Mission at Berlin to the Department of State," August 16, 1961, *FRUS*, 1961–1963, vol. 14, Doc. 117. For the assessment of the U.S. mission at Berlin, see "Telegram from the Mission at Berlin to the Department of State," August 16, 1961, *FRUS*, 1961–1963, vol. 14, Doc. 115.

38. Smyser, *Kennedy*, 114–16.

39. Smyser, *Kennedy*, 114–16, 125–27.

40. Smyser, *Kennedy*, 128.

41. Smyser, *Kennedy*, 117–23, 129–31; Kempe, *Berlin 1961*, 378–80, 383–90.

42. Smyser, *Kennedy*, 131–32.

43. Freedman, *Kennedy's Wars*, 89–91.

44. Smyser, *Kennedy*, 135–41; Kempe, *Berlin 1961*, 448–81; Freedman, *Kennedy's Wars*, 90–91.

45. Smyser, *Kennedy*, 145, 163–64.

46. Smyser, *Kennedy*, 165–66.

47. Some of these points are from Sestanovich, *Maximalist*, 107, 110.

48. Smyser, *Kennedy*, 172–76; Freedman, *Kennedy's Wars*, 112–16.

49. Smyser, *Kennedy*, 177–182 ("smorgasbord" at 178, "Chamberlain" umbrellas at 181).

50. May and Zelikow, *Kennedy Tapes*, 417.

51. May and Zelikow, *Kennedy Tapes*, li; Smyser, *Kennedy*, 187–88.

52. Smyser, *Kennedy*, 189–90. For the original source of Udall's conversation with Khrushchev, see "Memorandum of Conversation Between Secretary of the Interior Udall and Chairman Khrushchev," *FRUS*, 1961–1963, vol. 15, Berlin Crisis, 1962–1963, Doc. 112. For Khrushchev and the West German ambassador, Hans Kroll, see Aleksandr Fursenko and Timothy Naftali, *Khrushchev's Cold War: The Inside Story of an*

American Adversary (New York: W. W. Norton & Company, 2006), 458. For "rotten tooth," see "Memorandum of Conversation," *FRUS, 1961–1963*, vol. 15, Berlin Crisis, 1962–1963, Doc. 135.

53. The literature on the Cuban Missile Crisis is enormous. See, most important, Michael Dobbs, *One Minute to Midnight: Kennedy, Khrushchev, and Castro on the Brink of Nuclear War* (New York: Knopf, 2008); Aleksandr Fursenko and Timothy Naftali, *"One Hell of a Gamble": Khrushchev, Castro, and Kennedy, 1958–1964* (New York: W. W. Norton & Company, 1997); Mark J. White, *Missiles in Cuba* (Chicago: Ivan R. Dee, 1997); Max Frankel, *High Noon in the Cold War: Kennedy, Khrushchev, and the Cuban Missile Crisis* (New York: Ballantine Books, 2005); Sheldon M. Stern, *The Week the World Stood Still: Inside the Secret Cuban Missile Crisis* (Stanford, CA: Stanford University Press, 2007); Don Munton and David A. Welch, *The Cuban Missile Crisis: A Concise History* (New York: Oxford University Press, 2007); James G. Hershberg, "The Cuban Missile Crisis," in *The Cambridge History of the Cold War*, vol. 2, eds. Melvyn P. Leffler and Odd Arne Westad (New York: Cambridge University Press, 2010). The Berlin-Cuba connection is forcefully made by May and Zelikow in *Kennedy Tapes*, based on JFK's tapes and recent studies of Soviet sources. Freedman also points to the strategic balance and Berlin in *Kennedy's Wars* at 172–73. A growing recognition of the Berlin-Cuba connection is also evident in the differences between the first and second editions of Graham Allison's classic account. See Graham Allison, *Essence of Decision: Explaining the Cuban Missile Crisis* (Boston: Little, Brown, 1971); Graham Allison and Philip Zelikow, *Essence of Decision: Explaining the Cuban Missile Crisis* (New York: Longman, 1999).

54. See Smyser, *Kennedy*, 192–95 for "Berlin in Khrushchev's Cuba Plans," and 184–85 for pipelines and military plans in Germany; May and Zelikow, *Kennedy Tapes*, 427.

55. For details on the missile gap, the NIE, and Deputy Secretary Roswell Gilpatric's presentation, see Freedman, *Kennedy's Wars*, 82–83. For details on intelligence, see May and Zelikow, *Kennedy Tapes*, xlviii–xlix.

56. Freedman, *Kennedy's Wars*, 172; May and Zelikow, *Kennedy Tapes*, 416. For the original NIE, see "SNIE 11-19-62: Major Consequences of Certain US Courses of Action on Cuba," October 20, 1962, in *CIA Documents on the Cuban Missile Crisis, 1962*, ed. Mary S. McAuliffe (Washington, DC: History Staff, Central Intelligence Agency, 1992), 215.

57. May and Zelikow, *Kennedy Tapes*, 426–27, 429; Anatoly Dobrynin, *In Confidence: Moscow's Ambassador to America's Six Cold War Presidents* (New York: Times Books, 1995), 65, 54.

58. Smyser, *Kennedy*, 197 (Kennedy's speech) and 197–200 (Berliners' reaction); Freedman, *Kennedy's Wars*, 173 (Joint Chiefs) and 189 (quote, emphasis in original).

59. See, among others, Dobbs, *One Minute to Midnight*; Fursenko and Naftali, *"One Hell of a Gamble"*; May and Zelikow, *Kennedy Tapes*; Allison and Zelikow, *Essence of Decision*.

60. May and Zelikow, *Kennedy Tapes*, 305; Sestanovich, *Maximalist*, 97; Smyser, *Kennedy*, 197–98.

61. As May and Zelikow conclude, "For reasons that then remained obscure to Americans, the end of the missile crisis also became the end of the Berlin crisis." May and Zelikow, *Kennedy Tapes*, 410. For the impact on Berlin, see also Smyser, *Kennedy*, 201. For Clay's interesting private assessment, see ibid., 203–4.

62. Craig and Logevall, *America's Cold War*, 212–13; Sestanovich, *Maximalist*, 111.

63. Smyser, *Kennedy*, xv.

64. Smyser, *Kennedy*, 227.

65. Sestanovich, *Maximalist*, 84. Eisenhower quoted in Robert A. Divine, *The Sputnik Challenge: Eisenhower's Response to the Soviet Satellite* (New York: Oxford University Press, 1993), 17.

66. Paterson, *Kennedy's Quest for Victory*, 5.

67. Craig and Logevall, *America's Cold War*, 211.

68. Michael Beschloss and Strobe Talbott, *At the Highest Levels: The Inside Story of the End of the Cold War* (Boston: Little, Brown, 1993), 470.

69. Sestanovich, *Maximalist*, 111. For the original *Saturday Morning Post* article, see Stewart Alsop and Charles Bartlett, "In Time of Crisis," *Saturday Evening Post*, December 18, 1962, 15–20.

70. Gordon Goldstein, *Lessons in Disaster: McGeorge Bundy and the Path to War in Vietnam* (New York: Times Books, 2008), 239. Historians have long wrestled with the question of whether Kennedy would have escalated the war in Vietnam or devised an exit strategy. We will never know. Goldstein discusses his assessment at 229–48. Fredrik Logevall, a historian of both Kennedy and Vietnam, has written a number of thoughtful appraisals. See, e.g., "Kennedy and What Might Have Been," in *The Vietnam War: An Intimate History*, ed. Geoffrey C. Ward (New York: Alfred A. Knopf, 2017), an update of Logevall's earlier essay, "Vietnam and the Question of What Might Have Been," in *Kennedy: The New Frontier Revisited*, ed. Mark J. White (London: Palgrave Macmillan, 1998).

Chapter 14. Lyndon Johnson: Learning from Defeat

1. Fredrik Logevall, *Choosing War: The Lost Chance for Peace and the Escalation of War in Vietnam* (Berkeley, CA: University of California Press, 1999), 109, 142; Goldstein, *Lessons in Disaster*, 111–112.

2. Michael Beschloss, *Taking Charge: The Johnson White House Tapes, 1963–1964* (New York: Simon & Schuster, 1997), 362. For the original source of "the situation is going to hell," see Charles Mohr, "Johnson Directs Taylor to Press Vietnam on War," *New York Times*, December 2, 1964. For the war cabinet, see "Draft Memorandum from the President's Special Assistant for National Security Affairs (Bundy) to the President," May 25, 1964, *FRUS*, 1964–1968, vol. 1, Vietnam, 1964, Doc. 173.

3. Goldstein, *Lessons in Disaster*, 113–114. For the original, see "Draft Memorandum," May 25, 1964.

4. For all quotes, see Beschloss, *Taking Charge*, 362–73; Goldstein, *Lessons in Disaster*, 115. On Bundy's role, see ibid., 5, 231–34. Eisenhower first articulated what would become known as the domino theory at a news conference on Indochina on April 7, 1954: "[Y]ou have broader considerations that might follow what you would call the 'falling domino' principle. You have a row of dominoes set up, you knock over the first one, and what will happen to the last one is the certainty that it will go over very quickly. So you could have a beginning of a disintegration that would have the most profound influences." See Editorial Note, *FRUS*, 1952–1954, Indochina, vol. 8, Part 1, Document 716.

5. For LBJ's possible motives, see Beschloss, *Taking Charge*, 369-370.

6. Logevall, *Choosing War*, 392.

7. Joseph A. Califano Jr., *The Triumph and Tragedy of Lyndon Johnson: The White House Years* (New York: Simon & Schuster, 1991), 10.

8. Logevall, *Choosing War*, 335.

9. See, among others, Leslie H. Gelb and Richard K. Betts, *The Irony of Vietnam: The System Worked* (Washington, DC: Brookings Institution Press, 1979); George C. Herring, *America's Longest War: The United States and Vietnam, 1950–1975*, 5th ed. (New York: McGraw-Hill, 2013); Stanley Karnow, *Vietnam: A History* (New York: Viking, 1983); Larry Berman, *Lyndon Johnson's War: The Road to Stalemate in Vietnam* (New York: W. W. Norton, 1989); idem., *Planning a Tragedy: The Americanization of the War in Vietnam* (New York: W. W. Norton, 1982); David E. Kaiser, *American Tragedy: Kennedy, Johnson, and the Origins of the Vietnam War* (Cambridge, MA: Belknap Press of Harvard University Press, 2000); Max Hastings, *Vietnam: An Epic Tragedy, 1945–1975* (New York: Harper, 2018).

10. Logevall, *Choosing War*, 404–5. See also John Prados, *The Hidden History of the Vietnam War* (Chicago: Ivan R. Dee, 1995). Larry Berman's *Planning a Tragedy* also offers a powerful analysis of the decisions discussed in this chapter.

11. See Gelb and Betts, *Irony of Vietnam*.

12. Logevall, *Choosing War*, xvi–xxi.

13. Quoted in Berman, *Planning a Tragedy*, 153.

14. Halberstam, *Best and Brightest*. On Halberstam, see Logevall, *Choosing War*, 288, 377. On the "quagmire thesis," see Craig and Logevall, *America's Cold War*, 236. On Bundy and Halberstam, see Goldstein, *Lessons in Disaster*, 149.

15. Beschloss, *Taking Charge*, 248–50 (McNamara), 262–63 (Bundy, "status quo"), 266–67 (to Bundy regarding JCS), 265–66 (Rostow, emphasis in original).

16. Beschloss, *Taking Charge*, 337–38 (to McNamara on military plans), 401 (Lodge and Clay), 410–11 ("turn tail").

17. See Robert J. Hanyok, "Skunks, Bogies, Silent Hounds, and the Flying Fish: The Gulf of Tonkin Mystery, 2–4 August 1964," *Cryptologic Quarterly* (2001), National Security Agency, https://www.nsa.gov/Portals/70 /documents/news-features/declassified-documents/gulf-of-tonkin/articles/release-1/rel1_skunks _bogies.pdf. For this and other documents on the incident released in 2005–06, see National Security Agency, "Gulf of Tonkin," https://www.nsa.gov/news-features/declassified-documents/gulf-of-tonkin/.

18. For background on the Gulf of Tonkin and the phone conversations, see Beschloss, *Taking Charge*, 493–504. On the resolution, incident, and vote, see Goldstein, *Lessons in Disaster*, 116, 126–28 (including LBJ quote at 126, emphasis in original). See also Logevall, *Choosing War*, 196–205. More broadly, see Edwin Moise, *Tonkin Gulf and the Escalation of the Vietnam War* (Chapel Hill, NC: University of North Carolina Press, 1996).

19. Goldstein, *Lessons in Disaster*, 129–30.

20. May and Zelikow, *Kennedy Tapes*, xvii–xviii.

21. For the "Death of the Domino Theory" memo, see "Memorandum from the Board of National Estimates to the Director of Central Intelligence (McCone)," June 9, 1964, *FRUS*, 1964–1968, vol. 1, Doc. 209. Bundy quoted in Goldstein, *Lessons in Disaster*, 139–40. For reliance on worst-case scenarios, see Craig and Logevall, *America's Cold War*, 278. However, some revisionists argue that the Vietnam War was necessary to buy time for other vulnerable Asian states "to fortify their political, economic, and military capabilities." This view was shared by the first prime minister of Singapore, Lee Kuan Yew. See Green, *By More Than Providence*, 317. See also Michael Lind, *Vietnam, the Necessary War: A Reinterpretation of America's Most Disastrous Military Conflict* (New York: Free Press, 1999).

22. Doris Kearns Goodwin, *Lyndon Johnson and the American Dream* (New York: Harper and Row, 1976), 252–53. On LBJ's worry about the loss of public support for internationalism, see Lyndon Baines Johnson, *The Vantage Point: Perspectives of the Presidency, 1963–1969* (New York: Holt, Rinehart and Winston, 1971), 151–52. See also Green, *By More Than Providence*, 509.

23. Logevall, *Choosing War*, 386. For the Bundy quote, see Goldstein, *Lessons in Disaster*, 137–38.

24. Michael Beschloss, *Presidents of War: The Epic Story, from 1807 to Modern Times* (New York: Crown, 2018), 537–38.

25. Green, *By More Than Providence*, 322. On Mahan, see chapter 5. MacArthur quoted in Goldstein, *Lessons in Disaster*, 235.

26. On the regional perspective, Japan, "flying geese," India, and Mike Mansfield, see Green, *By More Than Providence*, 318–19.

27. Jeffrey Goldberg, "World Chaos and World Order: Conversations with Henry Kissinger," *Atlantic*, November 10, 2016, https://www.theatlantic.com/international/archive/2016/11/kissinger-order-and-chaos/506876/. See also James Sebenius et al., *Kissinger the Negotiator: Lessons from Dealmaking at the Highest Level* (New York: Harper, 2018), 80–81.

28. Bundy quoted in Goldstein, *Lessons in Disaster*, 166–67 (emphasis in original). On Kennan, see Green, *By More Than Providence*, 313.

29. Logevall, *Choosing War*, 272.

30. Bundy quoted in Goldstein, *Lessons in Disaster*, 158, 167.

31. Logevall, *Choosing War*, 244–45. I used to tell colleagues at the State Department, the Office of the U.S. Trade Representative, and the World Bank that the real danger was not the initial mistake, but failing to acknowledge the mistake and to fix it.

32. Logevall, *Choosing War*, 388, 391–95; Green, *By More Than Providence*, 309; Berman, *Planning a Tragedy*, 146.

33. Logevall, *Choosing War*, 297–98.

34. Goldstein, *Lessons in Disaster*, 207, including Bundy quote on LBJ as "Senate-Leader-of-a-Commander-in-Chief."

35. Goldstein, *Lessons in Disaster*, 28, 208 for "stagecraft."

36. Reedy quoted in Logevall, *Choosing War*, 78–79. For the original source, see George E. Reedy, *Lyndon B. Johnson: A Memoir* (New York: Andrews and McMeel, 1982), 25.

37. Logevall, *Choosing War*, 75, 79. In contrast, Secretary Baker applied his political antennae and skills to grasp the motivations of leaders from different political systems. His memoir, titled *The Politics of Diplomacy: Revolution, War, and Peace, 1989–1992* (New York: G. P. Putnam's Sons, 1995), highlights the fusion of political insights and diplomacy (see the preface for his explanation of political skills internationally).

38. Goldstein, *Lessons in Disaster*, 208, 219 (emphasis in original).

39. Goldstein, *Lessons in Disaster*, 182.

40. Logevall, *Choosing War*, 255–56; Goldstein, *Lessons in Disaster*, 150–53; Berman, *Planning a Tragedy*, 36, 53. Berman's account focuses on the decisions to escalate with ground forces in the summer of 1965.

41. Goldstein, *Lessons in Disaster*, 169–70; Berman, *Planning a Tragedy*, 8.

42. Francis M. Bator, "No Good Choices: LBJ and the Vietnam/Great Society Connection," *Diplomatic History* 32, no. 3 (June 2008), 309. For the roundtable on Bator's article, see ibid., 341–70.

43. Berman, *Planning a Tragedy*, 146; see Goldstein, *Lessons in Disaster*, 192–98 on Bundy's key break with the president, which was over Bundy's desire to debate the case for the Vietnam War publicly. Johnson explained bluntly why he did not want a public discussion of the escalation: "You mean that if your mother-in-law...has only one eye, and it happens to be right in the middle of her forehead, then the best place for her is in the livin' room with all the company!"

44. Bundy quoted in Goldstein, *Lessons in Disaster*, 179, 182 (emphasis in original); Berman, *Planning a Tragedy*, 91.

45. See H. R. McMaster, *Dereliction of Duty: Lyndon Johnson, Robert McNamara, the Joint Chiefs of Staff, and the Lies That Led to Vietnam* (New York: HarperCollins, 1997).

46. Logevall, *Choosing War*, 118, 336; Berman, *Planning a Tragedy*, 22.

47. Sebenius, *Kissinger the Negotiator*, 105.

48. Logevall, *Choosing War*, 243–46.

49. Logevall, *Choosing War*, 206, 247–48.

50. There was a debate over priorities at the top level in Hanoi. See Pierre Asselin, *Hanoi's Road to the Vietnam War, 1954–1965* (Berkeley, CA: University of California Press, 2013). See also Lien-Hang T. Nguyen, *Hanoi's War: An International History of the War for Peace in Vietnam* (Chapel Hill, NC: University of North Carolina Press, 2012).

51. Logevall, *Choosing War*, 155–66 (Hanoi deliberations, Canadian emissary), 366 (quotes), and 373 (180,000 troops). For LBJ's question, see Goldstein, *Lessons in Disaster*, 177–78.

52. Wicker quoted in Logevall, *Choosing War*, 390.

53. Eisenhower began the practice of appointing a chief of staff. JFK and LBJ abandoned the practice. Nixon revived the role. Carter tried to operate without one for a while. Other presidents have appointed chiefs of staff, although their roles and responsibilities have varied greatly. See Chris Whipple, *The Gatekeepers: How the White House Chiefs of Staff Define Every Presidency* (New York: Crown, 2017).

54. Goldstein, *Lessons in Disaster*, 183.

55. Logevall, *Choosing War*, 37.

56. Goldstein, *Lessons in Disaster*, 19.

57. Logevall, *Choosing War*, 165. On Taylor, see Berman, *Planning a Tragedy*, 36.

58. Logevall, *Choosing War*, 127–28. See Robert S. McNamara, *In Retrospect: The Tragedy and Lessons of Vietnam* (New York: Random House, 1995).

59. Logevall, *Choosing War*, 165–66, 242; Goldstein, *Lessons in Disaster*, 141.

60. Logevall, *Choosing War*, 243–46; see Goldstein, *Lessons in Disaster*, 131–32 on Bundy forwarding Ball's memo; Berman, *Planning a Tragedy*, 46 for a good discussion of how and why LBJ used the "devil's advocate" label.

61. Logevall, *Choosing War*, 346, 351; Craig and Logevall, *America's Cold War*, 238. For the original Humphrey memo, see Memorandum from Vice President Humphrey to President Johnson, February 17, 1965, *FRUS, 1964–1968*, vol. 2, Vietnam, January–June 1965, Doc. 134.

62. Goldstein, *Lessons in Disaster*, 179.

Chapter 15. Richard Nixon and Henry Kissinger: American Realpolitik

1. Margaret MacMillan, *Nixon in China: The Week That Changed the World* (Toronto: Penguin Canada, 2007), 7-8.

2. MacMillan, *Nixon in China*, 20. For "like going to the moon," see "An Interview with the President: 'The Jury Is Out,'" *Time*, January 3, 1972. For the best recent account of the U.S.-China relationship, see Pomfret, *Beautiful Country*.

3. MacMillan, *Nixon in China*, 22. On the Chinese navigator, radio operator, interpreters, and other Chinese officials joining the flight, see "Nixon in China Itinerary, Feb. 17–28, 1972," USC U.S.-China Institute, https://china.usc.edu/nixon-china-itinerary-feb-17-28-1972.

4. MacMillan, *Nixon in China*, 33, 111.

5. MacMillan, *Nixon in China*, 23–25.

6. MacMillan, *Nixon in China*, 67.

7. MacMillan, *Nixon in China*, 23, 66, 70–71.

8. MacMillan, *Nixon in China*, 72; Robert Dallek, *Nixon and Kissinger: Partners in Power* (New York: HarperCollins, 2007), 363.

9. MacMillan, *Nixon in China*, 73–75; Dallek, *Nixon and Kissinger*, 363–64.

10. MacMillan, *Nixon in China*, 74–75; Dallek, *Nixon and Kissinger*, 364.

11. MacMillan, *Nixon in China*, 75.

12. MacMillan, *Nixon in China*, 76–77; Dallek, *Nixon and Kissinger*, 364; Kissinger, *Diplomacy*, 327.

13. Dallek, *Nixon and Kissinger*, 364; MacMillan, *Nixon in China*, 72–76. For "seize the hour," see Richard Nixon, *RN: The Memoirs of Richard Nixon* (New York: Grosset & Dunlap, 1978), 563. For "no beating around the bush," see Li Zhisui, *The Private Life of Chairman Mao*, trans. Tai Hung-Chao (New York:

Random House, 1994), 565. For Mao's thoughts on Nixon and Kissinger, see Edward Heath, *The Course of My Life: My Autobiography* (London: Hodder & Stoughton, 1998), 495.

14. MacMillan, *Nixon in China*, 6, citing Nixon, *RN*, 580.

15. See Pomfret, *Beautiful Country*, for a history of ties; MacMillan, *Nixon in China*, 96–108; Sebenius, *Kissinger the Negotiator*, 191; Kissinger, *Diplomacy*, 719.

16. MacMillan, *Nixon in China*, 9.

17. Sestanovich, *Maximalist*, 180, citing Nixon, *RN*, 580. For comparison of approaches, see Joseph S. Nye, "Between Complacency and Hysteria," *China-US Focus*, January 18, 2019, https://www.chinausfocus .com/foreign-policy/between-complacency-and-hysteria.

18. MacMillan, *Nixon in China*, 191, citing Chen Jian, *Mao's China and the Cold War* (Chapel Hill, NC: University of North Carolina Press, 2001), 267.

19. Pomfret, *Beautiful Country*, 444–46, 450–51; MacMillan, *Nixon in China*, 115; Kissinger, *Diplomacy*, 730.

20. Sebenius, *Kissinger the Negotiator*, xxv; Kissinger, *Diplomacy*, 728; Pomfret, *Beautiful Country*, 445.

21. MacMillan, *Nixon in China*, 229; Professor Wu Xinbo of Fudan University made this point to me.

22. MacMillan, *Nixon in China*, 229–31.

23. Kissinger, *Diplomacy*, 723.

24. MacMillan, *Nixon in China*, 150–52 (quote at 152), citing "Memorandum of Conversation," January 7, 1972, National Security Archive, Electronic Briefing Book No. 70, "Negotiating U.S.-Chinese Rapprochement," Doc. 25, 4, https://nsarchive2.gwu.edu/NSAEBB/NSAEBB70/doc4.pdf.

25. Dallek, *Nixon and Kissinger*, 329.

26. Kissinger, *Diplomacy*, 726, 730 for quotes.

27. Nixon toyed a bit with his national security adviser about who should be the American trailblazer before letting Kissinger know, "Oh hell fire, I know that…[n]obody else can really handle it." Dallek, *Nixon and Kissinger*, 288–90; MacMillan, *Nixon in China*, 178–80; Pomfret, *Beautiful Country*, 452–54.

28. Dallek, *Nixon and Kissinger*, 290.

29. MacMillan, *Nixon in China*, 185–86; Pomfret, *Beautiful Country*, 452–54; Dallek, *Nixon and Kissinger*, 292–93.

30. MacMillan, *Nixon in China*, 186.

31. See Dallek, *Nixon and Kissinger*, 150–51 for quote.

32. See Dallek, *Nixon and Kissinger*, 295 for quotes.

33. Henry Kissinger, *White House Years* (Boston: Little, Brown and Company, 1979), 746; see Sestanovich, *Maximalist*, 177–78 for quotes, citing *FRUS, 1969–1976*, vol. 17, China, 1969–1972, Doc. 139.

34. See Sestanovich, *Maximalist*, 178 for quotes, citing "Memorandum of Conversation," July 9, 1971, *FRUS, 1969–1976*, vol. 17, China, 1969–1972, Doc. 139.

35. Sebenius, *Kissinger the Negotiator*, 192.

36. MacMillan, *Nixon in China*, 184, 191–92; Dallek, *Nixon and Kissinger*, 295–97; Pomfret, *Beautiful Country*, 454–55.

37. Pomfret, *Beautiful Country*, 454–55 draws attention to how far Kissinger moved on Taiwan. See also MacMillan, *Nixon in China*, 192–93; Sestanovich, *Maximalist*, 178.

38. Dallek, *Nixon and Kissinger*, 295–97, citing Kissinger, *White House Years*, 745–46; Sebenius, *Kissinger the Negotiator*, 192, citing Henry Kissinger, *On China* (New York: Penguin Press, 2011), 247–48.

39. Sestanovich, *Maximalist*, 178.

40. The secret U.S. opening to China was bound to shock Tokyo. The Japanese had held off overtures to China out of deference to Washington's wishes. Within another month, Nixon would shock Tokyo again by abandoning the dollar's gold-exchange standard of the Bretton Woods monetary regime and imposing an added 10 percent tax on imports. On occasion, the United States has to manage big differences with its allies, and Japan's trade protectionism warranted U.S. unhappiness. But Nixon and Kissinger failed to account for Japan's value as a political and security partner; moreover, Tokyo's "commercial power" strategy, which the United States had encouraged, could not change overnight. See John Farrell, *Richard Nixon: The Life* (New York: Doubleday, 2017), 444–48 on Nixon's economic moves.

41. MacMillan, *Nixon in China*, 194–98; Dallek, *Nixon and Kissinger*, 298, 300.

42. Farrell, *Nixon*, 442.

43. Dallek, *Nixon and Kissinger*, 293; MacMillan, *Nixon in China*, 196; Kissinger, *Diplomacy*, 727.

44. See Dallek, *Nixon and Kissinger*, 303–4 on reactions, including Reagan's.

45. MacMillan, *Nixon in China*, 205–10.

46. MacMillan, *Nixon in China*, 208–9; Sebenius, *Kissinger the Negotiator*, 174–75. For "the very novelty of the approach," see Kissinger, *White House Years*, 782. For "sharpest possible formulations," see "Memorandum of Conversation," October 24, 1971, *FRUS*, 1969–1976, vol. E-13, Documents on China, 1969–1972, Doc. 52.

47. See Kissinger, *Diplomacy*, 727–28 for quotes; MacMillan, *Nixon in China*, 209, 296 on Taiwan.

48. Kissinger, *Diplomacy*, 728. The full communique, also known as the "Shanghai Communique," is reprinted in MacMillan, *Nixon in China*, 330–34. The text is also available in "Joint Statement Following Discussions with Leaders of the People's Republic of China," February 27, 1972, *FRUS*, 1969–1976, vol. 17, China, 1969–1972, Doc. 203.

49. MacMillan, *Nixon in China*, 210, 253; Dallek, *Nixon and Kissinger*, 333.

50. MacMillan, *Nixon in China*, 293.

51. MacMillan, *Nixon in China*, 295. For "important changes and great upheavals," see Shanghai Communique. In 2018, China was America's largest trading partner with a two-way exchange of $737 billion of goods and services; after the United States imposed much higher barriers, and China's retaliation, Canada and Mexico have resumed the top positions. U.S. visitors to China amount to about two million per year, and America hosts about three million Chinese annually. About 363,000 Chinese study in the United States, including children of Party leaders and business executives. See Office of the United States Trade Representative, "The People's Republic of China: U.S.-China Trade Facts," https://ustr.gov/countries-regions/china-mongolia-taiwan/peoples-republic-china; U.S. Department of Commerce, "Fast Facts: United States Travel and Tourism Industry, 2018," https://travel.trade.gov/outreachpages/download_data_table/Fast_Facts_2018.pdf. According to one estimate, "Since 2013 [Chinese] inbound tourist rates from the US have remained steady at roughly 2.1 million visits per year." See "Is China Attracting Foreign Visitors?" China-Power, Center for Strategic and International Studies, February 2, 2016, updated May 14, 2019, https://chinapower.csis.org/tourism/. According to the Institute of International Education, in the 2017–18 academic year, the number of Chinese students in the United States was just over 363,300. See Institute of International Education, "International Student Totals by Place of Origin, 2012/13–2017/18," *Open Doors Report on International Educational Exchange*, https://www.iie.org/Research-and-Insights/Open-Doors/Data/International-Students/Places-of-Origin.

52. MacMillan, *Nixon in China*, 252–53 and Shanghai Communique. For "the trouble is that we disagree," see "Memorandum of Conversation," October 26, 1971, *FRUS*, 1969–1976, vol. E-13, Documents on China, 1969–1972, Doc. 55. For Taiwan, see Shanghai Communique.

53. MacMillan, *Nixon in China*, 300–303.

54. MacMillan, *Nixon in China*, 305–6, 312 (including Gallup), citing Rosemary Foot, *The Practice of Power: American Relations with China Since 1949* (Oxford: Clarendon Press, 1995), 107.

55. Kissinger, *Diplomacy*, 728–29 (for quotes, emphasis in original).

56. See Farrell, *Nixon*, 350 (fifth of nine Cold War presidents); Sebenius, *Kissinger the Negotiator*, xxv and Farrell, *Nixon*, 347 (on nuclear); Dallek, *Nixon and Kissinger*, 285 and MacMillan, *Nixon in China*, 14 for quotes.

57. Farrell, *Nixon*, 359, 361–63 for Haldeman, Eisenhower analogy, and casualties.

58. Kissinger, *Diplomacy*, 697 including quotes; last quote from Dallek, *Nixon and Kissinger*, 210.

59. Dallek, *Nixon and Kissinger*, 84; MacMillan, *Nixon in China*, 121.

60. Dallek, *Nixon and Kissinger*, 270.

61. Sestanovich, *Maximalist*, 168–69 (military data); see Green, *By More Than Providence*, 337 for Osgood quote (emphasis in original).

62. Dallek, *Nixon and Kissinger*, 99; MacMillan, *Nixon in China*, 12–13 (quotes). After long travel through Asia, Nixon published an article in the October 1967 issue of *Foreign Affairs* titled "Asia After Viet Nam." In the years that followed, most who recalled the article cited the future president's signal on China: "Taking the long view, we simply cannot afford to leave China forever outside the family of nations, there to nurture its fantasies, cherish its hates and threaten its neighbors." Yet Michael Green reminds us that the piece places China within the evolving nationalism and multipolarity in the wider region. Nixon said the United States needed a longer-term strategy—considering Japan and India, as well as Southeast Asia and China. This strategy should mesh multipolarity, U.S. interests, and American alliances. Mao read the article and shared it with Chou. See Richard Nixon, "Asia after Viet Nam," *Foreign Affairs* 46, no. 1 (October 1967); Kissinger, *Diplomacy*, 721; Green, *By More Than Providence*, 326–27; Farrell, *Nixon*, 437 on Mao reading.

63. See MacMillan, *Nixon in China*, 14 for the first two quotes; Sestanovich, *Maximalist*, 169, 192 for the next two.

64. See MacMillan, *Nixon in China*, 10, 12; Sestanovich, *Maximalist*, 169, 173; Green, *By More Than Providence*, 346 for all quotes.

65. Green, *By More Than Providence*, 327, 347; Farrell, *Nixon*, 437–38 (including White); MacMillan, *Nixon in China*, 51–52, 58; Niall Ferguson, *Kissinger*, vol. 1, *1923–1968: The Idealist* (New York: Penguin Press, 2015), especially 637–56 for HAK's trips to Vietnam. Kissinger would also point out that the Soviet-Chinese military clashes in 1969 created a shift in thinking in Beijing and the opportunity to pursue Nixon's bold approach.

66. Sebenius, *Kissinger the Negotiator*, 71 (strategic negotiator); Sestanovich, *Maximalist*, 170 ("marbles").

67. See Dallek, *Nixon and Kissinger*, 94, 285; Craig and Logevall, *America's Cold War*, 253. For the text of the first inaugural, see Richard Nixon, "First Inaugural Address of Richard Milhous Nixon," Avalon Project, Yale University, https://avalon.law.yale.edu/20th_century/nixon1.asp.

68. See Kissinger, *Diplomacy*, 705 for quotes.

69. See MacMillan, *Nixon in China*, 49 (for RN-HK differences); Kissinger, *Diplomacy*, 705–7 for quotes (emphasis in original).

70. See Kissinger, *A World Restored*; Ferguson, *Kissinger*; MacMillan, *Nixon in China*, 49–51.

71. MacMillan, *Nixon in China*, 122 (integration, "seamless web"); see Kissinger, *Diplomacy*, 719, where he analogizes diplomacy to chess: "[T]he more squares a player dominates, the greater his options and the more constrained become those of his opponent. Similarly, in diplomacy, the more options one side has, the fewer will be available to the other side and the more careful it will have to be in pursuing its objectives."

72. See MacMillan, *Nixon in China*, 49 on 1968 essay. The full essay, titled "Central Issues of American Foreign Policy," is reprinted in "Essay by Henry A. Kissinger," *FRUS*, 1969–1976, vol. 1, Foundations of Foreign Policy, 1969–1972, Doc. 4. Sestanovich, *Maximalist*, 170, citing Henry Kissinger, *The Necessity for Choice* (New York: Harper & Bros., 1961), 6. Green, *By More Than Providence*, 324. For the original source, see "White House Background Press Briefing by the President's Assistant for National Security Affairs (Kissinger)," December 18, 1969, *FRUS*, 1969–1976, vol. 1, Foundations of Foreign Policy, 1969–1972, Doc. 47.

73. Sestanovich, *Maximalist*, 170, citing "Essay by Henry A. Kissinger," *FRUS*, Doc. 4; Kissinger, *White House Years*, 66.

74. See MacMillan, *Nixon in China*, 49 for "folklore" and sentimental; Dallek, *Nixon and Kissinger*, 71; Kissinger, *Diplomacy*, 676, 709–10; Sebenius, *Kissinger the Negotiator*, 82–84 (on theology and psychiatric).

75. MacMillan, *Nixon in China*, 49–50; Dallek, *Nixon and Kissinger*, 71; Kissinger, *Diplomacy*, 683.

76. MacMillan, *Nixon in China*, 49; Kissinger, *Diplomacy*, 742, 744.

77. See Dallek, *Nixon and Kissinger*, 46, 370 for quotes at beginning and end; Kissinger, *Diplomacy*, 705 for his quote.

78. See Sebenius, *Kissinger the Negotiator*, 165 on Triangular Diplomacy; Kissinger, *Diplomacy*, 729 (emphasis in original).

79. Sebenius, *Kissinger the Negotiator*, 167, citing Henry Kissinger, "The White Revolutionary: Reflections on Bismarck," *Daedalus* 97, no. 3 (Summer 1968), 912–13.

80. Sebenius, *Kissinger the Negotiator*, 167, 178, 179, citing Kissinger, *White House Years*, 764–75; Kissinger, "Transcript of the American Secretaries of State Project: Henry A. Kissinger," interview with R. Nicholas Burns, Robert Mnookin, and James K. Sebenius, November 6, 2014; Kissinger, *Diplomacy*, 741.

81. Sebenius, *Kissinger the Negotiator*, xiv, xv.

82. Kissinger, *Diplomacy*, 711.

83. Kissinger, *Diplomacy*, 711.

84. All quotes from the report, titled "U.S. Foreign Policy for the 1970s: A New Strategy for Peace," reprinted as "Report by President Nixon to the Congress," February 18, 1970, *FRUS*, 1969–1976, vol. 1, Foundations of Foreign Policy, 1969–1972, Doc. 60.

85. MacMillan, *Nixon in China*, 15.

86. Dallek, *Nixon and Kissinger*, 81, 111; Walter Isaacson, *Kissinger: A Biography* (New York: Simon & Schuster, 1992), 209; Green, *By More Than Providence*, 325 ("intrigue and manipulation").

87. Kissinger, *Diplomacy*, 705, 712.

88. MacMillan, *Nixon in China*, 304–5.

89. MacMillan, *Nixon in China*, 261.

90. MacMillan, *Nixon in China*, 264; Sebenius, *Kissinger the Negotiator*, 134–35. MacMillan and Sebenius differ on Chinese support to North Vietnam at 264 and 135, respectively. See Green, *By More Than Providence*, 330 (on contradictions on Vietnam, emphasis in original).

91. MacMillan, *Nixon in China*, 313; Dallek, *Nixon and Kissinger*, 375; Sebenius, *Kissinger the Negotiator*, 137, 141 (including Arbatov).

92. Dallek, *Nixon and Kissinger*, 287; Sebenius, *Kissinger the Negotiator*, 136–41.

93. Sestanovich, *Maximalist*, 171, 182–83.

94. Sestanovich, *Maximalist*, 169–70; Green, *By More Than Providence*, 342 (Connally quote).

95. See Dallek, *Nixon and Kissinger*, 467 on China-Britain; Green, *By More Than Providence*, 372 on Taiwan Relations Act.

96. Sestanovich, *Maximalist*, 175.

97. Sestanovich, *Maximalist*, 199. This particular speech, titled "The Moral Foundations of Foreign Policy," was delivered by Kissinger in Bloomington, Minnesota. The speech is reprinted as "Address by Secretary of State Kissinger," July 15, 1975, *FRUS*, 1969–1976, vol. 39, Part 1, Foundations of Foreign Policy, 1973–1976, Doc. 59.

98. Dallek, *Nixon and Kissinger*, 305, 618.

99. Dallek, *Nixon and Kissinger*, 536; Craig and Logevall, *America's Cold War*, 280.

100. Sestanovich, *Maximalist*, 203 (Reagan quote); Dallek, *Nixon and Kissinger*, 617 (unreliable partner).

101. Kissinger, *Diplomacy*, 742–47; Sestanovich, *Maximalist*, 207.

Chapter 16. Ronald Reagan: The Revivalist

1. Robert C. Rowland and John M. Jones, *Reagan at Westminster: Foreshadowing the End of the Cold War* (College Station, TX: Texas A&M University Press, 2010), 63; Charles Moore, *Margaret Thatcher: The Authorized Biography*, vol. 1, *From Grantham to the Falklands* (New York: Alfred A. Knopf, 2013), 580. For the full address, see Ronald Reagan, "Address to Members of the British Parliament," June 8, 1982, Ronald Reagan Presidential Library & Museum (hereafter Reagan Library), https://www.reaganlibrary.gov /research/speeches/60882a.

2. See "The Royal Gallery," United Kingdom Parliament, https://www.parliament.uk/about/living-heritage /building/palace/architecture/palace-s-interiors/royal-gallery/.

3. Steven Hayward, *The Age of Reagan*, vol. 2, *The Conservative Counterrevolution, 1980–1989* (New York: Crown Forum, 2009), 254.

4. H. W. Brands, *Reagan: The Life* (New York: Anchor Books, 2015), 444; Rowland and Jones, *Reagan at Westminster*, 54.

5. Reagan, "Address to Members of the British Parliament."

6. James Graham Wilson, *The Triumph of Improvisation: Gorbachev's Adaptability, Reagan's Engagement, and the End of the Cold War* (Ithaca, NY: Cornell University Press, 2014), 38–41; Kiron Skinner et al., *Reagan: A Life in Letters* (New York: Free Press, 2003), 293; Moore, *Thatcher*, 576–78.

7. Rowland and Jones, *Reagan at Westminster*, 56–58.

8. On "triple audience," see Richard J. Cattani, "Reagan's European Agenda: Money, Guns, and Image," *Christian Science Monitor*, June 3, 1982, 1; Rowland and Jones, *Reagan at Westminster*, 56–60.

9. Rowland and Jones, *Reagan at Westminster*, 59.

10. Rowland and Jones, *Reagan at Westminster*, 63–64; Hayward, *Age of Reagan*, 256; see Moore, *Thatcher*, 581 on teleprompter; conversation with Lord Charles Powell, Thatcher's foreign policy adviser in March 2019, on RR's gift to MT.

11. In 1983, Congress created a new National Endowment for Democracy to pursue Reagan's vision, and the U.S. Agency for International Development added democracy-building to its mission. See Rowland and Jones, *Reagan at Westminster*, 16–17, 104–5.

12. All quotes from Reagan, "Address to Members of the British Parliament."

13. "We win...," quoted by Richard Allen, "Richard Allen Oral History," Presidential Oral Histories, Miller Center of Public Affairs, University of Virginia, May 28, 2002, https://millercenter.org/the -presidency/presidential-oral-histories/richard-allen-oral-history-assistant-president-national. On RR's first presidential press conference, see Editorial Note, *FRUS*, 1981–1988, vol. 3, Soviet Union, January 1981–January 1983, Document 7. For NSDD 32, see "U.S. National Security Strategy," May 20, 1982, Reagan Library, https://www.reaganlibrary.gov/sites/default/files/archives/reference/scanned-nsdds/nsdd32 .pdf. For the full address at Eureka College, see "Address at Commencement Exercises at Eureka College,

Eureka, Illinois," May 9, 1982, Ronald Reagan Presidential Foundation & Institute, https://www.reagan foundation.org/media/128700/eureka.pdf. See Brands, *Reagan*, 254, 278–79; Hal Brands, *Making the Unipolar Moment: U.S. Foreign Policy and the Rise of the Post–Cold War Order* (Ithaca, NY: Cornell University Press, 2016), 72; Sestanovich, *Maximalist*, 222, 224; Wilson, *Triumph of Improvisation*, 9.

14. Rowland and Jones, *Reagan at Westminster*, 49.

15. Rowland and Jones, *Reagan at Westminster*, 45–53; Lou Cannon, *President Reagan: The Role of a Lifetime* (New York: Simon & Schuster, 1991), 317; Lou Cannon and Carl M. Cannon, *Reagan's Disciple: George W. Bush's Troubled Quest for a Presidential Legacy* (New York: PublicAffairs, 2008), 324.

16. Hayward, *Age of Reagan*, 288.

17. Rowland and Jones, *Reagan at Westminster*, 86; John Lewis Gaddis, *The Cold War: A New History* (New York: Penguin Press, 2005), 198; see Sestanovich, *Maximalist*, 241 for change in terms.

18. Sestanovich, *Maximalist*, 228, 240; Rowland and Jones, *Reagan at Westminster*, 34; Kiron Skinner, Serhiy Kudelia, Bruce Bueno de Mesquita, and Condoleezza Rice, "The Strategy of Campaigning," *Hoover Digest*, no. 1 (2008), 101.

19. Rowland and Jones, *Reagan at Westminster*, 35, 75, 87; Cannon and Cannon, *Reagan's Disciple*, 31; Gaddis, *Cold War*, 198.

20. On initial media reaction, see Rowland and Jones, *Reagan at Westminster*, 89–102. "Hard line" quoted in Richard Reeves, *President Reagan: The Triumph of Imagination* (New York: Simon & Schuster, 2005), 110. For "oversimplified," see Steven Rattner, "Britons Reassured by Reagan's Visit," *New York Times*, June 12, 1982, A17. For "irrelevant," see Lou Cannon, "Soviets Assail Reagan's European Trip; President Gained His Major Goal," *Washington Post*, June 13, 1982, A1. For "mediocre," see Leslie Plommer, "Reagan Appeals to Brezhnev for Exchange of Views on TV," *Globe and Mail*, June 9, 1982, n.p. For "unmemorable," see Nancy Banks-Smith, "Speech Day," *Guardian*, June 9, 1982, 9.

21. For the *New York Times* headline, see Hayward, *Age of Reagan*, 256. For "more stagecraft than statecraft," see Tom Morganthau, Thomas M. DeFrank, and John Walcott, "The Upstaged Summit," *Newsweek*, June 21, 1982, 34. For "reckless," "hostile," "crude," see Richard Cohen, "Leadership," *Washington Post*, June 13, 1982, B1; "Getting to Know Reagan," *Christian Science Monitor*, June 9, 1982, 24; John F. Burns, "Soviet Says Crusade by Reagan May Risk Global Catastrophe," *New York Times*, June 10, 1982, A17. TV commentators quoted in Reeves, *President Reagan*, 109. On Cannon, see Rowland and Jones, *Reagan at Westminster*, 100; Lou Cannon, "President Calls for 'Crusade'; Reagan Proposes Plan to Counter Soviet Challenge," *Washington Post*, June 9, 1982, A1.

22. Rowland and Jones, *Reagan at Westminster*, 89; see Moore, *Thatcher*, 581 on Thatcher's hand note on Eisenhower.

23. Rowland and Jones, *Reagan at Westminster*, 97–99, including Soviet press, Reagan, and Diggins; Kiron Skinner, ed., *Turning Points in Ending the Cold War* (Stanford, CA: Hoover Institution Press, 2008), 97; John Lewis Gaddis, *Strategies of Containment: A Critical Appraisal of American National Security Policy During the Cold War*, rev. and exp. ed. (New York: Oxford University Press, 2005), 356.

24. Rowland and Jones, *Reagan at Westminster*, 15, 101, 103–4; Ronald Reagan, *Speaking My Mind: Selected Speeches* (New York: Simon & Schuster, 1989), 107, 108.

25. Brands, *Reagan*, 1, 741; Rowland and Jones, *Reagan at Westminster*, 30–31. Near the end of Reagan's presidency, Michael Mandelbaum and Strobe Talbott, two critics, tried to explain Reagan's method to the members of the Council on Foreign Relations. They pointed out that the president worked at fine-tuning speech announcements—as if they were policies on their own. Michael Mandelbaum and Strobe Talbott, *Reagan and Gorbachev* (New York: Vintage Books, 1987), 129.

26. Rowland and Jones, *Reagan at Westminster*, 26–29.

27. He also had newspaper columns but often relied on Peter Hannaford, a former aide, to pen those articles. Brands, *Making the Unipolar Moment*, 71; Brands, *Reagan*, 186–87; Kiron Skinner et al., eds., *Reagan, in His Own Hand: The Writings of Ronald Reagan That Reveal His Revolutionary Vision for America* (New York: Touchstone, 2002), xiv–xxi.

28. See George Shultz, foreword in Skinner, *Reagan, in His Own Hand*, x for MacFarlane; Brands, *Reagan*, 734.

29. Cannon, *President Reagan*, 26; Brands, *Reagan*, 734 (flattered); Rowland and Jones, *Reagan at Westminster*, 30 (themes).

30. Skinner, *Reagan, in His Own Hand*, especially 4–14.

31. Rowland and Jones, *Reagan at Westminster*, 38; see Skinner, *Reagan, in His Own Hand*, ix for Shultz.

32. Brands, *Reagan*, 734; see Skinner, *Reagan, in His Own Hand*, ix for Shultz.

33. Hayward, *Age of Reagan*, 3–4; Brands, *Reagan*, 157.

34. Hayward, *Age of Reagan*, 3; Brands, *Reagan*, 12, 725.

35. Brands, *Reagan*, 734; Cannon, *President Reagan*, 12.

36. See Wilson, *Triumph of Improvisation*, 9 for Spencer story; Brands, *Making the Unipolar Moment*, 25, 36 on détente and Carter; Skinner, *Life in Letters*, 396 for RR.

37. See Skinner, *Life in Letters*, 396 for four points; Wilson, *Triumph of Improvisation*, 5.

38. Brands, *Making the Unipolar Moment*, 22–29, 53; "Can Capitalism Survive?" *Time*, July 14, 1975, 52–63.

39. See Brands, *Reagan*, 734 for quote on FDR; Ronald Reagan, *An American Life* (New York: Simon & Schuster, 1990), 205 on the economy; idem., "Address to a Joint Session of Parliament in Ottawa, Canada," April 6, 1987, in *Public Papers of the Presidents of the United States: Ronald Reagan, January 1 to July 3, 1987* (Washington, DC: U.S. Government Printing Office, 1989), 339 on free markets; Skinner, *Life in Letters*, 391 on four wars. See also Brands, *Making the Unipolar Moment*, 175–76; Wilson, *Triumph of Improvisation*, 14, 26.

40. Skinner, *Life in Letters*, 372; see idem., *Reagan, in His Own Hand*, 9, 25 on reliable energy and credibility; Wilson, *Triumph of Improvisation*, 10 for Baker.

41. Note there are various measures of RR's military buildup. Gaddis, *Cold War*, 225; Sestanovich, *Maximalist*, 224, 240; Wilson, *Triumph of Improvisation*, 18; Brands, *Making the Unipolar Moment*, 73, citing Reagan to Edward Langley, January 15, 1980, Box 3, Ronald Reagan Subject Collection, Hoover Institution.

42. See Skinner, *Reagan, in His Own Hand*, 24 for arms as symptom; Brands, *Making the Unipolar Moment*, 78 for "break their backs," citing NSC Meeting, November 30, 1983, Box 91303, Executive Secretariat File, Reagan Library; Skinner, *Life in Letters*, 398; Brands, *Reagan*, 413 on SALT and buildup to negotiate down.

43. See Craig and Logevall, *America's Cold War*, 330 for SIOP story; Sestanovich, *Maximalist*, 224, 226, 234.

44. See Brands, *Making the Unipolar Moment*, 39–53 on human rights; Sestanovich, *Maximalist*, 231–33 on evolution; Wilson, *Triumph of Improvisation*, 21, 63–64. Will Inboden, who is writing a biography of Reagan, highlighted for me that Reagan sought to weaken the USSR by challenging the very legitimacy of its Communist system.

45. Brands, *Making the Unipolar Moment*, 41; Sestanovich, *Maximalist*, 231–33. For RR's full address, see "Text of the Reagan Message to Congress on Foreign Policy," *New York Times*, March 15, 1986, 4.

46. After a visit to NORAD's headquarters for strategic warfare at Cheyenne Mountain in 1979, Reagan's friend and adviser Martin Anderson persuaded him that the absence of defensive systems could be traced to a shortfall in new strategic thinking, not because of the lack of technology. In 1982, Edward Teller, the designer of America's hydrogen bomb, urged the exploration of missile defense, in part as a counter to the drive for a nuclear freeze. The president had brainstormed the idea with the Joint Chiefs of Staff early in 1983 and then announced his SDI in a speech of March 23, 1983. See Wilson, *Triumph of Improvisation*, 71–73; Hayward, *Age of Reagan*, 291–98.

47. Wilson, *Triumph of Improvisation*, 4, 70–71, 72–73 (insurance and uncertainty about nature of shield); Brands, *Making the Unipolar Moment*, 78 (cost for Soviets); Brands, *Reagan*, 608–9 for Shultz and "bargaining chip."

48. Brands, *Reagan*, 270.

49. Wilson, *Triumph of Improvisation*, 5; Sestanovich, *Maximalist*, 242.

50. George Shultz, *Turmoil and Triumph: My Years as Secretary of State* (New York: Scribner's, 1993).

51. See Wilson, *Triumph of Improvisation*, 2, 5, 6; Brands, *Making the Unipolar Moment*, 71; Shultz, *Turmoil and Triumph*, 263.

52. Wilson, *Triumph of Improvisation*, 5–6.

53. Shultz, foreword in Skinner, *Turning Points*, xx.

54. Wilson, *Triumph of Improvisation*, 6, 63; Sestanovich, *Maximalist*, 238 ("psychological warfare").

55. Wilson, *Triumph of Improvisation*, 64, 65, 75; Hayward, *Age of Reagan*, 448.

56. See Skinner, *Life in Letters*, 509 for RR on North America.

57. See Ronald Reagan, "Remarks at the Annual Convention of the National Association of Evangelicals in Orlando, Florida," March 8, 1983, Reagan Library, https://www.reaganlibrary.gov/research/speeches/30883b. For "malice aforethought," see Sestanovich, *Maximalist*, 222. However, Wilson notes that the phrase had not caught RR's eye. See Wilson, *Triumph of Improvisation*, 71. On speech staffing, see Hayward, *Age of Reagan*, 288–91. See also Shultz, *Turmoil and Triumph*, 267.

58. See Ronald Reagan, "Address to the Nation on Defense and National Security," March 23, 1983, Reagan Library, https://www.reaganlibrary.gov/research/speeches/32383d. On the origin of SDI idea and speech, see Wilson, *Triumph of Improvisation*, 71–73; Hayward, *Age of Reagan*, 291–98. Shultz learned of the president's initiative only a short time in advance and objected to the "destabilizing" assault on strategic

doctrines and alliance confidence in U.S. nuclear deterrence. See Hayward, *Age of Reagan*, 295 for Shultz reaction.

59. Ronald Reagan, *The Reagan Diaries*, vol. 1, ed. Douglas Brinkley (New York: HarperCollins, 2009), 212 (emphasis in original); Wilson, *Triumph of Improvisation*, 74.

60. Wilson, *Triumph of Improvisation*, 76–78; Brands, *Making the Unipolar Moment*, 69, 88–96; Hayward, *Age of Reagan*, 343 (on *1984*).

61. See Ronald Reagan, "Address to the Nation and Other Countries on United States–Soviet Relations," January 16, 1984, Reagan Library, https://www.reaganlibrary.gov/research/speeches/11684a; Skinner, *Turning Points*, 34–37; Hayward, *Age of Reagan*, 346–47.

62. Reagan, "Address to the Nation and Other Countries on United States–Soviet Relations"; Hayward, *Age of Reagan*, 346–47.

63. See Ronald Reagan, "Remarks on East-West Relations at the Brandenburg Gate in West Berlin," June 12, 1987, Reagan Library, https://www.reaganlibrary.gov/research/speeches/061287d; Sestanovich, *Maximalist*, 227 on RR quote; Wilson, *Triumph of Improvisation*, 85 on RR wanting to meet; Hayward, *Age of Reagan*, 1–2 on staff debate and RR decision and 593–94 on reusing phrase; Rowland and Jones, *Reagan at Westminster*, 116 on strategy. Nevertheless, in a meeting with Soviet foreign minister Eduard Shevardnadze on September 23, 1988, the president raised his speech in Berlin, recognizing "[i]t had perhaps been unrealistic to have suggested that the Berlin Wall be torn down in its entirety." He acknowledged the strength of Soviet feeling about the division of Germany. Reagan then reiterated his earlier proposals to allow the two parts of Berlin and Germany to work together. See "Memorandum of Conversation," September 23, 1988, *FRUS*, 1981–1988, vol. 6, Soviet Union, October 1986–1989, Doc. 177.

64. See Ronald Reagan, "Remarks and a Question-and-Answer Session with the Students and Faculty at Moscow State University," May 31, 1988, Reagan Library, https://www.reaganlibrary.gov/research/speeches/053188b; Sestanovich, *Maximalist*, 239–40 (including quote); Hayward, *Age of Reagan*, 606 (including bust of Lenin); Rowland and Jones, *Reagan at Westminster*, 116.

65. Sestanovich, *Maximalist*, 222; see Hayward, *Age of Reagan*, 606 on RR's quote.

66. For example, see Mandelbaum and Talbott, *Reagan and Gorbachev*, 129.

67. Sestanovich, *Maximalist*, 222–23; Reagan, *American Life*, 595; James Mann, *The Rebellion of Ronald Reagan: A History of the End of the Cold War* (New York: Viking, 2009), 260.

68. See Wilson, *Triumph of Improvisation*, 69–70 on the meeting; Hayward, *Age of Reagan*, 285–86 for more info on the Pentecostals.

69. Wilson, *Triumph of Improvisation*, 85–87.

70. Wilson, *Triumph of Improvisation*, 89, 92–93.

71. Wilson, *Triumph of Improvisation*, 81, 97–98.

72. Hayward, *Age of Reagan*, 449; Brands, *Reagan*, 505; Sestanovich, *Maximalist*, 241.

73. Wilson, *Triumph of Improvisation*, 108–9; Brands, *Reagan*, 510–18.

74. Wilson, *Triumph of Improvisation*, 104; Brands, *Reagan*, 518; Reagan, *American Life*, 641.

75. Sestanovich, *Maximalist*, 234.

76. Brands, *Reagan*, 522–23; Brands, *Making the Unipolar Moment*, 105, citing NSC Meeting, September 20, 1985, Box 91303, Executive Secretariat File, Reagan Library (emphasis in original).

77. Wilson, *Triumph of Improvisation*, 106–7.

78. Wilson, *Triumph of Improvisation*, 110–11, including Mitterrand quote. Mitterrand quoted in Anatoly Chernyaev, *My Six Years with Gorbachev*, trans. Robert English and Elizabeth Tucker (University Park, PA: Pennsylvania State University Press, 2000 [1993]), 76.

79. See, e.g., Kenneth L. Adelman, *Reagan at Reykjavik: Forty-Eight Hours That Ended the Cold War* (New York: Broadside Books, 2014); Sidney D. Drell and George P. Shultz, eds., *Implications of the Reykjavik Summit on Its Twentieth Anniversary: Conference Report* (Stanford, CA: Hoover Institution Press, 2007). The Reykjavik Summit also features prominently in Jack F. Matlock, *Reagan and Gorbachev: How the Cold War Ended* (New York: Random House, 2004); John Lewis Gaddis, *The United States and the End of the Cold War: Implications, Reconsiderations, Provocations* (New York: Oxford University Press, 1992); Raymond L. Garthoff, *The Great Transition: American-Soviet Relations and the End of the Cold War* (Washington, DC: Brookings Institution, 1994).

80. Brands, *Reagan*, 577–610, including 606 (not withdrawing proposals), 599 (insurance), 600–603 (promise to America and final try), and 610 (Gorbachev's first quote to Politburo). See "Russian Transcript of Reagan-Gorbachev Summit in Reykjavik," October 12, 1986 (afternoon), published in FBIS-USR-93-121,

September 20, 1993, in National Security Archive, Electronic Briefing Book No. 203, Document 16, https://nsarchive2.gwu.edu/NSAEBB/NSAEBB203/Document16.pdf. For "in a corner" and "waiting for us to drown," see Matlock, *Reagan and Gorbachev*, 260. At 341fn10, Matlock writes that these quotes are based on his notes from the meeting.

81. See Brands, *Reagan*, 674–75 on Thatcher's reaction.
82. On Soviet concessions, see Wilson, *Triumph of Improvisation*, 123, 130; Sestanovich, *Maximalist*, 238.
83. Brands, *Reagan*, 680–85; Wilson, *Triumph of Improvisation*, 135–38.
84. Hayward, *Age of Reagan*, 606–7.
85. Sestanovich, *Maximalist*, 240; Gorbachev quoted in Chernyaev, *My Six Years with Gorbachev*, 84.
86. Rowland and Jones, *Reagan at Westminster*, 115, 118; Gaddis, *Cold War*, 233.
87. Rowland and Jones, *Reagan at Westminster*, 116–17; Martin Anderson, *Revolution* (San Diego: Harcourt Brace Jovanovich, 1988), 72–75.
88. Brands, *Making the Unipolar Moment*, 73–74, citing Reagan, "Are Liberals Really Liberal?" circa 1963, in Skinner, *Reagan, in His Own Hand*, 442; Reagan, "Soviet Workers," undated, Box 8, Ronald Reagan Subject Collection, Hoover Institution.
89. See Rowland and Jones, *Reagan at Westminster*, 124 for Diggins; Brands, *Reagan*, 735 for his quote.
90. For a more critical assessment of Reagan's accomplishments and legacy from a "realist" perspective, see Norman A. Graebner, Richard Dean Burns, and Joseph M. Siracusa, *Reagan, Bush, Gorbachev: Revisiting the End of the Cold War* (Westport, CT: Praeger Security International, 2008), especially 105–13 (costs and reversion to détente) and 137–46 (a mistaken preoccupation with bipolarity, factors that prompted the end of the Cold War, and misapplied lessons).

Chapter 17. George H. W. Bush: Alliance Leader

1. For the NATO communique, see "NATO Summit: 'A Comprehensive Concept of Arms Control and Disarmament': Report Adopted by the Heads of State and Government of the North Atlantic Council, Brussels, May 30, 1989," in *American Foreign Policy: Current Documents, 1989*, eds. Nancy L. Golden and Sherrill Brown Wells (Washington, DC: Department of State, 1990), 283-292. For President Bush's Mainz speech, see "A Europe Whole and Free: Remarks to the Citizens in Mainz, President George Bush," May 31, 1989, U.S. Diplomatic Mission to Germany, https://usa.usembassy.de/etexts/ga6-890531.htm. For Secretary Baker's account of the NATO negotiations, see Baker, *Politics of Diplomacy*, 92–96. See also George Bush and Brent Scowcroft, *A World Transformed* (New York: Knopf, 1998), 79–83.
2. See George Bush, "Address Accepting the Presidential Nomination at the Republican National Convention in New Orleans," August 18, 1988, The American Presidency Project, UC Santa Barbara, https://www.presidency.ucsb.edu/node/268235.
3. In Baker's second memoir, he titles one chapter, "If You're So Smart, Jimmy, How Come I'm Vice President and You're Not?" See James A. Baker III with Steve Fiffer, *"Work Hard, Study...and Keep Out of Politics!" Adventures and Lessons from an Unexpected Public Life* (New York: G. P. Putnam's Sons, 2006).
4. Philip Zelikow and Condoleezza Rice, *To Build a Better World: Choices to End the Cold War and Create a Global Commonwealth* (New York: Twelve, 2019), 109–11. See Henry Kissinger, "A Memo to the Next President," *Newsweek*, September 19, 1988, 34; idem., "The Challenge of a 'European Home,'" *Washington Post*, December 4, 1988. See Bush and Scowcroft, *World Transformed*, 26–28.
5. Kissinger, "Challenge of a 'European Home.'"
6. See NIE 11-4-89, "Soviet Policy Toward the West: The Gorbachev Challenge," April 1989, reprinted in *At Cold War's End: U.S. Intelligence on the Soviet Union and Eastern Europe, 1989-1991*, ed. Benjamin B. Fischer (Washington, DC: Central Intelligence Agency, Center for the Study of Intelligence, 1999), 227–54.
7. For Bush's meeting in Ottawa, see Zelikow and Rice, *Better World*, 113–14; Bush and Scowcroft, *World Transformed*, 62–63; Baker, *Politics of Diplomacy*, 86; Brian Mulroney, *Memoirs, 1939–1993* (Toronto: McClelland & Stewart, 2007), 651.
8. It turned out that key NSC staff members—including Bob Blackwill, Phil Zelikow, and Arnie Kanter—were more forward leaning than General Scowcroft, who nevertheless permitted them to argue their positions. See Zelikow and Rice, *Better World*, 108–11, 117–19, 172–73 for a fuller account of the internal debates.
9. See Bush and Scowcroft, *World Transformed*, 91–96 for the trip to Japan and China, including the meeting with Deng.

10. Baker, *Politics of Diplomacy*, 85–90.

11. The secretary and the State Department need to keep their ideas within the regular flow into the Oval Office. Recall that Charles Evans Hughes employed a similar technique with President Harding—a daily morning meeting—during his months-long negotiation of the Washington Naval Conference. Hughes took that precaution even before the establishment of large White House and NSC staffs to "guide" presidential time, reading, and attention.

12. See "Our Purpose is to Improve the Security of Europe," in *American Foreign Policy: Current Documents*, 269–74 for Baker's speech in Vienna, including proposals on chemical weapons. See Baker, *Politics of Diplomacy*, 63–67 for meetings.

13. Baker, *Politics of Diplomacy*, 63–67.

14. Baker, *Politics of Diplomacy*, 67–68.

15. See Zelikow and Rice, *Better World*, 119–20 for Scowcroft note and the internal reviews; Baker, *Politics of Diplomacy*, 68.

16. Baker, *Politics of Diplomacy*, 68–70.

17. While waiting for the confirmation of our assistant secretary for inter-American affairs, Bernie Aronson, who had prepared our strategy, I led the discussions with congressional groups. I recall the frustrations of Republicans as we had to bargain with the Democrats who had the votes. About one-third of the Democrats seemed sympathetic, enough to create a majority with Republicans, but the Democrats held firm to a caucus position. Members from both sides, and especially their staffs, were more intent on settling old and bitter scores with one another. Without all sides' confidence in and respect for Baker—and his sense of when to yield a word, adapt a compromise idea, and hold firm—we would have never reached an agreement. The administration then worked with other Central Americans, the Organization of American States, the UN, Europeans, the Soviets, the National Endowment for Democracy, and former president Jimmy Carter to force the Sandinistas to hold fair elections with plenty of monitors. On February 26, 1990, Violeta Chamorro, the leader of the opposition, defeated Daniel Ortega and the Sandinistas in a democratic election. Baker, *Politics of Diplomacy*, 47–60. Sad to say, after the opposition to Ortega fell prey to infighting, corruption, and Ortega's ongoing manipulation of the security services, Ortega returned to the presidency in 2007 following his election in 2006, when I was back at the State Department as deputy secretary. As of this writing, public frustration with the abuse of power by Ortega and his wife, Rosario Murillo (the vice president), has erupted again.

18. Bush and Scowcroft, *World Transformed*, 43–45; Zelikow and Rice, *Better World*, 136–37.

19. Baker, *Politics of Diplomacy*, 70–83. On Secretary Cheney's comment about Gorbachev, Baker explains that he called the president, who directed Scowcroft to distance the White House from Cheney's comment. Baker adds that it was his only significant dispute with Cheney over "turf." His main message is that administrations that cannot discipline messages on foreign policy harm their own diplomacy.

20. Baker, *Politics of Diplomacy*, 83.

21. Bush and Scowcroft, *World Transformed*, 67–71; Baker, *Politics of Diplomacy*, 92. For the Texas A&M speech, see *American Foreign Policy: Current Documents*, 363–66.

22. Bush and Scowcroft, *World Transformed*, 73–74; Baker, *Politics of Diplomacy*, 93.

23. Zelikow and Rice, *Better World*, 137–38.

24. The president paid a political price for leading. Admiral Crowe, whom General Colin Powell succeeded as chair, harbored resentments. In 1992, when candidate Bill Clinton needed security credentials against the more experienced Bush, Crowe endorsed Clinton and actively supported him. Crowe was rewarded in 1993 with an appointment as U.S. ambassador to the United Kingdom. Zelikow and Rice, *Better World*, 137–38; Bush and Scowcroft, *World Transformed*, 73–74, 79–81; Baker, *Politics of Diplomacy*, 93–94.

25. Zelikow and Rice, *Better World*, 138–39.

26. Bush and Scowcroft, *World Transformed*, 82–83; Baker, *Politics of Diplomacy*, 95–96; for the NATO communique, see "A Comprehensive Concept of Arms Control and Disarmament."

27. When I was in Bonn, Foreign Minister Genscher's chief of staff, Frank Elbe, sought me out for a get-to-know-you chat. Elbe later told me that he and Genscher had watched my interactions with Baker at the NATO summit and decided to reach out. Our partnership—and friendship—would prove fruitful during the negotiations for German unification that were soon to come.

28. Bush and Scowcroft, *World Transformed*, 83; Bush, "A Europe Whole and Free."

29. For Bush's reference to unification, see Arnaud de Borchgrave, "Bush Would Love Reunited Germany," *Washington Times*, May 16, 1989, A1; Bush and Scowcroft, *World Transformed*, 83 for speech.

30. Bush and Scowcroft, *World Transformed*, 112–16; Zelikow and Rice, *Better World*, 126–28, 151–52.

31. Baker, *Politics of Diplomacy*, 75–76.

32. Bush and Scowcroft, *World Transformed*, 112–23.

33. Bush and Scowcroft, *World Transformed*, 121–22.

34. Bush and Scowcroft, *World Transformed*, 124–28.

35. Bush and Scowcroft, *World Transformed*, 125–26.

36. Bush and Scowcroft, *World Transformed*, 128–29; Zelikow and Rice, *Better World*, 151–53, 162–66. On the G-7 summit, see "Declaration on East-West Relations," July 15, 1989, Munk School of Global Affairs & Public Policy, Trinity College, University of Toronto, http://www.g8.utoronto.ca/summit/1989paris/east .html.

37. Zelikow and Rice, *Better World*, 152–53; Bush and Scowcroft, *World Transformed*, 129.

38. See Zelikow and Rice, *Better World*, 451fn33 for discussion of the historical commentary about the so-called pause. For an early reference, see Beschloss and Talbott, *At the Highest Levels*, 28–29, 41, 60, 165, 469. The viewpoint has persisted over decades, including in sympathetic accounts. See Jeffrey Engel, *When the World Seemed New: George H. W. Bush and the End of the Cold War* (New York: Houghton Mifflin Harcourt, 2017), 86–99, including a chapter on "The Pause." Authors who focus on the end of the Cold War through the prism of Gorbachev and the Soviets have always had this narrow view. See Jack F. Matlock, *Autopsy on an Empire: The American Ambassador's Account of the Collapse of the Soviet Union* (New York: Random House, 1995), 182–90, 195–200 ("Washington Fumbles") and the more recent biography by William Taubman, *Gorbachev: His Life and Times* (New York: W. W. Norton & Company, 2017), 465, 467–74 (including the view that the Cold War was "over," even though Germany and Europe remained divided).

39. Zelikow and Rice, *Better World*, 328–31, 482fn40.

40. See, e.g., Taubman, *Gorbachev*, 469–73; Beschloss and Talbott, *At the Highest Levels*, 470.

41. See Zelikow and Rice, *Better World*, 108–9, including references to "New Yalta" and to "Yalta II" at 448fn6.

42. See Baker's retrospective (2011) comment in Zelikow and Rice, *Better World*, 451fn33 on the effect of the Bush administration's approach to the USSR: "[W]e gave Gorbachev a little bit of grief because he couldn't figure out exactly what we were doing, but by May it was over. [He could see what the United States was doing.] After my meeting with Shevardnadze…in Vienna, and that may have been in March [March 7]… from about that time on [the United States was moving]….So do I think it cost the country anything? Absolutely not."

43. Jon Meacham, *Destiny and Power: The American Odyssey of George Herbert Walker Bush* (New York: Random House, 2015), 456. For Dr. Kissinger's ongoing interest in "world order," see his *World Order* (New York: Penguin Books, 2014).

44. Baker used this phrase all the time. To him, "getting things done" differentiated talkers from doers.

45. George H. W. Bush, "Agenda for American Renewal" (Bush-Quayle '92 General Committee, 1992).

Chapter 18. Five Traditions of American Diplomacy

1. For Lake's speech at SAIS, see "From Containment to Enlargement: Remarks of Anthony Lake, Assistant to the President for National Security Affairs," September 21, 1993, https://www.mtholyoke.edu/acad/intrel /lakedoc.html. For Clinton's address to the UN General Assembly, see "Address by President Bill Clinton to the UN General Assembly," September 27, 1993, U.S. Department of State, https://2009-2017.state.gov/p /io/potusunga/207375.htm. On the "Kennan Sweepstakes" and the development of "democratic enlargement," see Douglas Brinkley, "Democratic Enlargement: The Clinton Doctrine," *Foreign Policy* (Spring 1997), 111–27. See also chapter 3 in Derek Chollet and James Goldgeier, *America Between the Wars: From 11/9 to 9/11: The Misunderstood Years Between the Fall of the Berlin Wall and the Start of the War on Terror* (New York: PublicAffairs, 2008), especially at 65–71.

2. On grand strategy, see, e.g., Hal Brands, *What Good Is Grand Strategy? Power and Purpose in American Statecraft from Harry S. Truman to George W. Bush* (Ithaca, NY: Cornell University Press, 2014); idem., *American Grand Strategy in the Age of Trump* (Washington, DC: Brookings Institution Press, 2018); John Lewis Gaddis, *On Grand Strategy* (New York: Penguin Press, 2018); Nina Silove, "Beyond the Buzzword: The Three Meanings of 'Grand Strategy,'" *International Security* 27 (2018).

3. Baker, *Politics of Diplomacy*, 84.

4. Robert Merry, *A Country of Vast Designs: James K. Polk, the Mexican War, and the Conquest of the American Continent* (New York: Simon & Schuster, 2009), 361, 386, 408–10, 424–26.

5. Hendrickson, *Peace Pact*, 166–67, 174.

6. Irwin, *Clashing over Commerce*, 617. See also Gregg Lint, "John Adams on the Drafting of the Treaty Plan of 1776," *Diplomatic History* 2, no. 3 (July 1978); Gerard Clarfield, "John Adams: The Marketplace, and American Foreign Policy," *New England Quarterly* 52, no. 3 (September 1979).

7. Irwin, *Clashing over Commerce*, 68–69, citing "From Benjamin Franklin to John Adams, 19 May 1781," in *Papers of Benjamin Franklin*, vol. 35, *May 1 Through October 31, 1781*, ed. Barbara B. Oberg (New Haven: Yale University Press, 1999), 83; "From Thomas Jefferson to John Adams, 31 July 1785," in *Papers of Thomas Jefferson*, vol. 8, *25 February to 31 October 1785*, ed. Julian P. Boyd (Princeton, NJ: Princeton University Press, 1953), 332. See also Thomas Jefferson, *Notes on the State of Virginia*, ed. William Peden (Chapel Hill, NC: University of North Carolina Press, 1955 [1785]), 176.

8. Hendrickson, *Peace Pact*, 174, citing "From John Adams to John Jay, 10 August 1785," in *The Adams Papers: Papers of John Adams*, vol. 17, *April–November 1785*, eds. Gregg L. Lint et al. (Cambridge, MA: Harvard University Press, 2014), 321 (emphasis in original).

9. Irwin, *Clashing over Commerce*, 51–52, 62.

10. Irwin, *Clashing over Commerce*, 86, citing "The Continentalist No. V [18 April 1782]," in *The Papers of Alexander Hamilton*, vol. 3, 78–79; "The Federalist No. 35, [5 January 1788]," in *Papers of Alexander Hamilton*, vol. 4, 477; "Alexander Hamilton's Final Version of the Report on the Subject of Manufactures, [5 December 1791]," in *Papers of Alexander Hamilton*, vol. 10, 301. See discussion in chapter 10.

11. For many developing and smaller countries today, trade relations are their top foreign policy priority with the United States. I recall Secretaries of State Colin Powell and Hillary Clinton telling me that they were surprised that most fellow foreign ministers concentrated on trade topics in their meetings.

12. See Irwin, *Clashing over Commerce*, 101–13 for discussion of Jefferson's Embargo.

13. See Ian W. Toll, *Six Frigates: The Epic History of the Founding of the U.S. Navy* (New York: W. W. Norton & Company, 2006).

14. See Melvyn P. Leffler, *Safeguarding Democratic Capitalism: U.S. Foreign Policy and National Security, 1920–2015* (Princeton, NJ: Princeton University Press, 2017), chapters 1–3 on U.S. debt, reparations, and financial and trade policies of the 1920s.

15. See Robert Dallek, *Franklin D. Roosevelt: A Political Life* (New York: Viking, 2017), 289–91 for discussion of the Quarantine Speech.

Afterword. From Traditions to Today

1. Brown, a keen student of economic history, recalled that the London Economic Conference of 1933, which Cordell Hull attended, had failed dismally, contributing to the breakdown of the international economy in the Great Depression.

2. In his memoir, President Bush notes that he should have made immigration reform the first major initiative of his second term, instead of Social Security. George W. Bush, *Decision Points* (New York: Crown Publishers, 2010), 306.

3. Bush, *Decision Points*, 306.

4. My challenge for China—and for U.S. diplomacy—was to move beyond questions of Chinese participation to encouraging Beijing's behavior—attention to norms, not just forms. The United States, China, and many others have mutual interests in resisting protectionism, thwarting proliferation of weapons of mass destruction and missiles, and countering terrorism; they need to cooperate on energy security, climate change, diseases, exchange rate policies, economic growth, development, and regional security, including dangers in North Korea, Central Asia, and the Persian Gulf. Differences over Taiwan need to be managed peacefully. As Ronald Reagan demonstrated, the United States can speak up for its values—and for freedom—even as it works with China on mutual responsibilities and manages conflicts. For my recent assessment of accomplishments and challenges with China, see Robert B. Zoellick, "The China Challenge," *The National Interest*, no. 166 (March/April 2020), 10–20.

5. The text of the United Nations Framework Convention on Climate Change is available online at https://unfccc.int/resource/docs/convkp/conveng.pdf. Bush's Clean Air Act amendments also countered acid rain and ozone depletion in accord with the Montreal Protocol, a treaty that came into effect in 1989.

6. In 1997, the Senate voted 95–0 on the Byrd-Hagel Resolution, which expressed disapproval of any climate agreement that failed to demand that developing countries reduce their emissions. The resolution prevented ratification of the Kyoto Protocol the following year. On the Senate vote, see https://www.congress.gov/bill/105th-congress/senate-resolution/98.

7. Meacham, *Destiny and Power*, 466.

8. Quoted in Edward Luce, *Time to Start Thinking: America in the Age of Descent* (New York: Atlantic Monthly Press, 2012), 3. There are various translations of Alexis de Tocqueville's two-volume *Democracy in America* (in the original French, *De La Démocratie en Amérique*), the first volume of which was published in 1835. Another common English translation reads: "The great privilege of the Americans does not simply consist in their being more enlightened than others, but in their being able to repair the faults they may commit." See de Tocqueville, *Democracy in America*, vol. 1, trans. Henry Reeve (New York: J. & H. G. Langley, 1841), 250.

Photo Credits and Sources

1: Benjamin Franklin Historical Society. 2, 8: White House Historical Association. 3, 14, 15, 16, 20, 23: Library of Congress. 4: Yale University Art Gallery. 5: Winterthur Museum, Garden & Library. 6: New York City Public Design Commission, City Hall Portrait Commission. 7, 11: Wikimeda Commons. 9, 24, 25, 27, 36: Getty Images. 10: Metropolitan Museum of Art. 12: British Library. 13: Amanda Foreman, *World on Fire: An Epic History of Two Nations Divided* (London: Allen Lane, 2010). 17: Brown University Portrait Collection. 18: Encyclopedia Britannica. 19: John Milton Cooper, *The Warrior and the Priest: Woodrow Wilson and Theodore Roosevelt* (Cambridge, MA: Belknap Press of Harvard University Press, 1983). 21, 22: Philip C. Jessup, *Elihu Root*, vol. 2 (New York: Dodd, Mead & Company, 1938). 26: National Museum of Naval Aviation. 28: Truman Library. 29, 31: *Time* magazine. 30: MIT Museum. 32: *Globe and Mail*. 33: American Public Media. 34: *National Geographic*. 35: AFP/Getty Images. 37: Reagan Library. 38, 39: Robert B. Zoellick.

Index

Page numbers of maps appear in italics
Key to abbreviations: FDR = Franklin Delano Roosevelt; JFK = John F. Kennedy; LBJ = Lyndon Baines Johnson;
TR = Theodore Roosevelt

Acheson, Dean, 237, 243, 244, 246, 250–51, 253, 258, 268–70, 278, 288, 334, 335, 347, 359, 377, 449, 457; Berlin crisis and JFK, 322, 323; as diplomat, 286; the German question, 285–86, 507–8n158; Marshall Plan and, 270, 272, 273–74, 506n121; North Atlantic Treaty and, 288–89; postwar Greece and Turkey and, 259, 261–62; as secretary of state, 243, 244, 285, 336, 377, 504–5n60; Truman doctrine and, 263–64; Vandenberg Resolution and, 286–88

Adams, Brook, *American Economic Supremacy*, 99

Adams, Charles Francis, 75, 76, 78

Adams, Henry, 46, 102

Adams, John, 4, 5, 9, 22, 30, 139, 447, 448; free trade and, 448; Navy-building, 448; Quasi-Naval War with France, 22, 30; Treaty Plan of 1776, 447, 449

Adams, John Quincy, 50, 52–55, 64, 67, 89, 378, 453–55, 472; acquisition of Florida, 53; address, July 4, 1821, on far-ranging escapades, 67; ambitions and agenda, 52–54; anti-British views, 54, 55; Canning's proposal (on Latin America), 58–60, 104; Clay and, 56, 64–65; education in diplomacy, 52; election of, 64; famous words, 55; foreign policy doctrine, 50, 387; geopolitical republicanism, 67, 68, 73, 453, 454, 459; grand strategy, 54–55; Monroe Doctrine and, 289; as Monroe's secretary of state, 52; transcontinental expansion and, 9, 66–67; Treaty of Ghent, 48, 52; U.S. western border and, 53

Adams, Louisa, 56

Adams, Samuel, 65

Adenauer, Konrad, 283, 290, 324, 329, 330

Advanced Research Projects Agency (ARPA, later DARPA), 292

Afghanistan, 175, 342, 431, 466, 469

Africa, 100, 128, 222, 241, 261, 318, 390, 437, 442, 444, 453; G. W. Bush's global health initiative and, 470

African Growth and Opportunity Act, 465

Akira Iriye, 195

Alabama (Confederate ship), 87, 141, 201–2, 498n9

Alaska purchase, 90, 114, 445, 486n54

Albert, Prince Consort, 79, 81, 82

Alexander, Sir Michael, 419

Alexander I, Czar, 50, 58, 60, 63

Alexander II, Czar, 83

Alexander III, Czar, 121

Allen, Richard, 395

Alliance of Democracies, 57

Ambrosius, Lloyd, 162–63

American Diplomacy, 1900–1950 (Kennan), 7

American diplomacy and foreign policy, 63–64, 353, 478n19; activist diplomacy, 92, 317, 318, 319, 320, 329, 334–37, 429, 441; alliances, early, and avoiding entanglements, 12–13, 23, 30, 49, 50, 51, 64, 137, 152, 158, 219, 289, 378, 444, 451; alliance system, postwar, 132, 241–90, 334–35, 346–47, 349–50, 356, 357, 362, 449, 451–53, 457, 459, 466–70, 472; American exceptionalism and, 13–14, 383; anticolonialism of, 50, 54, 55, 61, 64, 461; applying standards of personal conduct to, 143; author on U.S. message, 372; balance of power politics, 112–28, 201, 208, 217, 319, 331, 349, 367, 387, 392, 399; cautions for, six factors in Vietnam War decisions, 346–62; congressional support and, 244, 247, 253–56, 261–62, 277–80, 287–89, 322, 416, 454–59, 470–71; containment policy, 7, 346, 347, 362, 396, 432, 443, 444; credibility and, 349–50, 354; crisis management, JFK and, 315–34; defining moment for (1947), 253, 259–80; détente, 374, 385, 390, 396, 401; economic interests, economic statecraft, 7, 12, 16–46, 97–111; five traditions, 12–14, 443–61; freedom and democracy infused in, 395, 440; "futurist" diplomacy, 27–46, 293; geopolitical republicanism, 50, 67, 68, 73, 241, 453, 454, 459, 460; global leadership, 132, 161, 163, 165, 175, 195, 217, 264, 382, 387, 418–42,

About the Author

Robert B. Zoellick has served as Deputy Secretary, Under Secretary, and Counselor of the State Department; Ambassador and U.S. Trade Representative; Counselor to the Secretary of the Treasury; Deputy Chief of Staff at the White House; and President of the World Bank. His experience spans six U.S. Presidencies—during the Cold War, in its closing chapter, and into the first decades of the twenty-first century. Zoellick is now a Senior Fellow at the Belfer Center for Science and International Affairs at Harvard University's Kennedy School of Government, where he contributes to the "Applied History" project.